Springer Texts in Business and Economics

Springer Texts in Business and Economics (STBE) delivers high-quality instructional content for undergraduates and graduates in all areas of Business/Management Science and Economics. The series is comprised of self-contained books with a broad and comprehensive coverage that are suitable for class as well as for individual self-study. All texts are authored by established experts in their fields and offer a solid methodological background, often accompanied by problems and exercises.

John D. Levendis

Time Series Econometrics
Learning Through Replication

Second Edition

John D. Levendis
Loyola University New Orleans
New Orleans, LA, USA

ISSN 2192-4333 ISSN 2192-4341 (electronic)
Springer Texts in Business and Economics
ISBN 978-3-031-37309-1 ISBN 978-3-031-37310-7 (eBook)
https://doi.org/10.1007/978-3-031-37310-7

1st edition: © Springer Nature Switzerland AG 2018
2nd edition: © The Editor(s) (if applicable) and The Author(s), under exclusive license to Springer Nature Switzerland AG 2023
This work is subject to copyright. All rights are solely and exclusively licensed by the Publisher, whether the whole or part of the material is concerned, specifically the rights of translation, reprinting, reuse of illustrations, recitation, broadcasting, reproduction on microfilms or in any other physical way, and transmission or information storage and retrieval, electronic adaptation, computer software, or by similar or dissimilar methodology now known or hereafter developed.
The use of general descriptive names, registered names, trademarks, service marks, etc. in this publication does not imply, even in the absence of a specific statement, that such names are exempt from the relevant protective laws and regulations and therefore free for general use.
The publisher, the authors, and the editors are safe to assume that the advice and information in this book are believed to be true and accurate at the date of publication. Neither the publisher nor the authors or the editors give a warranty, expressed or implied, with respect to the material contained herein or for any errors or omissions that may have been made. The publisher remains neutral with regard to jurisdictional claims in published maps and institutional affiliations.

This Springer imprint is published by the registered company Springer Nature Switzerland AG
The registered company address is: Gewerbestrasse 11, 6330 Cham, Switzerland

Paper in this product is recyclable.

To Catherine and Jack

Preface

What makes this book unique? It follows a simple ethos: it is easier to learn by doing. Or, "Econometrics is better taught by example than abstraction" (Angrist & Pischke, 2017, p. 2)

The aim of this book is to explain how to use the basic, yet essential, tools of time-series econometrics. The approach is to be as simple as possible so that real learning can take place. We won't try to be encyclopedic, nor will we break new methodological ground. The goal is to develop a practical understanding of the basic tools you will need to get started in this exciting field.

We progress methodically, building as much as possible from concrete examples rather than from abstract first principles. First we learn by doing. Then, with a bit of experience under our belts, we'll begin developing a deeper theoretical understanding of the real processes. After all, when students learn calculus, they learn the rules of calculus first and practice taking derivatives. Only after they've gained familiarity with calculus do students learn the Real Analysis theory behind the formulas. In my opinion, students should take applied econometrics before econometric theory. Otherwise, the importance of the theory falls on deaf ears, as the students have no context with which to understand the theorems.

Other books seem to begin at the end, with theory, and then they throw in some examples. We, on the other hand, begin where you are likely to be and lead you forward, building slowly from examples to theory.

In the first section, we begin with simple univariate models on well-behaved (stationary) data. We devote a lot of attention on the properties of autoregressive and moving-average models. We then investigate deterministic and stochastic seasonality. Then we explore the practice of unit root testing and the influence of structural breaks. The first section ends with models of non-stationary variance. In the second section, we extend the simpler concepts to the more complex cases of multi-equation multi-variate VAR and VECM models.

By the time you finish working through this book, you will not only have studied some of the major techniques of time-series, you will actually have worked through many simulations. In fact, if you work along with the text, you will have replicated some of the most influential papers in the field. You won't just know about some results, you'll have derived them yourself.

No textbook can cover everything. In this text, we will not deal with fractional integration, seasonal cointegration, or anything in the frequency domain. Opting for a less-is-more approach, we must leave these and other more complicated topics to other textbooks.

Nobody works alone. Many people helped me complete this project. They deserve thanks.

Several prominent econometricians dug up—or tried to dig up—data from their classic papers. Thanks, specifically, to Richard T. Baillie, David Dickey, Jordi Gali, Charles Nelson, Dan Thornton, and Jean-Michel Zakoian.

Justin Callais provided tireless research assistance, verifying Stata code for the entire text. Donald Lacombe, Wei Sun, and Jennifer Moreale reviewed early drafts of various chapters and offered valuable suggestions. Mehmet F. Dicle found some coding and data errors and offered useful advice. Matt Lutey helped with some of the replications. Daymler O'Farrill and Jaime Rodriguez Garzon kindly pointed out some errors in the first edition. Maximo Sangiacomo helped explain parts of his `xtcips` command. Regina Cati and Lorena Barberia worked through many of the exercises and kindly inflicted the first edition of the text on their students. Ralph Nyilas provided Matlab version of some of the Stata exercises.

The text was inflicted upon a group of innocent undergraduate students at Loyola University. These bright men and women patiently pointed out mistakes and typos, as well as passages that required clarification. For that, I am grateful and wish to thank (without implication) Justin Callais, Rebecca Driever, Patrick Driscoll, William Herrick, Christian Mays, Nate Straight, David Thomas, Tom Whelan, and Peter Wrobleski.

This project could not have been completed without the financial support of Loyola University, the Marquette Fellowship Grant committee, and especially Fr. Kevin Wildes.

Thanks to Lorraine Klimowich from Springer, for championing this project.

Finally, and most importantly, I'd like to thank my family. My son Jack: you are my reason for being; I hope to make you proud. My wife Catherine: you are a constant source of support and encouragement. You are amazing. I love you.

New Orleans, LA, USA   John D. Levendis

Contents

1	**Introduction**		1
	1.1	What Makes Time Series Econometrics Unique?.	1
	1.2	Notation.	2
	1.3	Statistical Review.	5
	1.4	Specifying Time in Stata.	7
	1.5	Installing New Stata Commands.	8
	1.6	Exercises.	9
2	**ARMA(p,q) Processes**.		11
	2.1	Introduction.	11
		2.1.1 Stationarity.	13
		2.1.2 A Purely Random Process.	15
	2.2	AR(1) Models.	15
		2.2.1 Estimating an AR(1) Model.	16
		2.2.2 Impulse Responses.	21
		2.2.3 Forecasting.	24
	2.3	AR(p) Models.	26
		2.3.1 Estimating an AR(p) Model.	27
		2.3.2 Impulse Responses.	29
		2.3.3 Forecasting.	31
	2.4	MA(1) Models.	33
		2.4.1 Estimation.	34
		2.4.2 Impulse Responses.	34
		2.4.3 Forecasting.	35
	2.5	MA(q) Models.	38
		2.5.1 Estimation.	38
		2.5.2 Impulse Responses.	40
	2.6	Nonzero ARMA Processes.	40
		2.6.1 Nonzero AR Processes.	41
		2.6.2 Nonzero MA Processes.	42
		2.6.3 Dealing with Nonzero Means.	43
		2.6.4 Example.	44

	2.7	ARMA(p,q) Models.	47
		2.7.1 Estimation.	47
	2.8	Conclusion.	47
3	**Model Selection in ARMA(p,q) Processes.**		**49**
	3.1	ACFs and PACFs.	50
		3.1.1 Theoretical ACF of an AR(1) Process.	50
		3.1.2 Theoretical ACF of an AR(p) Process.	54
		3.1.3 Theoretical ACF of an MA(1) Process.	59
		3.1.4 Theoretical ACF of an MA(q) Process.	61
		3.1.5 Theoretical PACFs.	65
		3.1.6 Summary: Theoretical ACFs and PACFs.	66
	3.2	Empirical ACFs and PACFs.	66
		3.2.1 Calculating Empirical ACFs.	70
		3.2.2 Calculating Empirical PACFs.	71
	3.3	Putting It All Together.	75
		3.3.1 Example.	75
		3.3.2 Example.	77
		3.3.3 Exercises.	79
	3.4	Information Criteria.	80
		3.4.1 Example.	81
		3.4.2 Exercises.	82
4	**Stationarity and Invertibility.**		**85**
	4.1	What Is Stationarity?.	85
	4.2	The Importance of Stationarity.	86
	4.3	Restrictions on AR Coefficients Which Ensure Stationarity.	87
		4.3.1 Restrictions on AR(1) Coefficients.	87
		4.3.2 Restrictions on AR(2) Coefficients.	88
		4.3.3 Restrictions on AR(p) Coefficients.	96
		4.3.4 Characteristic and Inverse Characteristic Equations.	97
		4.3.5 Restrictions on ARIMA(p,q) Coefficients.	98
	4.4	The Connection Between AR and MA Processes.	99
		4.4.1 AR(1) to MA(∞).	99
		4.4.2 AR(p) to MA(∞).	101
		4.4.3 Invertibility: MA(1) to AR(∞).	101
	4.5	What Are Unit Roots, and Why Are They Bad?.	103
5	**Nonstationarity and ARIMA(p,d,q) Processes.**		**105**
	5.1	Differencing.	105
	5.2	The Random Walk.	108
	5.3	The Random Walk with Drift.	110
	5.4	Deterministic Trend.	111
	5.5	Random Walk with Drift Versus Deterministic Trend.	112

	5.6	Differencing and Detrending Appropriately............................	113
		5.6.1 Mistakenly Differencing (Over-Differencing)............	118
		5.6.2 Mistakenly Detrending..	121
	5.7	Replicating Granger and Newbold (1974)..............................	122
	5.8	Conclusion...	126
6	**Seasonal ARMA(p,q) Processes**..		127
	6.1	Two Different Types of Seasonality......................................	127
		6.1.1 Deterministic Seasonality......................................	128
		6.1.2 Seasonal Differencing..	130
		6.1.3 Additive Seasonality..	132
		6.1.4 Multiplicative Seasonality.....................................	132
		6.1.5 MA Seasonality...	135
	6.2	Identification...	136
	6.3	Invertibility and Stability...	138
	6.4	How Common Are Seasonal Unit Roots?.............................	139
	6.5	Using Deseasonalized Data..	140
	6.6	Conclusion...	141
7	**Unit Root Tests**		143
	7.1	Introduction...	143
	7.2	Unit Root Tests...	144
	7.3	Dickey-Fuller Tests...	145
		7.3.1 A Random Walk Versus a Zero-Mean AR(1) Process...	145
		7.3.2 A Random Walk Versus an AR(1) Model with a Constant...	150
		7.3.3 A Random Walk with Drift Versus a Deterministic Trend...	152
		7.3.4 Augmented Dickey-Fuller Tests............................	155
		7.3.5 DF-GLS Tests...	157
		7.3.6 Choosing the Lag Length in DF-Type Tests................	157
	7.4	Phillips-Perron Tests...	160
	7.5	KPSS Tests...	162
	7.6	Replicating Nelson and Plosser..	164
	7.7	Testing for Seasonal Unit Roots...	172
	7.8	Conclusion and Further Readings..	172
8	**Structural Breaks**		175
	8.1	Structural Breaks and Unit Roots...	176
	8.2	Perron (1989): Tests for a Unit Root with a Known Structural Break..	177
	8.3	Zivot and Andrews' Test of a Break at an Unknown Date..........	188
		8.3.1 Replicating Zivot & Andrews (1992) in Stata.............	189
		8.3.2 The `zandrews` Command....................................	194
	8.4	Further Readings...	197

9 ARCH, GARCH, and Time-Varying Variance ... 201
- 9.1 Introduction ... 201
- 9.2 Conditional Versus Unconditional Moments ... 204
- 9.3 ARCH Models ... 205
  - 9.3.1 ARCH(1) ... 205
  - 9.3.2 AR(1)-ARCH(1) ... 212
  - 9.3.3 ARCH(2) ... 217
  - 9.3.4 ARCH(q) ... 221
  - 9.3.5 Example 1: Toyota Motor Company ... 225
  - 9.3.6 Example 2: Ford Motor Company ... 230
- 9.4 GARCH Models ... 233
  - 9.4.1 GARCH(1,1) ... 233
  - 9.4.2 GARCH(p,q) ... 236
- 9.5 Variations on GARCH ... 242
  - 9.5.1 GARCH-t ... 242
  - 9.5.2 GARCH-M or GARCH-IN-MEAN ... 248
  - 9.5.3 Asymmetric Responses in GARCH ... 251
  - 9.5.4 I-GARCH or Integrated GARCH ... 258
- 9.6 Exercises ... 260

10 Vector Autoregressions I: Basics ... 263
- 10.1 Introduction ... 263
  - 10.1.1 A History Lesson ... 264
- 10.2 A Simple VAR(1) and How to Estimate It ... 266
- 10.3 How Many Lags to Include? ... 270
- 10.4 Expressing VARs in Matrix Form ... 272
  - 10.4.1 Any VAR(p) Can Be Rewritten as a VAR(1) ... 274
- 10.5 Stability ... 276
  - 10.5.1 Method 1 ... 276
  - 10.5.2 Method 2 ... 279
  - 10.5.3 Stata Command Varstable ... 282
- 10.6 Long-Run Levels: Including a Constant ... 282
- 10.7 Expressing a VAR as an VMA Process ... 284
- 10.8 Impulse Response Functions ... 285
  - 10.8.1 IRFs as the Components of the MA Coefficients ... 286
- 10.9 Forecasting ... 292
- 10.10 Granger Causality ... 296
  - 10.10.1 Replicating Sims (1972) ... 298
  - 10.10.2 Indirect Causality ... 301
- 10.11 VAR Example: GNP and Unemployment ... 303
- 10.12 Exercises ... 308

Contents

11 Vector Autoregressions II: Extensions 311
  11.1 Orthogonalized IRFs 311
    11.1.1 Order Matters in OIRFs 313
    11.1.2 Cholesky Decompositions and OIRFs 315
    11.1.3 Why Order Matters for OIRFs 324
  11.2 Forecast Error Variance Decompositions 326
  11.3 Structural VARs 329
    11.3.1 Reduced Form vs Structural Form 329
    11.3.2 SVARs Are Unidentified 330
    11.3.3 The General Form of SVARs 332
    11.3.4 Cholesky Is an SVAR 333
    11.3.5 Long-Run Restrictions: Blanchard and Quah (1989)... 336
  11.4 VARs with Integrated Variables 338
  11.5 Conclusion 340

12 Cointegration and VECMs 343
  12.1 Introduction 343
  12.2 Cointegration 343
  12.3 Error Correction Mechanism 348
    12.3.1 The Effect of the Adjustment Parameter 350
  12.4 Deriving the ECM 350
  12.5 Engle and Granger's Residual-Based Tests of Cointegration 351
    12.5.1 MacKinnon Critical Values for Engle-Granger Tests... 352
    12.5.2 Engle-Granger Approach 354
  12.6 Multi-equation Models and VECMs 360
    12.6.1 Deriving the VECM from a Simple VAR(2) 360
    12.6.2 Deriving the VECM(k-1) from a Reduced-Form VAR(k) 362
    12.6.3 $\Pi = \alpha \beta'$ Is Not Uniquely Identified 363
    12.6.4 Johansen's Tests and the Rank of Π 364
  12.7 IRFs, OIRFs, and Forecasting from VECMs 375
  12.8 Lag Length Selection 375
  12.9 Cointegration Implies Granger Causality 377
    12.9.1 Testing for Granger Causality 377
  12.10 Conclusion 378
  12.11 Exercises 379

13 Static Panel Data Models 385
  13.1 Introduction 385
  13.2 Formatting the Data 386
    13.2.1 Wide and Long 387
  13.3 The Static Panel Model 388
    13.3.1 The Error Terms 389
    13.3.2 Pooled OLS 390
    13.3.3 Endogeneity 390
    13.3.4 First Differencing 391
    13.3.5 Demeaning 392

	13.4	Fixed Effects and Random Effects	393
		13.4.1 Random Effects Models	394
		13.4.2 Fixed Effects Models	394
		13.4.3 Estimating FE Models	394
		13.4.4 Two Equivalent Ways of Estimating FE Models	395
	13.5	Choosing Between RE and FE Models	396
		13.5.1 Hausman Test	396
		13.5.2 Mundlak Test	400
		13.5.3 You Must Estimate the Correct Model	401
	13.6	Time Fixed Effects	403
		13.6.1 Estimation	405
		13.6.2 Estimating FEs with Explicit Time Dummies in Stata	406
	13.7	Cross-Sectional Dependence	408
		13.7.1 Driscoll-Kraay Standard Errors	409
		13.7.2 If CSD Shocks Are Correlated with Regressors	410
		13.7.3 Testing for CSD in Stata	411
		13.7.4 Lagrange Multiplier CSD Test	412
		13.7.5 Estimation When You Have CSD	413
14	**Dynamic Panel Data Models**		**415**
	14.1	Dynamic Panel Bias	415
		14.1.1 Demeaning Does Not Fix This Problem	416
		14.1.2 First Differencing Does Not Fix This Problem	417
		14.1.3 GMM Estimators Fix This Problem	417
		14.1.4 Arellano-Bond-Type Estimators	418
		14.1.5 Forward Orthogonal Deviations	419
		14.1.6 Arellano-Bond in Stata	419
		14.1.7 Too Many Instruments	420
		14.1.8 Sargan's and Hansen's J-Test for Instrument Validity	423
		14.1.9 Difference-in-Hansen/Sargan Tests	424
		14.1.10 Blundell-Bond Test of Autocorrelation	424
	14.2	Replicating Arellano and Bond (1991)	426
	14.3	Replicating Thomson (2017)	429
	14.4	Stationarity and Panel Unit Root Tests	431
		14.4.1 First-Generation Tests	432
		14.4.2 Second-Generation Tests	439
	14.5	Structural Breaks	441
	14.6	Panel VARs	442
		14.6.1 Panel VAR Example	444
	14.7	Cointegration Tests	448
		14.7.1 Cointegration Test Example: The Permanent Income Hypothesis	451

	14.8	Further Reading.. 455
	14.9	Homework.. 455
15	**Conclusion**..	459
A	**Tables of Critical Values**..	465

References.. 471

Index.. 483

Introduction 1

Econometrics can be used to answer many practical questions in economics and finance:

- Suppose you own a business. How might you use the previous 10 years' worth of monthly sales data to predict next month's sales?
- You wish to test whether the "permanent income hypothesis" holds. Can you see whether consumption spending is a relatively constant fraction of national income?
- You are a financial researcher. You wish to determine whether gold prices lead stock prices, or vice versa. Is there a relationship between these variables? If so, can you use it to make money?

Answering each of these questions requires slightly different statistical apparatuses, yet they all fall under the umbrella of "time series econometrics."

1.1 What Makes Time Series Econometrics Unique?

Consider the differences in the two panels of Fig. 1.1. Panel (a) shows cross-sectional data, and panel (b), a time series. Standard econometrics—the econometrics of cross sections—relies on the fact that observations are independent. If we take a sample of people and ask whether they are unemployed today, we will get a mixture of answers. And even though we might be in a particularly bad spell in the economy, one person's unemployment status is not likely to affect another person's. It's not as though person A can't get a job just because person B is unemployed. But if we are focused on the unemployment rate, year after year, then this year's performance is likely influenced by last year's economy. The observations in time series are almost never independent. Usually, one observation is correlated with the previous observation.

© The Author(s), under exclusive license to Springer Nature Switzerland AG 2023
J. D. Levendis, *Time Series Econometrics*, Springer Texts in Business and Economics, https://doi.org/10.1007/978-3-031-37310-7_1

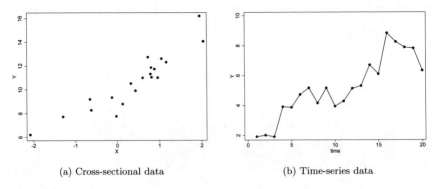

(a) Cross-sectional data (b) Time-series data

Fig. 1.1 Two different types of data. (**a**) Cross-sectional data. (**b**) Time series data

This isn't just a trivial difference. Perhaps a simpler example will illustrate why this distinction is so important. Suppose you want to know whether a coin is biased. You should flip it and record its value. Then, flip it again and record its value. Do this over and over, say one hundred times, and you will get a good idea of whether it is biased. An unbiased coin should give us roughly fifty heads and fifty tails, plus or minus random error. Under the null hypothesis of a fair coin, the probability of a head in the first flip is 1/2. Likewise, the probability of heads in the second flip is also 1/2, regardless of how the first flip turned out.

But things are different when the observations are not independent. Suppose you flip the coin once and record the outcome. Then, you immediately look back down, observe that it is still heads, and record a second observation of heads. You can do this one hundred times. But you don't have one hundred useful observations! No, you only have one good observation. Even though you recorded one hundred heads, you only had one coin flip.

Things in time series are never quite as bad as this example. But time series are far more like a situation where you flip the coin and record the observation sometimes after two flips and sometimes after four flips. There will be a lot of inertia in your observations which invalidates the simple formulas. We'll need new ones.

In fact, in one sense, this dependency makes some things easier in time series. In time series, we watch something unfold slowly over time. If the economy changes slowly, then we can use the past as a useful guide to the future. Want to know what next month's unemployment rate will be? It will very likely be close to this month's rate. And it will be changing by roughly the same amount as it changed in the recent past.

1.2 Notation

In what follows, we will try to maintain the following notational conventions: random variables will be denoted by capital letters (X, Y, Z). Particular realizations of the random variable will take lowercase letters (x, y, z). The value of X at a particular time period t will be denoted X_t or x_t.

1.2 Notation

Unknown parameters will be denoted with Greek letters such as β, γ, μ.

Estimates of these parameters will be denoted with the notation ˆ (ex: $\hat{\beta}$) except where the notation becomes cumbersome.

Sometimes we will speak of a "lag operator" or a "lag polynomial." You can think of "lagging" as a function, which takes a value of the independent variable X_t and gives the dependent variable X_{t-1}.

The lag operator is denoted with a capital L. The lagged value of X_t is X_{t-1}; it is denoted L.X in Stata's notation and is read "the lag of X." If we wish to refer to an observation two periods ago, a lag of two is called for. That is, we may lag the lagged value of X. For Stata commands, we will often denote X_{t-2} as LL.X or L2.X. Likewise, the third lag would be LLL.X or L3.X, and so on. When using mathematical notation, we will refer to the second lag as $L^2 X$, the third lag as $L^3 X$, the kth lag as $L^k X$, and so forth.

It is important to note that raising L to an exponent is a notational convention. L is not a number, it is an operator, so the exponent just signifies how many times an operation is to be carried out.

Often, we will wish to calculate the "first difference of a variable," or more simply "the difference": $X_t - X_{t-1}$. Stata's notation for the first difference of X is D.X where D is a "difference operator." The lag and difference operators are related. After all, the difference of X_t is simply X_t minus the lag of X_t:

$$X_t - X_{t-1} = \text{D.X} = (1 - L)X_t = \text{X-L.X}$$

We can raise the difference operator D or $(1 - L)$ to an exponent, just as we did with L. For example, we may want to difference a differenced series. That is, given X_t, we can calculate the first difference as $X_t - X_{t-1}$ which we will denote, here, Z_t. We can even calculate the first difference of Z_t; calling it, say Y_t:

$$\begin{aligned} Y_t &= Z_t - Z_{t-1} \\ &= (X_t - X_{t-1}) - (X_{t-1} - X_{t-2}) \\ &= X_t - 2X_{t-1} + X_{t-2}. \end{aligned}$$

That is, the first difference of a first difference is called a "second difference."

For notational simplicity, we denote the second difference as D^2. Thus, the second difference of X_t is $D^2 X_t$. The third difference of X_t is $D^3 X_t$. The kth difference is $D^k X_t$. As with L, raising D to a power denotes the number of times that differencing is to occur.

Likewise, the second difference of X_t is:

$$\begin{aligned} D^2 &= (1 - L)^2 X \\ &= (X_t - X_{t-1}) - (X_{t-1} - X_{t-2}) \\ &= X_t - 2X_{t-1} + X_{t-2}. \end{aligned}$$

Calculating second differences is quite easy in Stata: D.X for first differences, DD.X or D2.X for second differences, etc....

Quite often, the differenced variable has a financial interpretation. For example, if X_t is the price of a stock at time t, then $D.X = (1 - L)X = X_t - X_{t-1}$ is the return on the stock. In fact, differencing is the discrete-time analogue to "taking the derivative." If X is the position of an object, then D.X is its velocity, and D2.X is its acceleration. Likewise, if X is the price of an asset, D.X is its return, and D2.X is the rate at which the returns are increasing or decreasing.

For practice, let us open a very small dataset in Stata and calculate the first and second lags and the first and second differences using Stata.

```
. use DandL.dta, clear
. list

     +-----------+
     | time   X  |
     |-----------|
  1. |   1   10  |
  2. |   2   13  |
  3. |   3   10  |
  4. |   4    8  |
  5. |   5   15  |
     +-----------+

. gen LagX = L.X
(1 missing value generated)

. gen SecLagX = L2.X
(2 missing values generated)

. gen Y = D.X          //Y is the first difference of X
(1 missing value generated)

. gen Z = D.Y          //Z is the first difference of Y, and 2nd diff of X.
(2 missing values generated)

. list

     +------------------------------------------+
     | time   X   LagX   SecLagX    Y     Z  |
     |------------------------------------------|
  1. |   1   10    .        .       .     .  |
  2. |   2   13   10        .       3     .  |
  3. |   3   10   13       10      -3    -6  |
  4. |   4    8   10       13      -2     1  |
  5. |   5   15    8       10       7     9  |
     +------------------------------------------+
```

Notice that a lagged variable shifts the column of data down by one row.

1.3 Statistical Review

In this section, we dust off some cobwebs and refresh the basic rules of probability.

Given a random variable X, its probability distribution function f(x) is a function that assigns a probability to each possible outcome of X. For example, suppose you are flipping a coin; the random variable X is whether the coin shows heads or tails, and to these two outcomes, we assign a probability of Pr(X=heads) = 1/2, and Pr(X=tails) = 1/2.

Continuous variables are those that can take on any value between two numbers. Between 1 and 100, there is an infinite continuum of numbers. Discrete numbers are more like the natural numbers. They take on distinct values. Things that are not normally thought of as numeric can also be coded as discrete numbers. A common example is pregnancy, a variable that is not intrinsically numeric. Pregnancy status might be coded as a zero/one variable, one if the person is pregnant and zero otherwise.

Some discrete random variables in economics are a person's unemployment status, whether two countries are in a monetary union, the number of members in the OPEC, and whether a country was once a colony of the UK.[1] Some discrete random variables in finance include whether a company is publicly traded or not, the number of times it has offered dividends, or the number of members on the board.

Continuous financial random variables include the percent returns of a stock, the amount of dividends, and the interest rate on bonds. In economics, GDP, the unemployment rate, and the money supply are all continuous variables.

If the list of all possible outcomes of X has discrete outcomes, then we can define the mean (aka average or expectation) of X as:

$$E(X) = \sum x_i Pr(X = x_i).$$

If X is a continuous variable, then we generalize from summations to integrals and write:

$$E(X) = \int x f(x) \, dx.$$

The population mean of X will be denoted μ_X and the sample mean, $\bar{X}$. We will switch between the notations E(X) and μ_X as convenient.

The population variance of a random variable is the average squared deviation of each outcome from its mean:

$$Var(X) = \sigma_x^2$$

---

[1] Acemoglu et al. (2000) argue that a colonizing country might negatively affect a colony's legal and cultural institutions. To the extent that those institutions are still around today, the colonial history from dozens if not hundreds of years ago could have a lingering effect.

$$= E\left(X^2\right) - E(X)E(X)$$
$$= 1/N \sum (x_i - E(X))^2$$
$$= \int (x_i - E(X))^2 \, dx,$$

depending on whether X is discrete or continuous. The sample variance replaces N with $(n-1)$ and the notation changes from σ^2 to s^2.

The standard deviation is the square root of the variance:

$$\sigma = \sqrt{\sigma^2}$$
$$s = \sqrt{s^2}.$$

In either case, the standard deviation will often be denoted $Stdev(X)$.

The covariance of two random variables X and Y is defined as:

$$Cov(X, Y) = \frac{1}{N} \sum (x_i - E(X))(y_i - E(y)) = E(XY) - E(X)E(Y).$$

The correlation between X and Y would then be defined as:

$$Corr(X, Y) = \frac{Cov(X, Y)}{Stdev(X)\,Stdev(Y)}.$$

If X and Y are random variables, and a and b are constants, then some simple properties of the statistics listed above are:

$$E(a) = a$$
$$E(aX) = aE(X)$$
$$Stdev(aX) = a\,Stdev(X)$$
$$Var(a) = 0$$
$$Var(aX) = a^2 Var(X)$$
$$Var(X) = Cov(X, X)$$
$$Cov(X, Y) = Cov(Y, X)$$
$$Cov(aX, bY) = ab\,Cov(X, Y)$$
$$Corr(aX, bY) = Corr(X, Y) = Corr(Y, X).$$

Adding a constant to a random variable changes its mean, but not its variance:

1.4 Specifying Time in Stata

$$E(a + X) = a + E(X)$$
$$V(a + X) = Var(X).$$

If two random variables are added together, then it can be shown that

$$E(aX + bY) = E(aX) + E(bY) = aE(X) + bE(Y)$$
$$Var(aX + bY) = a^2 Var(X) + b^2 Var(Y) + 2ab Cov(X, Y).$$

Suppose that every realization of a variable e is drawn independently of each other from the same identical normal distribution:

$$e_t \sim N(0, \sigma^2)$$

so that $E(e_t) = 0$, and $Var(e_t) = \sigma^2$ for all t. In this case we say that e_t is distributed "iid normal", or "independently and identically distributed" from a normal distribution. If this is the case, then you should be able to show that:

$$Var(e_t) = E\left(e_t^2\right) - E(e_t)E(e_t) = E\left(e_t^2\right)$$
$$Cov(e_t, e_{j \neq t}) = E(e_t e_{j \neq t}) - E(e_t)E(e_{j \neq t}) = 0 - 0 = 0$$
$$Corr(e_t, e_{j \neq t}) = \frac{Cov\left(e_t, e_{j \neq t}\right)}{Stdev(e_t) \, Stdev\left(e_{j \neq t}\right)} = 0.$$

In other words, the variance formula simplifies, the variable does not covary with itself across any lag, and the variable is not correlated with itself across any lag.

1.4 Specifying Time in Stata

For time series, the order of observations is important. In fact, it is the defining feature of time series. Order matters. First, one thing happens, then another, and another still. This happens over time. You can't rearrange the order without changing the problem completely. If sales are trending down, you can't just rearrange the observations so that the line trends up. This is different from cross sections where the order of observations is irrelevant. You might want to know what the correlation is between heights and weight; whether you ask Adam before Bobby won't change their heights or weights.

Given that time is the defining feature of time series, Stata needs to have a time variable. It needs to know which observation came first and which came second. Suppose your observations were inputted with the first observation in, say, row one, and the second observation in row two, and so forth. Then it might be pretty obvious to you that the data are already in the proper order. But Stata doesn't know that. It needs a variable (a column in its spreadsheet) that defines time. In our case, we could just create a new variable called, say, `time` that is equal to the row number.

```
. generate time = _n
```

But just because we named the variable "`time`" doesn't mean that Stata understands what it is. To Stata, the variable `time` is just another variable. We need to tell it that `time` establishes the proper order of the data. We do this by using the `tsset` command:

```
. tsset time
```

Sometimes we might import a dataset that already has a variable indicating time. Stata needs to be told which variable is the time variable. To check whether a time variable has already been declared, you can type

```
. tis
```

and Stata will tell you which variable has been `tsset`, if any. If no variable has already been `tsset`, then you must do it yourself.

If you are certain that there are no gaps in your data (no missing observations), then you could simply just `sort` your data by the relevant variable and then `generate` a new time variable using the two commands above. This simple procedure will get you through most of the examples in this book.

If there are gaps, however, then you should be a bit more specific about your time variable. Unfortunately, this is where things get tricky. There are a myriad different ways to describe the date (ex: Jan 2, 2003; 2nd January 2003; 1/2/2003; 2-1-03; and so on). There are almost as many different ways to `tsset` your data in Stata. Alas, we must either show you specifics as they arise, or ask you to consult Stata's extensive documentation.

1.5 Installing New Stata Commands

Stata comes off the shelf with an impressive array of time series commands. But it is a fully programmable language, so many researchers have written their own commands. Many are downloadable directly from Stata.

In this book we'll make heavy use of three user-written commands to download data in Stata-readable format: `fetchyahooquotes` (Dicle & Levendis, 2011), `freduse` (Drukker, 2006), and `wbopendata` (Azevedo, 2011).

The first of these, `fetchyahooquotes`, downloads publicly available financial data from Yahoo! Finance. Macroeconomic data for the United States can be downloaded from FRED, the Federal Reserve Bank of St. Louis' economic database, using the `freduse` command. Finally, `wbopendata` downloads worldwide macroeconomic data from the World Bank's online database.

If these commands are not already installed on your computer, you can download and install them by typing the following:

```
. net install ///
    http://researchata.com/stata/203/fetchyahooquotes.pkg, force
. net install st0110_1.pkg    // freduse
. net install wbopendata.pkg  // wbopendata
```

The following commands will also be used as needed. Some students may wish to install them all at once; others will install as needed.

```
. net install sim_arma.pkg    // Generates ARIMA data
. net install sts15_2.pkg     // KPSS unit root test
. net install zandrews.pkg    // Zivot-Andrews
. net install st0085_2.pkg    // estout package
. net install st0455.pkg      // pvar estimation
. net install xtvar.pkg       // pvar estimation
. net install xtfisher        // Fisher panel unit root test
. net install st0159_1        // xtabond2
. net install st0439          // xtcips
. net install xtbreak         // xtbreak
```

1.6 Exercises

1. Given the time series: X = [2, 4, 6, 8, 10], where $X_1 = 2$, $X_2 = 4,\ldots$, and $X_5 = 10$. Calculate the first and second lags of X. Also calculate the first and second differences of X. Do these by hand.
2. Given the time series: X = [10, 15, 23, 20, 19], where $X_1 = 10$, $X_2 = 15,\ldots$ Calculate the first and second lags and the first and second differences of X. Do these by hand.
3. Enter into Stata the following time series: X = [10, 15, 23, 20, 19]. Create a time variable (with values 1 through 5) and tell Stata that these are a time series (tsset time). Using Stata, calculate first and second lags and the first and second differences of X.
4. Download the daily adjusted closing price of IBM stock from 1990-2012 using fetchyahooquotes. Take the natural logarithm of this price. Then, using Stata's D notation, generate a new variable containing the percentage returns of IBM's share price (the first difference of the logs is equal to the percentage change). What is the average daily rate of return for IBM during this period? On which date did IBM have its highest percentage returns? On which date did it have its lowest percentage returns?
5. Download the daily adjusted closing price of MSFT stock from 2000-2012 using fetchyahooquotes. Take the natural logarithm of this price. Then, using Stata's D notation, generate a new variable containing the percentage returns of Microsoft's share price. (The first difference of the logs is equal to the percentage change.) What is the average daily rate of return for Microsoft during this period? On which date did Microsoft have its highest percentage returns? On which date did it have its lowest percentage returns?
6. Suppose midterm grades were distributed normally, with a mean of 70 and a standard deviation of 10. Suppose further that the professor multiplies each

exam by 1.10 as a curve. Calculate the new mean, standard deviation, and variance of the curved midterm grades.

7. Suppose X is distributed normally with a mean of five and a standard deviation of two. What is the expected value of 10X? What is the expected value of 20X? What are the variance and standard deviations of 5X and of 10X?

8. Suppose that two exams (the midterm and the final) usually have averages of 70 and 80, respectively. They have standard deviations of 10 and 7, and their correlation is 0.80. What is their covariance? Suppose that the exams were not weighted equally. Rather, in calculating the course grade the midterm carries a weight of 40% and the final has a weight of 60%. What is the expected grade for the course? What is the variance and standard deviation for the course grade?

9. Suppose that an exam has an average grade of 75 and a standard deviation of 10. Suppose that the professor decided to curve the exams by adding five points to everyone's score. What are the mean, standard deviation, and variance of the curved exam?

10. Suppose that in country A, the price of a widget has a mean of $100 and a variance of $25. Country B has a fixed exchange rate with A, so that it takes two B-dollars to equal one A-dollar. What is the expected price of a widget in B-dollars? What is its variance in B-dollars? What would the expected price and variance equal if the exchange rate were three-to-one?

ARMA(p,q) Processes

2.1 Introduction

A long-standing dream of economists was to build a massive model of the economy: one with supply and demand equations for each of the thousands of inputs, intermediate goods, and final products. One would only need to estimate the relevant elasticities and a few simple parameters to construct an economic crystal ball. It would be able to make accurate forecasts and useful policy prescriptions. Most economists wished this at one point. Slowly, though, the era of optimism in structural macroeconomic forecasting during the 1950s and 1960s became an era of doubt during the 1970s and 1980s.

The Cowles Commission typified the large-scale systems-of-equations approach to macroeconomic forecasting. Founded in 1932 and currently at Yale University, it was staffed by the best and the brightest economists and statisticians.[1] Three economists earned their Nobel Prizes for research directly associated with the econometric project at the Cowles Commission: Tjalling Koopmans (in 1975), Lawrence Klein (in 1980), and Trygve Haavelmo (in 1989).

At its height, the Cowles model consisted of almost four hundred equations. For decades it was the method of choice for economic forecasting and policy analysis.

---

[1] The list of influential economists who have worked in some capacity at the Cowles Commission is astounding. All in all, 13 Nobel Prize-winning economists have worked at the commission including Maurice Allais, Kenneth Arrow, Gerard Debreu, Ragnar Frisch, Trygve Haavelmo, Lenoid Hurwicz, Lawrence Klein, Tjalling Koopmans, Harry Markowitz, Franco Modigliani, Edmund Phelps, Joseph Stiglitz, and James Tobin. Not all were involved in the econometric side of the Cowles Commission's work.

But by the 1970s, economists began to have doubts about the enterprise. Several factors worked to end the dominance of the Cowles Commission approach:[2]

First, the models stopped working well. To patch them up, the economists began adding ad hoc terms to the equations.[3]

Second, Robert Lucas (1976) levied a powerful theoretical critique. He argued that the estimated parameters for each of the equations weren't structural. For example, they might have estimated that the marginal propensity to consume, in a linear consumption function, was, say, 0.80. That is, on average people consume 80% of their income. Lucas argued that this might be the optimal consumption amount because of a particular set of tax or monetary policies. Change the tax structure, and people will change their behavior. The models, then, are not useful at all for policy analysis, only for forecasting within an unchanging policy regime.

Third, a series of papers compared revealed that large-scale econometric models were outperformed by far simpler models. These simple models—called ARIMA models—are the subject of the present chapter. Naylor et al. (1972) found that ARIMA outperformed Wharton's more complex model by 50% in forecasting GNP, unemployment, inflation, and investment. Cooper (1972) compared even simpler AR models with the forecasting ability of seven leading large-scale models. For almost all of the thirty-one variables he examined, the simpler models were superior. Charles R. Nelson (1972) examined critically the performance of a large-scale model jointly developed by the Federal Reserve Bank, MIT, and the University of Pennsylvania. By 1972 the FRB-MIT-Penn model used 518 parameters to investigate 270 economic variables (Ando et al., 1972). In fact, Nelson showed that this complex model was outperformed by the simplest of time series models, embarrassingly simple models. One variable regressed on itself usually produced better forecasts than the massive FRB model.

An ARIMA model is made up of two components: an autoregressive (AR) model and a moving average (MA) model. Both rely on previous data to help predict future outcomes. AR and MA models are the building blocks of all our future work in this text. They are foundational, so we'll proceed slowly.

In Chap. 10 we will discuss VAR models. These models generalize univariate autoregressive models to include systems of equations. They have come to be the replacement for the Cowles approach. But first, we turn to two subsets of ARIMA models: autoregressive (AR) models and moving average (MA) models.

---

[2] For a brief discussion of the Cowles approach, see Fair (1992). Epstein (2014) provides much more historical detail. Diebold (1998) provides some historical context, as well as a discussion of the more current macroeconomic forecasting models that have replaced the Cowles approach.

[3] This is reminiscent of adding epicycles to models of the geocentric universe. The basic model wasn't fitting the data right, so they kept adding tweaks on top of tweaks to the model, until the model was no longer elegant.

2.1.1 Stationarity

In order to use AR and MA models, the data have to be "well behaved." Formally, the data need to be "stationary." We will hold off rigorously defining and testing for stationarity for later chapters. For now, let us make the following loose simplifying assumptions. Suppose you have a time series on a variable, X, that is indexed by a time subscript t, so that $X_t = X_0, X_1, X_2$, and so forth. Then X is "mean stationary" if the expected value of X at a particular time does not depend upon the particular time period in which it is observed. Thus, the unconditional expectation of X is not a function of the time period t:

$$E(X_t) = E(X_1) = E(X_2) = \cdots = E(X) = \mu. \tag{2.1}$$

Likewise, X is said to be "variance stationary" if its variance is not a function of time, so that

$$Var(X_t) = Var(X_1) = Var(X_2) = \cdots = Var(X) = \sigma^2. \tag{2.2}$$

Figure 2.1 illustrates a time series that is mean stationary (it reverts back to its average value) but is not variance stationary (its variance fluctuates over time with periods of high volatility and low volatility).

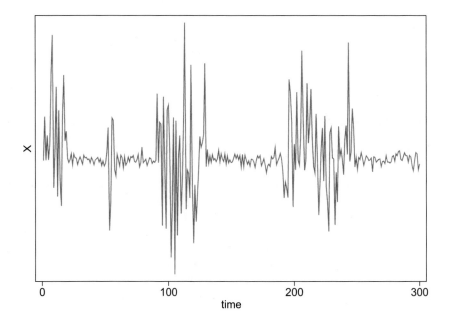

Fig. 2.1 X is mean stationary but not variance stationary

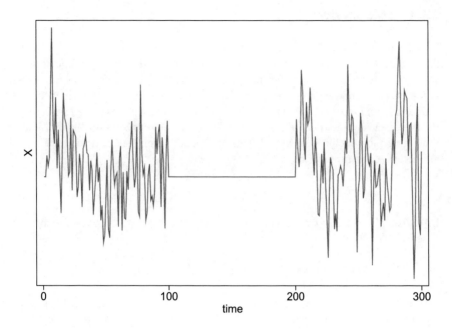

Fig. 2.2 X is mean stationary but neither variance nor covariance stationary

Finally, X is "covariance stationary" if the covariance of X with its own lagged values depends only upon the length of the lag, but not on the specific time period nor on the direction of the lag. Symbolically, for a lag length of one,

$$Cov(X_t, X_{t+1}) = Cov(X_{t-1}, X_t) \tag{2.3}$$

and for all lag lengths of k,

$$Cov(X_t, X_{t+k}) = Cov(X_{t+1}, X_{t+k+1}) = Cov(X_{t-1}, X_{t+k-1}). \tag{2.4}$$

An example of a time series that is not covariance stationary is one where there is seasonality, with the size of the seasonality fluctuating over time.

Figure 2.2 illustrates a different example of a time series that is not covariance stationary. In this example each value of X is weakly correlated with its previous value, at least in the first and final thirds of the dataset. In the middle third, however, each value of X is perfectly correlated with its previous value. This implies that its variance is also not stationary, since the variance in the middle third is zero.

2.1.2 A Purely Random Process

Suppose you are the manager at a casino, and one of your jobs is to track and predict the flow of cash into and from the casino. How much cash will you have on hand on Tuesday of next week? Suppose you have daily data extending back for the previous 1000 days.

Let X_t denote the net flow of cash into the casino on day t. Can we predict tomorrow's cash flow (X_{t+1}), given what happened today (X_t), yesterday (X_{t-1}), and before?

Consider a model of the following form:

$$X_t = e_t$$

where the errors are normally distributed with mean of zero and variance of one,

$$e_t \sim iidN(0, 1)$$

in all time periods. In other words, X is just pure random error. This is not a very useful, or even accurate, model of a Casino's cash flows, but it is a useful starting point pedagogically. Each day's cash flow is completely independent of the previous days' flow, and moreover, the amount of money coming into the casino is offset, on average, by cash outflow. In other words, the average cash flow is zero. That is,

$$E(X_t) = E(e_t) = 0$$

since the mean of e_t is zero for all t.

This process is mean stationary: the expected value of X is zero, no matter which time period we're in. This process is also variance stationary, because $V(X_t) = V(e_t) = 1$ for all t. And since the X_ts are all just independent draws from the same distribution, they are uncorrelated with each other; thus, $Cov(X_t = X_{t-k}) = 0$ making X covariance stationary.

Exercise
1. Using the definitions in Eqs. (2.3) and (2.4), show whether the purely random process

$$X_t = \beta_0 + e_t \quad \text{with} \quad e_t \sim iidN(0, 1)$$

is mean stationary, variance stationary, and covariance stationary.

2.2 AR(1) Models

Consider, now, a different type of model:

$$X_t = \beta X_{t-1} + e_t. \tag{2.5}$$

We'll look more closely at this simple random process. It is the workhorse of time series econometrics and we will make extensive use of its properties throughout this text.

Here, the current realization of X depends in part X's value last period plus some random error. If we were to estimate this model, we'd regress X on itself (lagged one period). This is why the model is called an "autoregressive model with lag one" or "AR(1)" for short. An autoregression is a regression of a variable on itself.

2.2.1 Estimating an AR(1) Model

One of the appeals of AR models is that they are quite easy to estimate. An AR(1) model consists of X regressed on its first lag. As expressed in Eq. (2.5), there is no constant in the model, so we can estimate it using the standard `regress` command with the `nocons` option. Let's try this on a simple dataset, `ARexamples.dta`.

```
. use "ARexamples.dta", clear

. regress X L.X, nocons

      Source |       SS           df       MS      Number of obs   =     2,999
-------------+----------------------------------   F(1, 2998)      =   1135.56
       Model |  1115.36604         1  1115.36604   Prob > F        =    0.0000
    Residual |  2944.69279     2,998  .982219076   R-squared       =    0.2747
-------------+----------------------------------   Adj R-squared   =    0.2745
       Total |  4060.05883     2,999  1.35380421   Root MSE        =    .99107

------------------------------------------------------------------------------
           X |      Coef.   Std. Err.      t    P>|t|     [95% Conf. Interval]
-------------+----------------------------------------------------------------
           X |
         L1. |   .5241678   .0155548    33.70   0.000     .4936685    .554667
------------------------------------------------------------------------------
```

The `nocons` option tells Stata not to include a constant term in the regression. Our estimated model is

$$X_t = 0.524 X_{t-1} + e_t.$$

The data were constructed specifically for this chapter and came from an AR(1) process where the true value of $\beta = 0.50$. Our estimate of 0.524 is fairly close to this true value.

Another way to estimate this model is to use Stata's `arima` command.

2.2 AR(1) Models

```
. arima X, ar(1) nocons nolog

ARIMA regression

Sample:  1 - 3000                         Number of obs    =       3000
                                          Wald chi2(1)     =    1138.20
Log likelihood = -4229.18                 Prob > chi2      =     0.0000

------------------------------------------------------------------------
             |                 OPG
         X   |    Coef.   Std. Err.     z    P>|z|   [95% Conf. Interval]
-------------+----------------------------------------------------------
ARMA         |
          ar |
         L1. |   .52404    .015533   33.74   0.000    .4935959   .5544842
-------------+----------------------------------------------------------
      /sigma |  .9907818   .0128047  77.38   0.000    .9656851   1.015878
------------------------------------------------------------------------
Note: The test of the variance against zero is one sided, and the two-sided
confidence interval is truncated at zero.
```

As before, the `nocons` option tells Stata not to include a constant. The `nolog` option declutters the output but does not affect the estimates in any way.

There are very small differences in the two estimates. The `arima` command uses an iterative procedure to maximize the likelihood function. This iterative procedure sometimes converges on an estimate that is slightly different from the one using the `regress` command. Another difference is that it uses one more observation than does `regress`.

Why does Stata use a more complicated procedure than OLS? Actually, OLS is a biased estimator of a lagged dependent variable. This bias goes away in large samples.

Problems with OLS in Models with LDVs

AR models explicitly have lagged dependent variables (LDVs). This implies that, even if the errors are iid and serially uncorrelated, OLS estimates of the parameters will be biased.

To see this, consider a simple AR(1) model:

$$X_t = \beta X_{t-1} + e_t \tag{2.6}$$

where $|\beta| < 1$ and $e_t \sim iidN(0, \sigma^2)$. (We will see shortly that this restriction on β implies that $E(X) = \bar{X} = 0$.) The variable X_{t-1} on the right-hand side is a lagged dependent variable. Running ordinary least squares (OLS) of X on its lag produces a biased (but consistent) estimate of β. To see this, recall from introductory econometrics that the OLS estimate of β is

$$\hat{\beta}_{OLS} = \frac{Cov(X_t, X_{t-1})}{Var(X_{t-1})} = \frac{\sum X_t X_{t-1}}{\sum X_{t-1}^2}.$$

Plugging in X_t from Eq. (2.6) gives

$$\hat{\beta}_{OLS} = \frac{\sum (\beta X_{t-1} + e_t) X_{t-1}}{\sum X_{t-1}^2}$$

$$= \frac{\sum \left(\beta X_{t-1}^2 + e_t X_{t-1}\right)}{\sum X_{t-1}^2}$$

$$= \frac{\sum \beta X_{t-1}^2}{\sum X_{t-1}^2} + \frac{\sum e_t X_{t-1}}{\sum X_{t-1}^2}$$

Since β is a constant, we can pull it out of the summation and simplify:

$$\hat{\beta}_{OLS} = \beta \frac{\sum X_{t-1}^2}{\sum X_{t-1}^2} + \frac{\sum e_t X_{t-1}}{\sum X_{t-1}^2}$$

$$= \beta + \frac{\sum e_t X_{t-1}}{\sum X_{t-1}^2}.$$

Thus, we can see that the OLS estimate $\hat{\beta}_{OLS}$ is equal to the true value of β plus some bias.[4] Fortunately, this bias shrinks in larger samples (that is, the estimate is said to be "consistent").

If the errors are autocorrelated, then the problem is worse. OLS estimates are biased and inconsistent. That is, the problem of bias doesn't go away even in infinitely large samples. We illustrate this problem with some simulated data and graph the sampling distribution of the OLS estimator. Figures 2.3 and 2.4 show the performance of OLS. Figure 2.3 shows that OLS estimates on LDVs are biased in small samples, but that this bias diminishes as the sample size increases. Figure 2.4 shows that OLS' bias does not diminish in the case where the errors are autocorrelated.

Below is the core part of the Stata code used to generate Figs. 2.3 and 2.4.

```
. drop _all
. set seed 123
. postfile buffer beta1 using filename, replace

. forvalues i = 1/1000   /*The number of replications*/ {
.         qui drop _all
.         qui set obs 20    /*The number of observations*/
.         qui gen time = _n
.         qui tsset time
.         qui gen double error = rnormal()
```

---

[4] I am indebted to Keele & Kelly (2005) who showed the algebra behind OLS' bias when used with lagged dependent variables.

2.2 AR(1) Models

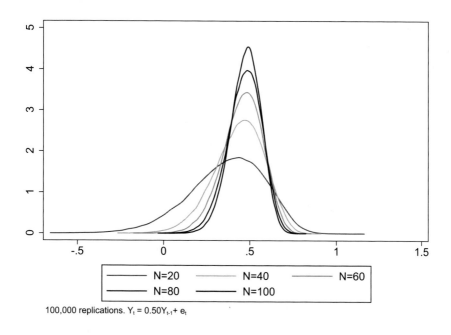

100,000 replications. $Y_t = 0.50Y_{t-1} + e_t$

Fig. 2.3 OLS on an LDV is biased but consistent

```
.           * Generate Y
.           qui gen double Y = .
.           qui replace Y = error in 1
.           qui replace Y = 0.50*L1.Y + error in 2/L

.           qui reg Y L1.Y   /*Estimates the regression*/
.           post buffer (_b[L.Y])  /*Saves the estimate*/
. }

. postclose buffer   /*Closes the file of the estimates*/

. * Kernel density graph
. use filename.dta , clear
. kdensity beta1
```

Summary stats for the OLS estimates of β are reported below for sample sizes of 20, 40, 60, 80, and 100:

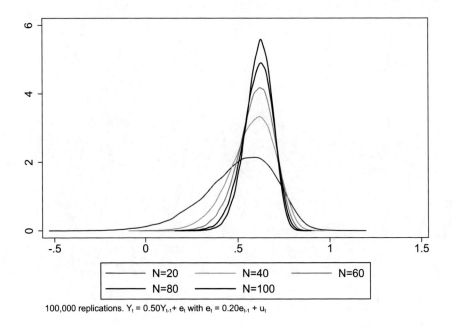

100,000 replications. $Y_t = 0.50Y_{t-1} + e_t$ with $e_t = 0.20e_{t-1} + u_t$

Fig. 2.4 OLS on a LDV with AR errors is inconsistent

```
. summarize beta1*
```

Variable	Obs	Mean	Std. Dev.	Min	Max
beta1_20	100,000	.3679739	.2153429	-.6380695	1.14319
beta1_40	100,000	.4358739	.145755	-.2541299	.8966309
beta1_60	100,000	.4570284	.1165173	-.1629504	.8422198
beta1_80	100,000	.4682731	.1001702	-.0235224	.8133429
beta1_100	100,000	.4741067	.0889166	-.0065295	.7684597

The table above and Fig. 2.3 shows that as the sample size increases, the OLS estimates get closer and closer to the true value of 0.50.

What about the case where the errors are autocorrelated? In this case, OLS estimates do not converge to 0.50 (see below and Fig. 2.4).

Variable	Obs	Mean	Std. Dev.	Min	Max
beta1_20	100,000	.5069872	.192547	-.5111647	1.179885
beta1_40	100,000	.5750127	.1241957	-.0797341	.9624402
beta1_60	100,000	.5956973	.0975625	-.02318	.9041315
beta1_80	100,000	.6065245	.0830323	.167726	.8898938
beta1_100	100,000	.6120668	.0733702	.1943227	.8459554

2.2 AR(1) Models

Rather, they get increasingly worse.

Now that we have estimated an AR(1) model, what does it mean? How do AR(1) models behave? We will answer these questions by examining the model's "impulse response function" or IRF.

2.2.2 Impulse Responses

If a time series X is known to be, or is well represented by, an AR(1) process, then we might ask: How does X respond to shocks? Does it dampen over time, or is the effect of the shock persistent? That is, we might want to know how X responds to an impulse shock over time. Or, in the language of time series analysis, "what is the impulse response function of X?"

An impulse response function (IRF) traces out the effect of a particular shock (say, e_0) on X_0, X_1, X_2, and subsequent values.

Given an estimated AR(1) model such as

$$X_t = 0.75 X_{t-1} + e_t,$$

let us trace out the estimated effects of a one-unit change in e_t. First, suppose that X has been constantly zero for each period leading up to the current period t.

$$X_{t-3} = 0.75\,(0) + 0 = 0$$
$$X_{t-2} = 0.75\,(0) + 0 = 0$$
$$X_{t-1} = 0.75\,(0) + 0 = 0$$

And now suppose that e receives a one-time shock of one unit in period t; that is, $e_t = 1$ in period t only.

$$X_t = 0.75 X_{t-1} + e_t = 0.75(0) + 1 = 1.$$

How will this shock affect subsequent values of X_t?

Plugging in this value into next period's function yields

$$X_{t+1} = 0.75 X_t + e_{t+1} = 0.75(1) + 0 = 0.75$$

Repeating this process, we get

$$X_{t+2} = 0.75 X_{t+1} + e_{t+2} = 0.75(0.75) + 0 = 0.75^2$$
$$X_{t+3} = 0.75 X_{t+2} + e_{t+3} = 0.75(0.75^2) + 0 = 0.75^3$$
$$X_{t+4} = 0.75 X_{t+3} + e_{t+4} = 0.75(0.75^3) + 0 = 0.75^4.$$

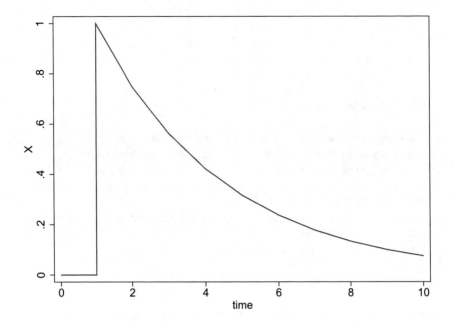

Fig. 2.5 The IRF of AR(1) process: $X_t = 0.75X_{t-1} + e_t$

Thus, we can see that a one-time one-unit shock onto X has a lingering, but exponentially decaying effect on X (Fig. 2.5).

So much for the theoretical IRF. What about an estimated—i.e., empirical—IRF? Stata can use the estimated model to calculate the IRF. Before we proceed, though, it would be beneficial to note that we were quite arbitrary in postulating a shock of one unit. The shock could have been any size we wished to consider. We could have considered a shock of, say, two or three units. A more common option would be to trace out the effect of a one standard deviation (of X) shock. In fact, this is the default in Stata.

Using Stata's `irf` post-estimation command, we can automatically graph the IRF of an estimated ARMA model. After estimating a model, you must first create a file to store the IRF's estimates and then ask for those estimates to be displayed graphically. We can do this by typing:

```
. use ARexamples.dta, clear
. arima X, ar(1) nocons
. irf create AR1, step(10) set(name)
. irf graph irf
. irf drop AR1
```

This creates the IRF as shown in Fig. 2.6.

2.2 AR(1) Models

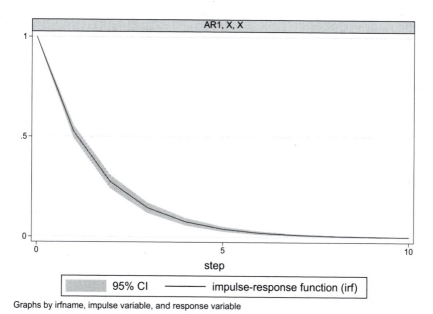

Fig. 2.6 The IRF of AR(1) process: $X_t = 0.52404 X_{t-1} + e_t$

Now let's get a little more general. Rather than assume $\beta = 0.75$, or 0.5236071, or some other particular number, let's keep β unspecified. To keep things simple, we will assume that Eq. (2.5) has $e_t \sim N(0, \sigma)$, and for stationarity, we'll assume that $-1 < \beta < 1$.

What is the average value of this process? Does the answer to this question depend upon the time period (i.e., is it mean stationary)? And how do previous shocks affect current realizations?

Rewriting Eq. (2.5) for period $t = 1$, we have

$$X_1 = \beta X_0 + e_1. \qquad (2.7)$$

Likewise, for periods $t = 2, 3, \ldots$

$$X_2 = \beta X_1 + e_2 \qquad (2.8)$$
$$X_3 = \beta X_2 + e_3 \qquad (2.9)$$

and so forth.

Substituting X_1 from (2.7) into X_2 (Eq. (2.8)), we have

$$X_2 = \beta X_1 + e_2$$

$$= \beta(\beta X_0 + e_1) + e_2$$
$$= \beta^2 X_0 + \beta e_1 + e_2.$$

Likewise, for X_3 and X_4, we have

$$X_3 = \beta X_2 + e_3$$
$$= \beta(\beta^2 X_0 + \beta e_1 + e_2) + e_3$$
$$= \beta^3 X_0 + \beta^2 e_1 + \beta e_2 + e_3$$
$$X_4 = \beta^4 X_0 + \beta^3 e_1 + \beta^2 e_2 + \beta e_3 + e_4.$$

Notice that the effect of the most recent shock (e_4) enters undiminished. The effect of the previous shock (e_3) is diminished since it is multiplied by the fraction β. The shock two periods earlier is diminished by a factor of β^2, and so forth. Since β is a number between -1 and 1, β^t can become quite small quite quickly.

A general pattern begins to emerge. In general, an AR(1) process can be expressed as

$$X_t = \beta X_{t-1} + e_t = \beta^t X_0 + \sum_{i=1}^{t} \beta^{t-i} e_i.$$

The impulse response k periods after the shock is

$$IRF(k) = \beta^k.$$

As we move farther away from X_0, the effect of X_0 becomes diminished since it is multiplied by β^t. All of the shocks have an effect, but their impact becomes negligible the farther back in time they occur. This would seem to be a nice feature for an economy. The economy gets hit by shocks all the time. But a healthy economy heals itself and re-equilibrates so that the negative effect of the shock fades into the distant past.

2.2.3 Forecasting

Let's suppose that X_t is evolves according to:

$$X_t = 0.75 X_{t-1} + e_t. \tag{2.10}$$

We do not usually know what the error terms are—we have to estimate them via the residuals—but let's pretend that we know them so we can better understand how the variable X_t evolves. For example, let's suppose that $X_0 = 100$ and that the first four error terms, drawn from a $N(0, 100)$ distribution, happen to be $e_t = [20, -30, 10, 15]$. Then the next four values of X_t are

$$X_1 = 0.75X_0 + e_1 = 0.75(100) + 20 = 95$$
$$X_2 = 0.75X_1 + e_2 = 0.75(95) - 30 = 41.25$$
$$X_3 = 0.75X_2 + e_3 = 0.75(41.25) + 10 = 40.9375$$
$$X_4 = 0.75X_3 + e_4 = 0.75(40.9375) + 15 = 45.7031$$

Forecasting out beyond where we have data, we can only comment on the expected value of X_5, conditional on all the previous data:

$$\begin{align} E(X_5 \mid X_4, X_3, \ldots) &= E(0.75X_4 + e_5 \mid X_4, X_3, \ldots) \\ &= E(0.75(45.7031) + e_5 \mid X_4, X_3, \ldots) \\ &= E(34.27725 + e_5 \mid X_4, X_3, \ldots) \\ &= 34.27725 + E(e_5 \mid X_4, X_3, \ldots). \end{align}$$

Since $e_t \sim iid N(0, 1)$, then its expectation is zero, and then

$$E(X_5 \mid X_4, X_3, \ldots) = 34.27725 + 0 = 34.27725.$$

What if we wanted to predict X two periods out? In other words, what if we had data only up to time $t = 4$ and wanted to predict X_6? In symbols, calculate: $E(X_6 \mid X_4, X_3 \ldots)$. The trick is to feed the forecast into itself:

$$\begin{align} E(X_6 \mid X_4, X_3 \ldots) &= E(\beta X_5 + e_6) \\ &= \beta E(X_5) + E(e_6) \\ &= 0.75(34.27725) + E(0) \\ &= 25.7079. \end{align}$$

Repeating the procedure, the two-periods-out forecast of X is

$$\begin{align} E(X_{t+2} \mid X_t, X_{t-1}, \ldots) &= E(\beta(\beta X_t + e_{t+1}) + e_{t+2}) \\ &= \beta\beta X_t + \beta E(e_{t+1}) + E(e_{t+2}) \\ &= \beta^2 X_t + \beta(0) + 0 \\ &= \beta^2 X_t \end{align}$$

and the three-periods-out forecast is

$$E(X_{t+3} \mid X_t, X_{t-1}, \ldots) = E(\beta X_{t+2} + e_{t+3})$$
$$= E(\beta X_{t+2}) + E(e_{t+3})$$
$$= \beta E(X_{t+2}) + 0$$
$$= \beta\left(\beta^2 X_t\right) + 0$$
$$= \beta^3 X_t.$$

Even more generally, given data up to period t, we can expect that the value of X_{t+a}, i.e., a periods ahead, will be

$$E(X_{t+a} \mid X_t, X_{t-1}, \ldots) = \beta^a X_t.$$

Since $|\beta| < 1$, this means that the one period ahead forecast is a fraction of today's X value. The forecast two periods ahead is twice as small; the three periods ahead forecast is smaller yet. In the limit, X is expected eventually to converge to its mean which, in this case, is equal to zero.

2.3 AR(p) Models

The idea of an autoregressive model can be extended to include lags reaching farther back than one period. In general, a process is said to be AR(p) if

$$X_t = \beta_1 X_{t-1} + \beta_2 X_{t-2} + \ldots + \beta_p X_{t-p} + e_t.$$

As before, we will assume that the process is stationary so that it has a constant mean, variance, and autocovariance.[5]

Usually, economic theory is silent on the number of lags to include. The matter is usually an econometric one: AR models with more lags can accommodate richer dynamics. Further, adding lags makes the residuals closer to white noise, a feature which aids in hypothesis testing. Occasionally, economic theory implies a model with a specific number of lags. Paul Samuelson's multiplier-accelerator model is an example of an AR(2) process from economic theory. Beginning with the GDP accounting identity for a closed economy with no governmental expenditure,

$$Y_t = C_t + I_t,$$

---

[5] For AR(p) models, the requirements for stationarity are a little more stringent than they are for AR(1) processes. Necessary conditions include that the βs each be less than one in magnitude, they must not sum to anything greater than plus or minus one, and they cannot be more than one unit apart. We will explore the stationarity restrictions at greater length in Chap. 4.

2.3 AR(p) Models

Samuelson adds the classic Keynesian consumption function with autonomous consumption (β_0) and marginal propensity to consume (β_1),

$$C_t = \beta_0 + \beta_1 Y_{t-1}$$

and an equation that models investment as depending on the amount of growth in consumption from last period to today:

$$I_t = \beta_2 (C_t - C_{t-1}) + e_t$$

These three equations imply an AR(2) model:

$$Y_t = \beta_0 + \beta_1(1 + \beta_2)Y_{t-1} - \beta_1\beta_2 Y_{t-2} + e_t$$

or

$$Y_t = \alpha_0 + \alpha_1 Y_{t-1} + \alpha_2 Y_{t-2} + e_t$$

with the α's properly defined. Samuelson's model accommodates different kinds of dynamics—dampening, oscillating, etc.—depending on the estimated parameters.

2.3.1 Estimating an AR(p) Model

Estimating an AR(p) model in Stata is just as easy as estimating an AR(1) model. Suppose we wanted to estimate an AR(3) model such as

$$X_t = \beta_1 X_{t-1} + \beta_2 X_{t-2} + \beta_3 X_{t-3} + e_t.$$

The following approaches will all estimate an AR(3) model:

- regress X L.X L2.X L3.X, nocons
- regress X L(1/3).X, nocons
- arima X, ar(1/3) nocons
- var X, lags(1/3) nocons

The first two are biased estimators. Notice also that Stata requires us to tell it which lags to include. The option ar(1/3) or lags(1/3) tells it that we want the first through third lags. If we had typed ar(3) or lags(3), it would have estimated an AR(3) model where the first two lags were set to zero:

$$\begin{aligned}X_t &= 0X_{t-1} + 0X_{t-2} + \beta_3 X_{t-3} + e_t \\ &= \beta_3 X_{t-3} + e_t.\end{aligned}$$

That is, ar(3) includes only the third lag.

Exercises

Let's practice estimating AR(p) models using the dataset `ARexamples.dta`. The dataset consists of a three variables (X, Y, and Z) and a time variable.

1. What is the equation of the AR(p) process corresponding to the following Stata estimation commands?
   (a) `arima X, ar(1/4) nocons`
   (b) `arima X, ar(1 2 4) nocons`
   (c) `arima X, ar(2 4) nocons`
2. Write out the `arima` estimation command you would use to estimate the following AR processes:
   (a) $X_t = \beta_1 X_{t-1} + \beta_2 X_{t-2} + \beta_3 X_{t-3} + \beta_4 X_{t-4} + e_t$
   (b) $X_t = \beta_1 X_{t-1} + \beta_2 X_{t-2} + \beta_3 X_{t-3} + e_t$
   (c) $X_t = \beta_1 X_{t-1} + \beta_4 X_{t-4} + e_t$
3. Using the `ARexamples.dta` dataset, graph the last 100 observations of X over time. Using all of the observations, estimate the AR(1) model,

$$X_t = \beta_1 X_{t-1} + e_t.$$

   Verify that the coefficient is approximately $\hat{\beta}_1 \approx 0.50$.

4. Using the `ARexamples.dta` dataset, graph the last 100 observations of Y over time. Using all of the observations, estimate the AR(2) model,

$$Y_t = \beta_1 Y_{t-1} + \beta_2 Y_{t-2} + e_t.$$

   Verify that the coefficients are approximately $\hat{\beta}_1 \approx 0.70$ and $\hat{\beta}_2 \approx 0.20$.

5. Using the `ARexamples.dta` dataset, graph the last 100 observations of Z over time. Using all of the observations, estimate the AR(3) model,

$$Z_t = \beta_1 Z_{t-1} + \beta_2 Z_{t-2} + \beta_3 Z_{t-3} + e_t.$$

   Verify that the coefficients are approximately $\hat{\beta}_1 \approx 0.60$, $\hat{\beta}_2 \approx 0.20$, and $\hat{\beta}_3 \approx 0.10$.

6. Using the `ARexamples.dta` dataset, estimate the AR(3) model,

$$Z_t = \beta_1 Z_{t-1} + \beta_3 Z_{t-3} + e_t.$$

   Notice that this is a restricted model, where the coefficient on the second lag is set to zero. Verify that the estimated coefficients are approximately $\hat{\beta}_1 \approx 0.70$, and $\hat{\beta}_3 \approx 0.20$.

2.3.2 Impulse Responses

The IRFs of AR(p) processes are only slightly more complicated than those for an AR(1) but the calculation procedure is essentially the same.

Suppose that X follows an AR(3) process,

$$X_t = \beta_1 X_{t-1} + \beta_2 X_{t-2} + \beta_3 X_{t-3} + e_t$$

and it has been estimated to be, say,

$$X_t = 0.60 X_{t-1} + 0.20 X_{t-2} + 0.10 X_{t-3} + e_t.$$

To calculate the IRF of this particular AR(3) model, let us assume as before, that X_t and e_t were equal to zero for every period up until and including period zero. Now, in period $t = 1$, X_1 receives a shock of one unit via e_1 (that is, $e_1 = 1$). Let us trace out the effect of this one-period shock on X_1 and subsequent periods:

$$\begin{aligned}
X_1 &= 0.60 X_0 + 0.20 X_{-1} + 0.10 X_{-2} + e_1 \\
&= 0.60(0) + 0.20(0) + 0.10(0) + 1 \\
&= 1 \\
X_2 &= 0.60 X_1 + 0.20 X_0 + 0.10 X_{-1} + e_2 \\
&= 0.60(1) + 0.20(0) + 0.10(0) + 0 \\
&= 0.60 \\
X_3 &= 0.60 X_2 + 0.20 X_1 + 0.10 X_0 + e_3 \\
&= 0.60(0.60) + 0.20(1) + 0.10(0) + 0 \\
&= 0.56 \\
X_4 &= 0.60 X_3 + 0.20 X_2 + 0.10 X_1 + e_4 \\
&= 0.60(0.56) + 0.20(0.60) + 0.10(1) + 0 \\
&= 0.556 \\
X_5 &= 0.60 X_4 + 0.20 X_3 + 0.10 X_2 + e_5 \\
&= 0.60(0.556) + 0.20(0.56) + 0.10(0.60) + 0 \\
&= 0.5056 \\
X_6 &= 0.60 X_5 + 0.20 X_4 + 0.10 X_3 + e_6 \\
&= 0.60(0.5056) + 0.20(0.556) + 0.10(0.56) + 0 \\
&= 0.47056
\end{aligned}$$

Just as in the case of the AR(1) process, the effect of the shock lingers on, but the effects decay.

We didn't estimate this model; we posited it, so we can't use `irf` after `arima` to automatically draw the impulse response functions. But we can get Stata to calculate the IRF's values by typing:

```
. drop _all
. set obs 25
. gen time = _n - 3
. tsset time
. gen X= 0                      //Initially, all observations
                                     are zero
. replace X = 1 in 3      //The one-unit shock
. replace X= 0.6*L.X + 0.2*LL.X + 0.1*LLL.X in 4/L
```

The last line above calculated the response, from the first period after the one-unit shock through to the last observation. (Stata denotes the last observation with a capital "L.") The results of this procedure are:

```
. list in 1/10
```

time	X
1. -2	0
2. -1	0
3. 0	1
4. 1	.6
5. 2	.56
6. 3	.556
7. 4	.5056
8. 5	.47056
9. 6	.439056
10. 7	.4081056

Stata's calculations verify our earlier by-hand estimates.

Exercises

1. Calculate by hand the IRFs out to five periods for the following AR models:
   (a) $X_t = 0.5X_{t-1} + e_t$
   (b) $X_t = -0.5X_{t-1} + e_t$
   (c) $X_t = 0.5X_{t-1} - 0.10X_{t-2} + e_t$
   (d) $X_t = 0.10 + 0.5X_{t-1} - 0.20X_{t-2} + e_t$
   (e) $X_t = X_{t-1} + e_t$

2.3 AR(p) Models

Explain how the dynamics change as the coefficients change, paying special attention to negative coefficients. Given the IRFs you calculated, do these all seem stationary? Why or why not?

2.3.3 Forecasting

Given that we have estimated an AR(p) model, how can we use it to forecast future values of X_t? In the same way that we did from an AR(1) model: iteratively. Let us work out a simple example by hand. Stata can calculate more extensive examples quite quickly—and we will see how to do this—but first it will be instructive to do it manually.

Suppose we estimated the following AR(3) model:

$$X_t = 0.75X_{t-1} + 0.50X_{t-2} + 0.10X_{t-3} + e_t. \quad (2.11)$$

Suppose further that $X_1 = 5$, $X_2 = -10$, and $X_3 = 15$. Given these values, what is the expected value of X_4? That is, what is $E(X_4 \mid X_3, X_2, X_1, \ldots)$? And rather than specifying all of those conditionals in the expectation, let's use the following notation: let $E_3(.)$ denote the expectation conditional on all information up to and including period 3.

$$
\begin{aligned}
E(X_4 \mid X_3, X_2, X_1, \ldots) &= E_3(X_4) \\
&= E_3\left(0.75X_3 + 0.50X_2 + 0.10X_1 + e_4\right) \\
&= 0.75X_3 + 0.50X_2 + 0.10X_1 + E_3(e_4) \\
&= 0.75(15) + 0.50(-10) + 0.10(5) + E_3(e_4) \\
&= 11.25 - 5 + 0.5 + 0 \\
&= 6.75.
\end{aligned}
$$

Given this expected value of $E(X_4)$, we use it to help us make forecasts farther out, at X_5 and beyond. We proceed in the same fashion as before. The expected value two periods out, at X_5, is

$$
\begin{aligned}
E(X_5 \mid X_3, X_2, X_1, \ldots) &= E_3\left(0.75X_4 + 0.50X_3 + 0.10X_2 + e_5\right) \\
&= 0.75E_3(X_4) + 0.50E_3(X_3) + 0.10E_3(X_2) + E_3(e_5) \\
&= 0.75(6.75) + 0.50(15) + 0.10(-10) + 0 \\
&= 11.5625.
\end{aligned}
$$

Stata can automate these calculations for us. If you'd like to forecast four periods out, add four blank observations to the end of your dataset. After estimating the model, use Stata's predict command to calculate the forecasts. For example, using the `ARexamples.dta` dataset, let's estimate an AR(3) model on the variable Z and then forecast out to four periods.

We begin by loading the data and estimating the model.

```
. use ARexamples.dta, clear

. arima Z, ar(1/3) nocons nolog

ARIMA regression

Sample:  1 - 3000                               Number of obs    =     3000
                                                Wald chi2(3)     =  9403.34
Log likelihood = -4305.155                      Prob > chi2      =   0.0000

------------------------------------------------------------------------------
             |                 OPG
           Z |      Coef.   Std. Err.      z    P>|z|     [95% Conf. Interval]
-------------+----------------------------------------------------------------
ARMA         |
          ar |
         L1. |   .6171596   .0181677    33.97   0.000     .5815516    .6527676
         L2. |   .1851499   .0204627     9.05   0.000     .1450438    .2252561
         L3. |   .1050058   .0180299     5.82   0.000     .0696679    .1403437
-------------+----------------------------------------------------------------
      /sigma |   1.015987   .0130895    77.62   0.000     .990332     1.041642
------------------------------------------------------------------------------
Note: The test of the variance against zero is one sided, and the two-sided
confidence interval is truncated at zero.
```

Next, we append four blank observations to the end of our dataset.

```
. tsappend, add(4)

. list Z in 2998/L

        +------------+
        |          Z |
        |------------|
 2998.  |  .68069001 |
 2999.  |  1.1054195 |
 3000.  |  .58345208 |
 3001.  |          . |
 3002.  |          . |
        |------------|
 3003.  |          . |
 3004.  |          . |
        +------------+
```

Finally, we use the `predict` command to have Stata calculate the forecasts:

```
. predict Zhat
(option xb assumed; predicted values)

. list Z Zhat in 2998/L

          +----------------------+
          |       Z       Zhat   |
          |----------------------|
   2998.  | .68069001   1.824737 |
   2999.  | 1.1054195   1.093875 |
   3000.  | .58345208    1.03031 |
   3001.  |        .    .6362278 |
   3002.  |        .    .6167556 |
          |----------------------|
   3003.  |        .       .5597 |
   3004.  |        .    .5264241 |
          +----------------------+
```

Exercises
1. Consider the model described in Eq. (2.11). In the text, we forecasted out to periods four and five. Now, forecast out from period six through period ten. Graph these first ten observations on X_t. Does X_t appear to be mean stationary?
2. Estimate an AR(3) model of the variable Z found in ARexamples.dta. Verify by hand Stata's calculations for the four-periods-out forecast of 0.526421 that was reported in our last example.

2.4 MA(1) Models

ARMA models are composed of two parts, the second of which is called a moving average (or "MA") model. AR models had autocorrelated Xs because current X depended directly upon lagged values of X. MA models, on the other hand, have autocorrelated Xs because the errors are, themselves, autocorrelated.

The simplest type of MA model is

$$X_t = e_t \tag{2.12a}$$

$$e_t = u_t + \beta u_{t-1} \tag{2.12b}$$

$$u_t \sim iidN(\mu, \sigma_u^2) \tag{2.12c}$$

which can be condensed to

$$X_t = u_t + \beta u_{t-1}. \tag{2.13}$$

It will be useful to differentiate between the errors (e_t) from the random shocks (u_t). The error terms (e_t) are autocorrelated. The shocks (u_t) are presumed to be white noise. That is, each u_t is drawn from the same normal distribution, independently of all the other draws of u in other time periods; thus, we say that the u_t's are independent and identically distributed from a normal distribution.

Such a model is called an MA(1) model because the shock shows up in Eq. (2.13) with a lag of one. The important thing to note is that the action in this model lies in the fact that the errors have a direct effect on X beyond the immediate term. They have some inertia to them.

Notice that $E(u_t u_{t-1})$ is equivalent to $E(u_{t-1} u_{t-2})$ because of stationarity. Also, recall that $u_t \sim iidN(\mu, \sigma_u^2)$, so that $E(u_t^2) = \sigma_u^2$. Since the u_t are all independent of each other, then it will always be the case that $E(u_t u_j) = 0$ for all $t \neq j$.

Since the errors (e_t) on X are autocorrelated, then X is also autocorrelated. What is the nature of this autocorrelation? At what lags is X autocorrelated? In other words, what is the autocorrelation function (ACF) of this MA(1) process?

2.4.1 Estimation

How does one estimate an MA(1) model in Stata? MA(1) models look like:

$$X_t = u_t + \beta u_{t-1}.$$

That is, X is a function, not of past lags of itself, but of past lags of unknown error terms. Thus, we cannot create a lagged-X variable to regress upon.

To estimate an MA(1) model in Stata, we can use the now-familiar `arma` command, with the `ma(1)` option:

```
. arima X, ma(1) nocons
```

Include `nocons` only in those cases where the AR or MA process has a mean of zero. If you graph the data and find that the observations doesn't hover around zero, then leave out the `nocons` option.

2.4.2 Impulse Responses

It is quite easy to calculate IRFs for MA processes. Presume X follows an MA(1) process that is equal to

$$X_t = u_t + 0.75 u_{t-1}$$

Let us presume that X and e have been equal to zero for every period, up until what we will call period $t = 1$, at which point X_1 receives a one-time shock equal to one unit, via u_1. In other words, $u_1 = 1$, $u_2 = 0$, $u_3 = 0$, and so forth. Let us trace out the effects of this shock:

2.4 MA(1) Models

$$X_1 = u_1 + 0.75(u_0) = 1 + 0.75(0) = 1$$
$$X_2 = u_2 + 0.75(u_1) = 0 + 0.75(1) = 0.75$$
$$X_3 = u_3 + 0.75(u_2) = 0 + 0.75(0) = 0$$
$$X_4 = u_4 + 0.75(u_3) = 0 + 0.75(0) = 0$$

and so forth.

Thus, we see that the IRF of an MA(1) process is quite short-lived. In fact, we will see shortly that the IRF of an MA(q) process is only nonzero for q periods. The practical implication of this is that a one-time shock to an MA process does not have lasting effects (unlike with an AR process). This has significant implications for economic policy. For example, if GDP follows an AR process, then the one-time shock of, say, the Arab oil embargo of 1973 will still influence the economy 35 years later in 2018. On the other hand, if memories are short, as in an MA process, then the economy recovers quickly, and we no longer suffer the effects of that economic shock. Once repealed, bad financial regulations, for example, will have a temporary—but only temporary—effect on financial markets if such markets are MA processes.

2.4.3 Forecasting

The iterative process for forecasting from MA(1) models is complicated by the fact that we are not able to directly use previous lagged Xs in helping us predict future Xs.

Let us work concretely with a simple MA(1) model:

$$X_t = u_t + \beta u_{t-1}.$$

And let us suppose that we have 100 observations of data on X, extending back from $t = -99$ through $t = 0$. Now we find ourselves at $t = 0$ and we wish to forecast next period's value, X_1. First, we estimate the parameter β, and let's suppose that $\hat{\beta} = 0.50$. Given the data and our estimated model, we can calculate the residuals from $t = -99$ through $t = 0$. These will be our best guess as to the actual errors (residuals approximate errors), and using these, we can forecast X_t. In other words, the procedure is as follows:

1. Estimate the model.

```
. arima X, ma(1) nocons
```

2. Calculate the fitted values from this model.

```
. predict Xhat
```

3. Calculate the residuals (r) between the data and the fitted values.

    . predict r, residuals

4. Feed these residuals, iteratively, into the estimated model: $X_t = r_t + \hat{\beta} r_{t-1}$,

$$E(X_1 \mid r_0) = E(r_1) + 0.5120095(r_0) = 0.5120095(r_0)$$

5. Return to step (3) and repeat.

We will work out an example "by hand" and in Stata.

```
. use MAexamples.dta, clear

. arima X, ma(1) nocons nolog

ARIMA regression

Sample:  1 - 3000                          Number of obs     =       3000
                                           Wald chi2(1)      =    1040.68
Log likelihood = -4230.101                 Prob > chi2       =     0.0000

------------------------------------------------------------------------------
             |                 OPG
           X |      Coef.   Std. Err.      z    P>|z|     [95% Conf. Interval]
-------------+----------------------------------------------------------------
ARMA         |
          ma |
         L1. |   .5120095   .0158716    32.26   0.000     .4809017    .5431172
-------------+----------------------------------------------------------------
      /sigma |   .9910838   .0127745    77.58   0.000     .9660463    1.016121
------------------------------------------------------------------------------
Note: The test of the variance against zero is one sided, and the two-sided
confidence interval is truncated at zero.

. predict Xhat              // Calculate the fitted values
(option xb assumed; predicted values)

. predict r, residuals      // Calculate the residuals

. list X Xhat r in 2996/3000 // Listing the last 5 periods

       +------------------------------------+
       |         X         Xhat           r |
       |------------------------------------|
 2996. | -1.448623    -1.292183    -.1564398 |
 2997. |  .94783365   -.0800986    1.027932  |
 2998. | -.92384487    .526311    -1.450156  |
 2999. | -1.0000537   -.7424936    -.2575602 |
 3000. | -.59472139   -.1318733    -.4628481 |
       +------------------------------------+
```

2.4 MA(1) Models

To forecast X in period 3001, we need to add an empty observation in our dataset. We need a blank for Stata to fill in using the `predict` post-estimation command.

```
. tsappend, add(1)            // Adding a blank observation

. list X Xhat r in 2996/3001  // Listing the last 6 periods
```

```
     +----------------------------------------+
     |          X         Xhat          r    |
     |----------------------------------------|
2996.|  -1.448623   -1.292183    -.1564398    |
2997.|   .94783365   -.0800986    1.027932    |
2998.|  -.92384487    .526311    -1.450156    |
2999.|  -1.0000537   -.7424936   -.2575602    |
3000.|  -.59472139   -.1318733   -.4628481    |
     |----------------------------------------|
3001.|       .            .            .     |
     +----------------------------------------+
```

```
. drop Xhat

. predict Xhat                 // Re-calculating the fitted values
(option xb assumed; predicted values)
```

Stata has filled in the missing observation with the predicted value:

```
. list X Xhat r in 2996/3001   // Listing the last 6
  periods
```

```
     +----------------------------------------+
     |          X          Xhat          r    |
     |----------------------------------------|
2996.|   -1.448623    -1.292183    -.1564398  |
2997.|    .94783365   -.0800986     1.027932  |
2998.|   -.92384487    .526311     -1.450156  |
2999.|   -1.0000537   -.7424936    -.2575602  |
3000.|   -.59472139   -.1318733    -.4628481  |
     |----------------------------------------|
3001.|        .       -.2369826         .     |
     +----------------------------------------+
```

In the last time period ($t = 3000$), the value of X_{3000} is -0.59472139, and the predicted value of X_{3000} is -0.1318733, so the residual is -0.4628481. We can use the residual as our best guess for the error, and calculate the expectation of X_{3001} conditional on the previous period's residual:

$$E\left(X_{3001} \mid r_{3000}\right) = 0.5120095\left(r_{3000}\right) = 0.5120095\left(-0.4628481\right) = -0.2369826.$$

2.5 MA(q) Models

Moving average models can be functions of lags deeper than 1. The general form of the moving average model with lags of one through q, an MA(q) model, is

$$X_t = u_t + \beta_1 u_{t-1} + \beta_2 u_{t-2} + \ldots + \beta_q u_{t-q} = \sum_{i=0}^{q} u_{t-i} \beta_i, \qquad (2.14)$$

where β_0 is implicitly equal to one.

2.5.1 Estimation

It is easy to see that the MA(1) process we were working with in the previous section is a special case of the general MA(q) process, where β_2 through β_q are equal to zero.

We can use Stata's `arima` command to estimate MA(q) models. The general format is

```
. arima X, ma(1/q)
```

which estimates an MA model with q lags. For example, to estimate an MA(4) model, we can type

```
. arima X, ma(1/4)
```

Equivalently, we can specify each of the four lags:

```
. arima X, ma(1 2 3 4)
```

If you want to exclude specific lags from estimation,

```
arima X, ma(1 2 4)
```

specifies an MA model with only β_1, β_2, and β_4 as nonzero coefficients; β_3 is set to zero.

Example

Using `MAexamples.dta`, let's calculate an MA(3) model on the variable Y.

2.5 MA(q) Models

```
. use MAexamples.dta, clear

. arima Y, ma(1/3) nocons nolog

ARIMA regression

Sample:  1 - 3000                              Number of obs    =      3000
                                               Wald chi2(3)     =   1713.32
Log likelihood = -4203.531                     Prob > chi2      =    0.0000

------------------------------------------------------------------------------
             |                 OPG
           Y |      Coef.   Std. Err.      z    P>|z|     [95% Conf. Interval]
-------------+----------------------------------------------------------------
ARMA         |
          ma |
         L1. |   .7038533   .0184673    38.11   0.000     .667658    .7400487
         L2. |   .2275206   .0217738    10.45   0.000     .1848448   .2701963
         L3. |   .0328569   .018113      1.81   0.070    -.002644    .0683578
-------------+----------------------------------------------------------------
      /sigma |   .9823166   .0130024    75.55   0.000     .9568323   1.007801
------------------------------------------------------------------------------
Note: The test of the variance against zero is one sided, and the two-sided
confidence interval is truncated at zero.
```

Stata estimated the following MA(3) model:

$$\hat{Y}_t = u_t + \hat{\beta}_1 u_{t-1} + \hat{\beta}_2 u_{t-2} + \hat{\beta}_3 u_{t-3}$$
$$= u_t + (.7038533)\, u_{t-1} + (.2275206)\, u_{t-2} + (.0328569)\, u_{t-3}.$$

Since the coefficient on u_{t-3} is not significant at the 0.05 significance level, a case could be made for dropping that lag and estimating an MA(2) model instead.

Exercises

Use `MAexamples.dta` to answer the following questions.

1. A moment ago we estimated an MA(3) model on Y and found that the third lag was statistically insignificant at the 0.05 level. Drop that lag and estimate an MA(2) model instead. Write out the estimated equation. You should be able to verify that $\hat{\beta}_1 \approx 0.69$ and $\hat{\beta}_2 \approx 0.20$.
2. Estimate an MA(3) model on Z. Write out the estimated equation. Are all the lags statistically significant? You should be able to verify that $\hat{\beta}_1 \approx 0.60$, $\hat{\beta}_2 \approx 0.20$, and $\hat{\beta}_3 \approx 0.05$.

2.5.2 Impulse Responses

Calculating the IRF for an MA(q) process is quite straightforward. Suppose that X follows an MA(q) process such as

$$X_t = e_t + \beta_1 e_{t-1} + \beta_2 e_{t-2} + \ldots + \beta_q e_{t-q} = \sum_{i=0}^{q} e_{t-i} \beta_i.$$

Suppose, as before, that all the es (and therefore all the Xs) are equal to zero, up until what we will call period k. In period k, $e_k = 1$, a one-time one-unit shock, after which the e's return to being zero (i.e., $e_{k+1} = e_{k+2} = e_{k+3} = \ldots = 0$). Let us trace out the effects of this one-time shock:

$$X_k = e_k + \beta_1 e_{k-1} + \beta_2 e_{k-2} + \ldots + \beta_q e_{k-q}$$
$$= (1) + \beta_1(0) + \beta_2(0) + \ldots + \beta_{q-1}(0)$$
$$= 1.$$

Advancing one period,

$$X_{k+1} = e_{k+1} + \beta_1 e_k + \beta_2 e_{k-1} + \ldots + \beta_q e_{k-q+1}$$
$$= 0 + \beta_1(1) + \beta_2(0) + \ldots + \beta_q(0)$$
$$= \beta_1.$$

Two periods ahead,

$$X_{k+2} = \beta_2.$$

Looking to the qth period ahead,

$$X_{k+q} = \beta_q$$

after which the series is once again at its equilibrium level of zero and the effects of the one-time shock are completely eradicated from the economy.

Absent any seasonality, the βs are usually smaller at further lags; for example, it would be odd for an event two periods ago to have a larger effect, on average, than events only one period ago.

2.6 Nonzero ARMA Processes

By now we have, hopefully, become familiar with zero-mean AR(p) processes. You might have been wondering, though, why do we pay so much attention to a process

2.6 Nonzero ARMA Processes

with zero mean? Isn't that assumption very restrictive? How many things in life have an average value of zero, anyway?!

While many processes have a zero mean, many more do not. Neither GDP nor GNP vary around zero, nor do the unemployment rate, the discount rate, and the federal funds' rate. It turns out that the zero-mean assumption makes understanding the crucial concepts behind time series modeling much clearer. It also turns out that the zero-mean assumption isn't all that critical, and it is really easy to drop that assumption altogether.

2.6.1 Nonzero AR Processes

Consider a stationary AR(1) process with an additional constant term, β_0:

$$X_t = \beta_0 + \beta_1 X_{t-1} + e_t.$$

Taking expectations of both sides, we have

$$\begin{aligned} E(X_t) &= E(\beta_0 + \beta_1 X_{t-1} + e_t) \\ &= \beta_0 + E(\beta_1 X_{t-1}) + E(e_t) \\ &= \beta_0 + \beta_1 E(X_{t-1}). \end{aligned}$$

Mean stationarity (i.e., $E(X_t) = E(X_{t-1})$) allows us to group terms and simplify further,

$$E(X_t) - \beta_1 E(X_t) = \beta_0$$
$$E(X_t)(1 - \beta_1) = \beta_0$$
$$E(X_t) = \frac{\beta_0}{1 - \beta_1}.$$

The mean of an AR process is proportional to the constant, but it is also influenced by X's correlation with its own lagged values.[6]

If the process were AR(p), then the expectation generalizes to

$$E(X_t) = \frac{\beta_0}{1 - \beta_1 - \beta_2 - \ldots \beta_p}.$$

What is the variance of a nonzero AR(1) process?

---

[6] Notice that it is critical that β_1 not be equal to one, as you'd be dividing by zero and the expectation would not be defined. This is a familiar result: stationarity requires that we not have a unit root. We will explore the consequences of such "unit roots" in Chap. 5.

$$Var(X_t) = Var(\beta_0 + \beta_1 X_{t-1} + e_t)$$
$$= Var(\beta_0) + Var(\beta_1 X_{t-1}) + Var(e_t)$$
$$= 0 + \beta_1^2 Var(X_{t-1}) + \sigma_e^2.$$

By stationarity, $Var(X_t) = Var(X_{t-1})$, so we can collect terms and simplify:

$$Var(X_t) = \beta_1^2 Var(X_t) + \sigma_e^2$$
$$= \frac{\sigma_e^2}{1 - \beta_1^2}. \qquad (2.15)$$

Notice that β_0 does not show up in Eq. (2.15). Thus, adding a constant (β_0) changes the mean but it does not affect the variance.

2.6.2 Nonzero MA Processes

Now, let's consider the following MA(1) process with an intercept, α:

$$X_t = \alpha + u_t + \beta u_{t-1}$$

with $u_t \sim N(0, \sigma_u^2)$. The constant, α, allows the mean of the error to be nonzero.

What are the features of this type of MA(1) model? What is the mean of such a process?

$$E(X_t) = E(\alpha + u_t + \beta u_{t-1})$$
$$= \alpha + E(u_t) + \beta E(u_{t-1})$$
$$= \alpha + 0 + \beta(0)$$
$$= \alpha.$$

The rather straightforward result is that mean of an MA(1) process is equal to the intercept. This generalizes to any MA(q) process:

$$E(X_t) = E\left(\alpha + u_t + \beta_1 u_{t-1} + +\beta_2 u_{t-2} + \cdots + \beta_q u_{t-q}\right)$$
$$= \alpha + E(u_t) + \beta_1 E(u_{t-1}) + \beta_2 E(u_{t-2}) + \cdots + \beta_q E\left(u_{t-q}\right)$$
$$= \alpha + 0 + \beta_1(0) + \beta_2(0) + \cdots + \beta_q(0)$$
$$= \alpha.$$

What is the variance of a nonzero MA(1) process?

$$Var(X_t) = Var(\alpha + u_t + \beta u_{t-1})$$
$$= Var(\alpha) + Var(u_t) + Var(\beta u_{t-1})$$
$$= 0 + Var(u_t) + \beta^2 Var(u_{t-1})$$
$$= \sigma_u^2 + \beta^2 \sigma_u^2$$
$$= \sigma_u^2 \left(1 + \beta^2\right)$$

We moved from the first to the second line because, since the u_t are white noise at all t, there is no covariance between u_t and u_{t-1}. We moved to the third line because α and β are not random variables.

Notice that the variance does not depend on the added constant (α). That is, adding a constant affects the mean of an MA process, but does not affect its variance.

2.6.3 Dealing with Nonzero Means

If we are presented with an AR process that does't have a mean of zero, how do we accommodate it? We could directly estimate a model with an intercept.

Alternatively, we could de-mean the data: estimate the average and subtract this average each of the observations. Then we can estimate an AR process in the de-meaned variables without an intercept. Let's see exactly why this is the case.

Suppose we have a random variable, X_t, which does not have a mean of zero, but a mean of, say, $\bar{X}$. The fact that there is no time subscript on $\bar{X}$ indicates that the mean is constant; it does not depend on the time period t. That is, X_t is a mean stationary process, with a nonzero mean.

If we subtract the mean ($\bar{X}$) from X_t,

$$\tilde{X}_t = X_t - \bar{X} \tag{2.16}$$

the resulting variable ($\tilde{X}_t$) will have a mean of zero:

$$E\left(\tilde{X}_t\right) = E\left(X_t - \bar{X}\right) = E\left(X_t\right) - E\left(\bar{X}\right) = \bar{X} - \bar{X} = 0 \tag{2.17}$$

but the same variance:

$$Var(\tilde{X}_t) = Var(X_t - \bar{X}) = Var(X_t) - 0 = Var(X_t).$$

Subtracting a constant shifts our variable (changes its mean) but does not affect the dynamics nor the variance of the process.

This has a deeper implication. We've been talking all along about zero-mean process X_t. We can now see that X_t can be thought of as the deviations of $\tilde{X}_t$ from its mean. That is, we've been modeling the departures from the average value all along.

It is easy to show that de-meaning the variables changes the model from an AR(1) with a constant to our more familiar zero-mean AR(1) process. Beginning with a nonzero AR(1) process,

$$X_t = \beta_0 + \beta_1 X_{t-1} + e_t \tag{2.18}$$

Replacing all the X_t terms in (2.18) with $\tilde{X}_t + \beta_0/(1-\beta_1)$:

$$\tilde{X}_t + \frac{\beta_0}{1-\beta_1} = \beta_0 + \beta_1 \left(\tilde{X}_{t-1} + \frac{\beta_0}{1-\beta_1} \right) + e_t$$

$$\tilde{X}_t = \beta_0 - \frac{\beta_0}{1-\beta_1} + \beta_1 \frac{\beta_0}{1-\beta_1} + \beta_1 \tilde{X}_{t-1} + e_t$$

$$\tilde{X}_t = \frac{\beta_0(1-\beta_1) - \beta_0 + \beta_1 \beta_0}{1-\beta_1} + \beta_1 \tilde{X}_{t-1} + e_t$$

$$\tilde{X}_t = 0 + \beta_1 \tilde{X}_{t-1} + e_t$$

$$\tilde{X}_t = \beta_1 \tilde{X}_{t-1} + e_t.$$

De-meaning the variables transforms the nonzero AR(1) process (i.e., one with a constant) to a zero-mean AR(1) process (i.e., one without a constant).

The moral is the following: whenever you are looking at a zero-mean AR(p) process, just remember that the Xs represent deviations of a variable $\hat{X}$ from its mean.

2.6.4 Example

We can illustrate these two "solutions" using some simulated data in Stata. First, let's generate our nonzero data:

```
. set more off
. drop _all
. clear all
. set obs 10000
. set seed 1234
. generate time = _n
. tsset time
. generate double error = rnormal()
. generate double X = error in 1
. replace X = 10 + 0.50*L.X + error in 2/L
. drop if _n <= 1000
```

We drop the first 1,000 observations.[7]

---

[7] We do this because the earlier data have not yet converged to their long-run level. By keeping only the later observations, we ensure that the earlier data do not contaminate our analysis. It is

2.6 Nonzero ARMA Processes

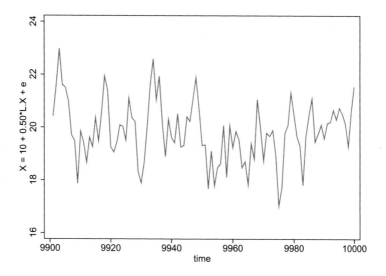

Fig. 2.7 The last 100 observations of simulated nonzero AR(1) data

The data were generated from an AR(1) model where $\beta_0 = 10$ and $\beta_1 = 0.50$. This means that the mean of the series should be $\mu_x = \beta_0/(1-\beta_1) = 20$. Of course, the sample mean is never exactly the same as the true population mean. Figure 2.7 graphs the last 100 observations of this dataset. Notice that the observations hover around 20.

The first approach to dealing with nonzero processes is to directly estimate a model that includes an intercept:

```
. arima X, ar(1) nolog      // We leave out the ''nocons'' option

ARIMA regression

Sample:  1001 - 10000                    Number of obs    =       9000
                                         Wald chi2(1)     =    3082.84
Log likelihood = -12813.62               Prob > chi2      =     0.0000

------------------------------------------------------------------------
             |                 OPG
           X |     Coef.   Std. Err.      z    P>|z|   [95% Conf. Interval]
-------------+----------------------------------------------------------
X            |
       _cons |  19.97985   .0214003   933.62   0.000    19.9379    20.02179
-------------+----------------------------------------------------------
```

probably overkill to drop so many of our initial observations, but we're playing with lots of fake data anyway.

```
ARMA      |
       ar |
       L1.|   .5050286    .0090958    55.52   0.000     .4872012    .522856
----------+----------------------------------------------------------------
   /sigma |   1.004792    .0075765   132.62   0.000     .9899423   1.019641
---------------------------------------------------------------------------
```

Note: The test of the variance against zero is one sided, and the two-sided confidence interval is truncated at zero.

The second approach is to estimate the sample mean ($\bar{X}$), subtract this mean from the data ($\tilde{X}_t = X_t - \bar{X}$) so that they are centered over zero, and then estimate the AR model without a constant:

$$\tilde{X}_t = \beta_1 \tilde{X}_{t-1} + e_t. \tag{2.19}$$

In Stata we do this as follows:

```
. sum X

    Variable |       Obs        Mean    Std. Dev.       Min        Max
-------------+--------------------------------------------------------
           X |     9,000    19.97968    1.164232    15.97467   24.58859

. local mean = r(mean)
. gen X_demeaned = X - 'mean'
. arima X_demeaned, ar(1) nolog nocons    //De-mean, but include ''nocons''

ARIMA regression

Sample:  1001 - 10000                           Number of obs   =      9000
                                                Wald chi2(1)    =   3083.49
Log likelihood = -12813.62                      Prob > chi2     =    0.0000

---------------------------------------------------------------------------
             |                 OPG
  X_demeaned |    Coef.    Std. Err.       z    P>|z|   [95% Conf. Interval]
-------------+-------------------------------------------------------------
ARMA         |
          ar |
         L1. |  .5050288    .0090948    55.53   0.000    .4872032   .5228544
-------------+-------------------------------------------------------------
      /sigma |  1.004791    .0075764   132.62   0.000    .9899412   1.01964
---------------------------------------------------------------------------
```

Note: The test of the variance against zero is one sided, and the two-sided confidence interval is truncated at zero.

Notice that the estimated coefficients are virtually identical in the two approaches. Which approach should you use? The first approach: directly estimate the constant. By manually de-meaning, Stata doesn't know that you've subtracted an estimate. It cannot adjust its standard errors to reflect this additional bit of uncertainty.

2.7 ARMA(p,q) Models

As if things weren't complicated enough, a process can be a mixture of AR and MA components. That is, there is a more general class of process called ARMA(p,q) models that consist of (a) an autoregressive component with p lags and (b) a moving average component with q lags.

An ARMA(p,q) model looks like the following:

$$X_t = \beta_1 X_{t-1} + \beta_2 X_{t-2} + \cdots + \beta_p X_{t-p} + \\ u_t + \gamma_1 u_{t-1} + \gamma_1 u_{t-1} + \cdots + \gamma_q u_{t-q}. \quad (2.20)$$

It has p lags of X and q lags of shocks. We did have a slight change of notation. Before, when we were discussing simple AR and MA models separately, all of our coefficients were βs. Now that we're estimating models that mix the two, it'll be easier for us to use β_i for the ith lagged AR coefficient and γ_j for the jth lagged MA coefficients.

2.7.1 Estimation

The general command for estimating ARMA(p,q) models is

. arima varname, arma(p,q)

or

. arima varname, ar(1/p) ma(1/q)

If for some reason we wished to leave out some lags, then we proceed as before: we list only the lags we want. For example, the command:

. arima X, ar(1 5) ma(1 4)

estimates:

$$X_t = \beta_1 X_{t-1} + \beta_5 X_{t-5} + e_t + \gamma_1 e_{t-1} + \gamma_4 e_{t-4}.$$

2.8 Conclusion

We have learned about AR and MA processes, the two basic components of ARMA models. We have learned what they are, how to estimate them, how they describe different reactions to shocks, and how to use them for forecasting. What we haven't figure out yet, however, is how to tell whether to estimate one type of model or another. Given a dataset, should we model it as an AR process, an MA process, or a combination of the two? To answer this question, we need to delve deeper into some additional characteristics of AR and MA processes. AR and MA processes imply different patterns of correlation between a variable and its own previous values. Once we understand the types of autocorrelation patterns associated with each type of process, we are in a better position to tell what type of model we should estimate. We turn to this in the next chapter.

Model Selection in ARMA(p,q) Processes   3

In practice, the form of the underlying process that generated the data is unknown. Should we estimate an AR(p) model, an MA(q) model, or an ARMA(p,q) model? Moreover, what lag lengths of p and q should we choose? We simply do not have good a priori reason to suspect that the data generating process is of one type or another, or a combination of the two. How is a researcher to proceed? Which sort of model should we estimate?

It is often impossible to tell visually whether a time series is an AR or an MA process. Consider Fig. 3.1 which shows four time series: an AR(1) process, an MA(1), and two ARMA(p,q). Which one is which? It is impossible to tell visually. We need something a bit more formal, something that relies on the differing statistical processes associated with AR and MA models.

The classic (Box & Jenkins, 1976) procedure is to check whether a time series mimics the properties of various theoretical models before estimation is actually carried out. These properties involve comparing the estimated autocorrelation functions (ACFs) and partial autocorrelation functions (PACFs) from the data, with the theoretical ACFs and PACFs implied by the various model types. A more recent approach is to use various "information criteria" to aid in model selection. We will discuss each of these in turn. We begin with deriving the theoretical ACFs and PACFs for AR(p) and MA(q) processes. Once we know the telltale signs of these processes, then we can check whether our data correspond to one or both of these processes. Then we estimate the model. The Box-Jenkins procedure is concluded by verifying that the estimated residuals are white noise. This implies that there is no leftover structure to the data that we have neglected to model. If the residuals are not white noise, then Box and Jenkins recommend modifying the model, reestimating, and reexamining the residuals. It is a complicated process. But the central part in their procedure comparing the autocorrelation structure from the data with what would is implied theoretically by various processes. We turn to this now.

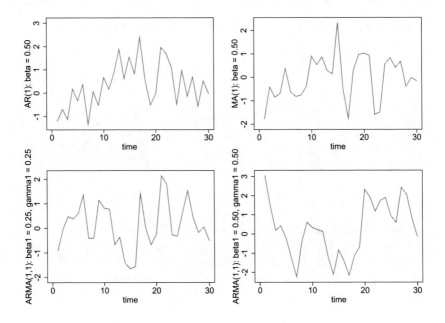

Fig. 3.1 Some various ARMA processes

3.1 ACFs and PACFs

ACFs and PACFs each come in two flavors: theoretical and empirical. The former is implied by a model; the latter is a characteristic of the data. We can compare (a) the empirical ACFs and PACFs that we estimate directly from the data without using a model, with (b) the theoretical ACFs and PACFs that are associated with a particular model. Then, we only need to see how they match up. That is, we can be fairly certain that the data were generated from a particular type of process (model) if the empirical ACF matches up with that of a particular model's theoretical ACFs.

We'll proceed as follows. First, we'll derive the theoretical ACFs and PACFs for AR processes and then for MA processes. Then we'll see how to estimate the ACFs and PACFs directly from the data. And then we'll see how we can match the two.

3.1.1 Theoretical ACF of an AR(1) Process

Let us now derive the theoretical ACF of an AR(1) process:

$$X_t = \beta X_{t-1} + e_t. \tag{3.1}$$

3.1 ACFs and PACFs

An ACF is a description of how X_t is correlated with its first lag, its second lag, through to its kth lag. To find the theoretical ACF for an AR(1) process, let's derive the values of $Corr(X_t, X_{t-1}), Corr(X_t, X_{t-2}), \ldots Corr(X_t, X_{t-k})$, under the assumption that Eq. (3.1) is true.

We will make use of the following:

$$E(e_t) = 0 \tag{3.2}$$

$$Var(e_t) = \sigma^2 \tag{3.3}$$

$$Cov(e_t, e_{t-k}) = 0, \tag{3.4}$$

which are implied by the assumption that $e_t \sim iidN(0, \sigma^2)$, and

$$E(X_t) = E(X_{t-k}) = 0 \tag{3.5}$$

which follows from the fact that X is a zero-mean process.

The autocorrelation at lag one is derived as follows. First, using the definition of correlation, the correlation of X with its own values lagged one period is

$$Corr(X_t, X_{t-1}) = \frac{Cov(X_t, X_{t-1})}{Stdev(X_t) Stdev(X_{t-1})}. \tag{3.6}$$

Since the AR(1) process is stationary, then $Stdev(X_t) = Stdev(X_{t-1})$, so Eq. (3.6) simplifies to

$$Corr(X_t, X_{t-1}) = \frac{Cov(X_t, X_{t-1})}{Var(X_t)}. \tag{3.7}$$

From the definition of covariance,

$$Cov(X_t, X_{t-1}) = E(X_t, X_{t-1}) - E(X_t) E(X_{t-1}), \tag{3.8}$$

and from the definition of variance,

$$Var(X_t) = E\left(X_t^2\right) - E(X_t) E(X_t). \tag{3.9}$$

Plugging (3.8) and (3.9) into (3.7),

$$Corr(X_t, X_{t-1}) = \frac{E(X_t, X_{t-1}) - E(X_t) E(X_{t-1})}{E\left(X_t^2\right) - E(X_t) E(X_t)}.$$

Since $E(X_t) = 0$, then

$$Corr(X_t, X_{t-1}) = \frac{E(X_t X_{t-1})}{E(X_t^2)}. \qquad (3.10)$$

Now, let's look further at the numerator in (3.10). Take $X_t = \beta X_{t-1} + e_t$ and multiply both sides by X_{t-1}:

$$X_t X_{t-1} = \beta X_{t-1} X_{t-1} + e_t X_{t-1}.$$

Taking expectations, the lag-1 autocovariance is

$$E(X_t X_{t-1}) = \beta E(X_{t-1} X_{t-1}) + E(e_t X_{t-1}) = \beta E(X_{t-1} X_{t-1}).$$

This allows us to simplify (3.10) further:

$$Corr(X_t, X_{t-1}) = \frac{\beta E(X_{t-1} X_{t-1})}{E(X_t^2)}. \qquad (3.11)$$

By stationarity, $E(X_{t-1} X_{t-1}) = E(X_t X_t) = E(X_t^2)$, so (3.11) simplifies to

$$Corr(X_t, X_{t-1}) = \frac{\beta E(X_t^2)}{E(X_t^2)} = \beta. \qquad (3.12)$$

What about the autocorrelation of X at lags deeper than one? The autocorrelation at lag $k = 2$, $Corr(X_t, X_{t-2})$, is

$$Corr(X_t, X_{t-2}) = \frac{Cov(X_t, X_{t-2})}{Stdev(X_t) Stdev X_{t-2}}.$$

By stationarity, $Stdev(X_t) = Stdev(X_{t-2})$, so

$$Corr(X_t, X_{t-2}) = \frac{Cov(X_t, X_{t-2})}{Var(X_t)}.$$

From the definition of covariance,

$$Corr(X_t, X_{t-2}) = \frac{E(X_t X_{t-2}) - E(X_t) E(X_{t-2})}{Var(X_t)}$$

and since X is a zero-mean process,

$$Corr(X_t, X_{t-2}) = \frac{E(X_t X_{t-2})}{Var(X_t)}. \qquad (3.13)$$

Let us now focus on the numerator. Since $X_t = \beta X_{t-1} + e_t$, then multiplying both sides by X_{t-2} gives

3.1 ACFs and PACFs

$$X_t X_{t-2} = \beta X_{t-1} X_{t-2} + e_t X_{t-2}.$$

Taking expectations of both sides,

$$E(X_t X_{t-2}) = \beta E(X_{t-1} X_{t-2}) + E(e_t X_{t-2}) = \beta E(X_{t-1} X_{t-2}).$$

By stationarity, $E(X_{t-1}X_{t-2}) = E(X_t X_{t-1})$, which we know from our work computing the lag-1 autocorrelation several lines previously is equal to $\beta E(X_t^2)$. Substituting, we get

$$E(X_t X_{t-2}) = \beta^2 E\left(X_t^2\right) = \beta^2 Var(X_t). \qquad (3.14)$$

Plugging (3.14) into (3.13), we have the theoretical autocorrelation at lag-2 of an AR(1) model:

$$Corr(X_t, X_{t-2}) = \frac{E(X_t X_{t-2})}{Var(X_t)} = \frac{\beta^2 Var(X_t)}{Var(X_t)} = \beta^2.$$

Notice that X_t is correlated with X_{t-2} even though it is not explicitly a function of X_{t-2}, i.e., even though X_{t-2} does not appear in the definition of an AR(1) process:

$$X_t = \beta X_{t-1} + e_t.$$

What about autocorrelation at further lags? If X follows an AR(1) process, then X_t has an autocorrelation function of

$$Cov(X_t, X_{t+k}) = \beta^k.$$

Thus,

$$Cov(X_t, X_{t+1}) = \beta$$
$$Cov(X_t, X_{t+2}) = \beta^2$$
$$Cov(X_t, X_{t+3}) = \beta^3$$
$$Cov(X_t, X_{t+4}) = \beta^4$$

and so forth.

Thus, even a simple AR process with one lag can induce an outcome where each observation of X will be correlated with long lags of itself.

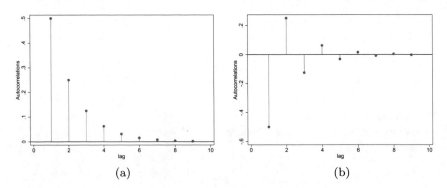

Fig. 3.2 Theoretical ACF of AR(1): $X_t = \beta_1 X_{t-1} + e_t$. (a) $\beta_1 = 0.50$. (b) $\beta_1 = -0.50$

Notice that the ACF of an AR(1) process decays exponentially. If β is a positive number, then it will decay toward zero.[1] If β is a negative number, then it will still converge toward zero, but it will oscillate between negative and positive numbers. (Raising a negative number to an even power makes it positive.) The ACF for a positive β_1 has the characteristic shape shown in Fig. 3.2a. The ACF for a negative β_1 oscillates, such as in Fig. 3.2b.

Regardless of whether the ACF oscillates or not, it is still the case that today's value of X_t is correlated with values from its past. That is, even though X_t is not directly determined by X_{t-2} or X_{t-3} (they are not terms in $X_t = \beta X_{t-1} + e_t$), X_t is correlated with its past, but old values have increasingly faint impact.

3.1.2 Theoretical ACF of an AR(p) Process

Let us now suppose that X_t follows an general AR(p) process:

$$X_t = \beta_1 X_{t-1} + \beta_2 X_{t-2} + \ldots + \beta_p X_{t-p} + e_t. \tag{3.15}$$

What is its autocorrelation function? That is, what are $Corr(X_t, X_{t-1})$, and $Corr(X_t, X_{t-2})$, through $Corr(X_t, X_{t-k})$?

Beginning with the definition of autocorrelation at arbitrary lag k, we can use the stationarity of the standard deviation, and the iid assumption for u_ts, to arrive at

$$Corr(X_t, X_{t-k}) = \frac{Cov(X_t, X_{t-k})}{Stdev(X_t) Stdev(X_{t-k})}$$

$$= \frac{E(X_t X_{t-k}) - E(X_t) E(X_{t-k})}{Stdev(X_t) Stdev(X_t)}$$

---

[1] A positive β must be between zero and one for stationarity.

3.1 ACFs and PACFs

$$= \frac{E(X_t X_{t-k})}{Var(X_t)}. \qquad (3.16)$$

Thus, our task is to derive expressions for each of these autocorrelations at each lag k.

We will attack this problem in pieces, focusing on the numerator and denominator of (3.16) separately. We will begin with the numerator, i.e., with the autocovariances.

We can solve this problem using a system of equations called Yule-Walker equations. To find the first such equation, multiply both sides of (3.15) by X_t and take the expectation:

$$\begin{aligned} E(X_t X_t) &= E\left[(\beta_1 X_{t-1} + \beta_2 X_{t-2} + \ldots + \beta_p X_{t-p} + e_t) X_t\right] \\ &= E\left[\beta_1 X_{t-1} X_t + \beta_2 X_{t-2} X_t + \ldots + \beta_p X_{t-p} X_t + e_t X_t\right] \\ &= \beta_1 E(X_{t-1} X_t) + \beta_2 E(X_{t-2} X_t) + \ldots + \beta_p E(X_{t-p} X_t) + E(e_t X_t) \end{aligned}$$
$$(3.17)$$

The only term in (3.17) that looks a little new is the last one, $E(e_t X_t)$; it is the only term that is not an autocovariance. Let's look at that term a bit more closely. Multiplying (3.15) by e_t and taking expectations:

$$\begin{aligned} E(X_t e_t) &= E\left(\beta_1 X_{t-1} e_t + \beta_2 X_{t-2} e_t + \ldots + \beta_p X_{t-p} e_t + e_t e_t\right) \\ &= \beta_1 E(X_{t-1} e_t) + \beta_2 E(X_{t-2} e_t) + \ldots + \beta_p E(X_{t-p} e_t) + E(e_t e_t) \end{aligned}$$

Since each e_t is independent of any past realizations of X_t, then

$$\begin{aligned} E(X_t e_t) &= \beta_1 E(0) + \beta_2 E(0) + \ldots + \beta_p E(0) + E(e_t e_t) \\ &= \sigma^2. \end{aligned}$$

Therefore, we can simplify (3.17) to be

$$E(X_t X_t) = \beta_1 E(X_{t-1} X_t) + \beta_2 E(X_{t-2} X_t) + \ldots + \beta_p E(X_{t-p} X_t) + \sigma^2. \qquad (3.18)$$

We can derive our second Yule-Walker equation by multiplying both sides of (3.15) by X_{t-1} and taking the expectation:

$$\begin{aligned} E(X_t X_{t-1}) &= E\left[(\beta_1 X_{t-1} + \beta_2 X_{t-2} + \ldots + \beta_p X_{t-p} + e_t) X_{t-1}\right] \\ &= E\left[\beta_1 X_{t-1} X_{t-1} + \beta_2 X_{t-2} X_{t-1} + \ldots + \beta_p X_{t-p} X_{t-1} + e_t X_{t-1}\right] \\ &= \beta_1 E(X_{t-1} X_{t-1}) + \beta_2 E(X_{t-2} X_{t-1}) + \ldots \\ &\quad + \beta_p E(X_{t-p} X_{t-1}). \end{aligned} \qquad (3.19)$$

Similarly, we can derive our third Yule-Walker equation by multiplying both sides of (3.15) by X_{t-2} and taking the expectation:

$$\begin{aligned} E\left(X_{t} X_{t-2}\right) &= E\left[\left(\beta_{1} X_{t-1}+\beta_{2} X_{t-2}+\ldots+\beta_{p} X_{t-p}+e_{t}\right) X_{t-2}\right] \\ &= E\left[\beta_{1} X_{t-1} X_{t-2}+\beta_{2} X_{t-2} X_{t-2}+\ldots+\beta_{p} X_{t-p} X_{t-2}+e_{t} X_{t-2}\right] \\ &= \beta_{1} E\left(X_{t-1} X_{t-2}\right)+\beta_{2} E\left(X_{t-2} X_{t-2}\right)+\ldots \\ &\quad + \beta_{p} E\left(X_{t-p} X_{t-2}\right). \end{aligned} \qquad (3.20)$$

Following a similar process, we can derive our final Yule-Walker equation by multiplying both sides of (3.15) by $X_{t-(p+1)}$ and taking the expectation:

$$\begin{aligned} E\left(X_{t} X_{t-p-1}\right) &= E\left[\left(\beta_{1} X_{t-1}+\beta_{2} X_{t-2}+\ldots+\beta_{p} X_{t-p}+e_{t}\right) X_{t-p-1}\right] \\ &= \beta_{1} E\left[X_{t-1} X_{t-p-1}\right]+\beta_{2} E\left[X_{t-2} X_{t-p-1}\right]+\ldots \\ &\quad + \beta_{p} E\left[X_{t-p} X_{t-p-1}\right]. \end{aligned} \qquad (3.21)$$

It is time to take stock. For notational simplicity, let's denote the variance and each of the autocovariances with ϕ's:

$$E(X_t X_t) = \phi_0$$
$$E(X_t X_{t-1}) = \phi_1$$
$$E(X_t X_{t-2}) = \phi_2$$
$$\vdots$$
$$E(X_t X_{t-k}) = \phi_k$$
$$\vdots$$

Using this notation, we can rewrite Eqs. (3.18)–(3.21) as

$$\begin{aligned} \phi_0 &= \beta_1 \phi_1 + \beta_2 \phi_2 + \ldots + \beta_p \phi_p + \sigma^2 \\ \phi_1 &= \beta_1 \phi_0 + \beta_2 \phi_1 + \ldots + \beta_p \phi_{p-1} \\ \phi_2 &= \beta_1 \phi_1 + \beta_2 \phi_0 + \ldots + \beta_p \phi_{p-2} \\ &\vdots \\ \phi_p &= \beta_1 \phi_{p-1} + \beta_2 \phi_{p-2} + \ldots + \beta_p \phi_0 \\ &\vdots \end{aligned} \qquad (3.22)$$

3.1 ACFs and PACFs

Thus, we have $(p+1)$ equations in $(p+1)$ unknowns so we can solve analytically for the autocovariances. The autocorrelations are then found by dividing each covariance ϕ_k by the variance ϕ_0. The last line above establishes a recursive formula for the autocovariance at any arbitrary lag length p.

For the simple case of an AR(2) process, the autocovariances are as follows:

$$\phi_0 = \beta_1 \phi_1 + \beta_2 \phi_2 + \sigma^2$$

$$\phi_1 = \beta_1 \phi_0 + \beta_2 \phi_1 \tag{3.23}$$

$$\phi_2 = \beta_1 \phi_1 + \beta_2 \phi_0. \tag{3.24}$$

The last two lines establish a recursive pattern: $\phi_s = \beta_1 \phi_{s-1} + \beta_2 \phi_{s-2}$. With these autocovariances, we are prepared to derive the autocorrelations.

Equation (3.23) simplifies to

$$\phi_1 = \frac{\beta_1}{1 - \beta_2} \phi_0, \tag{3.25}$$

so the autocorrelation at lag $k = 1$ is

$$Corr(X_t, X_{t-1}) = \frac{Cov(X_t, X_{t-1})}{Var(X_t)} = \frac{\phi_1}{\phi_0} = \frac{\frac{\beta_1}{1-\beta_2}\phi_0}{\phi_0} = \frac{\beta_1}{1 - \beta_2}. \tag{3.26}$$

Similarly, we can substitute (3.25) into (3.24), to yield

$$\phi_2 = \beta_1 \frac{\beta_1}{1 - \beta_2} \phi_0 + \beta_2 \phi_0 \tag{3.27}$$

which implies that the autocorrelation at lag $k = 2$ is

$$Corr(X_t, X_{t-2}) = \frac{Cov(X_t, X_{t-2})}{Var(X_t)} = \frac{\phi_2}{\phi_0} = \frac{\beta_1^2}{1 - \beta_2} + \beta_2. \tag{3.28}$$

Given the recursion, $\phi_s = \beta_1 \phi_{s-1} + \beta_2 \phi_{s-2}$, the autocorrelation at lag k can be found by

$$\frac{\phi_k}{\phi_0} = \beta_1 \frac{\phi_{k-1}}{\phi_0} + \beta_2 \frac{\phi_{k-2}}{\phi_0}. \tag{3.29}$$

Thus, the autocorrelation at lag $k = 3$ is

$$\frac{\phi_3}{\phi_0} = \beta_1 \frac{\phi_2}{\phi_0} + \beta_2 \frac{\phi_1}{\phi_0}$$

or

$$\text{Corr}(X_t, X_{t-3}) = \beta_1 \text{Corr}(X_t, X_{t-2}) + \beta_2 \text{Corr}(X_t, X_{t-1}). \tag{3.30}$$

For the more general case of an AR(k) process, we can employ a similar strategy, solving the Yule-Walker equations recursively.

Example
Using Eqs. (3.26)–(3.30), let's solve for the theoretical ACF implied by the following AR(2) process:

$$X_t = 0.50 X_{t-1} + 0.20 X_{t-2} + e_t.$$

The lag-1 autocorrelation is

$$\text{Corr}(X_t, X_{t-1}) = \frac{\beta_1}{1-\beta_2} = \frac{0.50}{1-0.20} = 0.625.$$

The lag-2 autocorrelation is

$$\text{Corr}(X_t, X_{t-2}) = \frac{\beta_1^2}{1-\beta_2} + \beta_2 = \frac{0.50^2}{1-0.20} + 0.20 = 0.5125$$

The lag-3 autocorrelation can be found using the recursion:

$$\text{Corr}(X_t, X_{t-3}) = \beta_1 \text{Corr}(X_t, X_{t-2}) + \beta_2 \text{Corr}(X_t, X_{t-1})$$
$$= 0.50(0.5125) + 0.20(0.625)$$
$$= 0.38125.$$

The lag-4 autocorrelation is

$$\text{Corr}(X_t, X_{t-4}) = \beta_1 \text{Corr}(X_t, X_{t-3}) + \beta_2 \text{Corr}(X_t, X_{t-2})$$
$$= 0.50(0.38125) + 0.20(0.5125)$$
$$= 0.293125$$

and so forth. Today's value of X is increasingly less correlated with values farther back in time.

Exercises
1. Using Eqs. (3.26)–(3.30), calculate the first three lags of the theoretical ACFs implied by the following AR(2) processes:
   (a) $X_t = 0.50 X_{t-1} - 0.20 X_{t-2} + e_t$
   (b) $X_t = -0.50 X_{t-1} - 0.20 X_{t-2} + e_t$

3.1.3 Theoretical ACF of an MA(1) Process

It is important to know the theoretical ACF of an MA(1) process, because we will need to compare our estimated ACF with the theoretical one, in order to assess whether we are, in fact, actually looking at an MA(1) process.

How are the Xs at different lags correlated with each other? Our MA(1) model, yet again, is

$$X_t = u_t + \beta u_{t-1} \qquad (3.31)$$

with $u_t \sim iidN(0, \sigma_u^2)$. That is, the u error terms are white noise, independent of each other. Therefore,

$$Cov(u_t, u_t) = Var(u_t) = \sigma_u^2 \qquad (3.32)$$

$$Cov(u_t, u_j) = E(u_t u_j) = 0, \ \forall t \neq j \qquad (3.33)$$

What is X's ACF at lag 1? In symbols, we need to figure out the value of

$$\begin{aligned} Corr\,(X_t, X_{t-1}) &= \frac{Cov\,(X_t, X_{t-1})}{Stdev\,(X_t)\,Stdev\,(X_{t-1})} \\ &= \frac{Cov(X_t, X_{t-1})}{Var\,(X_t)}. \end{aligned} \qquad (3.34)$$

In order to answer this question, we need to know the variance of X_t and the covariance of X_t and X_{t-1}. Let us take a brief detour to answer these intermediate questions.

We begin by calculating the variance of X_t:

$$\begin{aligned} Var\,(X_t) &= Var\,(u_t + \beta u_{t-1}) \\ &= Var\,(u_t) + Var\,(\beta u_{t-1}) + 2Cov\,(u_t, \beta u_{t-1}) \\ &= Var\,(u_t) + Var\,(\beta u_{t-1}) \\ &= Var\,(u_t) + \beta^2 Var\,(u_{t-1}) \\ &= \sigma_u^2 + \beta^2 \sigma_u^2 \\ &= \sigma_u^2 \left(1 + \beta^2\right). \end{aligned} \qquad (3.35)$$

Now let's calculate the covariance, $Cov(X, Y) = E(XY) - E(X)E(Y)$. And recall that X_t is a zero mean process, so $E(X_t) = 0$. Thus,

$$Cov\,(X_t, X_{t-1}) = E\,(X_t X_{t-1}) - E\,(X_t)\,E\,(X_{t-1})$$

$$= E(X_t X_{t-1})$$
$$= E[(u_t + \beta u_{t-1})(u_{t-1} + \beta u_{t-2})]$$
$$= E\left(u_t u_{t-1} + \beta u_t u_{t-2} + \beta u_{t-1}^2 + \beta^2 u_{t-1} u_{t-2}\right)$$
$$= E(u_t u_{t-1}) + \beta E(u_t u_{t-2}) + \beta E\left(u_{t-1}^2\right) + \beta^2 E(u_{t-1} u_{t-2}).$$

Using (3.33) the above expression simplifies to

$$Cov(X_t, X_{t-1}) = E(u_t u_{t-1}) + \beta E(u_t u_{t-2}) + \beta E\left(u_{t-1}^2\right) + \beta^2 E(u_{t-1} u_{t-2})$$
$$= 0 + 0 + \beta \sigma_u^2 + 0$$
$$= \beta \sigma_u^2. \tag{3.36}$$

Having calculated (3.35) and (3.36), we can substitute these into (3.34) to find the autocorrelation at lag= 1:

$$Corr(X, X_{t-1}) = \frac{Cov(X_t, X_{t-1})}{Var(X_t)}$$
$$= \frac{\beta \sigma_u^2}{\sigma_u^2 (1 + \beta^2)}$$
$$= \frac{\beta}{(1 + \beta^2)}. \tag{3.37}$$

What about autocorrelation at lags greater than one?

$$Cov(X_t, X_{t-2}) = E(X_t X_{t-2}) - E(X_t) E(X_{t-2})$$
$$= E(X_t X_{t-2})$$
$$= E[(u_t + \beta u_{t-1})(u_{t-2} + \beta u_{t-3})]$$
$$= E\left(u_t u_{t-2} + \beta u_t u_{t-3} + \beta u_{t-1} u_{t-2} + \beta^2 u_{t-1} u_{t-3}\right)$$
$$= E(u_t u_{t-2}) + \beta E(u_t u_{t-3}) + \beta E(u_{t-1} u_{t-2}) + \beta^2 E(u_{t-1} u_{t-3})$$
$$= (0) + \beta(0) + \beta(0) + \beta^2(0)$$
$$= 0$$

where we made extensive use again of the fact that $E\left(u_j u_t\right) = 0$ whenever $t \neq j$.
In fact, for an MA(1) process,

$$E(X_t X_j) = 0 \quad \forall j > (t+1).$$

In other words, if X follows an MA(1) process, then X_t and X_{t-1} will be correlated, but X_t will not be correlated with X_{t-2}, nor with longer lags of X.

3.1.4 Theoretical ACF of an MA(q) Process

In general, the ACF is defined as the set of all

$$Corr(X_t, X_{t-k}) = \frac{Cov(X_t, X_{t-k})}{Stdev(X_t)\,Stdev(X_{t-k})} = \frac{Cov(X_t, X_{t-k})}{Var(X_t)} \quad (3.38)$$

at each lag length k. To derive this sequence of correlations, let's take apart Eq. (3.38) piece by piece.

We begin with the denominator, deriving an expression for the variance of X_t. To do this, let's start with the definition of an MA(q) process:

$$X_t = u_t + \beta_1 u_{t-1} + \beta_2 u_{t-2} + \cdots + \beta_q u_{t-q} \quad (3.39)$$

where

$$u_t \sim iidN\left(0, \sigma_u^2\right). \quad (3.40)$$

Taking the variance of Eq. (3.39),

$$\begin{aligned}
Var(X_t) &= Var\left(u_t + \beta_1 u_{t-1} + \beta_2 u_{t-2} + \cdots + \beta_q u_{t-q}\right) \\
&= Var(u_t) + Var(\beta_1 u_{t-1}) + Var(\beta_2 u_{t-2}) + \cdots + Var\left(\beta_q u_{t-q}\right) \\
&= Var(u_t) + \beta_1^2 Var(u_{t-1}) + \beta_2^2 Var(u_{t-2}) + \cdots + \beta_q^2 Var\left(u_{t-q}\right) \\
&= \sigma_u^2 + \beta_1^2 \sigma_u^2 + \beta_2^2 \sigma_u^2 + \cdots + \beta_q^2 \sigma_u^2 \\
&= \sigma_u^2 \left(1 + \beta_1^2 + \beta_2^2 + \cdots + \beta_q^2\right).
\end{aligned} \quad (3.41)$$

This will be our term in the denominator. What about the numerator?

Beginning with the definition of covariance and using the fact that $E(X_t) = 0$,

$$\begin{aligned}
Cov(X_t, X_{t-k}) &= E(X_t X_{t-k}) - E(X_t)E(X_{t-k}) \\
&= E(X_t X_{t-k}).
\end{aligned} \quad (3.42)$$

Substituting (3.39) into (3.42),

$$E(X_t X_{t-k}) = E[(u_t + \beta_1 u_{t-1} + \beta_2 u_{t-2} + \cdots + \beta_q u_{t-q}) \\
(u_{t-k} + \beta_1 u_{t-k-1} + \beta_2 u_{t-k-2} + \cdots + \beta_q u_{t-k-q})].$$

Next, we multiply out the terms inside the brackets and get

$$\begin{aligned}E(X_t X_{t-k}) = E[&u_t\left(u_{t-k} + \beta_1 u_{t-k-1} + \beta_2 u_{t-k-2} + \cdots + \beta_q u_{t-k-q}\right) + \\ &\beta_1 u_{t-1}\left(u_{t-k} + \beta_1 u_{t-k-1} + \beta_2 u_{t-k-2} + \cdots + \beta_q u_{t-k-q}\right) + \\ &\beta_2 u_{t-2}\left(u_{t-k} + \beta_1 u_{t-k-1} + \beta_2 u_{t-k-2} + \cdots + \beta_q u_{t-k-q}\right) + \\ &\beta_3 u_{t-3}\left(u_{t-k} + \beta_1 u_{t-k-1} + \beta_2 u_{t-k-2} + \cdots + \beta_q u_{t-k-q}\right) + \\ &\cdots + \\ &\beta_q u_{t-q}\left(\cdots + \beta_{q-1} u_{t-k-q+1} + \beta_q u_{t-k-q}\right)].\end{aligned}$$
(3.43)

This equation includes many products of us. Since each u_i is independent of each u_j whenever their subscripts are different ($i \neq j$), then $E(u_i u_j) = 0$ and, mercifully, the equation above simplifies dramatically.

At $k = 1$, Eq. (3.43) reduces to

$$\begin{aligned}E(X_t X_{t-1}) =& E\left[\beta_1 u_{t-1}^2 + \beta_2 \beta_1 u_{t-2}^2 + \beta_3 \beta_2 u_{t-3}^2 + \cdots + \beta_q \beta_{q-1} u_{t-q}^2\right] \\ =& \beta_1 E\left(u_{t-1}^2\right) + \beta_2 \beta_1 E\left(u_{t-2}^2\right) + \beta_3 \beta_2 E\left(u_{t-3}^2\right) + \cdots \\ &+ \beta_q \beta_{q-1} E\left(u_{t-q}^2\right) \\ =& \beta_1 \sigma_u^2 + \beta_2 \beta_1 \sigma_u^2 + \beta_3 \beta_2 \sigma_u^2 + \cdots + \beta_q \beta_{q-1} \sigma_u^2 \\ =& \sigma_u^2 \left(\beta_1 + \beta_2 \beta_1 + \beta_3 \beta_2 + \cdots + \beta_q \beta_{q-1}\right).\end{aligned}$$
(3.44)

At $k = 2$, Eq. (3.43) reduces to

$$\begin{aligned}E(X_t X_{t-2}) &= E\left[\beta_2 u_{t-2} u_{t-k} + \beta_3 \beta_1 u_{t-3} u_{t-k-1} + \cdots + \beta_q \beta_{q-2} u_{t-q} u_{t-k-q+2}\right] \\ &= E\left[\beta_2 u_{t-2}^2 + \beta_3 \beta_1 u_{t-3}^2 + \beta_4 \beta_2 u_{t-4}^2 + \cdots + \beta_q \beta_{q-2} u_{t-q}^2\right] \\ &= \beta_2 \sigma_u^2 + \beta_3 \beta_1 \sigma_u^2 + \beta_4 \beta_2 \sigma_u^2 + \cdots + \beta_q \beta_{q-2} \sigma_u^2 \\ &= \sigma_u^2 \left(\beta_2 + \beta_3 \beta_1 + \beta_4 \beta_2 + \cdots + \beta_q \beta_{q-2}\right).\end{aligned}$$
(3.45)

At $k = 3$, Eq. (3.43) reduces to

$$E(X_t X_{t-3}) = \sigma_u^2 \left(\beta_3 + \beta_4 \beta_1 + \beta_5 \beta_2 + \beta_6 \beta_3 + \cdots + \beta_q \beta_{q-3}\right).$$
(3.46)

Notice that the sequence of βs begins later and later. Eventually, once k exceeds q, there are no longer any nonzero correlations. In other words, at $k = q$, Eq. (3.43) reduces to

3.1 ACFs and PACFs

$$E(X_t X_{t-k}) = \sigma_u^2 \beta_q, \qquad (3.47)$$

and at $k > q$, Eq. (3.43) reduces to

$$E(X_t X_{t-k}) = 0. \qquad (3.48)$$

We've calculated all of the autocovariances at each lag $k = 1, 2, \ldots$. We are now, finally, in a position to show the autocorrelations that comprise the ACF.

The autocorrelation at lag $k = 1$ is found by plugging in (3.44) and (3.41) into Eq. (3.38):

$$\begin{aligned}
Corr(X_t, X_{t-1}) &= \frac{Cov(X_t, X_{t-1})}{Var(X_t)} \\
&= \frac{\sigma_u^2 \left(\beta_1 + \beta_2 \beta_1 + \beta_3 \beta_2 + \cdots + \beta_q \beta_{q-1}\right)}{\sigma_u^2 \left(1 + \beta_1^2 + \beta_2^2 + \cdots + \beta_q^2\right)} \\
&= \frac{\beta_1 + \beta_2 \beta_1 + \beta_3 \beta_2 + \cdots + \beta_q \beta_{q-1}}{1 + \beta_1^2 + \beta_2^2 + \cdots + \beta_q^2}.
\end{aligned} \qquad (3.49)$$

The autocorrelation at lag $k = 2$ is found by plugging in (3.45) and (3.41) into Eq. (3.38):

$$\begin{aligned}
Corr(X_t, X_{t-2}) &= \frac{Cov(X_t, X_{t-2})}{Var(X_t)} \\
&= \frac{\sigma_u^2 \left(\beta_2 + \beta_3 \beta_1 + \beta_4 \beta_2 + \cdots + \beta_q \beta_{q-2}\right)}{\sigma_u^2 \left(1 + \beta_1^2 + \beta_2^2 + \cdots + \beta_q^2\right)} \\
&= \frac{\beta_2 + \beta_3 \beta_1 + \beta_4 \beta_2 + \cdots + \beta_q \beta_{q-2}}{1 + \beta_1^2 + \beta_2^2 + \cdots + \beta_q^2}.
\end{aligned} \qquad (3.50)$$

Using the same procedure, we can calculate the autocorrelation at lag $k = 3$:

$$Corr(X_t, X_{t-3}) = \frac{\beta_3 + \beta_4 \beta_1 + \beta_5 \beta_2 + \beta_6 \beta_3 + \cdots + \beta_q \beta_{q-3}}{1 + \beta_1^2 + \beta_2^2 + \cdots + \beta_q^2} \qquad (3.51)$$

the autocorrelation at lag $k = q$:

$$Corr(X_t, X_{t-q}) = \frac{\beta_q}{1 + \beta_1^2 + \beta_2^2 + \cdots + \beta_q^2} \qquad (3.52)$$

and the autocorrelation at lag $k > q$:

$$\operatorname{Corr}(X_t, X_{t-k}) = \frac{0}{\sigma_u^2 \left(1 + \beta_1^2 + \beta_2^2 + \cdots + \beta_q^2\right)} = 0. \qquad (3.53)$$

The ACF of an MA(q) process is given by the values of Eqs. (3.49), (3.50), (3.51),..., (3.52) and zeros thereafter.

This might seem a bit too abstract. It is time for an example.

Example

Suppose that somehow we knew that an MA(3) and was equal to

$$X_t = u_t + 0.40 u_{t-1} + 0.20 u_{t-2} + 0.10 u_{t-3}. \qquad (3.54)$$

Armed with the above formulas for the ACF of an MA(q) process, we can calculate the theoretical autocorrelations at lags $k = 0, 1, 2, 3$, and $k > 3$:

$$\begin{aligned}
AC(k=1) &= \frac{\beta_1 + \beta_2 \beta_1 + \beta_3 \beta_2 + \cdots + \beta_q \beta_{q-1}}{1 + \beta_1^2 + \beta_2^2 + \cdots + \beta_q^2} \\
&= \frac{\beta_1 + \beta_2 \beta_1 + \beta_3 \beta_2}{1 + \beta_1^2 + \beta_2^2 + \beta_3^2} \\
&= \frac{0.40 + (0.20)(0.40) + (0.10)(0.20)}{1 + (0.40)^2 + (0.20)^2 + (0.10)^2} \\
&= 0.4132
\end{aligned} \qquad (3.55)$$

$$\begin{aligned}
AC(k=2) &= \frac{\beta_2 + \beta_3 \beta_1 + \beta_4 \beta_2 + \cdots + \beta_q \beta_{q-2}}{1 + \beta_1^2 + \beta_2^2 + \cdots + \beta_q^2} \\
&= \frac{\beta_2 + \beta_3 \beta_1}{1 + \beta_1^2 + \beta_2^2 + \beta_3^2} \\
&= \frac{0.20 + (0.10)(0.40)}{1 + (0.40)^2 + (0.20)^2 + (0.10)^2} \\
&= 0.1983
\end{aligned} \qquad (3.56)$$

$$\begin{aligned}
AC(k=3) &= \frac{\beta_3 + \beta_4 \beta_1 + \beta_5 \beta_2 + \beta_6 \beta_3 + \cdots + \beta_q \beta_{q-3}}{1 + \beta_1^2 + \beta_2^2 + \cdots + \beta_q^2} \\
&= \frac{\beta_3}{1 + \beta_1^2 + \beta_2^2 + \beta_3^2} \\
&= \frac{0.10}{1 + (0.40)^2 + (0.20)^2 + (0.10)^2} \\
&= 0.0826
\end{aligned} \qquad (3.57)$$

3.1 ACFs and PACFs

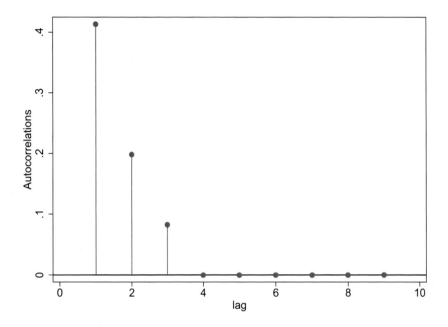

Fig. 3.3 Theoretical ACF of $X_t = u_t + 0.40u_{t-1} + 0.20u_{t-2} + 0.10u_{t-3}$

$$AC(k > 3) = 0. \tag{3.58}$$

Graphically, the ACF of this particular process is given in Fig. 3.3.

Exercises
1. Use the formulas for the ACFs of MA(3) processes derived above (i.e., (3.55)–(3.58)) to calculate the first five values of the ACF of the following processes:
   (a) $X_t = u_t + 0.50u_{t-1} - 0.10u_{t-2} + 0.05u_{t-3}$.
   (b) $X_t = u_t - 0.50u_{t-1} + 0.20u_{t-2} + 0.10u_{t-3}$.

3.1.5 Theoretical PACFs

Theoretical partial ACFs are more difficult to derive, so we will only outline their general properties. Theoretical PACFs are similar to ACFs, except they remove the effects of other lags. That is, the PACF at lag 2 filters out the effect of autocorrelation from lag 1. Likewise, the partial autocorrelation at lag 3 filters out the effect of autocorrelation at lags 2 and 1.

A useful rule of thumb is that theoretical PACFs are the mirrored opposites of ACFs. While the ACF of an AR(p) process dies down exponentially, the PACF has spikes at lags 1 through p and then is zero at lags greater than p. The ACF of an

MA(q) process has nonzero spikes up to lag q and zero afterward, while the PACF of dampens toward zero and often with a bit of oscillation.

3.1.6 Summary: Theoretical ACFs and PACFs

We have covered much ground thus far, so it will be useful to summarize what we have concluded about theoretical ACFs and PACFs of the various processes.

Theoretical ACFs and PACFs will show the following features:

1. For AR(p) processes:
   (a) The ACFs decays slowly.
   (b) The PACFs show spikes at lags $1 - p$ and then cut off to zero.
2. For MA(q) processes:
   (a) The ACFs show spikes at lags $1 - q$ and then cuts off to zero.
   (b) The PACFs decay slowly, often with oscillation.
3. For ARMA(p,q) processes:
   (a) The ACFs decay slowly.
   (b) The PACFs decay slowly.

Figures 3.4–3.15 graph the theoretical ACFs and PACFs of several different AR(p), MA(q), and ARMA(p,q) processes.

3.2 Empirical ACFs and PACFs

Theoretical ACFs and PACFs were implied by particular models. Empirical ACFs and PACFs, on the other hand, are the sample correlations estimated from data. As such, they are quite easy to estimate. We'll review the Stata syntax for estimating

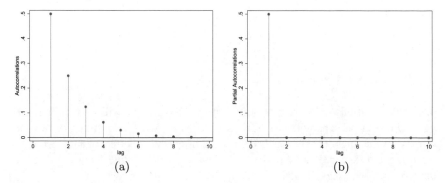

Fig. 3.4 Theoretical ACF and PACF of AR(1): $X_t = 0.50 X_{t-1} + e_t$. (**a**) Theoretical ACF. (**b**) Theoretical PACF

3.2 Empirical ACFs and PACFs

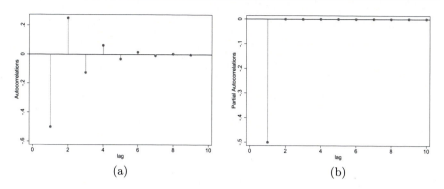

Fig. 3.5 Theoretical ACF and PACF of AR(1): $X_t = -0.50X_{t-1} + e_t$. (**a**) Theoretical ACF. (**b**) Theoretical PACF

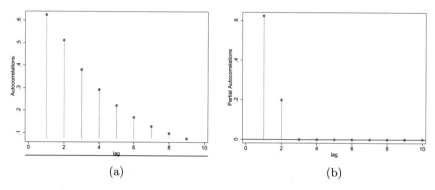

Fig. 3.6 Theoretical ACF and PACF of AR(2): $X_t = 0.50X_{t-1} + 0.20X_{t-2} + e_t$. (**a**) Theoretical ACF. (**b**) Theoretical PACF

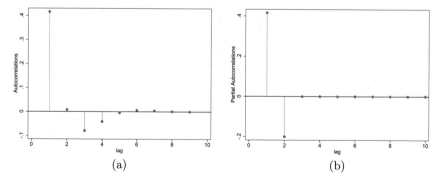

Fig. 3.7 Theoretical ACF and PACF of AR(2): $X_t = 0.50X_{t-1} - 0.20X_{t-2} + e_t$. (**a**) Theoretical ACF. (**b**) Theoretical PACF

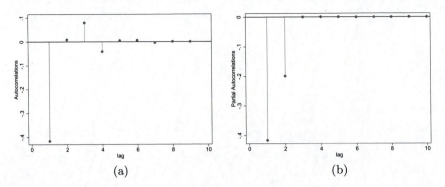

Fig. 3.8 Theoretical ACF and PACF of AR(2): $X_t = -0.50X_{t-1} - 0.20X_{t-2} + e_t$. (**a**) Theoretical ACF. (**b**) Theoretical PACF

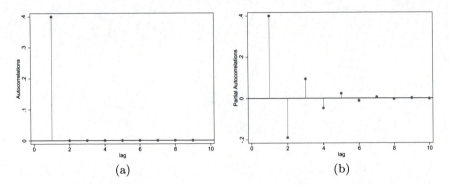

Fig. 3.9 Theoretical ACF and PACF of MA(1): $X_t = u_t + 0.50u_{t-1}$. (**a**) Theoretical ACF. (**b**) Theoretical PACF

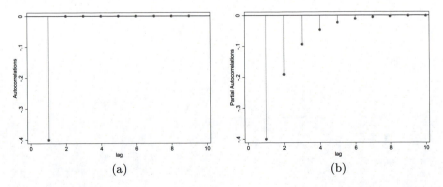

Fig. 3.10 Theoretical ACF and PACF of MA(1): $X_t = u_t - 0.50u_{t-1}$. (**a**) Theoretical ACF. (**b**) Theoretical PACF

3.2 Empirical ACFs and PACFs

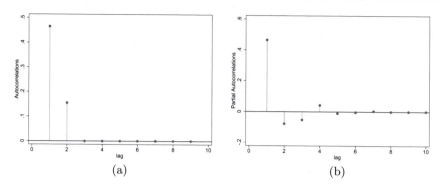

Fig. 3.11 Theoretical ACF and PACF of MA(2): $X_t = u_t + 0.50u_{t-1} + 0.20u_{t-2}$. (**a**) Theoretical ACF. (**b**) Theoretical PACF

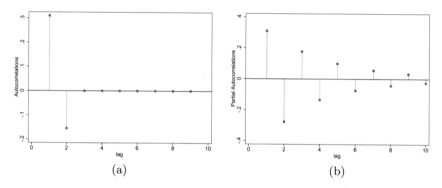

Fig. 3.12 Theoretical ACF and PACF of MA(2): $X_t = u_t + 0.50u_{t-1} - 0.20u_{t-2}$. (**a**) Theoretical ACF. (**b**) Theoretical PACF

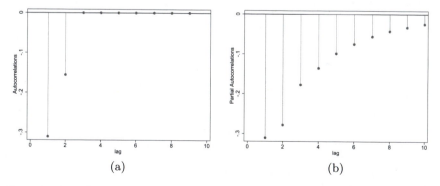

Fig. 3.13 Theoretical ACF and PACF of MA(2): $X_t = u_t - 0.50u_{t-1} - 0.20u_{t-2}$. (**a**) Theoretical ACF. (**b**) Theoretical PACF

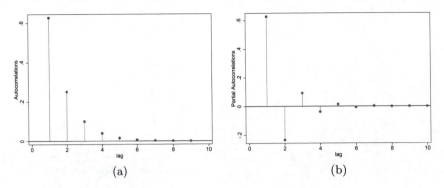

Fig. 3.14 Theoretical ACF and PACF of ARMA(1,1): $X_t = 0.40 X_{t-1} + u_t + 0.40 u_{t-1}$. (**a**) Theoretical ACF. (**b**) Theoretical PACF

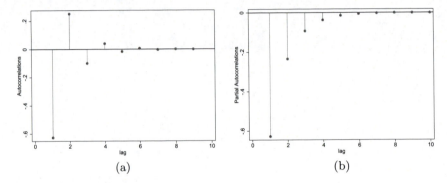

Fig. 3.15 Theoretical ACF and PACF of ARMA(1,1): $X_t = -0.40 X_{t-1} + u_t - 0.40 u_{t-1}$. (**a**) Theoretical ACF. (**b**) Theoretical PACF

simple correlations, and we'll explore in greater depth what was meant by a partial ACF.

3.2.1 Calculating Empirical ACFs

Empirical ACFs are not the result of a model. They are a description of data. They can be calculated much like any other correlation. To calculate an empirical ACF in Stata, create a new variable that is the lag of X—let us call it LagX. Treat this new variable like any other variable Y and calculate the correlation between X and Y. That is,

```
. gen LagX = L.X
. correlate X LagX
```

In fact, Stata is quite smart. There is no need to create the new variable. Rather, we may estimate the correlation between X and its lag more directly by

3.2 Empirical ACFs and PACFs

```
. correlate X L.X
```

which only calculates the autocorrelation at a lag of one. To calculate deeper lags,

```
. correlate X L.X L2.X L3.X L4.X L5.X
```

Alternatively,

```
. correlate X L(1/5).X
```

provides the empirical ACF (and PACF), as well as a text-based picture of the two. A nicer graph of the ACF is produced via the ac command:

```
. use ARexamples.dta, clear
. ac X
```

which produced the empirical ACF in Fig. 3.16a.

3.2.2 Calculating Empirical PACFs

The empirical partial autocorrelation function shows the correlation between sets of ordered pairs (X_t, X_{t+k}) while removing the effect of the intervening Xs. Regression analysis is perfectly suited for this type of procedure. After all, when one estimates $Y = \beta_0 + \beta_1 X + \beta_2 Z$, the coefficient β_1 is interpreted as the effect, or relationship, between X and Y, holding the effect of Z constant.

Let's denote the partial autocorrelation coefficient between X_t and X_{t+k} as ϕ_{kk} (following the notation in Pankratz (1991, 1983)).

Suppose we are given data on X. Then the PACF between X_t and X_{t-1} (or the "PACF at lag 1") is found by estimating, via linear regression,

$$X_t = \phi_{10} + \phi_{11} X_{t-1} + e_t.$$

The PACF between X_t and X_{t-2} (i.e., the PACF at lag 2) is found by estimating

$$X_t = \phi_{20} + \phi_{21} X_{t-1} + \phi_{22} X_{t-2} + e_t.$$

Likewise, we can find $\phi_{33}, \phi_{44}, \ldots \phi_{kk}$, by estimating

$$X_t = \phi_{30} + \phi_{31} X_{t-1} + \phi_{32} X_{t-2} + \phi_{33} X_{t-3} + e_t,$$

$$X_t = \phi_{40} + \phi_{41} X_{t-1} + \phi_{42} X_{t-2} + \phi_{43} X_{t-3} + \phi_{44} X_{t-4} + e_t,$$

$$\vdots$$

$$X_t = \phi_{k0} + \phi_{k1} X_{t-1} + \phi_{k2} X_{t-2} + \ldots + \phi_{kk} X_{t-k} + e_t.$$

The PACF of the series X is then

$$PACF(X) = \{\phi_{11}, \phi_{22}, \phi_{33}, \ldots \phi_{kk}\}.$$

Thus, much like a coefficient in a multiple regression is often termed a "partial correlation coefficient" (for suitably standardized data), we use these estimates to construct a partial autocorrelation function. That is, we construct a partial autocorrelation function from the partial correlation coefficients of a linear regression.

Example

We will show how to calculate PACFs "by hand" using a sequence of regressions. Then, we will estimate the PACF more quickly using Stata's built-in pac and corrgram commands, showing that the approaches—the long way and the quick way—are equivalent. Having shown this, we will thereafter rely on the easier short way in our subsequent calculations.

First, we will do this for a dataset which we know comes from an AR process (it was constructed to be so), and then we will repeat the process for data from an MA process. Then we will compare the ACFs and PACFs from the AR and MA processes. AR and MA processes have different ACFs and PACFs, so in practice, estimating these ACFs and PACFs will let us know what type of model we should estimate.

```
. use ARexamples, clear

. reg X L.X                       // reg1
. reg X L.X L2.X                  // reg2
. reg X L.X L2.X L3.X             // reg3
. reg X L.X L2.X L3.X L4.X        // reg4
```

The results of these regressions are summarized in Table 3.1

Stata's built-in command corrgram calculates these partial autocorrelation coefficients (PACs) automatically and even shows a text-based graph of the PACF:

Table 3.1 PACFs using regression

Variable	reg1	reg2	reg3	reg4
L1.X	**0.5236**	0.5283	0.5281	0.5285
L2.X		**−0.0087**	0.0018	0.0017
L3.X			**−0.0199**	−0.0305
L4.X				**0.0201**
_cons	0.0190	0.0189	0.0193	0.0188

3.2 Empirical ACFs and PACFs

```
. corrgram X, lags(4)

                                          -1       0       1 -1       0       1
  LAG       AC       PAC       Q      Prob>Q  [Autocorrelation]  [Partial Autocor]
  -------------------------------------------------------------------------------
  1       0.5235   0.5236   822.95   0.0000    |----              |----
  2       0.2677  -0.0087  1038.3    0.0000    |--                |
  3       0.1223  -0.0199  1083.2    0.0000    |                  |
  4       0.0693   0.0201  1097.6    0.0000    |                  |
```

Likewise, we could use Stata's built-in command pac to draw a nicer graph of the PACF, along with confidence bands in a shaded area:

```
. use ARexamples.dta, clear
. pac X
```

which produced the empirical PACF in Fig. 3.16b.

Next, we complete the same type of exercise, but with data from AR(2), MA(1) and MA(2) processes (Fig. 3.17–3.19).

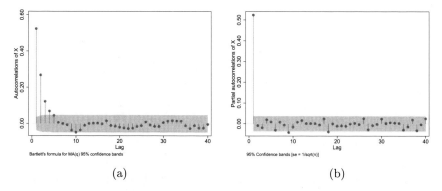

Fig. 3.16 Empirical ACF and PACF of data from an AR(1) process. (**a**) Empirical ACF. (**b**) Empirical PACF

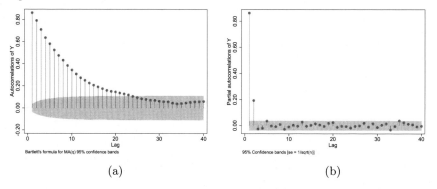

Fig. 3.17 Empirical ACF and PACF of data from an AR(2) process. (**a**) Empirical ACF. (**b**) Empirical PACF

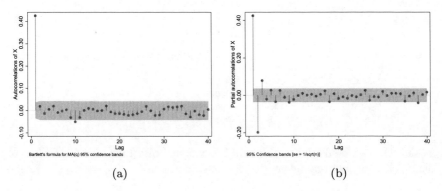

Fig. 3.18 Empirical ACF and PACF of MA(1) process. (**a**) ACF. (**b**) PACF

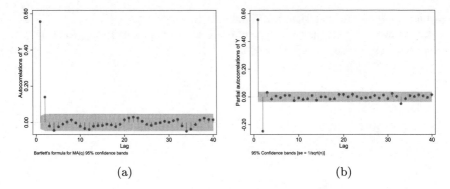

Fig. 3.19 Empirical ACF and PACF of MA(2) process. (**a**) ACF. (**b**) PACF

Exercises

1. Using `ARexamples.dta`, calculate the empirical PACFs (out to five lags) for variable Z using the regression approach. Do the same using `corrgram`. Verify that your answers are the same regardless of which approach you use.
2. Using `MAexamples.dta`, calculate the empirical PACFs (out to five lags) for variables X, Y, and Z using the regression approach and using `corrgram`. Verify that your answers are the same regardless of which approach you use.

3.3 Putting It All Together

Each type of process has its signature: its theoretical ACF and PACF. Each dataset has its own correlation structure: its empirical ACF and PACF. We can figure out which type of process to use to model the data by comparing the correlations in the data, with the correlations implied by the different models. The process is simple: calculate the empirical ACF and PACF from the data, and see whether it looks like the type of pattern predicted by a specific type of model. Do the empirical ACF and PACF look similar to the theoretical ACF/PACF from, say, an AR(2) process? Then, estimate an AR(2) model using the data.

3.3.1 Example

Suppose you were given data that produced the empirical ACF and PACF shown in Fig. 3.20. What type of process might have generated this data?

In Fig. 3.20a, the ACF has two significant spikes. In Fig. 3.20b, the PACF has a sequence of significant spikes, with dampening and oscillation. This looks similar to what might be expected from an MA(2) process as we see in Fig. 3.11.

Thus, we might estimate an MA(2) model, giving us output such as the following:

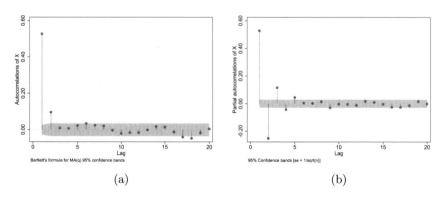

(a)   (b)

Fig. 3.20 Empirical ACF and PACF of Example data. (**a**) Empirical ACF. (**b**) Empirical PACF

```
. arima X, ma(1/2) nolog

ARIMA regression

Sample:  1 - 5000                             Number of obs    =      5000
                                              Wald chi2(2)     =   3158.05
Log likelihood = -7113.909                    Prob > chi2      =    0.0000

------------------------------------------------------------------------------
             |                 OPG
           X |      Coef.   Std. Err.      z    P>|z|     [95% Conf. Interval]
-------------+----------------------------------------------------------------
X            |
       _cons |  -.0128841   .0259289    -0.50   0.619    -.0637038    .0379356
-------------+----------------------------------------------------------------
ARMA         |
          ma |
         L1. |   .6954519   .0140585    49.47   0.000     .6678977    .7230061
         L2. |   .1299029   .0138403     9.39   0.000     .1027764    .1570294
-------------+----------------------------------------------------------------
      /sigma |   1.003802   .0100518    99.86   0.000     .9841009    1.023503
------------------------------------------------------------------------------
Note: The test of the variance against zero is one sided, and the two-sided
confidence interval is truncated at zero.
```

Since the constant is statistically insignificant, we can drop it and reestimate a zero-mean MA(2) model:

```
. arima X, ma(1/2) nolog nocons

ARIMA regression

Sample:  1 - 5000                             Number of obs    =      5000
                                              Wald chi2(2)     =   3161.78
Log likelihood = -7114.033                    Prob > chi2      =    0.0000

------------------------------------------------------------------------------
             |                 OPG
           X |      Coef.   Std. Err.      z    P>|z|     [95% Conf. Interval]
-------------+----------------------------------------------------------------
ARMA         |
          ma |
         L1. |   .6954989   .0140549    49.48   0.000     .6679519     .723046
         L2. |   .1299435   .0138441     9.39   0.000     .1028094    .1570775
-------------+----------------------------------------------------------------
      /sigma |   1.003825   .0100521    99.86   0.000     .9841228    1.023526
------------------------------------------------------------------------------
Note: The test of the variance against zero is one sided, and the two-sided
confidence interval is truncated at zero.
```

Thus, we can conclude that the data are reasonably described by

$$X_t = e_t + 0.6954989 e_{t-1} + 0.1299435 e_{t-2}.$$

3.3.2 Example

Suppose you are given the dataset rGDPgr.dta, which contains data on seasonally adjusted real GDP growth rates, quarterly, from 1947 Q2 through 2017 Q2. Alternatively, you can download it from the Federal Reserve's website and tsset the data:

- freduse A191RL1Q225SBEA, clear
- rename A19 rGDPgr
- gen time = _n
- tsset time

How should we model the real GDP growth rate? As an AR(p) process? An MA(q) or ARMA(p,q)? And of what order p or q? The standard approach is to calculate the empirical ACF/PACF exhibited by the data and compare them to the characteristic (i.e., theoretical) ACF/PACF implied by the various models.

So, our first step is to calculate the empirical ACF and PACF:

- ac rGDPgr, lags(20)
- pac rGDPgr, lags(20)

which produces the two panels in Fig. 3.21.

The empirical ACF shows two statistically significant spikes (at lags 1 and 2). The PACF has one significant spike at lag 1, after which the partial autocorrelations are not statistically different from zero (with one exception). The PACF at a lag of 12 is statistically significant. The data are quarterly, so this lag of 12 corresponds to an occurrence 48 months, or 4 years, previous. There does not seem to be any economically compelling reason why events 48 months previous should be important when events at 36, 24, and 12 months previous are insignificant. It seems as though this is a false-positive partial autocorrelation.

Given that the patterns in Fig. 3.21 look similar to those in Fig. 3.4, we conclude that the growth rate of real GDP is reasonably modeled as an AR(1) process.

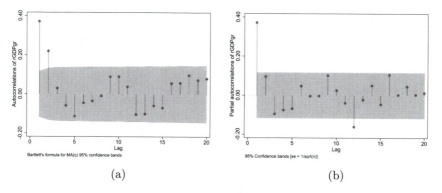

Fig. 3.21 Empirical ACF and PACF of the real GDP growth rate. (**a**) Empirical ACF. (**b**) Empirical PACF

Estimating the AR(1) model for rGDPgr,

```
. arima rGDPgr, ar(1) nolog

ARIMA regression

Sample:  1 - 281                              Number of obs     =        281
                                              Wald chi2(1)      =      61.21
Log likelihood = -759.3922                    Prob > chi2       =     0.0000

------------------------------------------------------------------------------
             |               OPG
      rGDPgr |     Coef.   Std. Err.      z    P>|z|     [95% Conf. Interval]
-------------+----------------------------------------------------------------
rGDPgr       |
       _cons |   3.211171   .349342     9.19   0.000     2.526473    3.895868
-------------+----------------------------------------------------------------
ARMA         |
          ar |
         L1. |   .3714602   .0474796    7.82   0.000     .2784018    .4645185
-------------+----------------------------------------------------------------
      /sigma |   3.608643   .1073432   33.62   0.000     3.398254    3.819032
------------------------------------------------------------------------------
Note: The test of the variance against zero is one sided, and the two-sided
confidence interval is truncated at zero.
```

One can make a case that

$$rGDPgr = 3.21 + 0.3715(rGDgr_t) + e_t$$

reasonably describes the dynamics of the real GDP growth rate.

We can use this information to forecast the real GDP growth rate over, say, the next five periods:

```
. tsappend, add(5)
. predict rGDPgrhat
```

We can graph the data and the forecast:

```
. twoway (connected rGDPgr time if time >=250,
  msymbol(none)) ///
  (connected rGDPgrhat time if time>= 250 &
  rGDPgr==., ///
  msymbol(none) lpattern(dash))
```

which produces Fig. 3.22.

3.3 Putting It All Together

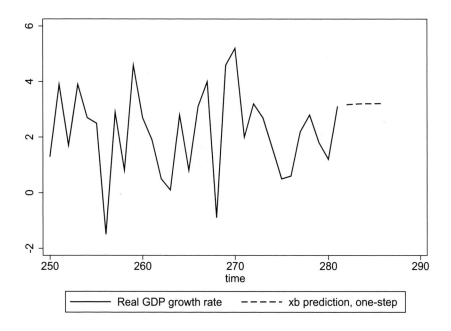

Fig. 3.22 Forecast of the growth rate of real GDP

3.3.3 Exercises

1. Load the dataset `ARMAexercises.dta`. Using the `ac` and `pac` commands in Stata, calculate the empirical ACF and PACF for each of the variables in the dataset. What type of process seems to have generated each variable?
2. For each of the variables in the question above, estimate the AR, MA, or ARMA model that seems to have generated the variable. Write out the estimated equation of each model. Pay special attention to whether the estimated constant is statistically significant. If it is not, drop the constant from the model and reestimate.
3. Download data from FRED on the seasonally adjusted growth rate of nominal GDP (this is series: `A191RP1Q027SBEA`). Use data from 1947 Q2 through 2017 Q2. Calculate its empirical ACF and PACF. What type of ARMA(p,q) process seems to best fit the ACF/PACF? Explain your reasoning. Estimate the ARMA process and report your results. If necessary, modify your model based on this output. Use your final estimated model to forecast out to five additional periods. Graph your results. Compare your forecasted GDP numbers with the real ones from FRED. Do you think your estimates are fairly good or not?

3.4 Information Criteria

Many of today's econometricians make use of various "information criteria" in much the same way as earlier econometricians compared models via the $\bar{R}^2$ statistic. In a nutshell, information criteria penalize the log-likelihood by various amounts, depending on the number of observations and the number of estimated statistics. That is, they are very similar to how the $\bar{R}^2$ penalized the R^2 by subtracting a function of the degrees of freedom.

Stata reports various information criteria after many estimation commands. The ARIMA command is no exception. To see Stata's estimate of the Akaike and Bayesian information criteria, simply type

```
. estat ic
```

after estimating an ARIMA model.

All information criteria (ICs) have, at their base, some version of the likelihood function. Many different econometric software programs use different variations of the information criteria formulas. Some of the software programs aim to maximize the likelihood, others the log-likelihood, and still others aim to minimize the negative of the log-likelihood, or the log-likelihood divided the sample size. Regardless of the particular way in which each program implements the idea, the basic idea is the same. We want a statistic that can give us an idea of how well a particular model fits a particular set of data. The most familiar such statistic is the R^2, but for many reasons, it is not the best statistic for comparing models (especially non-nested models).

Stata reports two information criteria after many estimation commands (in fact, after any likelihood-based estimation command).

Stata's version of the Akaike (1974) information criterion is defined as

$$AIC = -2ln(L) + 2k \qquad (3.59)$$

where $ln(L)$ is the maximized (natural) log-likelihood of the model and k is the number of parameters estimated.

Stata's Bayesian information criterion is

$$BIC = -2ln(L) + kln(N) \qquad (3.60)$$

where N is the sample size.

Both ICs penalize (-2 times the negative of) the likelihood function by adding a penalty; this penalty depends upon the number of estimated parameters and the sample size (much like the adjused-R2 does).

Everything else equal, the best model (the one that fits the data best) is the one associated with the greatest likelihood. Since Stata reports the negative of the likelihood (which is why the penalty is additive rather than subtractive), the best models have the *smallest* information criteria. Smaller is better, when dealing

3.4 Information Criteria

with Stata's ICs. To access these information criteria, type `estat ic` after any likelihood-based estimation command (such as `reg` or the `arma` command we have been using in this chapter).

3.4.1 Example

What type of model best fits X (from the dataset `ARexamples.dta`). We will consider AR and MA models up to three lags. To do this, calculate each of the models and compare AICs and BICs. The model with the lowest AIC and BIC is the preferred model.

First, estimate the AR models with three, two, and one lags, and compare their information criteria:

```
. use "ARexamples.dta", clear

. quietly arima X, ar(1/3) nocons

. estat ic

Akaike's information criterion and Bayesian information criterion

-----------------------------------------------------------------------------
       Model |        Obs    ll(null)   ll(model)      df         AIC        BIC
-------------+---------------------------------------------------------------
           . |      3,000           .   -4228.506       4    8465.013   8489.038
-----------------------------------------------------------------------------
Note: N=Obs used in calculating BIC; see [R] BIC note.

. quietly arima X, ar(1/2) nocons
. estat ic

Akaike's information criterion and Bayesian information criterion

-----------------------------------------------------------------------------
       Model |        Obs    ll(null)   ll(model)      df         AIC        BIC
-------------+---------------------------------------------------------------
           . |      3,000           .   -4229.076       3    8464.152   8482.171
-----------------------------------------------------------------------------
Note: N=Obs used in calculating BIC; see [R] BIC note.

. quietly arima X, ar(1) nocons
. estat ic

Akaike's information criterion and Bayesian information criterion

-----------------------------------------------------------------------------
       Model |        Obs    ll(null)   ll(model)      df         AIC        BIC
-------------+---------------------------------------------------------------
           . |      3,000           .    -4229.18       2     8462.36   8474.373
-----------------------------------------------------------------------------
Note: N=Obs used in calculating BIC; see [R] BIC note.
```

We can see that the AR model with the smallest information criteria is the last model, the AR(1). How do these compare to the MA models?

```
. quietly arima X, ma(1/3) nocons
. estat ic
```

Akaike's information criterion and Bayesian information criterion

```
-----------------------------------------------------------------------------
      Model |         Obs  ll(null)  ll(model)     df         AIC        BIC
------------+----------------------------------------------------------------
          . |       3,000         .  -4232.239      4    8472.478   8496.504
-----------------------------------------------------------------------------
```
Note: N=Obs used in calculating BIC; see [R] BIC note.

```
. quietly arima X, ma(1/2) nocons
. estat ic
```

Akaike's information criterion and Bayesian information criterion

```
-----------------------------------------------------------------------------
      Model |         Obs  ll(null)  ll(model)     df         AIC        BIC
------------+----------------------------------------------------------------
          . |       3,000         .  -4244.231      3    8494.463   8512.482
-----------------------------------------------------------------------------
```
Note: N=Obs used in calculating BIC; see [R] BIC note.

```
. quietly arima X, ma(1) nocons
. estat ic
```

Akaike's information criterion and Bayesian information criterion

```
-----------------------------------------------------------------------------
      Model |         Obs  ll(null)  ll(model)     df         AIC        BIC
------------+----------------------------------------------------------------
          . |       3,000         .  -4330.126      2    8664.252   8676.265
-----------------------------------------------------------------------------
```
Note: N=Obs used in calculating BIC; see [R] BIC note.

Of the MA models, the last one—the MA(1) model—fits best.

So, should we be fitting an AR(1) model or an MA(1) model? Since smaller information criteria indicate better fits, the AICs and BICs both indicate that an AR(1) model fits the data better than an MA(1) model. Since the data were, in fact, generated from an AR(1) process, the ICs have led us to the right conclusion.

3.4.2 Exercises

1. Load the dataset MAexamples.dta. Rather than using ACF and PACFs to determine which model to estimate, let's use information criteria (ICs) instead. For each of the three variables in the dataset estimate AR and MA models up to

3.4 Information Criteria

lag 3, calculate their corresponding AICs and BICs. Which type of model best fits each variable according to each information criterion. Do your results differ between the two ICs?

2. Load the dataset ARMAexercises.dta. For each of the variables in the dataset, calculate ICs for AR(1/4) down to AR(1) models and MA(1/4) down to MA(1) models. (The data were artificially generated from either an AR or MA process; they did not come from an ARMA process.) For each variable, which model is "preferred" by the AIC? By the BIC? Do your results differ between them? Do your results differ from what you deduced using ACFs and PACFs?

Stationarity and Invertibility   4

4.1 What Is Stationarity?

Most time series methods are only valid if the underlying time series is stationary. The more stationary something is, the more predictable it is. More specifically, a time series is stationary if its mean, variance, and autocovariance do not rely on the particular time period.[1]

The mean of a cross-sectional variable X is $E(X) = \mu$. When X is a time series, it is subscripted by the time period in which it is observed, with period t as the usual notation for an arbitrary time period. The mean of a time series X_t is $E(X_t) = \mu_t$; the subscript denotes that the mean could depend upon the particular time. For example, if X_t is growing, then its mean (or expected value) will also be growing. Tomorrow's X_{t+1} is expected to be greater than today's X_t. Likewise, the variance of X_t, denoted $Var(X_t)$ or σ_t^2, might depend upon the particular time period. For example, volatility might be increasing over time. More likely, volatility tomorrow might depend upon today's volatility.

Specifically, we say that X_t is "mean stationary," if

$$E(X_t) = \mu \qquad (4.1)$$

at all time periods t. It is "variance stationary" if

$$Var(X_t) = \sigma^2 \qquad (4.2)$$

---

[1] Stationarity of mean, variance, and covariance is called "weak stationarity." If all moments, including higher-order moments like skewness and kurtosis, area also constant, then we say the time series has "strong form stationarity," "strict stationarity," or "strong stationarity." For the purposes of this book, "stationarity" will refer to "weak stationarity."

no matter the time period t. A process is "autocovariance stationary" if the covariance between X and itself does not depend upon a phase shift:

$$Cov(X_t, X_{t+k}) = Cov(X_{t+a}, X_{t+k+a}) \qquad (4.3)$$

That is, the covariance between X_t and X_{t+k} does not depend upon which particular period t is; the time variable could be shifted forward or backward by a periods and the same covariance relationship would hold. What matters is the distance between the two observations.

For example, the covariance between X_1 and X_4 is the same as the covariance between X_5 and X_8, or between X_{11} and X_{14}. In symbols,

$$Cov(X_1, X_4) = Cov(X_5, X_8) = Cov(X_{11}, X_{14}) = Cov(X_t, X_{t+3}).$$

When a process satisfies all of the above conditions, we say that X is "stationary."[2]

At a first pass, testing for mean and variance stationarity seems fairly straightforward. We could test to see whether the series is increasing or decreasing. We could compare the mean or the variance between the first half and the second half of the series. Such methods are crude, however. (More formal and powerful tests—essential tests in the econometricians' toolbox—are the subject of Chap. 7.)

In the previous chapter we presumed stationarity. In this chapter, we derive the conditions under which a process is stationary and also show some further implications of this stationarity. In Chap. 5 we will weaken this assumption and begin exploring processes which are not stationary.

4.2 The Importance of Stationarity

Why do we care whether a series is stationary?

First, stationary processes are better understood than nonstationary ones, and we know how to estimate them better. The test statistics of certain nonstationary processes do not follow the usual distributions. Knowing how a process is nonstationary will allow us to make the necessary corrections.

Further, if we regress two completely unrelated integrated processes on each other, then a problem called "spurious regression" can arise. In a nutshell, if X and Y are both trending, then regressing Y on X is likely to indicate a strong relationship between them, even though there is no real connection. They both depend upon

---

[2] In this chapter, we will be exploring primarily stationarity in the means of processes. This is often called "stability" and is a subset of stationarity. Since we do not explore nonstationary variance until Chap. 9, though, we will treat "stability" and "stationarity" as synonyms and use them interchangeably.

4.3 Restrictions on AR Coefficients Which Ensure Stationarity

Not all AR processes are stationary. Some grow without limit. Some have variances which change over time. In this section we explore the restrictions on the parameters (the βs) of AR processes that render them stationary.

4.3.1 Restrictions on AR(1) Coefficients

Consider an AR(1) process:

$$X_t = \beta X_{t-1} + e_t. \tag{4.4}$$

It is easy to see that it will grow without bound if $\beta > 1$; it will decrease without bound if $\beta < -1$. The process will only settle down and have a constant expected value if $|\beta| < 1$.

This might be intuitively true, but we'd like to develop a method for examining higher-order AR processes.

First, rewrite Eq. (4.4) in terms of the lag operator L,

$$X = \beta L X + e_t.$$

Collecting the Xs to the left-hand side,

$$X - \beta L X = e_t$$
$$(1 - \beta L) X = e_t.$$

The term in parentheses is a polynomial in the lag operator. It is sometimes referred to as the "lag polynomial" or "characteristic polynomial" and is denoted by

$$\Phi(L) = (1 - \beta L).$$

Stationarity is ensured if and only if the roots of the lag polynomial are greater than one in absolute value.

Replacing the Ls with zs, we apply a little algebra and solve for the roots of the polynomial, i.e., solve for the values of z that set the polynomial equal to zero:

$$1 - z\beta = 0$$
$$1 = z\beta$$

$$z^* = 1/\beta.$$

Thus, our lag polynomial has one root, and it is equal to $1/\beta$.

The AR process is stationary if its roots are greater than 1 in magnitude:

$$|z^*| > 1,$$

which is to say that

$$|\beta| < 1.$$

To summarize, the AR(1) process is stationary if the roots of its lag polynomial are greater than one (in absolute value), and this is assured if β is less than one in absolute value.

4.3.2 Restrictions on AR(2) Coefficients

For an AR(2) process, stationarity is ensured if and only if the roots of the second-order lag polynomial $\Phi(L)$ lie outside the complex unit circle. We say the "complex unit circle" now because we have a second-degree polynomial. These polynomials might have imaginary roots. Plotting the root on the complex plane, it must have a length greater than one; it must lie outside a circle of radius = 1.

Suppose we estimated an AR(2) model,

$$X_t = \beta_1 X_{t-1} + \beta_2 X_{t-2} + e_t.$$

Collecting the Xs to the left-hand side,

$$X_t - \beta_1 L X_t - \beta_2 L^2 X_t = e_t.$$

This AR(2) process will be stationary if the roots of the second-order lag polynomial

$$\Phi(L) = 1 - L\beta_1 - L^2 \beta_2$$

are greater than one. Replacing Ls with zs, we set the polynomial equal to zero (to find its roots) and solve

$$1 - z\beta_1 - z^2 \beta_2 = 0$$

$$z^2 \beta_2 + z\beta_1 - 1 = 0.$$

A complementary approach is to work with the "inverse characteristic polynomial,"

4.3 Restrictions on AR Coefficients Which Ensure Stationarity

$$\beta_2 + z\beta_1 - z^2 = 0$$
$$0 = z^2 - z\beta_1 - \beta_2. \tag{4.5}$$

Working with the inverse characteristic polynomial will be a bit easier in this case. Many software programs such as Stata report their results in terms of the inverse characteristic polynomial. In this case, the AR process is stationary if the roots of the inverse polynomial lie inside the unit circle. This has caused a great deal of confusion with students. (In Sect. 4.3.4 we will derive the inverse characteristic polynomial and explore the relationship between the characteristic and inverse characteristic polynomials.)

To find these roots, use the quadratic formula. We're used to seeing the quadratic formula in terms of Ys and Xs, as in $Y = aX^2 + bX + c$, in which case the roots (X^*) are given by

$$X^* = \frac{-b \pm \sqrt{b^2 - 4ac}}{2a}.$$

So, to find the roots of Eq. (4.5), use the quadratic formula, replacing a with 1, b with $-\beta_1$, and c with $-\beta_2$:

$$z^* = \frac{\beta_1 \pm \sqrt{\beta_1^2 + 4\beta_2}}{2}.$$

Since we have presumably estimated the model, we simply plug in values for $\hat{\beta}_1$ and $\hat{\beta}_2$ to find the value of the roots. If these roots of the inverse characteristic polynomial are less than one, then the process is stable.

What values of β_1 and β_2 ensure that these roots of the inverse characteristic polynomial are less than one?

$$\left| \frac{\beta_1 \pm \sqrt{\beta_1^2 + 4\beta_2}}{2} \right| < 1. \tag{4.6}$$

We must consider a couple of different cases: (1) the term inside the square root of (4.6) is positive, in which case we are dealing with nice real numbers, or (2) the term inside the square root is negative, which means that we have imaginary roots.

Let's begin with the simpler case where the roots are real numbers. We can rewrite the absolute value condition as

$$-1 < \frac{\beta_1 \pm \sqrt{\beta_1^2 + 4\beta_2}}{2} < 1$$
$$-2 < \beta_1 \pm \sqrt{\beta_1^2 + 4\beta_2} < 2.$$

Since real square root terms are positive, then we can split the above into two inequalities. The first inequality is

$$\beta_1 + \sqrt{\beta_1^2 + 4\beta_2} < 2$$

$$\sqrt{\beta_1^2 + 4\beta_2} < 2 - \beta_1$$

$$\beta_1^2 + 4\beta_2 < (2 - \beta_1)^2$$

$$\beta_1^2 + 4\beta_2 < 4 - 4\beta_1 + \beta_1^2$$

$$4\beta_2 < 4 - 4\beta_1$$

$$\beta_2 < 1 - \beta_1$$

$$\beta_2 + \beta_1 < 1. \tag{4.7}$$

The second inequality is

$$-2 < \beta_1 - \sqrt{\beta_1^2 + 4\beta_2}$$

$$-2 - \beta_1 < -\sqrt{\beta_1^2 + 4\beta_2}$$

$$2 + \beta_1 > \sqrt{\beta_1^2 + 4\beta_2}$$

$$(2 + \beta_1)^2 > \beta_1^2 + 4\beta_2$$

$$4 + 4\beta_1 + \beta_1^2 > \beta_1^2 + 4\beta_2$$

$$4 + 4\beta_1 > 4\beta_2$$

$$1 + \beta_1 > 1\beta_2$$

$$1 > 1\beta_2 - \beta_1$$

$$\beta_2 - \beta_1 < 1. \tag{4.8}$$

If roots are complex, this is because $\sqrt{\beta_1^2 + 4\beta_2} < 0$, which can only happen if β_2 is negative.

$$z^* = \frac{\beta_1 \pm \sqrt{\beta_1^2 + 4\beta_2}}{2} < 1$$

$$\frac{\beta_1 \pm \sqrt{(-1)(-1)(\beta_1^2 + 4\beta_2)}}{2} < 1$$

$$\frac{\beta_1}{2} \pm i\frac{\sqrt{-\beta_1^2 - 4\beta_2}}{2} < 1.$$

4.3 Restrictions on AR Coefficients Which Ensure Stationarity

Complex numbers are usually expressed in the form $z^* = r \pm ci$ where r is the real part, and ci is the complex part. The length, or "modulus," of a complex number is equal to $\sqrt{r^2 + c^2}$, which for stationarity must be less than one, so

$$\sqrt{\frac{\beta_1^2}{4} + \frac{-\beta_1^2 - 4\beta_2}{4}} < 1$$

$$\sqrt{-\beta_2} < 1$$

$$-\beta_2 < 1$$

$$\beta_2 > -1. \tag{4.9}$$

Notice that adding restrictions (4.7) and (4.8) implies that

$$(\beta_2 + \beta_1) + (\beta_2 - \beta_1) < 2$$

$$2\beta_2 < 2$$

$$\beta_2 < 1.$$

When taken with (4.9) this implies that

$$|\beta_2| < 1. \tag{4.10}$$

In summary, there are three conditions on the βs of an AR(2) process that imply stability:

$$\beta_2 + \beta_1 < 1 \tag{4.11}$$

$$\beta_2 - \beta_1 < 1 \tag{4.12}$$

$$|\beta_2| < 1. \tag{4.13}$$

In words: (1) the coefficients cannot add up to a number greater than one, so that each successive X doesn't become greater and greater, (2) the coefficients cannot be too far apart, and (3) the coefficient on the deepest lag cannot be too big. If any of these conditions are violated, then the process is not stationary.

We can get a better understanding of the constraints by examining Fig. 4.1, a graph of the so-called Stralkowski triangle (Stralkowski & Wu, 1968). If we rewrite each of the constraints with β_2 as our "y" variable and β_1 as the "x" variable, then we see that constraints (4.11)–(4.13) define a triangle. Any set of βs that fall inside this triangle will result in a stable AR(2) process.

If the characteristic equation (or its inverse) has complex roots, this implies that the AR(2) process will have oscillations, fluctuating up and down. These complex roots will arise if the term in the square root of Eq. (4.6) is negative:

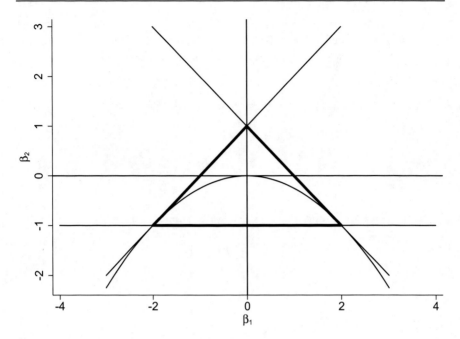

Fig. 4.1 The Stralkowski triangle for AR(2) process stability

$$\beta_1^2 + 4\beta_2 < 0$$
$$4\beta_2 < -\beta_1^2$$
$$\beta_2 < \frac{-\beta_1^2}{4}. \tag{4.14}$$

While Eq. (4.14) is not particularly illuminating in this form, it has a nice geometric interpretation within the Stralkowski triangle. Combinations of βs that fall below the upside-down parabola will result in oscillating patterns in the time series. If the βs are under the parabola, but still within the triangle, then we will have a stable oscillatory pattern. If the βs are under the parabola, but outside the triangle, then we will have an explosive oscillatory pattern.

Examples
Which of the following AR processes are stationary, and why?

1. $X_t = 1.10X_{t-1} + e_t$
2. $Y_t = 0.70Y_{t-1} + 0.10Y_{t-2} + e_t$
3. $Z_t = 0.80Z_{t-1} + 0.30Z_{t-2} + e_t$
4. $W_t = -0.80W_{t-1} + 0.30W_{t-2} + e_t$

Process (1) above is not stationary because $\beta_1 = 1.10 > 1$.

4.3 Restrictions on AR Coefficients Which Ensure Stationarity

Process (2) is stationary because its lead coefficient is less than one in absolute value ($|\beta_1| = 0.70 < 1$), its coefficients add up to less than one ($\beta_2 + \beta_1 = 0.10 + 0.70 = 0.80 < 1$), and the coefficients are less than one unit apart ($\beta_2 - \beta_1 = 0.10 - 0.70 = -0.60 < 1$).

Process (3) is not stationary as the coefficients add to more than one ($0.30 + 0.80 = 1.10 > 1$).

Process (4) is not stationary. While the first condition is met ($|0.80| < 1$), and the second condition is met ($0.30 - 0.80 = -0.50 < 1$), the third condition is not met ($0.30 - (-0.80) = 1.10 > 1$).

Figure 4.2 graphs each of the four examples above. You can verify visually which series seem stationary.

Exercises

1. Which of the following processes are stationary? Why? Express your answer in terms of the Stralkowski triangle inequalities.
   (a) $X_t = 1.05 X_{t-1} + e_t$
   (b) $X_t = 0.60 X_{t-1} + 0.10 X_{t-2} + e_t$
   (c) $X_t = 0.50 X_{t-1} + 0.30 X_{t-2} + e_t$
   (d) $X_t = 0.80 X_{t-1} - 0.10 X_{t-2} + e_t$

Example

Let's use Stata to estimate an AR(2) model and check whether it is stationary.

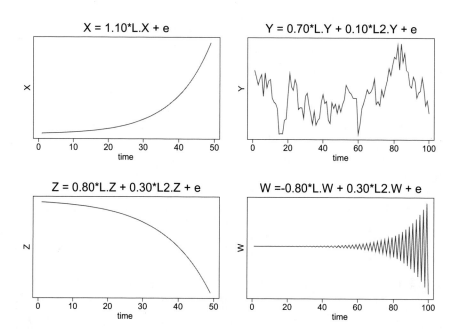

Fig. 4.2 Graphs of the stationarity condition examples

```
. use stationarity_ex.dta

. arima X, ar(1/2)  nolog nocons

ARIMA regression

Sample:  1 - 100                          Number of obs    =         100
                                          Wald chi2(2)     =     1.27e+08
Log likelihood = -604.5022                Prob > chi2      =      0.0000

------------------------------------------------------------------------------
             |                 OPG
           X |      Coef.   Std. Err.      z    P>|z|     [95% Conf. Interval]
-------------+----------------------------------------------------------------
ARMA         |
          ar |
         L1. |   1.99894   .0019518  1024.16   0.000     1.995114    2.002765
         L2. |  -.9989857  .0020413  -489.38   0.000    -1.002987   -.9949847
-------------+----------------------------------------------------------------
       /sigma|   91.29767  3.458993    26.39   0.000     84.51816    98.07717
------------------------------------------------------------------------------
Note: The test of the variance against zero is one sided, and the two-sided
confidence interval is truncated at zero.
```

After estimation, the command `estat aroots` calculates the roots of the inverse characteristic function and graphs them as well (see Fig. 4.3).

```
. estat aroots

  Eigenvalue stability condition
  +-----------------------------------------+
  |           Eigenvalue       |  Modulus   |
  |----------------------------+------------|
  |    .9994698 + .00677032i   |   .999493  |
  |    .9994698 - .00677032i   |   .999493  |
  +-----------------------------------------+
  All the eigenvalues lie inside the unit circle.
  AR parameters satisfy stability condition.
```

The two roots are complex. They have lengths that are quite close to, but less than, one. Having lengths of 0.999493, they are not technically "unit roots," but they are too close for comfort. "Near unit roots" pose their own problems. Visually inspecting Fig. 4.3a the roots seem to be on, not inside, the unit circle. The practical takeaway is that the estimated model may not be stationary. A more formal hypothesis test will be required to test whether the root is statistically close to the unit circle. (Such unit root tests are the subject of Chap. 7.)

Example
Working with the same dataset, let's estimate an AR(2) model on the variable Y.

4.3 Restrictions on AR Coefficients Which Ensure Stationarity

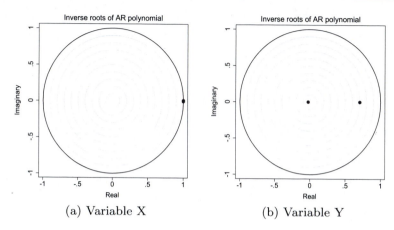

Fig. 4.3 Inverse roots of two estimated AR(2) models. (**a**) Variable X. (**b**) Variable Y

```
. arima Y, ar(1/2) nolog nocons

ARIMA regression

Sample:  1 - 100                          Number of obs     =         100
                                          Wald chi2(2)      =       98.49
Log likelihood = -151.1697                Prob > chi2       =      0.0000

------------------------------------------------------------------------------
             |                 OPG
           Y |      Coef.   Std. Err.      z    P>|z|     [95% Conf. Interval]
-------------+----------------------------------------------------------------
ARMA         |
          ar |
         L1. |   .6758953   .0945573     7.15   0.000     .4905664    .8612242
         L2. |    .018181   .0908963     0.20   0.841    -.1599725    .1963345
-------------+----------------------------------------------------------------
      /sigma |   1.093728   .0873323    12.52   0.000      .92256    1.264896
------------------------------------------------------------------------------
Note: The test of the variance against zero is one sided, and the two-sided
confidence interval is truncated at zero.

. estat aroots

Eigenvalue stability condition
  +----------------------------------------+
  |        Eigenvalue        |   Modulus   |
  |--------------------------+-------------|
  |         .7018015         |   .701802   |
  |        -.0259062         |   .025906   |
  +----------------------------------------+
All the eigenvalues lie inside the unit circle.
AR parameters satisfy stability condition.
```

Stata estimates the two inverse roots to be 0.701802 and 0.025906 and graphs them as in Fig. 4.3b. The estimated AR(2) model on Y seems to be stable and, therefore, stationary.

Exercises
1. For each of the remaining variables (Z, W, A, B, C, and D) in the stationarity_ex.dta dataset, answer the following:
   (a) Estimate a zero-mean AR(2) model using Stata's arima command.
   (b) Check for stationarity using Stata's estat aroots post-estimation command.
   (c) Check for stationarity by using the quadratic formula to compute the roots of the characteristic equation.
   (d) Check for stationarity by using the quadratic formula to compute the roots of the inverse characteristic equation.
   (e) Which variables are not stationary?
   (f) Do any of the variables seem to have roots on the unit circle (i.e., do they have "unit roots?")

Stata sometimes has problems estimating nonstationary ARIMA models. If it cannot find an estimate, this is one indication that the estimated model is not stationary. Still, if you want to force Stata into providing an estimate, you can try using the diffuse option at the end of the arima command. The diffuse estimates are suspect, though, so use this option sparingly. This will be necessary, however, for some of the exercises above.

4.3.3 Restrictions on AR(p) Coefficients

The stationarity restrictions on the coefficients of an AR(3) are much more complicated than those for AR(1) or AR(2). Moreover, there is no such thing as a "quadratic formula" for polynomials of order five or higher. Thus, for higher-order AR(p) processes, we cannot provide a set of explicit formulas for the βs that ensure stationarity. All is not lost however, as computers can solve for complicated (and complex) roots numerically. We're not stuck with analytical solutions from a quadratic formula type of solution.

Consider the AR(p) process:

$$X_t = \beta_1 X_{t-1} + \beta_2 X_{t-2} + \cdots + \beta_p X_{t-p} + e_t$$

Collecting the Xs to the left-hand side and using the lag operator L,

$$X\left(1 - \beta_1 L - \beta_2 L^2 - \cdots - \beta_p L^p\right) = e_t$$

$$X\Phi(L) = e_t$$

where $\Phi(L)$ is the lag polynomial.

4.3 Restrictions on AR Coefficients Which Ensure Stationarity

Substituting zs into the lag polynomial gives the characteristic polynomial:

$$1 - \beta_1 z - \beta_2 z^2 - \cdots - \beta_p z^p = 0.$$

If the roots of this characteristic polynomial (i.e., the values of z such that the polynomial is equal to zero) are greater than zero, then the AR process is stationary.

Alternatively, we could calculate the roots of the inverse characteristic polynomial:

$$z^p - \beta_1 z^{p-1} - \beta_2 z^{p-2} - \cdots - \beta_{p-1} z - \beta_p = 0$$

and verify whether they are inside the complex unit circle.

While there is no "quadratic formula" for an arbitrary pth-order polynomial, computers can still estimate the roots of such equations. Stata does this easily. Thus, to check for stationarity, we simply need to verify that the roots as provided by Stata are inside the unit circle.

4.3.4 Characteristic and Inverse Characteristic Equations

A linear difference equation is stable if the roots of its characteristic equation are greater than one in absolute value. Including the possibility of imaginary roots, the restriction is that the roots of the characteristic equation must have a "modulus greater than one" (i.e., they must lie outside the unit circle).

Some textbooks and econometric packages (such as Stata) express this stationarity as having roots *less than one* rather than greater than one. What gives? They are referring to roots of related, but different, equations. One is referring to the roots of the characteristic equation. The other is referring to the roots of the inverse equation. Still others talk about "inverse roots." What is the relationship between these?

For an AR(p) process,

$$X_t = \beta_1 X_{t-1} + \beta_2 X_{t-2} + \cdots + \beta_p X_{t-p} + e_t,$$

the characteristic equation is found by finding the lag polynomial, substituting zs for Ls, and setting it equal to zero (since we'll want to find its roots):

$$1 - \beta_1 z - \beta_2 z^2 - \cdots - \beta_p z^p = 0. \tag{4.15}$$

The inverse characteristic equation is found by substituting $z = 1/Z$:

$$1 - \beta_1 \frac{1}{Z} - \beta_2 \frac{1}{Z^2} - \cdots - \beta_p \frac{1}{Z^p} = 0$$

and multiplying both sides by Z^p:

$$Z^p\left(1 - \beta_1\frac{1}{Z} - \beta_2\frac{1}{Z^2} - \cdots - \beta_p\frac{1}{Z^p}\right) = 0$$

$$Z^p - \beta_1\frac{Z^p}{Z} - \beta_2\frac{Z^p}{Z^2} - \cdots - \beta_p\frac{Z^p}{Z^p} = 0$$

$$Z^p - \beta_1 Z^{p-1} - \beta_2 Z^{p-2} - \cdots - \beta_p = 0.$$

Multiplying both sides by a negative and rearranging,

$$\beta_p - \cdots - \beta_2 Z^{p-2} - \beta_1 Z^{p-1} - Z^p = 0. \tag{4.16}$$

Since $z = 1/Z$, the roots of the characteristic equation (z) are reciprocals (i.e., inverses) of the roots of the inverse characteristic equation (Z). The roots of the inverse equation happen to be inverses of the roots of the characteristic equation. Thus, the terms "inverse roots" and "the roots of the inverse equation" are synonyms.

Stata reports the inverse roots of the characteristic equation, so the stationarity condition is that these roots must lie *inside* the unit circle.

Exercises
1. For each of the following AR(2) process,
   (a) $X_t = 0.50X_{t-1} + 0.10X_{t-2} + e_t$
   (b) $X_t = -0.50X_{t-1} + 0.20X_{t-2} + e_t$
   (c) $X_t = 1.10X_{t-1} + 0.20X_{t-2} + e_t$
   write down the characteristic equation and use the quadratic formula to find its roots. Write down the inverse characteristic equation. Use the quadratic formula to find its roots. Show that the two roots are reciprocals of each other.
2. For the following general AR(2) process,

$$X_t = \beta_1 X_{t-1} + \beta_2 X_{t-2} + e_t$$

write down the characteristic equation; plug in the appropriate βs into the quadratic formula to describe its roots. Write down the inverse characteristic equation; plug in the appropriate βs into the quadratic formula to describe its roots. Show that the two roots are reciprocals of each other. (Hint: Reciprocals multiply to one.)

4.3.5 Restrictions on ARIMA(p,q) Coefficients

Consider a general ARIMA(p,q) model with p autoregressive terms and q moving average terms:

$$X_t = \left(\beta_1 X_{t-1} + \beta_2 X_{t-2} + \cdots + \beta_p X_{t-p}\right)$$
$$+ \left(u_t + \gamma_1 u_{t-1} + \gamma_2 u_{t-2} + \cdots + \gamma_q u_{t-q}\right). \tag{4.17}$$

What restrictions on the βs and γs ensure that the estimated model is stable?

After collecting terms and factoring, we can express Eq. (4.17) in terms of two lag polynomials:

$$X\left(1 - \beta_1 L + \beta_2 L^2 + \cdots + \beta_p L^p\right) = u\left(1 + \gamma_1 L + \gamma_2 L^2 + \cdots + \gamma_q L^q\right)$$

$$\Phi(L)X = \Theta(L)u$$

where $\Phi(L)$ is the lag polynomial on X:

$$\Phi(L) = \left(1 - \beta_1 L + \beta_2 L^2 + \cdots + \beta_p L^p\right)$$

and $\Theta(L)$ is the lag polynomial on u:

$$\Theta(L) = \left(1 + \gamma_1 L + \gamma_2 L^2 + \cdots + \gamma_q L^q\right).$$

The same restrictions apply here, as well. If the roots of the characteristic equation are outside the unit circle, the estimated model is stationary. Likewise, the model is stationary if the roots of the inverse characteristic equation are inside the unit circle.

4.4 The Connection Between AR and MA Processes

Under certain conditions, AR processes can be expressed as infinite order MA processes. The same is true for MA processes. They can be expressed as infinite order AR processes, under certain conditions.

To go from AR to MA, the AR process must be stationary. To go from MA to AR, the MA process must be invertible.

We will explore these connections with simple AR(1) and MA(1) models before making more general claims about AR(p) and MA(q) models.

4.4.1 AR(1) to MA(∞)

There is an important link between AR and MA processes. A stationary AR process can be expressed as an MA process, and vice versa.

It is easy to show that an AR(1) process can be expressed as an MA(∞) process under certain conditions. Consider the following AR(1) process:

$$X_t = \beta X_{t-1} + e_t. \tag{4.18}$$

Since the t subscript is arbitrary, we can write (4.18) as

$$X_{t-1} = \beta X_{t-2} + e_{t-1} \tag{4.19}$$

or as

$$X_{t-2} = \beta X_{t-3} + e_{t-2}. \tag{4.20}$$

Substituting (4.20) into (4.19) and (4.19) into (4.18),

$$\begin{aligned} X_t &= \beta\left[\beta\left(\beta X_{t-3} + e_{t-2}\right) + e_{t-1}\right] + e_t \\ &= \beta X_{t-3} + \beta^2 e_{t-2} + \beta e_{t-1} + e_t. \end{aligned}$$

Continuing the substitutions indefinitely yields

$$X_t = e_t + \beta e_{t-1} + \beta^2 e_{t-2} + \beta^3 e_{t-3} + \ldots \tag{4.21}$$

Thus, the AR(1) process is an MA(∞) process:

$$X_t = e_t + \gamma_1 e_{t-1} + \gamma_2 e_{t-2} + \gamma_3 e_{t-3} + \ldots \tag{4.22}$$

where $\gamma_1 = \beta$, $\gamma_2 = \beta^2$, $\gamma_3 = \beta^3$, and so forth.

Can an AR(1) process always be expressed in this way? No.

The reason why an AR(1) process is not always an MA(∞) lies in our ability to continue the substitution indefinitely. For X_t to be finite, then the infinite sum in (4.22) cannot be unbounded. How do we know whether the sum is bounded or not? We turn to that question next.

Proof Using Lag Operators

Above, we saw via direct substitution that an AR(1) process can be expressed as an MA(∞) process. We show the same now, but using the lag operator L:

$$\begin{aligned} X_t &= \beta X_{t-1} + e_t \\ X_t &= \beta L X_t + e_t \\ X - \beta L X &= e_t \\ X_t (1 - \beta L) &= e_t \end{aligned} \tag{4.23}$$

$$X_t = e_t \frac{1}{1 - \beta L}. \tag{4.24}$$

We can only move from line (4.23)–(4.24) if βL is not equal to one; otherwise we would be dividing by zero.

Continuing, recall the infinite sum formula: $1/(1-\alpha) = 1 + \alpha^1 + \alpha^2 + \ldots$ if $|\alpha| < 1$. In this context, and presuming $|\beta L| < 1$ holds, then we can substitute βL for α and reexpress the AR(1) process as

4.4 The Connection Between AR and MA Processes

$$X_t = e_t \left(1 + \beta L + \beta^2 L^2 + \beta^3 L^3 + \ldots\right)$$
$$= 1 + \beta L e_t + \beta^2 L^2 e_t + \beta^3 L^3 e_t + \ldots$$
$$= 1 + \beta e_{t-1} + \beta^2 e_{t-2} + \beta^3 e_{t-3} + \ldots$$

We could only make the infinite sum substitution as long as the terms in the infinite sum are appropriately bounded, which is ensured by $|\beta L| < 1$.

We have shown that an AR(1) can be expressed as an MA(∞) as long as it doesn't grow without bound: $|\beta L| < 1$.

4.4.2 AR(p) to MA(∞)

The ability to represent a stationarity AR process as an MA(∞) generalizes to higher-order AR(p) processes:

$$X_t = \beta_1 X_{t-1} + \beta_2 X_{t-2} + \cdots + \beta_p X_{t-p} + e_t$$

which we can write using the lag operator as

$$X = \beta_1 L X + \beta_2 L^2 X + \cdots + \beta_p L^p + e_t$$
$$X \Phi(L) = e_t$$

where

$$\Phi(L) = \left(1 - \beta_1 L - \beta_2 L^2 - \cdots - \beta_p L^p\right). \tag{4.25}$$

If $\Phi(L)$ is not equal to zero, then we can divide both sides of Eq. (4.25) by $\Phi(L)$:

$$X = \frac{e_t}{\Phi(L)}.$$

There is an analogous condition for MA processes, allowing us to go in the other direction: expressing an MA process as an infinite AR. That condition is called "invertibility."

4.4.3 Invertibility: MA(1) to AR(∞)

We saw how a stationary AR(1) process is equivalent to an MA(∞). Is it possible to go in the other direction, expressing an MA(1) process as an equivalent AR(∞). In short, yes it is possible as long as the MA process is "invertible."

Consider the MA(1) model,

$$X_t = u_t + \gamma u_{t-1} \qquad (4.26)$$

which can be rewritten as

$$u_t = X_t - \gamma u_{t-1}. \qquad (4.27)$$

This also implies that

$$u_{t-1} = X_{t-1} - \gamma u_{t-2} \qquad (4.28)$$
$$u_{t-2} = X_{t-2} - \gamma u_{t-3} \qquad (4.29)$$
$$u_{t-3} = X_{t-3} - \gamma u_{t-4} \qquad (4.30)$$

and so forth.

Substituting (4.30) into (4.29) into (4.28) into (4.27),

$$u_t = X_t - \gamma X_{t-1} + \gamma^2 X_{t-2} - \gamma^3 (X_{t-3} - \gamma u_{t-4})$$
$$= X_t - \gamma X_{t-1} + \gamma^2 X_{t-2} - \gamma^3 X_{t-3} + \gamma^4 u_{t-4}.$$

Repeating this process indefinitely yields

$$u_t = X_t - \gamma X_{t-1} + \gamma^2 X_{t-2} - \gamma^3 X_{t-3} + \ldots$$
$$= X_t + \sum_{i=1}^{\infty} \left(-\gamma^i\right) X_{t-i}.$$

Equivalently,

$$X_t = u_t - \sum_{i=1}^{\infty} \left(-\gamma^i\right) X_{t-i} \qquad (4.31)$$

which is an AR(∞) process, with $\beta_1 = \gamma$, $\beta_2 = -\gamma^2$, $\beta_3 = \gamma^3$, $\beta_4 = -\gamma^4$, and so on.

The condition that was required for us to continue the substitutions above indefinitely is analogous to what was required for stationarity when dealing with AR processes. The infinite sum in (4.31) must be finite. It must have a convergent infinite sum. To wit, the lag polynomial on the MA process must have roots greater than one, or inverse roots less than one.

This also applies to MA processes of higher order. Consider an MA(q) model such as

$$X_t = \left(u_t + \gamma_1 u_{t-1} + \gamma_2 u_{t-2} + \cdots + \gamma_q u_{t-q}\right)$$

$$= u_t \left(1 + \gamma_1 L + \gamma_2 L^2 + \cdots + \gamma_q L^q\right)$$
$$= \Theta(L)u_t.$$

What kinds of restrictions on the γs ensure that the estimated model is invertible? The invertibilty restrictions are directly analogous to the stationarity restrictions: the roots of $\Theta(L)$ must lie outside the unit circle. Equivalently, the inverse roots must lie inside the unit circle.

4.5 What Are Unit Roots, and Why Are They Bad?

As was hinted in the previous section, "unit roots" refer to the roots of the lag polynomial. In the AR(1) process, if there was a unit root, then $L^* = 1/\beta = 1$, so $\beta = 1$, which means that the AR process is actually a random walk.

Roots that lie on the unit circle are right at the threshold that marks the transition from stationarity.

The problem with unit root processes—that is, with processes that contain random walks—is that they look stationary in small samples. But treating them as stationary leads to very misleading results. Moreover, regressing one nonstationary process on another leads many "false positives" where two variables seem related when they are not. This important finding is due to Granger and Newbold (1974), whose paper we replicate in Sect. 5.7.

Unit roots represent a specific type of nonstationarity. We will explore unit root processes (such as a "random walk") in the next chapter. We will learn how to test for these processes in Chap. 7.

Nonstationarity and ARIMA(p,d,q) Processes 5

Up until now we have been looking at time series whose means did not exhibit long-run growth. It is time to drop this assumption. After all, many economic and financial time series do not have a constant mean. Examples include: the US GDP per capita and the US CPI (Fig. 5.1) or the Dow Jones Industrial Index and the share price of Google (Fig. 5.2).

Nonstationary ARIMA models include the "random walk" and the "random walk with drift." Simple univariate models such as these have proven to be very powerful forecasting tools. Nelson (1972) showed this with his comparison of ARIMA versus Cowles-type models. Meese and Rogoff (1983a,b) found that simple random walk models perform at least as well as structural univariate models and even vector autoregressions for forecasting exchange rates.[1]

5.1 Differencing

In calculus, integration and differentiation are inverses. Similarly, in time series integration and differencing are inverses; they undo each other.

In calculus, if $f(x) = ax + b$ is increasing linearly in x, then $f'(x) = a$ is not increasing at all. It is a constant. Likewise, if $f(x) = ax^2 + bx + c$ is increasing quadratically in x (over the relevant range), then its derivative, $f'(x) = 2ax + b$, is increasing linearly. Its second derivative, $f''(x) = 2a$, is a constant. It is "mean stationary." Something similar applies to time series.

Differencing is in time series what differentiation is in calculus. If we have a time series whose mean is increasing, we can apply the difference operator enough times to render the series stationary.

If a series needs to be differenced once in order to make it stationary, we say that the series is "integrated of order one" or "I(1)." A series that needs to be differenced

---

[1] The exchange rate market is very efficient and therefore notoriously hard to forecast.

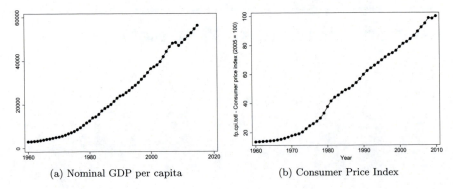

Fig. 5.1 Two nonstationary economic time series. (**a**) Nominal GDP per capita. (**b**) Consumer price index

twice is "integrated of order two" and is "I(2)." In general, if a series needs to be differenced d times, it is said to be "integrated of order d" and is "I(d)."

If a time series X is increasing, it is nonstationary. If its first (or higher) differences are stationary, then we say that it is "integrated." Differencing does not remove all nonstationarities; it only removes nonstationarity associated with integration.

We can easily build on the ARMA(p,q) framework that we used for stationary processes to include I(d) variables. The two can be integrated to make ARIMA(p,d,q) models. Really, there is little new here regarding estimation. We simply need to find out whether differencing a variable a small number of times renders a variable stationary. We then proceed with the ARMA(p,q) portion of the analysis.

In what follows, we'll explore how differencing affects three different nonstationary processes: a random walk, a random walk with drift, and a deterministic trend model. We will see that the difficulty lies in figuring out whether the variable is stationary after differencing d times. Mistakenly differencing adds to our problems, so it is not a costless and automatic solution.

Example of Differencing

We will show an example, using Stata, of how differencing a series can render it stationary. We would like to do the following: using `fetchyahooquotes`, download the daily Dow Jones Industrial Index from the beginning of 2000 through the end of 2010. (Alternatively, use the `ARIMA_DJI.dta` dataset.) Calculate the first difference of the DJIA. Graph the original series, as well as the differenced series. Using this visual information, what does the order of integration of the DJIA seem to be?

The stock ticker for the DJIA is "^DJI" so we enter:

5.1 Differencing

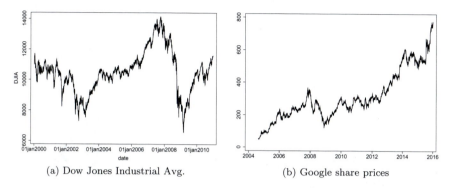

(a) Dow Jones Industrial Avg.   (b) Google share prices

Fig. 5.2 Two nonstationary financial time series. (**a**) Dow Jones Industrial Avg. (**b**) Google share prices

```
. fetchyahooquotes ^DJI, freq(d) start(1jan2000) end(31dec2010)
^DJI is downloaded.
time variable:  date, 03jan2000 to 31dec2010, but with gaps
delta:  1 day

. rename adjclose__DJI DJIA

. graph twoway line D1.DJIA date
```

In the original (not-differenced) series, the DJIA has some rather long swings (see Fig. 5.2a). The first-differenced DJIA series seems to have a constant mean, most likely a mean of zero (see Fig. 5.3). The variance might not be stationary, though, as there are certain patches of high volatility interspersed by periods of low volatility.

Exercises

1. For each of the following items listed below, you should be able to do the following: download the data, and calculate the first and second differences. Graph the original series and the two differenced series. Visually identify its possible order of integration.
   (a) The nominal US GDP per capita. The command to download the data into Stata is as follows:
   wbopendata, country(usa) indicator(ny.gdp.pcap.cd) year(1960:2015) long clear).
   (b) US CPI. The command to download the data into Stata is as follows:
   wbopendata , country(usa) indicator(fp.cpi.totl) year(1960:2015) long clear)

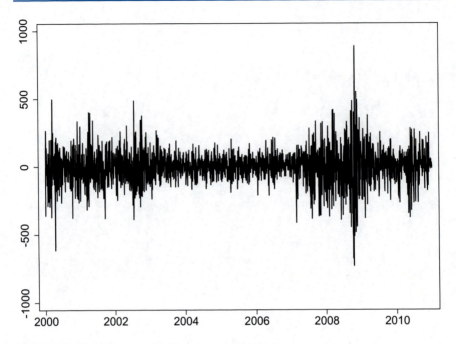

Fig. 5.3 The first difference of the Dow Jones Industrial Average

2. The dataset `integrated012.dta` contains two sets of three variables: (A, B, C) and (X, Y, Z). For each set, graph each variable. Calculate the first and second differences of each variable. Identify which variable is I(2), I(1), and I(0).

5.2 The Random Walk

The random walk process is one of the simpler examples of a nonstationary process. The random walk is

$$X_t = X_{t-1} + e_t \tag{5.1}$$

which is the usual AR(1) but with the coefficient on X_{t-1} equal to one. Whenever that coefficient is equal to, or greater than one (or less than negative one), the series either increases (or decreases) without bound. Thus, its expected value depends upon the time period, rendering the process nonstationary.

The Mean and Variance of the Random Walk

Before we show how to make the random walk stationary, let us first see why the random walk itself is not stationary. To do so, though, we will have to reexpress this process in a slightly different way.

Applying the backshift or lag operator onto both sides of Eq. (5.1) and substituting the result back into (5.1) yields

$$X_t = X_{t-1} + e_t$$
$$= (X_{t-2} + e_{t-1}) + e_t.$$

Continuing such substitution to period $t = 0$ allows us to write the random walk model as

$$X_t = X_0 + e_1 + e_2 + \ldots + e_{t-1} + e_t. \tag{5.2}$$

Written in this way, it will be easier for us to see what the mean and variance of this process is.

At period 0, taking the expectation of both sides of Eq. (5.2):

$$E(X_t \mid X_0) = E(X_0 + e_1 + e_2 + \ldots + e_t \mid X_0)$$
$$= X_0 + E(e_1 \mid X_0) + E(e_2 \mid X_0) + \ldots + E(e_t \mid X_0)$$
$$= X_0.$$

The random walk model is very unpredictable, so our best guess during period 0 of what X will be in period t is just X's value right now at period zero. The predicted value of a random walk tomorrow is equal to its value today.

Taking the variance of both sides of Eq. (5.2) gives

$$Var(X_t) = Var(X_0 + e_1 + e_2 + \ldots + e_{t-1} + e_t).$$

Since each of the error terms are drawn independently of each other, there is no covariance between them. And since X_0 was drawn before any of the es in (5.2), then there is no covariance between X_0 and the es. (Moreover, but incidentally, it is a seed term and is usually thought of as a constant.) Therefore, we can push the variance calculation through the additive terms:

$$Var(X_t) = Var(X_0) + Var(e_1) + Var(e_2) + \ldots + Var(e_{t-1}) + Var(e_t)$$
$$= 0 + \sigma^2 + \sigma^2 + \ldots + \sigma^2 + \sigma^2$$
$$= t\sigma^2.$$

Since the variance of X_t is a function of t, the process is not variance stationary.

Taking the First Difference Makes It Stationary

We can difference the random walk process once and the resulting differenced series is stationary. To see this, subtract X_{t-1} from both sides of Eq. (5.1) to yield

$$X_t - X_{t-1} = X_{t-1} - X_{t-1} + e_t$$
$$Z_t = e_t$$

where we call the new differenced series Z_t. The differenced series is now the strictly random process, in fact the first model we looked at in this chapter, a model which is stationary.

5.3 The Random Walk with Drift

The "random walk with drift" is another type of nonstationary process. It is a random walk process which trends upward (or downward) and is specified by

$$X_t = \beta_0 + X_{t-1} + e_t. \tag{5.3}$$

This process can be expressed in slightly different terms which we will find useful. Given an initial value of X_0, which we arbitrarily set to zero, then

$$X_0 = 0$$
$$X_1 = \beta_0 + X_0 + e_1 = \beta_0 + e_1$$
$$X_2 = \beta_0 + X_1 + e_2 = \beta_0 + (\beta_0 + e_1) + e_2 = 2\beta_0 + e_1 + e_2$$
$$X_3 = \beta_0 + X_2 + e_3 = \beta_0 + (2\beta_0 + e_1 + e_2) + e_3 = 3\beta_0 + e_1 + e_2 + e_3$$

$$X_t = t\beta_0 + \sum_{i=1}^{t} e_i. \tag{5.4}$$

The Mean and Variance of the Random Walk with Drift

In this section we see why a random walk with drift is neither mean stationary nor variance stationary.

Taking the mathematical expectation of Eq. (5.4), we see that at any point in time t, the mean of X is

$$E(X_t) = t\beta_0. \tag{5.5}$$

The variance of Eq. (5.4) is

$$Var(X_t) = Var\left(t\beta_0 + \sum_{i=1}^{t} e_i\right) = Var\left(\sum_{i=1}^{t} e_i\right) = t\sigma_e^2. \qquad (5.6)$$

As t increases, so do the mean and variance of X.

Taking the First Difference Makes It Stationary

Taking the first differences of Eq. (5.3):

$$X_t - X_{t-1} = \beta_0 + X_{t-1} + e_t - X_{t-1} \qquad (5.7)$$

$$\Delta X_t = \beta_0 + e_t. \qquad (5.8)$$

Let $Y_t = \Delta X_t$, and we see that

$$Y_t = \beta_0 + e_t. \qquad (5.9)$$

The variable Y_t is just white noise with a mean of β_0.

5.4 Deterministic Trend

A third example of a nonstationary process is

$$X_t = \beta_0 + \beta_1 t + e_t \qquad (5.10)$$

where t denotes the time elapsed and the βs are parameters; the only random component of the model is given e_t, the iid errors.

Mean and Variance

The mean of a deterministic trend model is

$$E(X_t) = E(\beta_0 + \beta_1 t + e_t) = \beta_0 + \beta_1 t.$$

The variance is

$$Var(X_t) = V(\beta_0 + \beta_1 t + e_t) = Var(e_t) = \sigma_e^2.$$

Thus, a deterministic trend process has a nonstationary mean (it grows linearly with time) and a stationary variance (equal to σ_e^2).

First Differencing Introduces an MA Unit Root

Taking the first difference of Eq. (5.10),

$$\begin{aligned} X_t - X_{t-1} &= (\beta_0 + \beta_1 t + e_t) - (\beta_0 + \beta_1(t-1) + e_{t-1}) \\ &= \beta_1 t + e_t - (\beta_1 t - \beta_1) - e_{t-1} \\ &= \beta_1 + e_t - e_{t-1}. \end{aligned}$$

Since this first-differenced series does not depend upon time, then the mean and variance of this first-differenced series also do not depend upon time:

$$E(X_t - X_{t-1}) = E(\beta_1 + e_t - e_{t-1}) = \beta_1$$
$$Var(X_t - X_{t-1}) = Var(e_t - e_{t-1}) = Var(e_t) + Var(e_{t-1}) = 2\sigma_e^2.$$

Notice that the first-differenced model now has an MA unit root in the error terms. Never take first differences to remove a deterministic trend. Rather, regress X on time, and then work with the residuals. These residuals now represent X that has been linearly detrended.

5.5 Random Walk with Drift Versus Deterministic Trend

There are many similarities between (a) random walks with drift and (b) deterministic trend processes. They are both nonstationary, but the source of the nonstationarity is different. It is worthwhile to look at these models side by side.

The "random walk with drift" is

$$X_t = \beta_0 + X_{t-1} + e_t = t\beta_0 + \sum_{i=1}^{t} e_i$$

with mean and variance of

$$E(X_t) = t\beta_0$$
$$Var(X_t) = t\sigma_e^2.$$

In order to make it stationary it needs to be differenced.

The deterministic trend model is

$$X_t = \beta_0 + \beta_1 t + e_t$$

with mean and variance of

$$E(X_t) = t\beta_1 + \beta_0$$
$$Var(X_t) = \sigma_e^2.$$

Both models have means which increase linearly over time. This makes it very difficult to visually identify which process generated the data. The variance of the random walk with drift, however, grows over time while the variance of the deterministic trend model does not.

Toward the end of the next section we will show some formal means of identifying which type of process generated a particular dataset.

5.6 Differencing and Detrending Appropriately

We have seen that we can take the first difference of an integrated process to make it stationary. Such a process is said to be "difference stationary."

A different type of process is called "trend stationary." Such a process has an increasing mean, so it is nonstationary in a sense. But it can be made stationary by "detrending," and so it is called "trend stationary." Confusingly, both differencing and detrending remove a trend, but they refer to two different things. When econometricians say they are "detrending" the data, they usually mean that there is a deterministic trend. That is, the variable "time" shows up in the data generating process. Its effect can be removed by including time in a regression and extracting the residuals.

So, why is it worthwhile understanding this difference? What would happen if we detrend a difference-stationary process, or difference a trend-stationary process? We will answer these two questions in this subsection. We will do so by simulating some data and seeing what happens.

First, let us generate two variables, one which is trend stationary (it has time as a right-hand-side variable) and another which is difference stationary (a random walk with drift).

```
. drop _all
. clear all
. set obs 100
. set seed 1234
. gen time = _n
. tsset time
. gen error = rnormal()

. * Generate a Difference Stationary process
(random walk with drift)
. gen y = error in 1
. replace y = 1 + L.y + error in 2/L
```

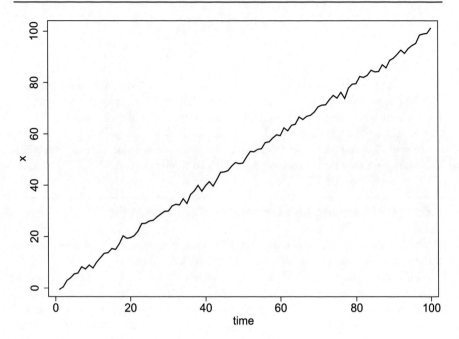

Fig. 5.4 x: A trend-stationary process

```
. * Generate a Trend Stationary process
. gen x = error in 1
. replace x = 1*time + error in 2/L
```

We can easily deal with first-differenced data by using the D. difference operator in Stata. We can detrend the data by regressing each variable on time. Let's call the resulting, detrended, variables "dtx" and "dty."

```
. quietly reg y time
. predict dty, resid
. quietly reg x time
. predict dtx, resid
```

These two series look very similar at the outset. Visually, they are nearly indistinguishable in their levels (Figs. 5.4 and 5.5) and in their first differences (Figs. 5.6 and 5.7). They also look similar when detrended (Figs. 5.8 and 5.9).

The detrended and differenced series at first blush look similar.

5.6 Differencing and Detrending Appropriately

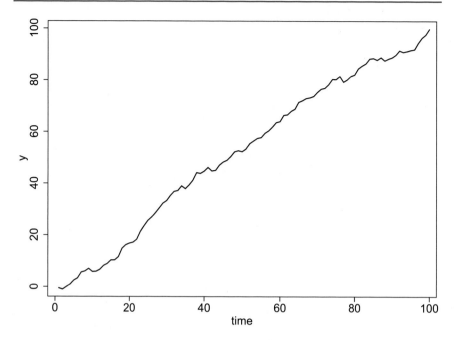

Fig. 5.5 y: A difference-stationary process (a random walk with drift)

```
. sum d.x d.y dtx dty

    Variable |      Obs        Mean    Std. Dev.       Min        Max
-------------+--------------------------------------------------------
           x |
         D1. |       99     1.02717    1.355538  -2.442459   4.081596
             |
           y |
         D1. |       99      1.0128    .9781713  -2.217911   3.284249
             |
         dtx |      100    2.28e-09     .983297  -3.167634   2.227478
         dty |      100    2.38e-09    3.262829  -7.455291   5.269494
```

Keep in mind that x is trend stationary; y is difference stationary (a random walk with drift).

We can see that the first-differenced variables both have means around 1.02. Their standard deviations, however, seem a bit different. The standard deviation when we differenced the trend-stationary variable, x, is a bit higher than the stdev when we differenced the difference-stationary variable y.

The detrended series also have similar means of zero. The standard deviation when we detrended the trend-stationary variable x is much lower than the standard deviation when we (inappropriately) detrended y, the difference-stationary variable.

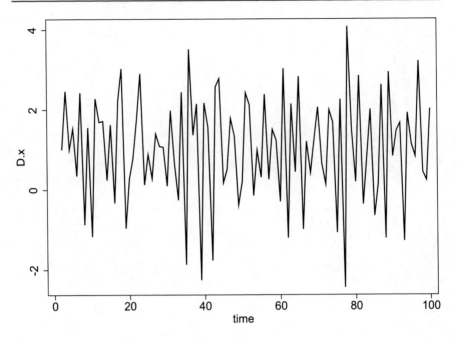

Fig. 5.6 D.x: A first-differenced trend-stationary process

By changing `observations` in the third line of the Stata code above, we can gauge the impact that sample size has on these distortions. Below, we show what the standard deviations would have been for a sample size of one million observations.

```
. sum d.x d.y dtx dty

    Variable |       Obs        Mean    Std. Dev.       Min        Max
-------------+--------------------------------------------------------
           x |
         D1. |   999,999    1.000001    1.415928       -5.5   8.300781
             |
           y |
         D1. |   999,999    .9989122     1.00149  -4.046875     5.9375
             |
         dtx | 1,000,000   -1.33e-11    1.001489  -5.043788   4.936587
         dty | 1,000,000    7.66e-10    322.1399  -755.6169   869.5712
```

The standard deviation of the inappropriately detrended variable (dty) is 322; this implies that its variance is 103,774. Thus, we see that the effect of inappropriately detrending a difference-stationary variable can be quite huge. It can be shown, though we will not do so here, that the variance increases to infinity as the sample size increases. Inappropriately including a time trend when the true process is a unit root with drift will induce ever escalating variance in the series.

5.6 Differencing and Detrending Appropriately

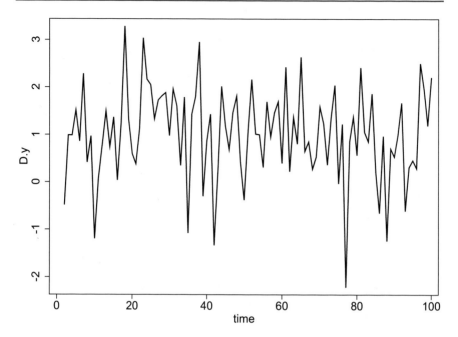

Fig. 5.7 D.y: A first-differenced difference-stationary process

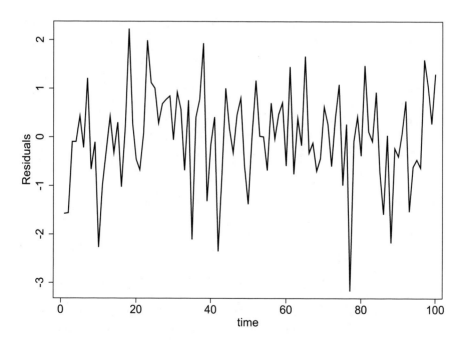

Fig. 5.8 dtx: A linearly detrended trend-stationary process

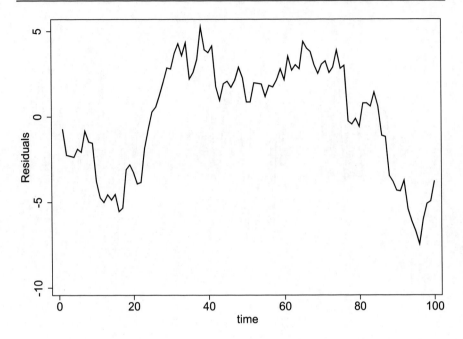

Fig. 5.9 dty: A linearly detrended difference-stationary process

Mistakenly differencing and mistakenly detrending introduce their own problems. We will continue exploring these in the next subsection.

Exercises

1. Redo the exercise above, slowly increasing the sample size from 100 to 1000, 10,000, and 100,000. Summarize your results. Especially important, what are the standard deviations? What conclusions do you draw?

5.6.1 Mistakenly Differencing (Over-Differencing)

Differencing integrated variables makes them stationary. Just to be safe, should we simply difference all variables to ensure stationarity? No. Just as you can underdifference, so that a variable becomes nonstationary, you can over-difference, so that the transformed variable becomes non-invertible. As with Goldilocks and her porridge, we need to make sure our differencing is just right.

Over-differencing causes several problems. First, over-differencing induces a unit root in the MA terms of the process. Such models can be challenging to

5.6 Differencing and Detrending Appropriately

estimate. It induces an artificial negative autocorrelation in the data. And as we saw in the previous few pages, it tends to increase the variance of the data. Finally, over-differencing unnecessarily throws away data. We lose an observation every time we difference. It also throws away information about the level of the data, as the constants are eliminated. And it throws away information about the medium and long term (the slowly changing levels of the data), privileging the short-term variation (the variation remaining from one period to the next).

Consider what would happen if you inappropriately first differenced a white noise process:

$$X_t = e_t.$$

White noise processes are already stationary. Lagging by one period and subtracting,

$$X_t - X_{t-1} = e_t - e_{t-1}$$
$$\tilde{X}_t = e_t - e_{t-1} \tag{5.11}$$

where we define $\tilde{X}_t$ to be equal to ΔX_t. Notice that (5.11) is a non-invertible MA(1) process with an MA-unit root.

We have increased the variance of the process. The variance of the untransformed variable was $Var(X_t) = Var(e_t)$. After over-differencing, the variance of the transformed variable is

$$\begin{aligned} Var\left(\tilde{X}_t\right) &= Var\left(e_t - e_{t-1}\right) \\ &= Var(e_t) - 2Cov(e_t, e_{t-1}) + Var(e_{t-1}) \\ &= Var(e_t) + Var(e_{t-1}) \\ &= Var(e_t) + Var(e_t) \\ &= 2Var(e_t). \end{aligned}$$

The variance has doubled. The process was already stationary. We didn't make it *more* stationary. What we did was make things worse: we added noise. Econometricians strive to find the signal through the noise, but here we've added more noise!

First differencing also introduces negative autocorrelation into the data. The ACF of a white noise process is zero at every lag. But now, after over-differencing, the ACF of $\tilde{X}_t$ at lag=1 is

$$\begin{aligned} Corr(\tilde{X}_t, \tilde{X}_{t-1}) &= \frac{Cov(\tilde{X}_t, \tilde{X}_{t-1})}{\sqrt{Var(\tilde{X}_t)Var(\tilde{X}_{t-1})}} \\ &= \frac{Cov(\tilde{X}_t, \tilde{X}_{t-1})}{Var(\tilde{X}_t)} \end{aligned}$$

$$= \frac{E(\tilde{X}_t \tilde{X}_{t-1}) - E(\tilde{X}_t)E(\tilde{X}_{t-1})}{2Var(e_t)}$$

$$= \frac{E(\tilde{X}_t \tilde{X}_{t-1})}{2Var(e_t)}$$

$$= \frac{E[(e_t - e_{t-1})(e_{t-1} - e_{t-2})]}{2Var(e_t)}$$

$$= \frac{E(e_t e_{t-1} - e_t e_{t-2} - e_{t-1}e_{t-1} + e_{t-1}e_{t-2})}{2Var(e_t)}$$

$$= \frac{E(e_t e_{t-1}) - E(e_t e_{t-2}) - E(e_{t-1}e_{t-1}) + E(e_{t-1}e_{t-2})}{2Var(e_t)}$$

$$= \frac{Cov(e_t, e_{t-1}) - Cov(e_t, e_{t-2}) - Var(e_{t-1}) + Cov(e_{t-1}, e_{t-2})}{2Var(e_t)}$$

$$= \frac{0 - 0 - Var(e_{t-1}) + 0}{2Var(e_t)}$$

$$= \frac{-Var(e_t)}{2Var(e_t)}$$

$$= \frac{-1}{2}$$

$$< 0.$$

Of course, if the process really were white noise, then a graph of the data would tend to look stationary; you wouldn't be tempted to difference in the first place. A more realistic example is a trend-stationary process, where the increasing values might tempt you to automatically first difference.

What would happen if you inappropriately first differenced a trend stationary process?

$$X_t = \alpha + \beta t + e_t.$$

If we take the first difference,

$$X_t - X_{t-1} = (\alpha + \beta t + e_t) - (\alpha + \beta(t-1) + e_{t-1})$$
$$= \alpha + \beta t + e_t - \alpha - \beta(t-1) - e_{t-1}$$
$$= \beta t + e_t - \beta t + \beta - e_{t-1}$$
$$\tilde{X}_t = \beta + e_t - e_{t-1}.$$

5.6 Differencing and Detrending Appropriately

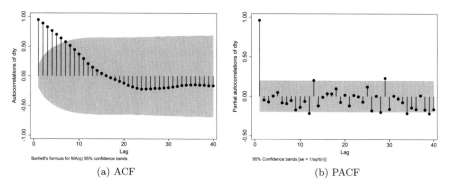

Fig. 5.10 ACF and PACF of a detrended random walk with drift. (**a**) ACF. (**b**) PACF

We have made this into an MA(1) process. Notice, too, that the coefficient on e_{t-1} is equal to one, so that there is a unit root in the MA terms. As such, it is non-invertible.[2]

5.6.2 Mistakenly Detrending

What happens if we mistakenly detrend a random walk with drift (which is a difference stationary variable)? Mistakenly detrending invalidates most hypothesis testing (Durlauf & Phillips, 1988). Detrending a random walk also induces spurious cyclicality or seasonality in the data. This is revealed in Fig. 5.10 by the "dampened sine wave" form of the ACF and spikes at somewhat regular intervals in the PACF.

Exercises

1. Use Stata to generate 1000 observations of a variable X, equal to random noise from a normal distribution with zero mean and a standard deviation of two.
   (a) Summarize X and verify that the mean is approximately zero and the variance is four (since it is the square of the standard deviation).
   (b) Use `corrgram X, lags(5)` to calculate the ACF and PACF of X out to five lags. Verify that this is white noise with no autocorrelation structure.
   (c) Summarize D1.X, the first difference of the variable. What is the mean? What is its variance? Did it increase or decrease? In what way? Is this what you expected?

---

[2] Plosser and Schwert (1977) explore the implications of such over-differencing and suggest a way to estimate such models.

(d) Use corrgram D1.X, lags(5) to calculate the ACF and PACF of the first difference of X out to five lags. Describe its autocorrelation structure. Is it positive or negative?
(e) Estimate an MA(1) model on D1.X using arima D1.X, ma(1).
(f) Use estat aroots to test graphically whether we have an MA unit root in D1.X.

5.7 Replicating Granger and Newbold (1974)

In 1974, Granger and Newbold published one of the most influential papers in econometrics. They showed via simulation that if two completely unrelated series are regressed on each other, but these series each have unit roots, then all of the standard methods will tend to show that the two series are related. They will have statistically significant coefficients between them (i.e., statistically significant βs), they will have low p-values, and they will have high R^2s. Even if the two series are independent random walks, having nothing to do with each other, in finite samples they will look similar.

This is easiest to understand if the two series, Y and X, are random walks with drift. Since they are both drifting, then regressing Y on X will find a linear relationship between them, simply because they are both drifting. If they both happen to be trending in the same direction, the coefficient will be positive; if they are trending in opposite directions, the coefficient will be negative. But the point is that there will be a statistically significant coefficient.

Granger and Newbold showed that this would be the case even if there was no drift in the variables. Two random walk without drift will wander aimlessly, but wander they will. And so it will look as though they have some sort of trend. Regressing one on the other then will indicate a statistically significant relationship between them. This phenomenon, of finding relationships between integrated variables where there are none is called "spurious regression."[3]

Phillips (1986) provides the theory explaining Granger and Newbold's findings. Phillips shows that this problem of spurious regression worsens as the sample size increases.

---

[3] The book by Tyler Vigen (2015) presents dozens of humorous instances of spurious correlations using real data. For example, there is a correlation of 66% between (a) films in which Nicolas Cage has appeared and (b) the number of people who drowned by falling into a pool. The correlation between (a) per capita cheese consumption and (b) the number of people who died by becoming tangled in their bedsheets is also quite large with a correlation of 95%. Vigen's website (TylerVigen.com) also provides many such spurious correlations.

5.7 Replicating Granger and Newbold (1974)

In this subsection, we will generate two simple random walks, regress one on the other, and show that Stata finds a spurious relationship between them. We follow this up with a more thorough simulation that mimics much of the original Granger and Newbold paper.

```
. drop _all
. set seed 1234
. set obs 100

. gen double e1 = rnormal()
. gen double e2 = rnormal()
. gen time = _n
. tsset time

. * Create the first random walk
. gen double X1 = e1 in 1
. replace X1= L.X1 + e1 in 2/L

. * Creating the second random walk
. gen double X2 = e2 in 1
. replace X2= L.X2 + e2 in 2/L

. graph twoway (line X1 time) (line X2 time, lpattern(dash))

. reg X1 X2
. predict X1hat
. graph twoway (scatter X1 X2) (line X1hat X2)
```

The regression output is shown below:

```
. reg X1 X2

      Source |       SS           df       MS      Number of obs   =       100
-------------+----------------------------------   F(1, 98)        =     34.51
       Model |   315.739019         1   315.739019 Prob > F        =    0.0000
    Residual |   896.556294        98   9.14853361 R-squared       =    0.2604
-------------+----------------------------------   Adj R-squared   =    0.2529
       Total |   1212.29531        99   12.2454072 Root MSE        =    3.0247

------------------------------------------------------------------------------
          X1 |      Coef.   Std. Err.      t    P>|t|     [95% Conf. Interval]
-------------+----------------------------------------------------------------
          X2 |  -.6671845   .1135684    -5.87   0.000    -.8925574   -.4418117
       _cons |   .8012785    .40697     1.97   0.052    -.0063402    1.608897
------------------------------------------------------------------------------
```

We can best understand what happened by looking at the graphs of the variables. The first graph above shows the two random walks over time. Just by random chance, there seems to be a negative correlation between them. This is further shown when we create a scatterplot of X1 vs X2 and overlay the regression line over the scatter (Fig. 5.11).

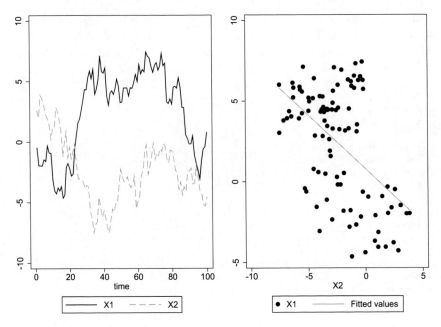

Fig. 5.11 Spurious correlation between two random walks

Stata finds a negative and statistically significant relationship between these two series. That is, even though the two series were created independently of each other, Stata estimates a relationship that is statistically significant even at the 1% level.

Of course, this was just for one pair of series. What if we had drawn a different set of numbers? Readers are encouraged to enter the code above once again into Stata, but removing the `set seed` command. With that command removed, you will draw a different set of random numbers each time you run the do file. You will find, however, that you reject the null of no relationship far too frequently, far more than 5% of the time.

In what follows, we show how to repeat this process thousands of times, each time storing the output, so that we can summarize the results. That is, we show how to run a simulation study of the "spurious regression" phenomenon, similar to what Granger and Newbold had done.

First, we define a program. This program describes what would happen with one run of a simulation.

```
. capture program drop GN
. program GN, rclass
. version 12.0
. drop _all
. set obs 50

. * Creating two pure random walk processes
```

5.7 Replicating Granger and Newbold (1974)

```
. gen double e1 = rnormal()
. gen double e2 = rnormal()
. gen time = _n
. tsset time

. gen double X1 = e1 in 1
. replace X1= L.X1 + e1 in 2/L

. gen double X2 = e2 in 1
. replace X2= L.X2 + e2 in 2/L

. reg X1 X2
. estat dwatson

. return scalar DWstat = r(dw)
. return scalar R2 = e(r2)
. return scalar Pval = (2 * ttail(e(df_r), ///
    abs(_b[X2]/_se[X2])))

. end
```

So that your random numbers look like my numbers, set the "seed" of Stata's random number generator to the same number I used:

```
. set seed 1234
```

Next, using the `simulate` command, we run 200 iterations of the simulation

```
. simulate DWstat = r(DWstat) R2=r(R2) Pval=r(Pval), ///
    reps(200) saving(GNtemp2, replace)///
    nodots nolegend: GN
```

and then we summarize the results:

```
. summarize
```

Variable	Obs	Mean	Std. Dev.	Min	Max
DWstat	200	.3334125	.1872522	.0470574	1.152255
R2	200	.24575	.2300506	5.09e-06	.9039305
Pval	200	.1498806	.2537258	4.59e-26	.9875988

We have just generated two random walks, each of length 50. We regressed one on the other and calculated the R^2, the p-value, and the Durbin-Watson statistic. We took note of these numbers and repeated the whole process another 199 times. We then summarized all of those results in the summary table above.

What we see is that the average R^2 is equal to 0.21. This is quite high, considering that there is no relationship between these variables. Furthermore,

```
. count if Pval < 0.05
130
```

One hundred and thirty (or 65%) of the 200 p-values are less than 0.05. That is, sixty-five percent of the time, we would believe that the two independent unit-root processes are statistically correlated. This is far more than we would normally expect, which shows us that Granger and Newbold were correct: regressing two unit root series on each other leads one to believe falsely that they are related.

5.8 Conclusion

In these first few chapters we have explored simple univariate models. We did this at length for two reasons. First, understanding these fundamental models helps us understand more complicated models. Second, these simple models are quite powerful. In fact, in forecasting competitions, these simple models hold their own against far more complicated ones.

For decades, Spiros Makridakis has run a series of competitions to assess the accuracy of various forecasting methods. In his paper (1979), he and Michele Hibon use 111 data series to compare various simple univariate methods (including exponential smoothing, AR, MA, ARMA, and ARIMA models). There is no clear "best method." The answer depends upon the definition of "best." Still, Makridakis and Hibon find that the simpler methods do remarkably well. They conjecture that the simpler methods are robust to structural breaks. The random walk model, for example, uses the most recent observation as its prediction. In the simplest of methods, data from earlier periods—data that may have come from an economy that was structurally different than it is today—do not enter into the forecast calculations. This competition was followed by what is now known as the M competition (Makridakis et al., 1982). This competition increased the number of data series to 1001 and included data sampled at different frequencies (yearly, quarterly, and monthly). Makridakis also outsourced the forecasting to individual researchers who were free to propose their own methods. No one used multivariate methods such as VARs. It was a competition among univariate methods. They find that simpler models hold their own, that the choice of "best model" still depends on the definition of "best," and that models that average other models do better than their constituent pieces.

The M2 competition focused on real-time updating of forecasts, but the conclusions were largely the same (Makridakis et al., 1993). The M3 competition increased the number of data series to 3003. This competition saw the inclusion of artificial neural networks. The earlier conclusions still hold, however: complex methods do not always outperform the simpler ones (Makridakis & Hibon, 2000). The M4 competition is being organized at the time of writing. It promises to extend the number of data series to 100,000 and incorporate more machine learning (neural network) algorithms.

Seasonal ARMA(p,q) Processes   6

Many financial and economic time series exhibit a regular cyclicality, periodicity, or "seasonality." For example, agricultural output follows seasonal variation, flower sales are higher in February, retail sales are higher in December, and beer sales in college towns are lower during the summers.

Of course, when we say "seasonality" here, we simply mean any sort of periodicity (ex: Fig. 6.1). A weekly recurring pattern is "seasonal," but at the weekly frequency.

Seasonality can arrive at different lengths. Retail sales vary seasonally with the holiday shopping season, but they also have "seasonality" at the weekly frequency: weekend sales are higher than weekday sales. Moreover, the two seasonal effects may be of different types (stochastic vs deterministic). If you had quarterly data on airline travel, what type of seasonal pattern might you expect to see? What if you had monthly data?

ACFs and PACFs will prove themselves especially useful in detecting seasonality, as fourth-quarter GDP in one year should tend to be correlated with fourth-quarter GDP in another year.

6.1   Two Different Types of Seasonality

Just as models of growth can be deterministic or stochastic, stationary or integrated, so too can models which exhibit seasonality.

Seasonality comes in two primary flavors: deterministic and stochastic.

1. The seasonal differences can vary by the same amount, or by the same percent, each year. Such deterministic seasonality is best captured with the use of seasonal dummy variables. If the dependent variable is in levels, then the dummies capture level shifts; if the dependent variable is logged, then they capture equal percentage changes. For example, if Christmas shopping shows deterministic

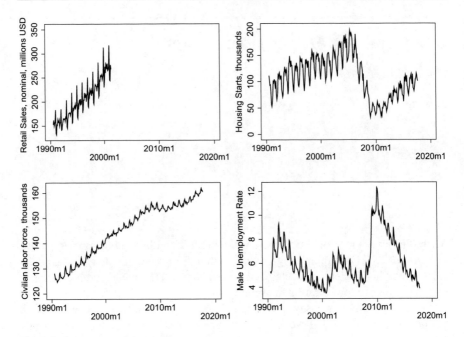

Fig. 6.1 Some seasonal time series

seasonality, then retail sales might show a spike of approximately 20% growth every Winter, for example.

2. On the other hand, seasonal differences may vary over time. In this case, Christmas shopping might be higher than other seasons, but some years the spike is much larger than 20%, other years much lower, with the differences evolving slowly over time. The best way to capture such evolution is to think of the seasonal spike as being a unit root process; a random walk Christmas sales might be unusually strong, followed by sequences of Christmas sales that are a bit weaker.

Which type of seasonality should we use? Solutions depend on the source of the problem. We need to properly examine the data.

If the seasonality is deterministic, then you should use dummy variables. If the seasonality varies stochastically, then a seasonal unit root process captures the evolving dynamics quite nicely, and seasonal differencing should be used.

6.1.1 Deterministic Seasonality

It is fairly easy to incorporate seasonality using dummy variables as exogenous variables.

6.1 Two Different Types of Seasonality

The simplest time series model with seasonality is a the white noise process, onto which a different deterministic amount is added each period. For example, consider the familiar white noise process:

$$X_t = e_t \quad \text{where} \quad e_t \sim iidN(0, \sigma^2)$$

where the data are now quarterly. To this we can add: 5 in the first quarter of every year, 10 in the second quarter, -3 in the third quarter, and 2 in the fourth. Let the dummy variables D_1, D_2, D_3, and D_4 denote first through fourth quarters of every year. This is modeled as

$$X_t = 5D_1 + 10D_2 - 3D_3 + 2D_4 + e_t.$$

An equivalent approach is to include a constant and exclude one of the seasonal dummies. In this case the coefficients represent deviations from the excluded baseline quarter:

$$X_t = 5 + 5D_2 - 8D_3 + 3D_4 + e_t.$$

In the first quarter, $E(X) = 5$. In the second, $E(X) = 5 + 5 = 10$. In the third, $E(X) = 5 - 8 = -3$, and in the fourth, $E(X) = 5 + 3 = 8$ (Fig. 6.2).

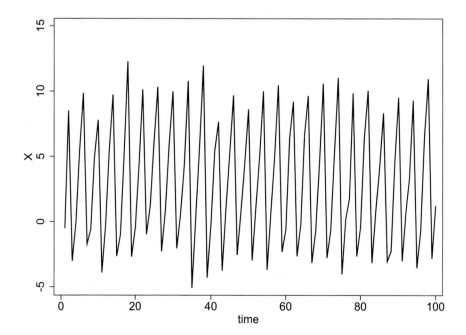

Fig. 6.2 A seasonal white noise process

6.1.2 Seasonal Differencing

Suppose you are examining retail sales with monthly data. Holiday sales in December are usually the strongest of the year. To see how strong this year's sales are, we should compare this December with last December. It is not terribly important or illuminating to say that retail sales this December were higher than in November. Of course they are! But are they bigger than what we'd expect December sales to be? Arguably, we should compare December sales with December sales, November with November, and so forth: X_t versus X_{t-12}. If we had a great Christmas season, then $X_t > X_{t-12}$, or

$$X_t - X_{t-12} > 0$$
$$X_t \left(1 - L^{12}\right) > 0.$$

Seasonal differencing means that an observation is subtracted from the previous one for the same season. If the data are quarterly and there is quarterly seasonality, then the seasonal first difference is $X_t - X_{t-4}$. If the data are monthly, then the seasonal first difference is $X_t - X_{t-12}$.

Thus, for nonstationary trending data with seasonality, two levels of differencing are required: first differences to remove the unit root in long-run growth and seasonal differences to remove seasonal unit roots.

We will need to establish some notation for seasonal differencing. We used superscripts such as D^2 to denote taking a first difference twice. We will use subscripts such as D_4 to denote quarterly differencing,

$$D_4 X = X\left(1 - L^4\right) = X - L^4 X$$

D_{12} for monthly differencing,

$$D_{12} X = X\left(1 - L^{12}\right) = X - L^{12} X$$

and so forth.

Let's apply seasonal differencing to a small dataset showing quarterly US unemployment rate for all persons, aged 15–64, not seasonally adjusted.

```
. use seasonal_unemp_rate.dta, clear
. gen temp = unemp - L4.unemp
(4 missing values generated)
```

6.1 Two Different Types of Seasonality

```
. list in 1/10

     +------------------------+
     |   date    unemp   temp |
     |------------------------|
  1. | 1960q1     6.1      .  |
  2. | 1960q2     5.4      .  |
  3. | 1960q3     5.2      .  |
  4. | 1960q4     5.8      .  |
  5. | 1961q1       8    1.9  |
     |------------------------|
  6. | 1961q2     7.1    1.7  |
  7. | 1961q3     6.3    1.1  |
  8. | 1961q4     5.7    -.1  |
  9. | 1962q1     6.5   -1.5  |
 10. | 1962q2     5.5   -1.6  |
     +------------------------+
```

The value for the differenced variable, temp, in the second quarter of 1962 is the difference between the unemployment rate in the second quarters of 1962 and 1961: $5.5 - 7.1 = -1.6$. Likewise, temp in 1962q1 is unemp(1962q1)–unemp(1961q1) = $6.5 - 8 = -1.5$. A graph of the original and seasonally differenced series is shown in Fig. (6.3).

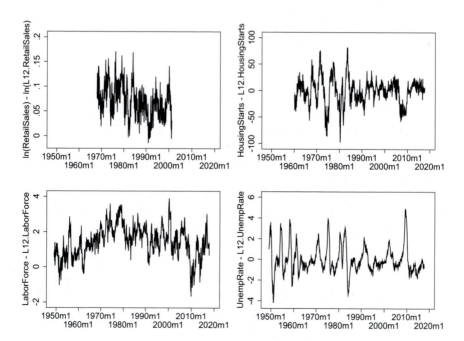

Fig. 6.3 Seasonal time series after seasonal differencing

The appropriate lag for differencing depends upon the frequency of the data and the type of seasonality. If we have quarterly data with quarterly seasonality, then the seasonal difference of a variable X can be obtained by subtracting its value from four previous periods:

. generate Xnew = X - L4.X

For monthly seasonal data, subtract its value 12 periods ago:

. generate Xnew = X - L12.X

6.1.3 Additive Seasonality

It is easy to add seasonal terms to an ARIMA model. Additive seasonality simply requires adding an AR term or an MA term at a seasonal frequency. If you have quarterly seasonality, then add a lag-4 AR term, or a lag-4 MA term.

Consider the following model for quarterly data:

$$X_t = \beta_4 X_{t-4} + e_t$$

$$X\left(1 - L^4 \beta_4\right) = e.$$

This is simply a stationary random noise model, with an additional quarterly AR term.

A simple additive MA model might be

$$X_t = u_t + \gamma_4 u_{t-4}$$

$$X_t = u\left(1 + L^4 \gamma_4\right).$$

6.1.4 Multiplicative Seasonality

December sales are not always independent of November sales. There is some inertial to human behavior. If November sales are unusually brisk, then we might expect this to carry over into December. For this reason, a purely additive seasonal model would be inadequate. Box & Jenkins (1976) propose a multiplicative model of seasonality.

Consider an ARIMA(1,0,0) model such as

$$X_t = \beta_1 X_{t-1} + e_t$$

$$X\left(1 - \beta_1 L\right) = e$$

$$X \Phi(L) = e$$

6.1 Two Different Types of Seasonality

where $\Phi(L)$ is the AR lag polynomial.

Now suppose that you want to include a seasonal lag polynomial such as

$$\phi\left(L^4\right) = \left(1 - \beta_4 L^4\right)$$

but you want to include it multiplicatively, so that

$$X\Phi(L)\phi(L^4) = e$$

$$X(1 - \beta_1 L)\left(1 - \beta_4 L^4\right) = e.$$

Multiplying this out,

$$X\left(1 - \beta_4 L^4 - \beta_1 L + \beta_1 \beta_4 LL^4\right) = e$$

$$X_t - \beta_4 X_{t-4} - \beta_1 X_{t-1} + \beta_1 \beta_4 X_{t-5} = e.$$

Modeled in this way, two parameters (β_1 and β_4) allow for lags at three different lengths (1, 4, and 5).

Multiplicative seasonality allows us to capture a lot of complexity with few parameters: parsimony. Such a model is often denoted as ARIMA(1, 0, 0) × (1, 0, 0)$_4$. The × symbol indicates that the seasonality is multiplicative. The second set of parentheses indicates that we have seasonal ARIMA terms. The subscript denotes the duration of seasonality. Our seasonality repeats every four observations (we have quarterly seasonality). The terms inside the parentheses have a similar interpretation to the terms in the first set. We have included one AR term at one seasonal lag, we do not need to take seasonal differences to induce stationarity (i.e., the number of seasonal differences is zero), and we have not included any seasonal MA terms in our model.

An ARIMA(1, 0, 1) × (2, 0, 0) model would be

$$X\Phi(L)\phi\left(L^4\right) = u\Theta(L)$$

which expands to

$$X(1 - \beta_1 L)\left(1 - L^4\beta_4 - L^8\beta_8\right) = u(1 + L\gamma_1)$$

$$X(1 - \beta_1 L)\left(1 - L^4\beta_4 - L^8\beta_8\right) = u(1 + L\gamma_1)$$

$$X\left(1 - \beta_1 L - \beta_4 L^4 - \beta_8 L^8 + \beta_1\beta_4 LL^4 + \beta_1\beta_8 LL^8\right) = u(1 + L\gamma_1)$$

$$X\left(1 - \beta_1 L - \beta_4 L^4 + \beta_1\beta_4 L^5 - \beta_8 L^8 + \beta_1\beta_8 L^9\right) = u(1 + L\gamma_1).$$

Example

What would an $ARIMA(1,0,0) \times (2,0,0)_{12}$ model look like? We have two AR polynomials. The nonseasonal polynomial,

$$\Phi(L) = 1 - L\beta_1, \qquad (6.1)$$

has one AR lag at length one. The seasonal polynomial,

$$\phi\left(L^{12}\right) = 1 - L^{12}\beta_{12} - L^{24}\beta_{24}, \qquad (6.2)$$

has two AR lags at seasonal length of 12: the powers on L in the seasonal polynomial are all multiples of 12. Since this is multiplicative seasonality we multiply the two lag polynomials:

$$\Phi(L)\phi\left(L^{12}\right) X = e_t. \qquad (6.3)$$

Substituting (6.1) and (6.2) into (6.3) and multiplying,

$$(1 - L\beta_1)\phi\left(1 - L^{12}\beta_{12} - L^{24}\beta_{24}\right) X = e_t$$

$$\left(1 - L\beta_1 - L^{12}\beta_{12} - L^{24}\beta_{24} + L^{13}\beta_1\beta_{12} + L^{25}\beta_1\beta_{24}\right) X = e_t.$$

Notice that the lag-1 term interacts with the two direct seasonal lags (12 and 24). The explicit form of this ARIMA model can be found by applying the lag operator:

$$X_t - \beta_1 X_{t-1} - \beta_{12} X_{t-12} + \beta_1\beta_{12} X_{t-13} - \beta_{24} X_{t-24} + \beta_1\beta_{24} X_{t-25} = e_t.$$

After moving terms to the other side of the equal sign,

$$X_t = \beta_1 X_{t-1} + \beta_{12} X_{t-12} - \beta_1\beta_{12} X_{t-13} + \beta_{24} X_{t-24} - \beta_1\beta_{24} X_{t-25} + e_t. \qquad (6.4)$$

Exercises

1. Generate 1000 observations from the model in Eq. (6.4), with $\beta_1 = 0.10$, $\beta_{12} = 0.40$, and $\beta_{24} = 40$. Graph the last 200 observations. Does the data appear seasonal? Examine the autocorrelation structure of the data. Can you detect seasonality?
2. What are the seasonal and nonseasonal AR and MA polynomials implied by the following models? Multiply out these polynomials and write out the explicit ARIMA model.
   (a) $ARIMA(1,0,1) \times (1,0,0)_{12}$
   (b) $ARIMA(2,0,0) \times (0,0,1)_4$
   (c) $ARIMA(0,0,1) \times (0,0,2)_{12}$
   (d) $ARIMA(0,0,2) \times (1,0,1)_4$

3. For each of the models listed above, what is the characteristic equation?
4. For each of the models listed above, what is the inverse characteristic equation?

6.1.5 MA Seasonality

This season's retail sales (X_t) might depend upon last year's sales (X_{t-12}) directly via an AR term, or they might instead be related via the error terms. That is, we might have seasonality by way of a moving average term. These can enter additively or multiplicatively.

Additive MA Seasonality

An example of additive MA seasonality is

$$X_t = e_t + \gamma_{12} u_{t-12}$$

where we simply add an additional error term at seasonal lengths. This can be estimated in Stata much like any other ARIMA model:

. arima X, ma(1 12)

Multiplicative MA Seasonality

We can also have multiplicative MA seasonality. Before we might have had nonseasonal MA(q) polynomial:

$$X_t = u_t + \gamma_1 u_{t-1} + \gamma_2 u_{t-2} + \cdots + \gamma_q u_{t-q} = u_t \Theta(L).$$

Now, we can multiply by a seasonal MA(Q) polynomial,

$$\theta(L^s) = 1 + \gamma_s L^s + \gamma_{2s} L^{2s} + \gamma_{3s} L^{3s} + \cdots + \gamma_{Qs} L^{Qs}$$

to produce

$$X_t = u_t \Theta(L) \theta(L^s).$$

We can estimate this model in Stata by

. arima X, sarima(0,0,1,12)

The seasonal option is sarima(P,D,Q,s) where P is the number of multiplicative seasonal AR lags (none, in this case); D is the number of seasonal differences required to induce stationarity (none, in this case); Q are the number of multiplicative MA lags (there is one), and s denotes the seasonal length (12 months). An equivalent command in Stata is

. arima X, mma(1,12)

The syntax of the option is mma(lags,s), so mma(1,12) denotes that we have a multiplicative moving average with one seasonal lag at a seasonal length of 12 months.

Example

What would an $ARIMA(0,0,1) \times (0,0,2)_{12}$ model look like? We have no AR terms at all. We have one nonseasonal MA term and two MA lags at a seasonal period of 12.

$$X_t = u_t \left(1 + L\gamma_1\right)\left(1 + L^{12}\gamma_{12} + L^{24}\gamma_{24}\right)$$
$$= u_t \left(1 + L\gamma_1 + L^{12}\gamma_{12} + L^{13}\gamma_1\gamma_{12} + L^{24}\gamma_{24} + L^{25}\gamma_1\beta_{24}\right).$$

Or, explicitly,

$$X_t = u_t + u_{t-1}\gamma_1 + u_{t-12}\gamma_{12} + u_{t-13}\gamma_1\gamma_{12} + u_{t-24}\gamma_{24} + u_{t-25}\gamma_1\gamma_{24}.$$

This would be estimated in Stata by

```
. arima X, arima(0,0,1) sarima(0,0,2,12)
```

Multiplicative ARIMA Seasonality in General

We can multiply any seasonal AR or MA lag polynomial onto any of our usual nonseasonal ARIMA processes. In general, on top of p AR terms, q MA terms, and d first differences, we can have P seasonal AR terms and Q seasonal MA terms and can require D number of seasonal differences of length s:

$$ARIMA(p,d,q) \times (P,D,Q)_s$$

or

$$\Phi(L)\phi\left(L^s\right)\Delta^d\Delta_s^D X = \Theta(L)\theta\left(L^s\right)u.$$

We can mix and match.

6.2 Identification

Given some dataset, what type of model should we estimate? We turn to familiar tools: ACFs and PACFs.

If a model only has seasonal terms, then the ACFs and PACFs will behave identically to nonseasonal ACFs/PACFs, only at seasonal frequencies, with all other terms equalling zero. For example, the ACF of the nonseasonal AR(1) process,

$$X_t = 0.50X_{t-1} + e_t, \tag{6.5}$$

6.2 Identification

is

$$Corr(X_t, X_{t-1}) = 0.50$$
$$Corr(X_t, X_{t-2}) = 0.50^2 = 0.25$$
$$Corr(X_t, X_{t-3}) = 0.50^3 = 0.125.$$

The analogous additively seasonal AR process (with quarterly seasonality)

$$X_t = 0.50 X_{t-4} + e_t \qquad (6.6)$$

has an ACF of

$$Corr(X_t, X_{t-1}) = 0$$
$$Corr(X_t, X_{t-2}) = 0$$
$$Corr(X_t, X_{t-3}) = 0$$
$$Corr(X_t, X_{t-4}) = 0.50$$
$$Corr(X_t, X_{t-5}) = 0$$
$$Corr(X_t, X_{t-6}) = 0$$
$$Corr(X_t, X_{t-7}) = 0$$
$$Corr(X_t, X_{t-8}) = 0.50^2 = 0.25$$
$$Corr(X_t, X_{t-9}) = 0.$$

The PACF of (6.5) is equal to 0.50 at lag one and zeros at all other lag lengths. Analogously, the PACF of (6.6) equals 0.50 at one seasonal length (i.e., at lag of four) and zeros otherwise. The two panels in Fig. 6.4 graph the ACF and PACF of Eq. (6.6).

The analogy extends to additively seasonal MA processes. The ACF will show a spike at the seasonal length, and the PACF will oscillate, declining exponentially at multiples of the seasonal length. The two panels in Fig. 6.5 graph the ACF and PACF of

$$X_t = u_{t-4},$$

an additively seasonal MA model.

Unfortunately, if a model has both seasonal and nonseasonal terms, then it is much harder to distinguish visually between competing processes using ACFs and PACFs.

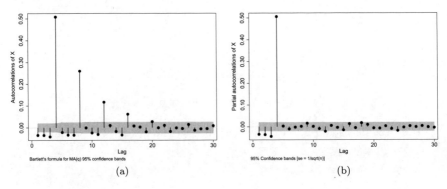

Fig. 6.4 ACF and PACF of $X_t = 0.50 X_{t-4} + e_t$. (a) Empirical ACF. (b) Empirical PACF

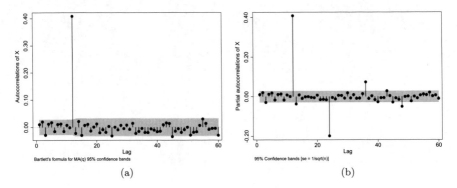

Fig. 6.5 ACF and PACF of $X_t = u_{t-4}$. (a) Empirical ACF. (b) Empirical PACF

6.3 Invertibility and Stability

The concepts of invertibility and stability generalize from nonseasonal to seasonal lags quite nicely. A seasonal ARIMA process is stable if the roots of its two characteristic polynomials ($\Phi(L)$ and $\phi(L^s)$) lie outside the unit circle. Equivalently, the roots of the inverse polynomial must lie inside the unit circle. The fact that the model now includes multiplicative seasonal lags does not change this. In fact, it helps. If a particular value of z makes $\phi(L^s)$ equal to zero, then it is also a zero of $\Phi(L)\phi(L^s)$, since anything times zero is also zero.

The Stata command is also the same:

```
. estat aroots
```

As before, the command provides a graph of the unit circle and plots the roots of the inverse characteristic polynomials. If the roots are inside the unit circle, then the function is invertible and stable.

What would happen if one of the seasonal roots is on the unit circle? Then we have seasonal unit roots, and we would have to estimate the model in differences.

6.4 How Common Are Seasonal Unit Roots?

That is, take seasonal differences until the model is stationary and then estimate. In practice, it is quite rare to take more than two seasonal differences. Usually one will suffice.

6.4 How Common Are Seasonal Unit Roots?

How common are seasonal unit roots? This is an open question.

Hylleberg et al. (1993) argue that it is common. Clements and Hendry (1997) argue that imposing a seasonal unit root, even when one is not present, helps increase forecast accuracy in the case when a structural break may occur in the economy.

On the other hand, an increasing body of evidence has argued that seasonal unit roots are not as present in the economy as nonseasonal unit roots.

Denise Osborn (1990) has examined at length the prevalence and nature of seasonality in 30 economic variables describing the UK economy. She finds evidence of a seasonal unit root in only 6 of the 30 variables. She also finds that more than half of the variables have at least 30% of their variation explained by deterministic seasonal dummy variables. Her conclusion is that deterministic seasonality accounted for via dummy variables is more than adequate to account for seasonality. Econometricians should not seasonally difference their variables unless there is evidence that they need to do so; otherwise, this results in over-differencing. On top of this, Osborn et al. (1999) examine eight measures of industrial production for each of three European countries and finds little evidence of unit roots. Rather, dummy variable models capture seasonality best.[1]

Ashworth and Thomas (1999) examine employment in the British tourism industry—a notoriously seasonal variable—and finds that its pattern of seasonality was best explained as consisting of two different periods of deterministic (dummy variable) seasonality. This repeats a finding that has become common in the literature: unit roots can often be confused with structural breaks.

Franses (1991) also warns against automatically taking seasonal differences. It is difficult to distinguish between deterministic and stochastic seasonality. If the seasonality is deterministic, seasonal differencing results in misspecification and poor forecasting ability.

Beaulieu and Miron (1990) examine the cross-country data and find that deterministic seasonality explains a large fraction of the variation in real GDP, industrial production, and retail sales. Beaulieu and Miron (1993) explore the aggregate US data and find only mixed support for seasonal unit roots. They warn against mechanically or automatically taking seasonal differences in an attempt to preclude possible unit root problems. Doing so runs the risk of misspecification. Ultimately, there should be strong economic reasons before estimating unit root seasonal models.

---

[1] The conclusions in Osborn et al. (1999) are tempered a bit by their finding that seasonal unit root models have good out-of-sample forecasting properties. This might have more to say about the low power of seasonal unit root tests, than about the existence of seasonal unit roots.

The evidence for seasonal unit roots has been weak. That doesn't mean such unit roots don't exist; seasonal unit root tests have serious deficiencies. For these reasons many researchers today simply choose to include seasonal dummy variables (even on deseasonalized data) and proceed with their analyses.

6.5 Using Deseasonalized Data

Most macroeconomic data are available in deseasonalized form. That is, you can download the raw data, or data that have been filtered so that the seasonal component has already been removed. Given this availability, many researchers take the easy route, use deseasonalized data, and ignore seasonality in their analyses. This might be useful, but there are no free lunches. Everything comes at a cost.

No pre-canned automatic routine will always be appropriate in all situations. Some seasonality may be additive. Some may be multiplicative. Some might be stochastic or deterministic. One size does not fit all. Relying on pre-canned deseasonalized data requires a lot of trust that the procedures being used by the statistical agency are appropriate. The procedures may be fancy, and they may test for and adjust for various contingencies, but they are never perfect.

Because of this, using deseasonalized data is bound to introduce some errors.

Ghysels (1990) explains that seasonal adjustment is an exercise in smoothing. Smoothing artificially brings values back down to trend after a shock, whereas a unit root would result in the shock's effect being persistent. When he tests US real GNP for a unit root using seasonally adjusted data, he finds support for unit roots, whereas using unadjusted data results in far weaker evidence of unit roots.

Ghysels and Perron (1993) find that using deseasonalized data lowers the power of unit root tests. They find that many of the standard de-seasonalizing procedures used by statistical agencies introduce an upward bias on the estimates of the AR coefficients and their sum. For example, if the true data-generating process were

$$X_t = 0.90 X_{t-1} + e_t$$

so that there was no seasonality, and the data were run through, say, the Census Bureau's X-11 filter, then OLS would estimate something closer to

$$X_t = 0.99 X_{t-1} + e_t.$$

This was the case for AR models of higher order: the sum of their coefficients was closer to one. This was also the case for data generated from different types of seasonal processes. Because of this upward bias, the standard unit root tests (such as Dickey-Fuller and Phillips-Perron tests, which we will discuss in Chap. 7) are less able to reject the null hypothesis of no unit roots. Using pre-filtered data reduces the power of the standard unit root tests. That is, the tests would indicate that there is a unit root even though there was none.

6.6 Conclusion

Little research is conducted these days using only univariate ARIMA models, but they are quite important. The concepts surrounding ARIMA modeling are foundational to time series; AR and MA processes are the component pieces of many more complicated models, and the problems of integration and nonstationarity must be dealt with in any time series setting. Mastering these ingredients ensures that the more complicated material will be more digestible.

Pankratz (1991, 1983) are two classic and gentle introductions to the theory and practice of ARIMA modeling. They are readable, insightful, and highly recommended. Of course it is hard to beat the time series textbook by Box and Jenkins (1976), especially regarding ARIMA modeling. Box and Jenkins are the two people most responsible for the popularity of ARIMA and seasonal ARIMA modeling. Their textbook should be on your bookshelf.

Hibon and Makridakis (1997) offers a skeptical voice regarding the mechanistically applied Box-Jenkins model-selection process, especially regarding the uncritical use of first-differencing to remove trends and seasonality. Mistakenly taking first differences results in decreased forecast accuracy. More formal testing is required before taking seasonal first differences.

The "frequency domain" (decomposing time series into the sum of sine and cosine waves of different frequencies) is a natural home for the study of periodic or seasonal time series. Unfortunately, this material is far beyond the scope of this book. However, for the interested and adventurous, the relevant chapters in Chatfield (2016) contain the gentlest introduction I have found to time series in the frequency domain. The book by Bloomfield (2004) is a popular and more in-depth introduction to frequency domain econometrics.

Franses (1996), Franses and Paap (2004), and Ghysels and Osborn (2001) provide book length treatments of seasonal time series models.

Unit Root Tests 7

7.1 Introduction

A process might be nonstationary without being a unit root. The two concepts are related, but they are not identical and it is common to confuse the two. A data series might be nonstationary because of a deterministic trend. Or it could be explosive. Or it can have a variance that is changing over time.

As we saw briefly in Chap. 5, the deterministic trend model and the random walk with drift share many features. They have a similar mean process that grows linearly over time, but they differ in the source of their nonstationarity. One has a stochastic trend. The other has a deterministic trend.

This is not mere semantics, and the source of the difference is of interest to more than just nerdy academics. Knowing the source of the nonstationarity has real-world policy implications.

For example, if the gross domestic product of the United States is the result of a deterministic trend model, then any shocks to the system will dampen over time and become irrelevant. A random walk processes, on the other hand, never gets over a shock. The shock lingers on, in full force, forever. Thus, the effects of a decades-old bad economic policy, even if the policy was short lived, would still be felt today. If GDP is a random walk with drift, we are doomed to suffer the full consequences of yesterday's mistakes; if it comes from a deterministic trend, then we will soon outgrow those mistakes.

If a company's stock price is the result of a stochastic growth process, then temporary shocks–mismanagement by the CEO, an unexpected energy crisis, or a small recession–will affect the stock price indefinitely into the future. If the stock price is determined by a deterministic trend model, then the stock will rebound; investors may profitably take a "this too will pass" attitude and invest countercyclically.

If we know why the economy is growing (stochastic '. deterministic trend), then we can better understand business cycles (the deviations from the trend). In the mid-twentieth century, it was quite common to study the business-cycle component of GDP, for example, by regressing the series on time, or a time polynomial, calculating the residuals (which by construction are zero mean) and studying the business cycle on this "detrended" time series. Detrending in this way, however, is only appropriate if a deterministic trend was the source of the nonstationarity in the first place. If the growth was stochastic, then first differencing the data would be the more appropriate approach.

In summary, knowing whether we have unit roots is important for policy-makers and academics alike.

7.2 Unit Root Tests

Any hypothesis test involves comparing the fit of the data with the results that would be expected if the null hypothesis were true and an implicit alternative hypothesis. Which hypothesis is the null is up to the researcher, but it is not an insignificant choice.

In what follows, we will discuss several unit root tests. These can be grouped as tests that have a null of a unit root and those whose null lacks a unit root.

1. Unit root tests (i.e., tests with nulls of unit roots):
   (a) Dickey-Fuller (DF)
   (b) Augmented Dickey-Fuller (ADF)
   (c) Dickey-Fuller GLS (DF-GLS)
   (d) Phillips-Perron
2. Stationarity tests (i.e., tests with nulls of no-unit roots):
   (a) Kwiatkowski, Phillips, Schmidt, and Shin test (KPSS)

We will work through some examples of each, paying extra attention to the Dickey-Fuller and augmented Dickey-Fuller tests.

After this, we will turn to a famous application of the DF unit root test on US macroeconomic data (Nelson & Plosser 1982). We will end by contrasting the results from all our various unit root tests.

If we need to analyze a dataset, we need to know whether it is stationary and what the source of nonstationarity is. Is it nonstationary because it is a random walk with drift? Or is it nonstationary because it has a deterministic trend?

In Chap. 5 we examined several stationary processes including (1) the AR processes (with and without a mean of zero) and some nonstationary processes, (2) the deterministic trend process (which is difference stationary), (3) the random walk process, and (4) the random walk with drift.

Let's combine all of the models listed above into one overarching model, so that we can make sense of how various statistical tests relate to each other. We write the following overarching model:

$$X_t = \beta_0 + \beta_1 X_{t-1} + \beta_2 t + e_t. \tag{7.1}$$

Table 7.1 Restrictions on the overarching model

Model			
Zero-mean stationary AR(1)	$\beta_0 = 0$	$|\beta_1| < 1$	$\beta_2 = 0$
Non-zero-mean stationary AR(1)	$\beta_0 \neq 0$	$|\beta_1| < 1$	$\beta_2 = 0$
Random walk (RW)	$\beta_0 = 0$	$\beta_1 = 1$	$\beta_2 = 0$
Random walk with drift (RWWD)	$\beta_0 \neq 0$	$\beta_1 = 1$	$\beta_2 = 0$
Deterministic trend (DT)		$|\beta_1| <= 1$	$\beta_2 \neq 0$

Notice that it nests the various models listed above. Table 7.1 lists all of the parameter restrictions required to yield each particular model.

How do we test whether a particular dataset came from an AR process? We need to specify the alternative hypothesis, and Table 7.1 makes clear that there are many possible alternative hypotheses.

With unit root testing, we're comparing one model with another. But there are so many different models to compare to. Unit root testing gets confusing because there are so many different alternatives. It's like that old joke: how's your wife? Compared to what?

The tests below differ–among other ways–in the specified alternative hypotheses. A test of an AR(1) versus an alternative of a deterministic trend (DT) model tests that $\beta_2 = 0$ against the alternative that $\beta_2 \neq 0$. A test of an RW model versus an alternative of an RWWD model tests whether $\beta_0 = 0$ against the alternative hypothesis that $\beta_0 \neq 0$. Testing between RW and DT models involves joint tests of several parameters.

7.3 Dickey-Fuller Tests

As we argued in the previous section, it is important to be able to identify whether the data come from a deterministic or stochastic process. Perhaps the most common type of unit root test is the Dickey-Fuller test (DF), or the augmented Dickey-Fuller test (ADF).

In all of the Dickey-Fuller and ADF tests below, the null hypothesis is that there is a unit root. Under the unit root hypothesis, the test statistics are not distributed as normal variables nor as t, but have a sampling distribution of their own. This distribution is now commonly called the Dickey-Fuller distribution. Dickey and Fuller (1979) estimated the distribution and provided critical values for various sample sizes. MacKinnon (1991, 2010) showed how to calculate its p-values for arbitrary sample sizes.

7.3.1 A Random Walk Versus a Zero-Mean AR(1) Process

A random walk process and a zero-mean AR(1) process are both nested by the overarching model (7.1):

$$X_t = \beta_0 + \beta_1 X_{t-1} + \beta_2 t + e_t$$

when $\beta_0 = 0$ (to make the process zero mean), $\beta_2 = 0$ and $|\beta_1| < 0$. We assume here that the error terms are iid$(0,\sigma^2)$, which is to say they are serially uncorrelated. If $\beta_1 = 1$ then the model is a random walk (it has a unit root). Alternatively, if $|\beta_2| < 0$, then the model is an AR(1).

A simple test of the random walk versus the zero-mean AR(1) model would seem to be the following. Estimate a regression of the form

$$X_t = \beta_1 X_{t-1} + e_t$$

and conduct a t-test of whether $\beta_1 = 1$. An alternative approach is to subtract X_{t-1} from both sides:

$$X_t - X_{t-1} = \beta_1 X_{t-1} - X_{t-1} + e_t$$
$$\Delta X_t = (\beta_1 - 1) X_{t-1} + e_t \qquad (7.2)$$
$$\Delta X_t = \gamma X_{t-1} + e_t \qquad (7.3)$$

and test whether $\gamma = 0$ (i.e., that $\beta = 1$). Equation (7.3) emphasizes the fact that if the model were a random walk, then first differencing would render the model stationary.

Unfortunately, under the null of a unit root, the sampling distribution of β_1 does not follow a t-distribution, or any other standard distribution, neither in finite samples nor asymptotically. The reason for this stems from the fact that X_{t-1} in the right-hand side of Eq. (7.3) is not stationary. This means that the test statistics do not converge along the usual lines of the central limit theorem.

Fortunately, Stata has done the hard work for us. We simply have to remember to ask it to do so.

Example

In this example, we will load up two artificial datasets, one where we know the data come from a RW process and another where the data come from a zero-mean AR(1). We will compare the results from the two datasets.

First, we load the random walk dataset:

. use RWdata.dta, clear

and graph the variable X (Fig. 7.1).

Second, the null hypothesis that we are testing is that the data came from a simple random walk:

$$H_0 : X_t = X_{t-1} + e_t$$

against the alternative that the process is

$$H_A : X_t = \beta X_{t-1} + e_t$$

7.3 Dickey-Fuller Tests

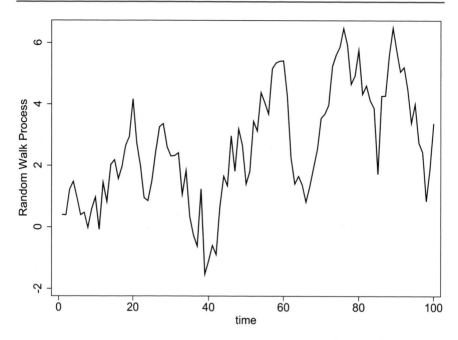

Fig. 7.1 Random walk data

with $|\beta| < 1$. Thus, there is neither constant nor trend in the null hypothesis nor the alternative. Therefore, we can implement a simple DF test by estimating (7.3) and comparing the test statistic with the appropriate critical values:

```
. dfuller X, noconstant regress

Dickey-Fuller test for unit root                   Number of obs   =        99

                           ---------- Interpolated Dickey-Fuller ---------
              Test         1% Critical       5% Critical      10% Critical
           Statistic          Value             Value             Value
------------------------------------------------------------------------------
Z(t)         -1.306          -2.600            -1.950            -1.610
------------------------------------------------------------------------------

------------------------------------------------------------------------------
     D.X |      Coef.   Std. Err.      t    P>|t|     [95% Conf. Interval]
-------------+----------------------------------------------------------------
       X |
      L1. |  -.0390038   .0298589    -1.31   0.195    -.0982579    .0202503
------------------------------------------------------------------------------
```

The `regress` option on `dfuller` tells Stata to report the coefficient estimates along with the Dickey-Fuller results.

When we usually undertake a hypothesis test, the most common null hypothesis is that the estimated coefficient is equal to zero. But looking back at the overarching model, the relevant coefficient value is that $\beta_1 = 1$. Recall, though, that we transform the model so that we are looking at first differences. This also transforms the relevant coefficient value from $\beta_1 = 1$ to $\beta_1 = 0$ so that we can run our usual hypothesis tests. Long story short, just check whether the dfuller coefficient values are equal to zero.

Resuming, Stata estimates the following model:

$$\Delta X_t = (-0.039)X_{t-1} + e_t.$$

Since $\hat{\gamma}_1 = -0.039$, then

$$\hat{\beta}_1 = 1 + \hat{\gamma}_1 = 1 - 0.039 = 0.96$$

which is quite close to one.

The test statistic (-1.306) is squarely in the "acceptance" region. Alternatively, the estimated *p*-value is greater than 0.10. Either way, the Dickey-Fuller test cannot reject the null hypothesis of a unit root, which is fortunate because we know the data were generated with a unit root (a random walk process).

Example

Let's contrast the performance of the Dickey-Fuller test when the data generating process does not have a unit root. Load up the dataset ARexamples.dta, keeping only the first 100 observations so that it has the same number of observations as the previous example. Graphing the variable indicates that the process is likely not a random walk (Fig. 7.2).

Indeed, the data on X were simulated from an AR(1) process, with coefficient equal to 0.50. Nevertheless, we conduct a formal Dickey-Fuller test:

```
. use ARexamples.dta, clear

. keep if _n <= 100
(2900 observations deleted)

. dfuller X, noconstant regress

Dickey-Fuller test for unit root                   Number of obs   =        99

                              ---------- Interpolated Dickey-Fuller ---------
                 Test        1% Critical      5% Critical     10% Critical
              Statistic         Value            Value            Value
------------------------------------------------------------------------------
Z(t)            -3.973          -2.600           -1.950           -1.610
------------------------------------------------------------------------------

------------------------------------------------------------------------------
     D.X |      Coef.   Std. Err.      t    P>|t|     [95% Conf. Interval]
---------+--------------------------------------------------------------------
       X |
      L1.|  -.2832969   .0713082    -3.97   0.000    -.4248057    -.141788
------------------------------------------------------------------------------
```

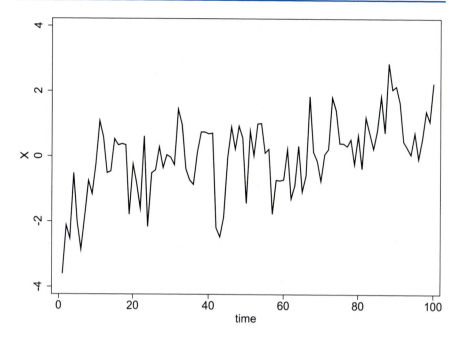

Fig. 7.2 Stationary AR data

The test statistic of -3.973 is far greater in magnitude than any of the critical values indicating a strong rejection of the null hypothesis of a unit root. This is encouraging, since the data were not from a random walk, but from a stationary AR process.

Exercises
1. Unit root tests have notoriously low power, especially if the AR coefficient is close to one. In this exercise you are asked to explore this for yourself. Generate 100 observations from a stationary zero-mean AR(1) process with $\beta = 0.95$. Draw the errors independently from a N(0,1) distribution. Conduct a dfuller test with the noconstant option. Are you able to reject the null of a unit root? Repeat the exercise another nine times for a total of ten experiments. In how many instances are you able to reject the null hypothesis?
2. Repeat the exercise above but with 1,000 observations and with $\beta = 0.99$. In how many of the ten instances are you able to reject the null hypothesis? (We should be rejecting 95% of the time, but we reject far less frequently than that.)
3. Repeat the previous exercise ($N = 1,000$ obs and $\beta = 0.99$) but write a loop to conduct the exercise 1,000 times. What proportion of the times are you able to reject the null hypothesis? Do you reject approximately 95% of the time? (Hint: you can't possibly count by hand the number of times the reported test statistic is greater than the critical value. Set up a counter to do this.)

7.3.2 A Random Walk Versus an AR(1) Model with a Constant

Many processes do not have a mean of zero. The zero-mean assumption is not problematic. As we saw before in Chap. 2, a stationary AR(1) process with a constant

$$X_t = \beta_0 + \beta_1 X_{t-1} + e_t \tag{7.4}$$

has a mean of

$$\mu = \frac{\beta_0}{1 - \beta_1}.$$

How do we test for a unit root? That is, how do we test whether our data came from a RW or a nonzero stationary AR(1) process? Begin again with our overarching model (7.1) but with no deterministic trend ($\beta_2 = 0$):

$$X_t = \beta_0 + \beta_1 X_{t-1} + \beta_2 t + e_t$$
$$= \beta_0 + \beta_1 X_{t-1} + e_t.$$

Subtracting X_{t-1} from both sides,

$$X_t - X_{t-1} = \beta_0 + \beta_1 X_{t-1} - X_{t-1} + e_t$$
$$= \beta_0 + (\beta_1 - 1) X_{t-1} + e_t \tag{7.5}$$
$$= \beta_0 + \gamma X_{t-1} + e_t. \tag{7.6}$$

Under the null hypothesis, the data generating process is a random walk (RW). As such, $\beta_1 = 1$, and $\gamma_0 = 0$. Under the alternative hypothesis, the data generating process is a stationary AR(1) with some potentially nonzero mean. As such, $|\beta_1| < 1$ and $\gamma < 0$.

The fact that the alternative hypothesis, the stationary AR(1) process, had a nonzero mean does not affect this. It affects the critical values only. Thus, to perform the Dickey-Fuller test where the alternative is a nonstationary process with nonzero mean, we simply add an intercept and proceed as before.

Example

We will do this version of the Dickey-Fuller test with two datasets. The first dataset will use data simulated from a random walk process, and the second will use data simulated from a nonzero AR(1) process.

The default setting for Stata's `dfuller` command is to include a constant. Previously, we had to specify a noconstant option. Here, the constant is called for because we are testing against an AR(1) process with a nonzero mean (i.e., one with a constant).

7.3 Dickey-Fuller Tests

```
. use RWdata.dta, clear

. dfuller X, regress

Dickey-Fuller test for unit root                   Number of obs   =        99

                              ---------- Interpolated Dickey-Fuller ---------
                    Test         1% Critical       5% Critical      10% Critical
                 Statistic          Value             Value             Value
------------------------------------------------------------------------------
 Z(t)             -2.723            -3.511            -2.891            -2.580
------------------------------------------------------------------------------
MacKinnon approximate p-value for Z(t) = 0.0701

------------------------------------------------------------------------------
       D.X |      Coef.   Std. Err.      t    P>|t|     [95% Conf. Interval]
-----------+------------------------------------------------------------------
         X |
       L1. |  -.1355355    .049772    -2.72   0.008    -.2343191   -.0367519
           |
     _cons |   .3844845   .1606448     2.39   0.019     .0656491    .7033199
------------------------------------------------------------------------------
```

The test statistic (-2.723) and p-value (0.0701) indicate that we cannot reject the null at the 1% of 5% levels.

Example

Let's now load up a dataset from a stationary AR(1) process with nonzero mean and compare the results. The data were generated according to $X_t = 10 - 0.50 X_{t-1}$.

```
. use AR1nonzero_b.dta, clear

. dfuller X, regress

Dickey-Fuller test for unit root                   Number of obs   =        99

                              ---------- Interpolated Dickey-Fuller ---------
                    Test         1% Critical       5% Critical      10% Critical
                 Statistic          Value             Value             Value
------------------------------------------------------------------------------
 Z(t)             -5.926            -3.511            -2.891            -2.580
------------------------------------------------------------------------------
MacKinnon approximate p-value for Z(t) = 0.0000

------------------------------------------------------------------------------
       D.X |      Coef.   Std. Err.      t    P>|t|     [95% Conf. Interval]
-----------+------------------------------------------------------------------
         X |
       L1. |   -.52943    .089347    -5.93   0.000    -.7067591   -.3521008
           |
     _cons |   10.5178   1.778593     5.91   0.000     6.987788    14.04782
------------------------------------------------------------------------------
```

In this case, we reject the null of a unit root at all the usual significance levels. We can see this in two ways. First, the estimated *p*-value is zero. Second, the test statistic (-5.926) is far more negative than any of the Dickey-Fuller critical values.

7.3.3 A Random Walk with Drift Versus a Deterministic Trend

What if our data are trending over time? How do we test between the RW with drift (a "stochastic trend") and the "deterministic trend" AR model? Visually, they look the same: they both trend upward linearly. And they are both nonstationary. We are not testing the stationarity assumption here, then. What we are testing is the *source* of the stationarity. Is it due to a stochastic or deterministic factor?

Both models are nested by the overarching model:

$$X_t = \beta_0 + \beta_1 X_{t-1} + \beta_2 t + e_t. \qquad (7.7)$$

The deterministic trend model has $|\beta_1| < 1$ and $\beta_2 \neq 0$, while the random walk with drift has $\beta_0 \neq 0$, $\beta_1 = 1$, and $\beta_2 = 0$.

Then a straightforward test of the unit root hypothesis –i.e., the hypothesis that the model is a random walk– is to run a regression of (7.7) and conduct an F-test of $\beta_1 = 1$ and $\beta_2 = 0$. The Dickey-Fuller approach is to rewrite (7.7) by subtracting X_{t-1} from both sides and estimating

$$\Delta X_t = \beta_0 + (\beta_1 - 1)X_{t-1} + \beta_2 t + e_t \qquad (7.8)$$

and testing whether $(\beta_1 - 1) = \beta_2 = 0$.

Again, under the unit root hypothesis, the test statistic is not distributed as normal variables nor as *t*, but has a sampling distribution all on its own.

Example

Let's load up our simulated random walk dataset, `RWdata.dta`, and focus on variable Y, the random walk with drift (see Fig. 7.3). The variable was generated according to $Y_t = 0.5 + Y_{t-1} + e_t$.

7.3 Dickey-Fuller Tests

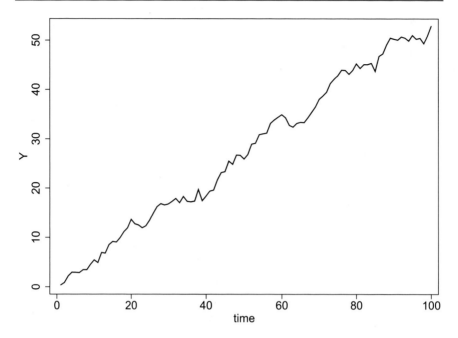

Fig. 7.3 Random walk with Drift: $Y_t = 0.50 + Y_{t-1} + t + e_t$

```
. use RWdata.dta, clear

. dfuller Y, regress trend

Dickey-Fuller test for unit root                   Number of obs   =        99

                               ---------- Interpolated Dickey-Fuller ---------
                  Test         1% Critical       5% Critical      10% Critical
               Statistic          Value             Value             Value
------------------------------------------------------------------------------
 Z(t)           -3.240            -4.042            -3.451            -3.151
------------------------------------------------------------------------------
MacKinnon approximate p-value for Z(t) = 0.0768


------------------------------------------------------------------------------
   D.Y     |      Coef.   Std. Err.      t    P>|t|     [95% Conf. Interval]
-----------+------------------------------------------------------------------
   Y       |
       L1. | -.2001429   .0617792    -3.24   0.002    -.3227737   -.0775122
    _trend |  .1071575   .0335155     3.20   0.002     .0406298    .1736852
    _cons  |  .5990923   .1879078     3.19   0.002     .2260983    .9720862
------------------------------------------------------------------------------
```

The output here is a bit ambiguous. Given the test statistic (-3.240) and p-value (0.0768), we can reject the null hypothesis of a unit root at the 10%, but not at the 1% and 5% levels.

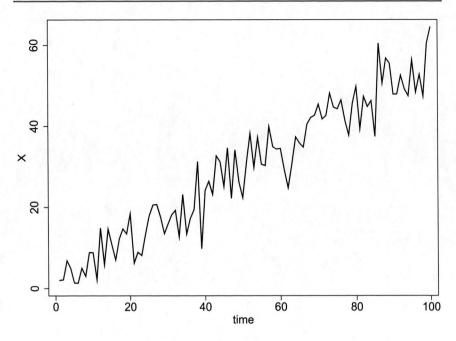

Fig. 7.4 Deterministic trend: $X_t = 1 + 0.10X_{t-1} + 0.50t + e_t$

Example

Let's see how the test performs when the true DGP does not have a unit root but rather has a deterministic trend (see Fig. 7.4).

```
. use DTdata.dta, clear

. dfuller X, regress trend

Dickey-Fuller test for unit root                   Number of obs   =        99

                              ---------- Interpolated Dickey-Fuller ---------
                Test         1% Critical      5% Critical     10% Critical
             Statistic          Value            Value            Value
------------------------------------------------------------------------------
 Z(t)         -10.078           -4.042           -3.451           -3.151
------------------------------------------------------------------------------
MacKinnon approximate p-value for Z(t) = 0.0000


------------------------------------------------------------------------------
  D.X    |      Coef.   Std. Err.      t    P>|t|     [95% Conf. Interval]
---------+--------------------------------------------------------------------
    X    |
    L1.  |  -1.043005   .1034907   -10.08   0.000    -1.248433   -.8375778
 _trend  |   .5734193   .0589168     9.73   0.000     .4564703    .6903682
 _cons   |   2.113389   .9940207     2.13   0.036     .1402734    4.086504
------------------------------------------------------------------------------
```

7.3 Dickey-Fuller Tests

The test statistic (-10.078) and p-value (0.0000) indicate that we can safely reject the null hypothesis of a unit root. This is fortunate, as the data were generated from a deterministic trend process, not a unit root with drift.

7.3.4 Augmented Dickey-Fuller Tests

The Dickey-Fuller test assumes that the error term was not serially correlated. This may not be a reasonable assumption. In fact, most of the times it is not. Most of the times, there is a lot of autocorrelation in the residuals. To account for this autocorrelation, Said and Dickey (1979) introduced the *augmented* Dickey-Fuller test. The ADF test adds k lagged difference terms onto the standard DF estimation equations.

Why did we just tack on some lagged difference terms to the standard DF equation? Dickey and Fuller (1979) presumed that the data generating process is AR(1) –i.e., that it has one lag (ex: $X_t = \beta_0 + \beta_1 X_{t-1} + e_t$)– and the question is whether it is stationary ($|\beta_1| < 0$) or nonstationary ($\beta_1 = 1$). Said and Dickey (1979) extended this to arbitrary AR(p) processes.

Let's see how this works for a simpler AR(2) process versus a RW without drift. Suppose that the data generating process is AR(2):

$$X_t = \beta_1 X_{t-1} + \beta_2 X_{t-2} + e_t \tag{7.9}$$

and we wish to check whether the process is stationary.

We can always add zero, so add and subtract $\beta_2 X_{t-1}$ to the right-hand side of (7.9) and simplify:

$$X_t = \beta_1 X_{t-1} + (\beta_2 X_{t-1} - \beta_2 X_{t-1}) + \beta_2 X_{t-2} + e_t$$
$$= (\beta_1 + \beta_2) X_{t-1} - \beta_2 (X_{t-1} - X_{t-2}) + e_t$$
$$= (\beta_1 + \beta_2) X_{t-1} - \beta_2 \Delta X_{t-1} + e_t.$$

As with the standard Dickey-Fuller procedure, subtract X_{t-1} from both sides:

$$X_t - X_{t-1} = (\beta_1 + \beta_2 - 1) X_{t-1} - \beta_2 \Delta X_{t-1} + e_t$$
$$\Delta X_t = \gamma X_{t-1} + c \Delta X_{t-1} + e_t$$

where $\gamma = (\beta_1 + \beta_2 - 1)$ and $c = -\beta_2$.

We test for stationarity by seeing whether

$$\gamma = (\beta_1 + \beta_2 - 1) = 0,$$

or equivalently whether

$$\beta_1 + \beta_2 = 1$$

which is one of our familiar stationarity conditions on an AR(2) process from Chap. 4.

A similar procedure applied to an AR(3) process yields

$$\Delta X_t = (\beta_1 + \beta_2 + \beta_3 - 1) X_{t-1} - \beta_2 \Delta X_{t-1} - \beta_3 \Delta X_{t-2} + e_t$$

$$= \gamma X_{t-1} + \sum_{i=1}^{2} c_i \Delta X_{t-i} + e_t.$$

And an arbitrary AR(p) process yields

$$\Delta X_t = \gamma X_{t-1} + \sum_{i=1}^{p-1} c_i \Delta X_{t-i} + e_t.$$

The regression equation for an ADF test of a RWWD versus a deterministic trend is equivalent to the standard DF equation but with additional lagged difference terms:

$$\Delta X_t = \beta_0 + \gamma X_{t-1} + \beta_2 t + \sum_{i=1}^{k} c_i \Delta X_{t-i} + e_t. \tag{7.10}$$

and we test whether $\gamma = (\beta_1 + \beta_2 + \cdots + \beta_p - 1) = 0$.

Adding $k - 1$ lagged difference terms allows us to test for unit roots in AR(k) processes. If the data generating process includes MA terms, then all is not lost. Recall that an invertible MA process can be expressed as an AR(∞) process. We could never estimate an infinite number of lagged differences, but if we estimate enough of them, we can adequately account for any number of MA terms.

In practice, however, we are never sure what the order of the ARMA(p,q) process is. And there are no definitive rules for how many lags to include in our estimating regressions. Some researchers add terms until the residuals exhibit no autocorrelation. Others begin with many lags and slowly remove insignificant terms, in a sort of general-to-specific methodology.

We will explore several of the more commonly used lag selection methods in Sect. 7.3.6. Ignoring this complication, though, the process for performing an ADF test in Stata is no different from performing the standard DF test. In fact, the command is the same. You must simply add a certain number of lagged differences via `lags(k)` as an option to `dfuller`. For example, an ADF for an AR(2) versus a random walk is `dfuller X, nocons lags(1)`.

7.3.5 DF-GLS Tests

Rather than using OLS to detrend the data, Elliot et al. (1992, 1996) propose a GLS detrending procedure. On the detrended data, $\hat{X}_t$, they then estimate

$$\Delta \hat{X}_t = \gamma \hat{X}_{t-1} + \sum_{i=1}^{p} c_i \Delta \hat{X}_{t-i} + e_t.$$

The mathematical details of generalized least squares are beyond the scope of this book; however, it is easy to implement the DF-GLS procedure in Stata using the command:

```
. dfgls varname [, maxlag(#) notrend ers]
```

The `maxlag(#)` option allows you to set the maximal number of lags to consider. (We will discuss lag selection in Sect. 7.3.6.) A trend is included by default; you can exclude the deterministic trend term by using the `notrend` option. Finally, `ers` uses critical values as calculated by Elliott, Rothenberg, and Stock (ERS), the original authors of the DF-GLS procedure. This option is seldom used, as the Cheung and Lai (1995a,b) critical values are considered superior. ERS calculated their critical values only for the case where the number of lags is zero. Cheung and Lai (1995a,b) find that finite-sample critical values depend on the number of lags and reestimated the critical values for various lag lengths.

The `dfgls` command reports the optimal lag choices of several different selection procedures. Specifically, it computes the optimal lag based upon Ng and Perron's (1995) sequential t-test, Ng and Perron's (2001) modified Akaike information criterion (the MIC), and Schwartz's (1978) information criterion (the SIC). We will discuss lag selection and work out an example in the next section.

7.3.6 Choosing the Lag Length in DF-Type Tests

Up to this point, we have left unspecified how many lags to include in the Dickey-Fuller tests. There are several different approaches to answering this problem, but all of them have as their centerpiece the idea that, once a model is properly specified, the residuals are white noise. Thus, a quick and easy answer to the question of lag length is simply this: choose as many lags as is required to leave the residuals as uncorrelated white noise.

There is, as usual, a trade-off to consider. If we have too few lags, then our residuals will be autocorrelated; the autocorrelation will throw off our hypothesis testing and bias our results. If we have too many lags, then we will have white noise residuals, but we will be estimating more coefficients (the ones on the extraneous lags) than we need to. This, in turn, means that our tests will have lower power; we will use up valuable degrees of freedom to estimate these extraneous coefficients, when they could be used to give us more precise estimates of the truly meaningful ones. (In general, econometricians believe the latter is less problematic. When in doubt, include the lag.)

Should you start with a few lags and keep adding more as needed? Or should you start with many lags and whittle them down as allowable? And if so, how many lags should you begin with before whittling? Can we use information criteria to directly choose the optimal lag length? Different econometricians have proposed different rules. In this subsection, we will review some of the more common ones.

Ng and Perron (1995) and Campbell and Perron (1991) suggest a sequence of t-tests, starting with a large number of lags, say k_{max}, and testing down. If the coefficient on the longest lagged term is insignificant (Stata uses a p-value greater than 0.10), then drop that term and reestimate the smaller model; repeat as necessary.

Ng and Perron (1995) compared their sequential t-tests method with the Akaike and Schwartz information criteria and found their sequential t-test approach to be optimal. They suffered less from size distortions, but had comparable power.

Of course, the Ng and Perron (1995) procedure leaves as unspecified the value of k_{max} from which to test down. Schwert provided one answer.

Schwert (1989, 2002) suggests that P_{max} should be calculated from

$$k_{max} = int\left[12\,(T/100)^{1/4}\right]$$

where T denotes the number of periods in your dataset, and "int" denotes the integer portion of the calculated number.

In its dfgls command, Stata implements a slight variation of this formula:

$$k_{max} = int\left[12\,[(T+1)/100]^{1/4}\right]$$

adding one to the number of periods.

Ng and Perron returned to the selection of lag length in their 2001 paper. They constructed a modified AIC, which is in many ways optimal to the traditional AIC and BIC which choose lag lengths that tend to be too small.

Cheung and Lai (1995a,b) found that the finite-sample critical values of the DF-GLS test depend upon the number of lags. Wu (2010) compared the performance of Ng and Perron's two methods –the sequential t-test and the modified AIC– and found that the sequential t-test approach performs best, especially when using the critical values computed by Cheung and Lai (as Stata does).

Fortunately, Stata has automated all the above calculations for us. It remains for the researcher to choose the most appropriate selection criteria. Of course, the ethical researcher will decide before testing, which procedure is the most appropriate. Do not run the tests first, choosing the answer that is the most convenient.

Example
This all gets quite dizzying. Let's turn to an example to solidify the material.

7.3 Dickey-Fuller Tests

First, we download and `tsset` some data: the seasonally adjusted civilian unemployment rate for the US (UNRATE).

```
. drop _all
. freduse UNRATE
. gen time = _n
. tsset time
```

If you're trying to work along, it would be best if our datasets were identical, beginning in Jan. 1948 and ending Oct. 2017.

Using `dfgls` on our data we get:

```
. dfgls UNRATE
```

DF-GLS for UNRATE   Number of obs =   817
Maxlag = 20 chosen by Schwert criterion

[lags]	DF-GLS tau Test Statistic	1% Critical Value	5% Critical Value	10% Critical Value
20	-3.424	-3.480	-2.826	-2.541
19	-3.247	-3.480	-2.828	-2.543
18	-3.035	-3.480	-2.830	-2.545
17	-3.013	-3.480	-2.832	-2.547
16	-3.002	-3.480	-2.834	-2.549
15	-2.945	-3.480	-2.836	-2.550
14	-2.833	-3.480	-2.838	-2.552
13	-2.750	-3.480	-2.840	-2.554
12	-2.796	-3.480	-2.842	-2.556
11	-3.206	-3.480	-2.844	-2.557
10	-3.120	-3.480	-2.846	-2.559
9	-3.517	-3.480	-2.847	-2.561
8	-3.559	-3.480	-2.849	-2.562
7	-3.604	-3.480	-2.851	-2.564
6	-3.814	-3.480	-2.853	-2.566
5	-3.813	-3.480	-2.855	-2.567
4	-3.378	-3.480	-2.856	-2.569
3	-3.075	-3.480	-2.858	-2.570
2	-2.548	-3.480	-2.860	-2.572
1	-1.975	-3.480	-2.861	-2.573

Opt Lag (Ng-Perron seq t) = 19 with RMSE   .1877671
Min SC   = -3.258017 at lag 5 with RMSE .1913537
Min MAIC = -3.283876 at lag 12 with RMSE .1886084

The output shows that Schwert's criterion suggests a maximum lag of 20. From there, we could test down, using Ng and Perron's sequential t-test procedure. If so, we would have arrived at 19 lags. Quite a lot of lags. If instead we opt to use an information criterion, we would have had chosen a different number of lags to use in our DF-GLS regressions. The Schwartz criterion chooses a lag length of five. This criterion tends to favor fewer lags. Ng and Perron's modified AIC, what Stata calls the MAIC, chooses 12 lags.

Our ultimate goal is not choosing the number of lags, but to conduct a unit root test. The lag selection is simply a preliminary.

If we had used 19 lags, then the DF-GLS test statistic is -3.247. This is greater than the critical values at the 5% and 10% levels. But we cannot reject the null at the 1% level.

If we had used the MAIC as our guiding principle for lag selection, then we would conduct a DF-GLS test with 12 lags. The test statistic from this would be -2.796. Given this test statistic, we would reject the null hypothesis of a unit root when testing at the 10% level. We cannot reject a unit root at the 5% or 1% levels.

Finally, if we had opted for the SIC, we would have estimated a DF-GLS model with five lags. This would have resulted in a test statistic of -3.813, which is greater in absolute value than all of the critical values. We would have rejected the null hypothesis of a unit root.

As you can see, the conclusions of these unit root tests depend upon the number of lags which you have estimated. Ideally, the various lag selection criteria would have recommended the same number of lags. Unfortunately, this is rarely the case.

Exercises
1. Apply DF-GLS to the Nelson and Plosser (1982) dataset. Allow for a trend. Use Ng and Perron's modified AIC for lag selection. Use 5% for hypothesis testing. Which of the variables are trend stationary? Which seem to be random walks with drift?

7.4 Phillips-Perron Tests

The Phillips-Perron (1988) test is an alternative to the ADF test. Rather than compensating for serial correlation in the error terms by adding lagged differences, Phillips and Perron correct the standard errors for heteroskedasticity and autocorrelation (HAC). That is, whereas ADF changes the regression equation, Phillips-Perron changes the test statistics. This is done in much the same way that Stata's `robust` option calculates HAC standard errors after the `reg` command (Newey & West 1986). The specifics of this correction will lead us too far afield; however, Stata estimates

$$X_t = \beta_0 + \rho X_{t-1} + \beta_2 t + e_t \tag{7.11}$$

and computes the HAC-corrected standard errors quite readily using the command:

```
. pperron varname [, noconstant trend regress lags(#)
```

The options `noconstant` and `trend` have the usual interpretation; `regress` shows the coefficient estimates of Eq. (7.11); and `lags(#)` indicates the number of lags used to calculate the Newey-West standard errors.

7.4 Phillips-Perron Tests

The `pperron` test produces two test statistics, $Z(\rho)$ and $Z(t)$. Phillips and Perron find that $Z(\rho)$ has higher power than $Z(t)$ or ADF tests when the error process has AR or positive MA components. The Phillips-Perron test is not suited to situations where the error has large, or even moderately sized, negative MA terms.

Example

```
. use RWdata.dta, clear

. pperron Y, regress trend

Phillips-Perron test for unit root              Number of obs   =         99
                                                Newey-West lags =          3

                            ---------- Interpolated Dickey-Fuller ---------
               Test         1% Critical      5% Critical     10% Critical
            Statistic          Value            Value            Value
------------------------------------------------------------------------------
Z(rho)       -22.332          -27.366          -20.682          -17.486
Z(t)          -3.427           -4.042           -3.451           -3.151
------------------------------------------------------------------------------
MacKinnon approximate p-value for Z(t) = 0.0478


------------------------------------------------------------------------------
     Y  |      Coef.   Std. Err.      t    P>|t|     [95% Conf. Interval]
---------+--------------------------------------------------------------------
       Y |
      L1.|   .7998571   .0617792    12.95   0.000     .6772263    .9224878
   _trend|   .1071575   .0335155     3.20   0.002     .0406298    .1736852
   _cons |   .5990923   .1879078     3.19   0.002     .2260983    .9720862
------------------------------------------------------------------------------
```

As with the other DF-type tests, the null hypothesis is that the data have a unit root (i.e., $\rho = 1$) and the alternative is that $\rho < 1$. Examining the test statistics, there is some evidence that Y has a unit root. The evidence is weak, though. As a further step, we can take the first difference and verify that there is no unit root in ΔY_t:

```
. pperron D.Y, trend

Phillips-Perron test for unit root              Number of obs   =         98
                                                Newey-West lags =          3

                            ---------- Interpolated Dickey-Fuller ---------
               Test         1% Critical      5% Critical     10% Critical
            Statistic          Value            Value            Value
------------------------------------------------------------------------------
Z(rho)      -117.038          -27.332          -20.664          -17.472
Z(t)         -11.125           -4.044           -3.452           -3.151
------------------------------------------------------------------------------
MacKinnon approximate p-value for Z(t) = 0.0000
```

Here, we reject the null of a unit root. That is, we conclude that there is no unit root in the first-differenced variable.

7.5 KPSS Tests

The null hypotheses in most unit root tests (certainly all the ones we have mentioned thus far) is that the process contains a unit root. Unfortunately, unit root tests have notoriously low power (i.e., they do not reject the null of a unit root often enough). Because of this, it is useful to run a complementary test, one that has stationarity as the null rather than the alternative. The KPSS test is such a test and provides a useful double-check. The test was developed by Kwiatkowski et al. (1992), which is, admittedly, a mouthful; everyone shortens this to "KPSS." The test is easy to execute in Stata, and researchers are encouraged to use it.[1] If it isn't already installed on your computer, install it by

```
. net install sts15_2.pkg
```

The KPSS test decomposes a time series variable into the sum of a deterministic trend, a random walk component, and a stationary error:

$$y_t = \beta t + r_t + e_t$$

where e_t is a stationary error, and the random walk component is

$$r_t = r_{t-1} + u_t.$$

The initial term in the random walk sequence, r_0, plays the role of the intercept.

The error terms on the random walk component (u_t) are presumed iid(0,σ^2).

If u_t has zero variance, its value is always zero. Thus, $r_1 = r_2 = r_3 = \cdots = r_0$. In other words, r_t is no longer a random walk, and y_t is a simple trend stationary model:

$$y_t = \beta t + r_0 + e_t.$$

The test is simply a Lagrange multiplier (LM) test that the random walk component has zero variance.

To implement the KPSS test, first estimate the model and calculate the residuals ϵ_t. Calculate the running sum of the residuals:

$$S_t = \sum_{i=0}^{t} \epsilon_i$$

Estimate the error variance of the regression:

---

[1] Sephton (2017) provides updated critical values for the KPSS test for use with small samples.

7.5 KPSS Tests

$$\hat{\sigma}_\epsilon^2 = \sum_{t=0}^{T} \epsilon_t^2$$

Finally, the test statistic is

$$LM = \sum_{t=0}^{T} S_t^2 / \hat{\sigma}_\epsilon^2$$

which is simply the ratio of two different estimates of the residual variance. In actuality, the denominator is a slightly different estimate of the "long-run" variance of e_t, calculated using the residuals ϵ_t, and weighted using a particular weighing method (the Bartlett kernel). The details of this are beyond the scope of this book.

In Stata, the whole process is quite easy:

. kpss y [, maxlag(k) notrend qs auto]

The maxlag(k) option allows you to specify the results using up to a maximal number of lags. notrend specifies that the null hypothesis is level stationary, rather than trend stationary. qs and auto allow Stata to use different methods for calculating autocovariances and maximal lags.

KPSS ran their stationarity tests on Nelson and Plosser's data and found that there was less evidence for unit roots than was originally believed. Their results can be replicated by running the following two commands for each variable in the dataset:

. kpss varname, maxlag(8) notrend
. kpss varname, maxlag(8)

Exercises

1. Kwiatkowski et al. (1992) applied their method to the Nelson and Plosser (1982) dataset and came to some different conclusions. In this exercise, you will now replicate KPSS' study using Stata on NelsonPlosserData.dta.
   (a) Calculate the KPSS test statistic for a model with no trend (notrend) and a maximal lag of eight periods (maxlag(8)). Which variables seem to have unit roots? (You can double-check your work by looking at Table 5a in the original KPSS paper.)
   (b) Calculate the KPSS test statistic for a model which allows for a trend (i.e., do not include the notrend option) and a maximal lag of eight periods (maxlag(8)). Which variables seem to have unit roots? (You can double-check your work by looking at Table 5b in the original KPSS paper.)
2. Redo both parts of the above exercise, but with the following modifications: let Stata pick the optimal lag length (using the auto option), and have Stata use a quadratic kernel to estimate the long-run variance of the series (using the qs option). Which variables seem to have unit roots?

7.6 Replicating Nelson and Plosser

In one of the most widely cited papers in modern macroeconomics, Nelson and Plosser (1982) examined several common macro datasets (data on GDP, per capita GDP, CPI, etc....) and tested them for unit roots. This question is important for two reasons, one statistical and one economic. Knowing whether the variables have a unit root tells us how we should model them statistically. Far more importantly, if economic variables such as GDP follow a unit root, then this tells us something quite meaningful about the economy. If GDP follows a unit root, then any shock to the economy will have a long-term impact. The shock's effects will be felt until a countervailing shock pushes the economy back onto its old path. Alternatively, if GDP does not follow a unit root, then the economy is resilient and self-healing. When GDP is affected by a shock, the effects of that shock are temporary: the economy adjusts so that it resumes its previous growth path.

Nelson and Plosser considered equations of the form

$$X_t = \mu + \rho X_{t-1} + \gamma t + u_t. \tag{7.12}$$

Using Dickey-Fuller tests, they found that almost all macroeconomic time series contain unit roots, or, more correctly, they found that they could not reject the null hypothesis of a unit root.

In this section, we will replicate the major tables in Nelson and Plosser's study. First, we download the data.

```
. use NelsonPlosserData.dta, replace
```

The variables are presented in their raw form and then once again in their logarithms. We will only use the logged versions, except for bond prices which are not logged. The logged variables are denoted with an "l" prefix.

```
. keep l* year bnd
```

To get the exact same numbers as Nelson and Plosser, we will need to define a new time variable for each variable. Each variable will begin at period 0, regardless of which year was the earliest date in the time series. It is easy to do so using a loop:

```
foreach v of var bnd-lsp500{
    gen time_`v' = .
    replace time_`v' = year if `v'~=.
    quietly summarize time_`v'
    replace  time_`v' = time_`v' - r(min)
    }
```

If we had not created new time variables and had simply used the calendar year, the substantive results would have not changed. However, we are aiming to replicate their study, so we follow their preference.

7.6 Replicating Nelson and Plosser

Table 7.2 Sample autocorrelations of the natural logs of annual data

Variable	r1	r2	r3	r4	r5	r6
bnd	0.84	0.72	0.60	0.52	0.46	0.40
lrgnp	0.95	0.90	0.84	0.79	0.74	0.69
lgnp	0.95	0.89	0.83	0.77	0.72	0.67
lpcrgnp	0.95	0.88	0.81	0.75	0.70	0.65
lip	0.97	0.94	0.90	0.87	0.84	0.81
lemp	0.96	0.91	0.86	0.81	0.76	0.71
lun	0.75	0.47	0.32	0.17	0.04	−0.01
lprgnp	0.96	0.93	0.89	0.84	0.80	0.76
lcpi	0.96	0.92	0.87	0.84	0.80	0.77
lwg	0.96	0.91	0.86	0.82	0.77	0.73
lrwg	0.96	0.92	0.88	0.84	0.80	0.75
lm	0.96	0.92	0.89	0.85	0.81	0.77
lvel	0.96	0.92	0.88	0.85	0.81	0.79
lsp500	0.96	0.90	0.85	0.79	0.75	0.71

Note: Reprinted from Nelson, Charles R. and Charles R. Plosser (1982), Trends and random walks in macroeconomic time series: Some evidence and implications, *Journal of Monetary Economics*, 10(2): 139–162, with permission from Elsevier

Nelson and Plosser then attempt to look at the autocorrelation structure of their data (in levels, differences, and from trend) in order to compare with what they would expect if the data had come from unit root processes. Such tests are not quite formal and have low power.

They first examine their data in levels (Table 7.2) and find they are highly autocorrelated, with the autocorrelation weakening slowly as the lag increases. This is indicative of a random walk.

In their Table 7.3, they then take the first differences of their data. About half of the variables in Table 7.3 (the differences) have large first-order AC components only. This is indicative of an MA process. Only the most contrived trend stationary process (one with serially uncorrelated errors) would give rise to an AC structure with large coefficients on the first-order terms only, and these terms would be negative. (We showed this in an earlier section.) This argues against trend stationarity.

The other half of the variables in Table 7.3 have more persistent autocorrelation. "The conclusion we are pointed toward is that if these series do belong to the TS class, then the deviations from trend must be sufficiently autocorrelated to make it difficult to distinguish them from the DS class on the basis of sample autocorrelations" (Nelson and Plosser 1982, p. 149).

In their Table 7.4, they show the autocorrelations of the deviations from a fitted trend. There, the autocorrelations for all but the unemployment series start high and decrease exponentially. NP refer to Nelson and Kang (1981) who showed that this

Table 7.3 Sample autocorrelations of the first difference of the natural log of annual data

Variable	r1	r2	r3	r4	r5	r6
bnd	0.18	0.31	0.15	0.04	0.06	0.05
lrgnp	0.34	0.04	−0.18	−0.23	−0.19	0.01
lgnp	0.44	0.08	−0.12	−0.24	−0.07	0.15
lpcrgnp	0.33	0.04	−0.17	−0.21	−0.18	0.02
lip	0.03	−0.11	−0.00	−0.11	−0.28	0.05
lemp	0.32	−0.05	−0.08	−0.17	−0.20	0.01
lun	0.09	−0.29	0.03	−0.03	−0.19	0.01
lprgnp	0.43	0.20	0.07	−0.06	0.03	0.02
lcpi	0.58	0.16	0.02	−0.00	0.05	0.03
lwg	0.46	0.10	−0.03	−0.09	−0.09	0.08
lrwg	0.19	−0.03	−0.07	−0.11	−0.18	−0.15
lm	0.62	0.30	0.13	−0.01	−0.07	−0.04
lvel	0.11	−0.04	−0.16	−0.15	−0.11	0.11
lsp500	0.22	−0.13	−0.08	−0.18	−0.23	0.02

Note: Reprinted from Nelson, Charles R. and Charles R. Plosser (1982), Trends and random walks in macroeconomic time series: Some evidence and implications, *Journal of Monetary Economics*, 10(2): 139–162, with permission from Elsevier

Table 7.4 Sample autocorrelations of the deviations from the time trend

Variable	r1	r2	r3	r4	r5	r6
bnd	0.85	0.73	0.62	0.55	0.49	0.43
lrgnp	0.87	0.66	0.44	0.26	0.13	0.07
lgnp	0.93	0.79	0.65	0.52	0.43	0.35
lpcrgnp	0.87	0.65	0.43	0.24	0.11	0.04
lip	0.84	0.67	0.53	0.40	0.29	0.28
lemp	0.89	0.71	0.55	0.39	0.25	0.17
lun	0.75	0.46	0.30	0.15	0.03	−0.01
lprgnp	0.92	0.81	0.67	0.54	0.42	0.30
lcpi	0.97	0.91	0.84	0.78	0.71	0.63
lwg	0.93	0.81	0.67	0.54	0.42	0.31
lrwg	0.87	0.69	0.52	0.38	0.26	0.19
lm	0.95	0.83	0.69	0.53	0.37	0.21
lvel	0.91	0.81	0.72	0.65	0.59	0.56
lsp500	0.90	0.76	0.64	0.53	0.46	0.43

Note: Reprinted from Nelson, Charles R. and Charles R. Plosser (1982), Trends and random walks in macroeconomic time series: Some evidence and implications, *Journal of Monetary Economics*, 10(2): 139–162, with permission from Elsevier

7.6 Replicating Nelson and Plosser

is the autocorrelation structure of the residuals that would be generated when fitting a random walk process to a trend.

Again, these comparative procedures provide a convenient starting point, but they lack the formality of a statistical test. To this end, Nelson and Plosser employ the unit root tests of Dickey and Fuller.

```
* NP's Table 2: Sample ACs of the natural logs of
    annual data foreach v of var bnd-lsp500 {
    display "The correlogram for variable `v' is: "
    corrgram `v', noplot lags(6)
    }

* NP's Table 3: Sample ACs of the first diff. of the
    annual data foreach v of var bnd-lsp500 {
    display "The correlogram of D.`v' is: "
    corrgram D.`v', noplot lags(6)
    }

* NP's Table 4: Sample ACs of the deviations from
    trend foreach v of var bnd-lsp500 {
    display "Correlogram of the deviations from trend
    of `v': "
    quietly reg `v' year
    quietly predict `v'devs, resid
    corrgram `v'devs, noplot lags(6)
    drop `v'devs
    }
```

Upon entering the above commands, you should get the following output:

. * NP's Table 2: Sample ACs of the natural logs of annual data

The correlogram for variable bnd is:

LAG	AC	PAC	Q	Prob>Q
1	0.8389	1.0759	52.108	0.0000
2	0.7178	-0.1514	90.815	0.0000
3	0.6003	-0.3514	118.29	0.0000
4	0.5244	-0.1986	139.56	0.0000
5	0.4561	0.0497	155.89	0.0000
6	0.4031	-0.0157	168.84	0.0000

The correlogram for variable lrgnp is:

```
LAG         AC         PAC          Q       Prob>Q
-----------------------------------------------------
 1        0.9508      1.0041      58.802    0.0000
 2        0.8954     -0.3451     111.82     0.0000
 3        0.8391      0.0805     159.18     0.0000
 4        0.7869      0.1931     201.54     0.0000
 5        0.7367      0.1297     239.32     0.0000
 6        0.6877      0.0946     272.83     0.0000
```

(some output omitted)

. * NP's Table 3: Sample ACs of the first diff. of the annual data

The correlogram of D.bnd is:

```
LAG         AC         PAC          Q       Prob>Q
-----------------------------------------------------
 1        0.1832      0.2189      2.4523    0.1174
 2        0.3061      0.3688      9.3982    0.0091
 3        0.1542      0.2028     11.187     0.0108
 4        0.0399     -0.0426     11.308     0.0233
 5        0.0608      0.0200     11.595     0.0408
 6        0.0459      0.0552     11.761     0.0675
```

The correlogram of D.lrgnp is:

```
LAG         AC         PAC          Q       Prob>Q
-----------------------------------------------------
 1        0.3394      0.3412      7.3761    0.0066
 2        0.0429     -0.0826      7.4961    0.0236
 3       -0.1753     -0.1880      9.5326    0.0230
 4       -0.2298     -0.1218     13.094     0.0108
 5       -0.1941     -0.0890     15.68      0.0078
 6        0.0142      0.0946     15.694     0.0155
```

(some output omitted)

. * NP's Table 4: Sample ACs of the deviations from trend

Correlogram of the deviations from trend of bnd:

```
LAG         AC         PAC          Q       Prob>Q
-----------------------------------------------------
 1        0.8484      1.0643     53.297     0.0000
```

7.6 Replicating Nelson and Plosser

```
2          0.7349   -0.1692    93.863   0.0000
3          0.6234   -0.3612   123.48    0.0000
4          0.5510   -0.2052   146.97    0.0000
5          0.4855    0.0424   165.48    0.0000
6          0.4348   -0.0218   180.55    0.0000

Correlogram of the deviations from trend of lrgnp:

LAG         AC        PAC        Q       Prob>Q
-------------------------------------------------
1          0.8710    0.8754    49.35    0.0000
2          0.6608   -0.4259    78.225   0.0000
3          0.4409   -0.0587    91.297   0.0000
4          0.2594    0.0597    95.901   0.0000
5          0.1341    0.0161    97.152   0.0000
6          0.0665    0.0036    97.466   0.0000

(some output omitted)
```

Nelson and Plosser's main results table (their Table 5) requires a different lag length for each variable. Below, you can see the commands for replicating the first variable from the table. The rest are left as an exercise; simply replace the variable name and lag length in the provided code. Table 7.5 shows the results from Stata's replication of Nelson and Plosser's final results table.

Table 7.5 Tests for autoregressive unit roots: $X_t = \mu + \rho X_{t-1} + \gamma t + u_t$

Variable	k	μ	t(μ)	γ	t(γ)	ρ_1	$\tau(\rho_1)$	s(u)	r1
lrgnp	2	0.813	3.04	0.006	3.03	0.825	−2.99	0.058	−0.03
lgnp	2	1.056	2.37	0.006	2.34	0.899	−2.32	0.087	0.03
lpcrgnp	2	1.274	3.05	0.004	3.01	0.818	−3.05	0.059	−0.03
lip	6	0.070	2.95	0.007	2.44	0.835	−2.53	0.097	0.03
lemp	3	1.414	2.68	0.002	2.54	0.861	−2.66	0.035	0.03
lun	4	0.515	2.76	−0.000	−0.23	0.706	−3.55	0.407	0.02
lprgnp	2	0.258	2.55	0.002	2.65	0.915	−2.52	0.046	−0.04
lcpi	4	0.088	1.74	0.001	2.84	0.968	−1.97	0.042	−0.14
lwg	3	0.558	2.30	0.004	2.30	0.910	−2.24	0.060	0.00
lrwg	2	0.484	3.10	0.004	3.14	0.831	−3.05	0.035	−0.02
lm	2	0.128	3.53	0.005	3.03	0.916	−3.08	0.047	0.03
lvel	4	0.042	0.72	−0.000	−0.40	0.946	−1.40	0.066	−0.02
bnd	3	−0.193	−0.97	0.003	1.75	1.032	0.69	0.284	−0.05
lsp500	3	0.089	1.63	0.003	2.39	0.908	−2.12	0.154	0.01

Note: Reprinted from Nelson, Charles R. and Charles R. Plosser (1982), Trends and random walks in macroeconomic time series: Some evidence and implications, *Journal of Monetary Economics*, 10(2): 139–162, with permission from Elsevier

```
. dfuller lrgnp, trend reg lags(1)
. local lags = r(lags)
. reg D.lrgnp L1.lrgnp L(1/'lags')D.lrgnp time_lrgnp
. local k = 'lags'+1
. display "K = 'k'"
. display "mu (the constant) = " _b[_cons]
. display "t(mu) = " _b[_cons]/_se[_cons]
. display "gamma (the coeff on time) = " _b[time]
. display "t(gamma) = " _b[time]/_se[time]
. display "rho_1 (coeff on lagged term) = " 1 + _b[L.1]
. display "tau(rho_1) = " _b[L.1]/_se[L.1]
. display "s(u) the std err of the regression = " e(rmse)
. predict errors, resid
. quietly corrgram errors, lags(1)
. drop errors
. local r1 = r(ac1)
. display "r1 is " 'r1'
```

We are a bit redundant in using both the `dfuller` and `reg` commands. Still, it is instructive to see how `dfuller` is really just a special type of regression. For example, the output from `dfuller` is

```
. dfuller lrgnp, trend reg lags(1)

Augmented Dickey-Fuller test for unit root        Number of obs   =      60

               ---------- Interpolated Dickey-Fuller ---------
                  Test       1% Critical      5% Critical     10% Critical
               Statistic        Value            Value            Value
------------------------------------------------------------------------------
 Z(t)           -2.994          -4.128           -3.490           -3.174
------------------------------------------------------------------------------
MacKinnon approximate p-value for Z(t) = 0.1338

------------------------------------------------------------------------------
  D.lrgnp  |      Coef.   Std. Err.      t    P>|t|     [95% Conf. Interval]
-----------+------------------------------------------------------------------
    lrgnp  |
      L1.  |  -.1753423   .0585665    -2.99   0.004    -.292665    -.0580196
      LD.  |   .4188873   .1209448     3.46   0.001    .1766058     .6611688
   _trend  |   .0056465   .0018615     3.03   0.004    .0019174     .0093757
    _cons  |   .8134145   .2679886     3.04   0.004    .2765688     1.35026
------------------------------------------------------------------------------
```

The output from the `reg` version of `dfuller` is

7.6 Replicating Nelson and Plosser

```
. reg D.lrgnp L1.lrgnp L(1/'lags')D.lrgnp time_lrgnp

      Source |       SS       df       MS              Number of obs =      60
-------------+------------------------------           F(  3,    56) =    5.93
       Model |  .060391061     3  .020130354           Prob > F      =  0.0014
    Residual |  .190201964    56  .003396464           R-squared     =  0.2410
-------------+------------------------------           Adj R-squared =  0.2003
       Total |  .250593025    59  .004247339           Root MSE      =  .05828

------------------------------------------------------------------------------
     D.lrgnp |      Coef.   Std. Err.      t    P>|t|     [95% Conf. Interval]
-------------+----------------------------------------------------------------
       lrgnp |
         L1. |  -.1753423   .0585665    -2.99   0.004    -.292665    -.0580196
         LD. |   .4188873   .1209448     3.46   0.001     .1766058    .6611688
             |
  time_lrgnp |   .0056465   .0018615     3.03   0.004     .0019174    .0093757
       _cons |   .8134145   .2679886     3.04   0.004     .2765688    1.35026
------------------------------------------------------------------------------
```

Recall from Eqs. (7.5) and (7.6) that we are estimated equations similar to

$$X_t - X_{t-1} = \beta_0 + (\rho - 1) X_{t-1} + e_t \tag{7.13}$$

$$= \beta_0 + \beta X_{t-1} + e_t. \tag{7.14}$$

Stata's `dfuller` or `reg` commands estimate $\beta = -0.175$. Table 7.5 reports $\rho = 1 + \beta = 1 - 0.175 = 0.825$. The estimates of the standard error $s(u)$ and the test statistic $\tau(\rho_1)$ are the same between `dfuller` and Table 7.5 as would be expected since one merely subtracts a constant from the other.

Nelson and Plosser may have discovered something quite meaningful. Looking at Table 7.5 we see that most of the variables seem to show evidence of a unit root. This is not readily apparent when looking at the table. We need to keep in mind that the relevant critical values are not 1.96. We need to use Dickey and Fuller's critical values which are approximately equal to -3.45. Almost all of the variables have a test statistic that is less than -3.45. Therefore, we should not reject the null hypothesis of $\rho = 1$ so we cannot reject the null hypothesis of a unit root. More plainly, we accept that these variables have a unit root.[2] This, in turn, means that the economy might carry the effects of negative (and positive) shocks with it forever. The economy might not be self-healing and might not always result its earlier growth path.

Exercises

1. Using the code provided in the text, replicate Table 7.5 containing Nelson and Plosser's main results.

---

[2] Please keep in mind that failure to reject does not mean that we "accept." Still, sometimes it is useful to think in these simpler terms.

2. Are the major stock market indexes unit root processes? Redo the Nelson and Plosser exercise, but with daily data on the NASDAQ index, the CAC-40 index, and the DAX for the period starting in 2013 and ending in 2017. (Use the Index.dta dataset or download the data using fetchyahooquotes ^IXIC ^FCHI ^GDAXI, freq(d) start(01012013) end(01012018).) What do you find?

7.7 Testing for Seasonal Unit Roots

Testing for seasonal unit roots follows the same lines as nonseasonal unit roots. If the roots of the characteristic polynomial are on the unit circle, then we have seasonal unit roots. But what if they are quite close to the unit circle? We need to perform a hypothesis test and verify whether we are statistically close or far away from the circle. That is, we need to employ a seasonal unit root test.

The most popular test for seasonal unit roots is the so-called HEGY test, named after the authors of the paper: Hylleberg et al. (1990). The HEGY test is a modification of a Dickey-Fuller test. It is implemented in Stata using the hegy4 command; however, the command is limited to quarterly data. Beaulieu and Miron (1993) developed the theory extending the HEGY procedure to monthly data, but there does not yet seem to be a Stata implementation of this.

Ghysels and Perron (1993) suggest carefully examining the data for the existence of different types of seasonality. And they suggest including at least as many lagged differences in the Dickey-Fuller and Phillips-Perron test as the length of seasonality. If there seems to be quarterly seasonality, use at least four lagged differences in the unit root test. Doing so decreases the size of the bias and increases the power of the unit root tests.

Ultimately, Ghysels et al. (1994) stress the difficulties in testing for stochastic seasonality. The AR unit roots and the MA terms often interfere with each other, resulting in low power and low size for the HEGY-type tests. Including deterministic seasonal terms in the regression models improves the power of the HEGY tests; however, "the picture drawn from our investigation is not very encouraging" (p. 436); there are too many problems with the size and power of the HEGY test.

7.8 Conclusion and Further Readings

In this chapter we have explored some of the more popular unit root tests.

There are two reasons why it is important to know whether your data have unit roots. First, from an econometric point of view, it is important to know the source of nonstationarity because we need to know how to correct for it. If the DGP is trend stationary (a deterministic trend), then we can detrend the model to render it stationary (and extract the business cycle components). If it is a stochastic trend (a RWWD), then the model is difference stationary. That is, we can take first (or second) differences and then proceed with our familiar ARMA(p,q) modeling.

7.8 Conclusion and Further Readings

Applying the wrong procedures and differencing a trend stationary process, i.e., over-differencing, introduces an MA unit root. That is, if you wrongly believe there is a unit root and take first differences to remove it, then you will inadvertently be *introducing* a unit root.

Second, from an economic point of view, it affects how we view the economy. A deterministic trend model shows the economy as self-healing and reverting back to its trend line. A stochastic trend shows the economy as nonhealing. It never recovers from a shock. It reverts back to its usual rate of growth, but from a lower level.

Despite its ubiquity, not everyone is convinced of the importance of unit root testing. Cochrane (1991) argues that the low power of unit root tests is inescapable. Christiano and Eichenbaum (1990) ponder unit roots in GNP and ask, "Do we know, and do we care?" They answer, "No, and maybe not." The evidence is too sensitive to various assumptions to draw any definitive conclusions. Further, they argue that evidence of a unit root does not answer more important questions like the prevalence of permanent technological versus temporary demand shocks.

The literature on unit root testing is vast and constantly increasing. Campbell and Perron (1991) provide a lengthy, if somewhat dated, review of the major issues involved in unit root testing and offer some very useful rules of thumb. The book by Maddala and Kim (1998) provides a more thorough yet readable discussion of univariate unit root testing and cointegration (which extends the unit root concept to the multivariate setting).

Unit root testing has been extended to panel datasets. This has proven quite useful as most macroeconomic data is available for multiple countries. Previously, researchers calculated a sequence of unit root tests, one for each country's GDP, for example. But this presumes the cross sections are independent. The profession demanded to be able to combine these into one panel model and test all countries simultaneously. Naturally, the quantity supplied of panel unit root tests has responded to the increased demand. Scores of papers have been written on this. Im et al. (2003) is an early and influential paper that developed a panel test where the cross sections are independent. Pesaran (2007) developed an extension, a modification of the standard ADF tests, to account for cross-sectional dependence. Stata implements some of the more popular panel unit root tests. These include the tests by Levin et al. (2002) and Im et al. (2003), which have unit roots as their null hypotheses (like DF-type tests), and Hadri (2000), which has stationarity as its null hypothesis (like KPSS). Panel unit root tests will occupy a lot of our attention in Chap. 14.

The concept of unit roots has been challenged by the concept of "structural breaks," a concept which we will explore next in Chap. 8.

Structural Breaks

8

In 1976, Robert Lucas offered one of the strongest criticisms of the Cowles Commission large-scale econometric modeling approach. Lucas critiqued Cowles' presumption that many economic phenomena are structural. They are not. They depend on the institutional and regulatory framework. For example, economists vigorously debated what was the "true" value of the marginal propensity to consume (MPC). A large MPC implies a large fiscal policy multiplier. A small MPC implies that fiscal policy will be ineffective. Lucas argued that the observed MPC is contingent on the economic and regulatory environment at the time. People consume more or less in response to the economic situation. They'll consume more if times are good, or if tax laws are favorable to consumption. The MPC is not a structural parameter. It is not a universal constant on par with Planck's constant or the gravitational constant. Essentially, Lucas argued that changes in the laws and regulations affect human behavior, and this will be revealed through the data. Change the rules of the game and you change the outcome. Change the economic landscape, and you change the ups and downs of the time series. Change the regulatory structure, and your econometric regressions should exhibit differences before and after the change. Lucas, in effect, argued that econometrics should be concerned with "structural breaks," the topic of this chapter.

"Structural breaks" is econometric jargon for "the world changed." At some point in the real world, there was a change in either the legal, institutional, or geopolitical rules of the game that resulted in a different process generating the data. If the practicing econometrician attempted to fit the whole dataset to one model, rather than two, he would be committing a serious misspecification error.

8.1 Structural Breaks and Unit Roots

Structural breaks complicate tests of unit roots.

Perron (1989) provides an interesting example of how small changes in modeling strategy can dramatically alter the econometric results. Perron reexamined Nelson and Plosser's dataset in light of a possible structural break in the data generating process. That is, Perron (1989) tested several periods separately. What he found cast some doubt on Nelson and Plosser's seemingly strong results.

An entire cottage industry testing for structural break has been developed, most of which are outside the scope of this text. However, it would be instructive to work through Perron's example of unit root testing in the face of structural breaks in his 1989 paper, as that paper has become canonical. That paper, along with his joint work with Phillips, are two of the most cited papers in econometrics.

A time series might be nonstationary, but its parts might be stationary. The term "structural breaks" refers to the possibility that the data were generated from two different processes, an old one and a new one. The world may have changed at some point.

What if we had spliced together two stationary series, with one large gap between them? It would look like the effect of the big one-time shock had not gone away. That is, it would look like a unit root process, even though it wasn't. Rather, it would have been two stationary processes, which, together, amount to a nonstationary process (the means and standard deviations would be different, etc.).

Consider Fig. 8.1. The final panel in the graph was generated from the following Stata code, where we just split the time series in half and shifted the latter half up by 20 units. Standard unit root tests do not take this exogenous shift into account and therefore misrepresent the data generating process.

```
. drop _all
. set obs 200
. set seed 1234
. gen time = _n
. tsset time
. gen error = rnormal()
. gen X = error in 1
. replace X = 0.50 * L.X + error in 2/L
. replace X = 20+X in 101/200
```

The other three panels in Fig. 8.1 also show some structural breaks. Panel (A) shows spliced data with the same trend, but with different intercepts, (B) shows two trend stationary processes with different trends spliced together, and (C) shows two trend stationary processes with different intercepts and trends spliced together.

The practicing econometrician needs to be aware that these are possibilities. In fact, they are very likely. A dutiful researcher must know the subject matter well enough to anticipate whether regulatory, legal, political, or other changes might have fundamentally altered the data generating process and resulted in a structural break.

8.2 Perron (1989): Tests for a Unit Root with a Known Structural Break

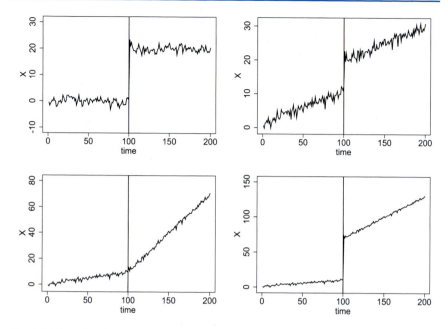

Fig. 8.1 Examples of structural breaks

How was Perron able to completely reverse Nelson and Plosser's conclusions? For the remainder of this section, we will work through a well-known paper by Perron which showed the importance of testing for structural breaks when testing for unit roots. It is important, not just because it pointed out the fragility of standard unit root tests, but also because it provided a method for dealing with structural breaks econometrically. (Perron's method is appropriate when the break happened only once, and the date of the single break is known. More recent research has relaxed these two assumptions.)

8.2 Perron (1989): Tests for a Unit Root with a Known Structural Break

In his 1989 paper, Perron postulated that there was a structural break in the economy in 1929, at least for the more common macroeconomic data. In other words, the world was different before and after 1929. Nelson and Plosser (1982), however, lumped all the data, pre- and post-1929, into the same group when performing their Dickey-Fuller tests. Perron investigates whether a structural break at 1929 could account for the time series properties of the data. He concluded that, in contrast to Nelson and Plosser, the data did not have a unit root. Rather a structural change in 1929 was confused with a unit root. That is, the effects of the 1929 shock had not dissipated, and so it looked like a unit root.

Perron begins with a casual analysis of the most major economic event of the twentieth century: the Great Depression. Perron notices that the Great Depression resulted in a drop in the values of most macroaggregates (a change in mean value). This observation will guide his choice of estimated unit root models.

Perron points out that, if it is known that only a subset of the parameters have changed after the structural break, then it does not make sense to estimate two separate regressions; doing so would require estimating the unchanged parameters twice, each time on smaller subsamples. Rather, Perron suggests estimating all of the parameters via one larger nested regression, where properly generated dummy or time variables allow for changes in the parameters, but only those parameters that are known to change. For example, why estimate the constant twice, each time with half the observations, when you could estimate it once with double the observations?

Let's suppose that we are looking at some data similar to the top right panel in Fig. 8.1 where there is a shift in the level of the series, whereas the slope has not changed. The mean changes so it seems nonstationary, but are its components stationary? The data could have come from one of two hypothesized models, a null and an alternative:

$$H_0 : y_t = \beta_0 + y_{t-1} + \mu D_P + e_t$$
$$H_A : y_t = \beta_0 + \beta_1 t + \mu D_L + e_t.$$

The null hypothesis is a unit root process. The alternative is a trend stationary process. Both models allow for some kind of parameter change (i.e., a structural change). Borrowing the terminology from Enders' (2014) textbook, we call "D_P" a pulse dummy variable; we construct it so that it has a value of zero, except in the one period directly following a shock. We call "D_L" a level dummy variable; it has a value equal to zero up to and including the shock and a value of one thereafter.

Let's see how these two equations act, step by step, "by hand," as it were. We'll do so in two stages: first, without random errors and then again with the errors. Since we're doing this by hand, let's choose some nice easy number $-\beta_0 = 1$, $\beta_1 = 1$, $\mu = 10$– and let the initial value of $y_0 = 1$.

At first, rather than generating error terms, let's treat these series as though they were deterministic. (In other words, ignore the error term for now by setting it equal to zero.) Suppose the structural break occurs in period 50, and the series runs for 100 periods.

If the null equation were true, then the equation reduces to

$$H_0 : y_t = 1 + y_{t-1} + 10 D_P$$

and the series would look like

$$y_0 \equiv 1$$
$$y_1 = 1 + y_0 + 10 D_P = 1 + 1 + 0 = 2$$

8.2 Perron (1989): Tests for a Unit Root with a Known Structural Break

$$y_2 = 1 + y_1 + 10D_P = 1 + 2 + 0 = 3$$
$$y_3 = 1 + y_2 + 10D_P = 1 + 3 + 0 = 4$$
$$y_{49} = 1 + y_{48} + 10D_P = 1 + 49 + 0 = 50$$
$$y_{50} = 1 + y_{49} + 10D_P = 1 + 50 + 0 = 51$$
$$y_{51} = 1 + y_{50} + 10D_P = 1 + 51 + 10 = 62$$
$$y_{52} = 1 + y_{51} + 10D_P = 1 + 62 + 0 = 63$$

If the alternative were true, then

$$H_A : y_t = 1 + t + 10D_L$$

and the series would look like

$$y_0 \equiv 1$$
$$y_1 = 1 + t + 10D_L = 1 + 1 + 0 = 2$$
$$y_2 = 1 + 2 + 0 = 3$$
$$y_3 = 1 + 3 + 0 = 4$$
$$y_{49} = 1 + 49 + 0 = 50$$
$$y_{50} = 1 + 50 + 0 = 51$$
$$y_{51} = 1 + 51 + 10 = 62$$
$$y_{52} = 1 + 52 + 10 = 63$$

A graph of the series under the null and alternative is given in Fig. 8.2.

Notice that when these are deterministic functions, the null and the alternative are equivalent. The processes differ by how they deal with shocks, those error terms which we had set equal to zero. In unit root processes (such as in the null), the effects of even small errors linger long into the future.

Let us now add some random errors and see how this changes things. We will simulate one column (variable) or random errors and use these same errors to simulate the two models, the null and the alternative.

```
. drop _all
. set obs 100
. set seed 3456
. gen t = _n-1
. tsset t
. gen DP = 0
. replace DP = 1 if t == 51
. gen DL = 0
```

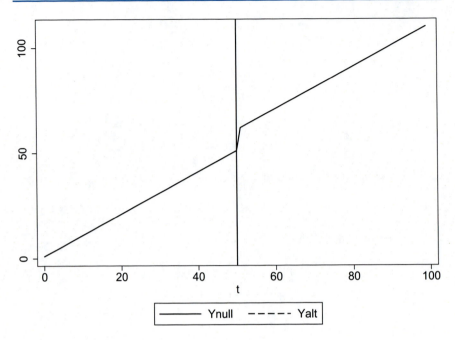

Fig. 8.2 The deterministic process

```
. replace DL = 1 if t > 50
. gen error = rnormal()
. gen Ynull = 1 in 1
. gen Yalt  = 1 in 1
. replace Ynull = 1 + L.Ynull + 10*DP + error in 2/L
. replace Yalt  = 1 + t + 10*DL + error in 2/L
```

Graphs of the processes under the null and alternative are given in Figs. 8.3 and 8.4.

Enders (2014) distills Perron's method into a few easy steps. Supposing that there seems to be a shift, but no change in the slope, then the null and alternative hypotheses that we are testing are

$$H_0 : y_t = \beta_0 + y_{t-1} + \beta_{DP} D_P + \epsilon_t$$

$$H_A : y_t = \beta_0 + \beta_1 t + \beta_{DL} D_L + \epsilon_t.$$

The estimation procedure is as follows:

1. Detrend the data. You can do this by estimating the model under the appropriate alternative hypothesis and then generating the residuals. Let's denote these detrended data $\bar{y}$.

8.2 Perron (1989): Tests for a Unit Root with a Known Structural Break

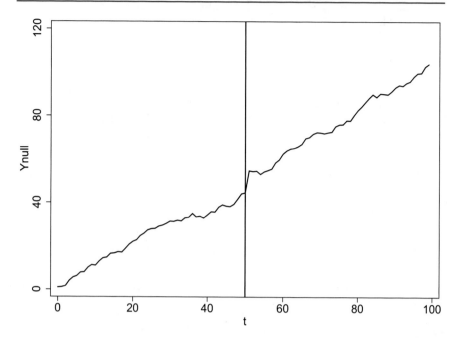

Fig. 8.3 The series under the null hypothesis

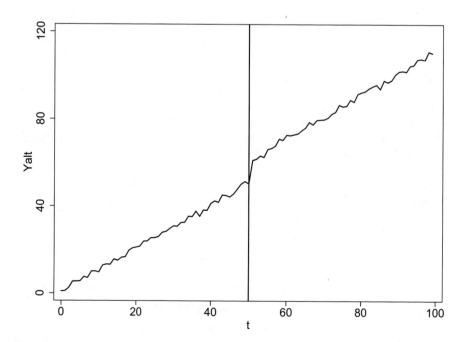

Fig. 8.4 The series under the alternative hypothesis

2. Does $\bar{y}$ (the detrended data) follow a unit root process? Estimate

$$\bar{y}_t = \alpha \bar{y}_{t-1} + \epsilon_t. \tag{8.1}$$

If $\bar{y}$ is a unit root, then α will be statistically indistinguishable from one. Perron derived the appropriate critical values for this test if the ϵs are IID.

3. What if the ϵs are not IID, but rather have some autocorrelation? If so, then reestimate the above model a la Dickey-Fuller, adding enough lagged differences to ensure non-autocorrelated residuals:

$$\bar{y}_t = \alpha \bar{y}_{t-1} + \sum_{i=1}^{k} \gamma_i \Delta \bar{y}_{t-i} + \epsilon_t. \tag{8.2}$$

Perron (1989) provides the appropriate critical values for testing $\alpha = 1$ here, too. If the test statistic is large enough, we can reject the null hypothesis of a unit root.

Finally, we should mention (following Enders 2014) that detrending does not have to occur as a separate step. In fact, all three steps can be collapsed into one big regression. For the more general case where we can have both a change of level and a change of slope, the model to be tested is

$$y_t = \beta_0 + \beta_{DP} D_P + \beta_{DL} D_L + \beta_3 t + \beta_4 NewSlope + \alpha y_{t-1} + \sum_{i=1}^{k} \gamma_i \Delta y_{t-i} + \epsilon_t \tag{8.3}$$

where

- $D_P = 1$ if $t =$ (BreakDate $+ 1$), and 0 otherwise. D_P models a one-time level shock after the break.
- $D_L = 1$ if $t >$ BreakDate, and 0 otherwise. D_L models a level shift.
- $NewSlope = t$ if $t >$ BreakDate, and 0 otherwise. $NewSlope$ models a change in the slope.

The unit root hypothesis ($\alpha = 1$) can be tested using Perron's critical values.

Perron uses Nelson and Plosser's own data to show that their results are suspect. So, let's reload their data, keeping only the variables we'll need.[1] With the exception of bond yields, we will look at the variables in their logarithms (hence the prefix "l").

```
. use NelsonPlosserData.dta, replace
. keep l* year bnd
```

Next, we need to create several special types of dummy and time variables.

---

[1] Perron also examines a real GNP variable from Campbell and Mankiw (1987b) and Campbell and Mankiw (1987a). We leave this variable out for the sake of brevity.

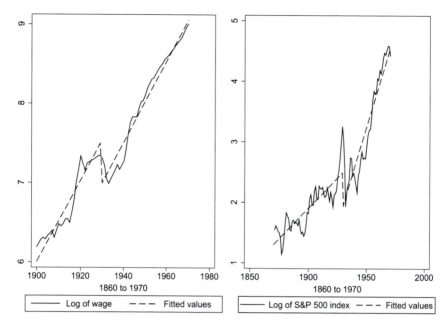

Fig. 8.5 Structural breaks in wages and stocks

```
. * Dummy variable indicating all periods after the
Great Depression
. gen DL = 0
. replace DL = 1 if year > 1929

. * Dummy variable indicating the one period after
the shock
. gen DP = 0
. replace DP = 1 if year == 1930

. gen NewSlope = year*DL
```

Perron points out that (almost) all of Nelson and Plosser's data could fit into one of several classes of stationary (but with structural break) models. There could be a change in intercept, a change in slope, or both. Perron fit wages and the S&P 500 into two such models, as can be seen in Fig. 8.5.

In replicating this study, be aware that Perron follows Stata's (and our) notation, where $k =$ lags; Nelson and Plosser have $k =$ lags $+ 1$.

The code below allows us to reconstruct Perron's Table 2, which shows the sample autocorrelations of the deterministically detrended data. Perron detrends most of the variables by fitting a regression with a constant, a trend, and an intercept and then extracting the residuals. The exceptions are the real wage and

S&P variables which he detrends by fitting a regression with a slope and intercept before extracting the residuals.

```
. foreach var of varlist lrgnp lgnp lpcrgnp lip lemp
lprgnp lcp lwg lm lvel bnd {
.       quietly reg 'var' year DL
.       quietly predict dt_'var', resid
.       label var dt_'var' "Detrended 'var'"
.       display "'var'"
.       corrgram dt_'var', lags(6) noplot
. }

. foreach var of varlist lrwg lsp500 {
.       quietly reg 'var' year DL NewSlope
.       quietly predict dt_'var', resid
.       label var dt_'var' "Detrended 'var'"
.       display "'var'"
.       corrgram dt_'var', lags(6) noplot
. }
```

Table 8.1 shows the autocorrelations of each variable after deterministic detrending. The autocorrelations decay fairly quickly, implying that the variables are trend stationary.

The heart of Perron's paper is his test for structural change. This is given in his Table 7, which we replicate with the code below for the real GNP variable.

Table 8.1 Sample autocorrelations of the detrended series

Series	Model	Period	T	Variance	r1	r2	r3	r4	r5	r6
Real GNP	A	1909–1970	62	0.010	0.77	0.45	0.23	0.11	0.05	0.04
Nominal GNP	A	1909–1970	62	0.023	0.68	0.31	0.12	0.08	0.11	0.12
Real per capita GNP	A	1909–1970	62	0.012	0.81	0.54	0.33	0.20	0.13	0.09
Industrial production	A	1860–1970	111	0.017	0.71	0.44	0.32	0.17	0.08	0.12
Employment	A	1890–1970	81	0.005	0.82	0.59	0.43	0.30	0.20	0.15
GNP deflator	A	1889–1970	82	0.015	0.82	0.63	0.45	0.31	0.17	0.06
Consumer prices	A	1860–1970	111	0.066	0.96	0.89	0.80	0.71	0.63	0.54
Wages	A	1900–1970	71	0.016	0.76	0.47	0.26	0.12	0.03	−0.03
Real wages	C	1900–1970	71	0.003	0.74	0.40	0.12	−0.12	−0.27	−0.33
Money stock	A	1889–1970	82	0.023	0.87	0.69	0.52	0.38	0.25	0.11
Velocity	A	1860–1970	102	0.036	0.90	0.79	0.70	0.62	0.57	0.52
Interest rate	A	1900–1970	71	0.587	0.77	0.58	0.38	0.25	0.15	0.11
Common stock prices	C	1871–1970	100	0.066	0.80	0.53	0.36	0.20	0.10	0.08

8.2 Perron (1989): Tests for a Unit Root with a Known Structural Break

```
. local var = "lrgnp"
. local lags = "8"

. reg `var' DL year DP L.`var' L(1/`lags')D.`var'

. display "Variable = `var'"
. display "          beta(DL)  = " %4.3f _b[DL]
. display "             t(DL)  = " %4.2f _b[DL]/_se[DL]
. display "        beta(time)  = " %4.3f _b[year]
. display "           t(time)  = " %4.2f _b[year]/_se[year]
. display "          beta(DP)  = " %4.3f _b[DP]
. display "             t(DP)  = " %4.2f _b[DP]/_se[DP]
. display "             alpha  = " %4.3f _b[L.`var']
. display "          t(alpha)  = " %4.2f (_b[L.`var']-1) ///
                                          /_se[L.`var']
. display "            S(e hat) = " %4.3f e(rmse)
```

The third line drives all of the results. The lines following simply pull out the appropriate statistics so they are not lost in a large regression table. To estimate the other variables, simply replace lnrgnp and lags in the first two lines and rerun.

The regression output from the code above is

```
. reg lrgnp DL year DP L.lrgnp   L(1/8)D.lrgnp

      Source |       SS       df       MS              Number of obs =      53
-------------+------------------------------           F( 12,    40) =  469.97
       Model |  14.5914744     12  1.2159562           Prob > F      =  0.0000
    Residual |  .103492465     40  .002587312          R-squared     =  0.9930
-------------+------------------------------           Adj R-squared =  0.9908
       Total |  14.6949668     52  .282595516          Root MSE      =  .05087


       lrgnp |      Coef.   Std. Err.      t    P>|t|     [95% Conf. Interval]
-------------+----------------------------------------------------------------
          DL |  -.1893632   .0442148    -4.28   0.000    -.2787247   -.1000018
        year |   .0267176    .00529      5.05   0.000     .0160262    .037409
          DP |  -.0184203   .0623849    -0.30   0.769    -.1445049    .1076643
             |
       lrgnp |
         L1. |   .2823267   .1427877     1.98   0.055    -.006258     .5709113
         LD. |   .5788573   .1261679     4.59   0.000     .3238624    .8338522
        L2D. |   .4104822   .1466318     2.80   0.008     .1141284    .7068361
        L3D. |   .2394301   .1478983     1.62   0.113    -.0594836    .5383438
        L4D. |   .1984957   .1345279     1.48   0.148    -.0733953    .4703867
        L5D. |   .1716997   .132337      1.30   0.202    -.0957635    .4391628
        L6D. |   .2057396   .125523      1.64   0.109    -.0479519    .4594311
        L7D. |   .2565997   .1262268     2.03   0.049     .0014859    .5117135
        L8D. |   .2577881   .1397218     1.85   0.072    -.0246002    .5401764
             |
       _cons |  -47.77706   9.469941    -5.05   0.000    -66.91652   -28.63759
-------------+----------------------------------------------------------------
```

(some output omitted)

```
Variable = lrgnp
    beta(DL)  = -0.189
       t(DL)  = -4.28
  beta(time)  = 0.027
     t(time)  = 5.05
    beta(DP)  = -0.018
       t(DP)  = -0.30
       alpha  = 0.282
    t(alpha)  = -5.03
    S(e hat)  = 0.051
```

Real wages and the S&P 500 are believed to have come from a different type of break. For these two series, Perron hypothesizes that the slope and intercept have changed. Thus, he adds a different dummy variable into the mix.

```
. local var = "lsp500"
. local lags = "1"

. quietly reg `var' DL year DP L.`var'  NewSlope  L(1/`lags')D.`var'

. display "Variable = `var'"
. display "      beta(DL)  = " %4.3f _b[DL]
. display "         t(DL)  = " %4.2f _b[DL]/_se[DL]
. display "    beta(time)  = " %4.3f _b[year]
. display "       t(time)  = " %4.2f _b[year]/_se[year]
. display "      beta(DP)  = " %4.3f _b[DP]
. display "         t(DP)  = " %4.2f _b[DP]/_se[DP]
. display "beta(NewSlope)  = " %4.3f _b[NewSlope]
. display "   t(NewSlope)  = " %4.2f _b[NewSlope]/_se[NewSlope]
. display "         alpha  = " %4.3f _b[L.`var']
. display "      t(alpha)  = " %4.2f (_b[L.`var']-1)/_se[L.`var']
. display "      S(e hat)  = " %4.3f e(rmse)
```

To actually see whether $t(\alpha)$ is statistically significant from 1 (i.e., it has a unit root), we need special critical values. In fact, part of Perron's purpose, similar to Dickey and Fuller's, is to provide new critical values. Perron's critical values depend upon, among other things, the position of the break relative to the sample. When there is no break, the critical values mimic those of Dickey-Fuller; otherwise, they are a bit larger. They are largest when the break occurs in the middle of the series. When conducting such tests, it is strongly recommended that the researcher consults the tables of critical values in Perron (1989).

Let's examine the results in Table 8.2. Recall that we estimated a model which controls for possible level shifts in all of the variables and for changes in the slopes in the case of common stocks and real wages. All of these structural change parameters are significant. After filtering out these effects, we can test for a unit root by examining the estimated value of α, the coefficient on y_{t-1}. If $\alpha = 1$, then we

8.2 Perron (1989): Tests for a Unit Root with a Known Structural Break

Table 8.2 Perron's tests for a unit root

Equation	k	β_2	β_3	β_4	β_1	α	$S(e)$
Real GNP	8	−0.189	0.027		−0.018	0.282	0.051
		(−4.28)	(5.05)		(−0.30)	(−5.03)	
Nominal GNP	8	−0.360	0.036		0.100	0.471	0.069
		(−4.77)	(5.44)		(1.09)	(−5.42)	
Real per capita GNP	7	−0.102	0.011		−0.070	0.531	0.056
		(−2.76)	(4.00)		(−1.09)	(−4.09)	
Industrial production	8	−0.298	0.032		−0.095	0.322	0.088
		(−4.58)	(5.42)		(−0.99)	(−5.47)	
Employment	7	−0.046	0.006		−0.025	0.667	0.030
		(−2.65)	(4.26)		(−0.77)	(−4.51)	
GNP deflator	5	−0.098	0.007		0.026	0.776	0.044
		(−3.16)	(4.01)		(0.53)	(−4.04)	
Consumer prices	2	−0.004	0.000		−0.036	0.978	0.045
		(−0.21)	(1.75)		(−0.79)	(−1.28)	
Wages	7	−0.190	0.020		0.085	0.619	0.053
		(−4.32)	(5.37)		(1.36)	(−5.41)	
Money stock	6	−0.071	0.012		0.033	0.812	0.044
		(−2.59)	(4.18)		(0.68)	(−4.29)	
Velocity	0	−0.005	−0.000		−0.136	0.941	0.066
		(−0.20)	(−0.35)		(−2.01)	(−1.66)	
Interest rate	2	−0.343	0.011		0.197	0.976	0.279
		(−2.06)	(2.64)		(0.64)	(−0.45)	
Common stock prices	1	−26.985	0.007	0.014	0.128	0.718	0.140
		(−3.992)	(4.431)	(3.976)	(0.759)	(−4.867)	
Real wages	8	−12.809	0.011	0.007	0.031	0.298	0.033
		(−3.341)	(3.787)	(3.332)	(0.776)	(−4.276)	

Note: The estimated model is $y_t = \beta_0 + \beta_1 D_P + \beta_2 D_L + \beta_3 t + \beta_4 NewSlope + ay_{t-1} + \sum_{i=1}^{k} \gamma_i \Delta y_{t-i} + \epsilon_t$. t-Statistics are in parentheses below their coefficients

have a unit root. Looking at the t-statistics on α, we see that none of the variables have a unit root with the exception of consumer prices, velocity, and the interest rate. Perron concludes that macroeconomic variables are not generally characterized by unit root processes, but rather by structural breaks. This completely reverses Nelson & Plosser's (1982) conclusion that US macro variables are unit root processes.

Perron's paper is important beyond what it implied for the specific macroeconomic data he examined. He proved that when undertaking ADF tests, the failure to allow for a structural break introduces a bias; this bias reduces the ability to reject a false unit root. There were a lot of double-negatives in that sentence. Here is the intuition. Suppose there was a structural break and no unit root, but that you forgot to account for that possibility in your ADF test. Then the structural break (a shock whose effects linger indefinitely) will be confused with a unit root process (a process of shocks whose effects linger indefinitely). In other words, it is more likely to look as though there is a unit root when, in fact, there is none. To abuse the terminology, we would be falsely led to "accept" the hypothesis of a unit root.

Perron (1989) showed how failing to account for the possibility of a structural break biases the standard unit root tests. Throughout the entire exercise above, however, we presumed we knew the date of the possible break. We cannot always be so certain. We now turn to the question of finding the date of the break when it is not known.

Exercises
1. Modify the code above to replicate the rest of Table 8.2.
2. Load the DJIA.dta dataset. This dataset reports the Dow Jones Industrial Average from the beginning of 1995 to the end of 2015. (Alternatively, download the data using `fetchyahooquotes`.) Take the natural log of the DJIA. Conduct a Dickey-Fuller test on ln(DJIA). Does there seem to be a unit root in the (log of the) DJIA? Graph the data. Visually, does there seem to be a structural break? If so, of what type (slope change, intercept change, or both)? Estimate the appropriate model, and conduct a unit root test following Perron's (1989) procedure as laid out in this chapter. Does there seem to be a unit root in the DJIA once a structural break has been accounted for?

8.3   Zivot and Andrews' Test of a Break at an Unknown Date

Perron's paper showed what to do if we know the date of the (one) possible structural break. This is often not the case. Rather, we might want to know which, if any, legal or institutional changes changed the behavior of the economy. In this case, we can employ a technique developed by Zivot and Andrews (1992). Their technique, like Perron's, can only identify the existence of a single structural break; different techniques are required if there may be more than one break.

A brief history might be useful. Dickey and Fuller (1979) showed how to test for a unit root, in the presence of AR(1) errors. Said and Dickey (1979) generalized this to account for AR(p) errors in their augmented Dickey-Fuller procedure by including additional lagged (differenced) terms. Perron investigated how the ADF results might change if a break point occurred at a known point in time. He did this by adding a dummy variable in the ADF procedure. Finally, Zivot and Andrews asked how to test for a break point at an unknown time. Their approach was to estimate many Perron-style equations, one for each year. Each regression includes an optimal number of lags (chosen via Schwarz' (1978) Bayesian information criterion or a sequence of t-tests). Finally, pick the one year which gives the most weight to the alternative hypothesis.

Zivot and Andrews' null hypothesis is of a unit root process –possibly with drift– and no structural break. Their basic idea is to estimate a sequence of Perron's trend stationary models, each with different break point. Which break point should be selected? The one which gives "the most weight to the trend stationary alternative" (Zivot and Andrews 1992, p. 254).

8.3 Zivot and Andrews' Test of a Break at an Unknown Date

The equation to be estimated is

$$y_t = \beta_0 + \beta_{DP} D_P + \beta_{DL} D_L + \beta_3 t + \beta_4 New Slope + \alpha y_{t-1} + \sum_{i=1}^{k} \gamma_i \Delta y_{t-i} + \epsilon_t.$$

This is Perron's equation. Testing that $\alpha = 1$ tests the unit root hypothesis. Testing $\beta_{DL} = 0$ tests for a level-shift structural break at a given year. Testing $\beta_4 = 0$ tests for a change-of-slope structural break at a given year. Zivot and Andrews suggest we estimate a sequence of these equations, one for each possible break year, and pick the most likely year under the alternative.

8.3.1 Replicating Zivot & Andrews (1992) in Stata

In this subsection, we will walk through implementing Zivot and Andrews' (1992) procedure, replicating the results from their paper. Again, recall that this is simply a Perron (1989) exercise, but with an extra step to choose the appropriate break date.

First, we download the familiar Nelson and Plosser data.

```
. use NelsonPlosserData.dta, replace
. keep l* year bnd
. order year lrgnp lgnp lpcrgnp lip lemp lprgnp ///
        lcpi lwg lm lvel bnd lrwg lsp500
. drop lun
```

Let's suppose, for just a second, that we knew the date of the break year and the number of lags. For RGDP we presume this break date is 1929 and the number of lags is 8.

```
. gen DL = 0
. replace DL = 1 if year > 1929
```

Given this, we can estimate the equation as:

```
. reg lrgnp DL year L.lrgnp LD(1/8).lrgnp
```

If we didn't have to worry about using the proper critical values, we could simply test for a level break by typing test DL. We can isolate particular estimates, their test statistics, and the equation's root mean squared error (RMSE) by

```
. display "Beta(DL): "  "%4.3f  _b[DL]        "   t(DL): "  "%4.2f _b[DL]/_se[DL]
. display "Beta(t): "   "%4.3f _b[year]       "   t(t): "   "%4.2f _b[year]/_se[year]
. display "Alpha:    "  "%4.3f _b[l1.lrgnp] "   t(alpha): " "%4.2f (_b[L1.lrgnp]-1)/_se[L1.lrgnp]
. display "S(e):     "  "%4.2f e(rmse)
```

The output of these commands is

```
. reg lrgnp DL year L.lrgnp LD(1/8).lrgnp

      Source |       SS       df       MS              Number of obs =      53
-------------+------------------------------           F( 11,    41) =  524.36
       Model |  14.5912488    11  1.32647716           Prob > F      =  0.0000
    Residual |  .103718036    41  .002529708           R-squared     =  0.9929
-------------+------------------------------           Adj R-squared =  0.9910
       Total |  14.6949668    52  .282595516           Root MSE      =   .0503

------------------------------------------------------------------------------
       lrgnp |      Coef.   Std. Err.      t    P>|t|     [95% Conf. Interval]
-------------+----------------------------------------------------------------
          DL |  -.1948966   .0395986    -4.92   0.000    -.2748676   -.1149256
        year |   .0273443   .0047912     5.71   0.000     .0176682    .0370203
             |
       lrgnp |
         L1. |   .2669447   .1314571     2.03   0.049     .0014618    .5324277
         LD. |   2.347314   .5457872     4.30   0.000     1.245074    3.449553
        LD2. |  -6.613034   1.935403    -3.42   0.001    -10.52166   -2.704409
        LD3. |   13.26996   4.123513     3.22   0.003      4.94236    21.59757
        LD4. |  -17.17223   5.738638    -2.99   0.005    -28.76164   -5.582813
        LD5. |   14.11228   5.210229     2.71   0.010     3.590005    24.63455
        LD6. |  -7.170474   2.971883    -2.41   0.020    -13.17231   -1.168635
        LD7. |   2.063456   .9689358     2.13   0.039     .1066502    4.020261
        LD8. |  -.2583127   .1381465    -1.87   0.069    -.5373052    .0206799
             |
       _cons |  -48.90544   8.567615    -5.71   0.000    -66.20809    -31.6028
------------------------------------------------------------------------------
```

(some output is omitted)

```
Beta(DL):  -0.195    t(DL):   -4.92
Beta(t):    0.027    t(t):     5.71
Alpha:      0.267    t(alpha): -5.58
S(e):       0.05
```

You will notice that, rather than having eight lags, we have eight differences. This is equivalent, actually, to the following formulation:

```
. reg d.lrgnp DL year  l.lrgnp L(1/8)D.lrgnp

. display "Beta(DL): " %4.3f  _b[DL]        " t(DL): " %4.2f _b[DL]/_se[DL]
. display "Beta(t): "  %4.3f  _b[year]      " t(t):  " %4.2f _b[year]/_se[year]
. display "Alpha:  "   %4.3f 1 + _b[l1.lrgnp] " t_alpha: " %4.2f (_b[L1.lrgnp])/_se[L1.lrgnp]
. display "S(e):  "    %4.2f e(rmse)
```

Notice that in this alternative formulation, α is equal to the estimated coefficient plus one. The output from this second (equivalent) formulation is

8.3 Zivot and Andrews' Test of a Break at an Unknown Date

```
. reg d.lrgnp DL year l.lrgnp L(1/8)D.lrgnp

      Source |       SS       df       MS              Number of obs =      53
-------------+------------------------------           F( 11,    41) =    4.88
       Model |  .135865089    11  .012351372           Prob > F      =  0.0001
    Residual |  .103718036    41  .002529708           R-squared     =  0.5671
-------------+------------------------------           Adj R-squared =  0.4509
       Total |  .239583125    52  .004607368           Root MSE      =   .0503

------------------------------------------------------------------------------
     D.lrgnp |      Coef.   Std. Err.      t    P>|t|     [95% Conf. Interval]
-------------+----------------------------------------------------------------
          DL |  -.1948966   .0395986    -4.92   0.000    -.2748676   -.1149256
        year |   .0273443   .0047912     5.71   0.000     .0176682    .0370203
             |
       lrgnp |
         L1. |  -.7330553   .1314571    -5.58   0.000    -.9985382   -.4675723
         LD. |   .5789596   .1247551     4.64   0.000     .3270116    .8309075
        L2D. |   .4205124   .1410459     2.98   0.005     .1356644    .7053603
        L3D. |   .2494641    .14233      1.75   0.087    -.0379771    .5369053
        L4D. |   .1996953   .1329612     1.50   0.141    -.0688254     .468216
        L5D. |   .1707963   .1308206     1.31   0.199    -.0934013    .4349939
        L6D. |   .2143065   .1207567     1.77   0.083    -.0295667    .4581796
        L7D. |   .2552669   .1247339     2.05   0.047     .0033617    .5071721
        L8D. |   .2583127   .1381465     1.87   0.069    -.0206799    .5373052
             |
       _cons |  -48.90544   8.567615    -5.71   0.000    -66.20809    -31.6028
------------------------------------------------------------------------------
```

(some output is omitted)

```
Beta(DL):  -0.195     t(DL):    -4.92
Beta(t):    0.027     t(t):      5.71
Alpha:      0.267     t(alpha):  -5.58
S(e):       0.05
```

Now, how did we know to include eight lags for 1929? Zivot and Andrews tested down from a max-lag of eight. If the test statistic on the maximal lag is insignificant (less than 1.60) at the 10% level, then we drop it and estimate the model with one fewer lags. We repeat the process until we no longer drop insignificant lags.

```
. local lags = 8            //This is the max-lag

. quietly reg lrgnp year DL Ld(0/`lags').lrgnp
. local tstat = _b[Ld`lags'.lrgnp]/_se[Ld`lags'.lrgnp]

. while abs(`tstat')<1.60 & `lags'>=0 {
.     local lags = `lags'-1
.     quietly reg lrgnp year DL Ld(0/`lags').lrgnp
```

```
.         local tstat = _b[Ld`lags'.lrgnp]/_se[Ld`lags'
                        .lrgnp]
. }

. display "Optimal lag for 1929:" `lags'
```

The idea is to repeat the above process for every candidate year. This requires creating an outer loop, one for every candidate break year. Be sure to drop the old break year dummy variable (1929) and create a new one for the new candidate year. Keep track of the t-stat on α for each year; we will keep regression for the year with the smallest test statistic on α.

Finally, we need to repeat this procedure for every variable, so let's create a final outer loop, looping over all of the variables. A complete implementation of this procedure on the Nelson and Plosser dataset is

```
. foreach var in lrgnp lgnp lpcrgnp lip lemp lprgnp lcpi lwg lm lvel bnd {
. quietly{
.         local optimal_t = 100
.         local optimal_year = 0

.         forvalues bp = 1860(1)1970{
.             capture drop DL
.             gen DL = 0
.             replace DL = 1 if year > `bp'

.             local lags = 8
.             reg `var' year DL Ld(0/`lags').`var'
.             local tstat = _b[Ld`lags'.`var']/_se[Ld`lags'.`var']
.             local alpha_tstat =   (_b[L1.`var']-1)/_se[L1.`var']
.             if `alpha_tstat' < `optimal_t' {
.                 local optimal_t = `alpha_tstat'
.                 local optimal_year = `bp'
.             }

.             while abs(`tstat')<1.60 & `lags'>=0 {
.                 local lags = `lags'-1
.                 reg `var' year DL Ld(0/`lags').`var'
.                 local tstat = _b[Ld`lags'.`var']/_se[Ld`lags'.`var']
.                 if `alpha_tstat' < `optimal_t' {
.                     local optimal_t = `alpha_tstat'
.                     local optimal_year = `bp'
.                 }
.             }
.         }
```

8.3 Zivot and Andrews' Test of a Break at an Unknown Date

```
. capture drop DL
. gen DL = 0
. replace DL = 1 if year > 'optimal_year'
. * Given the optimal year, what is the optimal K?
. local lags = 8
. reg 'var' year DL Ld(0/'lags').'var'
. local tstat = _b[Ld'lags'.'var']/_se[Ld'lags'.'var']
. while abs('tstat')<1.60 & 'lags'>=0 {
        local lags = 'lags'-1
        reg 'var' year DL Ld(0/'lags').'var'
        local tstat = _b[Ld'lags'.'var']/_se[Ld'lags'.'var']
        }
. }
. quietly reg 'var' year DL Ld(0/'lags').'var'

. display "'var'"
. display "   Breakpoint: " 'optimal_year'
. display "   K (lags):   " 'lags'
. display "   Beta(DL): " %4.3f _b[DL]         ///
          "   t(DL): (" %4.2f _b[DL]/_se[DL] ")"
. display "   Beta(t):  " %4.3f _b[year]       ///
          "   t(t):  (" %4.2f _b[year]/_se[year] ")"
. display "   Alpha:    " %4.3f _b[l1.'var']   ///
          "   t(alpha): (" %4.2f (_b[L1.'var']-1)/_se[L1.'var'] ")"
. display "   S(e):     " %4.2f e(rmse)
. display "----------------------------------------"
. display ""
. }
```

For the first three variables, the output from the code above is

```
            lrgnp
              Breakpoint: 1929
              K (lags):    8
              Beta(DL): -0.195    t(DL): (-4.92)
              Beta(t):   0.027    t(t):   (5.71)
              Alpha:     0.267    t(alpha): (-5.58)
              S(e):      0.05
            ----------------------------------------
```

```
lgnp
    Breakpoint: 1929
    K (lags):   8
    Beta(DL): -0.311    t(DL):  (-5.12)
    Beta(t):   0.032    t(t):   (5.97)
    Alpha:     0.532    t(alpha): (-5.82)
    S(e):      0.07
------------------------------------------

lpcrgnp
    Breakpoint: 1929
    K (lags):   7
    Beta(DL): -0.117    t(DL):  (-3.41)
    Beta(t):   0.012    t(t):   (4.69)
    Alpha:     0.494    t(alpha): (-4.61)
    S(e):      0.06
------------------------------------------
```

What does the output above tell us? We see that the most likely breakpoint is 1929, the date that Perron assumed for his structural break. The structural break variables (DL) and (t) are significant. More importantly, α does not seem to be equal to one. That is, unit roots do not describe Nelson and Plosser's data. Or, more accurately, there is less evidence for unit roots than Nelson and Plosser reported.

8.3.2 The zandrews Command

Kit Baum (2015) wrote a Stata command to implement Zivot and Andrews' (1992) technique. The command reports the period *after* the break rather than the year *of* the break. Also, I have been unable to fully replicate Nelson and Plosser's results using Kit Baum's zandrews program. Still, to install it, type the following in the command line:

```
. net install zandrews, from(http://fmwww.bc.edu/RePEc/bocode/z/)
```

A simplified syntax for zandrews is

```
. zandrews varname, maxlags(#) break() lagmethod() level(#)
```

Familiar questions keep arising: what types of breaks, and how many lags?

As in Perron's method, a break can occur in the intercept, the slope, or both. Accordingly, you must specify either break(intercept), break(trend), or break(both).

8.3 Zivot and Andrews' Test of a Break at an Unknown Date

How many lags should be included? As before, there are several different methods one might employ. You could find the number of lags that minimize your favorite information criterion (AIC or BIC). Alternatively, you could try a testing-down (sequential t-test) approach. The `lagmethod()` option allows you to choose one of the three options: `AIC`, `BIC`, or `TTest`. Alternatively, you can specify the maximum number of lags to consider, by using these two options in combination: `lagmethod(input) maxlags(#)`.

The following code uses `zandrews` to replicate most of Zivot and Andrews findings:

```
. foreach v of var lrgnp-lpcrgnp {
.     display ""
.     display "----------------------------------------"
.     zandrews 'v' , break(intercept) lagmethod(input) maxlags(8)
.   }
```

The output of this is

```
----------------------------------------

. zandrews lrgnp, break(intercept)  lagmethod(input) maxlags(8)

Zivot-Andrews unit root test for  lrgnp

Allowing for break in intercept

Lag selection via input: lags of D.lrgnp included = 8

Minimum t-statistic -5.576 at 1930  (obs 71)

Critical values: 1%: -5.34 5%: -4.80 10%: -4.58

----------------------------------------

. zandrews lgnp, break(intercept)  lagmethod(input) maxlags(8)

Zivot-Andrews unit root test for  lgnp

Allowing for break in intercept

Lag selection via input: lags of D.lgnp included = 8

Minimum t-statistic -5.824 at 1930  (obs 71)

Critical values: 1%: -5.34 5%: -4.80 10%: -4.58
```

(some output omitted)

```
. zandrews lsp500, break(both)  lagmethod(input)  maxlags(1)

Zivot-Andrews unit root test for   lsp500

Allowing for break in both intercept and trend

Lag selection via input: lags of D.lsp500 included = 1

Minimum t-statistic -5.607 at 1937  (obs 78)

Critical values: 1%: -5.57 5%: -5.08 10%: -4.82


. zandrews lrwg, break(both)  lagmethod(input)  maxlags(8)

Zivot-Andrews unit root test for   lrwg

Allowing for break in both intercept and trend

Lag selection via input: lags of D.lrwg included = 8

Minimum t-statistic -4.744 at 1941  (obs 82)

Critical values: 1%: -5.57 5%: -5.08 10%: -4.82
```

The final two variables (common stock prices a la the S&P-500 and real wages) were modeled with a break in both the intercept and the trend term. All other variables were modeled with a break in the intercept only.

The output of the `zandrews` command is summarized in Table 8.3. We were able to exactly replicate all but one of Zivot and Andrews' results.

Exercises
1. Repeat Perron's exercise on the Nelson and Plosser dataset, but use Stata's `zandrews` command and the AIC option to identify the existence and most likely location of a structural break. Ignore data before 1909. For each variable, which year is identified as the most likely for a structural break. Which of these are statistically significant? Are your results different from those identified by Perron? (Recall that real wages and the S&P-500 are thought to have a new intercept and slope after the break. All other variables have only a new intercept.) Are your results different from those in Zivot and Andrews' paper?
2. Repeat the exercise above, but use Stata's `zandrews` command and the sequential t-test option (at the 0.10 level) to identify the existence and most likely date of a structural break. Are your results different from those identified

Table 8.3 zandrews minimum t-statistics

Series	k (lags)	t-stat	Year-1
Real GNP	8	−5.576	1929
Nominal GNP	8	−5.824	1929
Real per capita GNP	7	−4.606	1929
Industrial production	8	−5.946	1929
Employment	7	−4.947	1929
GNP deflator	5	−4.122	1929
Consumer prices	2	−2.414	1880
Nominal wages	7	−5.302	1929
Money stock	6	−4.344	1929
Velocity	2	−3.262	1949
Interest rate	2	−0.983	1932
Common stock prices	1	−5.607	1936
Real wages	8	−4.744	1940

Source: Zivot & Andrews (1992); used with permission from Taylor & Francis Ltd (http://www.informaworld.com)

by Perron? Are your results different from those in the previous exercise? Are your results different from those in Zivot and Andrews' paper?

8.4 Further Readings

Structural breaks refer to a qualitative difference in the data before and after an event. For example, the economy might perform one way before a regulation is put into effect and differently afterward. Or investors might tolerate risk before the Great Depression and not tolerate it afterward.

The literature on structural breaks and unit root testing is its own cottage industry. An exhaustive review would be impossible.

Perron kicked off the research by providing a way to test for a structural break at a known date, specifically the Great Crash and the oil price shocks. Sometimes the date of a structural break is fairly certain. Germany's economy, for example, would certainly act differently pre- and post-unification (Lütkepohl & Wolters 2003).

The second wave of researchers relaxed the assumption that the date of the possible break is known. Rather, the possible number of breaks is known, and the algorithms check for the most likely dates of these changes. This wave is often called the "endogenous break" stream. This does not imply that the breaks occurred because of some endogenous economic process; rather the endogeneity refers to the calculation method. That is, the date is not given by the researcher exogenously. It is estimated by the statistical algorithm. Zivot and Andrews (1992), a paper we examined at length in this chapter, fits this molds. So, too, do the influential papers by Christiano (1992), Banerjee et al. (1992), Lanne et al. (2003), Perron and Vogelsang (1992), Perron (1997), and Vogelsang and Perron (1998).

Perron and Vogelsang (1992) propose a test for unknown structural break points. Their procedure should sound familiar if you have worked through this book. First, transform the series by removing its deterministic component. Then, calculate an augmented Dickey-Fuller-type regression with a possible structural break on the transformed series; similar in spirit to that of Zivot and Andrews, calculate t-statistics for a possible break at each date. The minimal t-statistic is then used to test the null hypothesis of a unit root. Perron (1997) expands on this.

Zivot and Andrews' asymptotic results rely on the assumption that structural breaks and unit roots are strict substitutes. That is, that a structural break occurs in a trend stationary process, but not in the null of a unit root process. Vogelsang and Perron (1998)–and Lee and Strazicich (2003) for two possible breaks–rectify this perceived deficiency. Since breaks are allowed under both the null (unit root) and the alternative (stationarity), "rejection of a null unambiguously implies stationarity" (Lee and Strazicich 2003, p. 1082).

It is informative to consider that Zivot and Andrews do not view their modeling assumptions as a deficiency, but rather as a feature. Unit roots can be thought of as the ultimate structural break; they are breaks that occur every period. Thus, the two relevant choices are (a) unit roots (which are themselves, continual structural breaks) versus (b) stationary processes with an occasional discrete structural break.

A third wave loosened the requirement that structural breaks are sharp, i.e., that the world was one way the day before an event and a completely different way starting the day after. Rather, there might be a smooth transition that takes place over several periods. Lanne et al. (2002) test for a known break point, but a flexible transition function. Leybourne et al. (1998) test for an endogenously dated structural break with a smooth transition.

Yet another wave extended the concept of structural breaks to include more than one break. Lumsdaine and Papell (1997) extend the procedure of Zivot and Andrews (1992) to include two distinct endogenous breaks. Lee and Strazicich (2003) also test for two endogenous breaks. The difference between them is that Lumsdaine and Papell tested trend stationary with breaks versus unit roots with no breaks; Lee and Strazicich test unit roots versus no unit roots, where there can be two endogenous breaks under both hypotheses. Bai and Perron (1998, 2003) offer a test for multiple structural changes at unknown dates. Narayan and Popp (2010) propose a Dickey-Fuller-type test for two structural breaks in level and slope at unknown dates with flexible transitions. As you can see, mixing and matching these concepts is a cottage industry.

If two economic variables are related, and one of them undergoes a structural change, it stands to reason that the other one would as well. Bai et al. (1998), for example, propose a test for a common structural break among a system of multiple time series. The idea is that if there is a structural break at a common date among multiple variables, then it will be easier to identify the break.

Research on structural breaks now include extensions to panel data. González et al. (2005), for example, extend the smooth transition literature to panels. They also now consider different break methods, such as Markov switching models, where the chances of switching from one type of system to another is itself a

8.4 Further Readings

probabilistic process depending on the characteristics of the economy at the time. Research has also extended the structural break tests to include multivariate models such as VARs and cointegration (ex: Saikkonen & Lütkepohl 2000), albeit with a known break point.

This literature is vast and increasing. The journal *Econometrics* devoted a special issue in 2017 exclusively to unit roots and structural change. Within that special issue, Clemente et al. (2017) test for cointegration evidence of the Fisher effect in a panel of countries while allowing for the possibility of structural breaks. Chang and Perron (2017) extend fractional unit root tests to allow for a structural change in trends, where the break is allowable under the null and alternative hypothesis. That is, the choice is not between unit roots and breaks, but between unit root with breaks and fractional unit roots with breaks.

For further reading, Hansen (2001) provides a wonderfully clear introduction to the logic and literature on structural breaks, including breaks with unit roots. Glynn et al. (2007) and Byrne and Perman (2007) provide a digestible overview of unit roots and structural breaks. More adventurous readers should consult Maddala and Kim (1998) for an in-depth treatment of unit roots, cointegration, and structural change.

ARCH, GARCH, and Time-Varying Variance 9

9.1 Introduction

To this point we have considered nonstationary means, but strictly speaking, nonstationarity could apply to any of the moments of a random variable: the mean, variance, skewness, kurtosis, etc... Finance especially is concerned with the nonstationarity of variance.[1] Most students will recall the issue of heteroskedasticity from their introductory econometrics classes. Heteroskedastiticy is a particular case of nonstationarity in the variance of a variable. (Skedasticity is a synonym for variance.) The traditional picture of heteroskedasticity is a scatterplot which spreads outward, growing proportionately as the value of X increases. Graphically, it looks like a funnel with the large part toward the right. Less common is heteroskedasticity with the variance decreasing in X; the funnel pointed in the other direction (see Fig. 9.1). But these are special cases, more common in cross sections. They are of limited use to the practicing financial econometrician.

Consider the stock market. Sometimes the markets are very volatile, and sometimes they are not. The volatility (variance) of stock market returns determines the riskiness of your investments. It is a truism in finance that risk and reward go together: they are positively correlated. When people take bigger risks with their investments (because the volatility of an asset's price was high), they demand to be compensated with higher reward. To make wise investments, it is crucial to understand and account for risk properly.

Before the introduction of ARCH and GARCH models, the most common—practically the only—method for incorporating volatility was to compute a rolling variance or rolling standard deviation. This, of course, brought up the practical

---

[1] Strictly speaking, it is the unconditional variance which can imply nonstationarity; conditional heteroskedasticity does not imply nonstationarity. The distinction between conditional and unconditional variance will be one of the focuses of this chapter.

© The Author(s), under exclusive license to Springer Nature Switzerland AG 2023
J. D. Levendis, *Time Series Econometrics*, Springer Texts in Business and Economics, https://doi.org/10.1007/978-3-031-37310-7_9

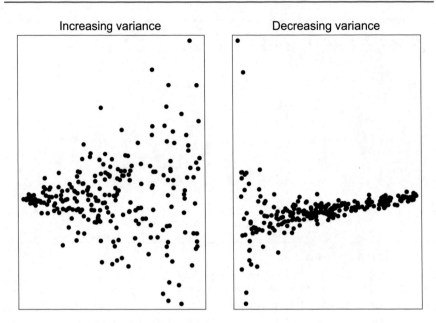

Fig. 9.1 Two cases of Classical Heteroskedasticity

question of choosing the best length of the window. Should you choose a rolling window of one week, or one month? A moving window effectively gives those observations outside the window a weight of zero and all observations inside the window an equal weight. Why should each observation be weighted equally? It seems reasonable that the more recent past contains more relevant information than the distant past, so more recent observations should be given more weight in our calculation of the rolling standard deviation. Moreover, if we choose one week as our window's length, should we ignore the information from a week and a half ago? Perhaps we should keep all the data points, but give distant observations exponentially diminished weight. The current practice avoids these issues by estimating the best weighting scheme, rather than taking an a priori approach.

In the 1980s, researchers turned seriously to the question of modeling volatility. Is it reasonable to predict that tomorrow's variance will equal last week's average, regardless of whether today's variance was particularly high? Volatility isn't seasonal—unfortunately it wasn't *that* predictable—but, like the weather, if one day happens to be particularly rainy, it is more likely that tomorrow will be rainy as well. Calm days tend to bunch into calm periods; volatile days tend to cluster into nerve-wracking turbulent periods. (See Fig. 9.2.)

The fact that the variance today depends, in some part, on the variance yesterday implies that it can be modeled quite easily by an autoregressive process such as an AR(1) process. Our standard AR(1) process from Chap. 2 was

9.1 Introduction

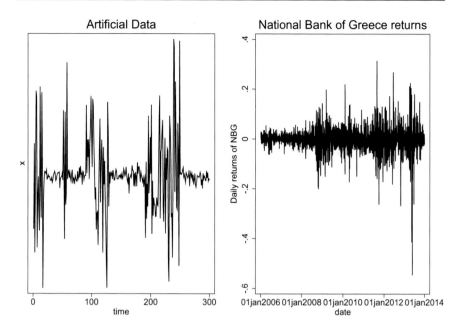

Fig. 9.2 Two cases of volatility clustering

$$X_t = \beta_0 + \beta_1 X_{t-1} + e_t.$$

Replacing X with σ^2, we have an AR(1) model of a variance:

$$\sigma_t^2 = \beta_0 + \beta_1 \sigma_{t-1}^2 + e_t. \tag{9.1}$$

An alternative representation would be a simple moving average process such as MA(1).

We will be assuming that the βs are such that σ_t^2 neither increases to infinity nor decreases to zero. Sometimes, though, its value is low, and sometimes it is high.

Our ultimate aim is to model a variable Y denoting, say, returns on the Dow Jones Index for example. The Dow might have average returns of 5% per year, but sometimes it is volatile, and sometimes it is calm. If the Dow's returns are distributed normally, then they can be modeled as

$$Y_t \sim N(0.05, \sigma_t^2).$$

Notice that Y_t is stationary in its mean, but not in its variance, σ_t^2, which is changing over time. (That's why it has the t subscript.)

The most common model used to capture varying variances is the generalized autoregressive conditional heteroskedasticity model (GARCH) developed by Bollerslev (1986) as a generalization of Engle's (1982) ARCH model. Since then, there have been countless generalizations of the GARCH model, comprising an alphabet soup of acronyms.

It has become standard for texts to jump directly to the general GARCH model. We will take a more incremental approach, building up slowly from a specific ARCH model to more general GARCH model. After we have established exactly what is going on inside general GARCH models, we will finish with a discussion of the many variants of GARCH. There are many, many variants of GARCH, so we will discuss a few and only briefly. But first, if ARCH stands for autoregressive conditional heteroskedasticity, what do we mean by "conditional heteroskedasticity?"

9.2 Conditional Versus Unconditional Moments

What exactly do we mean by "conditional" variance? Conditional on what? Let's look first at a very simple AR model to solidify this important distinction. After that, we will turn to the ARCH/GARCH models.

Suppose that Y_t follows a pure random walk without drift:

$$Y_t = Y_{t-1} + e_t \tag{9.2}$$

with the variance of e_t constant at σ^2. We can substitute recursively so that Eq. (9.2) can be rewritten as

$$Y_t = Y_0 + e_1 + e_2 + \ldots + e_t = Y_0 + \sum_{i=1}^{t} e_t.$$

Written this way we can see that Y_t is equal to the sum of a sequence of errors.

The unconditional variance of Y_t is

$$V(Y_t) = V(Y_0) + V(\sum_{i=1}^{t} e_t) = 0 + \sum_{i=1}^{t} V(e_t) = t\sigma^2.$$

Notice also how the unconditional variance changes: it increases unboundedly over time.

But what about the variance of Y_t, conditional on its previous value Y_{t-1}? That is, when we are curious to make a forecast of Y_t, we usually have some historical data to rely upon; we at least have Y's previous value. The variance of Y_t conditional on Y_{t-1} is

$$V(Y_t|Y_{t-1}) = 0 + 0 + 0 + \ldots + V(e_t) = \sigma^2.$$

Notice, in this case, the conditional variance is constant.

9.3 ARCH Models

We will spend a lot of time talking about conditional moments. We should make clear: "conditional on what?" For our purposes, we will condition on the entire set of outcomes previous to time t. That is, at time t, we will presume to know the realized values of all past variables.

9.3.1 ARCH(1)

ARCH and GARCH models of all stripes generally consist of two equations: (1) a mean equation describing the evolution of the main variable of interest, Y, and (2) a variance equation describing the evolution of Y's variance.

As promised, we will start out simple. Y_t will not even follow an AR(1) process, but will consist of a constant mean plus some error:

$$Y_t = \beta_0 + \epsilon_t. \tag{9.3}$$

More importantly, the error term operates as follows:

$$\epsilon_t = \left(\alpha_0 + \alpha_1 \epsilon_{t-1}^2\right)^{1/2} u_t \tag{9.4}$$

where $u_t \sim N(0, 1)$, $\alpha_0 > 0$, and $\alpha_1 > 1$. Equations (9.3) and (9.4) together define our ARCH(1) model.

This error term (Eq. 9.4) looks a bit unusual, but it isn't really. First, if you square both sides, you see that it is an expression for the mean equation's variance:

$$\epsilon_t^2 = \left(\alpha_0 + \alpha_1 \epsilon_{t-1}^2\right) u_t^2$$

and u_t^2 is a slightly different error term. Second, it is simply a multiplicative error term. This scales the variance up or down proportionately. While this all looks unnecessarily complicated, it simplifies the computation so it is quite useful.

Unconditional Moments

The unconditional mean of Y_t is

$$E(Y_t) = E(\beta_0 + \epsilon_t) = E(\beta_0) + E(\epsilon_t) = \beta_0.$$

The unconditional variance is

$$V(Y_t) = V(\beta_0 + \epsilon_t) = V(\beta_0) + V(\epsilon_t) = V(\epsilon_t) = E(\epsilon_t^2) - E^2(\epsilon_t) = E(\epsilon_t^2). \tag{9.5}$$

Now,

$$E(\epsilon_t^2) = E\left[\left(\alpha_0 + \alpha_1 \epsilon_{t-1}^2\right) u_t^2\right]$$
$$= E\left(\alpha_0 u_t^2 + \alpha_1 \epsilon_{t-1}^2 u_t^2\right)$$
$$= \alpha_0 E\left(u_t^2\right) + \alpha_1 E\left(\epsilon_{t-1}^2 u_t^2\right).$$

Independence implies that we can distribute the expectation operator, so

$$E(\epsilon_t^2) = \alpha_0 E\left(u_t^2\right) + \alpha_1 E\left(\epsilon_{t-1}^2\right) E\left(u_t^2\right).$$

Since $u_t \sim N(0, 1)$, then $E\left(u_t^2\right) = 1$ so

$$E(\epsilon_t^2) = \alpha_0 + \alpha_1 E\left(\epsilon_{t-1}^2\right). \tag{9.6}$$

If $E(\epsilon_t^2)$ is stationary,[2] then $E\left(\epsilon_t^2\right) = E\left(\epsilon_{t-1}^2\right) = E\left(\epsilon^2\right)$, so Eq. (9.6) simplifies to

$$E(\epsilon^2) = \frac{\alpha_0}{1 - \alpha_1}. \tag{9.7}$$

Finally, substituting Eq. (9.7) into (9.5) yields

$$V(Y_t) = \frac{\alpha_0}{1 - \alpha_1}, \tag{9.8}$$

so the unconditional variance is constant. So much for the unconditional variance. But ARCH refers to "conditional heteroskedasticity," so let's turn to the conditional moments.

Conditional Moments

We have several random variables (y_t, ϵ_t, and u_t) and we could condition on each of these or on their lags. So clearly, we could calculate an infinite number of conditional moments. Not all of them will be of interest. We need to be judicious.

First, an easy one. The mean of Y_t conditional on its previous value is

$$E(Y_t \mid Y_{t-1}) = E(Y_t) = \beta_0.$$

What about its variance? Since $Y_t = \beta_0 + \epsilon_t$, then $V(Y_t) = V(\epsilon_t)$.

$$V(\epsilon_t \mid \epsilon_{t-1}) = E\left(\epsilon_t^2 \mid \epsilon_{t-1}\right) - E^2\left(\epsilon_t \mid \epsilon_{t-1}\right)$$

---

[2] Refer back to Chap. 4 for the specific parameter restrictions.

9.3 ARCH Models

$$= E\left[\left(\left(\alpha_0 + \alpha_1 \epsilon_{t-1}^2\right)^{1/2} u_t\right)^2 \mid \epsilon_{t-1}\right] - E^2\left(\epsilon_t \mid \epsilon_{t-1}\right)$$

$$= E\left[\left(\alpha_0 u_t^2 + \alpha_1 \epsilon_{t-1}^2 u_t^2\right) \mid \epsilon_{t-1}\right]$$

$$= E\left(\alpha_0 u_t^2 \mid \epsilon_{t-1}\right) + E\left(\alpha_1 \epsilon_{t-1}^2 u_t^2 \mid \epsilon_{t-1}\right)$$

$$= \alpha_0 E\left(u_t^2 \mid \epsilon_{t-1}\right) + \alpha_1 E\left(\epsilon_{t-1}^2 u_t^2 \mid \epsilon_{t-1}\right).$$

Conditioning on ϵ_{t-1} means we treat it as a given constant. Therefore,

$$V(e_t \mid e_{t-1}) = \alpha_0 E\left(u_t^2 \mid \epsilon_{t-1}\right) + \alpha_1 \epsilon_{t-1}^2 E\left(u_t^2 \mid \epsilon_{t-1}\right).$$

Since the $u_t \sim N(0, 1)$, then $E(u_t^2) = 1$, regardless of whether it conditioned on ϵ_{t-1} or not. Therefore,

$$V(Y_t \mid Y_{t-1}) = V(\epsilon_t \mid \epsilon_{t-1}) = \alpha_0 + \alpha_1 \epsilon_{t-1}^2. \tag{9.9}$$

Notice from Eq. (9.9) that the conditional variance of Y_t depends upon time via ϵ_{t-1}. And since ϵ_t follows an AR(1) process, the conditional variance of Y exhibits time-varying volatility. But this is only true of the conditional variance. As we saw in Eq. (9.8), this was not a feature of the unconditional variance.

Kurtosis and Thicker Tails

Financial returns often have thicker tails than would be implied by normality. Some researchers believe these tails might be so thick as to have come from a Cauchy distribution, or some other distribution with no finite moments (Mandelbrot 1963). This would make any kind of statistical inference on returns completely invalid. This would also make much of finance completely irrelevant. ARCH and GARCH models actually reconcile the data with the self-interest of finance-oriented academics. It can be shown that the volatility clustering implied by ARCH and GARCH models also implies thicker tails than normal, even when the underlying error is itself normal.

We will show this analytically for the simple ARCH(1) model; we will show this only empirically when we simulate more complex models.

Before we begin computing, recall our assumptions about the ARCH(1) model:

$$Y_t = \beta_0 + \epsilon_t \tag{9.10}$$

$$\epsilon_t = \left(\alpha_0 + \alpha_1 \epsilon_{t-1}^2\right)^{1/2} u_t \tag{9.11}$$

$$u_t \sim N(0, 1). \tag{9.12}$$

The kurtosis of a variable X is defined as

$$K(X) = \frac{E[(X-\mu_x)^4]}{E^2(X-\mu_x)^2} = \frac{E(X^4)}{E^2(X^2)} \qquad (9.13)$$

where the second equality follows when the mean of X is zero. It is a standard exercise to show that the kurtosis of the normal distribution is 3. Thus, we aim to show that the kurtosis of $\epsilon_t \sim ARCH(1)$ is greater than three. Since u_t is standard normal, then (9.13) implies that

$$K(u_t) = \frac{E(u_t^4)}{[E(u_t^2)]^2} = 3. \qquad (9.14)$$

Using this information, let us calculate the kurtosis of ϵ_t:

$$\begin{aligned}
K(\epsilon_t) &= \frac{E[\epsilon_t^4]}{(E(\epsilon_t^2))^2} \\
&= \frac{E\left[(\alpha_0 + \alpha_1 \epsilon_{t-1}^2)^2 u_t^4\right]}{\left(E\left[(\alpha_0 + \alpha_1 \epsilon_{t-1}^2) u_t^2\right]\right)^2} \\
&= \frac{E\left[(\alpha_0 + \alpha_1 \epsilon_{t-1}^2)^2\right] E\left[u_t^4\right]}{\left[E(\alpha_0 + \alpha_1 \epsilon_{t-1}^2)\right]^2 \left[E(u_t^2)\right]^2} \\
&= \frac{E\left[(\alpha_0 + \alpha_1 \epsilon_{t-1}^2)^2\right] 3}{\left[E(\alpha_0 + \alpha_1 \epsilon_{t-1}^2)\right]^2}.
\end{aligned}$$

So, if we can prove that the expectation term in the numerator is greater than the denominator, we will have proven our case. To do this, we can rely on a mathematical theorem called Jensen's inequality. This theorem should be familiar to economics and finance students as it is the basis for risk aversion, which in turn is the basis of the theories of insurance and portfolio management. In words, the theorem states that if a function is concave, then the average of the function is greater than the function, evaluated at the average. In mathematics, if $f(x)$ is concave, then $E(f(x)) > f(E(x))$. Here, $f(x) = x^2$, which is a concave function, and $x = (\alpha_0 + \alpha_1 \epsilon_{t-1}^2)$. Therefore,

$$K(\epsilon_t) = \frac{3E(x^2)}{[E(x)]^2} = \frac{3E(f(x))}{f(E(x))} > 3.$$

Thus, we have shown that ARCH(1) processes have thicker tails than the normally distributed processes.

9.3 ARCH Models

Simulating the Process

So what does this type of process actually look like? We will generate some data and graph them to more intuitively understand the process. Then, we will use Stata's ARCH command to see if we can adequately estimate the parameters.

```
. drop _all
. set obs 1000
. set seed 12345
. gen time = _n
. tsset time
.
. * Enter the parameter values
. local beta0 = 10
. local alpha0 = 0.4
. local alpha1 = 0.5
.
. * Generate the data
. gen u = rnormal(0,1)
. gen e = .
. replace e = 0 in 1
. replace e = u*(`alpha0' + `alpha1'*(L.e^2))^(1/2)
   in 2/L
. gen Y = `beta0' + e
.
. * Graph data and estimate the model
. graph twoway line Y time
. arch Y, arch(1)
```

The data are graphed in Fig. 9.3.

We showed how an ARCH(1) process would have kurtosis that was greater than that of a normal process. We can show the same directly by calculating the empirical kurtosis:

```
. tabstat Y, statistics(kurtosis)

    variable |   kurtosis
-------------+-----------
           Y |   8.957432
-------------------------
```

Alternatively, we can approach the problem visually using a histogram (Fig. 9.4) or a QQ-plot (Fig. 9.5). The Stata commands for the graphs are

```
. qnorm Y
. histogram Y, normal
```

The output of the ARCH estimation is

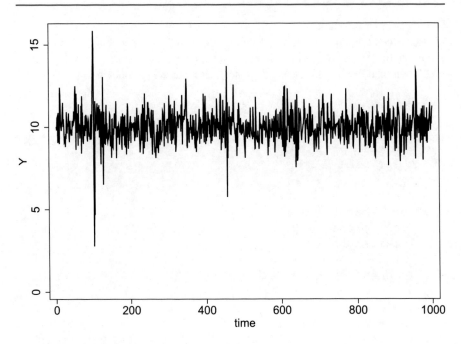

Fig. 9.3 Our simulated ARCH(1) data

```
ARCH family regression

Sample: 1 - 1000                                  Number of obs   =     1000
Distribution: Gaussian                            Wald chi2(.)    =        .

Log likelihood = -1251.018                        Prob > chi2     =        .

------------------------------------------------------------------------------
             |                 OPG
           Y |      Coef.   Std. Err.      z    P>|z|     [95% Conf. Interval]
-------------+----------------------------------------------------------------
Y            |
       _cons |   10.01859   .0236093   424.35   0.000     9.972319    10.06487
-------------+----------------------------------------------------------------
ARCH         |
        arch |
         L1. |   .5145089   .0678938     7.58   0.000     .3814394    .6475783
             |
       _cons |   .4229576   .0310762    13.61   0.000     .3620494    .4838659
------------------------------------------------------------------------------
```

The output of Stata's ARCH command is divided into two parts, corresponding to the two main component equations of any GARCH model: the mean and variance equations. We defined β_0 to be 10; it was estimated to be 10.0186. In the variance equation, α_0 and α_1, were defined to be 0.4 and 0.5, respectively; Stata estimated them to be 0.42 and 0.51.

9.3 ARCH Models

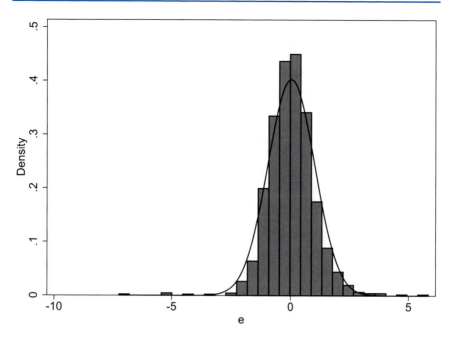

Fig. 9.4 Histogram of our simulated ARCH(1) data

Predicting the Conditional Variance

All econometric models are used to understand and to predict. ARCH models are no exception. Given that we have estimated an equation describing the variance, it is straightforward to generate a predicted variance, in the same way that we usually predict from the mean equation.

The "predicted values" can simply be fitted values or they can be true out-of-sample forecasts.

It is quite simple in Stata to calculate the estimated conditional variance. To calculate fitted values after a regression, you would simply use the `predict` command to calculate fitted values. You would use

```
. predict varname, residuals
```

to calculate the residuals (the estimates of the error and the means by which the squared errors are estimated for the variance equation).

Likewise, after an ARCH or GARCH estimation, you can predict the variance. The command is simply

```
. predict varname, variance
```

This is the estimated conditional variance, a graph of which is given in the first 1000 observations of Fig. 9.6.

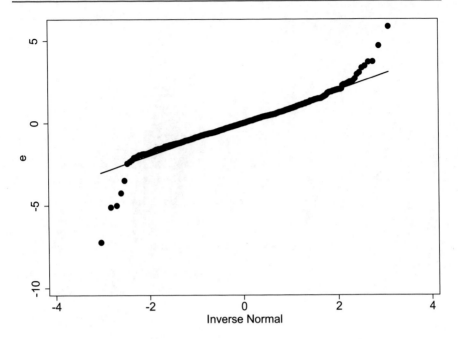

Fig. 9.5 Q-Q plot of our simulated ARCH(1) data

Predicting the Unconditional Variance

To predict the variance out into the future (rather than simply fitting the model to the data using "predicted values"), we can add some empty observations to the end of our dataset:

```
. tsappend, add(100)
. predict varhat, variance
```

After the first new observation, there is no data for the ARCH(1) process to pull from. Instead, it uses its own predicted values recursively, to generate more predicted values. That is, it predicts the variance in, say, period 1003 from its predicted value (not the realized value) in period 1002. Almost immediately, the predicted variance stabilizes to the estimated unconditional variance, a constant equal to $\hat{\alpha}_0/(1 - \hat{\alpha}_1) = 0.423/(1 - 0.515) = 0.87$. The final 100 observations in Fig. 9.6 show this convergence to the unconditional variance.

9.3.2 AR(1)-ARCH(1)

In the previous subsection, our mean equation was not particularly interesting; it was simply a constant plus some error. All of the dynamics were in the variance equation. In this subsection, we add some dynamics to the mean equation.

9.3 ARCH Models

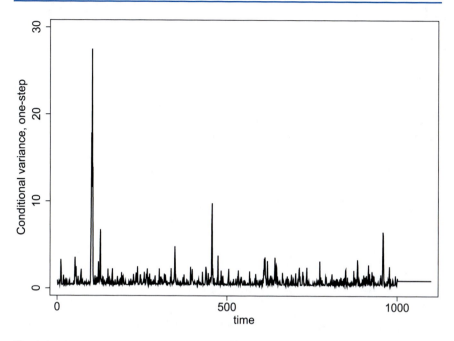

Fig. 9.6 The estimated variance from our simulated ARCH(1) data

We do this to make an important point: what makes the model an ARCH or GARCH model is the variance equation. The mean equation can be almost anything. Here, it will be an AR(1) process. (As this chapter progresses, the mean equation will usually be quite uninteresting. Sometimes, we won't even show it.)

To proceed, we replace the mean equation, (9.3), with

$$Y_t = \beta_0 + \beta_1 Y_{t-1} + \epsilon_t. \tag{9.15}$$

As before,

$$\epsilon_t = \left(\alpha_0 + \alpha_1 \epsilon_{t-1}^2\right)^{1/2} u_t, \tag{9.16}$$

with $u_t \sim N(0, 1)$ and the αs and βs defined such that each autoregressive process is stationary.

Unconditional Moments

First, we derive the unconditional moments. Y_t evolves as an AR(1) process. Presuming that β_0 and β_1 are such that Y_t is stationary, then

$$E(Y_t) = E(\beta_0 + \beta_1 Y_{t-1} + \epsilon_t)$$

$$= \beta_0 + \beta_1 E(Y_{t-1})$$
$$= \beta_0 + \beta_1 E(Y_t)$$
$$= \frac{\beta_0}{1-\beta_1}.$$

Given that this is simply an AR(1) process (with an unusual but still zero-mean error term), this equation should have been expected.

To derive the unconditional variance, let's begin with the mean equation (the AR(1) process) and substitute recursively into itself a couple of times:

$$Y_t = \beta_0 + \beta_1 Y_{t-1} + \epsilon_t$$
$$Y_t = \beta_0 + \beta_1 (\beta_0 + \beta_1 Y_{t-2} + \epsilon_{t-1}) + \epsilon_t$$
$$Y_t = \beta_0 + \beta_1 (\beta_0 + \beta_1 (\beta_0 + \beta_1 Y_{t-3} + \epsilon_{t-2}) + \epsilon_{t-1}) + \epsilon_t$$
$$Y_t = \beta_0 \sum_{i=0}^{2} \beta_1^i + \sum_{i=0}^{2} \epsilon_{t-i} \beta_1^i + \beta_1^3 Y_{t-3}$$

After repeated back-substitution, this becomes

$$Y_t = \beta_0 \sum_{i=0}^{\infty} \beta_1^i + \sum_{i=0}^{\infty} \epsilon_{t-i} \beta_1^i$$
$$= \frac{\beta_0}{1-\beta_1} + \sum_{i=0}^{\infty} \epsilon_{t-i} \beta_1^i. \qquad (9.17)$$

The unconditional variance can be found by using Eqs. (9.17) and (9.7):

$$V(Y_t) = V\left(\frac{\beta_0}{1-\beta_1} + \sum_{i=0}^{\infty} \epsilon_{t-i} \beta_1^i\right)$$
$$= V\left(\sum_{i=0}^{\infty} \epsilon_{t-i} \beta_1^i\right)$$
$$= \sum_{i=0}^{\infty} \beta_1^{2i} V(\epsilon_{t-i}) = \sum_{i=0}^{\infty} \beta_1^{2i} E\left(\epsilon_{t-i}^2\right) = \frac{\alpha_0}{1-\alpha_1} \sum_{i=0}^{\infty} \beta_1^{2i}$$
$$= \frac{\alpha_0}{1-\alpha_1} \frac{1}{1-\beta_1^2}.$$

Notice that adding a lagged Y_{t-1} term in the mean equation changed the unconditional variance of Y_t. Will it change the conditional variance as well?

9.3 ARCH Models

Conditional Moments

Below, we calculate the mean and variance of Y_t, conditional on the set of all previous information, Ω_{t-1}. This means that we know the values of $Y_{t-1}, Y_{t-2}, \ldots$, of $\epsilon_{t-1}, \epsilon_{t-1}, \ldots$, and of $u_t, u_{t-2}, \ldots$

$$
\begin{aligned}
E\left(Y_t \mid \Omega_{t-1}\right) &= E\left(\beta_0 + \beta_1 Y_{t-1} + \left(\alpha_0 + \alpha_1 \epsilon_{t-1}^2\right)^{1/2} u_t \mid \Omega_{t-1}\right) \\
&= \beta_0 + \beta_1 Y_{t-1} + E\left[\left(\alpha_0 + \alpha_1 \epsilon_{t-1}^2\right)^{1/2} u_t \mid \Omega_{t-1}\right] \\
&= \beta_0 + \beta_1 Y_{t-1} + \left(\alpha_0 + \alpha_1 \epsilon_{t-1}^2\right)^{1/2} E\left[u_t \mid \Omega_{t-1}\right] \\
&= \beta_0 + \beta_1 Y_{t-1} + \left(\alpha_0 + \alpha_1 \epsilon_{t-1}^2\right)^{1/2} [0] \\
&= \beta_0 + \beta_1 Y_{t-1}
\end{aligned}
$$

and

$$
\begin{aligned}
V\left(Y_t \mid \Omega_{t-1}\right) &= V\left(\beta_0 + \beta_1 Y_{t-1} + \left(\alpha_0 + \alpha_1 \epsilon_{t-1}^2\right)^{1/2} u_t \mid \Omega_{t-1}\right) \\
&= V\left(\beta_0 + \beta_1 Y_{t-1} \mid \Omega_{t-1}\right) + \left(\alpha_0 + \alpha_1 \epsilon_{t-1}^2\right) V\left(u_t \mid \Omega_{t-1}\right) \\
&= 0 + \left(\alpha_0 + \alpha_1 \epsilon_{t-1}^2\right)(1) \\
&= \alpha_0 + \alpha_1 \epsilon_{t-1}^2.
\end{aligned}
$$

Simulating the Process

We can simulate the data as follows:

```
. drop _all
. set obs 1000
. set seed 12345
. gen time = _n
. tsset time
.
. local beta0 = 10
. local beta1 = 0.10
. local alpha0 = 0.40
. local alpha1 = 0.50
.
. gen u = rnormal(0,1)
. gen e = .
. replace e = 0 in 1
. replace e = u*(`alpha0' + `alpha1'*(L.e^2))^(1/2)
```

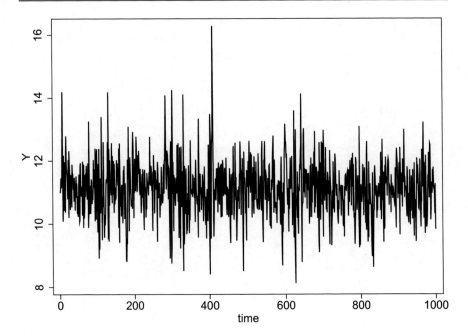

Fig. 9.7 Our simulated AR(1)-ARCH(1) data

```
   in 2/L
. gen Y = .
. replace Y = 11 in 1
. replace Y = `beta0' + `beta1'*L.Y + e in 2/L
```

Figure 9.7 graphs the data.

We can use Stata's tabstat command to calculate the unconditional kurtosis directly:

```
. tabstat Y, statistics(kurtosis)

    variable |  kurtosis
-------------+----------
           Y |  4.561622
------------------------
```

Stata allows us to estimate the AR(1)-ARCH(1) model quite readily, by typing the following command:

9.3 ARCH Models

```
. arch Y L.Y, arch(1)
```

the output of which is:

```
ARCH family regression

Sample:  2 - 1000                        Number of obs   =          999
Distribution: Gaussian                   Wald chi2(1)    =         9.74
Log likelihood = -1228.492               Prob > chi2     =       0.0018

------------------------------------------------------------------------------
             |                 OPG
           Y |      Coef.   Std. Err.      z    P>|z|     [95% Conf. Interval]
-------------+----------------------------------------------------------------
Y            |
           Y |
         L1. |   .1037784   .0332501     3.12   0.002     .0386094    .1689473
             |
       _cons |     9.9512   .3712735    26.80   0.000     9.223517    10.67888
-------------+----------------------------------------------------------------
ARCH         |
        arch |
         L1. |   .4650049   .0570121     8.16   0.000     .3532633    .5767466
             |
       _cons |   .4371298   .0297103    14.71   0.000     .3788988    .4953609
------------------------------------------------------------------------------
```

Stata does a good job estimating the parameters of this model, too. The mean equation's parameters, β_0 and β_1 were defined to be 10 and 0.10. Stata estimates them to be 9.95 and 0.103. The variance terms α_0 and α_1 were, as before, 0.40 and 0.50; Stata estimates them to be 0.437 and 0.465.

9.3.3 ARCH(2)

In the previous subsection we added complexity to our baseline model by adding an AR term to the mean equation. In this subsection we revert back to our constant-only mean Eq. (9.3), but add complexity in the variance Eq. (9.4). Specifically, the mean equation is still

$$Y_t = \beta_0 + \epsilon_t, \tag{9.18}$$

but the variance equation is now

$$\epsilon_t = \left(\alpha_0 + \alpha_1 \epsilon_{t-1}^2 + \alpha_2 \epsilon_{t-2}^2\right)^{1/2} u_t. \tag{9.19}$$

That is, we added an additional lagged ϵ term in the variance equation. If α_2 is positive, this essentially adds more inertia to the variance of Y.[3]

As before, we will first derive the features of this model mathematically. Then we will simulate the data and graph it so that we can see the features of the model visually. Then we will estimate the model empirically using Stata's ARCH command.

Conditional Moments

Let's look more closely at variance Eq. (9.19). The expectation of ϵ_t, conditional on its entire past history (which we denote as Ω_{t-1}), is

$$E(\epsilon_t \mid \Omega_{t-1}) = E\left[\left(\alpha_0 + \alpha_1 \epsilon_{t-1}^2 + \alpha_2 \epsilon_{t-2}^2\right)^{1/2} u_t \mid \Omega_{t-1}\right]$$

$$= \left(\alpha_0 + \alpha_1 \epsilon_{t-1}^2 + \alpha_2 \epsilon_{t-2}^2\right)^{1/2} E\left[u_t \mid \Omega_{t-1}\right]$$

$$= \left(\alpha_0 + \alpha_1 \epsilon_{t-1}^2 + \alpha_2 \epsilon_{t-2}^2\right)^{1/2} [0]$$

$$= 0.$$

The conditional variance of Y_t, however, is

$$V(Y_t \mid \Omega_{t-1}) = Var(\epsilon_t \mid \Omega_{t-1})$$

$$= E\left(\epsilon_t^2 \mid \Omega_{t-1}\right) - E^2(\epsilon_t \mid \Omega_{t-1})$$

$$= E\left(\epsilon_t^2 \mid \Omega_{t-1}\right)$$

$$= E\left[\left(\alpha_0 + \alpha_1 \epsilon_{t-1}^2 + \alpha_2 \epsilon_{t-2}^2\right) u_t^2 \mid \Omega_{t-1}\right]$$

$$= \left(\alpha_0 + \alpha_1 \epsilon_{t-1}^2 + \alpha_2 \epsilon_{t-2}^2\right) E\left[u_t^2 \mid \Omega_{t-1}\right]$$

$$= \left(\alpha_0 + \alpha_1 \epsilon_{t-1}^2 + \alpha_2 \epsilon_{t-2}^2\right)$$

$$= \alpha_0 + \alpha_1 V(Y_{t-1}) + \alpha_2 V(Y_{t-2}). \tag{9.20}$$

The second-to-last equality follows from the fact that $u_t \sim N(0, 1)$. The last equality follows from the fact that $V(Y_t) = V(\epsilon_t)$. We can easily see that the conditional variance depends upon its own past values.

---

[3] For ϵ_t^2 to be positive, as it must be since it is equal to the variance of Y, it is sufficient that all the αs are positive.

9.3 ARCH Models

Unconditional Moments

The unconditional expected value of Y_t is

$$E(Y_t) = E(\beta_0 + \epsilon_t) = \beta_0.$$

The stationarity of $V(Y_t)$ implies that $V(Y_t) = V(Y_{t-1}) = V(Y)$. Substituting this into Eq. (9.20),

$$V(Y) = \alpha_0 + \alpha_1 V(Y) + \alpha_2 V(Y)$$
$$= \frac{\alpha_0}{1 - \alpha_1 - \alpha_2}.$$

Simulating the Process

We can simulate the data by entering the code below.

```
. drop _all
. set obs 1000
. set seed 12345
. gen time = _n
. tsset time
.
. local beta0 = 10
. local alpha0 = 0.20
. local alpha1 = 0.30
. local alpha2 = 0.40
.
. gen u = rnormal(0,1)
. gen e = .
. replace e = 0 in 1/2
. replace e = u*(`alpha0' + `alpha1'*(L.e^2) + ///
            `alpha2'*(L2.e^2) )^(1/2) in 3/L
. gen Y = `beta0' + e
```

The data are graphed in Fig. 9.8. The volatility clustering is visually evident. The unconditional kurtosis is calculated to be

```
. tabstat Y, statistics(kurtosis)

    variable |  kurtosis
-------------+----------
           Y |  25.82196
-----------------------
```

Stata estimates the parameters quite accurately. The estimation command is

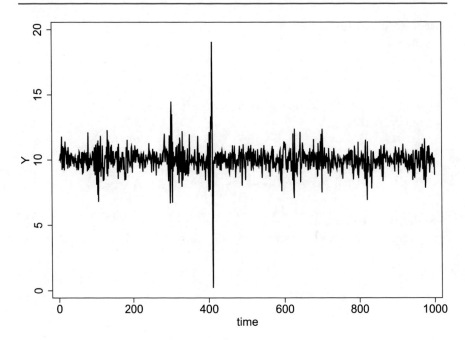

Fig. 9.8 Our simulated AR(0)-ARCH(2) data

```
. arch Y, arch(1/2)
```

and yields the following output:

```
ARCH family regression

Sample: 1 - 1000                               Number of obs    =      1,000
Distribution: Gaussian                         Wald chi2(.)     =          .
Log likelihood = -1072.506                     Prob > chi2      =          .

------------------------------------------------------------------------------
             |                 OPG
           Y |      Coef.   Std. Err.      z    P>|z|     [95% Conf. Interval]
-------------+----------------------------------------------------------------
Y            |
       _cons |   10.00629   .0192137   520.79   0.000     9.968632    10.04395
-------------+----------------------------------------------------------------
ARCH         |
        arch |
         L1. |   .288942    .0476651     6.06   0.000      .19552    .3823639
         L2. |   .424621    .0623969     6.81   0.000     .3023253   .5469167
             |
       _cons |   .21235     .0191894    11.07   0.000     .1747394   .2499606
------------------------------------------------------------------------------
```

9.3 ARCH Models

The estimates are very close to their true values. The constant in the mean function was equal to 10 and was estimated at 10.01. The parameters of the variance equation were 0.20, 0.30, and 0.40 and were estimated at 0.21, 0.29, and 0.43.

9.3.4 ARCH(q)

The General Model

By now, the relevant features of the ARCH(q) model should be apparent. It consists of two equations: (1) a mean equation,

$$Y_t = \beta + \epsilon_t,$$

and more importantly, (2) a variance equation with the form

$$\begin{aligned}\epsilon_t &= \left(\alpha_0 + \alpha_1 \epsilon_{t-1}^2 + \alpha_2 \epsilon_{t-2}^2 + \ldots + \alpha_p \epsilon_{t-q}^2\right)^{1/2} u_t \\ &= \left(\alpha_0 + \sum_{i=1}^{q} \alpha_i \epsilon_{t-i}^2\right)^{1/2} u_t.\end{aligned} \quad (9.21)$$

For the variance to be stationary—not to dampen to zero or explode to infinity—the coefficients must satisfy

$$-1 < \alpha_i < 1,$$

and

$$\sum_{i=1}^{q} \alpha_i < 1.$$

For the variance to be positive—there is no such thing as negative variance—then the αs must be nonnegative; this modifies the first constraint to be

$$0 < \alpha_i < 1.$$

The variance equation in an ARCH(q) process is simply an AR(q) process, just on the variance rather than the mean equation. Therefore, the stationarity constraints on the αs above are identical to those for any AR(q) process. (Refer to the AR chapter for a discussion of stationarity conditions.)

Conditional Moments

The conditional variance for the ARCH(q) process is

$$V(Y_t \mid \Omega_{t-1}) = \alpha_0 + \alpha_1 \epsilon_{t-1}^2 + \alpha_2 \epsilon_{t-2}^2 + \ldots + \alpha_p \epsilon_{t-q}^2.$$

Unconditional Moments

Using the now-familiar methods from earlier in this chapter, the unconditional variance for an ARCH(q) process is

$$V(Y) = \frac{\alpha_0}{1 - \alpha_1 - \alpha_2 - \ldots - \alpha_q}.$$

Testing for ARCH

How do you know that your data even exhibit ARCH in the first place? There are several different approaches to take. We will discuss two of tests of autocorrelation in the squared residuals. The squared residuals are an estimate of the variance, so any autocorrelation test of the squared residuals is a defensible test of autocorrelated variance. The two tests we will discuss are (1) the Ljung-Box test and (2) an autocorrelation (ACF) test using the test statistic proposed by Engle (1982), the so-called Engle LM test. Both of the tests relies on the same first steps: (1) estimate the mean equation: regressed on lags of itself or on some exogenous variables X, (2) investigate the properties of the residuals and the squared residuals.

(1) *The Ljung-Box (Q) test* investigates whether a variable is white noise. If variables are white noise, they cannot be autocorrelated. The Ljung-Box test is implemented in Stata using the command

```
. wntestq e, lags(4)
```

where e is the unconditional residual (if this is a test for ARCH effects in the raw data). After estimating the ARCH model, use the standardized residual (the residual divided by the conditional variance). The former is used to test for ARCH effects; the latter is used on the standardized residuals after ARCH estimation to make sure that all of the ARCH effects have been removed. We picked four lags just for the sake of illustration. Some researchers estimate an autocorrelation function (ACF) to help pick the Ljung-Box lag length.

(2) *The LM or ACF test* estimates the autocorrelation function of e^2, the squared residuals. This can be done by regressing e2 on an ample number of lags of itself:

```
. reg e2 L.e2 L2.e2 L3.e2 L4.e2
```
, or more compactly

```
. reg e2 L(1/4).e2
```

Then, test whether the coefficients are jointly significant. If so, then there is evidence of ARCH effects. A graphical alternative is to generate the ACF function using

```
. ac e2, lags(1/4)
```

(For a refresher on ACFs, see Chap. 3.)

Engle's (1982) Lagrange multiplier method relies on an χ^2 test; this is asymptotically identical to Stata's default F test from its test command. Engle's test statistic for the joint significance test is equal to TR^2 and is distributed χ^2 with q degrees of freedom. In Stata, after estimating the mean equation using reg, use the following post-estimation command:

9.3 ARCH Models

```
. estat archlm, lags(1/4)
```

As an example, we can download data on daily GM stock returns and perform the LM test.

```
. use ARCH-GM.dta, clear
. reg Y
. estat archlm, lags(1/10)
```

```
LM test for autoregressive conditional heteroskedasticity (ARCH)
-----------------------------------------------------------------------------
    lags(p)  |       chi2              df                Prob > chi2
-------------+---------------------------------------------------------------
       1     |       5.802              1                  0.0160
       2     |       6.996              2                  0.0303
       3     |       8.632              3                  0.0346
       4     |       9.426              4                  0.0513
       5     |      11.570              5                  0.0412
       6     |      56.410              6                  0.0000
       7     |      56.958              7                  0.0000
       8     |      57.151              8                  0.0000
       9     |      70.187              9                  0.0000
      10     |      70.625             10                  0.0000
-----------------------------------------------------------------------------
           H0: no ARCH effects    vs.   H1: ARCH(p) disturbance
```

Note the p-values. Even at one lag there is evidence of autocorrelation in the squared residuals, implying autocorrelation in the variance of GM stock returns.

It is tempting to go overboard when including lags. Often, one or two lags are sufficient. If you are using quarterly data, four lags should be included to capture seasonality. Daily data almost never require 365 lags, though. Such a model would be nearly impossible to estimate. As an exercise, you will be asked to show that the LM test will have significant p-values at all lags—even at a lag of one—when run on simulated ARCH(1) data.

Only if you suspect that the variance function is seasonal would you have an ARCH model which did not include earlier lags. For example, with quarterly data but no seasonality, you might have an

```
. arch Y, arch(1/4)
```

With seasonality, you might have

```
. arch Y, arch(4)
```

In the former case, an LM test with one lag would be sufficient to detect the ARCH effects. In the latter, the ARCH effects would not be apparent until the LM test reached lags = 4.

It should be pointed out that, in general, the LM tests will show decreasing p-values as the number of lags increases. This is because the sequence of tests just adds variables to a joint significance test. That is, the "lags(p) = 1" line shows results of

Table 9.1 AIC and BIC lag selection

Lags	AIC	BIC
1	−3674.506	−3660.658
2	−3675.836	−3657.371
3	−3674.654	−3651.574
4	−3677.691	−3649.994
5	−3677.990	−3645.678
6	−3694.836	−3657.908
7	−3698.461	−3656.916
8	−3697.910	−3651.75
9	**−3711.795**	**−3661.019**
10	−3709.825	−3654.432

a test that one lag is significant. The second line shows the result of a test that lags one or two are significant. Thus, the higher-lagged tests nest the previous tests.[4]

Finding the Optimal Lag Length

Of course, the above exercise presumes we know how many lags would belong in the Ljung-Box or LM tests in the first place. That is, we presumed that, if ARCH were to exist, it would be operative at a certain number of lags, and then we tested for ARCH given the lags. But how do we know what the number of lags would have been? While there is no universally accepted answer to this question, the most common approach is to estimate several models, each with different lags, and then compare them using either the Akaike information criterion, the Bayesian information criterion, or another such criterion.

We continue with our General Motors example, estimating a sequence of ARCH models, each with a different number of included lags.

```
. forvalues lags=1/10{
.     display "Lags = " `lags'
.     quietly arch Y, arch(1/`lags')
.     estat ic
. }
```

Table 9.1 summarizes the Stata output from above. In Stata, lower information criteria indicate a better fitting model. Therefore, the AIC and BIC indicate that nine lags would be preferred. A discrepancy between the two ICs is not uncommon. Generally, BICs choose smaller models than AICs. To the extent that parsimony is

---

[4] We are speaking loosely, here. The p-value would be guaranteed to drop by adding variables if we were adding variables to a test from the same regression. In this LM output, however, we are actually estimating and testing ten increasingly larger models and jointly testing the significance of each model's parameters, so "nesting" is not literally correct in the strict statistical sense of the term. Still, the point stands that adding lags to an LM test will almost always result in a p-value less than 0.05, so be judicious when adding lags.

9.3 ARCH Models

a virtue, the BICs are preferred. Others argue that the problem of omitted variable bias is more important than the usual gains in efficiency, so that AICs are preferred. The argument is an open one.

Estimating ARCH Models

Using the now-familiar `arch` command, it is perfectly within Stata's capabilities to estimate more interesting mean equations than we have above:

. arch *depvar* [*indepvars*], arch(*numlist*)

To estimate an ARCH(1) model with an exogenous X variable in the mean equation:

. arch Y X, arch(1)

To estimate an AR(1)-ARCH(6) model on Y:

. arch Y L.Y, arch(1 2 3 4 5 6)

or, more compactly,

. arch Y L.Y, arch(1/6)

To estimate an AR(2)-ARCH(20) model:

. arch Y L.Y L2.Y, arch(1/20)

To estimate the AR(1)-ARCH(6) model, Stata must estimate nine parameters (two in the mean equation and seven in the variance equation, intercepts included). To estimate an AR(2)-ARCH(12) model would require estimating 16 parameters. In practice, a well-fitting ARCH(q) model often requires estimating quite a large number of coefficients. It is not conceptually difficult, but the maximum likelihood procedures might not converge. Moreover, it requires a lot of data as each estimated coefficient eats up degrees of freedom. Or, to put it in English: when you have to estimate so many parameters, you can't estimate any of them very well.

9.3.5 Example 1: Toyota Motor Company

In this example, we will download some stock price data, test whether ARCH effects are present and estimate the appropriate ARCH model.

We will show several ways to accomplish the same task. In subsequent examples, we will proceed more quickly.

For this example, let's download the daily stock prices of Toyota Motor Company (ticker "TM") for 2000–2010.

. use ARCH-TM.dta, clear

The variable TM is the daily percentage returns of Toyota stock. A graph of the data is given in Fig. 9.9.

First, we performed Engle's LM test using `archlm`, which is a post-estimation command for `regress`. We arbitrarily chose ten lags as a starting point.

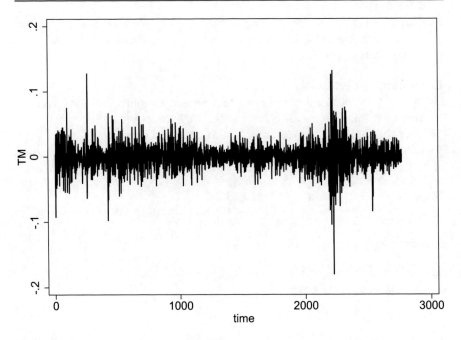

Fig. 9.9 The daily percent returns of Toyota stock

```
. quietly reg TM

. estat archlm, lags(1/10)

LM test for autoregressive conditional heteroskedasticity (ARCH)
---------------------------------------------------------------------
    lags(p)  |      chi2           df          Prob > chi2
-------------+-------------------------------------------------------
       1     |     14.059           1            0.0002
       2     |    124.791           2            0.0000
       3     |    169.760           3            0.0000
       4     |    183.493           4            0.0000
       5     |    252.112           5            0.0000
       6     |    266.300           6            0.0000
       7     |    383.974           7            0.0000
       8     |    396.482           8            0.0000
       9     |    401.532           9            0.0000
      10     |    401.705          10            0.0000
---------------------------------------------------------------------
           H0: no ARCH effects     vs.   H1: ARCH(p) disturbance
```

9.3 ARCH Models

Next, we perform Engle's LM test "by hand." This requires estimating a regression, extracting the residuals, squaring them, estimating an autoregressive model on the squared residuals, and then testing whether the coefficients on the AR model are jointly significant.

```
. quietly reg TM
. predict e, resid
. gen e2 = e^2
. reg e2 L(1/10).e2
```

```
      Source |       SS       df       MS              Number of obs =    2,756
-------------+------------------------------           F(10, 2745)   =    46.84
       Model |  .000468479     10   .000046848         Prob > F      =   0.0000
    Residual |  .002745643   2,745  1.0002e-06         R-squared     =   0.1458
-------------+------------------------------           Adj R-squared =   0.1426
       Total |  .003214122   2,755  1.1667e-06         Root MSE      =    .001


------------------------------------------------------------------------------
          e2 |      Coef.   Std. Err.      t    P>|t|     [95% Conf. Interval]
-------------+----------------------------------------------------------------
          e2 |
         L1. |  -.0339594    .019083    -1.78   0.075    -.0713778    .003459
         L2. |   .0982423    .019073     5.15   0.000     .0608433   .1356412
         L3. |   .0730985   .0191125     3.82   0.000     .0356222   .1105749
         L4. |   .0294145   .0187247     1.57   0.116    -.0073014   .0661304
         L5. |   .1271227   .0186934     6.80   0.000     .0904681   .1637772
         L6. |   .0634446   .0187012     3.39   0.001     .0267747   .1001145
         L7. |   .2141982   .0187327    11.43   0.000     .1774666   .2509299
         L8. |   .0654119   .0189155     3.46   0.001     .0283218    .102502
         L9. |   .0455213   .0188573     2.41   0.016     .0085454   .0824972
        L10. |   -.006043   .0188618    -0.32   0.749    -.0430279   .0309418
             |
       _cons |   .0001147    .000023     4.98   0.000     .0000696   .0001599
------------------------------------------------------------------------------
```

If the coefficients on the lagged squared residuals are statistically significant, then this is evidence of ARCH effects. A quick and easy way to do this is

```
. test L1.e2 L2.e2 L3.e2 L4.e2 L5.e2 ///
    L6.e2 L7.e2 L8.e2 L9.e2 L10.e2

 ( 1)    L.e2 = 0
 ( 2)    L2.e2 = 0
 ( 3)    L3.e2 = 0
 ( 4)    L4.e2 = 0
 ( 5)    L5.e2 = 0
 ( 6)    L6.e2 = 0
 ( 7)    L7.e2 = 0
 ( 8)    L8.e2 = 0
 ( 9)    L9.e2 = 0
 (10)    L10.e2 = 0
```

```
               F( 10,   2745) =    46.84
                     Prob > F =    0.0000
```

Engle preferred the χ^2 version of the test. An F-test is asymptotically χ^2 as the denominator degrees of freedom go toward infinity. The χ^2 test statistic is equal to $R^2 N$ and has q degrees of freedom:

```
. scalar teststat = e(r2)*e(N)

. display e(r2)*e(N)
401.70507

. display chi2tail(10,teststat)
4.082e-80
```

Notice that the test statistic that we calculated "by hand" is identical to that which Stata calculated via the `archlm` command. The p-value on this test is far below 0.05, so we reject the null hypothesis of "no ARCH."

The Ljung-Box test indicates that there is significant autocorrelation (the p-value is zero):

```
. wntestq e2

Portmanteau test for white noise
-----------------------------------------
  Portmanteau (Q) statistic =   1952.3569
  Prob > chi2(40)           =      0.0000
```

There is evidence of ARCH effects of length at least equal to 1. We should estimate an ARCH model, but what lag length? We calculated AICs and BICs of the ARCH models at various lag lengths (output not shown) and found that a lag length of ten fits the data best. We report this result.

```
. arch TM, arch(1/10) nolog

ARCH family regression

Sample: 2 - 2767                           Number of obs   =      2,766
Distribution: Gaussian                     Wald chi2(.)    =          .
Log likelihood =    7380.48                Prob > chi2     =          .
```

9.3 ARCH Models

```
             |              OPG
          TM |      Coef.   Std. Err.       z    P>|z|     [95% Conf. Interval]
-------------+----------------------------------------------------------------
TM           |
       _cons |   .0003909   .0002705     1.45    0.148    -.0001392    .000921
-------------+----------------------------------------------------------------
ARCH         |
        arch |
         L1. |   .0706262   .0175664     4.02    0.000     .0361967   .1050558
         L2. |   .1056462   .0182811     5.78    0.000      .069816   .1414764
         L3. |   .1317966    .021566     6.11    0.000     .0895279   .1740653
         L4. |   .0827439   .0220028     3.76    0.000     .0396191   .1258687
         L5. |   .0912129   .0191785     4.76    0.000     .0536238   .1288021
         L6. |   .0233804    .018131     1.29    0.197    -.0121557   .0589165
         L7. |   .0946893   .0175642     5.39    0.000     .0602642   .1291144
         L8. |   .0773595   .0202084     3.83    0.000     .0377518   .1169673
         L9. |   .0346793    .014553     2.38    0.017      .006156   .0632027
        L10. |   .0700995    .017391     4.03    0.000     .0360137   .1041853
             |
       _cons |   .0000844   7.57e-06    11.16    0.000     .0000696   .0000993
------------------------------------------------------------------------------
```

Finally, was the model that we estimated stationary? All of the ARCH coefficients are less than one. Do they add up to less than one?

```
. display [ARCH] L1.arch +   [ARCH] L2.arch +
[ARCH] L3.arch + ///
[ARCH] L4.arch + [ARCH] L5.arch + [ARCH] L6.arch +
[ARCH] L7.arch + ///
[ARCH] L8.arch + [ARCH] L9.arch + [ARCH] L10.arch

.78223389
```

The coefficients add to 0.78. Is this sufficiently far from one, statistically speaking? To test this, we run a formal hypothesis test:

```
. test [ARCH] L1.arch +   [ARCH] L2.arch + [ARCH] L3.arch + ///
[ARCH] L4.arch + [ARCH] L5.arch + [ARCH] L6.arch + [ARCH] L7.arch
    + ///
[ARCH] L8.arch + [ARCH] L9.arch + [ARCH] L10.arch = 1

 ( 1)   [ARCH] L.arch + [ARCH] L2.arch + [ARCH] L3.arch +
            [ARCH] L4.arch +
[ARCH] L5.arch + [ARCH] L6.arch + [ARCH] L7.arch + [ARCH] L8.arch +
[ARCH] L9.arch + [ARCH] L10.arch = 1

          chi2(  1) =    29.21
        Prob > chi2 =    0.0000
```

The hypothesis test verifies that 0.78 is sufficiently far from zero. Thus, our estimated ARCH model does not predict a variance that is growing without bound.

9.3.6 Example 2: Ford Motor Company

Download stock price data for Ford Motor Company (stock ticker "F") for the 1990s. Test whether it has ARCH effects. Estimate an AR(0)-ARCH(5) model on its pct daily returns. Is it stationary?

First, we download the data. A graph of the daily returns is given in Fig. 9.10.

```
. use ARCH-F.dta, clear
```

Are ARCH effects present? First, we calculate the Engle LM test:

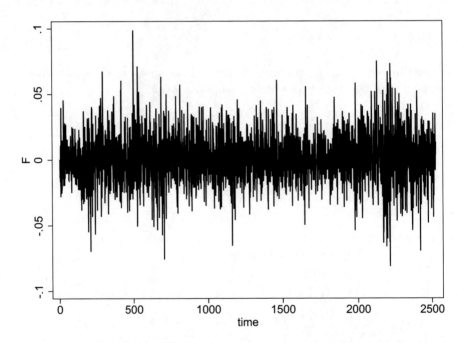

Fig. 9.10 The daily percent returns of Ford stock

9.3 ARCH Models

```
. quietly reg F
. estat archlm, lags(1/5)

LM test for autoregressive conditional heteroskedasticity (ARCH)
-----------------------------------------------------------------
    lags(p) |       chi2            df              Prob > chi2
------------+----------------------------------------------------
          1 |      13.335            1                 0.0003
          2 |      34.891            2                 0.0000
          3 |      38.215            3                 0.0000
          4 |      40.276            4                 0.0000
          5 |      43.009            5                 0.0000
-----------------------------------------------------------------
           H0: no ARCH effects    vs.   H1: ARCH(p) disturbance
```

For completeness, we also calculate the Ljung-Box test:

```
. quietly reg F
. predict e, resid
. gen e2 = e^2
. wntestq e2, lags(5)

Portmanteau test for white noise
---------------------------------------
Portmanteau (Q) statistic  =    53.5842
Prob > chi2(5)             =     0.0000
```

Both tests indicate strongly that there are ARCH effects present. We should estimate an ARCH model, but of what length?

We calculate AICs for models with lags of 1 through 20 (output not shown).

```
. forvalues lags=1/20{
.     display "Lags = " `lags'
.     qui arch F, arch(1/`lags')
.     estat ic
.     di ""
.     di ""
. }
```

The AIC indicates that a lag length of 15 fits best. Given this, we estimate the ARCH(15) model:

```
. arch F, arch(1/15) nolog

ARCH family regression

Sample: 3 - 2527                              Number of obs    =     2,525
Distribution: Gaussian                        Wald chi2(.)     =         .
Log likelihood =  6527.166                    Prob > chi2      =         .
```

	Coef.	OPG Std. Err.	z	P>|z|	[95% Conf. Interval]
F					
_cons	.000727	.0003592	2.02	0.043	.0000229 .0014311
ARCH					
arch					
L1.	.0600697	.0214917	2.80	0.005	.0179467 .1021927
L2.	.0629017	.0207973	3.02	0.002	.0221398 .1036637
L3.	.0136962	.0183856	0.74	0.456	-.0223388 .0497312
L4.	-.0159475	.0153219	-1.04	0.298	-.0459778 .0140828
L5.	.0233353	.0182654	1.28	0.201	-.0124642 .0591349
L6.	.0437856	.0186219	2.35	0.019	.0072874 .0802839
L7.	.0262186	.0183434	1.43	0.153	-.0097338 .0621711
L8.	.0141832	.0172145	0.82	0.410	-.0195565 .0479229
L9.	.061336	.0208329	2.94	0.003	.0205042 .1021678
L10.	.0256606	.018116	1.42	0.157	-.0098462 .0611674
L11.	.0193562	.014656	1.32	0.187	-.0093691 .0480815
L12.	.0793348	.0218597	3.63	0.000	.0364905 .122179
L13.	.0728871	.0179183	4.07	0.000	.0377678 .1080064
L14.	.0081259	.0182916	0.44	0.657	-.027725 .0439767
L15.	.0374053	.0200698	1.86	0.062	-.0019307 .0767413
_cons	.0001646	.0000166	9.89	0.000	.000132 .0001972

Finally, do the coefficients indicate stationarity?

```
. display [ARCH]L1.arch +   [ARCH]L2.arch + [ARCH]L3.arch + ///
>         [ARCH]L4.arch +   [ARCH]L5.arch + [ARCH]L6.arch + ///
>         [ARCH]L7.arch +   [ARCH]L8.arch + [ARCH]L9.arch + ///
>         [ARCH]L10.arch +  [ARCH]L11.arch + [ARCH]L12.arch + ///
>         [ARCH]L13.arch +  [ARCH]L14.arch + [ARCH]L15.arch
.53234879

. test [ARCH]L1.arch +    [ARCH]L2.arch + [ARCH]L3.arch + ///
>         [ARCH]L4.arch +   [ARCH]L5.arch + [ARCH]L6.arch + ///
>         [ARCH]L7.arch +   [ARCH]L8.arch + [ARCH]L9.arch + ///
>         [ARCH]L10.arch +  [ARCH]L11.arch + [ARCH]L12.arch + ///
>         [ARCH]L13.arch +  [ARCH]L14.arch + [ARCH]L15.arch = 1

 ( 1)   [ARCH]L.arch + [ARCH]L2.arch + [ARCH]L3.arch +
     [ARCH]L4.arch + [ARCH]L5.arch + [ARCH]L6.arch + [ARCH]L7.arch +
         [ARCH]L8.arch + [ARCH]L9.arch + [ARCH]L10.arch +
         [ARCH]L11.arch + [ARCH]L12.arch + [ARCH]L13.arch +
```

9.4 GARCH Models

```
[ARCH] L14.arch +
[ARCH] L15.arch = 1

   chi2(  1) =    73.66
 Prob > chi2 =    0.0000
```

Yes, the coefficients indicate a stationary model. The sum of the αs is less than one (it is 0.53) and is statistically different from one (we reject the null since $p < 0.05$).

As you can see, it is not uncommon to have to estimate very large ARCH models. We now turn to a related class of models, the so-called GARCH models, which are able to mimic many of the properties of large ARCH models without having to estimate quite as many parameters.

9.4 GARCH Models

ARCH models can capture many of the features of financial data, but doing so can require many lags in the variance equation. Bollerslev (1986) introduced a solution to this problem via a generalization of the ARCH model. This new model, called a GARCH(p,q) model, stands for "generalized autoregressive conditional heteroskedasticity," or "generalized ARCH." A GARCH model can mimic an infinite order ARCH model in the same way that an invertible MA process is equivalent to an infinite order AR process.

In the rest of this section we will explore the definition and estimation of a simple GARCH(1,1) model before turning to the more general GARCH(p,q) model.

9.4.1 GARCH(1,1)

Before we jump to the GARCH(1,1) model, let's rewrite the variance equation of our ARCH(1) model, usually

$$\epsilon_t = \left(\alpha_0 + \alpha_1 \epsilon_{t-1}^2\right)^{1/2} u_t, \tag{9.22}$$

as a two-equation model:

$$\epsilon_t = \left(\sigma_t^2\right)^{1/2} u_t = \sigma_t u_t \tag{9.23}$$

$$\sigma_t^2 = \alpha_0 + \alpha_1 \epsilon_{t-1}^2. \tag{9.24}$$

As we saw before, the conditional variance was equal to the term in parenthesis in (9.22), hence our choice of notation: $\sigma_t^2 = \left(\alpha_0 + \alpha_1 \epsilon_{t-1}^2\right)$.

The GARCH(1,1) model amounts to a small change in Eq. (9.24), adding the lagged variance:

$$\sigma_t^2 = \alpha_0 + \alpha_1 \epsilon_{t-1}^2 + \gamma \sigma_{t-1}^2. \tag{9.25}$$

This seemingly small addition actually captures an amazing degree of complexity over the ARCH(1) model. Lagging (9.25) by one period and substituting back into (9.25) several times yields

$$\sigma_t^2 = \alpha_0 + \alpha_1 \epsilon_{t-1}^2 + \gamma \left[\alpha_0 + \alpha_1 \epsilon_{t-2}^2 + \gamma \sigma_{t-2}^2 \right]$$

$$= \alpha_0 + \alpha_0 \gamma + \alpha_1 \epsilon_{t-1}^2 + \alpha_1 \gamma \epsilon_{t-2}^2 + \gamma^2 \left[\sigma_{t-2}^2 \right]$$

$$= \alpha_0 + \alpha_0 \gamma + \alpha_1 \epsilon_{t-1}^2 + \alpha_1 \gamma \epsilon_{t-2}^2 + \gamma^2 \left[\alpha_0 + \alpha_1 \epsilon_{t-3}^2 + \gamma \sigma_{t-3}^2 \right]$$

$$= \alpha_0 + \alpha_0 \gamma + \alpha_0 \gamma^2 + \alpha_1 \epsilon_{t-1}^2 + \alpha_1 \gamma \epsilon_{t-2}^2 + \alpha_1 \gamma^2 \epsilon_{t-3}^2 + \gamma^3 \left[\sigma_{t-3}^2 \right]$$

$$= \alpha_0 \sum_{i=0}^{2} \gamma^i + \alpha_1 \sum_{i=0}^{2} \gamma^i \epsilon_{t-i-1}^2 + \gamma^3 \left[\sigma_{t-3}^2 \right].$$

Repeating this procedure infinitely and changing notation appropriately yields

$$\sigma_t^2 = \hat{\alpha}_0 + \hat{\alpha}_1 \epsilon_{t-1}^2 + \hat{\alpha}_2 \epsilon_{t-2}^2 + \dots$$

$$= \hat{\alpha}_0 + \sum_{i=1}^{\infty} \hat{\alpha}_i \epsilon_{t-i}^2.$$

Thus, simply adding one term in (9.24) turns a finite order process into an infinite one. This allows us to capture a very complex process without needing to estimate tons of parameters; one special parameter pulls a lot of weight.

To summarize, the variance equations of the GARCH(1,1) model are

$$\epsilon_t = \sigma_t u_t \tag{9.26}$$

$$\sigma_t^2 = \alpha_0 + \alpha_1 \epsilon_{t-1}^2 + \gamma \sigma_{t-1}^2. \tag{9.27}$$

Simulating the Process
```
. drop _all
. set obs 5000
. set seed 12345
. gen time = _n
. tsset time

. * Defining the parameters
. local beta0 = 10
. local alpha0 = 0.2
. local alpha1 = 0.4
. local gamma = 0.6
```

9.4 GARCH Models

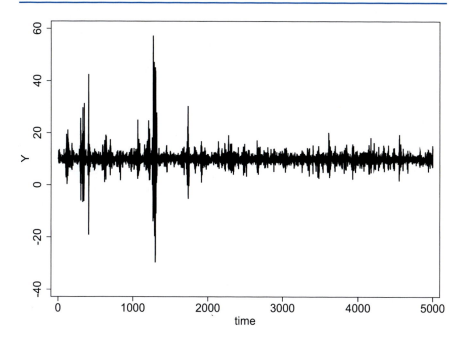

Fig. 9.11 Simulated GARCH(1,1) process

```
. * Initializing
. gen u = rnormal(0,1)
. gen e = .
. replace e = 0 in 1
. gen e2 = .
. replace e2 = e^2
. gen sigma2 = .
. replace sigma2 = 1 in 1

. * Generating the GARCH errors
. forvalues i=2/'=_N'{
     replace sigma2 = 'alpha0' + 'alpha1'*L.e2 +
   'gamma'*L.sigma2 in 'i'
     replace e = sqrt(sigma2)*u in 'i'
     replace e2 = e^2 in 'i'
. }

. * The mean equation
. gen Y = 'beta0' + e
```

The data are graphed in Fig. 9.11. We can estimate the model in Stata by

```
. arch Y , arch(1) garch(1)

ARCH family regression

Sample:  1 - 5000                               Number of obs   =       5,000
Distribution: Gaussian                          Wald chi2(.)    =           .
Log likelihood = -9828.683                      Prob > chi2     =           .

------------------------------------------------------------------------------
             |                 OPG
           Y |      Coef.   Std. Err.      z    P>|z|     [95% Conf. Interval]
-------------+----------------------------------------------------------------
Y            |
       _cons |   9.992245   .0177712   562.27   0.000     9.957415    10.02708
-------------+----------------------------------------------------------------
ARCH         |
        arch |
         L1. |   .4125879   .0221252    18.65   0.000     .3692232    .4559525
             |
       garch |
         L1. |   .5856877    .016295    35.94   0.000     .5537501    .6176253
             |
       _cons |   .1981093   .0210514     9.41   0.000     .1568492    .2393693
------------------------------------------------------------------------------
```

The true mean equation consisted of only $\beta_0=10$ plus error; it was estimated at 9.992. The constant in the variance equation, α_1, was set at 0.20 and was estimated as 0.198, $\alpha_1 = 0.40$ was estimated as 0.412, and $\gamma_1 = 0.60$ was estimated as 0.586.

9.4.2 GARCH(p,q)

In general, GARCH(p,q) models have the following variance equations:

$$\epsilon_t = \sigma_t u_t \tag{9.28}$$

$$\sigma_t^2 = \left[\alpha_0 + \alpha_1 \epsilon_{t-1}^2 + \alpha_2 \epsilon_{t-1}^2 \ldots + \alpha_p \epsilon_{t-p}^2\right] \tag{9.29}$$
$$+ \left[\gamma_1 \sigma_{t-1}^2 + \gamma_2 \sigma_{t-2}^2 + \ldots + \gamma_q \sigma_{t-q}^2\right]$$

In practice, it is rare for stock returns to require more than two lags in the ARCH and GARCH components (i.e., $p \leq 2$ and $q \leq 2$). Exceptions to this are often due to model misspecification. For example, if day-of-the-week effects are ignored, the standard model selection techniques will falsely prefer larger GARCH models (Bollerslev, Chou and Kroner 1992).

9.4 GARCH Models

Example: GARCH(2,1) on Simulated Data

First, we will go through the process of identifying and estimating a GARCH model with simulated data. This gives us the benefit of knowing exactly what the correct parameter values are. In this example, we will estimate 100,000 observations (a large number) from the following GARCH model:

$$Y_t = 0.10 + \epsilon_t$$

$$\epsilon_t = \sigma_t u_t$$

$$\sigma_t^2 = 0.10 + 0.20 e_{t-1}^2 + 0.30 e_{t-2}^2 + 0.20 \sigma_{t-1}^2$$

$$u_t \sim N(0, 1).$$

We simulate the data in Stata using

```
. drop _all
. set obs 100000
. set seed 345
. gen time = _n
. tsset time

. gen u = rnormal(0,1)
. gen e = .
. replace e = 0 in 1/3
. gen e2 = .
. replace e2 = e^2
. gen sigma2 = .
. replace sigma2 = 1 in 1/3

. quietly{
    forvalues i=4/`=_N'{
        replace sigma2 =  0.10 + 0.20*L.e2 + ///
            0.30*L2.e2 + 0.20*L1.sigma2 in `i'
        replace e = sqrt(sigma2)*u in `i'
        replace e2 = e^2 in `i'
    }
}

. gen Y = 0.10 + e
```

Of course in practice, we do not have the luxury of knowing what the true model is. We will continue as though we are agnostic of the true nature of the data.

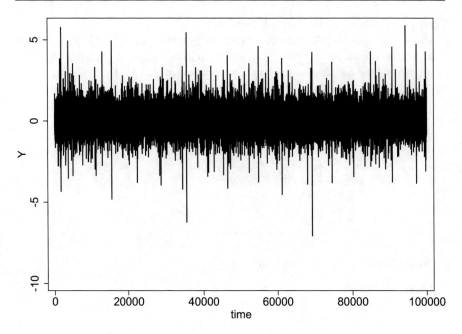

Fig. 9.12 Simulated GARCH(2,1) process

It is always best to begin by graphing the data. (See Fig. 9.12.) At least visually, there seems to be volatility clustering. We can formally test and confirm the presence of volatility clustering using the Ljung-Box:

```
. quietly reg Y
. predict v, resid
. gen v2 = v^2
. wntestq v2

Portmanteau test for white noise
---------------------------------------
Portmanteau (Q) statistic =   34352.3552
Prob > chi2(40)           =       0.0000
```

Given that there is volatility clustering, which type of model best fits our data? An ARCH(1)? A GARCH(2,1)? We estimate several such models and choose the one with the lowest AIC or BIC. The AICs and BICs are summarized in Table 9.2. Both information criteria choose the correct model, indicating that GARCH(2,1) fits best.

Now we can estimate the model.

9.4 GARCH Models

Table 9.2 Lag selection for simulated GARCH(2,1) data

p	q	AIC	BIC
1	0	163040.2	163068.7
1	1	153556.7	153594.7
1	2	152639.6	152687.2
2	0	152388.3	152426.3
2	**1**	**151739.6**	**151787.2**
2	2	151739.8	151796.9

```
. arch Y , arch(1/2) garch(1/1)

ARCH family regression

Sample: 1 - 100000                        Number of obs   =    100,000
Distribution: Gaussian                    Wald chi2(.)    =          .
Log likelihood = -75864.79                Prob > chi2     =          .

------------------------------------------------------------------------------
             |                 OPG
           Y |    Coef.    Std. Err.     z     P>|z|    [95% Conf. Interval]
-------------+----------------------------------------------------------------
Y            |
       _cons |  .0994767   .0014199    70.06   0.000    .0966936    .1022597
-------------+----------------------------------------------------------------
ARCH         |
        arch |
         L1. |  .1969713   .0046604    42.26   0.000    .187837    .2061056
         L2. |  .2997546   .0067189    44.61   0.000    .2865858   .3129234
             |
       garch |
         L1. |  .2003644   .0091497    21.90   0.000    .1824312   .2182975
             |
       _cons |  .1003524   .0018026    55.67   0.000    .0968193   .1038855
------------------------------------------------------------------------------
```

After estimation, it is best to conduct some post-estimation tests. Do the residuals indicate any leftover volatility clustering (via a Ljung-Box test)? If so, then a more flexible ARCH/GARCH model might have been preferred.

```
* Left-over volatility via Ljung-Box test:
. predict w, resid
. predict sigma2, variance
. gen w2 = (w^2)/sigma2

. wntestq w2

Portmanteau test for white noise
---------------------------------------
Portmanteau (Q) statistic =     39.7865
Prob > chi2(40)           =      0.4798
```

There does not seem to be any leftover autocorrelated variance.

Finally, is the model stationary?

```
. test    [ARCH]L1.arch + [ARCH]L2.arch + [ARCH]L1.garch = 1

 ( 1)    [ARCH]L.arch + [ARCH]L2.arch + [ARCH]L.garch = 1

            chi2( 1) =  1820.17
          Prob > chi2 =    0.0000
```

The model is stationary. We conclude that there were GARCH effects in the data and that our model has properly captured them.

Example: GARCH(p,q) on IBM Data

Let's try an example on some real data. Download the daily prices of IBM stocks for January 1st, 2000, through December 31st, 2010. From these calculate the percentage daily returns using the log-difference method. Use a Ljung-Box test to determine whether these daily returns exhibit volatility clustering. Given your results, estimate an appropriate GARCH(p,q) model for these; restrict your attention to $p \leq 2$ and $q \leq 2$. Defend your choice of model. Finally, test whether the ARCH and GARCH coefficients were jointly significant.

First, we download and format the data:

```
. drop _all
. fetchyahooquotes IBM, freq(d) start(01jan2001)
   end(31dec2010)
. gen time = _n
. tsset time
. gen IBM = ln(adjclose_IBM) - ln(L.adjclose_IBM)
```

We test for volatility clustering using a Ljung-Box test on the unstandardized squared residuals:

```
. quietly reg IBM
. predict e, resid
. gen e2 = e^2
. wntestq e2

Portmanteau test for white noise
---------------------------------------
  Portmanteau (Q) statistic =  1466.1900
  Prob > chi2(40)           =     0.0000
```

The Ljung-Box test indicates that there is volatility clustering: an ARCH or GARCH model would be useful.

Following this, we need to determine what lag lengths would best fit the ARCH/GARCH models. Thus, we estimate $p \times (q+1) = 2 \times 3 = 6$ GARCH(p,q) models and estimate their AICs and BICs. The results are summarized in Table 9.3. The AIC selects a GARCH(2,2) model, while the BIC selects a more

9.4 GARCH Models

Table 9.3 Lag selection for GARCH(p,q) model of IBM

ARCH(p)	GARCH(q)	AIC	BIC
1	0	−13686.909	−13669.420
1	1	−14223.317	**−14199.998**
1	2	−14222.660	−14193.512
2	0	−13873.394	−13850.075
2	1	−14224.870	−14195.722
2	2	**−14229.75**	−14194.772

parsimonious GARCH(1,1) model. (Stock returns are quite commonly found to resemble GARCH(1,1) processes.) We opt for parsimony here, but it would be useful in practice to estimate both models and see whether they provide conflicting results. Also, it is often the case that post-estimation tests will indicate a preference for one of the two models.

We are now ready to report the estimated GARCH(1,1) model:

```
. arch IBM, arch(1) garch(1) nolog
ARCH family regression

Sample: 2 - 2515                          Number of obs   =     2,514
Distribution: Gaussian                    Wald chi2(.)    =         .
Log likelihood =  7115.458                Prob > chi2     =         .

------------------------------------------------------------------------------
             |                 OPG
         IBM |      Coef.   Std. Err.      z    P>|z|     [95% Conf. Interval]
-------------+----------------------------------------------------------------
IBM          |
       _cons |   .0005984   .0002245     2.67   0.008     .0001584    .0010383
-------------+----------------------------------------------------------------
ARCH         |
        arch |
         L1. |   .1087662   .0081259    13.39   0.000     .0928397    .1246928
             |
       garch |
         L1. |   .8756493   .0084696   103.39   0.000     .8590493    .8922494
             |
       _cons |   4.76e-06   6.10e-07     7.81   0.000     3.57e-06    5.96e-06
------------------------------------------------------------------------------
```

As a standard post-estimation step, we perform another Ljung-Box test, this time on the standardized squared residuals. If there is no detectable leftover volatility clustering, this indicates that the estimated model is adequate.

```
. predict w, resid
(1 missing value generated)

. predict sigma2, variance
```

```
. gen w2 = (w^2)/sigma2
(1 missing value generated)

. wntestq w2

Portmanteau test for white noise
-----------------------------------------
 Portmanteau (Q) statistic =      27.1280
 Prob > chi2(40)           =       0.9399
```

The Ljung-Box Q^2 test indicates that there is no significant volatility clustering in the residuals. That is, the model is able to capture the vast majority of the conditional heteroskedasticity.

Finally, we test whether the estimated model is stationary.

```
. test [ARCH]L1.arch + [ARCH]L1.garch =1

 ( 1)  [ARCH]L.arch + [ARCH]L.garch = 1

         chi2( 1) =    12.07
       Prob > chi2 =    0.0005
```

Thus, we reject the null hypothesis that the true parameters add up to one or greater: the estimated model is stationary.

9.5 Variations on GARCH

In general, research has been pushing on the margins of GARCH modeling, not by adding additional lags onto the ARCH or GARCH components of the general model, but mainly by tweaking the restrictions on the coefficients. First, in Sect. 9.5.1 we present the GARCH-t model. This is a simple modification where the errors come from Student's t distribution, rather than from a normal distribution. Then, in Sect. 9.5.2 we present the GARCH-M model. This model alters the mean equation so that the mean depends directly upon the variance of the process. In Sect. 9.5.3, we turn to a class of models where positive and negative shocks have asymmetric responses (GJR-GARCH, E-GARCH, and T-GARCH). Finally, in Sect. 9.5.4 we close with the integrated GARCH model (I-GARCH).

9.5.1 GARCH-t

Up until this point, our models have presumed that the errors were drawn from a normal distribution. Bollerslev (1987) developed a version of his GARCH model

9.5 Variations on GARCH

where the errors come from a t-distribution. This was because previous research[5] had indicated that various financial time series—such as foreign exchange rates and major stock market indices—exhibited more leptokurtosis than the standard GARCH models were able to mimic.

It is quite easy to force Stata to draw its errors from a t rather than a normal distribution, by adding "distribution(t #)" as an option. For example, to estimate a GARCH(1,1)-t model, where the errors come from a t-distribution with five degrees of freedom, the command would be

. arch Y, arch(1) garch(1) distribution(t 5)

Alternatively, you can leave the degrees of freedom unspecified and have STATA estimate it:

. arch Y, arch(1) garch(1) distribution(t)

Replicating Bollerslev's (1987) GARCH(1,1)-t Model

In this subsection, we will replicate Bollerslev's results from his 1987 GARCH-t paper. Bollerslev estimates the following model:

$$Y_t = \beta_0 + \epsilon_t$$
$$\epsilon_t = \sigma_t u_t$$
$$\sigma_t^2 = \alpha_0 + \alpha_1 \epsilon_{t-1}^2 + \gamma \sigma_{t-1}^2$$
$$u \sim t(v)$$

where Y_t is either the Dollar-Pound or the Dollar-Deutsche Mark exchange rate.

We will replicate Bollerslev's results in the following order. For each variable, we will first establish that the variable likely has GARCH effects and excess kurtosis which justify estimating a GARCH-t model. Second, we estimate the model. From the model, we generate the residuals and predicted variance. We then show that the estimated GARCH-t model fits the data well, by establishing that the standardized residuals and standardized squared residuals do not exhibit any remaining GARCH effects or excess kurtosis.

First, we load the dataset and calculate the continuously compounded rate of return:

. use Bollerslev1987.dta, clear
. gen Y = ln(USUK) - ln(L.USUK)

---

[5] Bollerslev points to Milhøj (1987), Hsieh (1988), and McCurdy and Morgan (1985).

Then we test for GARCH effects and excess kurtosis:

```
. qui reg Y
. qui predict e, resid
. qui gen e2 = e^2
. wntestq e, lags(10)

Portmanteau test for white noise
---------------------------------------
 Portmanteau (Q) statistic =      7.6327
 Prob > chi2(10)           =      0.6647


. wntestq e2, lags(10)

Portmanteau test for white noise
---------------------------------------
 Portmanteau (Q) statistic =     74.8108
 Prob > chi2(10)           =      0.0000


. qui drop e e2

. tabstat Y, statistics(kurtosis)

    variable |  kurtosis
-------------+----------
           Y |  4.813832
------------------------
```

We should note that Bollerslev did not justify his choice of ten lags in the Ljung-Box tests, and we are simply following his choice. GARCH effects seem to be evident, and the large kurtosis implies that errors from a t-distribution would yield a better fit than a normal distribution.

We then estimate a GARCH(1,1) model with t-errors, calculate the residuals, and predict the variance:

```
. arch Y, arch(1) garch(1) distribution(t) nolog
. qui predict e, resid
. qui predict v, variance
```

9.5 Variations on GARCH

The output of the GARCH(1,1)-t estimation is

```
ARCH family regression

Sample: 2 - 1245                              Number of obs   =    1,244
Distribution: t                               Wald chi2(.)    =        .
Log likelihood =   4547.91                    Prob > chi2     =        .
```

	|	Coef.	OPG Std. Err.	z	P>|z|	[95% Conf. Interval]	
Y	|						
_cons	|	-.0004567	.0001672	-2.73	0.006	-.0007843	-.000129
ARCH	|						
arch L1.	| |	.0555282	.0161889	3.43	0.001	.0237986	.0872578
garch L1.	| |	.9235369	.022146	41.70	0.000	.8801316	.9669423
_cons	|	9.20e-07	4.48e-07	2.05	0.040	4.13e-08	1.80e-06
/lndfm2	|	1.809597	.2639147	6.86	0.000	1.292334	2.32686
df	|	8.107986	1.611987			5.641274	12.24572

Did GARCH(1,1)-t fit the data well? To answer this, we calculate the standardized residuals. We then subject the standardized residuals to the same tests (Q, Q^2, and kurtosis) to see whether we have properly accounted for time-varying volatility and thick-tailed returns.

```
. qui gen eSqrtV = e/sqrt(v)
. qui gen e2v = (e/sqrt(v))^2
. wntestq eSqrtV, lags(10)

Portmanteau test for white noise
-----------------------------------------
   Portmanteau (Q) statistic =     4.3287
   Prob > chi2(10)           =     0.9313

. wntestq e2v, lags(10)
```

```
Portmanteau test for white noise
-----------------------------------------
Portmanteau (Q) statistic =      8.5941
Prob > chi2(10)           =      0.5710

. tabstat eSqrtV, statistics(kurtosis)

    variable |   kurtosis
-------------+----------
      eSqrtV |   4.626597
------------------------
```

There is no leftover autocorrelation in the standardized squared residuals, so we draw the same conclusion as did Bollerslev: a GARCH(1,1) model with t-errors describes the dynamics of the Dollar-Pound exchange rate quite well.

We now undertake the same exercise on the Dollar-Deutsche Mark exchange rate.

```
. gen Y = ln(USDE) - ln(L.USDE)

. * Pre-tests: Unconditional Ljung-Box stats (Q and Q2) and Kurtosis
. qui reg Y
. qui predict e, resid
. qui gen e2 = e^2
. wntestq e, lags(10)

Portmanteau test for white noise
---------------------------------------
Portmanteau (Q) statistic =    9.1540
Prob > chi2(10)           =    0.5176

. wntestq e2, lags(10)

Portmanteau test for white noise
---------------------------------------
Portmanteau (Q) statistic =  133.1126
Prob > chi2(10)           =    0.0000

. qui drop e e2
```

9.5 Variations on GARCH

```
. tabstat Y, statistics(kurtosis)


    variable |  kurtosis
-------------+----------
           Y |   4.20499
------------------------


. * Garch(1,1)-t estimate
. arch Y, arch(1) garch(1) distribution(t) nolog

ARCH family regression

Sample: 2 - 1245                                Number of obs   =      1,244
Distribution: t                                 Wald chi2(.)    =          .
Log likelihood =   4471.78                      Prob > chi2     =          .

------------------------------------------------------------------------------
             |                 OPG
           Y |      Coef.   Std. Err.      z    P>|z|     [95% Conf. Interval]
-------------+----------------------------------------------------------------
Y            |
       _cons |  -.0005842   .0001782    -3.28   0.001    -.0009334    -.000235
-------------+----------------------------------------------------------------
ARCH         |
        arch |
         L1. |   .0949339   .0211911     4.48   0.000     .0534001    .1364676
             |
       garch |
         L1. |   .8802083   .0271853    32.38   0.000     .8269261    .9334904
             |
       _cons |   1.32e-06   5.92e-07     2.24   0.025     1.65e-07    2.48e-06
-------------+----------------------------------------------------------------
     /lndfm2 |   2.470069   .3592218     6.88   0.000     1.766007     3.17413
-------------+----------------------------------------------------------------
          df |   13.82326   4.247172                      7.847456    25.90602
------------------------------------------------------------------------------

. * Post-tests: Ljung-Box on stdized residuals and stdized-squared residuals.
. qui predict e, resid
. qui predict v, variance
. qui gen eSqrtV = e/sqrt(v)
. qui gen e2v = (eSqrtV)^2

. wntestq eSqrtV, lags(10)

Portmanteau test for white noise
---------------------------------------
 Portmanteau (Q) statistic =     7.6959
 Prob > chi2(10)           =     0.6585
```

```
. wntestq e2v, lags(10)

Portmanteau test for white noise
---------------------------------------
Portmanteau (Q) statistic =      9.5192
Prob > chi2(10)           =      0.4836

. * Conditional kurtosis?
. tabstat eSqrtV, statistics(kurtosis)

    variable |  kurtosis
-------------+----------
      eSqrtV |  3.762958
------------------------
```

The standardized residuals and squared standardized residuals are indistinguishable from white noise, indicating that the estimated GARCH-t model fits the data quite well.

Bollerslev also estimated a model on various stock indices including daily S&P-500 returns. We leave this as an exercise for the reader.

9.5.2 GARCH-M or GARCH-IN-MEAN

There are no free lunches in economics. This truism also holds in finance: higher rewards require higher risks. No one would undertake additional, unnecessary risk unless they were compensated with the prospect of additional returns. When purchasing stocks, for example, risk is a direct function of the conditional variance of the underlying stock. A regression that was attempting to estimate the returns on a stock must, therefore, have a term related to the conditional variance (σ^2) in its mean equation. In GARCH-M (aka GARCH-in-mean) models, the variance is an explicit term in the mean equation:

$$y_t = \beta X + \lambda \sigma_t + \epsilon_t \tag{9.30}$$

The variance equation can be any of the variance equations that we have seen.

The idea of including the variance in-mean is due to Engle et al. (1987) in the context of ARCH-M models, French et al. (1987) for GARCH-M models, and Bollerslev et al. (1988) for multivariate GARCH-M models.

To estimate the following GARCH(1,1)-in-mean model:

$$y_t = \beta_0 + \beta_1 X + \lambda \sigma_t + \epsilon_t$$

$$\epsilon_t = \sigma_t u_t$$

$$\sigma_t^2 = \alpha_0 + \alpha_1 \epsilon_{t-1}^2 + \gamma \sigma_{t-1}^2,$$

9.5 Variations on GARCH

the command is

. arch y X, arch(1) garch(1) archm

The `archm` option specifies that the mean equation includes the conditional variance.

More general GARCH-M models simply include more lags of the variance:

$$y_t = \beta X + \sum_{l=1}^{L} \lambda_l \sigma_{t-l} + \epsilon_t. \tag{9.31}$$

To estimate a model with two lags of the conditional variance in the mean equation, such as

$$y_t = \beta_0 + \beta_1 X + \lambda_1 \sigma_t + \lambda_2 \sigma_{t-1} + \epsilon_t$$

$$\epsilon_t = \sigma_t u_t$$

$$\sigma_t^2 = \alpha_0 + \alpha_1 \epsilon_{t-1}^2 + \gamma \sigma_{t-1}^2,$$

there are two options available:

. arch y X, arch(1) garch(1) archm archmlags(1)

where `archmlags(1)` specifies that one additional lag is to be included, or

. arch y X, arch(1) garch(1) archmlags(0/1).

Including zero inside the `archmlags()` option is redundant with `archm`.

It is quite uncommon to see lags of the conditional variance greater than two. Many models include only the first lag of the variance.

In the example below, we download return data for the Dow Jones Industrial Index, the S&P-500, and the NASDAQ Composite indexes, estimate a GARCH(1,1)-M(1) model, and compare their estimates of the coefficient of relative risk aversion.

Example: GARCH-M in Stock Index Returns

In this example, we will explore the performance and implications of the GARCH-M model in predicting excess returns in the major US equity markets. The reason why risk and return must balance each other is because people are generally averse to risk.

According to the standard capital asset pricing model,[6] there is a linear relationship between mean return and variance; this relationship is equivalent to the coefficient of relative risk aversion. In GARCH-M models where the dependent variable y_t is the mean equity return, λ estimates the linear relationship between mean return and variance and is therefore also an estimate of the coefficient of

---

[6] The standard references include Sharpe (1964), Lintner (1965), and Merton (1973, 1980).

relative risk aversion. Risk-averse investors will require higher average returns to compensate for volatility and will therefore have higher λs.

We begin by loading the dataset. The file contains the daily closing prices of the Dow Jones Industrial Average, the S&P-500, and the NASDAQ Composite, for January 1st, 1960, through December 31st, 2012. Also included is an estimate of the "risk-free rate" of return, as calculated by Kenneth French.

```
. use "GARCH-M example.dta", clear
```

Calculate the excess rates of return for the three stock market indices:

```
. gen retDJIA = log(DJIA) - log(L.DJIA) - ff3_RF
. gen retSP = log(SP) - log(L.SP)    - ff3_RF
. gen retNASDAQ = log(NASDAQ) - log(L.NASDAQ) - ff3_RF
```

And then estimate GARCH(1,1)-M models of these excess returns:

```
. qui arch retDJIA, arch(1) garch(1) archm
. estimates store DJIA
. qui arch retSP, arch(1) garch(1) archm
. estimates store SP
. qui arch retNASDAQ, arch(1) garch(1) archm
. estimates store NASDAQ
. esttab DJIA SP NASDAQ,   star(* 0.10 ** 0.05 *** 0.01)
```

	(1) retDJIA	(2) retSP	(3) retNASDAQ
main			
_cons	0.0000798	0.000141	0.000336***
	(0.79)	(1.55)	(3.50)
ARCHM			
sigma2	2.979**	2.633**	1.639*
	(2.36)	(2.23)	(1.86)
ARCH			
L.arch	0.0827***	0.0885***	0.111***
	(47.73)	(45.78)	(32.16)
L.garch	0.909***	0.907***	0.882***
	(350.56)	(361.21)	(240.99)
_cons	0.00000100***	0.000000755***	0.00000130***
	(11.05)	(10.23)	(13.18)
N	13309	13309	10564

t statistics in parentheses
* p<0.10, ** p<0.05, *** p<0.01

9.5 Variations on GARCH

We estimate the coefficient of relative risk aversion to be between 1.6 and 2.9, depending on which equity market is in our sample.

This relative consistency in the estimated in-mean risk-aversion parameter is a little uncommon. French et al. (1987) estimate a GARCH-M model on NYSE and S&P returns over several different time periods. Their estimates of λ vary considerably (between 0.6 and 7.8).[7] Baillie & DeGennaro (1990) reestimate the GARCH-M models of French, Schwert, and Stambaugh but assume a t-distributed error term. They find that the in-mean term is insignificant. In general, the evidence supporting CAPM has been mixed.

9.5.3 Asymmetric Responses in GARCH

In this subsection we discuss three variations to the standard GARCH model which are designed to capture an asymmetric response to new information. In finance, the arrival of new information is usually considered to be an unexpected event and is therefore a component of the error term. Many researchers, and investors for that matter, have noticed that volatility can rise quite rapidly and unexpectedly, but it does not dampen quite as quickly as it rises. That is, there is an asymmetric volatility response to the error term. The models that we discuss attempt to capture this phenomenon in slightly different ways.

GJR-GARCH

Our standard GARCH(1,1) variance equation was Eq. (9.24), which we repeat here for convenience:

$$\sigma_t^2 = \alpha_0 + \alpha_1 \epsilon_{t-1}^2 + \gamma_1 \sigma_{t-1}^2. \tag{9.32}$$

Glosten et al. (1993) altered this equation by decomposing the effect of ϵ_{t-1}^2 into the sum of two different effects via a dummy-variable interaction:

$$\sigma_t^2 = \alpha_0 + \alpha_1 \epsilon_{t-1}^2 + \alpha_2 D_{t-1} \epsilon_{t-1}^2 + \gamma_1 \sigma_{t-1}^2 \tag{9.33}$$

$$D_{t-1} = \begin{cases} 1, & \text{if } \epsilon \geq 0 \\ 0, & \text{otherwise.} \end{cases} \tag{9.34}$$

In this way, when the error is positive, the dummy variable D_{t-1} is equal to one, and

$$\sigma_t^2 = \alpha_0 + (\alpha_1 + \alpha_2) \epsilon_{t-1}^2 + \gamma_1 \sigma_{t-1}^2,$$

---

[7] In response, Chou et al. (1992) developed a variation of GARCH-M called TVP-GARCH-M that allows λ to vary over time, essentially modeling λ_t as a random walk.

and when the error is negative, $D_{t-1} = 0$ and

$$\sigma_t^2 = \alpha_0 + \alpha_1 \epsilon_{t-1}^2 + \gamma_1 \sigma_{t-1}^2.$$

To estimate a GJR-GARCH model in Stata, simply modify the usual `arch` command syntax by indicating which lags of the ARCH term require interacting with a dummy variable. This is done via the `tarch()` option in:

.arch depvar [indepvars], arch(numlist) garch(numlist) tarch(numlist)

For example, to estimate the GJR-GARCH(1,1) above,

. arch y, arch(1) garch(1) tarch(1)

To estimate a GJR-GARCH(2,1) model such as

$$\sigma_t^2 = \alpha_0 + \left(\alpha_1 \epsilon_{t-1}^2 + \alpha_2 D_{t-1} \epsilon_{t-1}^2\right) + \left(\alpha_3 \epsilon_{t-2}^2 + \alpha_4 D_{t-2} \epsilon_{t-2}^2\right) + \gamma_1 \sigma_{t-1}^2$$

$$D_{t-1} = \begin{cases} 1, & \text{if } \epsilon_{t-1} \geq 0 \\ 0, & \text{otherwise} \end{cases}$$

$$D_{t-2} = \begin{cases} 1, & \text{if } \epsilon_{t-2} \geq 0 \\ 0, & \text{otherwise} \end{cases}$$

the syntax would be

. arch y, arch(1/2) garch(1) tarch(1/2)

The syntax is sufficiently flexible to allow for the dummy variable to affect all or the ARCH terms, or only some of them. It would be difficult to find a theoretical justification as to why the asymmetry would only affect some time periods versus others, so on a priori grounds, the set of lags in the `tarch()` option should be the same as those in the `arch()` option. Occasionally, a researcher chooses to interact only the first lag and leave the other lagged ϵ^2 terms as symmetric. This is usually done if the researcher is trying to economize on degrees of freedom.

Thus, to estimate a GJR-GARCH(2,1) model where only the first lag is asymmetric:

$$\sigma_t^2 = \alpha_0 + \left(\alpha_1 \epsilon_{t-1}^2 + \alpha_2 D_{t-1} \epsilon_{t-1}^2\right) + \alpha_3 \epsilon_{t-2}^2 + \gamma_1 \sigma_{t-1}^2$$

$$D_t = \begin{cases} 1, & \text{if } \epsilon_t \geq 0 \\ 0, & \text{otherwise} \end{cases}$$

the syntax would be

. arch y, arch(1/2) garch(1) tarch(1)

9.5 Variations on GARCH

In this case, α_1 and α_3 are the coefficients from arch(1/2), α_2 is the coefficient from tarch(1), and γ_1 is the coefficient from garch(1).

E-GARCH

Another form of asymmetric GARCH model is Nelson's (1991) exponential GARCH, or "E-GARCH" model. E-GARCH(1,1) makes several changes to the standard variance equation (9.24), which we repeat here for convenience:

$$\sigma_t^2 = \alpha_0 + \alpha_1 \epsilon_{t-1}^2 + \gamma_1 \sigma_{t-1}^2. \tag{9.35}$$

First, it replaces the variances—the σ_t^2 terms—with their logarithms. Second, it a nonlinear response to news (i.e., the "shocks," error terms, or the ϵ_ts). Specifically, it replaces $\alpha_1 \epsilon_t^2$ with a function $g(z_{t-1})$:

$$g(z_{t-1}) = \alpha_{11} z_{t-1} + \alpha_{12} (|z_{t-1}| - E|z_{t-1}|) \tag{9.36}$$

where $z_{t-1} = \epsilon_{t-1}/\sigma_{t-1}$ so that $z_{t-1} \sim N(0, 1)$. Since z_{t-1} is a standard normal variable, its moments are well known.[8] For example, it is known that $E|z_{t-1}| = \sqrt{2/\pi}$. Therefore, after substitution, (9.36) becomes

$$g(z_{t-1}) = \alpha_{11} z_{t-1} + \alpha_{12} \left(|z_{t-1}| - \sqrt{2/\pi}\right) \tag{9.37}$$

and (9.35) becomes

$$\ln\left(\sigma_t^2\right) = \alpha_0 + \alpha_{11} z_{t-1} + \alpha_{12} \left(|z_{t-1}| - \sqrt{2/\pi}\right) + \gamma_1 \ln\left(\sigma_{t-1}^2\right). \tag{9.38}$$

Equation (9.37) models an asymmetric response to positive and negative shocks since

$$g(z_t) = \begin{cases} (\alpha_{11} + \alpha_{12}) z_t - \alpha_{12}\sqrt{2/\pi}, & \text{if } \epsilon_t \geq 0 \\ (\alpha_{11} - \alpha_{12}) z_t - \alpha_{12}\sqrt{2/\pi}, & \text{otherwise.} \end{cases}$$

To estimate the E-GARCH(1,1) model, whose variance equation is Eq. (9.38), the Stata command is

. arch depvar [indepvars], earch(1) egarch(1)

the output of which is presented in several parts. First, the parameters of the mean equation are shown. This is followed by the parameters from the variance equations. The parameters from Eq. (9.37) are shown as L1.earch and L1.earch_a. Specifically, L1.earch $= \alpha_{11}$ and L1.earch_a $= \alpha_{12}$.

---

[8] When $X \sim N(\mu, \sigma)$, $|X|$ has a "folded normal distribution." When $\mu = 0$, the distribution of $|X|$ is commonly known as the "half normal distribution."

E-GARCH models with more lags can be handled easily. The variance equation of a general E-GARCH(p,q) model is

$$\ln(\sigma_t^2) = \alpha_0 + \sum_{i=1}^{p}\left(\alpha_{i1}z_{t-i} + \alpha_{i2}\left(|z_{t-i}| - \sqrt{2/\pi}\right)\right) + \sum_{j=1}^{q}\gamma_j \ln(\sigma_{t-j}^2)$$
(9.39)

and is estimated with
- `arch depvar [indepvars], earch(1/p) egarch(1/q)`

That is, to add additional lags of the logged variance, just add terms to the `egarch` option. To add additional lags of z, the standardized residual, just add terms to the `earch` option.

Stata reports the coefficients of these in blocks. For each lag there are two `earch` components: the coefficient on lagged z (`L.earch`) and the coefficient on the absolute value of lagged z (`L.earch_a`).

This will make more sense with an example. Below, we generated data from the following model:

$$Y_t = \beta_0 + \epsilon_t$$

$$\epsilon_t = \sigma_t u_t$$

$$u_t \sim N(0,1)$$

with variance equation

$$\ln(\sigma_t^2) = \alpha_0 + \sum_{i=1}^{2}\left(\alpha_{i1}z_{t-i} + \alpha_{i2}\left(|z_{t-i}| - \sqrt{2/\pi}\right)\right) + \sum_{j=1}^{3}\gamma_j \ln(\sigma_{t-j}^2)$$

$$= \alpha_0 + \left(\alpha_{11}z_{t-1} + \alpha_{12}\left(|z_{t-1}| - \sqrt{2/\pi}\right)\right)$$

$$+ \left(\alpha_{21}z_{t-2} + \alpha_{22}\left(|z_{t-2}| - \sqrt{2/\pi}\right)\right)$$

$$+ \gamma_1 \ln(\sigma_{t-1}^2) + \gamma_2 \ln(\sigma_{t-2}^2) + \gamma_3 \ln(\sigma_{t-3}^2).$$

We generated the data using the following parameter values:

$\beta_0 = 0.10$ $\alpha_0 = 0.05$ $\alpha_{11} = 0.20$
$\alpha_{12} = 0.15$ $\alpha_{21} = 0.10$ $\alpha_{22} = 0.05$
$\gamma_1 = 0.15$ $\gamma_2 = 0.10$ $\gamma_3 = 0.05$

After generating the data (not shown), we estimate the model using
- `arch Y , earch(1/2) egarch(1/3)`

9.5 Variations on GARCH

the output of which is

```
ARCH family regression

Sample: 1 - 100000                              Number of obs   =     100000
Distribution: Gaussian                          Wald chi2(.)    =          .
Log likelihood = -144907.7                      Prob > chi2     =          .

------------------------------------------------------------------------------
             |                 OPG
           Y |      Coef.   Std. Err.      z    P>|z|     [95% Conf. Interval]
-------------+----------------------------------------------------------------
Y            |
       _cons |   .0947765   .0031957    29.66   0.000     .0885131    .1010399
-------------+----------------------------------------------------------------
ARCH         |
       earch |
         L1. |   .2103571   .0044889    46.86   0.000      .201559    .2191553
         L2. |   .1324385   .0219038     6.05   0.000     .0895079    .1753692
             |
     earch_a |
         L1. |   .1468577   .0073044    20.11   0.000     .1325414     .161174
         L2. |   .0610908   .0169639     3.60   0.000     .0278421    .0943394
             |
      egarch |
         L1. |   .0214899   .1031839     0.21   0.835    -.1807468    .2237267
         L2. |   .1651247   .0654789     2.52   0.012     .0367883     .293461
         L3. |   .0608116   .0226532     2.68   0.007     .0164122    .1052111
             |
       _cons |   .0453114   .0051388     8.82   0.000     .0352396    .0553832
------------------------------------------------------------------------------
```

The following should help you map the coefficients and the Stata output:

$$\hat{\beta}_0 = Y :_c = .0947765$$

$$\hat{\alpha}_0 = \text{ARCH} :_c \text{ons} = .0453114$$

$$\hat{\alpha}_{11} = \text{ARCH} : \text{L1.earch} = .2103571$$

$$\hat{\alpha}_{12} = \text{ARCH} : \text{L1.earch}_a = .1468577$$

$$\hat{\alpha}_{21} = \text{ARCH} : \text{L2.earch} = .1324385$$

$$\hat{\alpha}_{22} = \text{ARCH} : \text{L2.earch}_a = .0610908$$

$$\hat{\gamma}_1 = \text{ARCH} : \text{L1.egarch} = .0214899$$

$$\hat{\gamma}_2 = \text{ARCH} : \text{L2.egarch} = .1651247$$

$$\hat{\gamma}_3 = \text{ARCH} : \text{L3.egarch} = .0608116$$

T-GARCH or Threshold GARCH

As in GJR, Zakoian's (1994) T-GARCH model accounts for the possibility that shocks above a certain threshold value (the "T" in T-GARCH) have a qualitatively different effect than shocks below the threshold. In the simplest of T-GARCH models, this threshold is equal to zero. That is, when the error is positive, it has one type of impact on volatility, and when it is negative, it has another (usually larger) impact.

Zakoian's T-GARCH model is quite similar in spirit to GJR-GARCH in that shocks above and below some threshold value are separated via a dummy variable. In Zakoian's model, the effect of a shock, e_{t-k}, on σ depends upon the shock's sign and magnitude. Thus, T-GARCH is a version of GJR-GARCH where the volatility enters the mean equation, not via the variance but the standard deviation.

The terminology is confusing. In Stata, the `tgarch()` option invokes GJR-GARCH. Zakoian's T-GARCH model is invoked using a combination of Stata's `atarch()`, `abarch()`, and `sdgarch()` options. GJR-GARCH is far more commonly used in the literature.

Example: Comparing Asymmetric GARCH Models

Researchers will want to know whether to estimate asymmetric or standard (asymmetric) GARCH models. And if asymmetry is called for, which version?

In this example, we will estimate and compare three different GARCH models: a standard GARCH model, GJR-GARCH, and E-GARCH. Our data will be the Dow Jones Industrial Average (DJIA) for the beginning of 2005 to the end of 2012, a period that includes the worst of the financial crisis.

```
. * Get the data
. fetchyahooquotes ^DJIA, freq(d) start(01jan2005)
  end(31dec2012)
. gen DJIA = log(adj) - log(L.adj)

. * (1) Estimate a standard GARCH(1,1) model
. quietly arch DJIA, arch(1) garch(1) nolog
. estimates store GARCH
. predict GARCH_hat, variance

. * (2) Estimate a GJR-GARCH(1,1) model
. quietly arch DJIA, arch(1) garch(1) tarch(1) nolog
. estimates store GJR_GARCH
. predict GJR_GARCH_hat, variance

. * (3) Estimate an E-GARCH(1,1) model
. quietly arch DJIA, earch(1) egarch(1) nolog
. estimates store E_GARCH
. predict E_GARCH_hat, variance
```

9.5 Variations on GARCH

Now that we have estimated the models, we can report the results:

```
. esttab GARCH GJR_GARCH E_GARCH, not
```

	(1) DJIA	(2) DJIA	(3) DJIA
DJIA			
_cons	0.000476	0.000411	0.000298
ARCH			
L.arch	0.278***	0.314***	
L.garch	0.828***	0.871***	
L.tarch		-0.0825	
L.earch			-0.0830***
L.earch_a			0.437***
L.egarch			1.207***
_cons	-0.0000182	-0.0000220*	1.770*
N	1579	1579	1579

* p<0.05, ** p<0.01, *** p<0.001

```
. estimates stats GARCH GJR_GARCH E_GARCH
```

Model	Obs	ll(null)	ll(model)	df	AIC	BIC
GARCH	1579	.	4823.805	4	-9639.611	-9618.152
GJR_GARCH	1579	.	4824.555	5	-9639.111	-9612.288
E_GARCH	1579	.	4825.669	5	-9641.337	-9614.515

Note: N=Obs used in calculating BIC; see [R] BIC note

```
. correlate GARCH_hat E_GARCH_hat GJR_GARCH_hat
(obs=2013)
```

	GARCH_~t	E_GARC~t	GJR_GA~t
GARCH_hat	1.0000		
E_GARCH_hat	0.8967	1.0000	
GJR_GARCH_~t	0.9908	0.9262	1.0000

Which model fits best? We get conflicting results—a fact that is all too common in applied work. Model selection is often done by comparing information criteria. In this particular case, the AIC shows a slight preference for E-GARCH, while the BIC shows a slight preference for the standard GARCH model without asymmetry. A glance at the correlation table of the predicted variances shows that the differences between the models is fairly modest. The predicted variances are highly correlated, with the lowest correlation at almost 90%. The threshold term in the GJR-GARCH model is insignificant. Given this and the fact that neither information criterion indicates this as a preferred model, we can safely discard this model.

9.5.4 I-GARCH or Integrated GARCH

It is quite common to find that the sum of the estimated ARCH or GARCH parameters is quite close to one. That is, it would seem that the estimated model has a unit root or is integrated.

If this is the case, there is no finite conditional variance. While this presents some theoretical problems, it solves some other ones.

An I-GARCH(p,q) model restricts the standard GARCH(p,q) model by forcing a unit root:

$$\sum_{i=1}^{p} \alpha_i + \sum_{j=1}^{q} \gamma_j = 1.$$

Integrated GARCH models have the feature that their unconditional variance is not mean-reverting. The predicted variance from traditional GARCH models gets closer and closer to the long-run variance as the forecast horizon increases. That is, the one-step-ahead estimate is a bit closer to the long-run variance, σ^2. The two-step-ahead forecast is even closer. In the limit, the forecasted variance from a traditional GARCH model is simply the unconditional variance. This is not the same from an I-GARCH model. I-GARCH models share a similarity with other integrated processes, specifically that the effect of a shock does not dampen over time. Rather the effects of the shock linger indefinitely. A shock that increases the variance of a process will result in an increased variance indefinitely, or at least until a possible sequence of negative shocks draws it back down. The point, however, is that there is no guarantee that this will happen.

One of the fathers of Chaos Theory, Benoit Mandelbrot (1963), examined several financial time series and found that financial returns had thick tails, far thicker than a normal distribution would indicate. But so much of portfolio theory was based on the presumption that returns were normal. Further, Mandelbrot could not replicate his results in different time periods. The beta for a stock, for example, would have one value during one period and a far different value in another. He hypothesized that stock returns came from a distribution that did not have a finite variance. Thus, econometricians were trying to pin down values that did not exist. Mandelbrot found that processes drawn from the stable Paretian family of distributions—which, incidentally, do not have finite moments—seemed to mimic what he saw in the data.

9.5 Variations on GARCH

They were leptokurtic and had heavy tails.[9] Engle and Bollerslev (1986) developed the I-GARCH model which also seemed to share some of the same features that Mandelbrot saw in the data. (It was an attempt to mimic this leptokurtosis that also led Bollerslev (1987) to develop the GARCH-t model.)

Ghose and Kroner (1995) explored Mandelbrot's hypothesis and the performance of the I-GARCH model. The two models have many of the same features: they have infinite variances and fat tails, are leptokurtic, and aggregate similarly. However, they are not identical processes. Ghose and Kroner (1995) found that stable Paretian processes do not exhibit the volatility clustering that is so apparent in financial data. On these grounds, they rejected Mandelbrot's stable Paretian hypothesis in favor of I-GARCH processes.

Integrated GARCH processes are interesting for several reasons. First, they fit economic data very well. Second, they are a restricted model so they are more efficient. If you know, somehow, that the variance process is integrated, then restricting the coefficients to add to one means that we have one fewer parameter to estimate.

Example: I-GARCH on DJIA Data

Let's work through a simple example. The IGARCH-DJIA.dta dataset provides daily returns of the Dow Jones Industrial Average for January 1st, 1970, through December 31st, 2015.

```
. use IGARCH-DJIA.dta, clear
```

We can specify various constraints from within Stata. The syntax is

```
. constraint # eqn
```

We must provide a number as an identifier for each constraint. We will have only one constraint, so we'll call it constraint 1. We specify the constraint:

```
. constraint 1 [ARCH]_b[L1.arch] + [ARCH]_b[L1.garch]
  = 1
```

Finally, we estimate the constrained model:

---

[9] See also Gleick (1987) and Peters (1996) for accessible discussions on the relationships between Mandelbrot's Paretian hypothesis, chaos theory, and finance.

```
. arch DJIA_returns, arch(1) garch(1) nolog constraints(1)

ARCH family regression

Sample: 06jan1970 - 31dec2015, but with gaps      Number of obs    =     9,094
Distribution: Gaussian                            Wald chi2(.)     =         .
Log likelihood =  29213.81                        Prob > chi2      =         .

 ( 1)  [ARCH]L.arch + [ARCH]L.garch = 1
------------------------------------------------------------------------------
             |                 OPG
DJIA_returns |      Coef.   Std. Err.      z    P>|z|     [95% Conf. Interval]
-------------+----------------------------------------------------------------
DJIA_returns |
       _cons |   .0004095   .0000938     4.36   0.000     .0002256    .0005933
-------------+----------------------------------------------------------------
ARCH         |
        arch |
         L1. |   .1841262   .0089848    20.49   0.000     .1665165     .201736
             |
       garch |
         L1. |   .8158738   .0089848    90.81   0.000     .798264    .8334835
             |
       _cons |  -8.42e-08   4.74e-07    -0.18   0.859    -1.01e-06    8.45e-07
------------------------------------------------------------------------------
```

Notice how the ARCH and GARCH coefficients add to one (0.1841262 + 0.8158738 = 1), as we demanded in the constraint. Further, the ARCH and GARCH coefficients are statistically significant, implying that volatility in returns has a strong autoregressive component.

9.6 Exercises

1. Simulate 1,000 observations from a stationary ARCH(3) process by modifying the code given in the text above. Show that the variance is nonstationary.
2. Simulate 1,000 observations from a stationary ARCH(4) process. Using this data, estimate the appropriate ARCH model. Are the estimated coefficients close to those you specified?
3. Simulate a (stationary) ARCH(2) process with 10,000 observations. Using this data, graph the process, calculate the empirical kurtosis, and graph the histogram and qq-plot. Verify that the simulated data exhibit a large kurtosis.
4. Load the dataset `arch-1.dta`. This is an artificial dataset of 1,000 observations generated from an ARCH(1) process. Using this data, conduct an LM test for arch effects, using lags 1 through 10. Do you find evidence for ARCH effects at all lags?
5. Download the stock prices for Exxon-Mobil (stock ticker "XOM") for the beginning of January 2000 to the end of December 2010. Calculate the daily percentage returns using the log-difference approach. Use Engle's LM test and

the Ljung-Box Q^2 test to determine whether there are ARCH effects. If so, estimate the appropriate ARCH model and report your results. Defend your choice of model using some of the appropriate post-estimation specification tests.

6. Download the daily stock prices for the 3M Co. (stock ticker "MMM") for the beginning of January 2000 to the end of December 2010. Calculate the percentage returns using the log-difference approach. Calculate the AICs and BICs for an AR(0)-ARCH(20) and an AR(0)-ARCH(10) model of these daily returns. Which model is preferred by the AIC? Which model is preferred by the BIC?

7. We will compare the performance of a large ARCH model with a small GARCH model. Download the Ford dataset that we used earlier in this chapter, arch-F.dta, and reestimate the ARCH(10) model. Estimate a GARCH(1,1) model. Using the AIC, which model is preferred? Using BIC? Estimate the conditional variances from each model. What is the correlation between them?

8. What Stata command would you use to estimate the following model?

$$Y_t = \beta_0 + \beta_1 Y_{t-1} + \beta_2 Y_{t-2} + \beta_3 X_{1,t} + \beta_4 X_{2,t} + \sigma_t u_t$$

$$\ln\left(\sigma_t^2\right) = \alpha_0 + \sum_{i=1}^{2}\left(\alpha_{i1} z_{t-i} + \alpha_{i2}\left(|z_{t-i}| - \sqrt{2/\pi}\right)\right) + \sum_{j=1}^{3} \gamma_j \ln\left(\sigma_{t-j}^2\right)$$

9. What Stata command would you use to estimate the following model?

$$Y_t = \beta_0 + \beta_1 Y_{t-1} + \beta_2 X_{1,t} + \beta_3 X_{2,t} + \beta_4 X_{3,t} + \sigma_t u_t$$

$$\ln\left(\sigma_t^2\right) = \alpha_0 + \sum_{i=1}^{3}\left(\alpha_{i1} u_{t-i} + \alpha_{i2}\left(|u_{t-i}| - \sqrt{2/\pi}\right)\right) + \sum_{j=1}^{4} \gamma_j \ln\left(\sigma_{t-j}^2\right)$$

10. What Stata command would you use to estimate the following model?

$$Y_t = \beta_0 + \beta_1 Y_{t-1} + \beta_2 X_t + \beta_3 \epsilon_t + \beta_4 \epsilon_{t-1}$$

$$\epsilon_t = \sigma_t u_t$$

$$\sigma_t^2 = \alpha_0 + \alpha_1 \epsilon_{t-1}^2 + \gamma_1 \sigma_{t-1}^2$$

11. Write down the equations that describe the following models:
    a. GARCH(1,2) model
    b. AR(2)-ARCH(5)
    c. AR(3)-GARCH(2,1)

d. ARMA(2,3)-GARCH(1,1)
e. ARMA(4,3)-EGARCH(2,1)
f. ARMA(2,0)-GRJ-GARCH(1,1)

12. Continue replicating Bollerslev's (1987) paper, this time on S&P returns. Download the `BollerslevSP.dta` dataset. Generate the dependent variable using the following Stata commands:

```
. gen Y = .
. gen temp = log(adj/L.adj)
. sum temp
. replace Y = r(mean) in 1/5
. drop temp
. sum time
. local last = r(max)
. replace Y=log(adj/L.adj) - 0.268*L.Y - 0.0718*L2.Y ///
    + 0.0192*L3.Y - 0.0052*L4.Y in 6/`last'
```

Calculate the preestimation diagnostics (Q, Q^2, and kurtosis tests). Is there evidence of GARCH effects and leptokurtosis? Estimate a GARCH(1,1)-t model on Y. Conduct post-estimation diagnostics on the standardized residuals and squared standardized residuals. Does the GARCH(1,1)-t model provide a reasonable model of Y? How close are all of your estimates to those reported by Bollerslev?

Vector Autoregressions I: Basics   10

10.1 Introduction

If we take the notion of general equilibrium seriously, then everything in the economy is related to everything else. For this reason, it is impossible to say which variable is exogenous. It is possible that all variables are endogenous: they can all be caused by, and simultaneously be the cause of, some other variable. Introduced by Christopher Sims in (1980b), vector autoregressions or "VARs" attempt to model the many interdependencies between economic variables without imposing arbitrary assumptions on the data. The data are thought to "speak for themselves."[1]

Up until this point in the book, we have only looked at econometric models with one dependent variable (Y_t as a function of its lags as in an AR process); any other variables are exogenous or predetermined. In this chapter we will begin to work with multi-variable, multi-equation models. In this chapter we will rely on, and expand upon, some concepts we've already developed (e.g., AR processes, integration, and stationarity). Doing so will require developing our skills with vectors and matrices. We'll proceed slowly.

First, to provide context for what is to come, let's look at the history of the VAR. The historical development of the VAR roughly mirrors the outline of this chapter. Thus, looking at the road the field has traveled will also help the readers of this book see the road ahead.

---

[1] It was found not to be the case. There are many hidden assumptions in VARs; the researcher cannot stand outside the research process even in the case of VARs.

10.1.1 A History Lesson

The VAR is most closely associated with Christopher Sims' (1980b) article, "Macroeconomics and Reality." As with everything, there is nothing new under the sun. Sims' article relied on a long history among economists of estimating vector autoregressions, dynamic structural models, and dynamic reduced form models. But, as Qin (2011) outlines in his history of the VAR, Sims' work came at a unique time when the Cowles Commission's approach to large-scale structural econometric modeling was being questioned. Moreover, the emerging rational expectations revolution led by Thomas Sargent found a natural ally in the VAR, as the models frequently found themselves being expressed in terms of dynamic systems of equations, specifically, VARS.

Sims was inspired by Clive Granger's (1969) article which established what is now known as "Granger causality." To over-simplify, the key concept in Granger causality is that if variable X is observationally prior to another variable Y, this is statistically indistinguishable from true causation. Sims (1972) applied this concept to examine the relationship between the money supply and GNP. These weren't two arbitrarily chosen variables. In one elegant paper, Sims was able to test several major economic theories. First, it was a statistical test of Friedman and Schwartz' more narrative historical approach which concluded that misdirected monetary policy caused, or at least exacerbated, the Great Depression. That is, Sims seemed to confirm Friedman and Schwartz' (1963) contention that the money supply is to some extent exogenous and affects national income. Second, he did not find any Granger causality from income to money, calling into question the then-conventional approach of estimating money demand as a function of GNP. Finally, he tested Friedman's (1969) permanent income hypothesis, concluding that income responds to permanent but not current income. Incidentally, Sims revisited this question in his (1980a) "Monetarism Reconsidered" paper, but came to the opposite conclusion. There, he added prices and interest rates to his earlier model to estimate a 4-variable VAR. Causality is much harder to establish with more than two variables. Standard Granger causality is a test of direct causality. Sims used "innovation accounting" (what we now call impulse response functions) to examine any indirect causation. Sims ultimately concluded that, contrary to his conclusion in 1972, the money supply does not actually Granger-cause GNP after all.

Sims' VAR modeling approach was pitched as a direct attack on the Cowles Commission approach. There, economists would set up large systems of equations, trying to mimic general equilibrium. The problem with this approach was that there were far too many equations so that their parameters were unidentified. The Cowles solution was to set many of these variables to zero (with little or no solid theoretical reasons to do so) or to estimate the component equations one-by-one. (This second approach had two serious limitations. First, if the equations really were a system, then they needed to be estimated as a system or the parameter estimates would be biased. Second, estimation requires that variables change, but Lucas' famous (1976)

10.1 Introduction

critique argued that when policy variables change, the underlying parameters also change so that they are, in effect, a moving target that cannot be shot.)

The collaboration between Christopher Sims and Thomas Sargent was natural. While Sims was hard at work on the VAR from the econometric front, Sargent was hard at work on the theory of rational expectations, finding that the VAR was a natural outcome of this theory (Sargent 1976, for example). Both economists were working at the University of Minnesota and the Minnesota Federal Reserve. (They also shared the 2011 Nobel Prize in Economics.) At a 1975 conference hosted by the Minnesota Fed, they presented a paper on the VAR entitled "Business cycle modeling without pretending to have too much a priori economic theory," the title hinting at an imminent attack on the Cowles approach. The paper was published in the conference proceedings as Sargent et al. (1977).

Christopher Sims' (1980b) brashly titled paper "Macroeconomics and Reality" was "widely regarded as the manifesto to the VAR approach" (Qin 2011, p. 162–3). It is one of the most widely cited papers in all of economics.[2] In that paper, Sims laid out his vision for the VAR as a fully coherent substitute for, and improvement upon, the Cowles Commission approach. The paper was not received without controversy (see, e.g., Cooley and LeRoy 1985; Leamer 1985), but its eventual dominance was nearly absolute.

But if the major innovation in (Sims 1980b) was that it did not require making identifying restrictions, the subsequent history of the VAR has witnessed a retreat from this. No sooner was the atheoretical VAR in use that theoretical identifying restrictions began to be imposed. Responding to the criticism by Cooley and LeRoy (1985), the age of the VAR was quickly followed by the age of the structural VAR. This was not a reversion to the errors of the Cowles Commission—their identifying restrictions were considered ad hoc, "incredible," and without solid theoretical backing. Rather, it was the imposition of theory-based restrictions on formerly unrestricted VARs. This was required for VARs to be useful, not just for describing data, but for prescribing policy. What was needed is a structural model—one with current values of the policy variables showing up on both sides of the equal sign—and errors that are not cross-correlated. What was needed was a structural VAR.

There have been scores of different identifying assumptions proposed for SVARs. These primarily include short-run restrictions (Christiano et al. 1999) and long-run restrictions (Blanchard & Quah 1989). Though not discussed in this book, Uhlig (2005) introduced sign restrictions as a less restrictive sort of identifying restrictions.[3]

Other researchers have acknowledged that when a researcher imposes constraints—setting parameters to zero or requiring cross-equation restrictions—he imposes his beliefs on a parameter. The Bayesian VAR is an attempt to formalize and loosen this requirement. Rather than setting a parameter to zero, the Bayesian

---

[2] As of June 2017, it has been cited over 11,700 times.

[3] The book by Amisano and Giannini (2012) is considered a definitive guide to SVARs.

econometrician sets a soft constraint: a prior on the parameter which is centered over zero. Thus, it is allowed to vary from zero, but only if the data require it. Examples of this approach include Doan et al. (1984) and Litterman (1985).[4]

There have been many technical extensions and modifications to VARs. We'll begin learning about VARs by examining the simplest possible VAR, one with two variables and one lag.

10.2 A Simple VAR(1) and How to Estimate It

Suppose that X's value depends on its past, as well a past values of Y. Suppose the same could be said of Y. This is the essence of a vector autoregression.

The simplest vector autoregression has two variables and one lag:

$$X_t = \alpha_x + \beta_{x,1} X_{t-1} + \beta_{y,2} Y_{t-1} + \epsilon_{x,t} \tag{10.1}$$

$$Y_t = \alpha_y + \beta_{x,1} X_{t-1} + \beta_{y,2} Y_{t-1} + \epsilon_{y,t} \tag{10.2}$$

It is simple to estimate the above model. In fact nothing more fancy is required than ordinary least squares. So why do we make such a big deal out of it? Because we can do a lot of other things once we have estimated these parameters. We can graphically describe complex interactions; we can make statements about causality; we might even understand something about how the structure of the real economy works. But we're getting ahead of ourselves. Let's start simple: let's estimate a simple VAR model.

Suppose we want to know how two variables—the growth rates of the US's real GNP and money supply—are dynamically correlated. The data are graphed in Fig. 10.1. We will estimate the VAR between these variables using OLS and then again using Stata's `var` command and compare results.

```
. drop _all
. freduse GNPC96 MANMM101USQ189S

. gen time=yq(year(daten), quarter(daten))
. tsset time, quarterly

. gen GNPgr = ln(GNPC96) - ln(L.GNPC96)
. gen M1gr  = ln(MANMM)  - ln(L.MANMM)
. label var GNPgr "Growth rate of real GNP"
. label var M1gr "Growth rate of M1"
. drop GNPC MANMM date daten
```

---

[4] Valuable contributions were also made by Litterman (1985), DeJong et al. (2000), Otrok and Whiteman (1998), and Geweke and Whiteman (2006). Most of these researchers are connected to the University of Minnesota or the University of Iowa.

10.2 A Simple VAR(1) and How to Estimate It

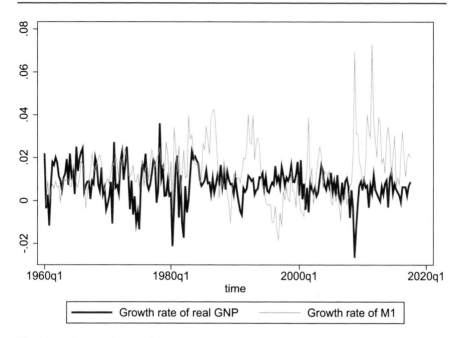

Fig. 10.1 The growth rates of GNP and M1

```
. drop if year(time)<1960

. reg GNPgr L.GNPgr L.M1gr  if time<yq(2017,3)
```
(some output omitted)

```
------------------------------------------------------------------------------
       GNPgr |      Coef.   Std. Err.      t    P>|t|     [95% Conf. Interval]
-------------+----------------------------------------------------------------
       GNPgr |
         L1. |   .3382094   .0628023     5.39   0.000     .2144535    .4619653
             |
        M1gr |
         L1. |   .0278705   .0410592     0.68   0.498    -.0530392    .1087802
             |
       _cons |   .0045657   .0009339     4.89   0.000     .0027254    .0064061
------------------------------------------------------------------------------
```

. reg M1gr L.GNPgr L.M1gr if time<yq(2017,3)

. reg M1gr L.GNPgr L.M1gr if time<yq(2017,3)

(some output omitted)

```
------------------------------------------------------------------------------
        M1gr |      Coef.   Std. Err.      t    P>|t|     [95% Conf. Interval]
-------------+----------------------------------------------------------------
       GNPgr |
         L1. |  -.135329    .0776424    -1.74   0.083    -.2883283    .0176704
             |
        M1gr |
         L1. |  .6334148    .0507614    12.48   0.000     .5333862    .7334434
             |
       _cons |  .0062374    .0011546     5.40   0.000     .0039622    .0085126
------------------------------------------------------------------------------
```

Compare this with the VAR estimates:

```
. var GNPgr M1gr if time<yq(2017,3), lags(1)

Vector autoregression

Sample: 1960q3 - 2017q2                          Number of obs     =        228
Log likelihood =   1517.885                      AIC               =  -13.26215
FPE            =   5.96e-09                      HQIC              =  -13.22573
Det(Sigma_ml)  =   5.66e-09                      SBIC              =   -13.1719

Equation          Parms      RMSE     R-sq      chi2     P>chi2
----------------------------------------------------------------
GNPgr                3      .007878   0.1143   29.4116   0.0000
M1gr                 3      .009739   0.4225  166.7801   0.0000
----------------------------------------------------------------


------------------------------------------------------------------------------
             |      Coef.   Std. Err.      z    P>|z|     [95% Conf. Interval]
-------------+----------------------------------------------------------------
GNPgr        |
       GNPgr |
         L1. |  .3382094    .0623877     5.42   0.000     .2159317    .4604871
             |
        M1gr |
         L1. |  .0278705    .0407882     0.68   0.494    -.0520728    .1078138
             |
       _cons |  .0045657    .0009277     4.92   0.000     .0027474    .0063841
-------------+----------------------------------------------------------------
M1gr         |
       GNPgr |
         L1. |  -.135329    .0771299    -1.75   0.079    -.2865008    .0158429
             |
        M1gr |
         L1. |  .6334148    .0504264    12.56   0.000     .5345809    .7322487
             |
       _cons |  .0062374     .001147     5.44   0.000     .0039894    .0084854
------------------------------------------------------------------------------
```

10.2 A Simple VAR(1) and How to Estimate It

Notice that the coefficients are identical in the two approaches. However, there is an important difference between the two. They differ in their standard errors. This is because the OLS approach presumes that the errors are not correlated across equations. When that isn't the case, and the shocks to the equations are correlated, then we need to adjust the standard errors to account for that. Fortunately, Stata's var and varbasic commands take care of that complication automatically. They do so by using seemingly unrelated regression (SUR). We leave it as an exercise for you to show that estimates using SUR are the same as those from var.

What does the output above tell us? It is hard to tell; there's a lot going on. It looks like increases in the growth rate of real GNP have some inertia from one quarter to the next (lagged X in the first equation is positive and statistically significant). It does not appear that changes in the growth rate of the money supply (Y) are correlated with next periods' GNP growth (Y is statistically insignificant in the first equation, with a p-value of 0.492).

Suppose that there is one solitary shock to $\epsilon_{1,t=1}$, and all other ϵ's are zero. How does this one shock affect the whole system? It affects $X_{t=1}$ immediately via Eq. (10.1). Then the shock propagates: $X_{t=1}$ affects $X_{t=2}$ via (10.1) and $Y_{t=2}$ via Eq. (10.2). The process doesn't stop there, and things get even more complicated. The newly affected variables $X_{t=2}$ and $Y_{t=2}$ now affect X_2 and Y_2 within and across equations. Specifically, $X_{t=2}$ affects $X_{t=3}$ via Eq. (10.1), and it affects $Y_{t=2}$ via (10.2); $Y_{t=2}$ also affects $X_{t=3}$ and $Y_{t=3}$ via Eqs. (10.1) and (10.1). This is dizzying.

It would be much easier if we could see visually how changes in each of the variables affect the other variables over time. We will get into the calculation of these impulse response functions (IRFs) later in the chapter. Indeed, when it comes to IRFs, the devil is truly in the details. But we're not ready for details yet. For now, let's see what VARs can do.

The Stata command to graph the IRF in Fig. 10.2 is

. irf graph irf

The headings at the top of each panel list the impulse variable first followed by the response. Thus, the top-left panel shows how a one standard deviation increase in GNP's growth rate affects itself over time. We see that the shock's effects dampen out and become indistinguishable from zero by around period 4. At the bottom left, we see that changes to the growth rate of the money supply do not seem to affect the growth rate of GNP. At the bottom right, we see that a one unit increase in the M1 growth rate dampens out over time until it reaches its usual rate by around period 5.

The top-right panel shows how a one standard deviation shock to GNPgr affects the money supply. It doesn't affect it by much, and the effect is statistically insignificant. You should always report the confidence intervals around your IRFs. In practice, these confidence intervals can be quite large. If you ignore this fact, you risk reporting insignificant results.[5]

---

[5] Runkle (1987) emphasizes the importance of including and properly calculating confidence intervals when reporting IRFs and FEVDs.

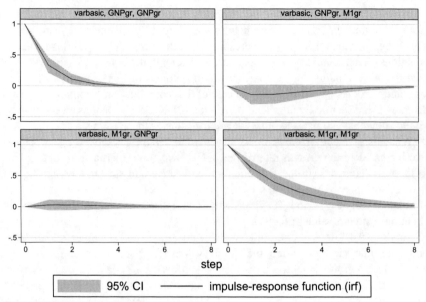

Fig. 10.2 Impulse response function

Exercises

1. Re-estimate the two-variable VAR(1) model on the growth rate of the money supply and the growth rate of RGNP, and show that the results from (a) Stata's var command and (b) seemingly unrelated regression (sureg) are equivalent. Specifically, estimate the following two commands:
   . sureg (GNPgr L.GNPgr L.M1gr) (M1gr L.GNPgr L.M1gr)
   . var GNPgr M1gr, lags(1)

10.3 How Many Lags to Include?

It is seldom the case that economic theory can tell us how many lags a model should include. We are faced with a very practical question: How many lags should we include in our model? Should it have one lag: VAR(1)? Two lags: VAR(2)? Eight lags: VAR(8)?

One approach is to estimate many VAR models with different numbers of lags and compare their fit. That is, estimate and compare a VAR(1), a VAR(2), etc. through VAR(p). You have to decide how large p is. You also need to decide on what the selection criterion or measure of fit you'll use. The standard set of lag length selection criteria includes Akaike information criterion (AIC), Schwarz's Bayesian information criterion (SBIC), and the Hannan and Quinn information criterion (HQIC). These are the same metrics that we used in choosing lags for

10.3 How Many Lags to Include?

ARMA(p,q) models, generalized to the multivariate cases. The details or formulas for these information criteria are not important here. They all adjust the log-likelihood function of the estimated VAR and penalize it by some function of model complexity. The three models differ by how, and how much, they penalize for the number of variables. (This makes them quite similar to the adjusted R^2, which penalizes the measure of fit (R^2) by a function of the number of parameters being estimated.)

Stata automates much of this task, so we don't need to manually estimate VAR(1) through VAR(p), nor do we have to manually calculate each VAR's information criteria. Stata's `varsoc` command automates all of this for us.

Using the same data as before, we type

```
. varsoc GNPgr M1gr if time<yq(2017,3), maxlag(8)
```

and Stata provides the following output:

```
Selection-order criteria
Sample:   1962q2 - 2017q2                       Number of obs     =        221
+---------------------------------------------------------------------------+
|lag |    LL      LR      df    p      FPE       AIC      HQIC      SBIC    |
|----+----------------------------------------------------------------------|
|  0 | 1397.68                        1.1e-08  -12.6306  -12.6182  -12.5998  |
|  1 | 1470.21  145.07    4   0.000  6.0e-09   -13.2508  -13.2136  -13.1585* |
|  2 | 1477.47   14.517   4   0.006  5.9e-09*  -13.2803* -13.2182* -13.1265  |
|  3 | 1480.65    6.3535  4   0.174  5.9e-09   -13.2728  -13.1859  -13.0576  |
|  4 | 1481.28    1.2643  4   0.867  6.1e-09   -13.2424  -13.1306  -12.9656  |
|  5 | 1486.22    9.8722* 4   0.043  6.0e-09   -13.2508  -13.1142  -12.9126  |
|  6 | 1490.74    9.0522  4   0.060  6.0e-09   -13.2556  -13.0942  -12.8558  |
|  7 | 1491.65    1.8073  4   0.771  6.2e-09   -13.2276  -13.0413  -12.7663  |
|  8 | 1492.56    1.8251  4   0.768  6.4e-09   -13.1996  -12.9885  -12.6768  |
+---------------------------------------------------------------------------+
Endogenous:  GNPgr M1gr
Exogenous:   _cons
```

The asterisks indicate which model is preferred by each selection criterion. Both the AIC and HQIC indicate that a two-lag VAR is preferred; the SBIC prefers a VAR with one lag.

How many lags should we include in our comparisons? That is, how high should we set `maxlag(p)`? You should pick p to be large enough that there are no gains from increasing it further. Brandt and Williams (2007) suggest setting p no larger than 5 for yearly data, 8 for quarterly, or 15 for monthly data.

Also, consider adding lags if the selection criteria choose the model with the maxlag. In our example above, if the information criteria had indicated that eight lags were best, then maybe nine would have been even better. In this case, we would have added a couple more lags and re-estimated information criteria.

What if the different ICs suggest different lag lengths? This is an unfortunate but extremely common problem. And there is no universally accepted answer. Some researchers go with the lag length preferred by the majority of selection criteria.

Others choose not to choose only one, reporting results from all VARs that are considered "best" by each selection criteria.

Braun and Mittnik (1993) investigate the effect of various types of misspecifications on VARs. These misspecifications include ignoring MA errors and selecting the wrong lag lengths. Since a finite MA process can be approximated by a sufficiently long AR(p) process, they argue for erring on the side of too many lags. Improper lag selection seriously affects the variance decompositions. A far greater problem is neglecting to include an important variable.

Lütkepohl (1985) studies two-variable and three-variable VARs and finds that the SBIC and HQIC perform best. However, Gonzalo and Pitarakis (2002) find that the AIC is, by far, the best metric in large dimensional models. A four-variable VAR has many more parameters than a three-variable VAR, so if your VAR has many equations, then the AIC seems to be the best tool for selecting lag lengths. There is no "last word" on this topic, and research is still underway.[6] Still, few research paper have been rejected for using the AIC for lag selection.

10.4 Expressing VARs in Matrix Form

The simplest vector autoregression has two variables and one lag:

$$X_t = \beta_{1,1} X_{t-1} + \beta_{1,2} Z_{t-1} + \epsilon_{1,t}$$

---

[6] As examples, Hatemi-J (2003) proposes a lag selection criterion that simply averages the SIC and HQIC; the theory is that this is a straightforward approach that is good enough for general use. Other approaches are tailored to more specific uses. Schorfheide (2005), for example, proposes a final prediction error approach to lag selection when the goal is multi-step forecasting.

There is no requirement that the number of lags in a VAR needs to be constant across equations nor variables. Ignoring irrelevant parameters means that the remaining parameters can be estimated more efficiently. Precisely estimated coefficients produce better IRFs and better forecasts. Hsiao (1979, 1981) developed a fully asymmetric VAR model to specifically address Sims' money/income causality question. Keating (2000) explores this concept within a class of VARs where each variable takes on different lags, but the lag structure is the same across equations. The AIC is known to select the correct symmetric lag lengths better than the other commonly used alternatives. Keating develops an alternative to the AIC for asymmetric lag length selection. In a Monte Carlo simulation, Ozcicek and McMillin (1999) examine the small-sample performance of the standard IC and Keating's versions of these. They find that the KAIC more frequently identified the correct number of asymmetric lags than did the other information criteria and had good forecasting properties. Ozcicek and McMillin (1999) conclude that the AIC and KAIC should be used over SIC when forecasting; their results are reversed when the IRFs are the focus of the study.

Ivanov and Kilian (2005) review much of the literature and conduct extensive Monte Carlo test of lag order's effect on IRFs. Their findings are sensitive to the observation frequency, with monthly data preferring AIC and quarterly data preferring SBIC and HQIC.

The most obvious conclusion that we can draw from all this is that the field has not yet reached a conclusion. But if we were to offer advice, it would be the following: if you wish to forecast, use AIC or KAIC. If you wish to construct IRFs, then BIC or SICs are preferred. IRFs will fit the data very well when they are fit with lots of lags.

10.4 Expressing VARs in Matrix Form

$$Z_t = \beta_{2,1} X_{t-1} + \beta_{2,2} Z_{t-1} + \epsilon_{2,t}$$

We could have added a constant but we're trying to keep things as simple as possible.

How might this be expressed in vector/matrix notation? Define the variables matrix

$$\mathbf{Y_t} = \begin{bmatrix} X_t \\ Z_t \end{bmatrix},$$

the coefficient matrix

$$\boldsymbol{\beta} = \begin{bmatrix} \beta_{1,1} & \beta_{1,2} \\ \beta_{2,1} & \beta_{2,2} \end{bmatrix},$$

and the error matrix

$$\boldsymbol{\epsilon}_t = \begin{bmatrix} \epsilon_{1,t} \\ \epsilon_{2,t} \end{bmatrix}.$$

Then we can rewrite the two-equation VAR in matrix form

$$\begin{bmatrix} X_t \\ Z_t \end{bmatrix} = \begin{bmatrix} \beta_{1,1} & \beta_{1,2} \\ \beta_{2,1} & \beta_{2,2} \end{bmatrix} \begin{bmatrix} X_{t-1} \\ Z_{t-1} \end{bmatrix} + \begin{bmatrix} \epsilon_{1,t} \\ \epsilon_{2,t} \end{bmatrix}$$

or more concisely as

$$\mathbf{Y_t} = \boldsymbol{\beta} \mathbf{Y_{t-1}} + \boldsymbol{\epsilon}_t. \tag{10.3}$$

Expressed this way, we can see where vector autoregressions get their name. Ignoring the bold font, they are an ordinary AR processes. The only difference is that the variable being examined is now a collection of other variables, i.e., it is a vector.

What about more complicated models? Ones with more variables, or more lags? A two-variable two-lag VAR such as

$$X_t = \beta_{1,1} X_{t-1} + \beta_{1,2} Z_{t-1} + \beta_{1,3} X_{t-1} + \beta_{1,4} Z_{t-2} + \epsilon_{1,t} \tag{10.4}$$

$$Z_t = \beta_{2,1} X_{t-1} + \beta_{2,2} Z_{t-1} + \beta_{2,3} X_{t-1} + \beta_{2,4} Z_{t-2} + \epsilon_{2,t} \tag{10.5}$$

can be expressed in matrix form as

$$\begin{bmatrix} X_t \\ Z_t \end{bmatrix} = \begin{bmatrix} \beta_{1,1} & \beta_{1,2} \\ \beta_{2,1} & \beta_{2,2} \end{bmatrix} \begin{bmatrix} X_{t-1} \\ Z_{t-1} \end{bmatrix} + \begin{bmatrix} \beta_{1,3} & \beta_{1,4} \\ \beta_{2,3} & \beta_{2,4} \end{bmatrix} \begin{bmatrix} X_{t-2} \\ Z_{t-2} \end{bmatrix} + \begin{bmatrix} \epsilon_{1,t} \\ \epsilon_{2,t} \end{bmatrix} \tag{10.6}$$

or more concisely as

$$\mathbf{Y_t} = \boldsymbol{\beta}_1 \mathbf{Y_{t-1}} + \boldsymbol{\beta}_2 \mathbf{Y_{t-2}} + \boldsymbol{\epsilon}_t. \qquad (10.7)$$

A three-variable two-lag VAR such as:

$$\begin{aligned}
X_t =& \beta_{1,1}X_{t-1} + \beta_{1,2}Z_{t-1} + \beta_{1,3}W_{t-1} + \\
& \beta_{1,4}X_{t-2} + \beta_{1,5}Z_{t-2} + \beta_{1,6}W_{t-2} + \epsilon_{1,t} \\
Z_t =& \beta_{2,1}X_{t-1} + \beta_{2,2}Z_{t-1} + \beta_{2,3}W_{t-1} + \\
& \beta_{2,4}X_{t-2} + \beta_{2,5}Z_{t-2} + \beta_{2,6}W_{t-2} + \epsilon_{2,t} \\
W_t =& \beta_{3,1}X_{t-1} + \beta_{3,2}Z_{t-1} + \beta_{3,3}W_{t-1} + \\
& \beta_{3,4}X_{t-2} + \beta_{3,5}Z_{t-2} + \beta_{3,6}W_{t-2} + \epsilon_{2,t}
\end{aligned}$$

can be expressed in matrix form as

$$\begin{bmatrix} X_t \\ Z_t \\ W_t \end{bmatrix} = \begin{bmatrix} \beta_{1,1} & \beta_{1,2} & \beta_{1,3} \\ \beta_{2,1} & \beta_{2,2} & \beta_{2,3} \\ \beta_{3,1} & \beta_{3,2} & \beta_{3,3} \end{bmatrix} \begin{bmatrix} X_{t-1} \\ Z_{t-1} \\ W_{t-1} \end{bmatrix} + \begin{bmatrix} \beta_{1,4} & \beta_{1,5} & \beta_{1,6} \\ \beta_{2,4} & \beta_{2,5} & \beta_{2,6} \\ \beta_{3,4} & \beta_{3,5} & \beta_{3,6} \end{bmatrix} \begin{bmatrix} X_{t-1} \\ Z_{t-1} \\ W_{t-2} \end{bmatrix} + \begin{bmatrix} \epsilon_{1,t} \\ \epsilon_{2,t} \\ \epsilon_{3,t} \end{bmatrix}$$

or more concisely as

$$\mathbf{Y_t} = \boldsymbol{\beta}_1 \mathbf{Y_{t-1}} + \boldsymbol{\beta}_2 \mathbf{Y_{t-2}} + \boldsymbol{\epsilon}_t. \qquad (10.8)$$

Notice that the matrix expression of a two-variable two-lag VAR (10.7) is the same as that of a three-variable two-lag VAR (10.8). For this reason, we can often ignore the number of variables in a VAR and just think of it as a two-variable model.

Many of the same old issues arise, even in this new context. We still want to know whether the estimated coefficient yields a stationary path for $\mathbf{Y_t}$ or whether it is explosive. We'd still like to be able to plot out the impulse response functions. We can also learn some new things. We can see how one variable affects *other* variables.

10.4.1 Any VAR(p) Can Be Rewritten as a VAR(1)

Matrices help us simplify equations by "stacking variables." Likewise, we can "stack matrices" to simplify matrix equations. It turns out that any VAR with p lags can be rewritten as a VAR with one lag. That is, we can rewrite Eq. (10.7) or (10.8) to look like Eq. (10.3).

Let's take the two-variable two-lag VAR as in Eq. (10.6). Define the "companion matrix" as

10.4 Expressing VARs in Matrix Form

$$\beta = \begin{bmatrix} \beta_1 & \beta_2 \\ I & 0 \end{bmatrix} = \begin{bmatrix} \begin{bmatrix} \beta_{1,1} & \beta_{1,2} \\ \beta_{2,1} & \beta_{2,2} \end{bmatrix} & \begin{bmatrix} \beta_{1,3} & \beta_{1,4} \\ \beta_{2,3} & \beta_{2,4} \end{bmatrix} \\ \begin{bmatrix} 1 & 0 \\ 0 & 1 \end{bmatrix} & \begin{bmatrix} 0 & 0 \\ 0 & 0 \end{bmatrix} \end{bmatrix} = \begin{bmatrix} \beta_{1,1} & \beta_{1,2} & \beta_{1,3} & \beta_{1,4} \\ \beta_{2,1} & \beta_{2,2} & \beta_{2,3} & \beta_{2,4} \\ 1 & 0 & 0 & 0 \\ 0 & 1 & 0 & 0 \end{bmatrix}.$$

Let

$$\mathbf{Y_t} = \begin{bmatrix} X_t \\ Z_t \\ X_{t-1} \\ Z_{t-1} \end{bmatrix}$$

and

$$\mathbf{e_t} = \begin{bmatrix} \epsilon_{1,t} \\ \epsilon_{2,t} \\ 0 \\ 0 \end{bmatrix}.$$

Then we can see that

$$\mathbf{Y_t} = \beta \mathbf{Y_{t-1}} + \mathbf{e_t} \tag{10.9}$$

is equivalent to

$$\begin{bmatrix} X_t \\ Z_t \\ X_{t-1} \\ Z_{t-1} \end{bmatrix} = \begin{bmatrix} \beta_{1,1} & \beta_{1,2} & \beta_{1,3} & \beta_{1,4} \\ \beta_{2,1} & \beta_{2,2} & \beta_{2,3} & \beta_{2,4} \\ 1 & 0 & 0 & 0 \\ 0 & 1 & 0 & 0 \end{bmatrix} \begin{bmatrix} X_{t-1} \\ Z_{t-1} \\ X_{t-2} \\ Z_{t-2} \end{bmatrix} + \begin{bmatrix} \epsilon_{1,t} \\ \epsilon_{2,t} \\ 0 \\ 0 \end{bmatrix} \tag{10.10}$$

or

$$X_t = \beta_{1,1} X_{t-1} + \beta_{1,2} Z_{t-1} + \beta_{1,3} X_{t-1} + \beta_{1,4} Z_{t-2} + \epsilon_{1,t}$$
$$Z_t = \beta_{2,1} X_{t-1} + \beta_{2,2} Z_{t-1} + \beta_{2,3} X_{t-1} + \beta_{2,4} Z_{t-2} + \epsilon_{2,t}.$$

In general, the companion matrix for an n-variable VAR(p) is the $np \times np$ matrix:[7]

---

[7] It is $np \times np$ because each component in matrix (10.11) is, itself, an $n \times n$ matrix.

$$\beta = \begin{bmatrix} \beta_1 & \beta_2 & \ldots & \beta_{p-1} & \beta_p \\ I & 0 & \ldots & 0 & 0 \\ 0 & I & \ldots & 0 & 0 \\ \vdots & \vdots & \ddots & \vdots & \vdots \\ 0 & 0 & \ldots & I & 0 \end{bmatrix}. \tag{10.11}$$

With the appropriately defined companion matrix, any VAR(p) can be written as a VAR(1). Thus we will often restrict our attention to simple VAR(1)s, knowing that what applies there also applies to more complicated VAR(p)s as well. The companion matrix will also prove useful in examining the stability of the VAR.

10.5 Stability

As with AR processes, there are two equivalent approaches to checking for stationarity.[8] For both approaches, we will build up slowly, beginning with a univariate autoregression and then building up by analogy to a bivariate and then multivariate vector autoregressive model.

What has caused confusion for countless econometrics students is that Method 1 requires the roots be less than one, while Method 2 requires they be greater than one. It turns out that the two sets of numbers are reciprocals of each other. The methods are, at their core, identical.

The entire discussion below mirrors that in Chap. 4 when we discussed the stability of AR(p) processes.

10.5.1 Method 1

In the univariate AR(1) case,

$$Y_t = \beta Y_{t-1} + \epsilon_t,$$

and Y_t is stable if

$$|\beta| < 1.$$

---

[8] We use "stability" and "stationarity" interchangeably. They are not the same thing. However, stability implies stationarity if the error process is stationary. Stability applies to the coefficients affecting the mean; stationarity is a broader concept that also demands that the autocovariances and the error variances do not change over time. Given that we do not address GARCH errors in this chapter, stability is enough to ensure stationarity.

10.5 Stability

If β is greater than one, then Y_t grows without limit; if it is less than one, it decreases without limit; and if it is equal to one, it is a nonstationary random walk process. How does this generalize to the vector-valued case?

Let's begin with a VAR in companion form, ignoring the error term:

$$\mathbf{Y_t} = \beta \mathbf{Y_{t-1}} \tag{10.12}$$

The system reaches a steady state if, as Y feeds into itself through β, it doesn't get bigger and bigger. $\mathbf{Y_t}$ is a vector. Any matrix can be thought to map a vector into another vector; alternatively, if we think of it as a change-of-basis, the matrix stretches space so that a vector becomes another vector. Here, β maps $\mathbf{Y_{t-1}}$ into $\mathbf{Y_t}$.

Every square matrix (like the companion matrix β) has at least one eigenvalue and associated eigenvector (if we allow for complex numbers). What are these eigen-things? Without getting too deeply into matrix algebra, a matrix β has an eigenvector $\mathbf{v}$ and associated eigenvalues λ if

$$\lambda \mathbf{v} = \beta \mathbf{v}, \tag{10.13}$$

i.e., if there is a vector $\mathbf{v}$ that keeps its direction and only changes its magnitude when transformed by the matrix β. Thus, if the original vector was say $\mathbf{v} = [1, 5]'$, then it might become $\mathbf{v} = [2, 10]'$. In other words, the relationships between the components stay proportional. As we iterate, constantly feeding $\mathbf{Y_t}$ or $\mathbf{v}$ through β, then it cannot get bigger and bigger if this system is to be stable. That is, $[1, 5]'$ cannot become $[2, 10]'$ and then $[4, 20]'$ and so forth. Rather, the vector needs to shrink. In matrix-speak, its eigenvalues must be less than one, so that each iteration is a fraction of the previous one. Since these eigenvalues might be complex numbers, then we say that they must have a length less than one when mapped on the complex plane; or, it must lie inside the unit circle; or, put yet another way, their modulus must be less than one.

Consider the two-variable VAR(1):

$$X_t = 0.50 X_{t-1} + 0.60 Y_{t-1} + \epsilon_{x,t}$$
$$Y_t = -0.50 X_{t-1} + 0.50 Y_{t-1} + \epsilon_{y,t}.$$

Its companion matrix

$$\beta = \begin{bmatrix} 0.50 & 0.60 \\ -0.50 & 0.50 \end{bmatrix} \tag{10.14}$$

has two eigenvalues: $(.5001246 + .54759i)$ and $(.5001246 - .54759i)$.

Fig. 10.3 Eigenvalues inside the unit circle

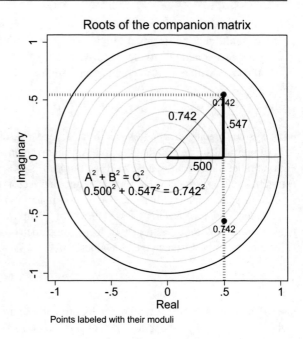

Roots can have real and complex (imaginary) components: $z^* = r \pm c\sqrt{-1}$. Using the Euclidian definition of length[9] (equivalent to the Pythagorean theorem), we need

$$\sqrt{r^2 + c^2} < 1. \tag{10.15}$$

In our example,

$$\sqrt{.500^2 + .547^2} \approx 0.742 < 1.$$

so our estimated VAR is stable. When graphed on the unit circle, such as in Fig. 10.3, we can see that their length (or "modulus") is less than one.

To summarize, a VAR is "stable" if the eigenvalues of the companion matrix lie inside the unit circle. As we'll see in a bit, Stata can easily calculate the eigenvalues of a matrix, letting us know whether the associated VAR is stable.

---

[9] Equivalently, the length of a complex vector is equal to the square root of the product of the vector and its complex conjugate: $\sqrt{(r+ci)(r-ci)} = \sqrt{(r^2 + rci - rci - ci^2)} = \sqrt{(r^2 + c^2)}$

10.5.2 Method 2

Let's return to the AR(1) case

$$Y_t = \beta Y_{t-1} + \epsilon_t.$$

and express this equation using the lag operator L. (Recall, $LY_t = Y_{t-1}$.)

$$Y_t = \beta L Y_t + \epsilon_t$$
$$Y_t - \beta L Y_t = \epsilon_t$$
$$Y_t (1 - \beta L) = \epsilon_t$$

From this, we can construct what is called the "characteristic equation" by replacing L with some variable (let's call it z) and set the equation equal to zero.

$$1 - \beta z = 0 \tag{10.16}$$

Now we solve for the roots of the characteristic equation, which we denote z^*. In this method, stability requires that $|z^*| > 1$, so

$$|z^*| = |\frac{1}{\beta}| > 1$$
$$|\beta| < 1.$$

Since Z and β are reciprocals, the requirement that $|z^*| > 1$ is equivalent to $|\beta| < 1$.

What if we had an AR(2) process? Then

$$Y_t = \beta_1 Y_{t-1} + \beta_2 Y_{t-2} + \epsilon_t.$$

This can be expressed using the lag operator as

$$Y_t - \beta_1 Y_{t-1} - \beta_2 Y_{t-2} = \epsilon_t$$
$$Y_t - \beta_1 L Y_t - \beta_2 L L Y_t = \epsilon_t$$
$$Y_t \left(1 - \beta_1 L - \beta_2 L^2\right) = \epsilon_t$$

and the characteristic equation is

$$\left(1 - \beta_1 z - \beta_2 z^2\right) = 0. \tag{10.17}$$

Since this is a second degree function in z, then we can find the roots by using the quadratic formula:

$$z^* = \frac{-(-\beta_1) \pm \sqrt{(-\beta_1)^2 - 4(1)(-\beta_2)}}{2(1)}$$

If these roots are greater than one in absolute value, then the equation is stable. In case that the roots are complex, the magnitude (a.k.a. modulus, length, size) of the root must be greater than one when measured on the complex plane.

For an AR(p) process,

$$Y_t = \beta_1 Y_{t-1} + \beta_2 Y_{t-2} + \cdots + \beta_p Y_{t-p} + \epsilon_t.$$

the lag form is

$$Y_t \left(1 - \beta_1 L - \beta_2 L^2 - \cdots - \beta_p L^p\right) = \epsilon_t$$

The characteristic equation is

$$\left(1 - \beta_1 z - \beta_2 z^2 - \cdots - \beta_p z^p\right) = 0, \qquad (10.18)$$

the roots of which must be greater than one for stability.

We're now ready to generalize from the univariate case to the multivariate or vector-valued case. After all, this is a chapter on *vector* autoregressions.

Consider our simple two-variable VAR(1) model:

$$\mathbf{Y_t} = \boldsymbol{\beta} \mathbf{Y_{t-1}} + \epsilon_t.$$

Here, $\mathbf{Y_t}$ and $\boldsymbol{\beta}$ are defined such that

$$\begin{bmatrix} X_t \\ Z_t \end{bmatrix} = \begin{bmatrix} \beta_{1,1} & \beta_{1,2} \\ \beta_{2,1} & \beta_{2,2} \end{bmatrix} \begin{bmatrix} X_{t-1} \\ Z_{t-1} \end{bmatrix} + \begin{bmatrix} \epsilon_{1,t} \\ \epsilon_{2,t} \end{bmatrix}.$$

As before, we apply the lag operator and move the lagged terms of $\mathbf{Y}$ to the left-hand side:

$$\mathbf{Y_t} = \boldsymbol{\beta} \mathbf{Y_{t-1}} + \epsilon_t$$
$$\mathbf{Y_t} - \boldsymbol{\beta} \mathbf{Y_{t-1}} = \epsilon_t$$
$$\mathbf{Y_t} - \boldsymbol{\beta} L \mathbf{Y_t} = \epsilon_t$$
$$(\mathbf{I} - \boldsymbol{\beta} L) \mathbf{Y_t} = \epsilon_t.$$

Replacing L with z, we solve for the roots of the characteristic equation

$$\left| \mathbf{I} - \hat{\boldsymbol{\beta}} z \right| = 0, \qquad (10.19)$$

10.5 Stability

where the vertical bars |.| denote the determinant of a matrix.

Let's work out an example. Suppose you estimated the VAR equation above and found that

$$\hat{\beta} = \begin{bmatrix} \hat{\beta}_{1,1} & \hat{\beta}_{1,2} \\ \hat{\beta}_{2,1} & \hat{\beta}_{2,2} \end{bmatrix} = \begin{bmatrix} 0.50 & 0.60 \\ -0.50 & 0.50 \end{bmatrix}$$

as we did before in Method 1. Is the estimated VAR(1) stable? Let's solve for the roots of the characteristic polynomial:

$$0 = \left| I - \hat{\beta}z \right|$$

$$0 = \left| \begin{bmatrix} 1 & 0 \\ 0 & 1 \end{bmatrix} - \begin{bmatrix} 0.50 & 0.60 \\ -0.50 & 0.50 \end{bmatrix} z \right|$$

$$0 = \left| \begin{bmatrix} 1 & 0 \\ 0 & 1 \end{bmatrix} - \begin{bmatrix} 0.50z & 0.60z \\ -0.50z & 0.50z \end{bmatrix} \right|$$

$$0 = \left| \begin{matrix} 1 - 0.50z & -0.60z \\ .50z & 1 - 0.50z \end{matrix} \right|$$

Since this is a 2 × 2 matrix, then we can calculate the determinant by hand:

$$(1 - 0.50z)^2 - (.50z)(-.60z) = 0$$

which simplifies to

$$0.55z^2 - z + 1 = 0.$$

This is a second-degree polynomial, so we can apply the quadratic formula to solve for $z*$, which yields a complex root:

$$z^* = 0.90909\ldots \pm 0.9959i.$$

These two roots have a length equal to $(0.90909^2 + 0.9959^2)^{.5} = 1.3484$. Since their lengths are greater than one, Method 2 agrees with Method 1 that the estimated VAR is stable.

The connection between the two methods is that

$$1/.3484 = 0.742.$$

That is, the eigenvalues in Method 1 are the inverses of the roots from Method 2.

Exercises

1. Suppose you are estimating a two-variable VAR(1) model. For each estimated coefficient matrix given below, determine whether the model is stable. Also, assuming starting values of $Y_0 = X_0 = 1$, use your favorite software to calculate the next ten values of Y and X. Graph these to verify whether the estimated model is stable.

   (a) $\hat{\beta} = \begin{bmatrix} .1 & -.2 \\ -.3 & .4 \end{bmatrix}$

   (b) $\hat{\beta} = \begin{bmatrix} .2 & .4 \\ .4 & .5 \end{bmatrix}$

   (c) $\hat{\beta} = \begin{bmatrix} 2 & 4 \\ 4 & 5 \end{bmatrix}$

2. Suppose you are estimating a three-variable VAR(1) model. For each estimated coefficient matrix given below, determine whether the model is stable. Also, assuming starting value of $Y_0 = X_0 = Z_0 = 1$, use your favorite software to calculate the next ten values of X, Y, and Z. Graph these to verify whether the estimated model is stable.

   (a) $\hat{\beta} = \begin{bmatrix} -0.2 & 0.4 & 0.35 \\ 0.3 & -0.2 & 0.15 \\ 0.2 & -0.3 & 0.4 \end{bmatrix}$

   (b) $\hat{\beta} = \begin{bmatrix} -0.1 & 0.3 & 0.4 \\ 0.9 & -0.2 & 0.1 \\ 0.2 & 0.3 & 0.8 \end{bmatrix}$

10.5.3 Stata Command Varstable

Fortunately, Stata has a built-in command to test for stability. After estimating the VAR, issue the following command:

. varstable

Stata estimates the eigenvalues from Method 1, reports their moduli, and even reports whether the estimated VAR is stable. Stata can also graph the eigenvalues on the complex unit circle (such as in Fig. 10.3) by typing

. varstable, graph

10.6 Long-Run Levels: Including a Constant

The previous example have focused on VARs with no constants. That was just for the sake of simplicity. But it also meant that the value of the series was centered around zero. There is no reason to be quite so limiting in real life. It is easy to change the mean of the series to be non-zero, simply by adding a constant.

Consider the following VAR(1):

10.6 Long-Run Levels: Including a Constant

$$X_t = 100 + 0.20X_{t-1} - 0.40Y_{t-1} + \epsilon_x$$
$$Y_t = 120 - 0.30X_{t-1} - 0.10Y_{t-1} + \epsilon_y.$$

To what values of X and Y does this process converge? We can solve this by hand by taking the unconditional expectation of both equations and solving for E(X) and E(Y). Equivalently, drop the random errors, set $X_t = X_{t-1} = X^*$, and $Y_t = Y_{t-1} = Y^*$, and solve for X^* and Y^*:

$$X^* = 100 + 0.20X^* - 0.40Y^*$$
$$Y^* = 120 - 0.30X^* - 0.10Y^*$$

Grouping terms:

$$0.80X^* = 100 - 0.40Y^*$$
$$1.10Y^* = 120 - 0.30X^*$$

or

$$X^* = \frac{1}{0.80}(100 - 0.40Y^*) = 125 - .50Y^* \tag{10.20}$$

$$Y^* = \frac{1}{1.10}(120 - 0.30X^*) \tag{10.21}$$

Substituting (10.21) into (10.20) yields

$$X^* = 125 - .50\left[\frac{1}{1.10}(120 - 0.30X^*)\right],$$

and solving for X^* yields

$$X^* \approx 81.579.$$

Similarly, substituting (10.20) into (10.21) and solving for Y^* yields

$$Y^* \approx 86.842.$$

The mean of the process is a complicated function of the constant and the other coefficients. If we express this problem in matrix-algebra form, then it doesn't look so complicated after all. Consider the general VAR(p) process

$$\mathbf{Y_t} = \boldsymbol{\beta_0} + \boldsymbol{\beta_1}\mathbf{Y_{t-1}} + \boldsymbol{\epsilon}_t. \tag{10.22}$$

where $\boldsymbol{\beta_1}$ is the companion matrix and $\boldsymbol{\beta_0}$ is a vector of constants. To solve for the long-run mean of the process, set $\mathbf{Y_t} = \mathbf{Y_{t-1}} = \mathbf{Y^*}$, set $\epsilon_t = 0$ and solve for $\mathbf{Y^*}$, the steady state of the system

$$\mathbf{Y^*} = \boldsymbol{\beta_0} + \boldsymbol{\beta_1}\mathbf{Y^*}$$
$$\mathbf{Y^*} - \boldsymbol{\beta_1}\mathbf{Y^*} = \boldsymbol{\beta_0}$$
$$\mathbf{Y^*}[\mathbf{I} - \boldsymbol{\beta_1}] = \boldsymbol{\beta_0}$$
$$\mathbf{Y^*} = \boldsymbol{\beta_0}[\mathbf{I} - \boldsymbol{\beta_1}]^{-1}$$

For $\mathbf{Y}$ to be stable, the matrix $[\mathbf{I} - \boldsymbol{\beta_1}]$ must be invertible. This does not depend on $\boldsymbol{\beta_0}$. Adding constants affects the mean of the process, but it does not affect whether the process is stable.

10.7 Expressing a VAR as an VMA Process

In Chap. 4 we learned that a stationary AR(1) process can be expressed as an MA(∞) process. In practice, this means that we can often switch back and forth between writing a process as an AR(1) and an MA(q) for large enough q.

The idea applies here, too, but for VAR processes. Consider a stationary VAR(1):

$$\mathbf{Y_t} = \boldsymbol{\beta}\mathbf{Y_{t-1}} + \epsilon_t,$$

then lag by one period and substitute

$$\mathbf{Y_t} = \boldsymbol{\beta}\left(\boldsymbol{\beta}\mathbf{Y_{t-2}} + \epsilon_{t-1}\right) + \epsilon_t$$
$$= \boldsymbol{\beta}^2\mathbf{Y_{t-2}} + \boldsymbol{\beta}\epsilon_{t-1} + \epsilon_t.$$

Repeating the process an infinite number of times

$$\mathbf{Y_t} = \sum_{j=0}^{\infty} \boldsymbol{\beta}^j \epsilon_{t-j}.$$

where $\boldsymbol{\beta}^0 = \mathbf{I}$.

In the MA representation, Y_t is equal to a weighted average of all its previous shocks. More recent shocks propagate through β and impact Y_t more forcefully; more distant shocks have fainter effects, having cycled through β several times.

The weights ($\boldsymbol{\beta}^j$) can be thought of as the values of the impulse response to a shock (ϵ_{t-j})

10.8 Impulse Response Functions

As we said earlier in this chapter, "when it comes to IRFs, the devil is truly in the details." We're now ready for some details. Let's calculate the first several values of an IRF by hand.

Suppose we estimated a simple 2-variable VAR(1):

$$X_t = 0.40 X_{t-1} + 0.10 Y_{t-1} + \epsilon_{x,t} \tag{10.23}$$

$$Y_t = 0.20 X_{t-1} - 0.10 Y_{t-1} + \epsilon_{y,t}. \tag{10.24}$$

Suppose that X_0 and Y_0 were equal to, say, zero. Let's see what happens to X_t and Y_t if there is a one-time one-unit shock to $\epsilon_{x,1}$, keeping all other ϵ's equal to zero.

In period 1

$$\hat{X}_1 = 0.40\,(0) + 0.10\,(0) + 1 = 1$$

$$\hat{Y}_1 = 0.20\,(0) - 0.10\,(0) + 0 = 0.$$

How does this affect the variables in the next period?

$$\hat{X}_2 = 0.40 X_1 + 0.10 Y_1 + 0 = 0.40\,(1) + 0.10\,(0) = 0.40$$

$$\hat{Y}_2 = 0.20 X_1 - 0.10 Y_1 + 0 = 0.20\,(1) - 0.10\,(0) = 0.20$$

In period 3

$$\hat{X}_3 = 0.40 X_2 + 0.10 Y_2 + 0 = 0.40\,(0.40) + 0.10\,(0.20) = 0.18$$

$$\hat{Y}_3 = 0.20 X_2 - 0.10 Y_2 + 0 = 0.20\,(0.40) - 0.10\,(0.20) = 0.06$$

and in period 4

$$\hat{X}_4 = 0.40 X_3 + 0.10 Y_3 + 0 = 0.40\,(0.18) + 0.10\,(0.06) = 0.078$$

$$\hat{Y}_4 = 0.20 X_3 - 0.10 Y_3 + 0 = 0.20\,(0.18) - 0.10\,(0.06) = 0.030.$$

We just calculated the impulse responses from X to X and X to Y (which are graphed in Fig. 10.4). Notice how a shock that directly affects only one variable ends up affecting both endogenous variables.

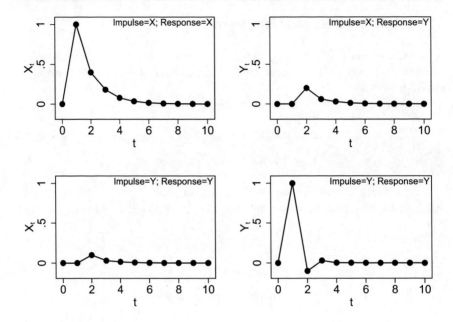

Fig. 10.4 Impulse response function

10.8.1 IRFs as the Components of the MA Coefficients

Let's return to the univariate AR(1) case for a second, with $\beta = 0.50$ for example:

$$Y_t = 0.50 Y_{t-1} + \epsilon_t$$

$$= \sum_{j=0}^{\infty} 0.50^j \epsilon_{t-j}$$

Now suppose that $Y = 0$ and $\epsilon = 0$ all along the infinite past up to period 0. Then, in period 0, ϵ_0 receives a one-time shock equal to one and then reverts back to zero. What is the impact of this on Y_t? That is, what is the IRF?

$$\hat{Y}_0 = 1$$
$$\hat{Y}_1 = 0.5$$
$$\hat{Y}_2 = 0.5^2 = 0.25$$
$$\hat{Y}_3 = 0.5^3 = 0.125.$$

10.8 Impulse Response Functions

Thus, at least for the univariate case, the slope coefficient of the AR(1) process provides the exponentially decreasing weights of the MA representation and is also equal to the IRF. We will see shortly that this generalizes to the vector case.

A stationary VAR(1) process

$$Y_t = \beta Y_{t-1} + \epsilon_t,$$

is equal to an MA(∞) process

$$Y_t = \sum_{j=0}^{\infty} \beta^j \epsilon_{t-j}. \tag{10.25}$$

Equation (10.25) shows that the values of Y_t are a weighted average of all its previous shocks. Last period's shock propagates through β and impacts Y_t more forcefully; a shock two periods ago cycles through β twice. Thus, a shock two periods ago has a proportionally (β^2) smaller effect. For this reason, the weights (β^j) can be thought of as the values of the impulse response to a shock to ϵ_{t-j}. The sequences of β^js are the IRFs. We will now verify this with an example.

Example 1: Two-Variable VAR(1)

Return to the IRF we calculated by hand from Eqs. (10.23) and (10.24). The companion matrix for that VAR is

$$\hat{\beta} = \begin{bmatrix} 0.4 & 0.10 \\ 0.20 & 0.10 \end{bmatrix}$$

The IRF of a 1-unit shock on ϵ_x as felt by X_t was 1, 0.40, 0.18, and 0.078. As felt by Y_t, it was 0, 0.20, 0.06, and 0.03.

Now consider the left-column entries in the following powers of β:

$$\hat{\beta}^1 = \begin{bmatrix} 0.40 & 0.10 \\ 0.20 & 0.10 \end{bmatrix}$$

$$\hat{\beta}^2 = \begin{bmatrix} 0.40 & 0.10 \\ 0.20 & 0.10 \end{bmatrix} \begin{bmatrix} 0.40 & 0.10 \\ 0.20 = 0.10 \end{bmatrix} = \begin{bmatrix} 0.18 & 0.03 \\ 0.06 & 0.03 \end{bmatrix}$$

$$\hat{\beta}^3 = \begin{bmatrix} 0.078 & 0.015 \\ 0.03 & 0.003 \end{bmatrix}.$$

Example 2: Two-variable VAR(1)

Let's work out another example. Using the method outlined above, calculate the first three values of the IRF a 1-unit shock on the errors in period zero.

$$X_t = 0.50X_{t-1} + 0.20Y_{t-1} + \epsilon_{x,t} \tag{10.26}$$

$$Y_t = 0.30X_{t-1} + 0.15Y_{t-1} + \epsilon_{y,t} \tag{10.27}$$

We begin by defining the companion matrix $\hat{\beta}$ and calculating its powers:

```
. matrix beta = (0.50, 0.20 \ 0.30, 0.15)

. matrix beta2 = beta*beta

. matrix beta3 = beta*beta*beta

. matrix beta4 = beta*beta*beta*beta

. matrix list beta

beta[2,2]
     c1   c2
r1   .5   .2
r2   .3  .15

. matrix list beta2

beta2[2,2]
       c1      c2
r1    .31     .13
r2   .195   .0825

. matrix list beta3

beta3[2,2]
         c1        c2
r1     .194     .0815
r2  .12225   .051375

. matrix list beta4

beta4[2,2]
           c1         c2
r1     .12145    .051025
r2  .0765375  .03215625
```

These show that a 1-unit shock to X will result in the following response in X: 1, 0.5, 0.31, 0.194, and 0.12145. The same shock will result in the following response in Y: 0, 0.3, 0.195, 0.12225, and 0.076537. Likewise, a 1-unit shock to Y will result

10.8 Impulse Response Functions

in the following response to X: 0, 0.2, 0.13, 0.0815, and 0.051025. The same shock to Y has the following response in Y: 1, 0.15, 0.0825, 0.051375, and 0.0321565.

Example 3: Three-variable VAR(1)
Suppose we estimated a three-variable VAR(1) such as

$$X_t = 0.25X_{t-1} + 0.20Y_{t-1} + 0.15Y_{t-1} + \epsilon_{x,t}$$
$$Y_t = 0.15X_{t-1} + 0.30Y_{t-1} + 0.10Y_{t-1} + \epsilon_{y,t}$$
$$Z_t = 0.20X_{t-1} + 0.25Y_{t-1} + 0.35Y_{t-1} + \epsilon_{z,t}$$

Setting the initial values of X, Y, and Z equal to zero, the IRF from a 1-unit shock to $\epsilon_{x,t}$ at period $t = 1$ is calculated as

$$\hat{X}_1 = 0.25X_0 + 0.20Y_0 + 0.15Z_0 + 1 = 0.25\,(0) + 0.20\,(0) + 0.15\,(0) + 1 = 1$$
$$\hat{Y}_1 = 0.15X_0 + 0.30Y_0 + 0.10Z_0 + 0 = 0.15\,(0) + 0.30\,(0) + 0.10\,(0) + 0 = 0$$
$$\hat{Z}_1 = 0.20X_0 + 0.25Y_0 + 0.35Z_0 + 0 = 0.15\,(0) + 0.30\,(0) + 0.10\,(0) + 0 = 0$$

At $t = 2$,

$$\hat{X}_2 = 0.25X_1 + 0.20Y_1 + 0.15Z_1 + 0 = 0.25\,(1) + 0.20\,(0) + 0.15\,(0) + 0 = 0.25$$
$$\hat{Y}_2 = 0.15X_1 + 0.30Y_1 + 0.10Z_1 + 0 = 0.15\,(1) + 0.30\,(0) + 0.10\,(0) + 0 = 0.15$$
$$\hat{Z}_2 = 0.20X_1 + 0.25Y_1 + 0.35Z_1 + 0 = 0.20\,(1) + 0.25\,(0) + 0.35\,(0) + 0 = 0.20$$

And after yet one more period,

$$\hat{X}_3 = 0.25X_2 + 0.20Y_2 + 0.15Z_2 + 0 = 0.25\,(0.25) + 0.20\,(0.15) + 0.15\,(0.20) + 0$$
$$= 0.1225$$

$$\hat{Y}_3 = 0.15X_2 + 0.30Y_2 + 0.10Z_2 + 0 = 0.15\,(0.25) + 0.30\,(0.15) + 0.10\,(0.20) + 0$$
$$= 0.1025$$

$$\hat{Z}_3 = 0.20X_2 + 0.25Y_2 + 0.35Z_2 + 0 = 0.20\,(0.25) + 0.25\,(0.15) + 0.35\,(0.20) + 0$$
$$= 0.1575$$

Now let's verify our matrix approach using Stata:

```
. matrix beta = (0.25, 0.20, 0.15 \ 0.15, 0.30, 0.10 \
    0.20, 0.25, 0.35)

. matrix beta2 = beta*beta
```

```
. matrix list beta

beta[3,3]
       c1    c2    c3
r1    .25    .2   .15
r2    .15    .3    .1
r3     .2   .25   .35

. matrix list beta2

beta2[3,3]
        c1      c2      c3
r1   .1225   .1475     .11
r2   .1025    .145   .0875
r3   .1575   .2025   .1775
```

We can extend a bit farther quite easily:

```
. matrix beta3 = beta*beta*beta

. matrix beta4 = beta*beta*beta*beta

. matrix list beta3

beta3[3,3]
           c1        c2        c3
r1    .07475    .09625   .071625
r2   .064875   .085875     .0605
r3    .10525   .136625      .106

. matrix list beta4

beta4[3,3]
             c1          c2          c3
r1      .04745   .06173125   .04590625
r2       .0412   .0538625    .03949375
r3   .06800625   .0885375      .06655
```

Example 4: Two-variable VAR(2)

This time let's work out an example with one more lag. This means that our coefficient matrix is no longer square, so that it can no longer be multiplied by itself. What do we do in this case? We work with the companion matrix. So, let's suppose that we estimated the following two-variable VAR(2) model:

$$X_t = 0.50X_{t-1} + 0.20Y_{t-1} + 0.10X_{t-2} + 0.10Y_{t-2} + \epsilon_{x,t}$$

10.8 Impulse Response Functions

$$Y_t = 0.30X_{t-1} + 0.15Y_{t-1} + 0.20X_{t-2} - 0.10Y_{t-2} + \epsilon_{y,t}$$

Let's set X and Y equal to zero for the first two periods ($t = 0$ and $t = 1$), and setting $\epsilon_{x,t} = 1$ in period $t = 2$ only, the IRF is calculated as

$$\hat{X}_2 = 0.50\,(0) + 0.20\,(0) + 0.10\,(0) + 0.10\,(0) + 1 = 1$$
$$\hat{Y}_2 = 0.30\,(0) + 0.15\,(0) + 0.20\,(0) - 0.10\,(0) + 0 = 0$$

In period $t = 3$,

$$\hat{X}_3 = 0.50\,(1) + 0.20\,(0) + 0.10\,(0) + 0.10\,(0) + 0 = 0.50$$
$$\hat{Y}_3 = 0.30\,(1) + 0.15\,(0) + 0.20\,(0) - 0.10\,(0) + 0 = 0.30$$

In period $t = 4$,

$$\hat{X}_4 = 0.50\,(0.50) + 0.20\,(0.30) + 0.10\,(1) + 0.10\,(0) + 0 = 0.41$$
$$\hat{Y}_4 = 0.30\,(0.50) + 0.15\,(0.30) + 0.20\,(1) - 0.10\,(0) + 0 = 0.395$$

and

$$\hat{X}_5 = 0.50\,(0.41) + 0.20\,(0.395) + 0.10\,(0.50) + 0.10\,(0.30) + 0 = 0.364$$
$$\hat{Y}_5 = 0.30\,(0.41) + 0.15\,(0.395) + 0.20\,(0.50) - 0.10\,(0.30) + 0 = 0.25225.$$

Now let's do this using matrices in Stata. The only wrinkle in this case is that the coefficient matrix is not square, so we can't square or cube it. However, we can work with the companion matrix:

$$\beta = \begin{bmatrix} 0.50 & 0.20 & 0.10 & 0.10 \\ 0.30 & 0.15 & 0.20 & -0.10 \\ 1 & 0 & 0 & 0 \\ 0 & 1 & 0 & 0 \end{bmatrix}$$

Thus, in Stata,

```
. matrix beta = (0.50, 0.20, 0.10, 0.10 \ ///
                0.30, 0.15, 0.20,-0.10 \ ///
                1,    0,    0,    0)

. matrix beta2 = beta*beta
```

```
. matrix beta3 = beta*beta*beta

. matrix list beta

beta[4,4]
        c1      c2      c3      c4
r1      .5      .2      .1      .1
r2      .3     .15      .2     -.1
r3       1       0       0       0
r4       0       1       0       0

. matrix list beta2

beta2[4,4]
          c1         c2         c3         c4
r1       .41        .23        .09        .03
r2      .395     -.0175        .06       .015
r3        .5         .2         .1         .1
r4        .3        .15         .2        -.1

. matrix list beta3

beta3[4,4]
            c1         c2         c3         c4
r1        .364      .1465       .087       .018
r2      .25225    .091375       .036     .04125
r3         .41        .23        .09        .03
r4        .395     -.0175        .06       .015
```

The IRF of X from shock to itself is given in the top-left entry of each matrix. The response to Y is given in the second entry of the left-most column.

10.9 Forecasting

A dynamic model—whether it is a univariate AR process or a multivariate VAR process—maps past values to present ones. It maps, say, X_{t-1} to X_t. But t is an arbitrary time period. We can use the same mapping, from old X to current X, to help us predict future X from current X. This exercise is one of the many reasons why VARs are so popular among economists.

Suppose we had data on X and Y covering 100 periods, and we wished to forecast X and Y for the subsequent 10 periods. Suppose we estimated a 1-lag VAR of X and Y. Does this mean that we can only predict out to one period? No! And for the same

10.9 Forecasting

reason that a VAR(1) still gives us an IRF out to many periods. The trick is to iterate on the function. To forecast for period 101, we must rely on the VAR model that was estimated for periods 1–100. The VAR's coefficients would tell us how to map from period 100's values to period 101. But to forecast further out, we must rely on our own forecasts. That is, to forecast period 102, we will need to rely on our forecast of period 101. To forecast period 103, we will need to rely on our forecasts of periods 101 and 102 and so forth.

And just in case you were wondering: what if we had a 4-lag VAR model? Could we estimate out four periods at a time? Nope. We would still need to do this one period at a time.

Let's see how this works for a two-variable VAR(2) processes.

Suppose we had the following data:

```
. list t X Y

     +----------------------------------+
     |   t           X              Y   |
     |----------------------------------|
  1. |   1    -.48685038      2.6062152 |
  2. |   2    -1.4760038      -.61448548|
  3. |   3    -.48222049      1.1561333 |
 (some output omitted)
 98. |  98     .51204487     -1.3839883 |
 99. |  99     .22059502     -.05463598 |
100. | 100     1.2968748      .97261489 |
     |----------------------------------|
101. | 101           .              .   |
102. | 102           .              .   |
103. | 103           .              .   |
104. | 104           .              .   |
105. | 105           .              .   |
     +----------------------------------+
```

from which we estimated the following VAR(2) process:

$$X_t = 0.30X_{t-1} + 0.20X_{t-2} + .10Y_{t-1} + .05Y_{t-2} + \epsilon_{1,t}$$
$$Y_t = 0.35X_{t-1} + 0.25X_{t-2} + .15Y_{t-1} + .01Y_{t-2} + \epsilon_{2,t}$$

Now suppose that we wanted to forecast X and Y for the next five periods.

We have data on X_{100}, X_{99}, Y_{100}, and Y_{99}, so we're on solid footing forecasting one period ahead. To be clear, all of the expectations below are conditional on data up to period 100. We forecast as follows:

$$E(X_{101}) = 0.30E(X_{100}) + 0.20E(X_{99}) + 0.10E(Y_{100}) + 0.05E(Y_{99}) + E(\epsilon_{1,101})$$
$$= 0.30X_{100} + 0.20X_{99} + 0.10Y_{100} + 0.05Y_{99} + 0$$
$$= 0.30(1.296\ldots) + 0.20(.220\ldots) + 0.10(.972\ldots) + 0.05(-.054\ldots)$$
$$= .5277111$$
$$E(Y_{101}) = 0.35E(X_{100}) + 0.25E(X_{99}) + 0.15E(Y_{100}) + 0.01E(Y_{99}) + E(\epsilon_{2,101})$$
$$= 0.35X_{100} + 0.25X_{99} + 0.15Y_{100} + 0.01Y_{99} + 0$$
$$= 0.35(1.296\ldots) + 0.25(.220\ldots) + 0.15(.972\ldots) + 0.01(-.054\ldots)$$
$$= .6544008$$

What about forecasting two periods ahead, to period 102? We only have data for X and Y up to period 100. We can plug these values in. But what about the values for period 101? We can plug in the expected value, the forecast from the previous step.

$$E(X_{102}) = 0.30E(X_{101}) + 0.20E(X_{100}) + 0.10E(Y_{101}) + 0.05E(Y_{100}) + E(\epsilon_{1,102})$$
$$= 0.30E(X_{101}) + 0.20X_{100} + 0.10E(Y_{101}) + 0.05Y_{100} + 0$$
$$= 0.30(.527\ldots) + 0.20(1.296\ldots) + 0.10(.654\ldots) + 0.05(.972\ldots)$$
$$= .53175912$$
$$E(Y_{102}) = 0.35E(X_{101}) + 0.25E(X_{100}) + 0.15E(Y_{101}) + 0.01E(Y_{100}) + E(\epsilon_{2,102})$$
$$= 0.35E(X_{101}) + 0.25X_{100} + 0.15E(Y_{101}) + 0.01Y_{100} + 0$$
$$= 0.35(.527\ldots) + 0.25(1.296\ldots) + 0.15(.654\ldots) + 0.01(.972\ldots)$$
$$= .61680386$$

The Stata command `fcast compute` is useful here, as it automates this process. We can use it to calculate the forecasted values out to period 105.

```
. fcast compute E, nose step(5)
```

The command creates several new variables, each with a given prefix. You can choose whichever prefix you want. I opted to use "E" since we're calculating expected values. The option `nose` might seem fishy, but it just instructs Stata not to calculate any standard errors (no SE's). Finally, the option `step(5)` tells Stata that we want to calculate the forecast five periods out. This is often called the "forecast window" or "forecast horizon."

The results of the `fcast` command are:

10.9 Forecasting

```
. list t X Y EX EY
```

	t	X	Y	EX	EY
1.	1	-.48685038	2.6062152	.	.
2.	2	-1.4760038	-.61448548	.	.
3.	3	-.48222049	1.1561333	.	.
(some output omitted)					
98.	98	.51204487	-1.3839883	.	.
99.	99	.22059502	-.05463598	.	.
100.	100	1.2968748	.97261489	1.2968748	.97261489
101.	101	.	.	.52771113	.6544008
102.	102	.	.	.53175912	.61680386
103.	103	.	.	.35947039	.41710806
104.	104	.	.	.28674394	.32748866
105.	105	.	.	.21152153	.24352235

which verifies our by-hand calculations and saves us further work.

Real-life forecasting requires that we use the most recent data. The farther out we are forecasting, the less certain we are of our forecasts. It is best to re-estimate the VAR and re-forecast every time new data arrives.

But sometimes we want to compare a couple of different formulas (say, two competing VARs), and we don't want to wait years for new data to arrive. Suppose we wanted to simulate the process of forecasting, say, five periods ahead. We can pretend that our data ended several periods ago, say in period 90, estimate the VAR using data up to period 90, and then estimate five periods ahead forecast for period 95. We then pretend that we just received data for period 91; repeat the process. That is, we re-estimate the VAR using all the data up to period 91 and forecast five periods ahead to period 96 and so forth. Such an exercise is called "pseudo out-of-sample forecasting."

One way to do this is to create a new set of columns each time we pretend to get new data. Something such as the following:

```
. var X Y, if t <= 90
. fcast compute E90, nose step(5)
. var X Y, if t <= 91
. fcast compute E91, nose step(5)
```

and so forth.

This method works, but it is clunky. It creates tons of new columns of data. (More elegant coding produces goes a long way here.)

10.10 Granger Causality

One of the more exciting things the time-series econometrician can explore is whether one variable "causes" another one. Strictly speaking, all we can explore is correlation, and as every student of statistics knows, correlation is not the same thing as causation. Still, if changes in X tend to predate changes in Y, then – at least, observationally speaking – X can be thought to cause Y. At least, if X actually does cause Y, then we should see that changes in X predate those in Y. If X really does cause Y, then X predating Y or even predicting Y is observationally indistinguishable from a correlation between Y and lagged X. Time-series econometricians are playing to role of a smoke detector. Where there is smoke, there isn't always fire, but it sure is a lot more likely.

Granger causality (1969) is a necessary condition for existential causality; but it is not a sufficient condition. It could be the case that Z causes X and after a much longer lag also causes Y. We would see a correlation between X and Y; we would say that X Granger-causes Y, even though X didn't really cause Y, Z did.

Econometricians don't want to be accused of mistaking correlation for causation, so they speak of "Granger causality" rather than strict "causality."

For all the associated jargon, and the Knighthood and Nobel Prize granted Sir Clive Granger, testing for Granger causality is really straightforward. A variable X is said to Granger-cause Y if accounting for earlier values of X helps us predict Y better than we could without it.

The concept of Granger causality is usually introduced to students only in the context of vector autoregressions, but the definition can be applied to simple autoregressions, with exogenous variables. For example, if the following AR(2) model:

$$Y_t = \beta_1 Y_{t-1} + \beta_2 Y_{t-2} + \beta_3 X_{t-1} + \epsilon_t \quad (10.28)$$

is (statistically significantly) better at predicting Y than is the more restricted regression

$$Y_t = \beta_1 Y_{t-1} + \beta_2 Y_{t-2} + \epsilon_t \quad (10.29)$$

then we say that X Granger-causes Y or that Y is Granger-caused by X. We would test for Granger causality by employing a simple t-test of $\beta_3 = 0$. If we had added more lags of X, then we would conduct a joint F-test of whether all of the coefficients on the lagged X variables are jointly different from zero.

The same concept generalizes to the multi-equation case of a VAR. If we have a two-variable VAR(2)

$$X_t = \beta_{1,1} X_{t-1} + \beta_{1,2} Y_{t-1} + \beta_{1,3} X_{t-1} + \beta_{1,4} Y_{t-2} + \epsilon_{x,t} \quad (10.30)$$

$$Y_t = \beta_{2,1} X_{t-1} + \beta_{2,2} Y_{t-1} + \beta_{2,3} X_{t-1} + \beta_{2,4} Y_{t-2} + \epsilon_{y,t} \quad (10.31)$$

10.10 Granger Causality

we would say that X Granger-causes Y if $\beta_{2,1}$ and $\beta_{2,3}$ are jointly significantly different from zero.[10]

Notice that testing whether X Granger-causes Y requires testing only the Y equation; really, all we're asking is whether lagged values of X are a statistically significant predictor of Y, given that we already control for lagged values of Y.

Tests of Granger causality are sensitive to omitted variables. An omitted third variable might make it seem as though X causes Y. In reality, perhaps Z causes X more quickly than it causes Y. In this case, failing to take Z into account will make it seems as though X causes Y, inducing a "false-positive" result to the tests. Omitted variables might also lead to "false negatives" (Lütkepohl 1982). For these reasons, researchers should make sure they have their economic theories straight, including all relevant variables in their analyses.

Example

Let's run a Granger causality test to see whether unemployment and inflation Granger-cause each other. (We should note at the outset that this simple example is only intended to illustrate the technique. We won't do any of the necessary pre-estimation or post-estimation tests; we aren't verifying whether the variables are integrated, cointegrated, etc.)

First we download and label the data:

```
. clear all
. freduse GNPDEF USAURHARMQDSMEI

. gen time=yq(year(daten), quarter(daten))
. tsset time, quarterly
. drop if year(daten)<1960 | year(daten)>=1980

. rename USAUR Unemp
. label var Unemp "Unemployment Rate"

. label var GNPDE "GNP Implicit Price Deflator"
. gen Infl = ln(GNPDE) - ln(L.GNPDE)
. label var Infl "Inflation rate"
```

After estimating the VAR, we employ Stata's built-in Granger causality command:

---

[10] Granger (1980) provides an interesting discussion on the philosophical nature and various definitions of causality. In that paper, he also generalizes his own definition of causality to include nonlinear models, providing a broader operational definition of causality.

```
. quietly var Infl Unemp if year(daten)< 1980, lag(1 2)

. vargranger

Granger causality Wald tests
  +---------------------------------------------------------------+
  |      Equation          Excluded |   chi2     df  Prob > chi2  |
  |---------------------------------+-----------------------------|
  |          Infl             Unemp |  5.0299     2      0.081    |
  |          Infl               ALL |  5.0299     2      0.081    |
  |---------------------------------+-----------------------------|
  |         Unemp              Infl |  7.6007     2      0.022    |
  |         Unemp               ALL |  7.6007     2      0.022    |
  +---------------------------------------------------------------+
```

The output above indicates that unemployment does not Granger-cause inflation at the 0.05 level (0.081 > 0.05), whereas inflation does Granger-cause unemployment (0.022 < 0.05).

Alternatively, we could estimate the joint significance by hand, replicating the statistics above:

```
. test [Infl] L1.Unemp [Infl] L2.Unemp

 ( 1)  [Infl]L.Unemp = 0
 ( 2)  [Infl]L2.Unemp = 0

       chi2(  2) =     5.03
     Prob > chi2 =    0.0809

. test [Unemp] L1.Infl [Unemp] L2.Infl

 ( 1)  [Unemp]L.Infl = 0
 ( 2)  [Unemp]L2.Infl = 0

       chi2(  2) =     7.60
     Prob > chi2 =    0.0224
```

The lagged values of unemployment in the inflation equation are statistically insignificant. The lagged values of inflation, on the other hand, are statistically significant predictors of unemployment, so we can conclude that inflation Granger-causes unemployment.

10.10.1 Replicating Sims (1972)

Chris Sims' first application of Granger's (1969) causality paper was his 1972 "Money, Income and Causality" paper. There, he tested whether changes in the money supply cause fluctuations in GNP or vice versa. Understanding the relation-

10.10 Granger Causality

ship between these two variables was highly relevant to one of the central economic debates of the time: monetarism vs Keynesianism. The debate centered over whether monetary policy could be effective in smoothing out the business cycle or whether business cycle fluctuations affected the money supply.

Sims' approach to Granger causality is different[11]—but mathematically equivalent[12]—from the current practice as established by Granger (1969). Thus, rather than replicating the paper closely using Sims unique method, we will replicate the main conclusions of Sims paper using the standard Granger causality tests.

Using quarterly data from 1947 to 1969, Sims tests whether changes in the money supply cause changes in GNP. Both variables are measured in logarithms.

We begin by downloading the data, creating the time variables, and logged versions of the monetary base (our estimate of the money supply) and of GNP:

```
. * Load the initial data
. freduse GNP AMBSL, clear
. drop if year(daten)< 1947 | year(daten)> 1969

. * Create quarterly versions of these variables
. gen year = year(daten)
. gen quarter = quarter(daten)
. collapse (mean) GNP AMBSL, by(year quarter)

. * Create time variables
. gen date = yq(year,quarter)
. format date %tq
. tsset date
. sort date
. gen time = _n

. * Generate log versions of the variables
. gen Y = log(GNP)
. gen MB = log(AMBSL)

. * Gen quarterly dummy variables
. gen q1 = 0
. gen q2 = 0
. gen q3 = 0
```

---

[11] Sims argued that if X causes Y (and not vice versa), then this should be evident in zero-coefficients in future values of X whenever regressing Y on past present and future values of X. Granger's approach was that if X causes Y, then there should be non-zero coefficients when regressing Y on past X and past Y. Ultimately, a string of research proved that the two approaches are identical.

[12] A sequence of papers by Hosoya (1977), Khon (1981), Chamberlain (1982), and Florens and Mouchart (1982) established the general conditions under which the two approaches are equivalent.

```
. gen q4 = 0
. replace q1 = 1 if quarter ==1
. replace q2 = 1 if quarter ==2
. replace q3 = 1 if quarter ==3
. replace q4 = 1 if quarter ==4
```

Next, we estimate the VAR. Following Sims, we include eight lags, a constant, a linear time trend, and seasonal dummies as exogenous variables. Including exogenous variables does not pose any problems. Even though the data are seasonally adjusted at their source, Sims still includes quarterly dummy variables to capture any remaining seasonality. (There was none.)

```
. quietly var Y MB, lags(1/8) exog(time q1-q4)

. vargranger

Granger causality Wald tests
+------------------------------------------------------------+
|       Equation        Excluded |   chi2     df  Prob > chi2 |
|--------------------------------+---------------------------|
|              Y              MB |  26.429     8     0.001    |
|              Y             ALL |  26.429     8     0.001    |
|--------------------------------+---------------------------|
|             MB               Y |  13.201     8     0.105    |
|             MB             ALL |  13.201     8     0.105    |
+------------------------------------------------------------+
```

Our results confirm those in Sims (1972). That is, we conclude that the money supply (monetary base) affects GNP; and GNP does not affect the money supply.[13]

One of the weaknesses in Sims' (1972) article was that he did not consider the effect of the interest rate. In his 1980a paper, Sims discovered that ignoring an important third variable can change the Granger causality results. Sims added an interest rate variable and discovered that the money supply no longer predicted national income.

This was hardly the last word on the matter. Sims' original results are sensitive to the choice of lag length and including a deterministic time trend.[14]

---

[13] To follow Sims' specific technique, we would estimate reg Y L(0/8).MB F(1/4).MB time quarter and then test F1.MB F2.MB F3.MB F4.MB to see whether MB causes Y. Then, we would estimate reg MB L(0/8).Y F(1/4).Y time quarter and test F1.Y F2.Y F3.Y F4.Y.

[14] Sims arbitrarily chose his lag length. Cheng Hsiao (1979, 1981) proposed using Akaike's FPE to select different lag lengths for each variable and each equation. He estimated such a fully asymmetric-lab VAR model to explore Sims' money/income causality results. He found bi-directional Granger causality for the USA and Canada. Thornton and Batten (1985) replicated Sims' paper on "Money, income and causality" using different lag lengths chosen by several different selection procedures. Different models give different results, so you should not choose a lag length arbitrarily. Thornton and Batten suggest relying on a lag selection method such as

Exercises
1. Redo the replication of Sims (1972) using data from 1970 through 2016. Do your conclusions change? If so, how?

10.10.2 Indirect Causality

Granger causality cannot detect indirect causality. For example, what if X causes Z and then Z causes Y (but X does not cause Y directly)? Then, logically speaking, changing X affects Y, and X causes Y. But the standard Granger causality test would not be able to detect this.[15] This is because a test for Granger causality occurs only on the coefficients of one equation. If we were looking for the variables that Granger-cause Y, then we would be restricted to testing the coefficients on X and Z only in the equation defining Y. That is, Granger causality tests are, ultimately, always single equation tests, whereas indirect causality operates through multiple equations.

Since we cannot use Granger causality tests to identify indirect causality, what are we to do if we want to know whether changes in X affect Y indirectly? This is the strength of IRFs, and especially OIRFs, as these show how changes in X – and only changes in X – affect all the other variables in the VAR system. This includes all of the indirect effects (as they propagate through powers of the companion matrix).

First, we generate the data.

```
. clear all
. set more off
. local obs = 10000
. set obs 'obs'
. gen time = _n-1
. tsset time

. matrix sigma = (1, 0, 0 \ 0, 1, 0 \ 0, 0, 1)
```

Akaike's FPE. You should never choose one simply because it gives you the results you were hoping for.

In their review of the money/income causality literature, Stock and Watson (1989) report that adding a deterministic time trend strengthens money's estimated effect on output. Further, the sample data can affect the results (e.g., Eichenbaum & Singleton 1986). (Structural breaks can often be confused with unit roots, leading to inappropriate detrending in the money/income regressions.) Stock and Watson's (1989) main econometric finding is that the initial method of detrending is responsible for the diverging results; detrending can cause the test statistics to have non-standard distributions. Their main economic finding is that shocks to the money growth rate that are greater than those predicted by the trend do have an effect on output.

Hall (1978) is also notable, reminding researchers that permanent rather than transitory income matters, so simple regressions of consumption on past income conflates two different effects. Dickey et al. (1991) revisited the money/income question, with interest rates added, in the context of cointegration analysis.

[15] This presumes that the lag-structure is correctly specified in the VAR.

```
. drawnorm e1 e2 e3, means(0,0,0) cov(sigma) double seed(1234)

. gen X = 0
. gen Z = 0
. gen Y = 0

. quietly{
.   forvalues i = 2/'obs' {
.       replace X = 0.00*L.Y + 0.00*L.X + 0.00*L.Z + e1 in 'i'
.       replace Z = 0.00*L.Y + 0.90*L.X + 0.00*L.Z + e2 in 'i'
.       replace Y = 0.00*L.Y + 0.00*L.X + 0.90*L.Z + e3 in 'i'
.       }
. }
```

Our simulated data comprise shocks to X, Y, and Z drawn so that they are uncorrelated with each other. Then we generated the values of X, Y, and Z with carefully selected coefficients such that (1) X does not depend on Z or Y; (2) X, and only X, affects Z; and (3) only Z affects Y.

Next, we estimate the VAR and run a Granger causality test:

```
. quietly varbasic X Z Y, lags(1)

. vargranger

Granger causality Wald tests
+------------------------------------------------------------------+
|      Equation          Excluded |   chi2     df Prob > chi2     |
|---------------------------------+--------------------------------|
|             X                 Z |  .81246     1    0.367        |
|             X                 Y |  1.6197     1    0.203        |
|             X               ALL |  2.4486     2    0.294        |
|---------------------------------+--------------------------------|
|             Z                 X |  8618.3     1    0.000        |
|             Z                 Y |  .12358     1    0.725        |
|             Z               ALL |  8618.6     2    0.000        |
|---------------------------------+--------------------------------|
|             Y                 X |  .4202      1    0.517        |
|             Y                 Z |  14864      1    0.000        |
|             Y               ALL |  14864      2    0.000        |
+------------------------------------------------------------------+
```

The Granger causality table shows that (1) nothing Granger-causes X, (2) X Granger-causes Z, and (3) Z Granger-causes Y. But, logically speaking, isn't it the case that an independent change in X will result in a change in Y? Yes, indirectly through X's effect on Z, but ultimately X did logically cause Y. This can be thought of as a failure of Granger causality tests, because when we tested, in the third panel above whether X caused Y, it was found not to ($p = 0.5176 > 0.05$). So X logically causes Y, but X didn't Granger-cause Y.

10.11 VAR Example: GNP and Unemployment

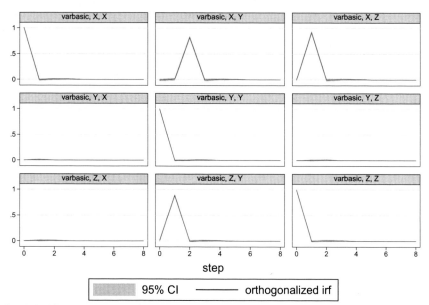

Fig. 10.5 Indirect Causality from X to Z to Y

Does the indirect effect of X on Y show up in the OIRFs? Thankfully, it does, as revealed in Fig. 10.5, where the top center panel indicates that a shock to X is followed by an ultimate response in Y.

10.11 VAR Example: GNP and Unemployment

We'll try to pull all of this information together by working out a full-scale example of a VAR analysis. We'll follow these steps:

1. Download and format the data.
2. Make sure our data are stationary.
3. Determine the number of lags.
4. Estimate the VAR.
5. Verify that the estimated VAR model is stable.
6. Investigate Granger causality and calculate IRFs and FEVDs.

We will estimate a VAR on the USA's unemployment rate and the GNP growth rate. Of course, this example is not meant to be definitive, only illustrative of the technique.

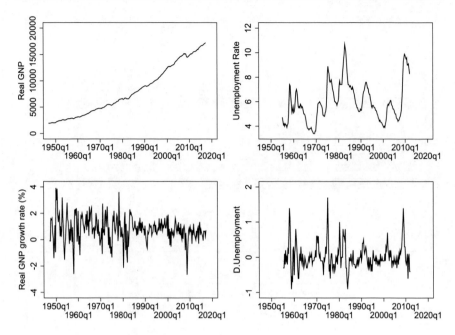

Fig. 10.6 VAR example: the data

First, we download and format the data:

```
. clear all
. freduse GNPC96 USAURHARMQDSMEI
. gen time=yq(year(daten), quarter(daten))
. tsset time, quarterly

. gen GNPgr = (ln(GNPC9) - ln(L.GNPC9))*100

. label var GNPC9 "Real GNP"
. label var USAUR "Unemployment Rate"
. label var GNPgr "Real GNP growth rate (%)"

. rename USAUR Unemp
```

A graph of the data is provided in Fig. 10.6.

Second, we use a KPSS test to ensure that the data are stationary around their levels.

10.11 VAR Example: GNP and Unemployment

```
. kpss GNPgr , notrend

KPSS test for GNPgr

Maxlag = 5 chosen by Schwert criterion
Autocovariances weighted by Bartlett kernel

Critical values for H0: GNPgr is level stationary

10%: 0.347   5% : 0.463   2.5%: 0.574   1% : 0.739

Lag order      Test statistic
0              .825
1              .603
2              .504
3              .463
4              .449
5              .449

. kpss Unemp, notrend

KPSS test for Unemp

Maxlag = 4 chosen by Schwert criterion
Autocovariances weighted by Bartlett kernel

Critical values for H0: Unemp is level stationary

10%: 0.347   5% : 0.463   2.5%: 0.574   1% : 0.739

Lag order      Test statistic
0              2.28
1              1.16
2              .789
3              .606
4              .499

. kpss D.Unemp , notrend

KPSS test for D.Unemp

Maxlag = 4 chosen by Schwert criterion
Autocovariances weighted by Bartlett kernel

Critical values for H0: D.Unemp is level stationary
```

```
               10%: 0.347    5% : 0.463    2.5%: 0.574    1% : 0.739

    Lag order      Test statistic
    0              .101
    1              .0622
    2              .0497
    3              .0442
    4              .042
```

Above, we see that the growth rate of GNP is stationary. On the other hand, the unemployment rate is not stationary; thus, we took the first difference and found that the change in the unemployment rate is stationary. Thus, we recast our VAR to look at the relationship between the growth rate of GNP and the change in the unemployment rate.

As our third step, we determine the number of lags by looking at the various information criteria.

```
. varsoc GNPgr D.Unemp, maxlag(8)

Selection-order criteria
Sample:  1957q2 - 2012q1                      Number of obs     =       220
  +---------------------------------------------------------------------------+
  |lag |    LL      LR      df    p      FPE       AIC      HQIC      SBIC   |
  |----+----------------------------------------------------------------------|
  |  0 | -312.625                      .059873   2.86023   2.87269   2.89108  |
  |  1 | -244.737  135.78   4  0.000   .033496   2.27943   2.3168    2.37198* |
  |  2 | -236.876   15.722  4  0.003   .032341*  2.24432*  2.30662*  2.39858  |
  |  3 | -236.089    1.5732 4  0.814   .033301   2.27354   2.36075   2.48949  |
  |  4 | -232.935    6.3087 4  0.177   .033559   2.28122   2.39335   2.55888  |
  |  5 | -230.654    4.5608 4  0.335   .034091   2.29296   2.4339    2.63622  |
  |  6 |  -230.1     1.1088 4  0.893   .035179   2.32818   2.49014   2.72925  |
  |  7 | -228.575    3.0492 4  0.550   .035985   2.35068   2.53756   2.81345  |
  |  8 | -220.659   15.832* 4  0.003   .034733   2.31508   2.52688   2.83955  |
  +---------------------------------------------------------------------------+

Endogenous:  GNPgr D.Unemp
Exogenous:   _cons
```

The Akaike information criterion and the Hannan-Quinn information criterion indicate that two lags are preferred; the Schwarz Bayesian information criterion disagrees slightly, preferring a single lag. Such a disagreement between the three statistics is not uncommon. We follow the AIC and estimate our VAR with two lags.

As our fourth and fifth steps, we estimate the VAR(2) and calculate the eigenvalues of the companion matrix to make sure our VAR is stable.

```
. quietly varbasic D.Unemp GNPgr , lag(1/2) irf

. varstable , graph modlabel

Eigenvalue stability condition
```

10.11 VAR Example: GNP and Unemployment

```
+---------------------------------------+
|       Eigenvalue        |   Modulus   |
|-------------------------+-------------|
|   .5151559 +  .3106396i |   .601567   |
|   .5151559 -  .3106396i |   .601567   |
|  -.2367879 +  .144781i  |   .277543   |
|  -.2367879 -  .144781i  |   .277543   |
+---------------------------------------+
All the eigenvalues lie inside the unit circle.
VAR satisfies stability condition.
```

All of the roots have a length (modulus) less than one. Thus, we are inside the unit circle (see Fig. 10.7), and our estimated VAR is stable.

As a final post-estimation check, we verify that our residuals to not exhibit any left-over autocorrelation:

```
. varlmar

Lagrange-multiplier test
+--------------------------------------+
| lag |    chi2     df   Prob > chi2   |
|-----+--------------------------------|
|  1  |   1.1463    4      0.88686     |
|  2  |   2.3625    4      0.66941     |
+--------------------------------------+
```

Fig. 10.7 VAR example: stability

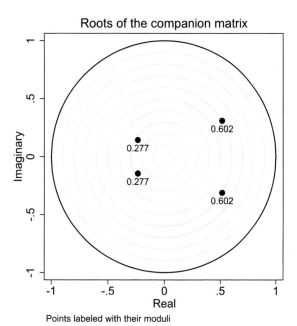

Points labeled with their moduli

HO: no autocorrelation at lag order

Is there any Granger causality? The output below reveals that both variables Granger-cause each other.

```
. vargranger

Granger causality Wald tests
  +------------------------------------------------------------------+
  |        Equation          Excluded |   chi2     df  Prob > chi2  |
  |-----------------------------------+------------------------------|
  |         D_Unemp             GNPgr |  27.023     2      0.000    |
  |         D_Unemp               ALL |  27.023     2      0.000    |
  |-----------------------------------+------------------------------|
  |           GNPgr          D.Unemp  |  17.785     2      0.000    |
  |           GNPgr               ALL |  17.785     2      0.000    |
  +------------------------------------------------------------------+
```

Finally, we examine the graphs of the IRFs and FEVDs (see Figs. 10.8 and 10.9) to better understand the dynamics between the two variables. The IRF indicates that a shock to D.Unemp dampens gently to zero by the third or fourth quarter. The same shock to D.Unemp decreases the GNP growth rate for a quarter, before GNPgr returns to its baseline level. Shocks to the GNP growth rate have a much more muted effect. They decrease the unemployment growth rate only slightly; a positive shock to the GNP growth rate also tends to dampen out and reaches its baseline within one to three periods.

The first column of Fig. 10.9 shows how much of the forecast error variance in D.Unemp is due to D.Unemp and to GNPgr. The top left panel shows that initially 100% of the variance in D.Unemp is due to earlier shocks to D.Unemp. This decreases slightly to approximately 80% by period 3 or 4. The bottom left panel shows that, initially, very little of the variation in D.Unemp is due to shocks in the growth rate of GNP; the impact of GNPgr on D.Unemp increases to approximately 20% by period 3 or 4.

10.12 Exercises

1. Suppose you estimated the following two-variable VAR(1) model:

$$X_t = 0.30 X_{t-1} + 0.10 Y_{t-1} + \epsilon_{x,t}$$
$$Y_t = 0.40 X_{t-1} - 0.20 Y_{t-1} + \epsilon_{y,t}$$

   with $X_0 = 0$ and $Y_0 = 0$.
   (a) Express the VAR in matrix form using the companion matrix.
   (b) Calculate the first five values of the IRF of a 1-unit shock to X_1 on X_t and Y_t.
   (c) Calculate the first five values of the IRF of a 1-unit shock to Y_1 on X_t and Y_t.
2. Suppose you estimated the following two-variable VAR(2) model:

$$X_t = 0.30 X_{t-1} - 0.20 Y_{t-1} + 0.15 X_{t-2} + 0.05 Y_{t-2} + \epsilon_{x,t}$$
$$Y_t = 0.30 X_{t-1} - 0.10 Y_{t-1} + 0.05 X_{t-2} + 0.01 Y_{t-2} + \epsilon_{y,t}$$

10.12 Exercises

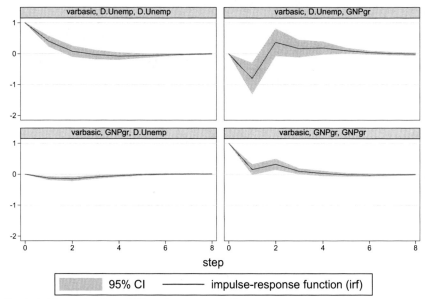

Fig. 10.8 VAR example: impulse response function

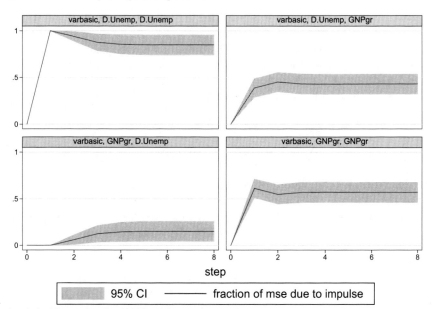

Fig. 10.9 VAR example: forecast error variance decomposition

(a) Write out this system in matrix form.
(b) Write out this system in companion form, showing each entry of the companion matrix (as we did in Eq. (10.10)).
(c) Calculate the eigenvalues of the companion matrix and determine whether the estimated VAR is stable.
(d) Using the companion matrix, calculate the first four values of the impulse response function following a one-unit shock to $\epsilon_{x,t}$. Do the same for a one-unit shock to $\epsilon_{y,t}$.

3. Suppose you estimated the following two-variable VAR(3) model:

$$X_t = 0.30X_{t-1} + .10Y_{t-1} - 0.15X_{t-1} + 0.15Y_{t-2} - 0.05X_{t-3} + 0.07Y_{t-3} + \epsilon_{x,t}$$

$$Y_t = 0.10X_{t-1} + 0.30Y_{t-1} - 0.12X_{t-1} + 0.15Y_{t-2} + 0.05X_{t-3} + 0.09Y_{t-3} + \epsilon_{y,t}.$$

with the first two values of X_t and Y_t equal to zero.
(a) Express the VAR in matrix form using one coefficient matrix per lag.
(b) Express the VAR in matrix form using the companion matrix.
(c) Calculate the eigenvalues of the companion matrix and determine whether the VAR is stable.
(d) Using the companion matrix, what are the first five values of the IRF from a one-unit shock to $\epsilon_{x,2}$.

4. Calculate the first five values of the IRF from Eqs. (10.23) and (10.24), given a one-unit shock to Y_1 (or $\epsilon_{2,1}$). That is, verify the values in the second row of Fig. 10.4.

5. Consider the two-variable VARe(1) model:

$$X_t = 100 + 0.20X_{t-1} - 0.40Y_{t-1} + \epsilon_{x,t}$$
$$Y_t = 120 - 0.30X_{t-1} - 0.20Y_{t-1} + \epsilon_{y,t}$$

with $X_0 = 85.71429$ and $Y_0 = 78.57143$:
(a) Express the VAR in matrix form using the companion matrix.
(b) Calculate the first five values of the IRF of a 1-unit shock to X_1 on X_t and Y_t.
(c) Calculate the first five values of the IRF of a 1-unit shock to Y_1 on X_t and Y_t.

Vector Autoregressions II: Extensions

11

In the previous chapter we covered the basics of reduced-form VARs on stationary data. In this chapter we continue learning about VARs, but we extend the discussion to structural VARs (SVARs) and VARS with integrated variables. In the process, we will go through some additional examples and in-depth replication of an SVAR paper by Blanchard and Quah (1989).

Many students begin estimating SVARs without even realizing it: by estimating "orthogonalized IRFs." Thus, we begin there.

11.1 Orthogonalized IRFs

We were able to calculate IRFs in Sect. 10.8 because we presumed there was a one-time shock to one variable that did not simultaneously affect the other endogenous variable. In practice, however, random shocks affect many variables simultaneously. They are not always independent of each other. Rather, they are often contemporaneously correlated. This is why a VAR is estimated using SUR (which allows for contemporaneously correlated errors across equations) rather than using separate OLS regressions (which presume independence or orthogonality).

IRFs indicate in general how a shock to one variable affects the other variables. But this is not particularly useful for policy purposes if we rely on errors which are correlated across variables. We'd like to identify an exogenous change in a policy variable and track its effect on the other variables. That is, for policy purposes, we can't have those shocks be correlated. So how do we uncorrelate those shocks? How can we make them orthogonal to each other?

After we estimate a VAR, we must impose a certain type of assumption or constraint to draw the corresponding orthogonalized IRF. There are several such assumptions that allow us to draw OIRFs. The most common such constraint is to impose sequential orthogonality via something called a "Cholesky decomposition."

To see how orthogonalization changes things, let's generate an artificial dataset—one where the shocks are highly correlated across equations—and show how the IRFs and OIRFs differ. We will generate observations for the following VAR(1):

$$Y_t = 0.30 Y_{t-1} - 0.50 X_{t-1} + \epsilon_{y,t} \quad (11.1)$$

$$X_t = -0.40 Y_{t-1} + 0.30 X_{t-1} + \epsilon_{x,t} \quad (11.2)$$

where the errors have the following variance/covariance matrix:

$$\Sigma = \begin{bmatrix} 1 & .75 \\ .75 & 1 \end{bmatrix} \quad (11.3)$$

so that shocks are correlated cross-equations.

```
. clear all
. local T = 10000
. set obs 'T'
. gen time = _n-1
. tsset time
. set seed 1234

. matrix sigma = (1,.75 \.75, 1)
. drawnorm epsilon_y epsilon_x, means(0,0) cov(sigma)
   double

. gen Y = 0
. gen X = 0

. quietly{
      forvalues i = 2/'T'{
         replace Y = 0.30*L.Y - 0.50*L.X ///
               + epsilon_y in 'i'
         replace X = -0.40*L.Y + 0.30*L.X ///
               + epsilon_x in 'i'
      }
.}
```

Then we estimate the VAR and calculate the impulse response functions. We'll ask Stata to calculate two sets of IRFs, (a) the simple IRFs, similar to the ones we calculated by hand, and (b) orthogonalized IRFs, where we take into account the correlation between $\epsilon_{x,t}$ and $\epsilon_{x,t}$.

```
. var Y X , lags(1) nocons
. irf create irf , set(name1)
. irf graph irf oirf, noci
```

11.1 Orthogonalized IRFs

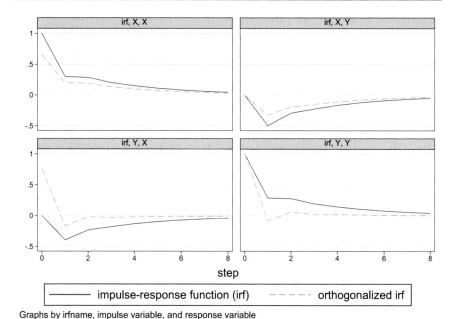

Fig. 11.1 Simple IRFs vs orthogonalized IRFs

The IRFs are drawn in Fig. 11.1, where you can see that IRFs can vary significantly when we take into account the fact that the errors hitting both equations might be correlated. IRFs are usually not the same as OIRFs.

11.1.1 Order Matters in OIRFs

Orthogonalized IRFs allow for the shocks to one equation to be correlated in the others. Thus, they are (a) arguably more realistic and (b) better describe the causal effects. Unfortunately, there are no free lunches. The process of orthogonalization depends upon something that we've been able to ignore thus far: the order in which the variables are listed in the VAR. That is, the OIRFs from

```
. var Y X
```

are not the same as those from

```
. var X Y
```

In Fig. 11.2 we show the OIRFs from two different orderings of the VAR, which we created from:

```
. quietly var Y X , lags(1) nocons
. irf create order1, step(10) order(Y X) set(myirf1,
```

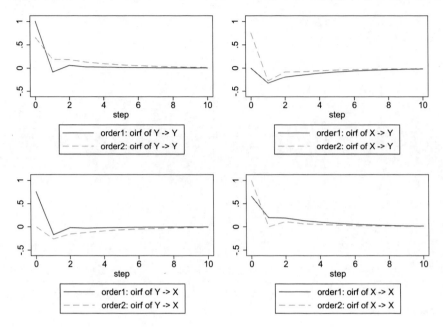

Fig. 11.2 Order matters with OIRFs

```
replace)
. irf create order2, step(10) order(X Y)
```

The first irf command specified a causal ordering giving Y primacy (order Y X). The second irf reversed the order, giving X primacy over Y (order X Y).

As you can see in Fig. 11.2, then estimated OIRFs can be quite different. So, what are we to do? If you want to report the OIRF, then you will need to justify the ordering. That is, you will have to determine—hopefully with the aid of solid economic theory—which variable is more likely to be causal and independent, and list it first. Then list the second most, third most, etc.

Sometimes, as in our example when the shocks were highly correlated across equations, order is important. Other times, order is negligible. But there is only one way to tell, and that means estimating the OIRFs from many different orderings and comparing them. If there are only two variables, then this is easy. But if there are, say, four variables, then there are $4 \times 3 \times 2 \times 1 = 24$ orderings. With K variables, there are K! orderings. One popular approach is to estimate your preferred ordering, where you list the variables in decreasing order of exogeneity and then reverse the order. The idea is that if the OIRFs from these two extremes are in agreement, then the other orderings can be ignored.

We saw above that order matters when drawing OIRFs, but we still don't know *why*. To better understand this, we'll need to take detour into Cholesky decompositions.

Exercises

1. Re-estimate the OIRFs from the VAR(1) described in Eqs. (11.1) and (11.2), but change the variance/covariance matrix to

$$\Sigma = \begin{bmatrix} 1 & .15 \\ .15 & 1 \end{bmatrix}$$

so that the shocks are not as highly correlated across equations. Use this to show that the Cholesky ordering has a negligible impact when the variables are relatively uncorrelated. (Hint: reuse the Stata code provided in Sect. 11.1, changing the definition of Σ.)

11.1.2 Cholesky Decompositions and OIRFs

Orthogonalization of the errors is done by a process called Cholesky decomposition.

Every legitimate variance/covariance matrix is symmetric and positive definite. And every positive definite matrix A can be expressed as the product of a lower triangular matrix L and its transpose L':

$$A = LL'.$$

A Cholesky decomposition can be thought of as decomposing a matrix into the product of its two square roots. This is quite useful. Just as we often need to work with the standard deviation (the square root of the variance), we might want to work with L which is the square root of the variance/covariance matrix.

For example, the variance/covariance matrix Σ can be decomposed into

$$\Sigma = \begin{bmatrix} 1 & .75 \\ .75 & 1 \end{bmatrix} = \begin{bmatrix} 1 & 0 \\ .75 & .66143783 \end{bmatrix} \begin{bmatrix} 1 & .75 \\ 0 & .66143783 \end{bmatrix}.$$

Likewise

$$\Sigma = \begin{bmatrix} 1 & .30 & .20 \\ .30 & 1 & .10 \\ .20 & .10 & 1 \end{bmatrix} = \begin{bmatrix} 1 & 0 & 0 \\ .3 & .953939 & 0 \\ .2 & .0419314 & .9788982 \end{bmatrix} \begin{bmatrix} 1 & .3 & .2 \\ 0 & .954949 & .0419314 \\ 0 & 0 & .9788982 \end{bmatrix}$$

There is often some confusion as to the notation of a Cholesky decomposition. Some authors define the Cholesky decomposition in terms of upper triangular matrices, $A = U'U$. Cholesky decomposes a matrix into the product of a lower triangular matrix and its transpose. The transpose of a lower triangular matrix is upper triangular ($L' = U$); and the transpose of an upper triangular matrix is lower triangular ($U' = L$). So $A = U'U$ is equivalent to our $A = LL'$.

We are used to standardizing a variable by dividing it by its standard deviation. For example, if $X \sim N\left(0, \sigma^2\right)$, then $X/\sigma \sim N(0, 1)$. The rescaled variable now has a standard deviation of one. This also requires rescaling our coefficients. We will use a similar procedure when we deal with matrices, too.

Variables should be ordered in increasing order of relative endogeneity. That is, list the variable most likely to be exogenous first. Your second variable should be the second most exogenous. Your final variable should be the one most likely to be endogenous. (None of the variables are truly exogenous. We're talking relative exogeneity: more or less exogenous).

Re-ordering our variables results in a completely different Cholesky decomposition. The ordering is, thus, a statement about economic theory. It doesn't test a theory; it imposes it. (Thus the data do not "speak for themselves.") The best research relies on solid economic theory to justify imposing particular constraints (your ordering). There is no substitute for solid economic theory here.

Using Cholesky to Orthogonalize Variables

The issue with the standard IRFs is that they are drawn presuming that shocks to X are independent of shocks to Y. But in reality, shocks are usually correlated. We would like some way of transforming our estimated IRFs so that they correspond to independent shocks, i.e., from shocks with a variance/covariance matrix a little bit more like

$$\mathbf{I} = \begin{bmatrix} 1 & 0 \\ 0 & 1 \end{bmatrix}$$

than from, say,

$$\Sigma = \begin{bmatrix} 1 & 0.75 \\ 0.75 & 1 \end{bmatrix}. \tag{11.4}$$

Recall from introductory statistics that we can standardize a variable by diving it by its standard deviation. That is, if $X \sim N\left(0, \sigma^2\right)$, then $X/\sigma \sim N(0, 1)$. It turns out we can do something similar with matrices, using the Cholesky decomposition. Multiplying by the inverse of a Cholesky factor accomplishes two things. First, it standardizes the shocks, so that a one-unit shock is also a one standard deviation shock. Second, it orthogonalizes the shocks, i.e., it makes them uncorrelated.

Let's work out an illustration. We'll generate two variables, where

$$\begin{bmatrix} \epsilon_1 \\ \epsilon_2 \end{bmatrix} \sim N(\begin{bmatrix} 0 \\ 0 \end{bmatrix}, \begin{bmatrix} 1 & 0.75 \\ 0.75 & 1 \end{bmatrix}),$$

transform them, and then verify that the transformed variables have the correlation structure that we wanted.

11.1 Orthogonalized IRFs

First, let's define the original variance/covariance matrix and get its Cholesky factors (as well as their inverses):

```
. matrix sigma = (1 , .75 \ .75, 1)
. matrix L = cholesky(sigma)   /* The lower triangular factor */
. matrix Lt = L'               /* L-transpose, the upper factor */
. matrix LInv = inv(L)         /* The inverse of L */
```

Generate the untransformed variables:

```
. set obs 10000
. gen time = _n-1
. tsset time
. drawnorm eps1 eps2, means(0,0) cov(sigma) double
  seed(1234)
```

Verify that they have the appropriate variance/covariance structure:

```
. correlate eps1 eps2, covariance
(obs=10,000)

     |     eps1       eps2
-----+-------------------
eps1 |   1.0123
eps2 |   .761498    1.004
```

Now, pre-multiply the error matrix by the inverse of the lower Cholesky factor to generate the transformed errors:

```
. gen e1 = LInv[1,1]*eps1 + LInv[1,2]*eps2
. gen e2 = LInv[2,1]*eps1 + LInv[2,2]*eps2
```

This is the matrix analogue of standardizing a variable by dividing it by its standard deviation. Notice, the transformed errors have the appropriate variance/covariance structure:

```
. correlate e_x e_y, covariance
(obs=10,000)

     |       e1         e2
-----+-------------------
  e1 |   1.00013
  e2 |  -.000276   1.00061
```

The original two variables eps1 and eps2 were correlated (not orthogonal) to each other (Fig. 11.3). The two transformed variables, e1 and e2, are orthogonal to each other (Fig. 11.4).

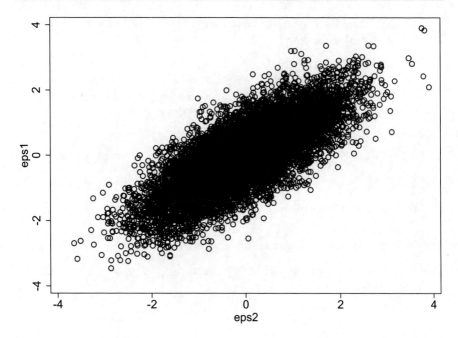

Fig. 11.3 Correlated errors

Expressing OIRFs as the Coefficients of the MA Representation

Recall that a stationary VAR(1) process

$$\mathbf{Y_t} = \boldsymbol{\beta} \mathbf{Y_{t-1}} + \boldsymbol{\epsilon}_t$$

can be expressed as an MA(∞) process.

$$\mathbf{Y_t} = \sum_{j=0}^{\infty} \boldsymbol{\beta}^j \boldsymbol{\epsilon}_{t-j} = \boldsymbol{\beta}^0 \boldsymbol{\epsilon}_t + \boldsymbol{\beta}^1 \boldsymbol{\epsilon}_{t-1} + \boldsymbol{\beta}^2 \boldsymbol{\epsilon}_{t-2} + \dots \qquad (11.5)$$

where $\boldsymbol{\beta}^0$ is equal to the Identity matrix. We saw earlier how the sequence of $\boldsymbol{\beta}^j$s were the IRFs of the VAR. How do we get the OIRFs?

The challenge is to rearrange the expression in (11.5) without altering the equation: we wish to change the way we see the data; we don't want to change the data. Thus, we can't just go about multiplying something on the right without multiplying something on the left. What we can do, however, is judiciously multiply by one; in matrices we can multiply by the identity matrix **I**. We can rewrite (11.5) as

11.1 Orthogonalized IRFs

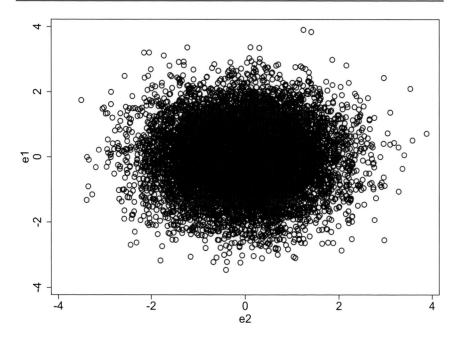

Fig. 11.4 Orthogonalized errors via Cholesky

$$\mathbf{Y_t} = \sum_{j=0}^{\infty} \beta^j \mathbf{L}\mathbf{L}^{-1}\epsilon_{t-j} = \beta^0 \mathbf{L}\mathbf{L}^{-1}\epsilon_t + \beta^1 \mathbf{L}\mathbf{L}^{-1}\epsilon_{t-1} + \beta^2 \mathbf{L}\mathbf{L}^{-1}\epsilon_{t-2} + \ldots \quad (11.6)$$

where $\mathbf{L}$ and $\mathbf{L}^{-1}$ are the lower Cholesky factor and its inverse. Thus, $\mathbf{Y_t}$ can be seen as a weighted average of orthogonal shocks. The weights – the OIRFs – are given by the sequence of $\beta^j \mathbf{L}^{-1}$s, and the orthogonal errors are given by the sequence of $\mathbf{L}^{-1}\epsilon_{t-j}$s.

Multiplying the error by L^{-1} orthogonalizes the error. Multiplying β by $\mathbf{L}$ transforms the coefficients in an offsetting (inverse) yet complementary direction. Thus, the βL's trace out the IRFs from orthogonal shocks $\mathbf{L}^{-1}\epsilon$. This is why OIRFs are different from IRFs. The errors get fed through transformed β's. There are other ways to multiplying by one. And there are unfortunately also other ways to orthogonalize. The Cholesky decomposition is merely the most popular (popularized by Chris Sims himself).

To solidify this concept, we will estimate a VAR from artificial data. Then we will have Stata estimate the IRFs and OIRFs. Then we'll perform the Cholesky multiplication as in Eq. (11.6) by hand and compare the results. We should be able to replicate Stata's answers. Then, we will redo the orthogonalization, but we'll change the order, and we'll show how this changes the estimated OIRFs.

We begin by generating the data

```
. clear all
. local obs = 10000
. set obs 'obs'
. gen time = _n
. tsset time
. matrix sigma = (1 , .75 \ .75, 1)
. drawnorm eps_x eps_y, means(0,0) cov(sigma) double
  seed(1234)
. gen X = 0
. gen Y = 0
. forvalues i = 2/'obs' {
.       quietly replace X = 0.40*L.X + 0.10*L.Y + eps_x
          in 'i'
.       quietly replace Y = 0.20*L.X + 0.10*L.Y + eps_y
          in 'i'
.     }
```

Then we estimate the VAR and extract the estimated coefficient matrix ($\hat{\beta}$) and variance/covariance matrix ($\hat{\Sigma}$).

```
. quietly var X Y, lags(1)
. irf create varXY, step(10) set(myirf1) replace
. irf table irf, noci
. irf table oirf, noci

. matrix sigmahat = e(Sigma)
. quietly varstable, amat(betahat)

. matrix L = cholesky(sigmahat)
. matrix LInv = inv(L)
```

Stata' estimates of the IRF and OIRF are:

11.1 Orthogonalized IRFs

```
. irf table irf, noci

Results from varXY
```

step	(1) irf	(2) irf	(3) irf	(4) irf
0	1	0	0	1
1	.39704	.205562	.104143	.104868
2	.179049	.103173	.05227	.032405
3	.081834	.047625	.024128	.014143
4	.037451	.021816	.011053	.006443
5	.017142	.009986	.005059	.002948
6	.007846	.004571	.002316	.001349
7	.003591	.002092	.00106	.000618
8	.001644	.000958	.000485	.000283
9	.000752	.000438	.000222	.000129
10	.000344	.000201	.000102	.000059

(1) irfname = varXY, impulse = X, and response = X
(2) irfname = varXY, impulse = X, and response = Y
(3) irfname = varXY, impulse = Y, and response = X
(4) irfname = varXY, impulse = Y, and response = Y

```
. irf table oirf, noci

Results from varXY
```

step	(1) oirf	(2) oirf	(3) oirf	(4) oirf
0	1.00612	.75688	0	.656501
1	.478294	.286191	.06837	.068846
2	.219707	.128331	.034316	.021274
3	.100597	.058621	.01584	.009285
4	.046046	.026826	.007256	.00423
5	.021076	.012279	.003322	.001935
6	.009647	.00562	.00152	.000886
7	.004415	.002572	.000696	.000405
8	.002021	.001177	.000319	.000186
9	.000925	.000539	.000146	.000085
10	.000423	.000247	.000067	.000039

(1) irfname = varXY, impulse = X, and response = X
(2) irfname = varXY, impulse = X, and response = Y
(3) irfname = varXY, impulse = Y, and response = X
(4) irfname = varXY, impulse = Y, and response = Y

We can replicate the IRF by reporting the powers of the estimated coefficient matrix:

```
. matrix betahat0 = I(2)

. matrix betahat1 = betahat

. matrix betahat2 = betahat*betahat

. matrix betahat3 = betahat*betahat*betahat

. matrix betahat4 = betahat*betahat*betahat*betahat

. matrix list betahat0

symmetric betahat0[2,2]
    c1  c2
r1   1
r2   0   1

. matrix list betahat1

betahat1[2,2]
           c1          c2
r1   .39704043   .10414341
r2   .20556151   .10486756

. matrix list betahat2

betahat2[2,2]
           c1          c2
r1   .17904898   .05227041
r2   .10317297   .03240508

. matrix list betahat3

betahat3[2,2]
           c1          c2
r1   .08183447   .02412824
r2   .04762508   .01414303

. matrix list betahat4

betahat4[2,2]
           c1          c2
r1   .03745143   .01105279
r2   .02181634   .00644298
```

11.1 Orthogonalized IRFs

The OIRs are the estimated coefficients multiplied by the lower Cholesky factor:

```
. matrix phi_0 = L

. matrix phi_1 = betahat1*L

. matrix phi_2 = betahat2*L

. matrix phi_3 = betahat3*L

. matrix phi_4 = betahat4*L

. matrix list phi_0

phi_0[2,2]
          X            Y
X  1.0061183            0
Y   .75687962    .65650145

. matrix list phi_1

phi_1[2,2]
          X            Y
r1   .47829365     .0683703
r2   .28619131     .0688457

. matrix list phi_2

phi_2[2,2]
          X            Y
r1   .21970686     .0343156
r2   .12833095     .02127398

. matrix list phi_3

phi_3[2,2]
          X            Y
r1   .10059733     .01584023
r2   .05862103     .00928492

. matrix list phi_4

phi_4[2,2]
          X            Y
r1    .0460462     .00725617
```

r2   .02682638   .00422983

Thus far, we have shown how to find the OIRFs automatically and "by hand" using matrix multiplication. Now, we will show, yet again, that the order matters for OIRFs.

```
. quietly var Y X, lags(1)

. irf create varYX, step(10) set(myirf2) replace

. irf table oirf, noci

Results from varYX

+-------------------------------------------------------------+
|       |   (1)    |   (2)    |   (3)    |   (4)    |
| step  |   oirf   |   oirf   |   oirf   |   oirf   |
|-------+----------+----------+----------+----------|
|0      | 1.00193  | .760045  | 0        | .659247  |
|1      | .261306  | .406113  | .135516  | .261748  |
|2      | .110884  | .188456  | .068016  | .118037  |
|3      | .050367  | .086373  | .031397  | .053949  |
|4      | .023037  | .039539  | .014382  | .02469   |
|5      | .010543  | .018098  | .006584  | .011301  |
|6      | .004826  | .008284  | .003013  | .005172  |
|7      | .002209  | .003791  | .001379  | .002367  |
|8      | .001011  | .001735  | .000631  | .001084  |
|9      | .000463  | .000794  | .000289  | .000496  |
|10     | .000212  | .000364  | .000132  | .000227  |
+-------------------------------------------------------------+
(1) irfname = varYX, impulse = Y, and response = Y
(2) irfname = varYX, impulse = Y, and response = X
(3) irfname = varYX, impulse = X, and response = Y
(4) irfname = varYX, impulse = X, and response = X
```

Notice that we reversed the order in the VAR, and the new OIRFs reflect this change. Now, why does order matter?

11.1.3 Why Order Matters for OIRFs

We've shown graphically and numerically *that* order matters for OIRFs, but we haven't been very explicit about *why* order matters. We're now in a position to explain this. Ultimately, the reason order matters is because when we take the Cholesky decomposition of $\hat{\Sigma}$, the error's estimated variance/covariance matrix, we create two triangular matrices, **L** and **L'**. We multiply the coefficients in the companion matrix by **L**, which is a lower triangular matrix. We also multiply the errors by the inverse of **L**, but this is also a lower triangular matrix. So there are systematic zeros in our equations that limit the effect in the earlier, higher up equations; the fewer zeros at the bottom of the lower triangular matrices allow for

11.1 Orthogonalized IRFs

more interactions with these later equations. But this is all quite vague. Let's work out the math of a simple example.

Suppose we estimated a VAR where we listed X first, such as in

$$\begin{bmatrix} X_t \\ Y_t \end{bmatrix} = \begin{bmatrix} \hat{\beta}_{xx} & \hat{\beta}_{xy} \\ \hat{\beta}_{yx} & \hat{\beta}_{yy} \end{bmatrix} \begin{bmatrix} X_{t-1} \\ Y_{t-1} \end{bmatrix} + \begin{bmatrix} \epsilon_{x,t} \\ \epsilon_{y,t} \end{bmatrix}$$

where, as usual, $\hat{\beta}$s are estimated parameters. And suppose that the estimated variance/covariance matrix of the error terms is

$$\hat{\Sigma} = \begin{bmatrix} \hat{\sigma}_x^2 & \hat{\sigma}_{x,y} \\ \hat{\sigma}_{y,x} & \hat{\sigma}_y^2 \end{bmatrix}.$$

Let's express the Cholesky decomposition of $\hat{\Sigma}$ as

$$\hat{\Sigma} = \hat{L}\hat{L}' = \begin{bmatrix} \hat{L}_{xx} & 0 \\ \hat{L}_{yx} & \hat{L}_{yy} \end{bmatrix} \begin{bmatrix} \hat{L}_{xx} & \hat{L}_{yx} \\ 0 & \hat{L}_{yy} \end{bmatrix}$$

and the inverse of the estimated lower Cholesky factor as

$$\hat{L}^{-1} = \begin{bmatrix} \hat{l}_{xx} & 0 \\ \hat{l}_{yx} & \hat{l}_{yy} \end{bmatrix}.$$

Presuming the VAR is invertible, we can express it as an MA(∞) process:

$$\mathbf{Y} = \boldsymbol{\beta}\mathbf{Y} + \boldsymbol{\epsilon}$$
$$= \boldsymbol{\beta}^0 \boldsymbol{\epsilon}_t + \boldsymbol{\beta}^1 \boldsymbol{\epsilon}_{t-1} + \boldsymbol{\beta}^2 \boldsymbol{\epsilon}_{t-2} + \ldots$$
$$= \boldsymbol{\beta}^0 \mathbf{L}\mathbf{L}^{-1}\boldsymbol{\epsilon}_t + \boldsymbol{\beta}^1 \mathbf{L}\mathbf{L}^{-1}\boldsymbol{\epsilon}_{t-1} + \boldsymbol{\beta}^2 \mathbf{L}\mathbf{L}^{-1}\boldsymbol{\epsilon}_{t-2} + \ldots$$

The OIRFs are the sequence of $\boldsymbol{\beta}^j \mathbf{L}$'s. Recalling that $\boldsymbol{\beta}^0 = \mathbf{I}$, the OIRFs are

$$\hat{\beta}^0 \hat{L} = \begin{bmatrix} 1 & 0 \\ 0 & 1 \end{bmatrix} \begin{bmatrix} \hat{L}_{xx} & 0 \\ \hat{L}_{yx} & \hat{L}_{yy} \end{bmatrix} = \begin{bmatrix} \hat{L}_{xx} & 0 \\ \hat{L}_{yx} & \hat{L}_{yy} \end{bmatrix}, \tag{11.7}$$

$$\hat{\beta}^1 \hat{L} = \begin{bmatrix} \hat{\beta}_{xx} & \hat{\beta}_{xy} \\ \hat{\beta}_{yx} & \hat{\beta}_{yy} \end{bmatrix} \begin{bmatrix} \hat{L}_{xx} & 0 \\ \hat{L}_{yx} & \hat{L}_{yy} \end{bmatrix} = \begin{bmatrix} \hat{\beta}_{xx}\hat{L}_{xx} + \hat{\beta}_{xy}\hat{L}_{yx} & \hat{\beta}_{xy}\hat{L}_{yy} \\ \hat{\beta}_{yx}\hat{L}_{xx} + \hat{\beta}_{yy}\hat{L}_{yx} & \hat{\beta}_{yy}\hat{L}_{yy} \end{bmatrix},$$

and so forth. Please note the zero entry in the top right of Eq. (11.7); it is important.

The entries in these matrices get complicated rather quickly. To simplify, let's denote entries in $\hat{\beta}^j \hat{L}$ as

$$\hat{\beta}^j \hat{\mathbf{L}} = \begin{bmatrix} b_{xx}^j & b_{xy}^j \\ b_{yx}^j & b_{yy}^j \end{bmatrix}.$$

The orthogonalized errors come from the sequence of

$$\hat{\mathbf{L}}^{-1}\epsilon_t = \begin{bmatrix} \hat{l}_{xx} & 0 \\ \hat{l}_{yx} & \hat{l}_{yy} \end{bmatrix} \begin{bmatrix} \epsilon_{x,t} \\ \epsilon_{y,t} \end{bmatrix} = \begin{bmatrix} e_{x,t} \\ e_{y,t} \end{bmatrix}$$

where we define the e's to denote the orthogonalized errors.

We're now in a position to put Humpty Dumpty back together again.

$$\mathbf{Y} = \beta^0 \mathbf{L}\mathbf{L}^{-1}\epsilon_t + \beta^1 \mathbf{L}\mathbf{L}^{-1}\epsilon_{t-1} + \beta^2 \mathbf{L}\mathbf{L}^{-1}\epsilon_{t-2} + \ldots$$

$$\begin{bmatrix} X_t \\ Y_t \end{bmatrix} = \begin{bmatrix} b_{xx}^0 & 0 \\ b_{yx}^0 & b_{yy}^0 \end{bmatrix} \begin{bmatrix} e_{xt} \\ e_{y,t} \end{bmatrix} + \begin{bmatrix} b_{xx}^1 & b_{xy}^1 \\ b_{yx}^1 & b_{yy}^1 \end{bmatrix} \begin{bmatrix} e_{x,t-1} \\ e_{y,t-1} \end{bmatrix} + \ldots$$

Multiplying out the matrices, and defining new coefficients (a's and d's) to get rid of some clutter, the two equations above are

$$X_t = a_0 e_{x,t} + a_1 e_{x,t-1} + a_2 e_{y,t-1} + \ldots$$
$$Y_t = d_0 e_{x,t} + d_1 e_{y,t} + d_2 e_{x,t-1} + d_3 e_{y,t-1} + \ldots$$

Notice that X_t depends upon $e_{x,t}$; but Y_t depends upon $e_{y,t}$ and $e_{x,t}$.

If we had ordered Y-then-X in the Cholesky ordering (and redefined the a's and d's appropriately), we would have had something different:

$$Y_t = d_0 e_{y,t} + d_1 e_{y,t-1} + d_2 e_{x,t-1} + \ldots$$
$$X_t = a_0 e_{y,t} + a_1 e_{x,t} + a_2 e_{y,t-1} + a_3 e_{x,t-1} + \ldots$$

and Y_t would depend upon $e_{y,t}$, while X_t would depend upon $e_{x,t}$ and $e_{y,t}$.

11.2 Forecast Error Variance Decompositions

Impulse response functions tell us how a shock to one variable propagates through the system and affects the other variables. What they can't do, however, is tell us how important each shock is. How much of the variation in X is due to shocks in Y? What we need is something like an R^2, but that can be split up among different variables, decomposing each shock's effects on a variable. It would also be useful to know how X affects Y across different lags. The forecast error variance decomposition (FEVD) satisfies all of these criteria.

Suppose we estimate a VAR on X and Y, after which we draw some forecasts 1, 2, or k periods out. Those forecasts are never perfect, so there will be some forecast

11.2 Forecast Error Variance Decompositions

error. The "forecast error" is simply the residual: the difference between what we expected Y to be after a certain number of periods, given the results of our VAR. The "variance decomposition" splits up the variance of this residual into its component causes and expresses the result as a percent.

Thus, the FEVD tells us: What percent of the variation in X from its forecasted value is due to shocks directly affecting X? And what percent is due to shocks from Y? Since they are percents, they will add to one.

Let's see how this works using the same data from Sect. 10.2:

```
. drop _all
. freduse GNPC96 MANMM101USQ189S
. gen time=yq(year(daten), quarter(daten))
. tsset time, quarterly
. gen GNPgr = ln(GNPC96) - ln(L.GNPC96)
. gen M1gr  = ln(MANMM)  - ln(L.MANMM)
. label var GNPgr "Growth rate of real GNP"
. label var M1gr "Growth rate of M1"
. drop GNPC MANMM date daten
. drop if year(time)<1960

. quietly varbasic GNPgr M1gr if time<yq(2017,3),
  lags(1/2) nograph
. irf table fevd, noci
```

Which produces the following table of FEVDs (leaving out their confidence intervals):

```
Results from varbasic
```

step	(1) fevd	(2) fevd	(3) fevd	(4) fevd
0	0	0	0	0
1	1	.01331	0	.98669
2	.999097	.031231	.000903	.968769
3	.996202	.049556	.003798	.950444
4	.99386	.062587	.00614	.937413
5	.991834	.071759	.008166	.928241
6	.990474	.077555	.009526	.922445
7	.989595	.08109	.010405	.91891
8	.989072	.083141	.010928	.916859

(1) irfname = varbasic, impulse = GNPgr, and response = GNPgr
(2) irfname = varbasic, impulse = GNPgr, and response = M1gr
(3) irfname = varbasic, impulse = M1gr, and response = GNPgr
(4) irfname = varbasic, impulse = M1gr, and response = M1gr

Column (1) of the first table shows the proportion of forecast error variance of GNPgr attributable to its own shocks. As it is listed first in the Cholesky ordering, it does not initially depend upon shocks from the other variable. Thus, 100% of the FE variance at lag one is attributable to its own shocks; column (3) correspondingly shows that 0% of GNPgr's FEV comes from M1gr. Eight periods out, the story is not much changed. Nearly 98.9% of our inability to accurately forecast GNPgr is attributable to shocks to GNPgr itself; 1% is attributable to shocks in the money growth rate.

Columns (2) and (4) decompose the FEV of M1gr into the effects of shocks on GNPgr and M1gr. Column (4) shows that 98.6% of the lag = 1 FEV of the money growth rate is attributable to own shocks. Or, loosely speaking, 98.6% of our inability to forecast M1gr one period out is attributable to changes in M1gr itself. Correspondingly, 1.33% comes from shocks to the growth rate of GNP. The money growth rate was the second variable in our Cholesky ordering, so it is allowed to immediately suffer from shocks to the first variable.

Eight periods out, the story is only slightly different. The 91.6% of M1gr's FEV comes from own shocks; 8.3% comes from shocks to GNPgr.

FEVDs rely on the Cholesky order of the VAR. If we reverse the Cholesky ordering, then we get a slightly different FEVD:

```
. quietly varbasic M1gr GNPgr if time<yq(2017,3), lags(1/2) nograph

. irf table fevd, noci

Results from varbasic
```

step	(1) fevd	(2) fevd	(3) fevd	(4) fevd
0	0	0	0	0
1	1	.01331	0	.98669
2	.991706	.012395	.008294	.987605
3	.980806	.012365	.019194	.987635
4	.972006	.013568	.027994	.986432
5	.965364	.014934	.034636	.985066
6	.960984	.016044	.039016	.983956
7	.958229	.016829	.041771	.983171
8	.956594	.017331	.043406	.982669

```
(1) irfname = varbasic, impulse = M1gr, and response = M1gr
(2) irfname = varbasic, impulse = M1gr, and response = GNPgr
(3) irfname = varbasic, impulse = GNPgr, and response = M1gr
(4) irfname = varbasic, impulse = GNPgr, and response = GNPgr
```

The columns in the two tables are presented in a different order. More importantly, the values in the tables are slightly different. The more exogenous variable in this Cholesky ordering is the money growth rate, so at lag=1 GNPgr does not affect our ability to properly forecast M1gr; 100% of the FEV of M1gr is from own shocks.

The two tables happen to look a bit similar in this example because the estimated shocks between the two variables were not highly correlated. Thus the Cholesky transformation does not have much to uncorrelate. Often in practice, the estimated FEVDs from different orderings vary more than this.

11.3 Structural VARs

What is a structural VAR? And how is it different from the "reduced-form" VARs that we've discussed so far? In short, a structural VAR has contemporaneous terms, X_t and Y_t, as dependent variables in each equation. Reduced-form VARs have only lagged values as dependent variables. Why the difference? And why is it a big deal?

Consider the simple model of supply and demand. The supply price of a widget is a function of, say, the prices of inputs and the quantity supplied. The demand price of a widget is a function of, say, the prices of competing products and the quantity demanded. Prices and quantities are endogenous variables. They determine each other. In a SVAR, X and Y also determine each other. They are both endogenous variables; they both show up as the dependent variables in their respective equations. You can't just regress one on the other; they must be considered as a system. Or, as we do with supply and demand models, we must derive a reduced-form representation of the system and try to back out the parameter values of the structural model.

For structural VARs we need X to be a function of exogenous things—things we can change via policy, too. This is why reduced-form VARs are best suited for data description and ill-suited for policy. We need structural models to figure out what happens if we change the structure of the economy.

11.3.1 Reduced Form vs Structural Form

VARs can be used to describe data or to estimate a structural model. The former is easier than the latter, so we began there, with reduced-form VARs. Now it is time to turn to "structural form" VARs.

The VARs that we have looked at thus far have been "reduced form" such as

$$X_t = \beta_{xx} X_{t-1} + \beta_{xy} Y_{t-1} + \epsilon_{xt} \tag{11.8}$$

$$Y_t = \beta_{yx} X_{t-1} + \beta_{yy} Y_{t-1} + \epsilon_{yt} \tag{11.9}$$

or

$$\mathbf{Y_t} = \beta \mathbf{Y_{t-1}} + \epsilon_t \tag{11.10}$$

with

$$Var(\epsilon_t) = \Sigma_\epsilon = \begin{bmatrix} \sigma_x^2 & \sigma_{x,y} \\ \sigma_{y,x} & \sigma_y^2 \end{bmatrix}.$$

Each variable affects the other with a lag; effects are not simultaneous but shocks can be correlated; identification is not a problem.

A structural var (SVAR), on the other hand, is

$$X_t = \alpha_{y0} Y_t + \alpha_{xx} X_{t-1} + \alpha_{xy} Y_{t-1} + e_{xt} \tag{11.11}$$

$$Y_t = \alpha_{x0} X_t + \alpha_{yx} X_{t-1} + \alpha_{yy} Y_{t-1} + e_{yt}. \tag{11.12}$$

or, in vector notation,

$$\mathbf{A}\mathbf{Y_t} = \boldsymbol{\alpha}\mathbf{Y_{t-1}} + \mathbf{e_t} \tag{11.13}$$

because the contemporaneous terms (the ones with a t subscript) can be moved over to the left-hand side.

11.3.2 SVARs Are Unidentified

What's the important difference between Eqs. (11.10) and (11.13)? What's the big deal about the matrix A that it requires its own section? The big deal is that the model, as expressed, is unidentified. That is, we can't estimate the parameters of (11.13) using the estimates of (11.10).

What does it mean to be "unidentified?" First, notice that we can transform an SVAR such as (11.13) into a reduced-form VAR (RF-VAR) such as (11.10)

$$\mathbf{A}\mathbf{Y_t} = \boldsymbol{\alpha}\mathbf{Y_{t-1}} + \mathbf{e_t} \tag{11.14}$$

$$\mathbf{A}^{-1}\mathbf{A}\mathbf{Y_t} = \mathbf{A}^{-1}\boldsymbol{\alpha}\mathbf{Y_{t-1}} + \mathbf{A}^{-1}\mathbf{e_t}$$

$$\mathbf{Y_t} = \mathbf{A}^{-1}\boldsymbol{\alpha}\mathbf{Y_{t-1}} + \mathbf{A}^{-1}\mathbf{e_t}$$

$$\mathbf{Y_t} = \boldsymbol{\beta}\mathbf{Y_{t-1}} + \boldsymbol{\epsilon}_t \tag{11.15}$$

where $\boldsymbol{\beta} = \mathbf{A}^{-1}\boldsymbol{\alpha}$ and $\boldsymbol{\epsilon}_t = \mathbf{A}^{-1}\mathbf{e_t}$. We know how to estimate the RF-VAR parameters in (11.15). But we can't use these estimates to figure out the SVAR parameters in (11.14). It is the same problem we might find ourselves in if we need to figure out a and b if we know that, say, $a/b = 10$. There's an infinite combination of a's and b's that divide to 10. Likewise, there's an infinite combination of $\mathbf{A}^{-1}$ and $\boldsymbol{\alpha}$ that multiply to $\boldsymbol{\beta}$. In other words, if somehow we know the parameters of (11.14), then we can figure out (11.15); but if we know (11.15), we can't figure out (11.14).

11.3 Structural VARs

In practical terms, this means that there are multiple structural form models that are compatible with an estimated reduced-form model. That is, multiple economic theories are compatible with the data. Our reduced-form regressions would not cast any light on which theory – say, New Keynesian vs Real Business Cycles – is correct.

To make this "unidentification problem" a bit more concrete, let's see why Eqs. (11.11) and (11.12) are unidentified. Notice that X and Y are truly endogenous in (11.11) and (11.12). Thus, we cannot estimate each equation separately; they are jointly determined. They are part of a system, so they need to be estimated as part of a system. We can, however, estimate the reduced-form equations. Could we then back out the coefficients of (11.11) and (11.12) with our estimates of (11.8) and (11.9)? No. We'd have four reduced-form estimates (the $\hat{\beta}$s) and six unknowns (the αs).

To see why, suppose we estimated (11.8) and (11.9) and found

$$\hat{\beta}_{xx} = 0.40 \quad \text{and} \quad \hat{\beta}_{xy} = 0.30$$
$$\hat{\beta}_{yx} = 0.20 \quad \text{and} \quad \hat{\beta}_{yy} = 0.10$$

We have four known values (the $\hat{\beta}$'s) from the reduced-form equations. Unfortunately, there are six unknowns (the α's) in the structural form equations.

One set of α's that satisfy these equations would be

$$\hat{\alpha}_{y0} = 0 \quad \hat{\alpha}_{xx} = 0.40 \quad \text{and} \quad \hat{\alpha}_{xy} = 0.30$$
$$\hat{\alpha}_{x0} = 0 \quad \hat{\alpha}_{yx} = 0.20 \quad \text{and} \quad \hat{\alpha}_{yy} = 0.10$$

but so does

$$\hat{\alpha}_{y0} = 1 \quad \hat{\alpha}_{xx} = 0.20 \quad \text{and} \quad \hat{\alpha}_{xy} = 0.20$$
$$\hat{\alpha}_{x0} = -1 \quad \hat{\alpha}_{yx} = 0.60 \quad \text{and} \quad \hat{\alpha}_{yy} = 0.40$$

as well as

$$\hat{\alpha}_{y0} = 2 \quad \hat{\alpha}_{xx} = 0 \quad \text{and} \quad \hat{\alpha}_{xy} = 0.10$$
$$\hat{\alpha}_{x0} = 1 \quad \hat{\alpha}_{yx} = -0.2 \quad \text{and} \quad \hat{\alpha}_{yy} = -0.20.$$

Once we know two of the α's, we can figure out the rest.

Estimating a structural VAR boils down to pegging down some of the coefficients—the so-called identifying restrictions - so that we can back out the rest of them from the reduced-form estimates. The statistical software takes care of the initial estimation and the "backing out." The hard part for the econometrician is coming up with a defensible set of identifying restrictions. This is where the action is at with SVARs; this is where macro-econometricians argue. How do we come up with such a defensible set of identifying restrictions? Theory. VARs were supposed to let us ignore economic theory and let the data speak for themselves; but SVARs reintroduced theory into the VAR methodology. The data cannot "speak for themselves."

11.3.3 The General Form of SVARs

In what follows, we will switch notation to match that in Stata. This will help us map our equations with Stata's commands.

A reduced-form VAR in companion form is

$$\mathbf{Y_t} = \beta Y_{t-1} + \epsilon_t \tag{11.16}$$

with

$$Var(\epsilon_t) = \Sigma_\epsilon = \begin{bmatrix} \sigma_x^2 & \sigma_{x,y} \\ \sigma_{y,x} & \sigma_y^2 \end{bmatrix}.$$

An SVAR with p lags such as

$$\mathbf{AY_t} = \mathbf{A_1}\mathbf{Y_{t-1}} + \mathbf{A_2}\mathbf{Y_{t-2}} + \cdots + \mathbf{A_p}\mathbf{Y_{t-p}} + \mathbf{e_t} \tag{11.17}$$

can be expressed more compactly in companion form as

$$\mathbf{A_0 Y_t} = \mathbf{A Y_{t-1}} + \mathbf{e_t} \tag{11.18}$$

with

$$\mathbf{e_t} = \mathbf{B u_t}$$

and

$$Var(e_t) = \Sigma_e = \begin{bmatrix} 1 & 0 \\ 0 & 1 \end{bmatrix}.$$

In the reduced form, the two equations are related by the correlation across equations via ϵ. In the SVAR, the two equations are related explicitly via $\mathbf{A}$, but the structural shocks (e's) are uncorrelated.

11.3 Structural VARs

We can also express the SVAR to emphasize its long-run levels:

$$\mathbf{A_0 Y_t} = \mathbf{A Y_{t-1}} + \mathbf{B u_t}$$
$$\mathbf{A_0 Y_t} - \mathbf{A Y_{t-1}} = \mathbf{B u_t}$$
$$(\mathbf{A_0} - \mathbf{A}(L)) \mathbf{Y_t} = \mathbf{B u_t}$$
$$(\mathbf{A_0} - \mathbf{A}(L))^{-1} (\mathbf{A_0} - \mathbf{A}(L)) \mathbf{Y_t} = (\mathbf{A_0} - \mathbf{A}(L))^{-1} \mathbf{B u_t}$$
$$\mathbf{Y_t} = (\mathbf{A_0} - \mathbf{A}(L))^{-1} \mathbf{B u_t}$$
$$\mathbf{Y_t} = \mathbf{C u_t}$$

where $\mathbf{C}$ is defined to be equal to $(\mathbf{A_0} - \mathbf{A}(L))^{-1}$. This $\mathbf{C}$ matrix describes the long-run responses to the structural shocks.

To be able to estimate the parameters of the SVAR, we need to impose some identification restrictions; that is, we need to specify some values in the entries of $\mathbf{A}$, $\mathbf{B}$, and $\mathbf{C}$ or otherwise adequately constrain them.

Incidentally, if $\mathbf{A_0} = \mathbf{I}$ and $\mathbf{B} = \mathbf{L}$ (the lower Cholesky factor), then our SVAR becomes the reduced-form VAR.

11.3.4 Cholesky Is an SVAR

Our motivation for SVARs was twofold: (1) to see what would happen if we exogenously changed a particular variable via policy and (2) to trace out the effects of such policy shocks via IRFs. You might be asking: isn't this what we accomplished via reduced from VARs and OIRFs via Cholesky? Actually, yes. The Cholesky factorization imposes a recursive structure on the unrestricted VAR. This makes it a type of SVAR, but SVARs are more general. Still, it might prove useful to see more formally how Cholesky is a type of SVAR. We'll do this using Stata, so it will prove useful to switch to Stata's notation.

Using Stata's notation, an SVAR can be written as

$$\mathbf{A}\left(\mathbf{I} - \mathbf{A_1} L^2 - \cdots - \mathbf{A_p} L^p\right) \mathbf{Y_t} = \mathbf{A} \epsilon_t = \mathbf{B} e_t \tag{11.19}$$

The SVAR corresponding to the Cholesky orthogonalized VAR sets $\mathbf{A}$ so that it has ones along its main diagonal and zeros in the entries above the diagonal. The $\mathbf{B}$ matrix constrains the $\mathbf{e_t}$'s so that there is zero covariance between the errors across equations. Thus, it is constrained to have zero elements off the diagonal.

For a three-variable VAR, **A** can be the lower triangular matrix

$$A = \begin{bmatrix} 1 & 0 & 0 \\ a_{21} & 1 & 0 \\ a_{31} & a_{32} & 1 \end{bmatrix} \quad (11.20)$$

and

$$B = \begin{bmatrix} b_{11} & 0 & 0 \\ 0 & b_{22} & 0 \\ 0 & 0 & b_{33} \end{bmatrix}$$

where the a's and b's need to be estimated.

The **A** matrix in (11.20) says that only the first endogenous variable shows up in the first equation. The second and third endogenous variables are multiplied by zero, so they cancel out of the first equation. In the second equation, the first and second variables show up. The third row of **A** allows for all three endogenous variables to appear in the third equation of the VAR. This recursive system is indicative of the Cholesky ordering.

It is easy to define these matrices in Stata

```
. matrix A = (1, 0, 0 \ ., 1, 0 \ ., ., 1)
. matrix B = (., 0, 0 \ 0, ., 0 \ 0, 0, .)
```

where the "." indicates that the entry is not constrained and needs to be estimated. Then, estimate the SVAR:

```
. svar Y1 Y2 Y3, aeq(A) beq(B)
```

Example

Next, we will show with an example how OIRFs derived via the SVAR approach and the Cholesky approach are equivalent. To do so, we need to generate some data. First we set up 10,000 empty observations:

```
. set obs 10000
. gen time = _n
. tsset time
```

Then we specify a variance/covariance matrix (Σ) and draw random data from the multivariate normal distribution $N(\mathbf{0}, \Sigma)$:

```
. matrix sigma = (1 , .75 \ .75, 1)
. drawnorm eps_x eps_y, means(0,0) cov(sigma) double seed(1234)
```

11.3 Structural VARs

Then we generate time series on X and Y:

```
. gen X = 0
. gen Y = 0
. forvalues i = 2/`obs'{
        quietly replace X = 0.40*L.X + 0.10*L.Y + eps_x in `i'
        quietly replace Y = 0.20*L.X + 0.10*L.Y + eps_y in `i'}
```

Next, we calculate a simple reduced-form VAR and instruct Stata to calculate the OIRFs with the ordering X Y.

```
. quietly var X Y, lags(1)
. irf create orderXY, step(10) set(myirf, replace) replace
. irf table oirf, noci

Results from orderXY

+------------------------------------------------------------+
|        |   (1)    |   (2)    |   (3)    |   (4)    |
| step   |  oirf    |  oirf    |  oirf    |  oirf    |
|--------+----------+----------+----------+----------|
|0       | 1.00612  | .75688   | 0        | .656501  |
|1       | .478294  | .286191  | .06837   | .068846  |
|2       | .219707  | .128331  | .034316  | .021274  |
|3       | .100597  | .058621  | .01584   | .009285  |
|4       | .046046  | .026826  | .007256  | .00423   |
|5       | .021076  | .012279  | .003322  | .001935  |
|6       | .009647  | .00562   | .00152   | .000886  |
|7       | .004415  | .002572  | .000696  | .000405  |
|8       | .002021  | .001177  | .000319  | .000186  |
|9       | .000925  | .000539  | .000146  | .000085  |
|10      | .000423  | .000247  | .000067  | .000039  |
+------------------------------------------------------------+
(1) irfname = orderXY, impulse = X, and response = X
(2) irfname = orderXY, impulse = X, and response = Y
(3) irfname = orderXY, impulse = Y, and response = X
(4) irfname = orderXY, impulse = Y, and response = Y
```

Next, we calculate the OIRF via a SVAR with the proper restrictions on the A and B matrices.

```
. matrix A = (1, 0 \ ., 1)
. matrix B = (., 0 \ 0, .)
. quietly svar X Y, aeq(A) beq(B) lags(1)
. irf create orderXY, step(10) set(myirf, replace) replace
. irf table oirf, noci

Results from orderXY
```

```
+-----------------------------------------------------------+
|        |   (1)    |   (2)    |   (3)    |   (4)    |
| step   |   oirf   |   oirf   |   oirf   |   oirf   |
|--------+----------+----------+----------+----------|
|0       | 1.00612  | .75688   | 0        | .656501  |
|1       | .478294  | .286191  | .06837   | .068846  |
|2       | .219707  | .128331  | .034316  | .021274  |
|3       | .100597  | .058621  | .01584   | .009285  |
|4       | .046046  | .026826  | .007256  | .00423   |
|5       | .021076  | .012279  | .003322  | .001935  |
|6       | .009647  | .00562   | .00152   | .000886  |
|7       | .004415  | .002572  | .000696  | .000405  |
|8       | .002021  | .001177  | .000319  | .000186  |
|9       | .000925  | .000539  | .000146  | .000085  |
|10      | .000423  | .000247  | .000067  | .000039  |
+-----------------------------------------------------------+
(1) irfname = orderXY, impulse = X, and response = X
(2) irfname = orderXY, impulse = X, and response = Y
(3) irfname = orderXY, impulse = Y, and response = X
(4) irfname = orderXY, impulse = Y, and response = Y
```

As you can see, the results are the same whether we calculated a reduced-form VAR and then imposed the Cholesky transformation or instead specified the appropriately restricted SVAR.

11.3.5 Long-Run Restrictions: Blanchard and Quah (1989)

Olivier Blanchard and Danny Quah (1989) introduced the long-run restriction to the estimation of SVARs. David Schenck (2016) wrote a detailed tutorial on the Stata Blog estimating Blanchard and Quah's SVAR in Stata. We follow Schenck closely, explaining a few more steps along the way.

Blanchard and Quah estimated a two-variable eight-lag SVAR between the GNP growth rate (YGR) and the unemployment rate (UNEMP)

$$Y_t = Cu_t$$

or

11.3 Structural VARs

$$\begin{bmatrix} YGR_t \\ UNEMP_t \end{bmatrix} = \begin{bmatrix} C_{1,1} & C_{1,2} \\ C_{2,1} & C_{2,2} \end{bmatrix} \begin{bmatrix} u_{y,t} \\ u_{u,t} \end{bmatrix}$$

Blanchard and Quah argue that the an unemployment shock has zero long-run impact on GNP growth. Therefore, setting $C_{1,2} = 0$ is a proper identifying restriction on **C** so that

$$YGR_t = C_{1,1} u_{y,t}$$

$$UNEMP_t = C_{2,1} u_{y,t} + C_{2,2} u_{u,t}.$$

First, we download and format the data.

```
. freduse GNPC96 UNRATE, clear

. gen year = year(daten)
. gen quarter = quarter(daten)

. collapse (mean) GNP UNRATE (first) daten, by(year
  quarter)
. sort year quarter
. gen time = _n
. tsset time
```

The data were quarterly, but we want annualized growth rates expressed as a percent, so we create a new variable:

```
. gen GNPgr = 4*100*(log(GNPC96) - log(L.GNPC96))
```

In their paper, Blanchard and Quah estimate their SVAR on data from the second quarter of 1952 through the fourth quarter of 1987. In his replication, Schenck includes the first quarter of 1952. You can switch between the two sets of estimates by commenting out the appropriate part below.

```
. *This follows Blanchard and Quah
.       gen quarterly = yq(year,quarter)
.       format quarterly %tq
.       keep if quarterly >= yq(1952,2) & quarterly <=
        yq(1987,4)

. *This follows Schenck
.       *keep if year>=1952 & year <= 1987
```

Blanchard and Quah take some ad hoc steps to ensure their data are stationary. They detrend the unemployment rate by regressing on a deterministic trend and extracting the residuals.

```
. quietly regress UNRATE time
```

```
. predict unemp, residual
```

Also, they perceive a break point in the GNP growth data at 1974, so they de-mean that variable by regressing on pre- and post-1974 dummy variables.

```
. gen Pre1974 = 0
. gen Post1974 = 0
. replace Pre1974 = 1 if year < 1974
. replace Post1974 = 1 if year >=1974
. quietly reg GNPgr Pre1974 Post1974, noconstant
. predict Ygr, residual
```

The data are now properly set up.

Finally, we impose our restriction on the **C** matrix, estimate the SVAR, and draw our IRFs.

```
. matrix C = (., 0 \ ., .)
. svar Ygr unemp , lags(1/8) lreq(C)

. irf create Blanchard_Quah, set(lrirf, replace) step(40)
  replace
. irf graph sirf, yline(0) byopts(yrescale)
```

The output of the SVAR is not really of interest, but we report it below to show that the **C** matrix was properly constrained.

```
. Structural vector autoregression

( 1)  [c_1_2]_cons = 0

Sample: 30 - 164                     Number of obs    =         135
Exactly identified model             Log likelihood   =   -338.2436

------------------------------------------------------------------------
             |    Coef.   Std. Err.      z    P>|z|   [95% Conf. Interval]
-------------+----------------------------------------------------------
       /c_1_1 |  1.393601   .0848119    16.43  0.000    1.227373    1.55983
       /c_2_1 | -.4643275   .3833661    -1.21  0.226   -1.215711    .2870564
       /c_1_2 |         0 (constrained)
       /c_2_2 |  4.442195   .2703434    16.43  0.000    3.912332    4.972058
------------------------------------------------------------------------
```

The IRFs are reported in Fig. 11.5.

11.4 VARs with Integrated Variables

Can we establish Granger causality if our variables are integrated? After all, if you look back at the examples thus far, you'll notice that the variables have all been differenced so that they are I(0). But what if we don't want to estimate a VAR in differenced variables? What if we want to estimate the VAR in levels, and these levels are I(d)? Toda and Yamamoto (1995) showed that there is a simple way to

11.4 VARs with Integrated Variables

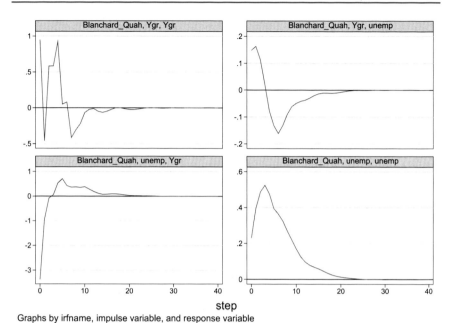

Fig. 11.5 IRF from Blanchard and Quah SVAR

estimate the VAR in levels, so that the usual asymptotic formulas for calculating standard errors and p-values still apply.[1] In fact, their method applies regardless of whether the variables have unit roots and are stationary around a deterministic trend (i.e., that t is an explicit variable in the regression), integrated of order d, or even cointegrated of order d.

The procedure is as follows:

1. Determine the number of lags k using one of the standard information criteria (such as with Stata's `varsoc` command). Let's suppose that k = 4.
2. Determine d_{max}, the largest order of integration of the variables. For example, if Y is I(1) and X is I(2), then $d_{max} = 2$. (Up until now, we might have differenced Y once, and differenced X twice, and then estimated the VAR in differences: `var d1.y d2.x, lags(1/k)`.)
3. Estimate the var in levels with $k + d_{max}$ lags. For example, `var y x, lags(1/6)`.

---

[1] Dolado & Lütkepohl (1996) derived many of the same results for the simpler case that the variables are I(1). The paper by Toda and Yamamoto (1995) is more general, showing the case for variables integrated up to an arbitrary order d.

4. In all further testing (e.g., stability tests, Granger causality tests) ignore the additional $d_{max} = 2$ lags, as these are zero. Restrict your tests to the first k lags.

Adding the extra d_{max} lags to the VAR ensures that the asymptotic formulas for test statistics are correct. Granger causality tests will then have to be done "by hand" using the `test` command rather than Stata's `vargranger` command, as the latter automatically uses the extra lags.

As a caveat to the discussion above, this method is useful for establishing Granger causality when variables are integrated (or even cointegrated). If the variables are cointegrated, however, we should not stop there. Rather, you should proceed with estimating and interpreting a vector error correction mechanism (VECM). VECMs are the topic of the next chapter.

11.5 Conclusion

The VAR is the workhorse of empirical macroeconomics and Granger causality is a standard topic of study. Before you run off and calculate Granger causal relationships between variables willy-nilly, it might be instructive to heed Clive Granger's warning from his Nobel acceptance speech:

> my definition [of causality] was pragmatic and any applied researcher with two or more time series could apply it, so I got plenty of citations. Of course, many ridiculous papers appeared. (Granger 2004, p. 425)

Try not to write ridiculous papers. You should have a solid theory in mind that would relate one variable to another. Get the theory in mind first. Don't form a theory to fit the data. Further, Granger causality is sensitive to many of the choices that you'll have to make while writing the paper. Your decisions to keep or discard variables might be justified by their *p*-values, but these decisions might affect the validity of your conclusions further in the process. Model mis-specification is a sure way to find spurious—or even "ridiculous"—Granger causal relations.

We've barely scratched the surface of VARs, but we'll forgo looking further into VARs and SVARs in favor of turning to VECMs. These are a related type of time-series model which are designed to look simultaneously at long-run and short-run relationships between variables.

For those who wish to explore VAR models in further detail, we recommend the book by Enders (2014). It is a modern classic, providing a more technical but still gentle and practitioner-oriented introduction into the application of VARs. The two chapters on VARs in Rachev et al. (2007) add some mathematical complexity.

Tsay (2013) adds moving average errors to the coverage of VARs, exploring vector-MA (VMA) and VARMA models in some depth. Shumway and Stoffer (2006) extend the topics in this book to cover state-space and frequency-domain models.

11.5 Conclusion

The next step up in difficulty is Kilian and Lütkepohl (2017); the book is forthcoming as of now, but drafts of the chapters are available online. Adventurous students wishing to leap fully down the rabbit hole of VARs can do no better than to explore Lütkepohl (2005) and Amisano and Giannini (2012). These offer in-depth examinations of the issues and techniques involved in estimating structural VARs. Both of these books are thorough and require a technical mastery of matrix calculus and asymptotics.

Cointegration and VECMs 12

12.1 Introduction

The VARs that we looked at in the last chapter were very well suited for describing the short-run relationship between variables, especially if they are stationary. Most economic variables are not stationary, however. This required us to transform the variables, taking first differences, so that they are stationary. In this chapter we show how to model the long-run relationship between variables in their levels, even if they are integrated. This is possible if two or more variables are "cointegrated." If two variables are cointegrated then, rather than taking the first difference of each variable, we can essentially model the difference between the two variables. Loosely speaking.

When we take first differences, we lose a lot of important information. We might know how a variable is changing; but we don't know its actual value (its level). We are not modeling the variables we are really interested in, but their rates of change. Similarly, when we model the difference between two variables, we are estimating the statistical properties of a new variable, not the original two variables we are interested in. While this is better than nothing, Engle and Granger (1987) showed how we can do much better than that.

12.2 Cointegration

Econometrician and textbook author Michael Murray (1994) wrote a humorous, but very useful piece, analogizing cointegration with a drunk walking her dog. The small paper is an underground classic among econometricians; everyone has read it, but not enough cite it. A drunk staggering out of a bar follows a random walk. An unleashed dog might also follow a random meander. But if the drunk staggers out of the bar with her dog, even without a leash, the distance between the drunk and her dog will be relatively stable. If the dog meanders too far away, the drunk will

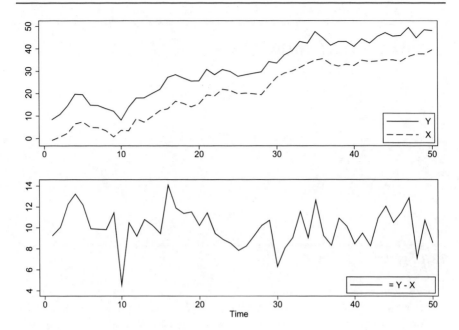

Fig. 12.1 Two cointegrated variables, X and Y

randomly call out to her dog, and it will move closer to its owner. Sometimes the dog will randomly bark for its owner, drawing her closer to it. If you see the drunk, the dog will not be too far away. Likewise, if you see the dog, its drunk owner should be nearby. The barking and calling—and the staggering toward each other—is the error correction mechanism, whereby when the two diverge, they begin to converge again. We might not know where they'll go as a pair, but we can be fairly certain they'll be close to each other. That is the essence of cointegration.

Suppose Y and X are two integrated but otherwise unrelated variables. Granger and Newbold (1974) showed us that if we were to regress Y on X, we are likely to find a statistically significant correlation between these variables even though none actually exists.

Now, consider the two variables in Fig. 12.1. They are both integrated. More importantly, there seems to be a relationship between these two variables. They never stray too far from each other. In the second panel of Fig. 12.1, we graph the difference between the two variables. (We also shifted them down by ten units so the new series fluctuates around zero). Even though X and Y are nonstationary, the difference between X and Y *is* stationary. Granger and Newbold may have made us skittish about regressing the levels of X and Y on each other, but with this new differenced variable, we can apply all of the techniques we learned in the VAR chapter. In fact, we will see that if the variables are cointegrated, we can estimate the levels and differenced relationship simultaneously. But we're getting ahead of ourselves.

12.2 Cointegration

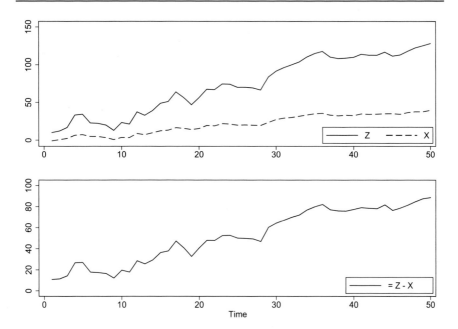

Fig. 12.2 Two cointegrated variables, X and Z

Let's turn to a slightly more subtle example. Consider a new set of variables, X and Z, in Fig. 12.2. They are both integrated. But are they cointegrated? The gap between them is increasing; that is, their difference is not stationary, so at first glance they do not seem to be cointegrated. But there does seem to be a relationship between X and Z. Ignoring their different slopes, when X dips so does Z. When X spikes so does Z. The problem is with their slopes. What would make the difference between X and Z stationary is if we could either tilt X up (as in Fig. 12.3) or tilt Z down (as in Fig. 12.4). This insight allows us to formally define cointegration: two more nonstationary variables are cointegrated if a linear combination of them is stationary.[1]

Many economic and financial theories provide conclusions in terms that relate to cointegration. They seldom speak about the speed of convergence to an equilibrium, but they do make equilibrium predictions about the levels of variables and that the relationship between them should be steady (i.e., cointegrated). For example, according to the permanent income hypothesis, consumption should be a relatively stable function of income (see Fig. 12.5).

---

[1] More precisely, two more variables which are integrated of order I(b) are cointegrated if a linear combination of them is integrated of a lower order than b.

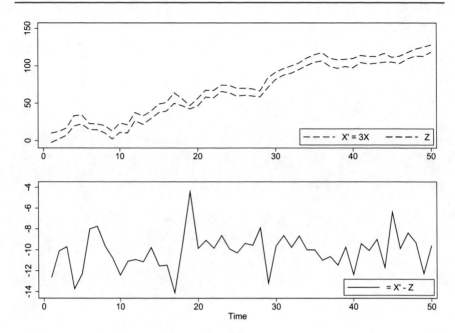

Fig. 12.3 Two cointegrated variables, 3X and Z

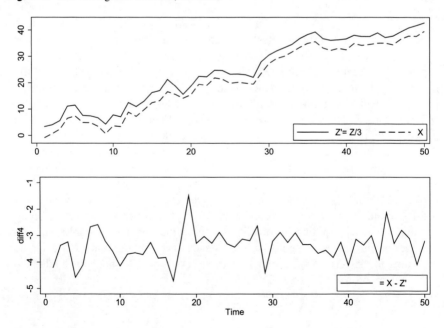

Fig. 12.4 Two cointegrated variables, X and Z/3

12.2 Cointegration

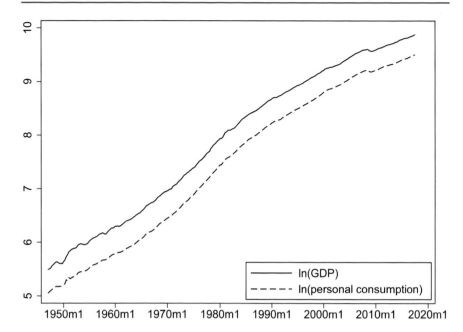

Fig. 12.5 Two arguably cointegrated variables, log(GDP) and log(C)

Most no-arbitrage theories in finance imply cointegration. Examples include neighborhood price levels, the theory of purchasing power parity, and the relationship between short-term and long-term interest rates.

House prices in two similar neighborhoods should be cointegrated, separated by the value of amenities differential and the costs of moving. Their prices shouldn't diverge indefinitely. If they did, then people would move from one neighborhood to another to re-establish the original price difference.

According to the theory of purchasing power parity (PPP), the exchange rate between two countries' currencies should equal the ratio of their price levels. Otherwise, one could exploit the difference in prices between them, buying low and selling high, to make unlimited profit. Thus, the theory of PPP is a no-arbitrage theory that predicts a cointegrated relationship between three variables: exchange rate between X and Y is equal to the prices in X divided by the prices in Y. Or, expressed in logarithms,

$$ln\,(e) = ln\,(P_{US}) - ln\,(P_{CA}) \tag{12.1}$$

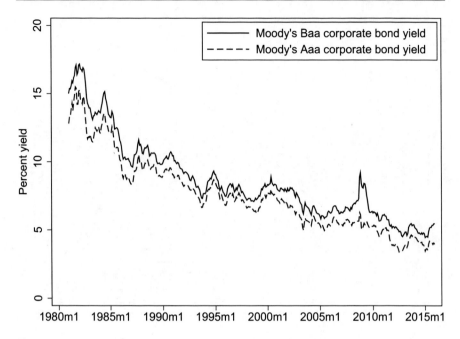

Fig. 12.6 Two arguably cointegrated variables, Aaa and Baa bond yields

The no-arbitrage condition in finance predicts that short-term and long-term interest rates should have a stable relationship (see Figs. 12.6 and 12.7) and arguably are cointegrated.[2]

12.3 Error Correction Mechanism

If two variables Y and X are cointegrated, then there is a steady relationship between them in their levels. In this case, we are justified in regressing Y on X because their relationship isn't spurious; it is a real thing. (We'll leave aside for now how we would know that the relationship isn't spurious.) The question arises: What is the statistical mechanism that keeps these variables moving together?

Suppose that X_t follows a random walk,

$$X_t = X_{t-1} + u_t \tag{12.2}$$

---

[2] Testing the theory of purchasing power parity is a classic use of cointegration analysis. Notable examples include Juselius et al. (1992), Corbae and Ouliaris (1988), Taylor (1988), and Kim (1990). Pedroni (2001) provides a cointegration test of PPP for panel data.

12.3 Error Correction Mechanism

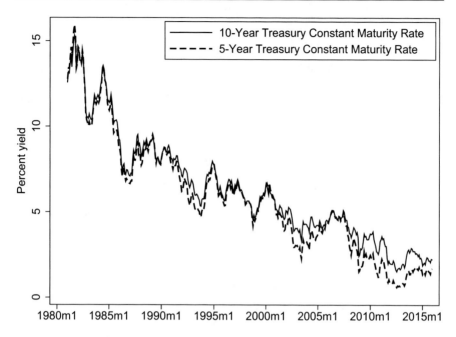

Fig. 12.7 Two arguably cointegrated variables, 10-year and 5-year Treasuries

and that Y_t and X_t are cointegrated in their levels, so that, say

$$Y_t = \beta X_t + \epsilon_t. \tag{12.3}$$

According to Granger's representation theorem, two variables X and Y are cointegrated if and only if they have an ECM representation.

The simplest error correction mechanism (ECM) for X and Y looks like

$$\Delta Y_t = \gamma \Delta X_t - \alpha \left(Y_{t-1} - \beta X_{t-1} \right) + e_t \tag{12.4}$$
$$= \gamma \Delta X_t - \alpha \left(\epsilon_{t-1} \right) + e_t \tag{12.5}$$

where Δ denotes the first difference of a variable, i.e., its change.

Equation (12.4) models the change in Y_t as a function of the change in X_t and another term in parentheses. That term in parenthesis is simply the error from the cointegrating relationship from Eq. (12.3), lagged by one period. That is, if we rearrange and lag the terms from Eq. (12.3), Eq. (12.4) becomes Eq. (12.5). Notice that ϵ_t is the deviation of X and Y from their cointegrating relationship. Further, notice that the term in parenthesis shows up with a lag. This reflects the reasonable assumption that it takes at least one period for the economy to notice the disequilibrium and begin adjusting. The ECM model says that when Y_{t-1} is above the level predicted by βX_{t-1} (so that $\epsilon_{t-1} > 0$), then the change in Y_t must go down by an amount equal to $\alpha\epsilon_t$. If, instead, Y is below its expected level, then ΔY_t will tend to increase by $\alpha\epsilon_t$.

All of the terms in Eqs. (12.4) or (12.5) are stationary. X_t is I(1), so ΔX_t is stationary. Likewise, Y_t is I(1), so ΔY_t is stationary. Finally, e_t is a stationary iid shock, so $Y_t - \beta X_t = e_t$ is stationary. Since all the terms are stationary, estimation should not be a problem.

12.3.1 The Effect of the Adjustment Parameter

How are we to interpret the parameter α in (12.4) or (12.5)? In short, α tells us how quickly the two variables adjust to re-establish equilibrium. Remember, ϵ_t is the amount by which we are out of equilibrium. Suppose that "error" was equal to, say, positive 30 so that Y was 30 units bigger than the amount warranted by βX. Something will have to give. Perhaps Y should drop by a bit or at least not grow by as much as it did last period, so that we may re-establish equilibrium. Suppose that $\alpha = 0.50$. This means that we need to reduce ΔY_t by 15 units, so that we get closer to where we should be. If, instead, $\alpha = 0.10$ then we would only decrease the change in Y by 10 percent of its disequilibrium (three units). In the most extreme case, $\alpha = 0$. In this case, there is nothing to decrease the rate of growth of Y; we are out of equilibrium, and we never move to re-establish equilibrium. We have no mechanism by which to correct this error, and we have no business calling the model an "error correction mechanism." This is why α is called the "speed of adjustment factor."

12.4 Deriving the ECM

The error correction model (ECM) seems useful. But where does it come from? Below we show that ECM models can be derived from the very VAR models we studied in Chap. 10.

Consider the dynamic equation:

$$Y_t = \alpha_{11}X_t + \lambda_1 Y_{t-1} + \lambda_2 X_{t-1} + e_t \qquad (12.6)$$

This is an ARDL model; alternatively, it is one equation pulled from a multi-equation SVAR(1) model. We will show how to manipulate this equation to arrive at an ECM model.

First, subtract Y_{t-1} from both sides:

$$Y_t - Y_{t-1} = \alpha_{11}X_t + \lambda_1 Y_{t-1} - Y_{t-1} + \lambda_2 X_{t-1} + e_t$$
$$\Delta Y_t = \alpha_{11}X_t + (\lambda_1 - 1)Y_{t-1} + \lambda_2 X_{t-1} + e_t.$$

Next, add and subtract $\alpha_{11}X_{t-1}$ on the right-hand side:

$$\Delta Y_t = \alpha_{11}X_t + \lambda_1 Y_{t-1} - Y_{t-1} + \lambda_2 X_{t-1} - \alpha_{11}X_{t-1} + \alpha_{11}X_{t-1} + e_t$$
$$= \alpha_{11}X_t - \alpha_{11}X_{t-1} + \lambda_1 Y_{t-1} - Y_{t-1} + \lambda_2 X_{t-1} + \alpha_{11}X_{t-1} + e_t$$
$$= \alpha_{11}(X_t - X_{t-1}) + \lambda_1 Y_{t-1} - Y_{t-1} + \lambda_2 X_{t-1} + \alpha_{11}X_{t-1} + e_t$$
$$= \alpha_{11}\Delta X_t - (1-\lambda_1)Y_{t-1} + (\lambda_2 + \alpha_{11})X_{t-1} + e_t.$$

The coefficients are starting to look a bit complicated. To make things easier to read, define

$$\alpha = 1 - \lambda_1$$
$$\theta = \lambda_2 + \alpha_{11}.$$

This allows us to simplify further to

$$\Delta Y_t = \alpha_{11}\Delta X_t - \alpha Y_{t-1} + \theta X_{t-1} + e_t$$
$$= \alpha_{11}\Delta X_t - \alpha\left(Y_{t-1} - \frac{\theta}{\alpha}X_{t-1}\right) + e_t$$

If we define $\beta = \theta/\alpha$, then

$$\Delta Y_t = \alpha_{11}\Delta X_t - \alpha(Y_{t-1} - \beta X_{t-1}) + e_t. \tag{12.7}$$

The stationary long-term (i.e., cointegrated) relationship between Y and X shows up in the parenthesis, with adjustment factor α. They enter lagged by one period since adjustment is presumed to take at least one period. All of the terms are stationary (the integrated terms are first-differenced, the cointegrated terms are subtracted from each other, and the error term is stationary).

Notice, too, that the original model had one lag, while the VECM had one fewer (no lags, in this particular instance).

12.5 Engle and Granger's Residual-Based Tests of Cointegration

How can we know if two more variables are cointegrated? Let's return to the definition. Two or more variables are cointegrated if (1) they are integrated and (2) if a linear combination of them is integrated of lower order. In the case of I(1) variables, like most economic variables, this means that (1) the variables X and Y are both I(1), but (2) a linear combination of them, such as

$$Y = \beta_0 + \beta_1 X$$

is not integrated. This implies that to test whether X and Y are cointegrated, we can follow a two-step procedure, attributed to Engle and Granger (1987):

1. Check whether X and Y are both I(1) using, say, a Dickey-Fuller or an augmented Dickey-Fuller test.
2. Regress Y on X, and estimate the residuals. The residuals are a linear combination of Y and X. Thus, the second step is to see test whether the estimated residuals are I(0).

There are several complications in the second stage unit root test. First, in the second-stage DF/ADF test, you should not include a constant if one was already included in the regression of Y on X. (If you typed `reg Y X`, then Stata automatically included a constant, and you should not include another one in the second-stage Dickey-Fuller test.) Second, unit root tests have low power, especially when the true data generating processes have near unit roots. Since unit roots are used to test for cointegration, this low power also affects cointegration tests (Elliott 1998). Third, this second stage must rely on the residual-based critical values provided by Engle and Yoo (1987), MacKinnon (1991), or MacKinnon (2010), rather than the usual DF/ADF critical values. These will be different from the standard AD and ADF critical values to reflect the fact that the second step relies on estimated residuals from the first step. That is, there is more uncertainty involved in step 2 dealing with estimates than in step 1 when we are dealing with the raw data. In step 2, we are dealing with estimates, so the critical values are adjusted to account for this added uncertainty.

12.5.1 MacKinnon Critical Values for Engle-Granger Tests

The Engle-Granger two-step test uses an augmented Dickey-Fuller (ADF) test as its second step, but it cannot use the ADF test's usual test statistics or p-values. Why? The standard ADF test presumes that the data are actual data. The EG test, however, relies on an ADF test on estimated residuals. These estimated residuals necessarily contain error that the usual ADF test statistics fail to take into account. What to do? Use different critical values from which to calculate p-values.

Engle and Yoo (1987) calculated critical values for the Dickey-Fuller[3] and ADF(4) tests of stationary residuals. These critical values depend upon the number of variables (they consider up to five variables) and the sample size (they consider samples of sizes 50, 100, and 200).

The latest and most accurate critical values were calculated by MacKinnon (2010). These are updated estimates of those in MacKinnon (1991).[4] MacKinnon presents his results as a "response surface." This is jargon for something fairly

---
[3] That is, ADF with zero lags.

[4] MacKinnon (2010) repeated his Monte Carlo simulations from MacKinnon (1991) using many more replications. This allowed him to provide a more accurate third-degree response surface rather than his earlier second-degree surface.

12.5 Engle and Granger's Residual-Based Tests of Cointegration

simple. The critical values were calculated for various sample sizes and number of variables. But what about intermediate sample sizes? Essentially, MacKinnon provides a formula which interpolates between these values so that we can estimate the appropriate critical value for any sample size.

The MacKinnon critical value for a test at level-p with sample size T can be calculated from

$$C(p, T) = \beta_\infty + \frac{\beta_1}{T} + \frac{\beta_2}{T^2} + \frac{\beta_3}{T^3} \tag{12.8}$$

The terms β_∞, β_1, and β_2 are not estimated coefficients from any of our regressions, but are rather parameters given by MacKinnon in his tables. There are three versions of his tables: one each for the no-trend (only a constant for drift), linear-trend, and quadratic-trend cases. These tables are provided in the Appendix of this textbook.

Example

Suppose we ran an Engle-Granger two-step test, that we estimated a (possible) cointegrating equation, and that we wanted to verify using an ADF test that the resulting residuals were stationary. How can we calculate the MacKinnon (2010) critical values? We need several piece of information: What kind of ADF test did we run? What is the sample size? How many variables were in the cointegrating equation? And what level test are we interested in? Suppose that we had estimated a cointegrating equation with N = 2 variables; that the ADF test had a constant but no trend; that our sample size was T = 100; and that we wanted to test at the 5% level. Then it is simply a matter of looking at MacKinnon's tables for the correct βs and plugging them into Eq. (12.8) to get

$$C(p = 0.05, T = 100) = -3.33613 + \frac{-6.1101}{100} + \frac{-6.823}{100^2} + \frac{0}{100^3}$$
$$= -3.33613 - 0.061101 - 0.0006823 + 0$$
$$= -3.3979133.$$

Example

Suppose we needed the MacKinnon critical values for an estimated first-step regression with N = 3 variables; that the ADF test had a constant but no trend; that our sample size was T = 50; and that we wanted to test at the 1% level. Using the βs from MacKinnon's tables, the correct critical value is

$$C = -4.29374 + \frac{-14.4354}{50} + \frac{-33.195}{50^2} + \frac{47.433}{50^3} = -4.5953465.$$

Example

As our final example, suppose we needed the MacKinnon critical values for an estimated first-step regression with four variables; that the ADF test had a constant and a trend; that our sample size was 150; and that we wanted to test at the 10% level. Using the βs from MacKinnon's tables, the correct critical value is

$$C = -4.42871 + \frac{-14.5876}{150} + \frac{-18.228}{150^2} + \frac{39.647}{150^3} = -4.5267591.$$

The user-written Stata command egranger by Schaffer (2010) automates much the work in conducting the Engle-Granger two-step and calculating the MacKinnon critical values.[5]

12.5.2 Engle-Granger Approach

Estimating an error correction model is quite simple. Single-equation ECMs can be estimated using OLS using Stata's reg command. Before long, we will estimate multi-equation ECMs, so-called vector ECMs; these can be estimated using Stata's vec command. But we'll begin with the simpler single-equation case.

Engle and Granger (1987) provide a straightforward, two-step procedure, to estimate an ECM. Suppose that we have two cointegrated variables, X and Y. An ECM for these variables is

$$\Delta Y_t = \delta + \gamma \Delta X_t - \alpha \left(Y_{t-1} - \beta X_{t-1} \right) + e_t \tag{12.9}$$

A constant can be included either as a term in parenthesis or outside of it as we have with δ.

To estimate this equation in Stata

```
. reg D.Y D.X L.Y L.X
```

While this is straightforward, you would need to back out the estimate of β by hand. (It is equal to the estimated coefficient on L.X divided by the estimated coefficient on L.Y. Can you see why?) Alternatively, Engle and Granger (1987) suggest a two-step procedure. Once we have established that the variables are cointegrated, then:

1. Estimate the cointegrating equation, and get the residuals.
2. Estimate a model in differences, but include the lagged residuals as a regressor.

---

[5] Since it is user-written and not an official Stata command, you must install it. You can do this by typing ssc install egranger.

12.5 Engle and Granger's Residual-Based Tests of Cointegration

In Stata

```
. reg Y X, nocons
. predict e, residuals
. reg D.Y D.X L.e
```

The first regression provides the estimate of the long-run or cointegrating equation (the term in parentheses in Eq. 12.9). The second equation estimates the short-run coefficients (δ and γ) and the speed-of-adjustment factor (α).

This approach is easy to implement, but it does have some deficiencies. First of all, if the variables are cointegrated, then we cannot say that X causes Y or Y causes X. Which variable should we have put on the left-hand side? By putting Y on the left, we are assuming that any deviation from the long-run relationship would show up directly in changes in Y rather than in X. Further, this approach only works well when we have two variables. But what if we have more than two variables? With three variables, X, Y and Z, there can be up to two cointegrating relationships. If there are four variables, there can be as many as three cointegrating relationships. Johansen's approach is well-suited for these cases, and we turn to it in the next section.

Engle-Granger Example

In this section, we will generate some simple cointegrated data, apply the Engle-Granger method to verify that are indeed cointegrated, and estimate an ECM for these variables.

First, we generate the data. This is the same data used to create Fig. 12.1.

```
. clear all
. set obs 50
. set seed 4321
. gen time = _n
. tsset time

. * Draw some random errors
. gen ex = rnormal(0,2)
. gen ey = rnormal(0,2)

. * Generate the variables, X and Y
. gen X = ex in 1
. replace X = 1 + L.X + ex in 2/L
. gen Y = 10 + X + ey
```

Let's suppose that we were confronted by the data on X and Y and that we didn't know they were cointegrated. Let's follow the Engle-Granger procedure to test for cointegration and then estimate an ECM.

First we test whether the variables are I(1). We begin with augmented Dickey-Fuller (ADF) tests on X and Y.

```
. dfuller X, drift

Dickey-Fuller test for unit root                    Number of obs   =         49

                          ---------- Z(t) has t-distribution ----------
                Test         1% Critical      5% Critical     10% Critical
             Statistic          Value            Value            Value
---------------------------------------------------------------------------
Z(t)           -0.927          -2.408           -1.678           -1.300
---------------------------------------------------------------------------
p-value for Z(t) = 0.1793

. dfuller Y, drift

Dickey-Fuller test for unit root                    Number of obs   =         49

                          ---------- Z(t) has t-distribution ----------
                Test         1% Critical      5% Critical     10% Critical
             Statistic          Value            Value            Value
---------------------------------------------------------------------------
Z(t)           -1.240          -2.408           -1.678           -1.300
---------------------------------------------------------------------------
p-value for Z(t) = 0.1105
```

The *p*-values for both X and Y in their levels are above 0.10, so we cannot reject the null hypothesis that these are two random walks with drift. What if we take the first differences?

```
. dfuller D.X

Dickey-Fuller test for unit root                    Number of obs   =         48

                          ---------- Interpolated Dickey-Fuller ---------
                Test         1% Critical      5% Critical     10% Critical
             Statistic          Value            Value            Value
---------------------------------------------------------------------------
Z(t)           -6.851          -3.594           -2.936           -2.602
---------------------------------------------------------------------------
MacKinnon approximate p-value for Z(t) = 0.0000

. dfuller D.Y

Dickey-Fuller test for unit root                    Number of obs   =         48

                          ---------- Interpolated Dickey-Fuller ---------
                Test         1% Critical      5% Critical     10% Critical
             Statistic          Value            Value            Value
---------------------------------------------------------------------------
Z(t)           -7.744          -3.594           -2.936           -2.602
---------------------------------------------------------------------------
MacKinnon approximate p-value for Z(t) = 0.0000
```

12.5 Engle and Granger's Residual-Based Tests of Cointegration

The zero *p*-values from the ADF tests lead us to easily reject the null hypothesis of a unit root for the first differences of X and of Y. Since X and Y seem to have a unit root, but ΔX and ΔY do not, then we conclude that X and Y are both I(1).

So, X and Y are integrated. Are they cointegrated? The next step is to see if there is a linear combination of X and Y that is stationary. If so, then they are cointegrated. So, let's regress Y on X and get the residuals:

```
. reg Y X

      Source |       SS           df       MS        Number of obs   =        50
-------------+------------------------------         F(1, 48)        =   2334.81
       Model |  7671.90154         1    7671.90154   Prob > F        =    0.0000
    Residual |   157.72195        48    3.28587396   R-squared       =    0.9799
-------------+------------------------------         Adj R-squared   =    0.9794
       Total |  7829.62349        49    159.788235   Root MSE        =    1.8127


           Y |      Coef.   Std. Err.      t    P>|t|     [95% Conf. Interval]
-------------+----------------------------------------------------------------
           X |   .9849859   .0203847    48.32   0.000     .9439998    1.025972
       _cons |   10.35948   .498132     20.80   0.000     9.357915    11.36104


. predict ehat, residuals
```

The Stata output above indicates that $\hat{Y}_t = 10.35 + 0.98 X_t$ describes the long-run relationship between X and Y; the residuals are the deviations from this long-run relationship. This is close to what we know to be the true relationship: $Y = 10 + X + e$; we know this to be true because that's how we generated the data.

The final step is to verify that this particular linear combination of X and Y is stationary. Recall that the residuals are equal to $\hat{Y}_t - \hat{\beta}_0 - \hat{\beta}_1 X_t$, so they are our linear combination of X and Y. Are the residuals stationary?

We can get our test statistics from

```
. dfuller ehat, nocons
```

or

```
. reg d.ehat L.ehat, nocons
```

These will give you the correct test statistics but the wrong critical values. Remember, we are now working with estimates rather than data, so the usual critical values no longer apply. We need to use the MacKinnon critical values.

To repeat, we can get our test statistic from
or we can run the Dickey-Fuller test "by hand" and get

```
. dfuller ehat, nocons

Dickey-Fuller test for unit root                    Number of obs   =          49

                            ---------- Interpolated Dickey-Fuller ---------
                   Test         1% Critical       5% Critical      10% Critical
                Statistic          Value             Value             Value
------------------------------------------------------------------------------
 Z(t)            -6.227           -2.622            -1.950            -1.610
```

or we can run the Dickey-Fuller test "by hand" and get:

```
. reg d.ehat L.ehat, nocons

      Source |       SS           df       MS      Number of obs   =        49
-------------+------------------------------       F(1, 48)        =     38.77
       Model |   124.9718          1     124.9718  Prob > F        =    0.0000
    Residual |   154.70814        48   3.22308624  R-squared       =    0.4468
-------------+------------------------------       Adj R-squared   =    0.4353
       Total |   279.67994        49   5.70775387  Root MSE        =    1.7953

------------------------------------------------------------------------------
      D.ehat |      Coef.   Std. Err.      t    P>|t|     [95% Conf. Interval]
-------------+----------------------------------------------------------------
        ehat |
         L1. |  -.8941409   .1435939    -6.23   0.000    -1.182856   -.6054261
------------------------------------------------------------------------------
```

For the hypothesis that the residuals are stationary, the test statistic is -6.227 or -6.23 after rounding. We did not include a constant in these regressions since we already included a constant in the first step.

What are our critical values? We can calculate this a couple of different ways. First, we can look at the appropriate table in MacKinnon and plug in the corresponding values into Eq. (12.8):

$$C(p=0.05, T=49) = -3.33613 + \frac{-6.1101}{49} + \frac{-6.823}{49^2} + \frac{0}{49^3}$$

$$= -3.4636677$$

Alternatively, we can use the pre-canned `egranger` command:

```
. egranger Y X

Engle-Granger test for cointegration                   N (1st step)   =       50
N (test)      =        49
------------------------------------------------------------------------------
                   Test         1% Critical       5% Critical      10% Critical
                Statistic          Value             Value             Value
------------------------------------------------------------------------------
 Z(t)            -6.227           -4.129            -3.464            -3.132

Critical values from MacKinnon (1990, 2010)
```

12.5 Engle and Granger's Residual-Based Tests of Cointegration

Since the test statistic (-6.227) is greater in absolute value than the critical value (-3.464), we reject the null hypothesis of a unit root and conclude that the residuals are stationary.

Finally, now that we know that X and Y are cointegrated, we can estimate an ECM model describing their short-run behavior. (Their long-run behavior was given by the regression in the previous step.)

```
. reg D.Y D.X L.ehat
```

Source	SS	df	MS		Number of obs	=	49
					F(2, 46)	=	33.09
Model	222.204393	2	111.102196		Prob > F	=	0.0000
Residual	154.429276	46	3.35715818		R-squared	=	0.5900
					Adj R-squared	=	0.5721
Total	376.633669	48	7.84653478		Root MSE	=	1.8323

D.Y	Coef.	Std. Err.	t	P>|t|	[95% Conf. Interval]	
X						
D1.	.9452758	.1430951	6.61	0.000	.6572402	1.233311
ehat						
L1.	−.8863005	.1493682	−5.93	0.000	−1.186963	−.5856378
_cons	.0528712	.286782	0.18	0.855	−.524391	.6301334

The ECM for X and Y is estimated to be

$$\Delta Y_t = 0.945 \Delta X_t - 0.886\,(Y_{t-1} - 10.35 - 0.98 X_{t-1}) + 0.0528 + \text{error}_t \quad (12.10)$$

It is easy to lose sight of the forest. Let's run through a streamlined version of the process. First check whether X and Y are I(1):

```
. dfuller X, drift
. dfuller Y, drift
. dfuller D.X
. dfuller D.Y
```

They are integrated, but are they cointegrated? Estimate the long-run linear relationship between X and Y, and extract the residuals:

```
. reg Y X
. predict ehat, residuals
```

Use a Dickey-Fuller test with MacKinnon critical values to verify that the residuals are I(0):

```
. egranger Y X
```

Since the residuals are found to be I(0), then X and Y are cointegrated, and we estimate an ECM model of X and Y:

    . reg D.Y D.X L.ehat

The Engle-Granger test tables show the critical values for various number of variables N. Don't let this fool you into thinking that you are testing for multi-cointegration. The Engle-Granger test still relies on a single first-step regression. The researcher arbitrarily chooses one of the N variables as the dependent variable, call it X_{1t}, for example, and regresses it on all other variables. With four variables the first Engle-Granger step in Stata is

    . reg X1 X2 X3 X4

But we are still only testing whether there is one cointegrating vector: one set of coefficients that render the residuals from this regression stationary. The Johansen test can actually test whether there are different (linearly independent) sets of coefficients (combinations) of the Xs which yield stationary residuals.

12.6 Multi-equation Models and VECMs

While the Engle-Granger approach is intuitive, it is not suited to examining cointegration among more than two variables. Johansen's procedure, while mathematically more difficult, shines with more than two variables. It allows for the simultaneous estimation of all cointegrating relationships.

Engle and Granger's two-step procedure builds on regression. Johansen's procedure builds on VARs and circumvents many of the problems in the two-step approach.

One of the strengths of cointegration analysis is that it is a convenient way to marry the short-term predictive power of VARs with the long-term predictive power of ECMs. We now turn to expanding the modeling approach from the one equation Engle-Granger two-step approach to the more general Johansen multi-equation VECM approach.

Johansen's (1988) approach has become the default method for estimating VECM models.[6]

12.6.1 Deriving the VECM from a Simple VAR(2)

Up until now we have looked at cointegration and ECMs using one-equation models. Next, we turn to a more general approach which can accommodate more equations and more left-hand-side variables.

---

[6] There are many features which recommend Johansen's (1988) approach. For example, Gonzalo (1994) shows that Johansen's method outperforms four rival methods—asymptotically and in small samples—at estimating cointegrating vectors. This is the case even when the errors are not normal or when the correct number of lags is unknown.

12.6 Multi-equation Models and VECMs

Consider the following two-variable, two-lag structural VAR model:

$$Y_t = \alpha_1 X_t + \beta_{11} Y_{t-1} + \beta_{12} X_{t-1} + \beta_{13} Y_{t-2} + \beta_{14} X_{t-2} + e_y \quad (12.11)$$

$$X_t = \alpha_2 Y_t + \beta_{21} Y_{t-1} + \beta_{22} X_{t-1} + \beta_{23} Y_{t-2} + \beta_{24} X_{t-2} + e_x \quad (12.12)$$

Which we can write in matrix form as

$$\begin{bmatrix} Y_t \\ X_t \end{bmatrix} = \begin{bmatrix} \alpha_1 & \alpha_2 \end{bmatrix} \begin{bmatrix} X_t \\ Y_t \end{bmatrix} + \begin{bmatrix} \beta_{11} & \beta_{12} \\ \beta_{21} & \beta_{22} \end{bmatrix} \begin{bmatrix} Y_{t-1} \\ X_{t-1} \end{bmatrix} + \begin{bmatrix} \beta_{13} & \beta_{14} \\ \beta_{23} & \beta_{24} \end{bmatrix} \begin{bmatrix} Y_{t-2} \\ X_{t-2} \end{bmatrix} + \begin{bmatrix} e_y \\ e_x \end{bmatrix} \quad (12.13)$$

or as

$$\mathbf{Y_t} = \mathbf{A} \mathbf{Y_t} + \boldsymbol{\beta}_1 \mathbf{Y_{t-1}} + \boldsymbol{\beta}_1 \mathbf{Y_{t-2}} + \mathbf{e_t} \quad (12.14)$$

where the bold-font variable $\mathbf{Y_t} = \begin{bmatrix} Y_t & X_t \end{bmatrix}'$.

Notice that Eqs. (12.11) and (12.12) follow the same form (albeit with one lag) as did Eq. (12.6). Thus, we should be able to construct an ECM representation of this SVAR.

Of course, an SVAR reduces to a reduced-form VAR

$$\mathbf{Y_t} - \mathbf{A} \mathbf{Y_t} = \boldsymbol{\beta}_1 \mathbf{Y_{t-1}} + \boldsymbol{\beta}_2 \mathbf{Y_{t-2}} + \mathbf{e_t}$$

$$(\mathbf{I} - \mathbf{A}) \mathbf{Y_t} = \boldsymbol{\beta}_1 \mathbf{Y_{t-1}} + \boldsymbol{\beta}_2 \mathbf{Y_{t-2}} + \mathbf{e_t}$$

$$\mathbf{Y_t} = (\mathbf{I} - \mathbf{A})^{-1} \boldsymbol{\beta}_1 \mathbf{Y_{t-1}} + (\mathbf{I} - \mathbf{A})^{-1} \boldsymbol{\beta}_2 \mathbf{Y_{t-2}} + (\mathbf{I} - \mathbf{A})^{-1} \mathbf{e_t}$$

$$\mathbf{Y_t} = \boldsymbol{\beta}'_1 \mathbf{Y_{t-1}} + \boldsymbol{\beta}'_2 \mathbf{Y_{t-2}} + \mathbf{e}'_t \quad (12.15)$$

where we define $\boldsymbol{\beta}'_1 = (\mathbf{I} - \mathbf{A})^{-1} \boldsymbol{\beta}_1$ and the other parameters analogously.

As we did with the single-equation derivation, we begin by subtracting $\mathbf{Y_{t-1}}$ from both sides of (12.15):

$$\mathbf{Y_t} - \mathbf{Y_{t-1}} = \boldsymbol{\beta}'_1 \mathbf{Y_{t-1}} + \boldsymbol{\beta}'_2 \mathbf{Y_{t-2}} - \mathbf{Y_{t-1}} + \mathbf{e}'_t \quad (12.16)$$

$$\Delta \mathbf{Y_t} = \boldsymbol{\beta}'_1 \mathbf{Y_{t-1}} + \boldsymbol{\beta}'_2 \mathbf{Y_{t-2}} - \mathbf{Y_{t-1}} + \mathbf{e}'_t \quad (12.17)$$

Next, we add and subtract $\boldsymbol{\beta}_1 \mathbf{Y_{t-2}}$ and $\mathbf{Y_{t-2}}$ from the right-hand side:

$$\Delta \mathbf{Y_t} = \boldsymbol{\beta}'_1 \mathbf{Y_{t-1}} + \boldsymbol{\beta}'_2 \mathbf{Y_{t-2}} - \mathbf{Y_{t-1}} + \\ \left(\boldsymbol{\beta}'_1 \mathbf{Y_{t-2}} - \boldsymbol{\beta}'_1 \mathbf{Y_{t-2}} \right) + \left(\mathbf{Y_{t-2}} - \mathbf{Y_{t-2}} \right) + \mathbf{e}'_t.$$

Re-arranging terms

$$\Delta \mathbf{Y_t} = \left(\boldsymbol{\beta}'_2 + \boldsymbol{\beta}'_1 - \mathbf{I} \right) \mathbf{Y_{t-2}} + \left(\boldsymbol{\beta}'_1 - \mathbf{I} \right) \left(\mathbf{Y_{t-1}} - \mathbf{Y_{t-2}} \right) + \mathbf{e}'_t$$

$$\Delta \mathbf{Y_t} = \boldsymbol{\Gamma} \mathbf{Y_{t-2}} + \mathbf{B} \Delta \mathbf{Y_{t-1}} + \mathbf{e}'_t \quad (12.18)$$

where

$$\Gamma = (\beta_2' + \beta_1' - I)$$
$$B = (\beta_1' - I).$$

Equation (12.18) is the VECM representation of the VAR (12.15) or SVAR (12.14).

The lagged term in levels describes the long-run relationship between the variables. To see this, consider the expected value of Eq. (12.18) in a steady-state equilibrium. In a steady state, the variables do not change so that $\Delta Y = 0$. The expected value of the error term is zero, so that term also drops out. Consequently, Eq. (12.18) simplifies to

$$\Gamma Y_{t-2} = 0. \tag{12.19}$$

Notice that the original VAR model had two lags; the corresponding VECM model had only one lag (in the ΔY term). This is a general relationship between VARs and their corresponding VECMs. The VECM always has one fewer lag than the VAR. When estimating a VECM in Stata, you specify the number of lags of the VAR rather than the number of lags in the VECM; Stata is smart enough to know to subtract one.

12.6.2 Deriving the VECM(k-1) from a Reduced-Form VAR(k)

Suppose we have an n-variable k-lag reduced-form VAR of the form

$$Y_t = \beta_0 + \beta_1 Y_{t-1} + \beta_2 Y_{t-2} + \cdots + \beta_2 Y_{t-k} + e_t. \tag{12.20}$$

According to the Engle and Granger (1987) representation theorem, if the variables in Y_t are cointegrated, the VAR can be re-written as a VECM of the form

$$\Delta Y_t = \beta_0 + \Gamma_1 \Delta Y_{t-1} + \Gamma_2 \Delta Y_{t-2} + \cdots + \Gamma_{k-1} \Delta Y_{t-k} + \Pi Y_{t-k} + e_t \tag{12.21}$$

with

$$\Pi = \alpha \beta' \tag{12.22}$$

and where α is an $n \times r$ matrix containing the speed of adjustment parameters and β is an $n \times r$ matrix containing the coefficients of the cointegrating vectors.

If our VECM was a two-variable one-lag model, then (12.21) would look like

$$\Delta Y_t = \delta + \Gamma_1 \Delta Y_{t-1} + \Pi Y_{t-k} + e_t \tag{12.23}$$

12.6 Multi-equation Models and VECMs

or

$$\begin{bmatrix} \Delta Y_t \\ \Delta X_t \end{bmatrix} = \begin{bmatrix} \delta_1 \\ \delta_2 \end{bmatrix} + \begin{bmatrix} \Gamma_{11} & \Gamma_{12} \\ \Gamma_{21} & \Gamma_{22} \end{bmatrix} \begin{bmatrix} \Delta Y_{t-1} \\ \Delta X_{t-1} \end{bmatrix} + \begin{bmatrix} \alpha_1 \\ \alpha_2 \end{bmatrix} (Y_{t-1} - \beta_0 - \beta_1 X_{t-1}) + \begin{bmatrix} e_{1t} \\ e_{2t} \end{bmatrix}. \quad (12.24)$$

The cointegrating vector is

$$\boldsymbol{\beta}' = \begin{bmatrix} 1 & -\beta_0 & -\beta_1 \end{bmatrix}$$

and the adjustment parameter matrix $\boldsymbol{\alpha}$ determines how deviations from the long-run relationship between Y and X gets transferred to ΔY_t and ΔX_t.

12.6.3 $\Pi = \alpha \beta'$ Is Not Uniquely Identified

If we estimate Eq. (12.23), then we can get an estimate of Π. However, without additional information, we will not be able to separate this out into its components $\hat{\alpha}$ and $\hat{\beta}$. In the single-equation case, where we aren't dealing with vectors, we would know that $\hat{\Pi}$ was estimated to be ten, for example, but there are an infinite number of ways that two numbers $\hat{\alpha}$ and $\hat{\beta}$ can multiply to ten

$$10 = 1 \times 10 = 2 \times 5 = 3 \times \frac{10}{3} = 3.1415 \times \frac{10}{3.1415} = \ldots$$

and so forth. That is, we cannot uniquely identify $\hat{\alpha}$ and $\hat{\beta}$, because we can always multiply and divide them by any constant c and get a new set of numbers that multiply to $\hat{\Pi}$:

$$10 = \hat{\alpha} \times \hat{\beta} = \hat{\alpha} c \times \frac{1}{c} \hat{\beta}.$$

This is true for matrices and vectors, too:

$$\hat{\Pi} = \hat{\alpha} \mathbf{c} \mathbf{c}^{-1} \hat{\boldsymbol{\beta}}'.$$

Johansen's Normalization
So, if $\hat{\alpha}$ and $\hat{\beta}$ are not identified, what are we to do? Johansen (1988) proposed a straightforward normalization, and this is the default in Stata. When we think of cointegrating vectors, we usually think in terms where the Y variable has a coefficient of one. That is, we think in terms of:

$$Y_{t-1} = \beta_0 + \beta_1 X_{t-1} + \epsilon$$

or, after rearranging,

$$Y_{t-1} - \beta_0 - \beta_1 X_{t-1} = \epsilon$$

rather than, say,

$$3Y_{t-1} - 3\beta_0 - 3\beta_1 X_{t-1} = 3\epsilon$$

or

$$cY_{t-1} - c\beta_0 - c\beta_1 X_{t-1} = c\epsilon.$$

All of the above cointegrating vectors "work." Return to the variables X and Z from Figs. 12.2, 12.1, and 12.4. Recall that two different linear operations could establish cointegration between X and Z: multiplying X by 3 or dividing Z by 3. Suppose you multiplied X by 3 to establish cointegration between X' and Z. Now that X' and Z are parallel, they would stay parallel if we were to multiply X' and Z by the same constant (c). We would be tilting the pair up or down, but they would be tilting in parallel. And while all of the above cointegrating vectors "work" equally well mathematically, they are not equally intuitive.

Johansen's normalization essentially insists that we write the cointegrating vectors like we instinctively want to: with a one in front of all of our Y variables. With the components of $\hat{\beta}$ pinned down like this, and with $\hat{\Pi}$ known, then $\hat{\alpha}$ is identified and can be backed out by $\hat{\alpha} = \hat{\Pi}\hat{\beta}^{-1}$.

12.6.4 Johansen's Tests and the Rank of Π

The Engle-Granger residual-based tests of cointegration are intuitive, and they are well-suited to testing for one cointegrating equation between two variables. But it is not particularly suited to finding more than one cointegrating equation, as might be the case if we are considering systems with more than two variables. In such a case, we need a better approach, such as the one pioneered by Helmut Johansen.

Johansen developed his approach to estimating the rank of $\hat{\Pi}$ in a series of papers. In Johansen (1988) he developed his eigenvalue tests for the case where there are no constants or seasonal dummy variables in the long-run cointegrating equations. Ultimately, including these dummy terms is important for empirics and affects the distribution of the relevant test statistics. Johansen (1991) showed how to include these important terms. Johansen (1995b) expanded these tests to include the case where the variables are I(2) rather than I(1).[7] Johansen (1994) summarizes these results in slightly less technical language.

---

[7] We do not consider the I(2) case in this book. A workable but incomplete solution is to difference the I(2) variables once to render them I(1) and then follow the procedures as outlined below.

12.6 Multi-equation Models and VECMs

The cointegrating equations (i.e., the long-run relationships) between the variables in Eq. (12.21) are all contained in ΠY_{t-k}. How many cointegrating equations are there? In matrices, this is equivalent to asking, what is r, the rank of the matrix Π?

If there are n variables in the system, then there could be anywhere from zero to $n - 1$ linearly independent cointegrating equations. If there are none, then these variables aren't cointegrated, and we should just estimate a VAR. The VAR will be in levels if the variables in Y_t are I(0); the VAR will be in first differences if the variables are all I(1).

If you have n variables that are I(1), then you can have up to $n - 1$ linearly independent cointegrating vectors between them. Why not n cointegrating vectors? You can't have n *linearly independent* cointegrating vectors between n variables. If we had two variables, X_t and Y_t, then the residuals from

```
. reg X Y
```

might be stationary. And if that is the case, then so will be the residuals from

```
. reg Y X
```

That is, if $e_t = Y_t - a - bX_t$ is stationary, then you could just rewrite this equation as $e_t/b = X_t + a/b - Y_t/b$ which will also be stationary. (Can you see why? You are asked to prove this as an exercise.) To know one equation is to know the other. They are just linear recombinations of the other.

Moreover, if each shock in the system is a unit root process, then necessarily the variables cannot be cointegrated. In a two-variable system, we would need one, say X, to be a unit root, and Y to depend on X. If they're both unit riots, then they'll drift independently of each other. They would not be cointegrated.

The interesting case for a chapter on VECMs is when the number of cointegrating equations, r, is at least one and less than n.

Johansen provides two different test for the rank of Π:

1. the maximum eigenvalue test, and
2. the trace test.

They aren't just different test statistics for the same hypothesis. They are different procedures that test different hypotheses. And in practice, they often lead the researcher to different conclusions. This is unfortunate, but a fact of econometric life. Ultimately, you should choose the specification that yields economically reasonable results.

The mathematics behind each of these tests can be rather complicated and beyond the scope of this introductory book. Instead, we'll outline the two test procedures below and illustrate with an example.

Any statistical test rests on some assumptions. Johansen's tests are no exception. They both build upon variations of a specific form of VECM model:

$$\Delta Y_t = \Gamma_1 \Delta Y_{t-1} + \Gamma_2 \Delta Y_{t-2} + \cdots + \Gamma_{k-1} \Delta Y_{t-k} \\ + \Pi Y_{t-k} + (\gamma + \tau t) + e_t \tag{12.25}$$

Recall that $\Pi = \alpha\beta'$. If we allow a constant and trend along with the adjustment parameter, then

$$\Delta Y_t = \Gamma_1 \Delta Y_{t-1} + \Gamma_2 \Delta Y_{t-2} + \cdots + \Gamma_{k-1} \Delta Y_{t-k}$$
$$+ \alpha (\beta Y_{t-k} + \mu + \rho t) + (\gamma + \tau t) + e_t \qquad (12.26)$$

Thus, Johansen allows for drift (via the constant terms μ and γ) and deterministic trend (via ρt and τt). If the differenced variables follow a linear trend, then the un-differenced variables will follow a quadratic trend.

Each of Johansen's two tests has five variations; the variations rely on different restrictions on these trend and drift terms:

1. $\mu = \gamma = \rho = \tau = 0$. This is the simplest, but least flexible case, where Eq. (12.26) simplifies to Eq. (12.21). Here, there are no drift or deterministic trends either in the first differences or the cointegrating equations. Thus, the (cointegrated) levels and the first differences are stationary with zero mean. In Stata this is the trend(none) option.
2. $\gamma = \rho = \tau = 0$, but μ is unrestricted. Since $\gamma = 0$, then the variables in first differences do not have drift. Since $\tau = 0$, then the variables in first differences do not follow a linear trend; thus, they also do not follow a quadratic trend in levels. Since $\rho = 0$ then the cointegrating equations do not follow a trend. They are, however, allowed to have non-zero mean since $\mu \neq 0$. This corresponds to Stata's trend(rconstant) option.
3. $\rho = \tau = 0$, but μ and γ are unrestricted. Again, since $\rho = 0$ then the cointegrating equations are not stationary around a deterministic trend. And since $\tau = 0$, then first-differenced terms also do not follow a deterministic linear trend; this implies that the variables in levels are constrained not to follow a quadratic trend. The fact that μ may not equal zero implies that the cointegrating equations are allowed to have a non-zero mean. And the fact that γ may not equal zero implies that the first differenced variables are also allowed to have a non-zero mean. This is the trend(constant) option in Stata and is the default.
4. $\tau = 0$, while the remaining variables (μ, γ, and ρ) are unrestricted. Since $\tau = 0$ then there is no linear trend in first differenced variables, so there is no quadratic trend in the un-differenced variables. We allow for a non-zero mean in the first-differenced variables via γ; we allow for non-zero mean in the cointegrating equations via μ, and we allow the cointegrating equations to follow a linear trend via ρ. This is the trend(rtrend) option in Stata.
5. In the most flexible case, there are no restrictions on μ, γ, ρ, or τ. Here, we use the trend(trend) option in Stata.

Which case should you use? You'll have to look at the data and verify whether the various assumptions (zero mean, etc.) seem reasonable. That said, Cases 1 and

12.6 Multi-equation Models and VECMs

5 are not really used in practice. Case 1 is rather extreme in that it would require that all variables have a mean of zero; but how often do economies exhibit zero or negative growth? Or zero inflation and deflation? Case five is also extreme in the sense that the levels follow a quadratic trend. But even exponential growth of, say, your bank account at a fixed interest rate, is linear (in logarithms).[8]

The website for the software program EViews recommends that: "As a rough guide, use case 2 if none of the series appear to have a trend. For trending series, use case 3 if you believe all trends are stochastic;[9] if you believe some of the series are trend stationary, use case 4."

For macroeconomic variables (GDP and its components, the price level, etc.) and financial asset prices (stock prices, bond prices, etc.), Zivot and Wang (2007) recommend using Case 3, as the assumption of deterministic growth in these variables is untenable. (GDP doesn't *have* to grow at a specific deterministic amount.)

Thus far we know that there are two different Johansen cointegration tests, and we have established that there are five (but in econ and finance, really three) different test statistics for these tests that we might consider. Presuming we know which case we are dealing with, how can we actually carry out either one of the Johansen tests? We turn to this right now.

Both tests rely on the eigenvalues of the Π matrix. Why? Recall that $\Pi = \alpha\beta'$ includes the matrix of cointegrating coefficients. If all of the n variables are cointegrated, then there can be $n-1$ linearly independent cointegrating relationships between them. The number of cointegrating relationships is equal to the number of eigenvalues of Π. Likewise if there is cointegration, then Π is not of full rank; it will have a rank of $r < n$. A square matrix that is not of full rank has a determinant of zero. Further, the determinant of a matrix is equal to the product of its eigenvalues. Thus, if there is at least one eigenvalue that is zero, the determinant is zero. Likewise, if we add eigenvalues and one of them is zero, then the sum wouldn't increase. The two tests essentially ask: At what point are we adding or multiplying zero eigenvalues? This will reveal the rank of Π and thereby will also reveal r, the number of cointegrating relationships.

To repeat, *the number of cointegrating vectors is equal to the rank of Π which is equal to the number of non-zero eigenvalues of Π*.

Why not directly calculate the eigenvalues of Π and be done with it? Because we don't have access to the true values of Π nor of its eigenvalues; we only have the estimate $\hat{\Pi}$ from a sample. Thus, we need to perform statistical tests on whether

---

[8] The online help for the Eviews econometric software also warns against using Cases 1 and 5 (http://www.eviews.com/help/helpintro.html#page/content/coint-Johansen_Cointegration_Test.html). Likewise, Zivot and Wang (2007) warn against using Case 1. Sjö (2008, p.18) calls Case 4 "the model of last resort" (since including a time in the vectors might induce stationarity) and Case 5 as "quite unrealistic and should not be considered in applied work." Thus, we are left with Cases 2 and 3 as reasonable choices.

[9] That is, the trend is due to drift from a random walk.

any of the estimated eigenvalues are close to zero (or, alternatively, whether they are statistically significantly different from zero).

Johansen's Maximum Eigenvalue Test

The "maximum eigenvalue test" is a sequential test that the rank of $\hat{\Pi}$ is r vs the alternative that it is $r + 1$.

Suppose that we estimated a n-variable VECM, calculated $\hat{\Pi}$, and its estimated eigenvalues. Suppose that we sort these eigenvalues in decreasing order, so that $\hat{\lambda}_1 \leq \hat{\lambda}_2 \leq \ldots \hat{\lambda}_n$.

The test procedure is as follows. We begin with the null hypothesis that $r = 0$ vs the alternative that $r = 1$. We calculate the test statistic, compare it to the appropriate critical value, and decide whether to reject the null. If we do not reject the null, then we can stop there and conclude that there is no cointegration among the variables. If, instead, we reject the null, then we update the null and alternative hypotheses and repeat the procedure. The new null hypothesis is that $r = 1$ and the alternative is that $r = 2$. We compare the test statistic and critical values and decide whether to reject the null. If we do not reject, then we conclude that $r = 1$, and we stop the process. If, instead, we do not reject the null, then we add one to the null hypothesis and repeat. That is, our new null is that $r = 2$ vs the alternative that $r = 3$, and we repeat the process, adding one to the null until we can no longer reject the null hypothesis.

The test statistic for the null hypothesis that the rank $= r$ vs the alternative that the rank $= r + 1$ is

$$LR(r, r+1) = -Tln\left(1 - \lambda_{r+1}\right)$$

Notice, we start with the largest and next-largest eigenvalues; this tests the hypothesis that r is smallest versus smallest plus one.

To summarize, we slowly increase our hypothesized rank r bit by bit until we can no longer reject the null hypothesis.

Johansen's Trace Test

The trace test[10] is also a sequential test, but with different alternative hypothesis. Here, the null hypothesis is that the rank is r vs the alternative that the rank is greater than r. We begin with the null hypothesis that the rank is equal to zero; i.e., that $r = 0$. The test statistic is calculated and compared with the appropriate critical value. If we reject the null that $r = 0$, then it must be greater than zero. But this doesn't tell us what r is, just that it is greater than we thought. Now we update and repeat the process. The updated null is that $r = 1$ vs the alternative that $r > 1$. Again, we calculate the test statistic and compare with the critical value. Rejecting the null means that r must be greater still. We repeat the process until we can no

---

[10] Dwyer (2014, p.6) explains that the trace statistic does not refer to the trace of $\hat{\Pi}$ but refers instead to the "trace of a matrix based on functions of Brownian motion." It also shares the similarity with the trace of the matrix in that both involve the sum of terms (here the sum of the eigenvalues); more specifically, we sum $ln(1 - \lambda) \approx \lambda$ when $(\lambda \approx 0)$.

12.6 Multi-equation Models and VECMs

longer reject the null hypothesis. Strictly speaking, we won't have "accepted the null" (we never "accept the null," only "fail to reject"), but we will use it as our working assumption and calculate the r cointegrating vectors.

The test statistic for the null hypothesis that rank = r vs the alternative that the rank > r is

$$LR(r, n) = -T \sum_{i=r+1}^{n} \ln(1 - \lambda_i)$$

As with the max eigenvalue test, we slowly increase our hypothesized rank r bit by bit until we can no longer reject the null hypothesis.

Johansen in Stata

Fortunately, Stata's `vecrank` command automates much of the tedium in testing for the cointegration rank. If we had five variables (X1 through X5) that we wanted to test for cointegration, we could type

```
. vecrank X1 X2 X3 X4 X5
```

which would show the trace statistic for the default Case 3 at the 5% level.

Adding the `notrace` option suppresses the trace statistic. Thus, typing

```
. vecrank X1 X2 X3 X4 X5, max  notrace
```

shows Johansen's maximum eigenvalue statistic, but not the trace statistic.

The safer bet is to ask for both statistics and compare. This is done by including the `max` option and excluding the `notrace` option.[11]

```
. vecrank X1 X2 X3 X4 X5, max
```

Johansen Example

We now turn to an example with simulated data. First, we simulate 1000 errors:

```
. clear all
. set obs 1000
. set seed 4321
. gen time = _n
. tsset time

. * Draw some random errors
. gen ex = rnormal(0,1)
. gen ey = rnormal(0,1)
. gen ez = rnormal(0,1)
. gen ev = rnormal(0,1)
```

Next, we generate the variables.

---

[11] It is unclear to me why Stata opted not to have `trace` and `max` options.

```
. gen X = ex in 1
. replace X = 1 + L.X + ex in 2/L
. gen Y = 10 + 2*X + ey
. gen Z =  5 + 3*X + ez
. gen V = ev in 1
. replace V = 2 + L.V + ev in 2/L
```

Here, X follows a random walk with drift, so it is I(1). By construction, Y and X are cointegrated, with cointegrating equation

$$Y_t = 10 + 2X_t + e_{yt} \quad (12.27)$$

Z and X are cointegrated, with cointegrating equation

$$Z_t = 5 + 3X_t + e_{zt} \quad (12.28)$$

and as a check, we also generate variable V

$$V_t = 2 + V_{t-1} + e_{vt} \quad (12.29)$$

which is a random walk with drift that is not cointegrated with X.

The first 100 observations of the data are graphed in Fig. 12.8.

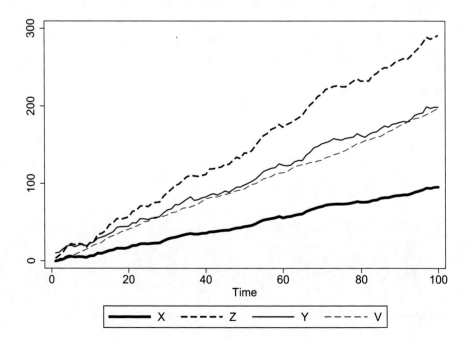

Fig. 12.8 Three cointegrated variables and one that is not

12.6 Multi-equation Models and VECMs

Now, we see whether the Johansen tests work. We'll examine the output for the trace and max eigenvalue statistics. In both cases the procedure is to select the smallest r where the test statistic is smaller than the corresponding critical value.

```
. vecrank X Y Z V, trend(constant) max
```

```
                    Johansen tests for cointegration
Trend: constant                                       Number of obs =   998
Sample:   3 - 1000                                    Lags          =     2
-----------------------------------------------------------------------------
                                                              5%
maximum                                            trace    critical
  rank     parms      LL        eigenvalue       statistic    value
    0        20    -6079.5292        .           823.7007    47.21
    1        27    -5864.6991    0.34983         394.0405    29.68
    2        32    -5671.3066    0.32129           7.2554*   15.41
    3        35    -5668.2982    0.00601           1.2387     3.76
    4        36    -5667.6789    0.00124
-----------------------------------------------------------------------------
                                                              5%
maximum                                             max     critical
  rank     parms      LL        eigenvalue       statistic    value
    0        20    -6079.5292        .           429.6602    27.07
    1        27    -5864.6991    0.34983         386.7851    20.97
    2        32    -5671.3066    0.32129           6.0167    14.07
    3        35    -5668.2982    0.00601           1.2387     3.76
    4        36    -5667.6789    0.00124
-----------------------------------------------------------------------------
```

Both the trace statistic and the max-eigenvalue statistics indicate (correctly) that there are two cointegrating equations (X and Y; and X and Z). We can see this by comparing the test statistics with their corresponding critical values.

The trace statistic for $r = 0$ is 823, whereas the critical value is 47.21. Since the test statistic is bigger than the critical value, we reject the null hypothesis and "accept" the null (that $r > 0$). Then we update to a new null hypothesis (that $r = 1$ vs the alternative that $r > 1$). The trace statistic is 394 which is greater than the critical value of 29.68, so we reject the null that $r = 1$. What about $r = 2$? The trace statistic is 7.26 which is smaller than the critical value (15.41). Thus, we cannot reject the null and we conclude that $r = 2$. Stata even indicates this for us with an *.

What about the maximum eigenvalue test? Beginning with a null hypothesis that $r = 0$ vs the alternative that $r = 1$, the test statistic is 429.6. Since the test statistic is greater than the critical value of 27.07, we reject the null of $r = 0$. Now we update. The test statistic for $r = 1$ is 386 which is greater than the critical value of 20.97, so we reject $r = 1$. What about $r = 2$? Here, the max eigenvalue statistic is 6.02 which is smaller than 14.07. Thus, we cannot reject the null hypothesis that $r = 2$.

Both tests indicate that there are two cointegrating equations. (It is not always the case that the two tests agree.)

The next step is to estimate these long-run cointegrating equations as well as the short-run adjustment terms.

```
. vec Z Y X , rank(2) trend(constant)
Vector error-correction model

Sample:  3 - 1000                          Number of obs   =        998
                                           AIC             =    8.56465
Log likelihood = -4253.76                  HQIC            =   8.602019
Det(Sigma_ml)  = 1.010999                  SBIC            =   8.662962
```

Equation	Parms	RMSE	R-sq	chi2	P>chi2
D_Z	6	3.17065	0.4685	874.5377	0.0000
D_Y	6	2.22674	0.4804	917.2352	0.0000
D_X	6	1.00808	0.4687	875.2629	0.0000

		Coef.	Std. Err.	z	P>|z|	[95% Conf.	Interval]
D_Z							
_ce1	L1.	-.9249586	.1384184	-6.68	0.000	-1.196254	-.6536635
_ce2	L1.	.0848118	.144498	0.59	0.557	-.1983991	.3680228
Z	LD.	.0665333	.097943	0.68	0.497	-.1254314	.2584981
Y	LD.	-.1933857	.1029971	-1.88	0.060	-.3952563	.008485
X	LD.	.2203036	.3599633	0.61	0.541	-.4852116	.9258187
_cons		.0422761	.5569334	0.08	0.939	-1.049293	1.133845
D_Y							
_ce1	L1.	.0705043	.0972111	0.73	0.468	-.1200259	.2610346
_ce2	L1.	-.8649982	.1014808	-8.52	0.000	-1.063897	-.6660994
Z	LD.	.0365918	.0687853	0.53	0.595	-.0982248	.1714084
Y	LD.	-.1603326	.0723348	-2.22	0.027	-.3021061	-.018559
X	LD.	.2468558	.2528019	0.98	0.329	-.2486267	.7423383

12.6 Multi-equation Models and VECMs

```
         _cons |   .086509    .3911337    0.22   0.825    -.680099    .853117
---------------+----------------------------------------------------------------
D_X            |
          _ce1 |
           L1. |  .0284979    .044009     0.65   0.517    -.0577581   .114754
               |
          _ce2 |
           L1. |  .0615169    .045942     1.34   0.181    -.0285277   .1515616
               |
             Z |
           LD. |  .0195993    .0311402    0.63   0.529    -.0414343   .080633
               |
             Y |
           LD. | -.0804207    .0327471   -2.46   0.014    -.1446039  -.0162376
               |
             X |
           LD. |  .1157547    .1144475    1.01   0.312    -.1085582   .3400676
               |
         _cons | 1.158131     .1770725    6.54   0.000     .8110753  1.505187
--------------------------------------------------------------------------------
```

Cointegrating equations

```
Equation           Parms      chi2      P>chi2
-----------------------------------------------
_ce1                  1     6.06e+08    0.0000
_ce2                  1     2.83e+08    0.0000
-----------------------------------------------
```

Identification: beta is exactly identified

Johansen normalization restrictions imposed

```
--------------------------------------------------------------------------------
         beta |    Coef.    Std. Err.      z     P>|z|    [95% Conf. Interval]
--------------+-----------------------------------------------------------------
_ce1          |
           Z  |      1         .          .       .          .          .
           Y  |      0      (omitted)
           X  |  -2.999701   .0001219   -2.5e+04  0.000    -2.99994    -2.999462
        _cons |  -8.315004     .          .       .          .          .
--------------+-----------------------------------------------------------------
_ce2          |
           Z  |      0      (omitted)
           Y  |      1         .          .       .          .          .
           X  |  -1.99998    .0001189   -1.7e+04  0.000    -2.000213   -1.999747
        _cons | -12.24858      .          .       .          .          .
--------------------------------------------------------------------------------
```

This produces a lot of output. What does it all mean?

Let's try to map this output back to the vector notation we've been using in this chapter:

$$\Delta Y_t = \Gamma_1 \Delta Y_{t-1} + \alpha \left(\beta Y_{t-1} + \mu \right) + e_t \tag{12.30}$$

First, the vectors of variables are

$$\mathbf{Y_t} = [Z_t, Y_t, X_t]'$$

and

$$\mathbf{\Delta Y_t} = \begin{bmatrix} \Delta Z_t \\ \Delta Y_t \\ \Delta X_t \end{bmatrix} = \begin{bmatrix} Z_t - Z_{t-1} \\ Y_t - Y_{t-1} \\ X_t - X_{t-1} \end{bmatrix}.$$

Stata estimates the cointegration matrix

$$\hat{\beta} = \begin{bmatrix} 1 & 0 & -2.9997012 \\ 0 & 1 & -1.9999803 \end{bmatrix},$$

with the matrix of constants

$$\hat{\mu} = \begin{bmatrix} -8.3150036 \\ -12.248583 \end{bmatrix}.$$

The adjustment matrix is estimated to be

$$\hat{\alpha} = \begin{bmatrix} -.92495862 & .08481184 \\ .07050434 & -.86499818 \\ .02849794 & .06151691 \end{bmatrix}.$$

And the coefficients on the differenced variables are estimated to be

$$\hat{\Gamma} = \begin{bmatrix} .06653331 & -.19338567 & .22030356 & .04227607 \\ .03659180 & -.16033256 & .24685581 & .08650901 \\ .01959932 & -.08042072 & .11575474 & 1.1581311 \end{bmatrix}.$$

Economically speaking, the most important part of the output is the last Stata table: the cointegrating equations. The first cointegrating equation expresses Z as a function of X

$$Z + 0Y - 2.999701X - 8.3150036 = 0,$$

or, after rearranging and rounding,

$$Z = 3X + 8.32. \tag{12.31}$$

The second cointegrating equation has Y as a function of X

$$0Z + Y - 1.99998X - 12.248583 = 0,$$

or

$$Y = 2X + 12.25. \qquad (12.32)$$

The slopes on these lines are almost identical to the true cointegrating Eqs. (12.27) and (12.28).[12]

Incidentally, if we had ordered our variables differently, such as with

```
. vec X Y Z
```

then the Johansen normalization would have expressed X as a function of Z and Y as a function of Z. We could then algebraically rearrange terms to give us the equations expressed as (12.31) and (12.32).

12.7 IRFs, OIRFs, and Forecasting from VECMs

Since VECMs have an underlying VAR, then we can estimate impulse response functions and OIRFs after estimating a VEC. The same apples for forecasting and for calculating forecast error decompositions. In fact, the same Stata command calculates the IRFs, OIRFs, and FEVDs after estimating a VECM, so there's no need to repeat ourselves. The accuracy of the IRFs, OIRFs, and FEVDs often depends critically on the lag length chosen in estimating the underlying VAR.

12.8 Lag Length Selection

How many lags should be included in the initial VAR? In other words, what is k in Eqs. (12.20) or (12.21)? Economic theory usually doesn't have much to say about such questions. But it is an important question for the econometrician, as the estimated number of cointegrating relationships is found to depend upon k.

Since a VECM comes from a VAR, it stands to reason that there is a connection between lag order selection for a VAR and lag order selection for a VECM. In short, we can use the same information criteria that we used in VARs to select the lag lengths in VECMs. VECMs should have one fewer lags than the levels-VAR. (One less because that extra lag is captured via differencing in the VECM.)

Lütkepohl and Saikkonen (1999) recommend using some form of information criteria for lag order selection as they balance the size and power trade-offs associated with having too few or too many lags. The command in Stata for estimating k in a VECM is the same command as for VARs: `varsoc`. This

---

[12] Cointegration merely requires that a linear combination of the variables is stationary. In practical terms, this means that the two variables can be tilted up or down until their difference is stationary. Two parallel lines are stationary, regardless of the constant difference between them. Or, what we care about is the slopes that establish stationarity; econometrically, we are less concerned with the constant. Economically, the constant term seldom has practical significance.

command calculates the common Information Criteria (the Akaike Information Criteria being the most common) to guide lag selection.

Unfortunately, the various information criteria often disagree as to the optimal lag length. Researchers are quite relieved when various information criteria choose the same lag length. If they disagree, however, which information criteria should you look at? This is an open question, and there are trade-offs with any such choice. As a general rule of thumb, the AIC and FPE (final prediction error) are better suited if the aim of the VAR model is forecasting. More parsimonious models tend to have better predictive power. If the aim, however, is in proper estimation of the true number of lags in the data generating process, then an argument can be made that Schwartz IC (SBIC) or Hannan-Quin information criterion (HQIC) should be used (Lütkepohl 2005).

It is common for practitioners to rely on the following sequential approach: use an information criterion to determine the lag length, and then use Johansen (1991) to estimate the cointegrating rank. Sequential approaches such as this, though intuitive, tend to accumulate problems. Properly estimating the lag length (k) affects the ability to estimate the rank (r). So, making a small mistake early on in the lag length step can lead to bigger errors in the rank estimation step. Gonzalo and Pitarakis (1998) compared the various information criteria in a Monte Carlo experiment to test their ability to properly choose r. They find that the BIC is better able than AIC or HQIC to identify r correctly. They find the AIC to be particularly weak. Thus, we face a trade-off. The AIC chooses k quite well, but when it doesn't it has large consequences for r.

The AIC and BIC tend to prefer few lags. Too few lags and the errors might be autocorrelated. The test statistics in use rely on uncorrelated errors. Thus, in practice, people add lags until the errors are white noise. Having too few leads to a model that is misspecified. Anything produced from this misspecified model, then, is suspect including the IRFs and variance decompositions. Adding too many lags spreads out the available observations over too many parameters, leading to inefficient estimates of the coefficients. These noisy estimates result in poor IRFs and variance decompositions (Braun and Mittnik 1993), as well as poor forecasting properties from the estimated VARs and VECMs (Lütkepohl 2005). This is an important problem with any finite sample, but especially in small samples.

Lag length for VARs and VECMs continues to be an active area of research. Researchers continue to investigate the small-sample properties of the various selection methods. Others consider methods where different equations take different lags. Still others consider whether the lag lengths have gaps in them. That is, whether to include, for example, lags 1, 3, and 4 but exclude lag=2. The general goal is to avoid estimating more parameters than necessary. Otherwise, we will waste valuable degrees of freedom. This, in turn, will result in more noisy parameter estimates which is the root cause of the bad forecasting ability of more longer-lagged models.

In practice, most practitioners opt for an eclectic approach. Many decide to emulate a democracy, and they choose the lag length that is preferred by the most information criteria. Others will estimate models with different lag lengths and show that their results are robust to the different lags. Ultimately, few papers are rejected because of lag length. Still, it is best to have a procedure and stick to it; otherwise you might be tempted to hunt for a particular outcome. This would invalidate your results and, more importantly, would be unethical.

12.9 Cointegration Implies Granger Causality

Given the close connection between VECMs and VARs, you may be wondering whether VECMs have a connection with Granger causality. Indeed, they do. If two variables X and Y are cointegrated, then there must exist Granger causality in at least one direction. That is, X must Granger-cause Y, or Y must Granger-cause X, or both (Granger 1988). That is, VECMs imply Granger causality. It is not always the case in the other direction, however. Granger causality does not imply that there exists some linear combination of variables that is stationary.

Without getting into the mathematical details of why cointegration implies causality, the intuition is as follows. Let's refer back to the example of a drunk walking her dog from Murray (1994) that we discussed at the beginning of this chapter. But suppose that the drunk is really fat, the dog is a miniature poodle, and the drunk has her dog on a leash. The leash is the linear relationship between the two. They never stray farther than the length of the leash. They might cross paths, but they would never drift apart. That is, there is a stationary relationship in the distance between the two. What about Granger causality? Well, if the owner is large, then she moves the dog. The dog is too small to move the owner. Thus, causality runs from the drunk to the dog. If the drunk and her dog are both similarly sized, then they each pull the other. There would be Granger causality from the drunk to the dog and from the dog to the drunk.

Why doesn't Granger causality necessarily imply cointegration? Well, suppose there were no leash, and the dog hated its owner. Each time the owner would yell "Fido!" looking for her dog, the dog might run farther away. There is a causal relationship, but there is no stationary relationship between the distance of the dog and the owner.

12.9.1 Testing for Granger Causality

A VECM can be used as the basis for a Granger causality test. However, this is not recommended. Instead, estimate a VAR model in levels using the Toda and Yamamoto (1995) procedure. For a refresher, refer to Sect. 11.4 on "VARs with Integrated Variables" where this procedure is laid out. If the variables are integrated—regardless of whether the variables are also cointegrated—use the Toda-Yamamoto procedure to test for Granger causality. Then proceed with tests of cointegration. Recall that cointegration implies Granger causality, so if you did not find causality in the first stage, this would provide some evidence that you do not have cointegration, regardless of what any particular cointegration test might say.

The problem of "pre-testing" arises when testing for cointegration first, then estimating a VECM, and then testing for causality from the VECM. In such a case, the Granger causality test and its test statistics are contingent on the estimate of the previous cointegration test. The usual test statistics for Granger causality do not reflect this pre-testing.[13] Clarke and Mirza (2006) find that pre-testing for cointegration results in a bias toward finding Granger causality where none exists.

To repeat, if you are interested in Granger causality, estimate a VAR augmented with additional lags as suggested by Toda and Yamamoto (1995), and test for Granger causality. After this, proceed to test for cointegration and estimate a VEC using Johansen's method.

12.10 Conclusion

No textbook can be encyclopedic, as the field advances with hundreds of papers published every year. Indeed, we have barely scratched the surface of VECMs. An introductory book such as this can only hope to outline the general themes and common procedures.

And as we've seen before, researchers are constantly mixing and matching many of the familiar concepts we've studied, such as cointegration, seasonality, and structural breaks. A procedure developed by Quintos and Phillips (1993), for example, detects breaks in the cointegrating vectors themselves. Campos et al. (1996) examine various cointegration tests in the presence of structural breaks. They find that the Johansen procedure works well in the face of endogenously known break-dates.

Engle et al. (1993) extend the Engle and Granger (1987) cointegration test to seasonal cointegration. They examine Japanese consumption and income data and—although they admit that the consumption's seasonality might be deterministic—they find some evidence that the two are seasonally cointegrated. Ghysels and Osborn (2001) provide a book-length treatment of seasonality with a discussion of seasonal cointegration among two more variables.

There are scores of books on cointegration analysis. The chapter in Brooks (2014) is accessible and shows how to estimate simple VECMs using the EViews software. As always Enders' (2014) book is highly recommended. I have found no better book-length introduction to the subject than Harris and Sollis (2003). Rao (2007) offers practical advice on performing cointegration analysis.

A number of longer, more mathematical treatments of cointegration and VECMs are published by Oxford University Press' *Advanced Texts in Econometrics* series. These include Banerjee et al. (1993), Hansen and Johansen (1998), Johansen

---

[13] I am indebted to David Giles and his popular "Econometrics Beat" blog for bringing this and the Toda-Yamamoto procedure to my attention. The blog piece can be found at http://davegiles.blogspot.com/2011/10/var-or-vecm-when-testing-for-granger.html. Readers are encouraged to read the cited references in that blog entry, especially the work by Clarke and Mirza (2006).

(1995a), and Juselius (2006). Also included in the Oxford series, Engle and Granger (1991) collect many of the most important references on ECMs and VECMs in one volume.

12.11 Exercises

1. We will explore how the cointegrating vector is only identified up to a particular normalization. Consider X_t and Y_t, two cointegrated variables where

$$Y_t = 10 + X_t + e_t$$
$$X_t = 1 + X_{t-1} + \epsilon_t$$
$$e_t \sim iidN(0, 1)$$
$$\epsilon_t \sim iidN(0, 1)$$

   as in Fig. 12.1. Generate 100 observations of this data. Graph these two variables, and verify visually that they seem cointegrated. Estimate the long-run relationship between them and verify that the cointegrating vector is $[1, -1]'$. Now, generate $Y'_t = 2Y_t$ and $X'_t = 2X_t$. Graph these two new variables. Verify graphically that X'_t and Y'_t are cointegrated. Perform Engle-Granger two-step tests to verify formally that X_t and Y_t are cointegrated and that X'_t and Y'_t are cointegrated. If X'_t and Y'_t are cointegrated, then we have shown that $[2, -2]'$ is also a valid cointegrating vector.
2. Suppose that e_t is stationary. Show that be_t is stationary, where b is a constant. (Hint: recall that the definition of stationarity requires that $E(e_t)$ and $V(e_t)$ not be functions of t.)
3. Calculate the MacKinnon (2010) critical values for an estimated first-step regression with the following characteristics:
   (a) 5 variables; with a sample size of 200 observations; that the ADF test had a constant and but no trend; and that we wanted to test at the 1% level.
   (b) 7 variables; with a sample size of 100 observations; that the ADF test had a constant and a linear trend; and that we wanted to test at the 5% level.
   (c) 9 variables; with a sample size of 50 observations; that the ADF test had a constant and a trend; and that we wanted to test at the 10% level.
4. Suppose you used Stata to estimate a VEC model on X and Y. Write out the estimated equations in Matrix notation, using Eq. (12.24) as a guide. Do any of the estimated coefficients look out of line? Explain.

```
. vec X Y, rank(1) trend(constant) alpha
```

Vector error-correction model

Sample: 3 - 500   Number of obs   =   498
                                                    AIC   =   7.090944
Log likelihood = -1756.645   HQIC   =   7.120809
Det(Sigma_ml) =   3.97111   SBIC   =   7.167039

Equation	Parms	RMSE	R-sq	chi2	P>chi2
D_X	4	.998896	0.5586	625.0948	0.0000
D_Y	4	2.26332	0.5213	537.9354	0.0000

	Coef.	Std. Err.	z	P>|z|	[95% Conf.	Interval]
D_X						
_ce1 L1.	.0453532	.0310574	1.46	0.144	-.0155181	.1062245
X LD.	-.1227547	.0510064	-2.41	0.016	-.2227255	-.022784
Y LD.	.0199489	.0221849	0.90	0.369	-.0235326	.0634305
_cons	1.167229	.0780659	14.95	0.000	1.014223	1.320236
D_Y						
_ce1 L1.	1.128215	.0703705	16.03	0.000	.9902912	1.266139
X LD.	-.4256927	.1155716	-3.68	0.000	-.6522089	-.1991766
Y LD.	.126372	.0502671	2.51	0.012	.0278504	.2248936
_cons	-.0469215	.1768837	-0.27	0.791	-.3936072	.2997642

12.11 Exercises

```
Cointegrating equations

Equation          Parms    chi2      P>chi2
-----------------------------------------------
_ce1                1    3746380    0.0000
-----------------------------------------------

Identification:  beta is exactly identified
Johansen normalization restriction imposed
--------------------------------------------------------------------------
         beta |     Coef.   Std. Err.       z    P>|z|   [95% Conf. Interval]
--------------+-----------------------------------------------------------
_ce1          |
            X |         1          .         .       .           .          .
            Y | -1.000194   .0005167  -1935.56   0.000   -1.001206  -.9991807
        _cons |  1.273441          .         .       .           .          .
--------------------------------------------------------------------------

Adjustment parameters

Equation          Parms    chi2      P>chi2
-----------------------------------------------
D_X                 1    2.132487   0.1442
D_Y                 1    257.0408   0.0000
-----------------------------------------------

--------------------------------------------------------------------------
        alpha |     Coef.   Std. Err.       z    P>|z|   [95% Conf. Interval]
--------------+-----------------------------------------------------------
D_X           |
        _ce1  |
          L1. |  .0453532   .0310574     1.46   0.144   -.0155181   .1062245
--------------+-----------------------------------------------------------
D_Y           |
        _ce1  |
          L1. |  1.128215   .0703705    16.03   0.000    .9902912   1.266139
--------------------------------------------------------------------------
```

5. Suppose you used Stata to estimate a VEC model on X and Z. Write out the estimated equations in matrix notation, using Eq. (12.24) as a guide. Do any of the estimated coefficients look out of line? Explain.

```
. vec X Z, rank(1) trend(constant)
```

Vector error-correction model

Sample: 3 - 500   Number of obs =   498
                                             AIC   =   7.79766
Log likelihood = -1932.617   HQIC   = 7.827524
Det(Sigma_ml) = 8.050715   SBIC   = 7.873755

Equation	Parms	RMSE	R-sq	chi2	P>chi2
D_X	4	.999118	0.5584	624.5982	0.0000
D_Z	4	3.04757	0.5132	520.8436	0.0000

	Coef.	Std. Err.	z	P>|z|	[95% Conf. Interval]	
D_X						
_ce1 L1.	-.0164664	.0224147	-0.73	0.463	-.0603985	.0274657
X LD.	-.0797503	.0475907	-1.68	0.094	-.1730263	.0135258
Z LD.	-.021304	.0157298	-1.35	0.176	-.0521339	.0095259
_cons	1.244905	.0720248	17.28	0.000	1.103739	1.386071
D_Z						
_ce1 L1.	1.07436	.0683709	15.71	0.000	.9403558	1.208365
X LD.	-.2210096	.1451641	-1.52	0.128	-.5055261	.0635069
Z LD.	.0566547	.0479801	1.18	0.238	-.0373847	.150694
_cons	.0190803	.2196946	0.09	0.931	-.4115132	.4496738

Cointegrating equations

Equation	Parms	chi2	P>chi2
_ce1	1	1874883	0.0000

12.11 Exercises

```
Identification:  beta is exactly identified

Johansen normalization restriction imposed
------------------------------------------------------------------------------
        beta |      Coef.   Std. Err.      z    P>|z|     [95% Conf. Interval]
-------------+----------------------------------------------------------------
_ce1         |
           X |          1          .        .       .            .           .
           Z |  -1.000134   .0007304 -1369.26   0.000    -1.001565    -.998702
       _cons |   3.272736          .        .       .            .           .
------------------------------------------------------------------------------
```

Static Panel Data Models

13

13.1 Introduction

In previous chapters, we looked at data where one thing—a country, a company, a person, or a generic "unit"—changed over time. Now it is time to generalize a bit. What if we have time-series observations on more than one unit? What if we have yearly data on, wait for it, two countries? Or three? We could observe a whole group of countries, measured repeatedly over time. In public health, we might measure a group of people's blood pressures before and after receiving a medication. In finance, we might have daily stock prices for the 30 companies in the Dow Jones Industrial Average. Or we might have quarterly population figures for the 50 US states.

Many datasets have this panel structure, where the dataset varies across units, indexed by i, that also vary over time t. Such data are called "panel data," "longitudinal data," or "cross-sectional time series."

Special data requires special methods, hence this chapter and the next. Figure 13.1 illustrates some of the generic patterns of stationary panel data.

In the best case, panel datasets offer a second chance to look at a time series. This is a bit naive, but it is a great starting place. We might think of "country A" as our first look at a specific data generating process. With only one such look at the data, we are squarely back in time-series mode. We can get better estimates of the process if we had a second, completely independent look at the data. Country B. At best, there is no spillover between, say, income in country A and income in country B. At best, they are not trading partners. With two completely independent views on the data generating process, we can get more precise estimates. In this case, it is as though we rewound time and let the process unfold again. We get twice the data on exactly the same process. This would correspond to the top-left panel in Fig. 13.1.

A second-best, and still naive, assumption is that the two countries share the same data generating process—their economies follow the same type of dynamics—but they differ by a constant pre-determined amount. One country remains richer than

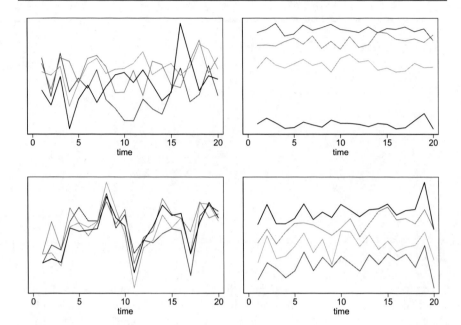

Fig. 13.1 Examples of stationary panel data

the other. We will see that this leads to what is called the "fixed effects" estimator. This type of process corresponds to the top-right panel in Fig. 13.1.

We can also model situations where all countries are hit by a similar shock in the same time period, moving them up or down simultaneously. These kind of "time effects" can happen on countries with similar levels (the bottom left panel) or with different levels (the bottom right panel of Fig. 13.1).

13.2 Formatting the Data

As with time-series data, we must first inform Stata what type of data we have. Before, we had to `tsset` the data, telling Stata what our time variable is. Now, we must specify one more bit of information: the variable that tells Stata what our observational units are.

This is easy enough. Rather than `tsset` (time series set), we `xtset` (cross-sectional time series set) our data. All panel data analysis begins with a statement such as

```
. xtset countrycode year
```

We simply need a numeric time variable (`year`) and a numeric country variable (`countrycode`). If your dataset only lists countries by their name, then you'll

13.2 Formatting the Data

need to create your own numeric variable that identifies each country. The `encode` command makes quick work of this.

13.2.1 Wide and Long

Panel data can be presented in one of two forms: wide form and long form. The information is the same, but the layout of the dataset is different.

Here is an example of GDP data, in trillions of Euros, in wide form:

```
+-----------------------------------------------------+
| country        GDP2018        GDP2019        GDP2020 |
|-----------------------------------------------------|
|  France      2.7909569      2.7288702      2.6390087 |
| Germany      3.9744434       3.888226      3.8896689 |
|   Italy      2.0919324      2.0113022      1.8967553 |
|   Spain      1.4217027      1.3943201      1.2769627 |
+-----------------------------------------------------+
```

The defining feature of a wide-form panel dataset is that, for each country i, the data along the time dimension is spread widthwise in separate columns. The same data can be presented in long form:

```
. use xtGDPlong.dta, clear
. list
```

```
+--------------------------------+
| country    year          GDP   |
|--------------------------------|
|  France    2018    2.7909569   |
|  France    2019    2.7288702   |
|  France    2020    2.6390087   |
|--------------------------------|
| Germany    2018    3.9744434   |
| Germany    2019     3.888226   |
| Germany    2020    3.8896689   |
|--------------------------------|
|   Italy    2018    2.0919324   |
|   Italy    2019    2.0113022   |
|   Italy    2020    1.8967553   |
|--------------------------------|
|   Spain    2018    1.4217027   |
|   Spain    2019    1.3943201   |
|   Spain    2020    1.2769627   |
+--------------------------------+
```

While not as compact, it is often easier to work with long-form data. It is easy to xtset your data when it is in long form; there is only one column that defines i and one that defines t.

Stata's reshape command allows one to switch between these forms with relative ease. For example, we can convert back to wide form by issuing the following command:

    . reshape wide GDP, i(country) j(year)

If we were to list our data, we would get back the wide-from dataset above.

In the reshape command above, we specify that we want the wide format, where GDP is the variable that goes wide. If you think of your wide-form dataset as a matrix X, you indicate the components of a matrix with i and j subscripts: $X_{i,j}$. So when we specify i(country) j(year), we're saying that the row of the matrix of GDPs will correspond to a country and the columns will correspond to the year. You can reshape all kinds of datasets, not merely panels; in this context, though, it is easy to wish that Stata's syntax were t() rather than j().

Once we've reshape-ed our data, it is even easier to switch back and forth. Stata keeps track of all of the internals, so we just need to specify the format.

    . reshape long
    . reshape wide

The above sequence takes an already reshaped dataset and converts it to long and then back to wide format.

13.3 The Static Panel Model

Suppose we want to know the relationship between GDP and the top marginal income tax rate. Obviously, there is more to GDP than mere tax policy. Aside from the standard economic variables, each country's culture, history, and institutions are also important. These types of characteristics are not easily quantifiable and are therefore "unobserved." Being unobserved, we denote them with a "u." Presumably, each country is different (so they vary over country i), but their culture doesn't change much over time t. Therefore, the u's get i subscripts but they don't get t subscripts.

Thus, we may think of the process as

$$Y_{i,t} = \beta_0 + \beta_1 X_{i,t} + u_i + \epsilon_{i,t} \tag{13.1}$$

Notice that we are also presuming that each country's tax policy has the same effect on GDP, regardless of culture. This is a simplifying assumption.

More importantly, notice that Y does not depend on its own previous values. Thus, it shares more in common with a cross-sectional regression models (reg Y X) than with the dynamic time-series models that we have been working with so far. That will change; we will add dynamics. But not yet. First, we crawl. Then we run. Then we soar! Then we fall. Then we so sore.

13.3.1 The Error Terms

In the standard OLS case, we presume our error term is homoskedastic, serially uncorrelated, etc. We need to do something similar, here, too, for the panel data case.

The most simplifying (and restrictive and unrealistic) assumptions we can make about the error terms are that:

1. The $\epsilon_{i,t}$'s are serially uncorrelated within units:

$$E\left(\epsilon_{i,t}\epsilon_{i,t+k}\right) = 0 \text{ for all } k \neq 0 \text{ and for all } i$$

2. The $\epsilon_{i,t}$'s are cross-sectionally uncorrelated:

$$E\left(\epsilon_{i,t}\epsilon_{j,t}\right) = 0 \text{ for all } i \neq j \text{ and for all } t$$

(This does not preclude the possibility that a global shock affects more than one country at the same time. It is possible that a global pandemic affects all countries' GDP at the same time. But this is also assumed to happen only randomly. If you want to include COVID in such a regression, you should create a COVID dummy variable and include that as an X variable. You just can't roll it into the error term.)

3. The errors are not correlated with X (i.e., not endogenous):

$$E\left(u_i X_{i,t}\right) = 0$$

and

$$E\left(\epsilon_{i,t} X_{i,t}\right) = 0.$$

4. The error terms have constant variances (i.e., no heteroskedasticity).

The $\epsilon_{i,t}$'s are definitely random variables. But what about the u_i's?

There is definitely serial correlation in the u_i's. Within each unit i—within each country, for example—the value of u is a constant. That's why we don't even bother to put a t subscript on u_i. One large shock at the beginning will persist fully throughout the entire process. Since the u's are part of the error term, and this error term is serially correlated, we must make adjustments for this. In Stata, it is usual to include robust at the end of the regress command.

If the u_i are random variables, then they need to be handled as such. If the u_i's are random and if we could somehow rewind the clock, each country would get a different u_i the second time around. In this case, we cannot attach too much meaning to the variable; its value was random luck. In this case, we don't estimate it, and we fold it into the error term, using a "random effects regression."

If they are fixed constants (i.e., if they couldn't have been anything else if we could rewind the clock), then we should treat them as such. They now have economic meaning. Each country has a specific value, and it couldn't have been another value. In this case, we will often want to estimate these more structural parameters, precisely because they have meaning. We will estimate a "fixed effects regression." If we want to estimate u_i, we can treat this like a fixed dummy variable, each country getting its own intercept (its own β_0, if you will).

13.3.2 Pooled OLS

Why can't we simply run an OLS regression on our panel dataset?

```
. reg Y X1 X2 X3
```

If we use OLS to estimate a panel, we are ignoring the fact that we have serial correlation within countries, merely from the effect of u_i. Within a country, a high u in the first period is followed by a high u in the next period, because u is constant within each country.

As long as u_i is independent of the $X_{i,t}$'s (i.e., it is not endogenous), then we get consistent estimates from OLS. Unfortunately, our standard errors are wrong, so any hypothesis test we run will be misleading.

One correction is to estimate cluster-robust standard errors, where we cluster across countries. In Stata,

```
. reg Y X, vce(cluster ccode)
```

where `ccode` is the numeric code denoting a country—the same variable we used when to `xtset` our data.

13.3.3 Endogeneity

The third simplifying assumption on the error terms was that there is no endogeneity. This is seldom the case. For example, it is entirely possible that culture is correlated with tax policy. Perhaps collectivist cultures tolerate higher taxes for the purposes of redistribution. Since an error term (u_i) is correlated with a regressor (X, taxes), then we have an endogeneity problem. We need to fix this. We can do that by re-expressing our model to get rid of the unobserved components, the u_i's.

We can get rid of the unobserved u_i's in one of three methods:

1. first-differencing,
2. demeaning, or
3. dummy variables for each panel.

13.3 The Static Panel Model

The first two methods involve subtracting things (the mean, or the previous value for country i), and both have the effect of subtracting u_i from itself. The last two are effectively identical.

13.3.4 First Differencing

Taking first differences of panel data is similar to the pure time-series case. Only, you must take care to not subtract across units. That is,

$$\Delta X_{i,t} = X_{i,t} - X_{i,t-1} \tag{13.2}$$

Once the dataset has been xtset, Stata calculates first differences just as before, using the D differencing operator:

```
. use "xtGDPlong.dta", clear
. gen FirstDiffGDP = D.GDP

. list country year GDP FirstDiffGDP, noobs sepby
 (country)
```

```
+------------------------------------------------+
| country    year         GDP     FirstDi~P |
|------------------------------------------------|
|  France    2018    2.7909569             . |
|  France    2019    2.7288702    -.0620866 |
|  France    2020    2.6390087    -.0898615 |
|------------------------------------------------|
| Germany    2018    3.9744434             . |
| Germany    2019     3.888226    -.0862173 |
| Germany    2020    3.8896689     .0014429 |
|------------------------------------------------|
|   Italy    2018    2.0919324             . |
|   Italy    2019    2.0113022    -.0806302 |
|   Italy    2020    1.8967553    -.1145469 |
|------------------------------------------------|
|   Spain    2018    1.4217027             . |
|   Spain    2019    1.3943201    -.0273827 |
|   Spain    2020    1.2769627    -.1173574 |
+------------------------------------------------+
```

Notice that there are missing values in the dataset. That is because there is nothing to subtract from each person's first observation. Since our dataset starts in year 2018, we cannot subtract a 2017 value from it.

We can first difference Y_{it} just as easily:

$$\Delta Y_{i,t} = \Delta Y_{i,t-1}$$
$$= \left(\beta_0 + \beta_x X_{i,t} + u_i + \epsilon_{i,t}\right) - \left(\beta_0 + \beta_x X_{i,t-1} + u_i + \epsilon_{i,t-1}\right)$$
$$= \beta_x X_{i,t} + \epsilon_{i,t} - \beta_x X_{i,t-1} - \epsilon_{i,t-1}$$
$$= \beta_x X_{i,t} - \beta_x X_{i,t-1} + \epsilon_{i,t} - \epsilon_{i,t-1}$$
$$= \beta_x \Delta X_{i,t} - \Delta \epsilon_{i,t}$$

So first differencing can get rid of unwanted constants and can save the day.

First differencing is not without costs, though: you can lose a lot of observations. You can't estimate the first value of the first difference. If you have lots of time periods, this isn't much of a loss. But if you have only two observations for each country, then first differencing reduce the number of observations by half!

13.3.5 Demeaning

With panel data, we have several means: the "overall mean," the "between" mean, and the "within mean." In this context, we will subtract off the unit-specific mean: the within mean.

Let's return to our basic model:

$$Y_{i,t} = \beta_0 + \beta_x X_{i,t} + u_i + \epsilon_{i,t} \tag{13.3}$$

We can calculate the within-country mean for arbitrary country i:

$$\bar{Y}_i = \frac{1}{T} \sum_t^T Y_{i,t}.$$

Likewise, for the other variables,

$$\bar{X}_i = \frac{1}{T} \sum_t^T X_{i,t} \quad \text{and} \quad \bar{\epsilon}_i = \frac{1}{T} \sum_t^T \epsilon_{i,t}.$$

Using Eq. (13.3), we can derive an expression for the country-specific mean:

$$\bar{Y}_i = \frac{1}{T} \sum_t^T Y_{i,t}$$
$$= \frac{1}{T} \sum_t^T \left(\beta_0 + \beta_x X_{i,t} + u_i + \epsilon_{i,t}\right)$$

$$= \frac{1}{T}\sum_t^T \beta_0 + \frac{1}{T}\sum_t^T \beta_x X_{i,t} + \frac{1}{T}\sum_t^T u_i + \frac{1}{T}\sum_t^T \epsilon_{i,t}.$$

Since β_0 and u_i do not vary over time, then $\sum_t^T \beta_0 = T\beta_0$, and $\sum_t^T u_i = Tu_i$, so

$$\bar{Y}_i = \frac{1}{T}T\beta_0 + \beta_x \frac{1}{T}\sum_t^T X_{i,t} + \frac{1}{T}Tu_i + \frac{1}{T}\sum_t^T \epsilon_{i,t}$$

$$= \beta_0 + \beta_x \frac{1}{T}\sum_t^T X_{i,t} + u_i + \frac{1}{T}\sum_t^T \epsilon_{i,t}$$

$$= \beta_0 + \beta_x \bar{X}_i + u_i + \bar{\epsilon}_i.$$

We are finally in a position to subtract off the unit-specific means from our data:

$$Y_{i,t} - \bar{Y}_i = \left[\beta_0 + \beta_x X_{i,t} + u_i + \epsilon_{i,t}\right] - \left[\beta_0 + \beta_x \bar{X}_i + u_i + \bar{\epsilon}_i\right]$$

$$= \beta_x X_{i,t} + \epsilon_{i,t} - \beta_x \bar{X}_i - \bar{\epsilon}_i$$

$$= \beta_x \left(X_{i,t} - \bar{X}_i\right) + \left(\epsilon_{i,t} - \bar{\epsilon}_i.\right) \quad (13.4)$$

The term on the left is the within deviation for Y; the first term in parentheses on the right of the equal sign is the within deviation on X; and the last term in parentheses is the within-deviation on the error term (all for country i).

Notice that by expressing the model in terms of within-deviations, we have removed the effect of the country-specific error term (u_i), the variable that was introducing endogeneity.

13.4 Fixed Effects and Random Effects

There are two main models in the Panel Data toolkit: fixed effects (FE) and random effects (RE). They yield slightly different results, so choosing between the two models is one of the first orders of business for the applied researcher.

Both models involve estimating equations of the following form:

$$Y_{i,t} = \beta X_{i,t} + u_i + \epsilon_{i,t} \quad (13.5)$$

Where they differ is in their identifying assumptions. Estimating the above model requires making assumptions about the error terms. Both RE and FE models presume that the time-varying error term, $\epsilon_{i,t}$, is conditionally exogenous:

$$E\left(\epsilon_{i,t} | X_{i,1}, X_{i,2}, \ldots X_{i,T}, u_i\right) = 0 \quad (13.6)$$

Notice that this exogeneity restriction applies over all past and future values of the exogenous X terms.

13.4.1 Random Effects Models

Random effects models assume the country-specific intercept, u_i, is also conditionally exogenous and independent of the X variables.

$$E\left(u_i | X_{i,1}, X_{i,2}, \ldots X_{i,T}\right) = 0. \tag{13.7}$$

13.4.2 Fixed Effects Models

The difference between FE models and the RE model above is that we drop (13.7), the assumption that country-specific intercept (u_i) is independent of the X variables. Instead, we allow the intercepts to be correlated with the X's. Thus, the RE model is a restricted version of the FE model. This additional assumption means we can get different estimates between RE and FE. But it also means that we can use these differences to detect which model might be the more appropriate one. This is the key insight of the Hausman (1978) test which we'll encounter later in this chapter.

13.4.3 Estimating FE Models

When estimating an FE model, two methods are equivalent: (a) the demeaned (aka "within") estimator and (b) the dummy variable method.

First, we can demean our data as we did in the Sect. 13.3.5 and then re-insert the overall mean. Continuing from Eq. (13.4),

$$Y_{i,t} - \bar{Y}_i = \beta_x \left(X_{i,t} - \bar{X}_i\right) + \left(\epsilon_{i,t} - \bar{\epsilon}_i\right)$$
$$Y_{i,t} - \bar{Y}_i + \bar{Y} = \beta_x \left(X_{i,t} - \bar{X}_i + \bar{X}\right) + \left(\epsilon_{i,t} - \bar{\epsilon}_i + \bar{\epsilon}\right).$$

As we saw in Sect. 13.3.5, demeaning isn't rude. It is a way of eliminating our time-invariant variables (the u_i's) and making our estimation problem easier. If the model is well-described by the FE assumptions, then demeaning also eliminates one source of endogeneity.

Automatically demeaning comes at a slight loss. If we are really interested in obtaining values of the country-specific intercepts (the u_i's), then eliminating is a problem. We can't get estimates for these terms. More often than not, though, we don't really want values for these variables. Rather, they are additional regressors, variables that we need to control for in our analysis. They serve a purpose, but we don't really need specific estimates for their values.

13.4 Fixed Effects and Random Effects

The dummy variable method estimates a set of N dummy variables, one for each country. This would seem to be a fairly inefficient method that quickly loses degrees of freedom. It turns out this is equally the case of both dummy variable and demeaning methods. The demeaning costs just as many degrees of freedom and gives equivalent results.

The two methods are equivalent, because they actually estimate the same number of parameters. In the dummy variable estimator, we estimate N different intercepts, one for each country. In the "within" estimator, we subtract off country-specific means—one for each of the N countries—and then run the regression on this demeaned data.

13.4.4 Two Equivalent Ways of Estimating FE Models

Don't believe me that "within" and dummy variables are equivalent? A formal proof would take us too far afield, but perhaps it is just as powerful to see the equivalent result for yourself. Load the "Thomson2017.dta" dataset and estimate the following equation using dummy variables and the FE-within estimator:

$$ln\,RnD = \beta_0 + \beta_1 ln\,ValueAdded_{i,t-1} + \beta_2 ln\,TaxPrice_{i,t-1} + \sum_i \beta_i EntityDummy_i + \epsilon_{i,t}$$

For the time being, let's just use it to verify the equality of the LS dummy variable and FE-within estimators. There is a set of time-invariant dummy variables. (Because of colinearity, we need to drop one of the unit-dummies.) The time variable is t, and the country variable is i. We also use the "i." prefix to automatically create the necessary dummies.

```
. use FEequivalence.dta, clear

. quietly xtreg y x, fe
. estimates store FEa

. quietly reg y x i.country
. estimates store FEb

. estimates table FEa FEb, t(%9.7f)


----------------------------------------
    Variable |     FEa          FEb
-------------+--------------------------
           x |  .91579147     .91579147
             |  1.16e+01      1.16e+01
```

```
   country |
         2 |                 -4.0110653
           |                  -7.12e+00
         3 |                  17.079983
           |                   3.03e+01
         4 |                 -43.227326
           |                  -7.70e+01
           |
      _cons |  -9.0877557    -1.5481538
           |   -4.13e+01     -3.82e+00
-------------------------------------------
```

Legend: b/t

The dummy variable estimator explicitly reports the country dummies and drops one because it is colinear with the intercept. The "within" estimator reports an intercept, but not the country dummies. Otherwise, the slope and standard error on X are identical between the two estimators.

13.5 Choosing Between RE and FE Models

13.5.1 Hausman Test

Recall that the critical feature distinguishing RE and FE DGPs is that, in the RE model, the country-specific intercept, u_i, is independent of the X variables (Eq. 13.7).

If this is true, and the u_i's are independent of the X's, then the FE (within) estimator and the RE estimator are both consistent; however, the RE estimates are more efficient. That is, they both give good, unbiased estimates as the sample size grows, but the RE estimates are more precise.

Why is this the case? Because RE is based upon the assumption of independence. FE is more general and allows independence. But this extra wiggle room in the correlation structure between the u_i's and the $X_{i,t}$'s translates to more wiggle room in the estimates of the βs. Put another way, the RE is optimized to take advantage of an assumption that may or may not be true. If it is actually true, then RE's estimates are unbiased and more precise than the FE's estimates.

If the RE model is true, then the RE and FE estimates will be the same, at least on average. But we don't get to run tons of estimates on thousands of samples and look at the averages of a bunch of estimates. We usually only have one sample. However, in any one sample, the two estimates can be different: the FE ("within") estimate will usually be a little farther than the RE estimate from the true value, because FE is less efficient in this case than the RE estimator. The Hausman (1978) test exploits this difference.

On the other hand, what if the data actually came from an FE DGP, and the unobserved errors are correlated with the $X_{i,t}$s? Then we should prefer the FE

13.5 Choosing Between RE and FE Models

Table 13.1 Performance of different estimators

	FE Estimator	RE Estimator	Conclusion
FE DGP	Consistent	Inconsistent	The two estimates are different
RE DGP	Consistent	Consistent and efficient	The two estimates are the same

model. Under the case that the data are truly FE, then the FE estimates are consistent. However, the RE estimates will be inconsistent. That is, the RE estimates will be biased, and this bias will not go away even if we have very large samples. That's because RE is a restricted version of the FE model, and the restrictions are not met. The RE model is misspecified (we have omitted variables bias), and large samples can't fix a broken model.

The four possibilities are summarized in Table 13.1. If the data are actually FE, then the RE estimates will be far from the FE estimates because of RE's bias. That is, if they are different, then we opt for FE because it is consistent (asymptotically unbiased, etc.). If the data are actually RE, then the RE and FE estimates will be the same on average, although in a particular sample the RE estimates will be a little different from the FE estimates because FE is a little less precise. In this case, if the estimates are similar, we opt for the RE estimator because it is known to be more precise.

So, we have our data. We don't know whether they were created from a RE process or an FE process. So we don't know which model to estimate, RE or FE. We can run both estimators and we might get two different estimates.

Hausman (1978) proposed a test statistic that is equal to the squared distance between the two estimates, each normalized by the variances of the two estimators. The null hypothesis assumes that the two estimates are the same (their distance is zero).

The Hausman test has become standard and comes prepackaged in most statistical software. Stata is no exception.

Stata's `hausman` command does this. We merely need to estimate the two different models and feed the estimates into the command. (Alas, `hausman` does not estimate the two versions for us. But estimation is easy enough.)

```
. hausman name-consistent name-efficient [, options]
```

First, we estimate the consistent model (the FE model) and save the results under a name. Then we estimate the efficient model (the RE model) and save the result under a different name. Then we pass the two set of results into the `hausman` command, usually with the `sigmamore` option.

Let's see this at work, first on data generated under the FE assumptions and then under the RE assumptions. We'll see how well it does.

Ex: Hausman Test on FE Data

First, load the data:

```
. use HausmanMundlak.dta, clear
```

The dataset is comprised of a $Y_{i,t}$ variable constructed from an FE process and another constructed from an RE process. The goal is to see whether we can statistically detect which is which.

In this subsection we'll work with $Y_{i,t}$'s generated from an FE process. First, we estimate an RE model and store the results:

```
. quietly xtreg Y_fe X, re
. estimates store m1
```

Then, we estimate an FE model and store the results:

```
. quietly xtreg Y_fe X, fe
. estimates store m2
```

We can look at the two sets of estimates to see how close they are:

```
. estimates table m1 m2
```

```
-----------------------------------------
    Variable |      m1            m2
-------------+---------------------------
           X |  1.0168256     1.0038198
       _cons | -.87777062    -.30034568
-----------------------------------------
```

The two estimates seem fairly similar. Finally, we feed the two sets of results into the Hausman command:

```
. hausman m2 m1, sigmamore
```

```
                ---- Coefficients ----
             |     (b)          (B)            (b-B)     sqrt(diag(V_b-V_B))
             |     m2           m1           Difference       Std. err.
-------------+-----------------------------------------------------------
           X |  1.00382      1.016826        -.0130057         .002221
------------------------------------------------------------------------
                     b = Consistent under H0 and Ha; obtained from xtreg.
         B = Inconsistent under Ha, efficient under H0; obtained from xtreg.

Test of H0: Difference in coefficients not systematic

    chi2(1) = (b-B)'[(V_b-V_B)^(-1)](b-B)
            =   34.29
Prob > chi2 =  0.0000
```

The p-value on the null is quite small ($p = 0.0000$). Therefore, we reject the null at any of the standard significance levels. That is, we reject the null that the

13.5 Choosing Between RE and FE Models

coefficients are the same and (loosely speaking) opt for the alternative that they are different. Looking at Table 13.1, the fact that we got two different estimates means that it is likely the data came from an FE process. This is, in fact, the case. We know it, because we used simulated data. So the Hausman test led us to the correct conclusion.

Ex: Hausman Test on RE Data

In this subsection, we'll work with data simulated from an RE process. The procedure is the same as before:

```
. quietly xtreg Y_re X, re
. estimates store m3
. quietly xtreg Y_re X, fe
. estimates store m4
```

These give the following two sets of estimates:

```
. estimates table m3 m4

------------------------------------------
    Variable |      m3            m4
-------------+----------------------------
           X |   1.0044778     1.0038198
       _cons |    .17408617     .20329641
------------------------------------------
```

and the following Hausman test output:

```
. hausman m4 m3, sigmamore

             ---- Coefficients ----
          |     (b)          (B)            (b-B)        sqrt(diag(V_b-V_B))
          |     m4           m3             Difference   Std. err.
----------+-----------------------------------------------------------------
        X |   1.00382       1.004478       -.0006579       .0010625
-----------------------------------------------------------------------------
                    b = Consistent under H0 and Ha; obtained from xtreg.
     B = Inconsistent under Ha, efficient under H0; obtained from xtreg.

Test of H0: Difference in coefficients not systematic

    chi2(1) = (b-B)'[(V_b-V_B)^(-1)](b-B)
            =    0.38
Prob > chi2 = 0.5358
```

Here, the coefficients are almost identical (1.004 vs 1.003). The p-value is 0.5358 on the null that the two coefficients are equal. Therefore, we cannot reject the null hypothesis that the two coefficients are identical. Looking at Table 13.1, we are more likely to get similar results from RE and FE if the data are RE (they're both consistent). So, it doesn't really matter which estimator we use. The coefficients are statistically identical, after all. However, the standard errors and p-values between the two models will be different. We opt for the more precise estimates and the smaller p-values of the RE estimator. This is the correct conclusion, as the data were in fact generated by an RE process.

13.5.2 Mundlak Test

The Mundlak (1978) test is another method for choosing between RE and FE models. It has the added benefit that we can allow the data to be heteroskedastic and serially correlated.

Here, as before, we need to detect whether the country-specific error terms (the u_i's) are correlated with the $X_{i,t}$'s.

If two variables are correlated, then regressing one on the other should yield a statistically significant slope coefficient between them. Unfortunately, the two variables here are the u_i's and $X_{i,t}$'s, and the first of these is not observable.

If the country-specific intercepts (the u_i's which do not vary over time) are correlated with the $X_{i,t}$'s, then they are correlated in their means: the u_i's don't vary over time, so if they are correlated with the $X_{i,t}$'s, it must be that they are correlated with the part that doesn't vary over time. So we can average out the time dimension of the $X_{i,t}$'s and use $\bar{X}_i$, the country-specific means of the $X_{i,t}$'s as a proxy for the u_i's.

Then, we merely estimate the model using our proxies. That is, rather than estimating

$$Y_{i,t} = \beta X_{i,t} + u_i + \epsilon_{i,t}$$

we estimate

$$Y_{i,t} = \beta X_{i,t} + \gamma \bar{X}_i + \epsilon_{i,t}. \tag{13.8}$$

What allowed us to do this is that we are presuming the u_i's and $X_{i,t}$'s are correlated. If they aren't, then adding the proxy for u_i will amount to adding noise, and γ will be insignificant. If there are several X variables, then Mundlak proposes jointly testing the hypothesis that all of the γ's are zero.

In summary, we regress $Y_{i,t}$ on the $X_{i,t}$'s and their country-specific means ($\bar{X}_i$) and test whether the coefficients (γ's) on the latter are equal to zero. If the γ's are zero, then the u_i's and $X_{i,t}$'s are not correlated, in which case the assumptions of the RE model are met. Otherwise, we reject the null that $\gamma = 0$, and conclude that the regressors ($X_{i,t}$'s) and the country-specific errors (u_i's) are correlated; we should estimate an FE model.

Example: Mundlak Test on FE Data
We continue using the same dataset, and we calculate the country-specific averages for the X variable:

13.5 Choosing Between RE and FE Models

```
. use HausmanMundlak.dta, clear
. bysort i: egen double meanX = mean(X)
```

Then we run an RE regression of Y on the Xs and the means of the Xs and test whether the coefficient on meanX is significantly different from zero:

```
. quietly xtreg Y_fe X meanX
. test meanX

 ( 1)  meanX = 0

       chi2(  1) =    41.26
       Prob > chi2 =   0.0000
```

The coefficient on meanX is statistically significant (p-value = 0.000), so the estimated meanX's are different from zero. We conclude that the u_i's and the $X_{i,t}$'s are correlated, so we should have estimated an FE model. And this is the correct conclusion, as we used Y_fe, the Y generated from an FE process.

Example: Mundlak Test on RE Data

Here, we'll run the Mundlak (1978) test on data generated from an RE process. We don't need to re-calculate the means of the Xs; we did that already in the subsection above. We can proceed directly to the regression and testing stage. Suppressing the regression output, we get

```
. quietly xtreg Y_re X meanX, vce(robust)
. test meanX

 ( 1)  meanX = 0

       chi2(  1) =     0.38
       Prob > chi2 =   0.5364
```

The p-value is quite large, so meanX is insignificant, implying that the u_i's and the $X_{i,t}$'s are uncorrelated. This implies that the best model for the data is an RE model. This is the proper conclusion, because Y_re was generated by an RE process.

13.5.3 You Must Estimate the Correct Model

So, which model should you estimate? The RE or FE? The preceding discussion might lead you to answer FE, because it requires fewer assumptions. And this is true. However, it isn't enough of a reason to make your selection of RE vs FE so automatic. You must estimate the correct model—the one corresponding to the true data generating process—in order to get good estimates. We've seen this before. Estimating a RW with deterministic drift (which we remove by including time as an X variable) and estimating a RW with stochastic drift (which we remove by first differencing, like demeaning here) give you different results. Estimate the wrong model, and you'll get the wrong results. The same applies here, with a warning against reflexive uncritical demeaning.

In this section, I'd like to drive the point home. We'll generate fake data from RE and FE processes and estimate RE and FE models. We'll see that it is important to know which model to report.

First, we define and run the simulation:

```
drop _all
program drop _all
set seed 12345

program define REvsFE, rclass

    drop _all
    clear
    set obs 20

    * Make time-invariant country-varying data
    generate i  = _n
    generate t  = 1
    generate nu = rnormal()
    generate u_re = rnormal() /* u1 is uncorrelated with X */
    generate u_fe = nu        /* u2 is correlated with X */

    * Add a time dimension
    expand 10
    bysort i:  replace t = _n
    xtset i t, yearly
    generate X = runiform(0,100) + 50*nu /* correlated to u_fe via nu*/

    * Generate Y's from RE and FE processes
    generate epsilon = rnormal()
    generate Y_re  = 1*X + u_re + epsilon /* Y from RE DGP */
    generate Y_fe  = 1*X + u_fe + epsilon /* Y from FE DGP */

    * Estimating RE models
    xtreg Y_re X*, re
    return scalar RERE  = _b[X]
    xtreg Y_fe X*, re
    return scalar FERE = _b[X]

    * Estimating FE models
    xtreg Y_re X*, fe
    return scalar REFE = _b[X]
    xtreg Y_fe X*, fe
return scalar FEFE = _b[X]
end

simulate REdataREmodel = r(RERE) FEdataREmodel = r(FERE) ///
         REdataFEmodel = r(REFE) FEdataFEmodel = r(FEFE) ///
         , reps(3000): REvsFE
```

13.6 Time Fixed Effects

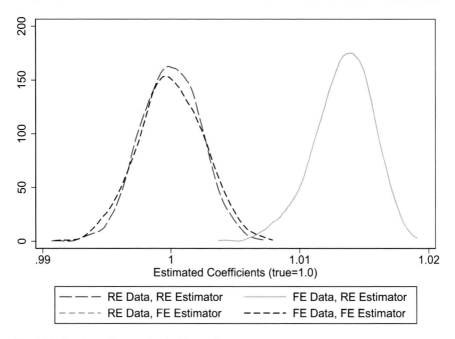

Fig. 13.2 Random effects vs fixed effects estimators

Next, we summarize the 3000 replications and graph their distribution in Fig. 13.2.

```
. summarize

    Variable |        Obs        Mean    Std. dev.       Min        Max
-------------+---------------------------------------------------------
REdataREmodel|      3,000    .9999904    .0023173    .9906914   1.007293
FEdataREmodel|      3,000    1.013385    .0022957    1.003647   1.019123
REdataFEmodel|      3,000    1.000021    .0025751    .9909078   1.007903
FEdataFEmodel|      3,000    1.000021    .0025751    .9909078   1.007903
```

The true value of the coefficient is one. Table 13.1 shows that we expect the RE estimator to perform poorly on FE data. The simulation verifies this.

13.6 Time Fixed Effects

Sometimes there is a random event that affects everyone at the same time. For example, in a macroeconomic study, you may have to account for the large random event such as COVID; it affected all countries simultaneously. Such a shock is not captured well by $\epsilon_{i,t}$ because these shocks are independent across countries. Instead,

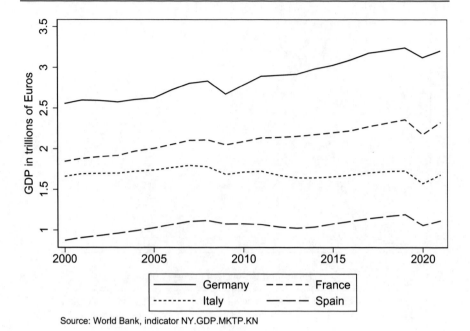

Fig. 13.3 European countries exhibit simultaneous shocks

we may model this one-off global event by including a dummy variable, to "dummy out" its effects.

When there is an interesting, well-defined, and identifiable shock (such as a global pandemic, a war, etc.), we may want to remove its effect and also estimate its impact. That is, we may want to isolate its effect and actually estimate its coefficient. In this case, our model should look like

$$Y_{i,t} = \beta_0 + \beta_x X_{i,t} + \beta_v v_t + u_i + \epsilon_{i,t} \tag{13.9}$$

where $v_t = 1$ for the COVID years and 0 otherwise.

At the more extreme end of things, we might consider that global shocks routinely affect the countries in our panel every year. For example, European countries all face similar exchange rate shocks or simultaneous regulatory changes. While Germany might be richer than Italy, they both may move up and down simultaneously, as in Fig. 13.3.

Rather than dummying out one particular event, we might need to include a dummy variable for each year in our sample in order to model the countries' co-movements. If our time periods are numbered 1 through T, then we create T time dummies, and we have

13.6 Time Fixed Effects

$$Y_{i,t} = \beta_0 + \beta_x X_{i,t} + \sum_{t=1}^{T} \beta_t v_t + u_i + \epsilon_{i,t} \quad (13.10)$$

where $v_t = 1$ for year t and 0 otherwise.

On the other hand, we might not want to estimate the coefficients on each of these shocks, because the shocks are all different. More often than not, we are just happy to model its effect and move on. No need for coefficients. In this case, our model is:

$$Y_{i,t} = \beta_0 + \beta_x X_{i,t} + v_t + u_i + \epsilon_{i,t} \quad (13.11)$$

where the v_t's are interpreted as a sequence of random "global" events.

Both of the models above are called "time fixed effects" models.

Really, all we've done is add another error. We have a bunch of them now. We have $\epsilon_{i,t}$ which are sprinkled across countries and time. We have u_i which affects single countries for their entire time duration. u_i shifts the entire line for a country up or down. And now we have v_t, which occurs randomly at a particular time, but affects all countries simultaneously.

Including both time-invariant and unit-invariant terms in our regression equation captures—and eliminates—the effect of all variables that either (1) don't change over time or (2) affect every unit equally.

13.6.1 Estimation

So, how should we estimate such equations? The answer depends on what you want out of your model. Do you want to control for an event, or do you want to quantify it? If the latter, then you need to estimate its coefficient.

Estimating a regression with both time FEs and country FEs can get expensive. That's a lot of parameters. If we have N countries observed over T periods, then we have $N + T$ parameters to estimate. Estimating this many parameters quickly eats up valuable degrees of freedom.

Earlier, we removed the impact of u_i by taking first differences. A moment's reflection should convince you that we can't do that for v_t. When we took first differences across time, there was an obvious ordering, and we knew what to subtract from what. But we can't take first differences between countries to remove v_t because there is no proper ordering of countries. Do we subtract Albania from Bolivia because they are alphabetically ordered this way? Nope, we can't do that. Instead, we can take time-differences of our Y's and Xs to remove u_i and then regress demeaned Y on demeaned X and a set of time dummy variables.

Just like with u_i, v_t may just represent an effect whose impact we simply want to get rid of. In this case, we can remove its impact by demeaning. For country i, we have a sequence of observations $1, 2, \ldots, T$. So we can take the mean of country i averaged over time, such as

$$\bar{Y}_i = \sum_{t=1}^{T} Y_{i,t}.$$

Likewise, we can take the mean at time t, averaged over countries:

$$\bar{Y}_t = \sum_{i=1}^{N} Y_{i,t}.$$

We then transform all of our $Y_{i,t}$'s and $X_{i,t}$'s by double-demeaning them

$$\widehat{Y_{i,t}} = Y_{i,t} - \bar{Y}_i - \bar{Y}_t$$
$$\widehat{X_{i,t}} = X_{i,t} - \bar{X}_i - \bar{X}_t$$

and then regress $\widehat{Y_{i,t}}$ on $\widehat{X_{i,t}}$.

13.6.2 Estimating FEs with Explicit Time Dummies in Stata

We can adjust for country fixed effects by including a set of country dummy variables. We can do the same for time-fixed effects: including a set of dummy variables, one for each time period.

Here, we'll take another look at the dataset from Thomson (2017) and re-estimate the within and dummy variable FE models, this time including time FEs.

That is, we will estimate

$$ln RnD = \beta_0 + \beta_1 ln ValueAdded_{i,t-1} + \beta_2 ln TaxPrice_{i,t-1} +$$
$$\sum_i \beta_i EntityDummy_i + \sum_t \gamma_t TimeDumy_t + \epsilon_{i,t}$$

```
. use Thomson2017.dta, clear

. reg lnRnD L.lnValueAdded L.lnTaxPrice i.t i.i
. estimates store LSDV

. qui xtreg lnRnD L.lnValueAdded L.lnTaxPrice i.t, fe
. estimates store FE

. estimates table LSDV FE, drop(i.i) t(%9.7f)

-------------------------------------------------
    Variable |      LSDV              FE
-------------+-----------------------------------
```

13.6 Time Fixed Effects

```
 lnValueAdded |
          L1. |   .66044928      .66044928
              |   1.75e+01       1.75e+01
              |
   lnTaxPrice |
          L1. |  -.42014906     -.42014906
              |  -3.46e+00      -3.46e+00
              |
            t |
         1989 |  -.06164228     -.06164228
              |  -0.7521604     -0.7521604
         1990 |  -.05591711     -.05591711
              |  -0.6872244     -0.6872244
         1991 |  -.05816525     -.05816525
              |  -0.7199691     -0.7199691
         1992 |    -.057648       -.057648
              |  -0.7111099     -0.7111099
         1993 |  -.06108312     -.06108312
              |  -0.7539777     -0.7539777
         1994 |   .00965022      .00965022
              |   0.1187609      0.1187609
         1995 |  -.00901411     -.00901411
              |  -0.1113468     -0.1113468
         1996 |   .02453807      .02453807
              |   0.3041132      0.3041132
         1997 |   .04690471      .04690471
              |   0.5830160      0.5830160
         1998 |   .09858715      .09858715
              |   1.2267638      1.2267638
         1999 |    .1343228       .1343228
              |   1.6681762      1.6681762
         2000 |   .12786899      .12786899
              |   1.5955774      1.5955774
         2001 |   .14176109      .14176109
              |   1.7605565      1.7605565
         2002 |   .12212412      .12212412
              |   1.5114383      1.5114383
         2003 |    .1429183       .1429183
              |   1.7628925      1.7628925
         2004 |   .17007732      .17007732
              |   2.0806451      2.0806451
         2005 |   .18964236      .18964236
              |   2.3000485      2.3000485
         2006 |   .32588337      .32588337
```

```
            |   3.7999975      3.7999975
            |
       _cons|  -2.4498072     -1.6699265
            |  -7.09e+00      -5.23e+00
------------------------------------------
Legend: b/t
```

We can see that adding time FEs is as easy as adding an additional set of dummy variables. (We also see that, as before, the within and dummy variable versions of the FE estimator are identical.)

13.7 Cross-Sectional Dependence

An unstated assumption up until now is that shocks are independent across countries. But what if a shock affects some countries and not others? This feature is known as "cross-sectional dependence." It is a form of correlation that can be quite common. It also complicates our usual estimation procedures.

Countries may have correlated shocks for a variety of reasons. An event may have different effects on different groups of countries. Perhaps some countries are gold exporters, and only these countries vary whenever there is a gold shock. This might be accounted for by including a gold production variable into our set of $X_{i,t}$. If we do not include a gold production variable in our regressions, this omission will get subsumed into the error term, resulting in an error term that is correlated with gold production, which is in turn correlated with membership on a particular cross section of gold-producing countries.

Similarly, neighboring agricultural countries will have weather shocks that are correlated. It is common practice in empirical macro to include dummy variables for large geographic clusters of countries (e.g., continents), but this easily over-aggregates dissimilar countries. It is also hard to believe that all countries in a region would respond in identical ways to common shocks. We need more nuance than this. We need the shocks to be correlated, without being identical. (Alternatively, we need to force estimated coefficients to be similar, not identical.)

Yet another source of cross-sectional dependence is when the economic activity of one country spills over into another. In this case of economic interdependence, we need $Y_{i,t}$ to depend on $Y_{j,t}$.

More nuance is needed to analyze cases where shocks are asymmetric across sets of countries. There are many different types of tests for cross-sectional dependence. We have to tailor our approaches for cases where (a) the errors are correlated with the regressors and cases where (b) the errors are not correlated with regressors. We also should consider that asymptotic formulas for cross sections used to rely on increases in sample size. But with panel data, we can increase N or T or both. So we must consider various combinations of small and large N or T or both. The various combinations are dizzying.

13.7.1 Driscoll-Kraay Standard Errors

If groups of countries face similar shocks, and these countries have similar responses to these shocks (i.e., $\beta_i = \beta$ for all countries i in the group), and if these shocks are uncorrelated with the included regressors (the $X_{i,t}$), then we can continue to use random effects and fixed effects regressions for our estimated coefficients. We merely need to modify the estimated standard errors using Driscoll and Kraay (1998) standard errors via Stata's `xtscc` command (Hoechle 2007). This is the simplest case.

```
. use "DKraay.dta", clear

. xtreg y x, fe

Fixed-effects (within) regression               Number of obs     =        100
Group variable: ivar                            Number of groups  =         20

R-squared:                                      Obs per group:
     Within  = 0.7811                                         min =          5
     Between = 0.5591                                         avg =        5.0
     Overall = 0.6924                                         max =          5

                                                F(1,79)           =     281.91
corr(u_i, Xb) = 0.1133                          Prob > F          =     0.0000

------------------------------------------------------------------------------
           y | Coefficient  Std. err.      t    P>|t|     [95% conf. interval]
-------------+----------------------------------------------------------------
           x |   .9439491   .0562202    16.79   0.000     .8320456    1.055853
       _cons |  -.0703849   .1277629    -0.55   0.583    -.3246906    .1839208
-------------+----------------------------------------------------------------
     sigma_u |   1.216035
     sigma_e |  1.2165031
         rho |  .49980759   (fraction of variance due to u_i)
------------------------------------------------------------------------------
F test that all u_i=0: F(19, 79) = 4.93                      Prob > F = 0.0000

. xtscc y x, fe

Regression with Driscoll-Kraay standard errors   Number of obs     =       100
Method: Fixed-effects regression                 Number of groups  =        20
Group variable (i): ivar                         F(  1,     4)     =   2008.29
maximum lag: 2                                   Prob > F          =    0.0000
within R-squared   =    0.7811

------------------------------------------------------------------------------
             |              Drisc/Kraay
           y | Coefficient   std. err.     t    P>|t|     [95% conf. interval]
-------------+----------------------------------------------------------------
           x |   .9439491    .0210637   44.81   0.000     .8854668    1.002431
       _cons |  -.0703849    .1068623   -0.66   0.546    -.3670824    .2263125
------------------------------------------------------------------------------
```

Notice that the coefficients are the same, but the standard errors are different. The data were generated from model with a coefficient of 1; therefore we should easily reject a null of zero. The Driscoll-Kraay test statistic is 44.81 vs the unadjusted test statistic of 16.79. Both models therefore reject the null of zero, but more emphatically so with the Driscoll-Kraay standard errors.

13.7.2 If CSD Shocks Are Correlated with Regressors

If the unobserved cross-sectionally correlated shocks (what we'll call CSD shocks) *are* correlated with the $X_{i,t}$'s, then we have an endogeneity problem. We cannot have regressors correlated with errors. We need a solution, usually in the form of an instrumental variable (IV) that is correlated with $X_{i,t}$ and uncorrelated with the unobserved CSD shock.

CSD Shocks Are Correlated with X and N<T

If the number of panels (N) is small relative to the number of time periods (T), then we can test for the presence of CSD using the Lagrange multiplier test implemented in Stata's xttest2 command (Baum 2001).

CSD Shocks Are Correlated with X and N>T

If the number of panels (N) is large relative to the number of time periods (T), then we can test for the presence of CSD using the Stata command xtcsd. This command implements three different tests of cross-sectional dependence.

With our baseline equation,

$$Y_{i,t} = \beta X_{i,t} + v_t + u_i + \epsilon_{i,t} \tag{13.12}$$

we usually assume that the $\epsilon_{i,t}$ are *iid*. There are two dimensions to look after. We can easily account for independence over time (e.g., with AR(1) errors). But what is more important here is the possibility that shocks are not independent across panels. Ideally,

$$Corr(\epsilon_{i,t}, \epsilon_{j,t}) = 0 \quad \text{when} \quad i \neq j. \tag{13.13}$$

In other words, it is usually assumed that a shock to country i is not usually associated with a similar shock to country j. But as we've argued above, this is easily not the case.

If the null hypothesis is given in Eq. (13.13), then what is the alternative hypothesis? The most common alternative is that there is *some* correlation between *some* countries; not necessarily that most countries are correlated or even that they are all correlated. (In fact, if they are all correlated, then a dummy variable would capture most of this correlation.) Thus, the alternative is

13.7 Cross-Sectional Dependence

$$Corr(\epsilon_{i,t}, \epsilon_{j,t}) = 0 \quad \text{for some} \quad i \neq j. \tag{13.14}$$

None of the tests immediately show you *which* countries' shocks are correlated, only that some of them are. If only two countries have correlated shocks, then the null will be rejected. This may make a mountain out of a mole hill.

There are three tests packaged into the Stata command: Pesaran's CD, the Friedman test, and the Frees test. The various tests differ in how they estimate the possible correlations in the shocks.

Pesaran (2021) proposed a test that is applicable for a wide range of situations, including after FE and RE estimation of dynamic panel data models, nonstationary processes, and even processes with multiple structural breaks. (We will see in Chap. 14 that RE and FE provide biased estimates of dynamic panel data models. Surprisingly, this bias does not invalidate Pesaran's test of CSD.)

Milton Friedman's (1937) test is a non-parametric test of correlation using ranks. (Yes, that Milton Friedman.) Neither of these two tests should be used after including time FEs. (See the explanation in De Hoyos and Sarafidis (2006)).

Frees (1995) developed a test that transforms the rank-correlation statistic used by Friedman in such a way that it can be used after estimating a model with time FEs.

Of the three tests, Pesaran's is the most commonly used in the macro literature.

13.7.3 Testing for CSD in Stata

In this section we will implement the trio of cross-sectional dependence tests incorporated into Stata's `xtcsd` command.

First, load the data:

```
. webuse abdata, clear
```

This dataset is associated with the Arellano-Bond estimator that we will explore in depth in Sect. 14.2. For now, it is just a dataset. Briefly, the dataset contains 9 yearly observations on a panel of 140 UK companies. Many of these companies are in the same industry (the variable `ind` classified companies into one of nine industries). It is reasonable to presume that companies in the same industry should be hit by similar shocks. But we cannot merely presume cross-sectional dependence; we must test for it.

Let us, for the time being, presume that we want to model employment as

$$n_{i,t} = \beta_1 w_{i,t} + \beta_2 w_{i,t-1} + \beta_3 k_{i,t} + \beta_4 w_{i,t-1} + \beta_5 y s_{i,t} + \beta_6 y s_{i,t-1} + \epsilon_{i,t} \tag{13.15}$$

where $n_{i,t}$ denotes the natural logarithm of employment in company i at time t; w is the log of real wages; k is the log of gross capital.

We quietly estimate Eq. (13.15) using a fixed effect model, allowing for the variance to cluster by company.

```
. quietly xtreg n L(0/1).(w k ys), cluster(id) fe
```

Now that we have estimated a panel model, we can test for cross-sectional dependence. Since $N > T$ we should use xtcsd rather than xttest2. We try the three different versions:

```
. xtcsd, pesaran

Pesaran's test of cross sectional independence =      1.812, Pr = 0.0700

. xtcsd, friedman

Friedman's test of cross sectional independence =     9.243, Pr = 1.0000

. xtcsd, frees

  Frees' test of cross sectional independence =     30.375
|----------------------------------------------------------|
  Critical values from Frees' Q distribution
                  alpha = 0.10 :    0.5822
                  alpha = 0.05 :    0.8391
                  alpha = 0.01 :    1.4211
```

The null hypothesis for each of these tests is that there is no cross-sectional dependence. Thus, a small *p*-value will reject the null, leading us to conclude that there *is* cross-sectional dependence.

Unfortunately, we get conflicting results from the three tests. Pesaran's test rejects the null of no-CSD at the 0.10 level (though not at the 0.05 level).

Friedman's test has a *p*-value of 1.000, so we cannot reject the no-CSD null hypothesis. Since we "cannot reject the null," this means that we must, in a manner of speaking, "accept it." That is, we must accept the hypothesis (it isn't a fact) that there is no cross-sectional dependence. This is surprising, considering the nature of our data.

Finally, Frees' test has a test statistic of 30.375. This is far in excess of any of the critical values provided above. Thus, we would reject the null at any level of significance. What do we conclude? Since we reject the null, we must conclude that there is evidence of cross-sectional dependence.

To summarize, we had three tests of CSD, and we got three different results: Frees says we should definitely reject no-CSD, Friedman says to definitely not reject no-CSD, and Pesaran's test is right in the middle depending on the significance level of the test.

13.7.4 Lagrange Multiplier CSD Test

The Lagrange multiplier test for cross-sectional dependence is the preferred test when $N < T$. First we generate some data:

```
. xtarsim y x eta, n(30) t(5) g(0) beta(1) rho(0) ///
    one(corr 1) sn(9) seed(1234)
```

13.7 Cross-Sectional Dependence

This user-written command generates data from a panel of $N = 200$ units, over $T = 5$ time periods. Specifically, it generates data from

$$Y_{i,t} = \beta X_{i,t} + u_i + \epsilon_{i,t} \tag{13.16}$$

where `beta(1)` specifies that the coefficient on $X_{i,t}$ is equal to one; `rho(0)` specifies that X is not auto-correlated; and `one(corr)` specifies that we generate a one-way FE (i.e., only country FEs, not time FEs) and allows for the errors to be correlated with the regressors. The signal-to-noise ratio is set to 9. Setting the seed ensures that the results below are reproducible.

Now that we have data, let's quietly estimate the model and run the test:

```
. quietly xtreg y x, fe
. xttest2
```

Which gives the following output:

```
Breusch-Pagan LM test of independence: chi2(190) =   227.189, Pr = 0.0337
Based on 5 complete observations
```

The null hypothesis is that there is no cross-sectional dependence. Since the *p*-value is 0.03, we can reject the null at the 0.05 level of significance. That is, we conclude that there is cross-sectional dependence.

13.7.5 Estimation When You Have CSD

If you have cross-sectional dependence, then the usual standard estimators are biased. In fact, all of the estimators in this chapter, and all of the first-generation unit root and cointegration tests in the next chapter, presume a lack of CSD and are not valid. If the Driscoll-Kraay assumptions are not met, then we must consider a couple different approaches. The first requires some economic insight; the second requires some mathematical sophistication.

First, consider what might be the source of the CSD. If a group of countries responds similarly to specific types of shocks, then you can isolate their dependence by including a dummy variable for group membership. For example, if you believe that, due to their common currency, European Union countries respond as a group to exchange rate fluctuations, then you can include a dummy variable that encodes EU membership. As another example, perhaps oil-producing countries respond to a geopolitical event that threatens to interrupt the flow of oil. Then you can include an oil production variable in your list of regressors.

After including the regressors, you will need to test again whether you have captured all of the CSD. This type of approach is not obvious. The CSD tests tell you that some cross-sectional dependence is present, but it doesn't tell you among which countries it is present. This also presumes that there is only one source of CSD. Perhaps both shocks examples we listed above are in effect. There is no way of knowing this a priori. It requires experimentation, and that, in turn, invites *p*-hacking.

All of this multiple-testing invites experimentation and running multiple hypothesis tests. This, in turn, invalidates the standard hypothesis testing approach (see the discussion in Chap. 15 on p-hacking.) It also invites ad-hoc analysis, and a proliferation of dummy variables, some of which may be extraneous, and all of which can alter the results.

The second approach is to employ estimators that explicitly allow for CSD. Pesaran's (2006) common correlated effects mean group estimator, and Teal & Eberhardt's (2010) augmented mean group estimators allow for estimating panel models when cross-sectional dependence is present. They are available in the Stata command xtmg developed by Eberhardt (2012). These are advanced techniques. The interested reader is invited to read the original literature, as well as the discussions in Pesaran (2015).

Dynamic Panel Data Models 14

You may have noticed that the previous chapter was missing a key ingredient that was in almost all the models in this book. The main feature of time-series econometrics—and of this book until the previous chapter—was that the value of a variable $Y_{i,t}$ depends upon events from the past, either from $Y_{i,t-p}$ as in an AR(p) process or through an autocorrelated error process as in an MA(q) processes. There has been none of that, so far, in this chapter. That ends now. We will finally introduce a lagged dependent variable, $Y_{i,t-p}$, and explore dynamic panel data models.

We will encounter two main problems. The first problem is a new one: dynamic panel models have a built-in endogeneity problem. The second is more familiar: nonstationarity. Individual variables may be nonstationary (i.e., integrated), and combinations of variables may be cointegrated. The fact that our data is now in panels doesn't make that problem go away. It makes the problem more complicated.

In this chapter, we will discuss the various tests for stationarity and cointegration. And we will show how to estimate a panel vector autoregression.

14.1 Dynamic Panel Bias

Let's begin with a simple dynamic model:

$$Y_{i,t} = \beta Y_{i,t-1} + u_i + \epsilon_{i,t}. \quad (14.1)$$

This is basically an AR(1) process, but the dataset is over a panel of countries, rather than just one country over time. We've subsumed the constant into the country FEs (u_i). And we've removed the $X_{i,t}$'s for simplicity. (We'll include them later.)

Nickell (1981) showed analytically what Nerlove (1967, 1971) showed using Monte Carlo: that the fixed effects estimator is biased for dynamic panel data models. In other words, if we have a lagged dependent variable in our model, we must look for a different estimation strategy.

But why is this the case? OLS is a biased estimator of dynamic panel data models like (14.1) because the error term ($u_i + \epsilon_{i,t}$) is correlated with the control variable ($Y_{i,t-1}$). This is because the error term itself is autocorrelated via u_i. Within country i, the error term is perfectly autocorrelated; it takes on the same value period after period.

More mathematically, $Y_{i,1}$ is correlated with u_i. Next period, $Y_{i,2}$ depends on $Y_{i,1}$ which we just said is correlated with u_i. So when we're estimating $Y_{i,2}$, $Y_{i,1}$ is a control variable that is correlated with the u_i part of the error.

As an example, let's suppose that we're modeling a country's GDP and that its level depends in part on the type of legal system it has. The legal system is fairly constant over time, so it is captured by u_i, the time-invariant variable. So, this year's GDP depends on the legal system u_i. But next period's GDP depends upon this period's GDP, which we just said depends on the error term u_i.

14.1.1 Demeaning Does Not Fix This Problem

Since the problem lies in u_i, can't we just demean and eliminate the problem? Unfortunately, no. To see why, let's take Eq. (14.1) and subtract off the means for each country:

$$Y_{i,t} - \bar{Y}_i = \left(\beta Y_{i,t-1} + \epsilon_{i,t}\right) - \left(\beta \bar{Y}_i + \bar{\epsilon}_i\right)$$
$$= \beta \left(Y_{i,t-1} - \bar{Y}_i\right) + \left(\epsilon_{i,t} - \bar{\epsilon}_i\right).$$

This gets rid of one source of endogeneity (the u_i), but it has sneakily introduced a new one.

Since $\bar{\epsilon}_i$ is an average that contains $\epsilon_{i,t-1}$, and since $Y_{i,t-1}$ is correlated with $\epsilon_{i,t-1}$, then we still have a situation where a regressor (the $Y_{i,t-1}$ part of $\left(Y_{i,t-1} - \bar{Y}_i\right)$) is correlated with the error (the $\bar{\epsilon}$ part of $\left(\epsilon_{i,t} - \bar{\epsilon}_i\right)$).

Again, the problem was that $\epsilon_{i,t-1}$ is a component of the demeaned error term, and it is correlated with $Y_{i,t-1}$. This becomes less and less of a problem as T increases, though. This is because $\epsilon_{i,t-1}$ becomes a smaller and smaller component of $\bar{\epsilon}_i$. (It is averaged over T time periods, so that one pesky time period become an insignificantly small portion of this average.)

The problem remains, though: What do we do if we have a small number of time periods? First differencing is not an ideal solution when we have small T, because we lose all of those first observations. (Remember, we can't subtract anything from our first observations; there is no "before the first" observation.) More importantly, it doesn't remove the endogeneity either!

14.1.2 First Differencing Does Not Fix This Problem

First differencing also removes the direct source of endogeneity and re-introduces it again in a different place. To see how, take Eq. (14.1) and subtract off the first lag:

$$Y_{i,t} - Y_{i,t-1} = \left(\beta Y_{i,t-1} + u_i + \epsilon_{i,t}\right) - \left(\beta Y_{i,t-2} + u_i + \epsilon_{i,t-1}\right)$$

$$Y_{i,t} - Y_{i,t-1} = \beta \left(Y_{i,t-1} - Y_{i,t-2}\right) + \left(\epsilon_{i,t} - \epsilon_{i,t-1}\right) \tag{14.2}$$

$$\Delta Y_{i,t} = \beta_y \Delta Y_{i,t-1} + \Delta \epsilon_{i,t}. \tag{14.3}$$

If we tried to estimate this first-differenced equation with OLS, it would still be the case that a regressor $(\Delta Y_{i,t-1})$ is correlated with the error $(\Delta \epsilon_i, t)$: the $Y_{i,t-1}$ part of $(\Delta Y_{i,t-1} = Y_{i,t-1} - Y_{i,t-2})$ is correlated with the $\epsilon_{i,t-1}$ part of $(\Delta \epsilon_{i,t} = \epsilon_{i,t} - \epsilon_{i,t-1})$.

First differencing a dynamic panel data model does not eliminate the endogeneity problem.

14.1.3 GMM Estimators Fix This Problem

Whenever a control variable is correlated with the error, we say there is "endogeneity." This endogeneity biases almost all estimators, because we cannot separate out the effects of the lagged variable and the unobserved error term. Since we can't observe the error term, we inadvertently lump the two effects together and attribute the whole to the observable term.

The classic econometric solution to this endogeneity problem is to use "instrumental variables" or "IV." That'll be our solution, here, too. The challenge is to find a variable, or a set of variables, that can act as a substitute for our control variable. It needs to be correlated with the regressor, but not correlated with the error term. This type of surrogate variable is called an "instrument." Good instruments are hard to find.

So, how do we estimate dynamic panel data models when there seems to be endogeneity problems at every turn and good instruments are hard to find? A string of research papers by Manuel Arellano, Richard Blundell, Stephen Bond, and Olympia Bover cracked this problem for the large-N small-T datasets. These types of large-N small-T situations are very common in economics and business. In macro, we often have 50 years' worth of annual data for no more than 200 countries. In public health or medicine, researchers often can measure before a treatment and after, or perhaps a couple of periods after. Even a long-term survey such as the National Longitudinal Survey of Youth has large-N small-T. It tracks roughly 10,000 people annually since 1979; even after over 40 years of tracking, T is much smaller than N.

Arellano and his colleagues proposed using two different variations of an estimation method developed by Holtz-Eakin et al. (1988) for estimating dynamic panel data called the "generalized method of moments." The details of GMM are too advanced for this book, so a brief sketch will have to suffice. The idea is that there are always hidden assumptions in regression models: assumptions about the expectation of the error term (it is equal to zero, in expectation), or about the variance of the error term (constant variance implies a homoskedastic error), or assumptions about the covariance between the error term and the regressor (they should have a zero covariance; otherwise there is endogeneity), and so forth. Such assumptions involve moments of variables (their means, variances, and covariances). It turns out that when enough of these moments are specified, there is a unique "best" set of coefficients that also satisfies the equation we're trying to model. If there are more moment restrictions than necessary, then we are "overidentified," and we can exploit these excess moments to test various aspects of our models.

14.1.4 Arellano-Bond-Type Estimators

The two variations of GMM proposed by Arellano et al. are called "difference GMM" and "system GMM." The "difference GMM" estimator models Eq. (14.3), the first difference of Eq. (14.1). As we showed above, this first differencing re-introduces endogeneity, so we must use some set of instrumental variables to correct for this.

What makes these IV's different from the IV's you've probably seen in 2SLS is that there is a different set of instruments for each time period. We're instrumenting particular observations rather than the complete set of observations of a variable.

Let's recall the exact cause of the endogeneity problem in the first-differenced Eq. (14.3): $\Delta Y_{i,t-1}$ is correlated with $\Delta \epsilon_{i,t}$ via $\epsilon_{i,t-1}$. But it is uncorrelated with deeper lags. So, for example, we can instrument $\Delta Y_{i,t}$ with $Y_{i,t-2}$. We can instrument, say, $\Delta Y_{i,3}$ with $Y_{i,1}$. In fact, we can use lags all the way back to the beginning of our sample. So we can instrument $\Delta Y_{i,4}$ with $Y_{i,2}$ and $Y_{i,1}$. We can instrument $\Delta Y_{i,5}$ with $Y_{i,3}$, $Y_{i,2}$, and $Y_{i,1}$. And we can instrument $\Delta Y_{i,6}$ with $Y_{i,4}$, $Y_{i,3}$, $Y_{i,2}$, and $Y_{i,1}$, and so forth.

System GMM estimators were introduced by Arellano and Bover (1995) and Blundell and Bond (1998). These estimate Eqs. (14.1) and (14.3) simultaneously. Essentially, this is done by creating a new dataset that stacks the data for Equations (14.1) and (14.3); the data column for the dependent variable will have a dataset of $Y_{i,t}$'s stacked on top of a set of $\Delta Y_{i,t}$'s. The variables in levels are instrumented by lagged differences; and the differences are instrumented by lagged levels. Often, only one lag is used, rather than the whole sequence extending back to the original observation.

14.1.5 Forward Orthogonal Deviations

An alternative form of differencing was proposed by Arellano and Bover (1995). With "forward orthogonal deviations," we subtract off the mean of all future observations and then multiply by a scaling factor so that the magnitudes are the same as before. This particular transformation has the nice property that if the variables were independent (i.e., orthogonal) before the transformation, they remain so afterward. This method subtracts the average of future values, while retaining orthogonality, hence "forward orthogonal deviations."

This transformation has an even more important property: we can use much more of the available dataset. If our dataset has gaps, then first differencing is impossible for the observation immediately after then gap (you can't subtract off the previous value, because it is missing). And you can't calculate the first difference of the missing observations, because you'd be trying to subtract a lagged value from a missing one. So gaps expand when we first-difference. But forward orthogonal deviations merely subtract off the mean of all *available* future observations, missing observations be damned. If there are four future time periods, but we have data for only three of them, then we subtract off the mean of the three available observations.

Which differencing technique should we use, then: first differences or forward orthogonal deviations? The Monte Carlo study by Hayakawa et al. (2009) provides evidence for the superiority of forward orthogonal deviations.

14.1.6 Arellano-Bond in Stata

With the ubiquity of panel datasets, it should not be surprising that there are many different software packages to model dynamic panel models. Even Stata has different versions. There is `xtabond`, an official Stata command that estimates difference GMM models. This was superseded by `xtabond2`, a user-written command by Roodman (2009a) that allowed for estimating difference and system GMM. Then Stata introduced two general commands `xtdpd` to estimate cross-sectional time-series dynamic panel data models using difference GMM and `xtdpdsys` to estimate such models using system GMM.

Choosing between the user-written and official commands is largely a matter of taste. Their syntaxes and defaults are a bit different, though. To keep the exposition simple, we'll be using `xtabond2` for the rest of the chapter. The default is the "system" estimator. To get the "difference" estimator, we must add the option `noleveleq`. This excludes the levels equations that are instrumented by first differences.

Each X variable that we want to include must have an associated instrument. This instrument list gets quite long. Still, we must specify what type of moment restriction we are assuming of the data and imposing on the estimator. Variables should be listed in either `ivstyle()` or `gmmstyle()`, but not in both. Strictly exogenous variables should be listed under `ivstyle()`. Time dummy variables belong here. Predetermined or endogenous variables should be listed under `gmmstyle()`.

14.1.7 Too Many Instruments

In difference GMM, we instrument differences with lagged levels. In system GMM we instrument differences with lagged levels and, simultaneously, levels with lagged differences. We can also include instruments for any endogenous control variables. Clearly, there is a proliferation of instruments. And this set of instruments explodes with T. It is a well-known result in econometrics that the performance of IV instruments declines when we have "too many instruments" (see Roodman 2009b, and the references therein). For example, including too many instruments has the paradoxical result that it actually overfits the data, replicates the original dataset (endogenous warts and all), and ends up not removing the endogeneity. We may as well have done nothing, saved ourselves the trouble, and economized on degrees of freedom; we would have gotten the same biased estimates, and our standard errors would have been smaller. To remove the endogeneity, a small number of good instruments works better than too many.

Roodman (2009b) describes a procedure where the set of instruments is "collapsed" to a smaller set. The instrument matrix is a sparse matrix with instruments for each observation. Collapsing eliminates some of the sparsity; the number of non-zero entries is unchanged, but the number of zero terms is diminished by adding columns together. This allows one to specify a fewer number of GMM moment conditions, one for each lag rather than one for each observation.

Unfortunately, there is no widely accepted guidance for the optimal number of instruments. In practice, researchers present results with different sets of interest to show that their results are robust to these variations.

If we have too many instruments in our GMM estimation, then we are right back where we started: with a biased estimator. In fact, the bias can be even worse. Rather than providing a lengthy proof, let's settle for an illustration. In this small Monte Carlo experiment, I've generated 2000 datasets from the following model:

$$Y_{i,t} = \gamma Y_{i,t-1} + \beta X_{i,t-1} + u_i + \epsilon_{i,t}$$
$$= (0.30)Y_{i,t-1} + (1)X_{i,t-1} + u_i + \epsilon_{i,t},$$

where $X_{i,t}$ is endogenous and $\epsilon_{i,t}$ follows an AR(1) process.

We then compare the performance of four different estimators:

1. Fixed effects (within) estimator
2. System GMM via `xtabond2`
3. System GMM but with a collapsed instrument set
4. System GMM but with the instrument set limited to lags of only two time-periods deep

14.1 Dynamic Panel Bias

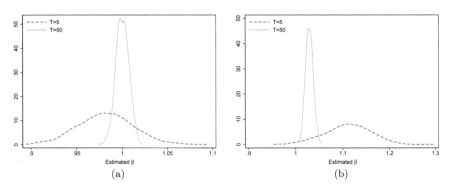

Fig. 14.1 FE and GMM estimates of βX_{t-1}; true $\beta = 1$. (**a**) Fixed effects estimator. (**b**) System GMM estimator

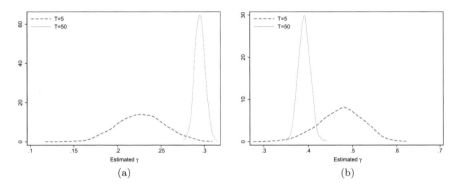

Fig. 14.2 FE and GMM estimates of γY_{t-1}; true $\gamma = 0.30$. (**a**) Fixed effects estimator. (**b**) System GMM estimator

Figure 14.1 illustrates nicely several properties of our two favorite estimators (FE and GMM). First, though the FE estimator is biased, the size of this bias is often negligible, and the estimates can be quite precise as T increases. Second, while the GMM estimator is asymptotically unbiased, its finite sample properties often leave much to be desired: when $T = 5$ the estimates were far from the true value of one, and this was true even when T increased to 50.

Figure 14.2 illustrates the ability of FE and GMM to estimate the coefficient on the lagged dependent variable. Here, the true value is $\gamma = 0.30$. The FE estimator is quite biased in small samples but shoots very close to the mark when $T = 50$. What is more troubling is the poor performance of the system GMM estimator. This is quite surprising, in fact, since GMM was developed to address this very problem of dynamic panel bias for models with lagged dependent variables. As Fig. 14.2b shows, GMM performed worse than FE for small T and large T as well. The reason for this is the proliferation of instruments.

So why did we spend so much time on GMM if it is such a bad estimator? Because there is a fix! We merely need to limit the number of instruments. A few good instruments is better than a large set of good and bad instruments together. There are two common ways of limiting the instrument set. First, we may collapse the instrument set. Second, we may limit how far back we use observations as instruments. For example, to instrument the levels equation in the 50th time period, we could use first differences in the 48th, 47th, etc. periods, all the way back to the $t = 0$ time period. This is too much of a good thing! Rather, we can merely discard those farther back time periods and only use, say, the observation two periods earlier, $t = 48$.

Figure 14.3 shows the performance of these two restricted GMM estimators in estimating β and Fig. 14.4 in estimating γ.

Once we've limited the number of instruments, the GMM estimator is very good at estimating the coefficient on endogenous regressors, including the coefficient on the lagged dependent variable.

This simple Monte Carlo study offers two rules of thumb for estimating dynamic panel data models. (1) Do not disregard the FE estimator off-hand. Its bias is often

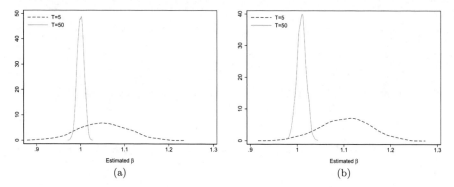

Fig. 14.3 Restricted GMM estimators of βX_{t-1}; true $\beta = 1$. (**a**) GMM with collapsed instrument set. (**b**) GMM with lag-limited instrument set

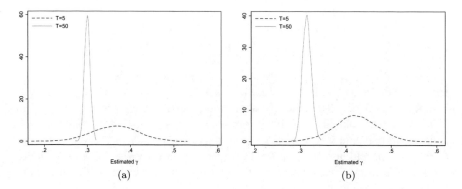

Fig. 14.4 Restricted GMM estimators of βX_{t-1}; true $\gamma = 0.30$. (**a**) GMM with collapsed instrument set (**b**) GMM with lag-limited instrument set

small, and it offers good precision. (2) If you will use an Arellano-Bond-type GMM estimator, you should restrict the number of instruments. The collapsed instrument option is a good default, as we often do not have a good a priori reason for limiting the instrument set to a particular number of lags.

We showed above that there is an inevitable correlation between one regressor (the lagged Y) and the error term, leading to endogeneity bias. But really, how bad can this bias be? It is known that the bias is proportional to $1/T$, where T is the number of time periods in our panel. So, if our dataset extends far enough, this bias asymptotically vanishes. But it can be quite large in small panels. In this subsection, we showed this empirically.

On the other hand, there is often a trade-off between accuracy and precision. Estimators that are unbiased (correct on average) can nevertheless be very imprecise. Their estimates can wildly undershoot on one sample and wildly overshoot on another. On average, they are correct; but they seldom hit their target. This is a similar situation. When we have a lagged dependent variable, an FE model estimated with OLS tends to be biased when T is small, but the estimates can be pretty precise. High precision may compensate for small bias. The bias usually affects the coefficient on the lagged dependent variable the most, rather than the coefficient on the $X_{i,t}$'s. OLS is also easy carry out. We don't have to worry about whether a variable belongs in one set of instruments or another. Some authors argue that the simplicity and precision of OLS makes it the superior choice (e.g., Bailey 2020; Beck & Katz 2011).

14.1.8 Sargan's and Hansen's J-Test for Instrument Validity

The GMM method works by specifying moment conditions. Whenever we have more moment restrictions than parameters to be estimated, we are said to be "overidentified." Sargan (1958) proposed a statistical test of whether overidentifying restrictions (in the context of instrumental variables) are valid. Hansen (1982) invented the generalized method of moments (GMM), groundbreaking work that earned him the 2013 Nobel Prize in Economics. In that same (1982) paper, he constructed an extension of Sargan's test which applied to this new GMM method.

The null hypothesis of Sargan/Hansen J-tests is that the overidentifying restrictions are valid. In this case, we'd prefer that our restrictions are appropriate. We do not want to reject the null, so higher p-values are better.

Windmeijer (2005) demonstrated that the J-test is weakened by many instruments. And what's more disappointing is that, if the number of instruments reaches the number of panels, we can even get a false $p = 1$ (Roodman 2009b). We'd like a test that can tell us if we have valid instruments, because the results of GMM depend on it. But this test doesn't work if we have too many instruments. Roodman (2009b) suggests that a p-value greater than 0.05 is to be desired, but not to much higher. P-values greater than 0.25 may imply that the large number of instruments has invalidated the test.

14.1.9 Difference-in-Hansen/Sargan Tests

Whereas the null on Hansen tests is that the entire set of overidentifying restrictions is valid, so-called "difference in Hansen" tests check whether a subset of instruments/restrictions is valid. To do this, they calculate two J-statistics: one when a particular subset is included and another when the subset is not included. The difference between the two J-statistics is distributed χ_k^2 where k is the number of additional instruments. As with the Hansen test, the difference-in-Hansen test also becomes invalid when the instrument count is large.

The Difference-in-Sargan test is an alternative to Hansen's test that is not as sensitive to the number of instruments. It does require the errors to be homoskedastic, though. It is usual in practice to provide both sets of results. Hopefully they are consistent with each other. This is not always the case.

14.1.10 Blundell-Bond Test of Autocorrelation

In the full dynamic model,

$$Y_{i,t} = \beta_y Y_{i,t-1} + \beta_x X_{i,t} + v_t + u_i + \epsilon_{i,t}, \tag{14.4}$$

we have three errors: u_i, country-specific errors that apply uniformly over time; v_t, time-specific errors that affect all countries uniformly at the same time; and $\epsilon_{i,t}$ errors that apply randomly over individual countries at random times. These latter errors are not supposed to be autocorrelated within countries. If they are even AR(1) within panels, then we cannot use the full set of instruments.

It is necessary, then, as a post-estimation check, to see whether there is any within-panel autocorrelation in the residuals, after estimation. Arellano and Bond (1991) derive a test of this, within the GMM framework, that is now standard output in many software implementations of their estimator. It is part of the output in xtabond2, for example.

First, let's suppose that there is no autocorrelation in $\epsilon_{i,t}$. It is pure white noise, sprinkled *iid* on $Y_{i,t}$. This is a best-case scenario. Now, let's suppose that we estimate the model in first differences. What will the residuals from this estimated first-differenced equation look like? They'll look like the first-differenced errors in (14.4). But recall from Chap. 5 that taking the first difference can sometimes introduce autocorrelation. Even though $\epsilon_{i,t}$ is independent of $\epsilon_{i,t-1}$, if we take first differences, then

$$\Delta \epsilon_{i,t} = \epsilon_{i,t} - \epsilon_{i,t-1}$$

is not independent of

$$\Delta \epsilon_{i,t-1} = \epsilon_{i,t-1} - \epsilon_{i,t-2}$$

14.1 Dynamic Panel Bias

because $\epsilon_{i,t}$ shows up in both equations. So, if we're estimating a first-differenced model, first-order autocorrelation in the residuals is not cause for concern. (We can adjust for it by using robust standard errors.)

But not so for second-order autocorrelation. We should not expect this from well-behaved $\epsilon_{i,t}$'s because there are no common terms between

$$\Delta \epsilon_{i,t} = \epsilon_{i,t} - \epsilon_{i,t-1}$$

and

$$\Delta \epsilon_{i,t-2} = \epsilon_{i,t-2} - \epsilon_{i,t-3}$$

and, by assumption, the $\epsilon_{i,t}$'s themselves are *iid*. So, to repeat, if the $\epsilon_{i,t}$'s are *iid*, then we should expect first-order autocorrelation in the residuals. This not the case for second-order autocorrelation.

On the other hand, if the $\epsilon_{i,t}$'s are, themselves, autocorrelated, then this will carry over into correlation in the second-order residuals. For the sake of concreteness, let's suppose that $\epsilon_{i,t}$ are AR(1), so that they can be modeled by

$$\epsilon_{i,t} = \rho \epsilon_{i,t-1} + e_{i,t}.$$

Then

$$\Delta \epsilon_{i,t} = \epsilon_{i,t} - \epsilon_{i,t-1}$$
$$= \epsilon_{i,t} - \rho \epsilon_{i,t-2} + e_{i,t-1}$$

is correlated with

$$\Delta \epsilon_{i,t-2} = \epsilon_{i,t-2} - \epsilon_{i,t-3}$$

via their common $\epsilon_{i,t-2}$ term.

To summarize, autocorrelated $\epsilon_{i,t}$'s can limit our use of instrumental variables. We must test for this. Arellano and Bond propose checking for autocorrelated error, by checking for autocorrelation in the residuals of the estimated differenced equation. First-order autocorrelation in these residuals are to be expected. But we have a problem if we find autocorrelated residuals in the 2nd differences.

The null hypothesis for this test is that there is no autocorrelation. Thus, if we have a *p*-value that is small, we can reject the null of no-autocorrelation; rather, we have evidence of autocorrelation. So, we should look for *p*-values greater than, say, 0.05 for AR(1) in first differences and *p*-values greater than 0.05 for AR(2).

Including time-FEs is a convenient, albeit blunt, way of removing an important source of autocorrelation in the error term and capturing panel-wide shocks.

14.2 Replicating Arellano and Bond (1991)

In their seminal 1991 paper, Arellano and Bond developed their estimator, derived some of its theoretical properties, conducted Monte Carlo experiments to explore its small-sample performance, and then used their estimator to investigate employment dynamics from an annual sample of 140 UK companies from 1976 to 1984. The model they estimated was

$$n_{i,t} = \alpha_1 n_{i,t} + \alpha_2 n_{i,t-2} + \beta'(L) X_{i,t} + v_t + u_i + \epsilon_{i,t} \qquad (14.5)$$

The variables include $n_{i,t}$, the logarithm of employment in company i in year t. $\beta(L)$ is a set of polynomials in the lag operator applied to a vector $X_{i,t}$ of control variables. This vector includes wages in the current and previous year, capital in the current and previous 2 years, and industrial production in the current and previous 2 years, all measured in logarithms. Dummy variables for all years are also included as control variables. Like before, there is a time-specific error term v_t affecting all companies at the same instant; a company-specific fixed effect, u_i, and an idiosyncratic error term, $\epsilon_{i,t}$.

First, make sure we have the xtabond2 command installed in our version of Stata. Then we load up the Arellano-Bond dataset and declare our panel and time variables:

```
. capture ssc install xtabond2
. webuse abdata, clear
. xtset id year
```

First, let's be naive about it and estimate Eq. (14.5) using Pooled OLS:

```
. reg n nL1 nL2 w wL1 k kL1 kL2 ys ysL1 ysL2 yr*, cluster(id)
. estimates store PooledOLS
```

Next, we estimate a fixed effects model:

```
. xtreg n nL1 nL2 w wL1 k kL1 kL2 ys ysL1 ysL2 yr*, cluster(id) fe
. estimates store FE
```

Now let's use xtabond2 to estimate Eq. (14.5). We try the one-step version of the Arellano-Bond estimator first

```
. xtabond2 n nL1 nL2 w wL1 k kL1 kL2 ys ysL1 ysL2 yr*, ///
    gmmstyle(nL1) ivstyle(w wL1 k kL1 kL2 ys ysL1 ysL2 yr*) ///
    nolevel robust small
. estimates store GMM_1
```

which gives the following output:

14.2 Replicating Arellano and Bond (1991)

```
Dynamic panel-data estimation, one-step difference GMM
------------------------------------------------------------------------------
Group variable: id                              Number of obs      =      611
Time variable : year                            Number of groups   =      140
Number of instruments = 41                      Obs per group: min =        4
F(0, 140)         =      .                                    avg =     4.36
Prob > F          =      .                                    max =        6
------------------------------------------------------------------------------
             |              Robust
           n | Coefficient  std. err.      t    P>|t|     [95% conf. interval]
-------------+----------------------------------------------------------------
         nL1 |   .6862261   .1469312     4.67   0.000     .3957352    .9767171
         nL2 |  -.0853582   .0569209    -1.50   0.136    -.1978938    .0271774
           w |  -.6078208   .1810857    -3.36   0.001    -.965837    -.2498047
         wL1 |   .3926237   .1707083     2.30   0.023     .0551242    .7301231
           k |   .3568456   .0599742     5.95   0.000     .2382734    .4754178
         kL1 |  -.0580012   .0743625    -0.78   0.437    -.2050197    .0890174

         kL2 |  -.0199475   .0332414    -0.60   0.549    -.0856674    .0457725
          ys |   .6085073   .1753198     3.47   0.001     .2618907    .9551239
        ysL1 |  -.7111651   .2354613    -3.02   0.003    -1.176685   -.2456454
        ysL2 |   .1057969   .1434843     0.74   0.462    -.1778792    .389473
      yr1978 |  -.0095545   .0104559    -0.91   0.362    -.0302263    .0111174
      yr1980 |   .0124607   .013474      0.92   0.357    -.014178     .0390994
      yr1981 |  -.0213288   .0255286    -0.84   0.405    -.0718003    .0291427
      yr1982 |  -.0366133   .0260865    -1.40   0.163    -.0881877    .0149612
      yr1983 |  -.0308749   .0281669    -1.10   0.275    -.0865624    .0248126
      yr1984 |  -.0172578   .0295624    -0.58   0.560    -.0757043    .0411887
------------------------------------------------------------------------------
Instruments for first differences equation
  Standard
    D.(w wL1 k kL1 kL2 ys ysL1 ysL2 yr1976 yr1977 yr1978 yr1979 yr1980 yr1981
    yr1982 yr1983 yr1984)
  GMM-type (missing=0, separate instruments for each period unless collapsed)
    L(1/8).nL1
------------------------------------------------------------------------------
Arellano-Bond test for AR(1) in first differences: z =  -3.60  Pr > z =  0.000
Arellano-Bond test for AR(2) in first differences: z =  -0.52  Pr > z =  0.606
------------------------------------------------------------------------------
Sargan test of overid. restrictions: chi2(25)   =  67.59  Prob > chi2 =  0.000
  (Not robust, but not weakened by many instruments.)
Hansen test of overid. restrictions: chi2(25)   =  31.38  Prob > chi2 =  0.177
  (Robust, but weakened by many instruments.)

Difference-in-Hansen tests of exogeneity of instrument subsets:
iv(w wL1 k kL1 kL2 ys ysL1 ysL2 yr1976 yr1977 yr1978 yr1979 yr1980 yr1981 yr19
> 82 yr1983 yr1984)
    Hansen test excluding group:     chi2(11)   =  12.01  Prob > chi2 =  0.363
    Difference (null H = exogenous): chi2(14)   =  19.37  Prob > chi2 =  0.151
```

As expected, we reject the null of no AR(1) errors, but are unable to reject the null of AR(2) errors. The Sargan and Hansen tests of overidentification give conflicting results. Recall that a p-value greater than 0.05 is considered "good" in this context, but that a value that is too high (Roodman suggested a p of 0.25 is too high) is itself an indicator that we have too many instruments. Thus, this moderately sized *p*-value of 0.177 is encouraging.

Next, we estimate the two-step version of the same equation and a version with a smaller set of control variables:

```
. xtabond2 n nL1 nL2 w wL1 k kL1 kL2 ys ysL1 ysL2 yr*, ///
    gmm(nL1) iv(w wL1 k kL1 kL2 ys ysL1 ysL2 yr*)   ///
    nolevel robust small twostep
. estimates store GMM_2

. xtabond2 n nL1 nL2 w wL1 k ys ysL1 yr*, ///
    gmm(nL1) iv(w wL1 k ys ysL1 yr*) ///
    nolevel robust small twostep
. estimates store GMM_3
```

The collected sets of estimates (ignoring the yearly dummies) are

```
. estimates table PooledOLS FE GMM_1 GMM_2 GMM_3, ///
    b(%7.3f) se(%7.3f)  keep(n* w* k* ys*)
```

Variable	Poole~S	FE	GMM_1	GMM_2	GMM_3
nL1	1.045	0.733	0.686	0.629	0.474
	0.052	0.060	0.147	0.197	0.188
nL2	-0.077	-0.139	-0.085	-0.065	-0.053
	0.049	0.078	0.057	0.046	0.052
w	-0.524	-0.560	-0.608	-0.526	-0.513
	0.174	0.160	0.181	0.157	0.148
wL1	0.477	0.315	0.393	0.311	0.225
	0.172	0.143	0.171	0.206	0.144
k	0.343	0.388	0.357	0.278	0.293
	0.049	0.057	0.060	0.074	0.063
kL1	-0.202	-0.081	-0.058	0.014	
	0.065	0.054	0.074	0.094	
kL2	-0.116	-0.028	-0.020	-0.040	
	0.036	0.043	0.033	0.044	
ys	0.433	0.469	0.609	0.592	0.610
	0.179	0.171	0.175	0.176	0.158
ysL1	-0.768	-0.629	-0.711	-0.566	-0.446
	0.251	0.207	0.235	0.265	0.220
ysL2	0.312	0.058	0.106	0.101	
	0.132	0.133	0.143	0.164	

Legend: b/se

Pooled OLS, which ignores the panel nature of the data, results in a much larger coefficient on the first lag of employment. The one-step and two-step difference GMM estimators provide comparable results, mostly different in the second decimal places. Comparing the last two sets of estimates, we see that small changes in the set of regressors can have outsized effects on the estimated coefficients.

The coefficients on the first and second lagged dependent variables (nL1 and nL2) were quite large under the biased Pooled OLS estimator. In fact, their sum of 0.968 (1.045−0.077) is almost close to 1, implying a unit root and nonstationarity. The coefficients from the GMM estimators are much more reasonable, summing to between 0.421 and 0.601.

14.3 Replicating Thomson (2017)

Russell Thomson (2017) uses system GMM estimator to investigate whether R&D tax credits are effective in stimulating research. Historically, the problem was examined by looking at cross-country regressions. However, endogeneity may be a problem with these types of investigations, because not only do firms respond to the tax credit, but the very existence of the tax credit may be due to the (lack of) R&D investment in the first place. To circumvent the endogeneity problem, Thomson (2015) constructs a panel dataset consisting of annual observations on 29 industries in 26 OECD countries. He then uses a GMM estimator, with its barrage of instrumental variables, to correct for the potential endogeneity.

Thomson theorizes that the (log of) R&D expenditure depends upon the log of industry value added and the log of the after-tax cost of R&D, as well as industry-specific, time-specific, and idiosyncratic error terms. Many of the tax credits only subsidize *increased* expenditure, so that the previous year's expenditure must be taken into account. Therefore, Thomson also includes a lagged dependent variable to contend with, which raises the specter of dynamic panel bias.

The equation that Thomson estimates is

$$ln\, RnD_{i,t} = \beta_1 ln\, RnD_{i,t-1} + \beta_2 ln\, TaxPrice_{i,t-1} + \\ \beta_3 ln\, ValueAdded + v_t + u_i + \epsilon_{i,t}. \quad (14.6)$$

Thomson compares several different estimation strategies. To follow along, download the Thomson2017.dta dataset. We will replicate his Table 4, where his main results are reported.

First, Thomson estimates (14.6) using a Pooled OLS model in first differences. He includes a time-dummy and clusters his standard errors by industry i.

```
. reg d.lnRnD ld.lnRnD ld.lnValueAdded ld.lnTaxPrice i.t ///
    , vce(cluster i)
. gen fdsample = e(sample)
. estimates store FD
```

Next, Thomson tries a fixed effects panel data model with time fixed effects while clustering standard errors by industry. To keep the estimations comparable, he limits his FE sample to only those observations that were available from the Pooled first-differenced estimation above. (That is the function of fdsample in the line below.)

```
. xtreg lnRnD L.lnRnD L.lnValueAdded L.lnTaxPrice i.t ///
        if fdsample, fe vce(cluster i)
. estimates store FE
```

Then Thomson turns to system GMM estimation. Here, he tries three different versions. The main structure of the model is the same (same dependent variable, lags on independent variables). Variables that are either endogenous or predetermined belong in the set of GMM-style instruments. Truly exogenous variables belong in the set of IV-style instruments. Aware of the "too many instruments" problem, Thomson limits his instrument set in a couple of different ways. First, recall that it is easy to have too many instruments. The Arellano-Bond method allows us to instrument a variable with lags reaching all the way back to the beginning of the sample. Instead, Thomson limits his lag length to three. Thomson also collapses the instrument set. He specifies that he wants robust standard errors, the two-step estimator, with the forward orthogonal deviations for instruments. Again, to keep the samples consistent so that we can better compare estimators, he limits his sample to the same observations as from the Pooled OLS estimator.

```
. xtabond2 lnRnD L.lnRnD L.lnValueAdded L.lnTaxPrice i.t if fdsample, ///
        gmm(L.lnRnD L.lnValueAdded L.lnTaxPrice, laglimit(. 3) collapse) ///
        iv(i.t) twostep orthog robust
. estimates store GMM4
```

Thomson then repeats the previous estimation, but further restricts his sample to include only manufacturing sectors.

```
. xtabond2 lnRnD L.lnRnD L.lnValueAdded L.lnTaxPrice i.t ///
        if fdsample & manuf == 1 , ///
        gmm(L.lnRnD L.lnValueAdded L.lnTaxPrice, laglimit(. 3) collapse) ///
        iv(i.t) twostep orthog robust
. estimates store GMM5
```

Finally, he runs his estimates on the whole sample:

```
. xtabond2 lnRnD L.lnRnD L.lnValueAdded L.lnTaxPrice i.t, ///
        gmm(L.lnRnD L.lnValueAdded L.lnTaxPrice, laglimit(. 3) collapse) ///
        iv(i.t) twostep orthog robust
. estimates store GMM6
```

We report all of the results in the following table:

14.4 Stationarity and Panel Unit Root Tests

```
. estimates table FE FD GMM4 GMM5 GMM6, ///
    b(%6.3g) se(%7.4f) drop(i.t _cons) stats(N)
```

Variable	FE	FD	GMM4	GMM5	GMM6
lnRnD					
L1.	.660		.876	.844	.871
	0.0279		0.0294	0.0414	0.0340
LD.		-.0746			
		0.0399			
lnValueAdded					
L1.	.206		.204	.289	.201
	0.0427		0.0480	0.0698	0.0576
LD.		.195			
		0.0666			
lnTaxPrice					
L1.	-.357		-.500	-.477	-.605
	0.1292		0.2119	0.2268	0.2249
LD.		-.442			
		0.1421			
N	5681	5681	5681	4621	6355

Legend: b/se

The main variable of interest is the coefficient on lnTaxPrice. Estimates range from −0.357 to −0.605.

The results from the first-differenced pooled OLS estimator indicate a short-run tax-price elasticity of R&D investment of −0.357.

Turning to the GMM estimates, we have a short-run tax-price elasticity of −0.50. This implies that a reduction of 10% in the tax price of R&D would increase R&D expenditure by 5%. This may be slightly smaller in magnitude for manufacturing firms (the GMM5 column). Finally, using the whole sample, we get an estimated short-run tax-price elasticity of R&D investment of −0.605, which is much larger in magnitude than earlier estimates. In fact, it is almost double the FE estimate. This implies that a 10% reduction in research and development taxes would increase R&D by 6.5%. Thomson reports that this estimate is two to three times higher than previous estimates.

14.4 Stationarity and Panel Unit Root Tests

We spent a lot of time in this book—especially in Chaps. 5 and 7—learning about unit roots. Processes with unit roots are nonstationary and harder to estimate.

Over the years, econometricians learned that the standard barrage of tests (e.g., Dickey-Fuller and Phillips-Perron) required many observations to have decent power.

It is generally hard to gather more data; we either have to wait more years for more annual data, or we have to do some historical archaeology to figure out earlier observations. Nobody has time for that. In general, we're stuck with the data we have. And even if we did the hard work of extending the time series, is it really reasonable to believe that the data-generating process in, say, the late twentieth century is really the same as it was before the Great Depression? Structural breaks are a legitimate concern. Is there really no good way to test for unit roots?

Perhaps, reasoned the econometricians, perhaps we can get more observations by exploiting the cross-sectional dimension. Rather than testing whether, say, US GDP has a unit root or not, we look at the UK's and Canada's GDPs too and test whether GDP in general has unit roots.

In the early 1990s, several tests were developed that became hugely popular. These so-called "first-generation" unit root tests will be discussed next. The topic is massively important and is still being explored. We'll briefly touch on "second-generation tests"; however, their properties are still being investigated, and there have not emerged any clear "favorites" yet among this new class of tests.

14.4.1 First-Generation Tests

Most of the tests we'll look at can be thought of as extensions of the Dickey-Fuller (DF) test, so let's take a moment and reacquaint ourselves with that classic test. Recall that the standard DF test begins with a simple dynamic model and allows for a deterministic trend (and possibly with exogenous variables):

$$X_t = \beta_0 + \beta_x X_{t-1} + \beta_t t + e_t. \tag{14.7}$$

If we subtract X_{t-1} from both sides

$$X_t - X_{t-1} = (\beta_0 + \beta_x X_t + \beta_t t + e_t) - X_{t-1}$$
$$\Delta X_t = \beta_0 + (\beta_x - 1) X_{t-1} + \beta_t t + e_t$$
$$\Delta X_t = \beta_0 + \gamma X_{t-1} + \beta_t t + e_t \tag{14.8}$$

where $\gamma = (\beta_x - 1)$. We can test for the unit root by testing whether $\beta_x = 1$ or $\gamma = 0$. (This is generalization of the approach in Eq. 7.8.)

To convert this to panels, we need to add the cross-sectional subscript i. We can also allow for fixed effects (replacing the constant β_0 with an individual constant for each country, u_i) and time fixed effects, v_t.

We can make this into an augmented Dickey-Fuller test—allowing for serial autocorrelation via an AR(p) process—by adding $(p-1)$ lags of differenced dependent variables:

14.4 Stationarity and Panel Unit Root Tests

$$\Delta X_{i,t} = \gamma X_{i,t-1} + \sum_{j=1}^{p-1} \beta_j \Delta X_{i,t-j} + \beta_t t + u_i + v_t + \epsilon_{i,t} \qquad (14.9)$$

This equation might look complicated, but we've estimated such models several times already in this chapter. There is a lagged dependent variable, so it is a dynamic panel data model; it just happens that the lagged dependent variable is the first difference of some other variable ($X_{i,t}$). It may include an exogenous time variable, country fixed effects, and time fixed effects.

LLC Test
The LLC or Levin-Lin-Chu test (Levin et al. 2002) estimates Eq. (14.9) as a standard fixed effects model (xtreg, fe in Stata).

The test assumes that the countries are cross-sectionally independent of each other. It also assumes that, except for the country FEs, the coefficients of the remaining variables are the same across countries. Most importantly, it assumes that the value of γ is the same for all countries.

Thus, the LLC test boils down to a test of the value of a single parameter:

$$H_0 : \gamma = 0$$
$$H_a : \gamma < 0$$

If it is greater than 1, it is an explosive, nonstationary series. Under the null, and the given assumptions, the value of γ is normal, so the usual test statistics apply.

The LLC test therefore tests the unit root hypothesis for the entire group of countries at once.

There is usually no strong a priori reason for including a set number of lags in Eq. (14.9). They are included by ADF-type tests to account for autocorrelation. In practice, the number of lags is determined by performing the regressions under different lags and then comparing how well each fits using some information criterion such as AIC or BIC.

The asymptotics of the LLC test requires that N and T both go to infinity but also that T grows faster than N. In practice, N should be large and T even larger. This is often not possible for macroeconomic panels. And where it is, we still face the potential for structural breaks to complicate matters (Im et al. 2023).

It might seem surprising at first that LLC's unit root test is based on a standard fixed effect regression, considering that (14.9) has a lagged dependent variable. OLS-based estimators such as FEs are known to have dynamic panel bias, which is why we explored Arellano-Bond-type GMM estimators in the first place, right? Under the null, though, there is no dynamic panel bias. To see this in the simplest case, substitute the null hypothesis ($H_0 : \gamma = 0$) into Eq. (14.8):

$$\Delta X_t = \beta_0 + \gamma X_{t-1} + \beta_t t + e_t$$

$$\Delta X_t = \beta_0 + \beta_t t + e_t$$

So, under the null, there is no lagged dependent variable at all! (Things are more complicated with the ADF case rather than DF because we've forcefully included lagged differences. We brush this complication aside.)

IPS Test

One may object to the assumption that all countries have the same value of γ. That is, some countries may have unit roots, and others may not. In this case, we might consider testing something like

$$\Delta X_{i,t} = \gamma_i X_{i,t-1} + \sum_{j=1}^{p-1} \beta_j \Delta X_{i,t-j} + \beta_t t + u_i + v_t + \epsilon_{i,t} \qquad (14.10)$$

where we've added the i subscript on γ_i.

This raises a complication, though. What are testing? Do all the countries have to be free of unit roots? Some of them? How many?

Instead, Im, Pesaran, & Shin (2003) proposed treating this like a bunch of separate univariate ADF tests. Essentially, to estimate Eq. (14.8) N times, and then creating an aggregate summary statistic for whether the overall sample of countries is, on the whole, characterized by a unit root.

To spell it out, they suggest estimating N single-country ADF equations:

$$\Delta X_t = \beta_0 + \gamma X_{t-1} + \beta_t t + e_t. \qquad (14.11)$$

Next, they suggest averaging the N t-statistics on γ. Their final test statistic is a transformation of this average of t-stats.

As with the LLC test, the number of lags is not usually known ahead of time. The optimal number of lags is determined by comparing different lags using some information criterion such as AIC or BIC. Unlike LLC, the number of lags can vary by country, as each country's equation is estimated separately, and the lags merely control for autocorrelation.

Likewise, since each country's regression is run separately, there is no requirement that the panel is balanced. We can have a different number of observations for each country. The aggregate test statistic will be a weighted average of the individual country-level statistics; but software takes care of that.

The null and alternative hypotheses for the IPS test are:

$H_0 : \gamma_i = 0$ for all i (all countries have unit roots)

$H_a : \gamma_i < 0$ for some i (some countries are stationary)

Rejecting the null merely indicates that some countries are stationary. It does not tell us which ones, nor does it tell us how many.

14.4 Stationarity and Panel Unit Root Tests

Univariate unit root tests have low power. LLC proposed leveraging the additional data from more countries and estimating a single regression coefficient – an average coefficient, so to speak. IPS proposed estimating many such individual coefficients and then averaging them. IPS took low-power univariate ADF tests and figured out that averaging them gives you much higher power. In fact, various Monte Carlo tests have shown that the IPS approach has higher power than the LLC approach.

It has been shown that the IPS test has better finite sample properties than does the LLC test (Im et al. 2003). Both IPS and LLC, however, have low power when deterministic terms are included in the regressions.

Maddala & Wu or "Fisher" Tests

Rather than taking the IPS approach and averaging the t-statistics, Maddala and Wu (1999) suggest averaging the p-values. More specifically, their test statistic is (-2 times) the sum of the natural logs of the p-values, a value which is asymptotically χ^2_{2N}.

Maddala and Wu (1999) argue that their test is more robust to the presence of cross-sectional dependence than the IPS test is. Since the test is an aggregation of individual-country ADF (or Phillips-Perron) tests, it can be applied to unbalanced panels and can accommodate different lag lengths on the individual-country unit root tests.

Harris Tzavalis Test

Rather than estimating a first-differenced ADF-type model like Eq. (14.9), Harris and Tzavalis (1999) propose estimating the panel version of Eq. (14.7) directly:

$$X_{i,t} = \gamma X_{i,t-1} + \beta_t t + u_i + \epsilon_{i,t}.$$

The lagged dependent variable creates bias, but Harris and Tsavalis were still able to derive the mean and variance of the estimator, so that a hypothesis test is possible.

Hadri Test

The Hadri (2000) test can be thought of as the panel version of the KPSS test. Unlike the panel tests above, the null and alternative are switched:

$$H_0 : \gamma_i < 0 \text{ for all } i \text{ (all countries are stationary)}$$

$$H_a : \gamma_i = 0 \text{ for some } i \text{ (some countries have unit roots)}$$

Since the null hypothesis for Hadri is stationarity, it is technically a "stationarity test." The null hypotheses for the other tests above were that a unit root is present, making them "unit root tests." (The point is semantic and pedantic.)

Hadri (2000) tests are best suited to datasets with large T and moderate N. Hadri's own simulations show that his test has unacceptably low size when $N \geq 50$

and $T \leq 50$. On the other hand, Hadri tests allow for cross-sectional dependence, so they are useful tests to have in your toolkit.

Examples

Stata implements many first-gen panel unit root tests with their xtunitroot command. In this section, we'll use some of them, but we will not explore all of the options for each command.

First, let's download some data on per capita real GDP for the European Union countries:

```
. use "PanelUnitRoot.dta", clear
```

We begin by conducting an LLC test, allowing for a deterministic trend. We do this because the GDPs of EU countries have tended to grow. Thus, we must compare deterministic vs stochastic growth.

```
. xtunitroot llc Y if EU==1, trend

Levin-Lin-Chu unit-root test for Y
---------------------------------
H0: Panels contain unit roots          Number of panels  =    25
Ha: Panels are stationary              Number of periods =    26

AR parameter: Common                   Asymptotics: N/T -> 0
Panel means:  Included
Time trend:   Included

ADF regressions: 1 lag
LR variance:    Bartlett kernel, 9.00 lags average (chosen by LLC)
------------------------------------------------------------------
                Statistic      p-value
------------------------------------------------------------------
Unadjusted t    -11.3722
Adjusted t*      -2.6777       0.0037
------------------------------------------------------------------
```

The p-value indicates that we reject the null hypothesis that all panels contain unit roots. Rather, we conclude that some panels are stationary: maybe one country, maybe all countries.

The default here was that there was only one lag for the augmented Dickey-Fuller test. Perhaps we should have included more? In a HW exercise, you are asked to repeat this, but allowing for an "optimal" lag selection using AIC.

Next, we run an IPS test allowing for a deterministic trend. We allow the number of ADF lags to be determined by the Akaike information criterion, with a maximum lag length of five:

14.4 Stationarity and Panel Unit Root Tests

```
. xtunitroot ips Y if EU==1, trend lags(aic 5)

Im-Pesaran-Shin unit-root test for Y
------------------------------------
H0: All panels contain unit roots          Number of panels  =     25
Ha: Some panels are stationary             Number of periods =     26

AR parameter: Panel-specific               Asymptotics: T,N -> Infinity
                                                        sequentially
Panel means:   Included
Time trend:    Included

ADF regressions: 0.84 lags average (chosen by AIC)
------------------------------------------------------------------------
                   Statistic      p-value
------------------------------------------------------------------------
W-t-bar             -2.2118       0.0135
------------------------------------------------------------------------
```

The small p-value indicates that we are still to reject the null hypothesis that all panels contain unit roots. Instead, at least some of them are stationary.

The Maddala and Wu (1999) test averages a sequence of univariate p-values, one for each country. These can be from univariate Phillips–Perron tests or Dickey–Fuller tests:

```
. xtunitroot fisher Y if EU==1, trend lags(3) pperron
. xtunitroot fisher Y if EU==1, trend lags(3) dfuller
```

The user-written `xtfisher` command provides some cleaner output:

```
. xtfisher Y if EU==1, trend lags(1) pp

Fisher Test for panel unit root using Phillips-Perron test (1 lags)

Ho: unit root

chi2(50)     =     52.4357
Prob > chi2  =      0.3797

. xtfisher Y if EU==1, trend lags(1)

Fisher Test for panel unit root using an augmented Dickey-Fuller test (1 lags)

Ho: unit root

chi2(50)     =     55.4857
Prob > chi2  =      0.2756
```

Above, we arbitrarily specified a lag of 1. (We also tried lags of up to five. For this dataset, the conclusions did not depend on the lag length.)

Next, we run the Harris–Tzavalis test:

```
. xtunitroot ht Y if EU==1, trend

Harris-Tzavalis unit-root test for Y
-----------------------------------
H0: Panels contain unit roots              Number of panels  =      25
Ha: Panels are stationary                  Number of periods =      26

AR parameter: Common                       Asymptotics: N -> Infinity
Panel means:  Included                                  T Fixed

Time trend:   Included
------------------------------------------------------------------------
                   Statistic       z         p-value
------------------------------------------------------------------------
rho                0.7885        1.6651      0.9521
------------------------------------------------------------------------
```

Then null hypothesis for the Harris-Tzavalis test is that the panels contained unit roots. The *p*-value is 0.9521, so we cannot reject this hypothesis at any level. In other words, this test indicates the presence of unit roots.

Finally, we switch gears and estimate a Hadri test. This allows the null hypothesis to be that all panels are stationary. Use the `robust` option to allow for cross-sectional dependence.

```
. xtunitroot hadri Y if EU==1, trend robust

Hadri LM test for Y
--------------------
H0: All panels are stationary              Number of panels  =      25
Ha: Some panels contain unit roots         Number of periods =      26

Time trend:         Included               Asymptotics: T, N -> Infinity
Heteroskedasticity: Robust                              sequentially
LR variance:        (not used)
------------------------------------------------------------------------
                   Statistic       p-value
------------------------------------------------------------------------
z                  25.8153         0.0000
------------------------------------------------------------------------
```

Here, we reject the null hypothesis that all panels are stationary.

So, what can we conclude? It seems that it is neither the case that all panels have unit roots, nor is it the case that no panels have unit roots. Rather, some do and some do not. The critical point is that there seem to be differences between these countries that should prevent us from lumping them together. That is, we should be hesitant to treat each country as though it is merely a different instance of the same type of economic dynamic.

Which Test Should You Use?

There is an entire menagerie of panel unit root tests. Which ones should you use?

So, which test should you use? A combination of tests seems best. Hlouskova and Wagner (2006) conducted an exhaustive Monte Carlo study of the various estimators. They find that the LLC tests have the highest power and sizes closest to nominal. There are combinations of parameters and model specifications, however, that favor various different tests over the others. The takeaway from their simulation is that (1) LLC deserves its place among the more popular unit root tests and (2) Hadri's stationarity test shows very poor performance except for the most extreme of cases. When T is very small relative to N (think $T = 5$), the Harris test performs well. Hlouskova and Wagner (2006) admit that the data generating process in their simulations specifically does not allow for the type of heterogeneity that IPS was designed for. This biases their simulations against IPS.

If your panel is unbalanced, you should use the IPS test. If the panel is balanced, the best choice depends largely on the sizes of N and T. Whenever $T > N$, LLC and Hadri are good choices. On the other hand, use the Harris-Tsavalis test if your panel has $N > T$.

The safest approach for applied researchers is to provide results from different tests with the hope that they reach similar conclusions.

Finally, all of the tests thus far are considered "first-generation tests" in the sense that they presume cross-sectional independence. If you believe there is a strong CSD component, then use none of the above tests, and opt for a "second-generation test."

14.4.2 Second-Generation Tests

As we mentioned earlier, panel unit root tests were developed in an attempt to increase the power of earlier time-series unit root tests by increasing the available amount of data. We can use data on, say, 38 OECD countries, or 193 UN member countries. However, to make full use of this data, we have to assume that each country's dynamics are the same as each other's. We can maybe have different fixed effects for each country, but if we also allow the slopes to vary, then we're back in a situation where each country has its own slope and intercept: we should run an individual regression on each country. But that puts us back in time-series land, with individual low-power tests on individual countries.

Another big limitation in first-generation unit root tests is that they all assume cross-sectional independence. Pesaran (2007) proposed an extension of the IPS unit root test (of which he is a co-author) that allows for cross-sectional dependence (CSD).

The ADF test was a time-series unit root test which augments the standard Dickey-Fuller test by including lagged difference terms to account for serial correlation. The IPS test extended the ADF test to panels by estimating N different ADF tests, one for each country, and then averaging their test statistics. Pesaran (2007) extended the IPS unit root test by allowing for CSD. He proposed to eliminate the CSD from the IPS regressions by augmenting even more, this time by including cross-sectional averages of lagged levels and first differences of the individual series.

Let's see how this works. Pesaran takes the original IPS equation

$$\Delta X_{i,t} = \beta_i X_{i,t-1} + \beta t + u_i + \epsilon_{i,t}$$

and augments it with two additional terms

$$\Delta X_{i,t} = \beta_i X_{i,t-1} + c_i \bar{X}_{t-1} + d_i \Delta \bar{X}_t + \beta t + u_i + \epsilon_{i,t}$$

where

$$\bar{X}_{t-1} = \frac{1}{N} \sum_{j=1}^{N} X_{j,t-1}$$

is the average, in the previous period, of all the countries' values of X, and

$$\Delta \bar{X}_t = \sum_{j=1}^{N} X_{j,t} - \sum_{j=1}^{N} X_{j,t-1}$$

is the change in the cross-sectional average from one period to the next.

Augmenting the regression in this way corrects for cross-sectional dependence. If there is cross-sectional dependence, then the value of $X_{i,t}$ is correlated with its value in another country, $X_{j,t}$. The IPS test aggregates a bunch of separate univariate ADF regressions, which are then averaged together to arrive at a single composite test statistic. But these IPS regressions on country i did not contain information from other countries, even if in real life, there is correlation between countries. The CIPS regression formally adds a term to correct for this. It does not add a term relating to a specific country j, but rather an aggregate of all countries. If there is cross-sectional dependence between many of these countries, then adding the value of the aggregate term will be significant and will appropriately influence the estimates of the β_i's.

Pesaran called these "CADF" or "cross-sectionally augmented Dickey-Fuller" tests. Pesaran's test statistic is an average of these individual CADF statistics t-tests. The null hypothesis is that all series have a unit root (are not stationary).

Pesaran's test has been implemented in the user-written `xtcips` and `pescadf` commands, written by Burdisso and Sangiácomo (2016) and Lewandowski (2007), respectively. Since each country's equation is estimated separately, there is not absolute requirement that the dataset is balanced. The test statistics in the Stata command `xtcips` requires balanced data; Burdisso and Sangiácomo (2016) explain how to construct a Monte Carlo simulation to estimate the test statistics for unbalanced samples.

14.5 Structural Breaks

The detection and estimation of structural breaks are far more complicated in a panel data setting. First, the number of breaks may, or may not, be known. Their (suspected) location may, or may not, be known. There can be breaks in intercept or slope. The breaks may affect some or all of the slopes. And the breaks may affect all panels or only subsets of the panels. Two of the simpler scenarios are shown in Fig. 14.5.

The user-written command xtbreak by Ditzen et al. (2021) provides some tools to simplify this process. Given the complexity of the issue, we will only give the most cursory example of the command.

First, we load and graph a dataset consisting of monthly unemployment rates for each US state.

```
. use panelUNRATE.dta, clear
. xtline lnUR if year >= 2010, overlay legend(off)
```

We can see quite clearly from Fig. 14.6 that there is a break around 2019–2020, resulting from the COVID pandemic. We model the unemployment rate as an AR(1) process with no exogenous variables. Let's see if the xtbreak command detects the obvious break:

```
. xtbreak estimate lnUR L.lnUR if year >= 2010 , breaks(1)

Estimation of break points
                                               N   =      50
                                               T   =     158
                                               SSR =   88.17
                                               Trimming =  0.15
--------------------------------------------------------------
 #      Index     Date              [95% Conf. Interval]
--------------------------------------------------------------
 1       122      2020m2            2019m4        2020m12
--------------------------------------------------------------
```

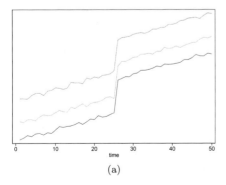
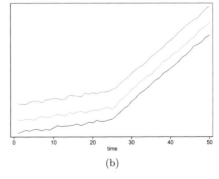

(a) (b)

Fig. 14.5 Two simpler examples of panel structural breaks. (**a**) Structural break in intercepts (**b**) Structural break in slopes

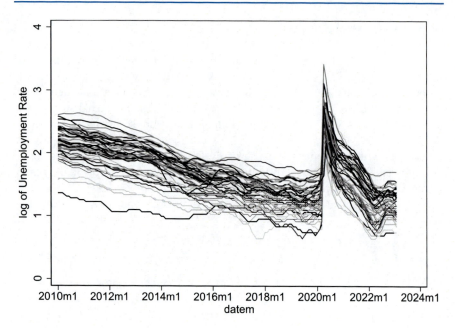

Fig. 14.6 State-level unemployment rates

Sure enough, the 95% confidence interval contains the tail end of 2019 (the beginning of the COVID-19 pandemic) and runs through the end of 2020. The most likely date for the break is February 2020, which is the data of the visible unemployment spike.

14.6 Panel VARs

The vector autoregressive model can be extended to estimate the dynamic relations in panels in many interesting ways. A panel VAR (pVAR) can estimate the average response of one economic quantity and another. These quantities can be, for example, the money supply and the price level. But the pVAR can be extended to estimate the response of one country's variables with another's. In principle, a pVAR can model almost any economic dynamics. But with great power comes great responsibility. And much difficulty. So we'll start simple and work our way up bit by bit.

From Chap. 10 we might have encountered a single-country two-variable VAR such as

$$X_t = \beta_1 + \beta_2 X_{t-1} + \beta_3 Y_{t-1} + e_t$$
$$Y_t = \beta_4 + \beta_5 Y_{t-1} + \beta_6 X_{t-1} + u_t.$$

14.6 Panel VARs

We can generalize by one level, allowing our variables to be panel-data:

$$X_{i,t} = \beta_1 + \beta_2 X_{i,t-1} + \beta_3 Y_{i,t-1} + e_{i,t} \tag{14.12}$$

$$Y_{i,t} = \beta_4 + \beta_5 Y_{i,t-1} + \beta_6 X_{i,t-1} + u_{i,t}. \tag{14.13}$$

Implicit above is that the β's are average effects. They are not country-specific. If they were, the β's would have i subscript.

There are two common ways to estimate the two equations in (14.12): (1) ordinary least squares FE estimation as done in the xtvar command and (2) an Arellano-Bond-type GMM estimator, as implemented in the pvar command. The first method is relatively straightforward. Its estimates are relatively stable but biased. The second method is, in principle, unbiased, but the estimates can depend greatly on instrumentation.

We can generalize a step further by allowing the coefficients to be country-specific. Let's suppose now that we have two countries in our panel (countries A and B). Then we might write

$$X_{A,t} = \beta_1 + \beta_2 X_{A,t-1} + \beta_3 Y_{A,t-1} + e_{A,t} \tag{14.14}$$

$$Y_{A,t} = \beta_4 + \beta_5 Y_{A,t-1} + \beta_6 X_{A,t-1} + u_{A,t} \tag{14.15}$$

and

$$X_{B,t} = \beta_7 + \beta_8 X_{B,t-1} + \beta_9 Y_{B,t-1} + e_{B,t} \tag{14.16}$$

$$Y_{B,t} = \beta_{10} + \beta_{11} Y_{B,t-1} + \beta_{12} X_{B,t-1} + u_{B,t}. \tag{14.17}$$

Here, the economic variables from country A only affect country A. Since there are no country-A variables in equations (14.16) and (14.17), we cannot capture any spill-overs from country A to country B. Effectively, we have two independent VARs, and we are back on relatively safe univariate ground.

Panels also allow us to model how one country's economy affects another's:

$$X_{A,t} = \beta_1 + \beta_2 X_{A,t-1} + \beta_3 X_{B,t-1} + \beta_4 Y_{A,t-1} + \beta_5 Y_{B,t-1} + e_{A,t}$$

$$Y_{A,t} = \beta_6 + \beta_7 Y_{A,t-1} + \beta_8 Y_{B,t-1} + \beta_9 X_{A,t-1} + \beta_{10} X_{B,t-1} + u_{A,t}$$

$$X_{B,t} = \beta_{11} + \beta_{12} X_{B,t-1} + \beta_{13} Y_{B,t-1} + \beta_{14} X_{B,t-1} + \beta_{15} Y_{B,t-1} + e_{B,t}$$

$$Y_{B,t} = \beta_{16} + \beta_{17} Y_{B,t-1} + \beta_{18} X_{B,t-1} + \beta_{19} Y_{B,t-1} + \beta_{20} X_{B,t-1} + u_{B,t} \tag{14.18}$$

The important innovation in (14.18) is that we now have explicit cross-country causation, with a lag, where variables from one country directly affect different variables from a different country. And we can still have instantaneous correlation by modeling the covariance between the e and u error terms.

For example, let $X_{A,t}$ be country A's GDP in time t, and let $Y_{A,t}$ be A's money supply. Then the first equation in (14.18) says that A's GDP in this period depends on its own GDP in the previous period, as well as B's GDP in the previous period. Perhaps they are trading partners and increases in income in B leads to increased purchases of A's products, thereby increasing A's GDP in the subsequent year.

Of course, this more complex model is harder to estimate. The number of parameters to estimate can grow out of hand quite easily. Panels allow us to bring more data to our estimations, allowing us to get more precise estimates of coefficients. But we don't get to enjoy this benefit if we have to estimate separate VARs. We face a trade-off between complex models estimated imprecisely and simple models estimated with great precision.

In practice, it is common to use economic theory to set specific coefficients to zero, making this a structural panel VAR. An alternative is to employ a "shrinkage estimator"—such as the LASSO—that statistically sets small coefficients to zero, freeing up degrees of freedom. Finally, Bayesian methods can constrain the parameters enough that estimation is possible.

14.6.1 Panel VAR Example

In the following few pages, we will work through a panel VAR exercise using the pvar suite of commands by Abrigo and Love (2016). Specifically, we want to investigate the relationship between economic output (real GDP in Euros) and air pollution (kilotons of CO_2 emissions).

First, we load the GDP and CO_2 data on the original eleven Euro countries (plus Greece, which joined shortly after):

```
. wbopendata, indicator(NY.GDP.MKTP.KN ; EN.ATM.CO2E.KT) ///
    country(AUT;BEL;DEU;ESP;FIN;FRA;GRC;IRL;ITA;LUX;NLD;PRT) ///
    year(2001:2019) clear long
```

Then we create a numeric identifier for each country and xtset the data:

```
. encode countrycode, gen(i)
. xtset i year
```

We rename our variables to something more readable:

```
. rename ny_gdp_mktp_kn GDP
. rename en_atm_co2e_kt CO2
```

and calculate the percentage change of these two variables:

```
. gen pctGDP = log(GDP) - log(L.GDP)
. gen pctCO2 = log(CO2) - log(L.CO2)
```

With those preliminaries out of the way, we are ready to begin our analysis. First, we need to figure out how many lags to include in our panel VAR model. The pvarsoc command extends to panels the varsoc command we saw in Chap. 10. It provides the panel versions of the common lag selection statistics (BIC, AIC, and HQIC) that were developed by Andrews and Lu (2001). As before, we choose

14.6 Panel VARs

the lag that minimizes these criteria. And as before, the information criteria seldom agree with each other. Hopefully, they only specify slightly different models.

We must contend with dynamic panel bias from having a lagged dependent variable. Our solution to this was the GMM-type estimators which remove bias by exploiting instruments. And as we saw before, the choice of instruments is tricky and has a potentially large effect on the final model. There is no elegant way around this. We'll ignore this problem for now, but in practice you will estimate different versions using different instruments, report all results, and hopefully be able to show that your results are consistent across these subtle changes to the model instrumentation.

Below, we consider lags up to length 4, and we specify that we will estimate our model using the 1st through 4th lags of our variables as instruments.

```
. pvarsoc pctGDP pctCO2 , maxlag(4) pvaropts(instlags(1/4))

Running panel VAR lag order selection on estimation sample
....

Selection order criteria
Sample:  2006 - 2018                       No. of obs    =     156
No. of panels   =        12
Ave. no. of T   =    13.000

+----------------------------------------------------------------------+
| lag |    CD         J       J pvalue    MBIC        MAIC      MQIC   |
|-----+----------------------------------------------------------------|
|  1  | .2142155    25.511    .0125786  -35.08727   1.510997  -13.35364|
|  2  | .3644327    10.71396  .2184394  -29.68489  -5.286044  -15.1958 |
|  3  | .3644676     2.630964 .621348   -17.56846  -5.369036  -10.32391|
|  4  | .380841         .         .         .         .          .     |
+----------------------------------------------------------------------+
```

The BIC-based selection statistic is minimized with one lag; the AIC is minimized with three lags, and the HQIC is minimized with two lags. It is not unusual to get mixed messages like this.

The three information criteria are based on Hansen's J-statistic. The fact that the p-value on the J statistic (0.012) is smaller than 0.05 is an indication that the model may be misspecified at two lags. For this reason, we estimate the larger lag-3 panel VAR model, keeping the same instrumentation:

```
. pvar pctGDP pctCO2 , lags(3) instlags(1/4)

Panel vector autoregresssion

GMM Estimation

Final GMM Criterion Q(b) =      .0169
Initial weight matrix: Identity
GMM weight matrix:     Robust
No. of obs       =         156
No. of panels    =          12
Ave. no. of T    =      13.000
```

	Coefficient	Std. err.	z	P>|z|	[95% conf.	interval]
pctGDP						
pctGDP						
L1.	.365789	.1949453	1.88	0.061	-.0162969	.7478748
L2.	-.0984745	.1157336	-0.85	0.395	-.3253081	.1283592
L3.	.1606883	.088879	1.81	0.071	-.0135113	.334888
pctCO2						
L1.	.0905422	.0763528	1.19	0.236	-.0591065	.240191
L2.	.0728497	.0720127	1.01	0.312	-.0682926	.213992
L3.	.0830113	.0775902	1.07	0.285	-.0690628	.2350853
pctCO2						
pctGDP						
L1.	.45337	.2281496	1.99	0.047	.0062051	.900535
L2.	.333369	.1449988	2.30	0.021	.0491766	.6175615
L3.	.1912476	.1934014	0.99	0.323	-.1878121	.5703073
pctCO2						
L1.	-.4279843	.146313	-2.93	0.003	-.7147524	-.1412162
L2.	-.2577303	.1276576	-2.02	0.043	-.5079346	-.0075261
L3.	.01425	.1186214	0.12	0.904	-.2182437	.2467437

```
Instruments : l(1/4).(pctGDP pctCO2)
```

Lagged pctCO2 seems to have no statistically significant effect on pctGDP, at least when we test each individual lag separately.

Next, we check whether the estimated VAR is stable by checking whether the eigenvalues of the companion matrix (inverse roots of the characteristic polynomial) are inside the unit circle:

```
. pvarstable

  Eigenvalue stability condition
```

14.6 Panel VARs

```
+---------------------------------+
|       Eigenvalue        |         |
|    Real      Imaginary  | Modulus |
|-------------------------+---------|
|  .7697733           0   | .7697733|
| -.2672641    .4902924   | .5584055|
| -.2672641   -.4902924   | .5584055|
| -.0566442    .5515007   | .554402 |
| -.0566442   -.5515007   | .554402 |
|  -.184152           0   | .184152 |
+---------------------------------+
```

All the eigenvalues lie inside the unit circle.
pVAR satisfies stability condition.

The output indicates that all eigenvalues lie inside the unit circle, implying the estimated VAR is stable.

We can draw the orthogonalized impulse response function to see visually how shocks to one variable propagate to affect the others:

. pvarirf, oirf mc(200)

We indicated that confidence intervals should be estimated using 200 Monte Carlo draws. The orthogonalized impulse response function is presented in Fig. 14.7.

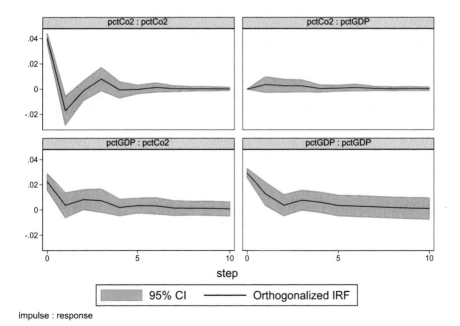

Fig. 14.7 Orthogonalized impulse response function

Finally, we can test whether `pctGDP` affects `pctCO2` pollution or vice versa using a Granger causality test:

```
. pvargranger

panel VAR-Granger causality Wald test
Ho: Excluded variable does not Granger-cause Equation variable
Ha: Excluded variable Granger-causes Equation variable

+--------------------------------------------------------+
|  Equation \ Excluded |   chi2     df    Prob > chi2   |
|----------------------+---------------------------------|
| pctGDP               |                                 |
|               pctCO2 |   1.686    3        0.640      |
|                  ALL |   1.686    3        0.640      |
|----------------------+---------------------------------|
| pctCO2               |                                 |
|               pctGDP |   7.550    3        0.056      |
|                  ALL |   7.550    3        0.056      |
+--------------------------------------------------------+
```

The *p*-value on `pctCO2` in the GDP equation is not significant (0.640). Remember that this is, strictly speaking, a Granger non-causality test: the null hypothesis is that the lagged variables do not affect current values. Thus, a *p*-value larger than, say, 0.05 indicates that we cannot reject the null hypothesis of non-causality. That's a lot of double negatives. "Not rejecting non-causality" translates loosely to "accepting non-causality" or even better: lagged CO_2 does not predict current GDP.

Likewise in the second equation, the fact that the *p*-value is (ever so slightly) greater than 0.05 implies that we cannot reject the null of non-causality: lagged GDP has no predictive power on current CO_2. If, for the sake of pedagogy, we took a permissive stance and were testing at the 0.10 level, then we would reject the null of non-causality. Or, more simply, there is evidence that lagged GDP is a predictor of current pollution.

14.7 Cointegration Tests

The danger of spurious regression applies to panels just as it does for time series. If two variables are each integrated of the same order, then regressing one on the other often results in a spurious relationship: finding a statistically significant relationship even when there is no true underlying relationship between the two variables. We will need to determine whether the variables are cointegrated before we begin reporting multivariate panel regressions. If two variables are integrated of the same order, then it is still possible that a linear combination of them is stationary. Panel cointegration tests can be quite complicated. Only some of the variables may cointegrate. Only some of the countries may form a group which is cointegrated. There may be different cointegrating groups.

14.7 Cointegration Tests

Most tests build on the Engle-Granger approach (there are some that rely on Johansen tests, but we won't really get into that). In the first stage, we estimate a regression of $Y_{i,t}$ on the set of $X_{i,t}$ variables. By definition, if the variables are cointegrated, then there is a linear combination of these variables that is stationary. In the second stage, we generate the residuals from this regression. These residuals are a linear combination of Ys and Xs. Finally, we test whether this linear combination is stationary.

One of the most popular panel cointegration tests was proposed by Pedroni (1999; 2004). Suppose there are M cointegrating variables. Then Pedroni proposes estimating the following first-stage regression:

$$Y_{i,t} = \beta_{1,i} X_{1,i,t} + \beta_{2,i} X_{2,i,t} + \ldots \beta_{M,i} X_{M,i,t} + u_i + \delta_i t + \epsilon_{i,t} \tag{14.19}$$

Pedroni allows for including country fixed effects as well as a deterministic time trend. The distinguishing feature in Pedroni's setup is that the slopes – on the time variable t and the M different X variables – are different for each country. This allows us to test whether the variables from all countries form a cointegrating relationship, or some of the countries, or none of them.

It becomes especially complicated if one set of variables forms one cointegrating relationship for one group of countries, and another set forms a second cointegrating relationship for a second group.

Regardless, we estimate Eq. (14.19) and then calculate the residuals. After this, we perform an augmented Dickey-Fuller regression on the residuals. The regression is augmented with a set of lagged differences; the number of lags L is allowed to differ by country. If there is no cointegration, then we are prone to spurious regression, and the estimated residuals will be nonstationary. On the other hand, if the variables are cointegrated, then the regression is correct, and the estimated residuals will be stationary.

The null hypothesis is that there is no cointegration, in which case the ADF test should indicate a unit root. That is, if the null is correct, the coefficients on the lagged residual are all equal to one, so that $\gamma_i = 1$ for all i.

The alternative hypothesis is a little more complicated. There is only one way that all the γ_i's equal 1. But there are several different ways that some can be less than 1. (Remember, we cannot have $\gamma > 1$ as this would make the series explosive.) In the simplest case, all of the coefficients are the same, and they are less than one:

$$H_a : \gamma_i = \gamma < 1 \text{ for all } i$$

In the more complicated case, all the coefficients are less than one, but they each have different values:

$$H_a : \gamma_i < 1 \text{ for all } i$$

Pedroni derived different test statistics for whether an intercept or trend (or neither or both) is included in the ADF regression.

Kao (1999) proposed a simplification of Pedroni's test, where the estimated slopes are forced to be the same for each country.

$$Y_{i,t} = \beta X_{i,t} + u_i + \epsilon_{i,t} \tag{14.20}$$

From this regression, calculate the residuals, $\hat{e}_{i,t}$, and then run a Dickey-Fuller type test on the residuals

$$\hat{e}_{i,t} = \rho \hat{e}_{i,t-1} + v_{i,t} \tag{14.21}$$

or an augmented Dickey-Fuller test on the residuals and lagged differences:

$$\hat{e}_{i,t} = \rho \hat{e}_{i,t-1} + \sum_{k=1}^{K} \rho_k \Delta \hat{e}_{i,t} + v_{i,t}.$$

The constraint that the β's are the same for each country is not always economically appropriate. However, when it is safe to assume that the coefficients are homogeneous across panels, forcing the estimate to be the same conserves valuable degrees of freedom and allows the test to be more efficient than Pedroni's tests. Kao constructs several different test statistics, depending on whether the $X_{i,t}$ are endogenous or exogenous.

Westerlund (2005) proposed estimating panel-specific versions of Eq. (14.21)

$$\hat{e}_{i,t} = \rho_i \hat{e}_{i,t-1} + v_{i,t}$$

and constructing a test based on the estimated long-run variance of process. (Unit root processes such as random walks have unbounded variances. Stationary processes have stationary variances.)

At least two commands in Stata conduct Pedroni (1999, 2004) tests: `xtpedroni` and `xtcointtest`. The former is a user-written program written by Neal (2014). The latter is an official Stata command and performs several tests beyond Pedroni. For example, it can also perform Kao (1999) and Westerlund (2005) tests.

The null hypothesis in Pedroni, Kao, and Westerlund tests is that there is no cointegration. The alternative for Pedroni and Kao is that all panels are cointegrated; Westerlund's alternative is that only some of the panels are cointegrated.

Wagner and Hlouskova (2009) conducted a set of Monte Carlo studies and found that tests which had null hypotheses of cointegration—such as a test by McCoskey and Kao (1998)—likewise performed quite poorly. This is analogous to their finding that tests where the null was integration—such as the Hadri test—also performed quite poorly. Their simulations indicate that Westerlund tests were found to be under-sized.

Larsson et al. (2001) developed a panel generalization of the Johansen cointegration test. The additional complexity is a bit daunting, and the test has not yet found a broad audience among applied econometricians.

14.7 Cointegration Tests

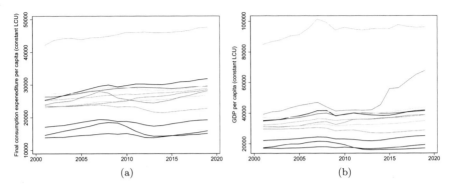

Fig. 14.8 Consumption and GDP per capita. (**a**) Consumption per capita. (**b**) GDP per capita

Wagner and Hlouskova (2009) provide a discussion of several "second-generation" cointegration tests that allow for cross-sectional dependence. There is no clear consensus on how to estimate cointegration in the face of CSD.

Pedroni (1999, 2004) tests perform best among single-equation cointegration tests (Wagner & Hlouskova 2009).

14.7.1 Cointegration Test Example: The Permanent Income Hypothesis

The "permanent income hypothesis" posits that people spread their consumption over their lifetime based on how much income they expect to earn. Therefore, consumption and income should, on average, move similarly. Let's test this hypothesis using national-level data.

First, load the data (which is graphed in Fig. 14.8)

```
. use xtcoint.dta, clear
```

Given that the data is from European Union countries, we have strong reason to suspect there is cross-sectional dependence. They are neighboring countries. And they are subject to the same exchange rate, monetary, and regulatory shocks. Still, we should conduct a formal test of cross-sectional dependence:

```
.   quietly xtreg Cpc GDP, fe
.   xtcsd, pesaran

Pesaran's test of cross sectional independence =     9.679, Pr = 0.0000
```

The low *p*-value indicates that we reject the null of cross-sectional independence. In other words, we have evidence of cross-sectional dependence.

Next, we conduct a Pedroni test of cointegration between consumption and income (both per capita). We specify the demean option since this mitigates the effect of cross-sectional dependence. We allow for different autoregressive terms for each country, and ADF tests with lags up to a depth of five, as selected by the Akaike information criterion:

```
. xtcointtest pedroni Cpc GDPpc, lags(aic 5) ar(panelspecific) demean

Pedroni test for cointegration
------------------------------
H0: No cointegration                      Number of panels    =    12
Ha: All panels are cointegrated           Number of periods   =    18

Cointegrating vector: Panel specific
Panel means:          Included            Kernel:             Bartlett
Time trend:           Not included        Lags:               1.00 (Newey?West)
AR parameter:         Panel specific      Augmented lags:     3 (AIC)

Cross-sectional means removed
--------------------------------------------------------------------------------
Statistic             p-value
--------------------------------------------------------------------------------
Modified Phillips-Perron t                2.9341              0.0017
Phillips-Perron t                         2.1930              0.0142
Augmented Dickey-Fuller t                 3.6182              0.0001
--------------------------------------------------------------------------------
```

For the sake of robustness, we also run the test requiring the same autoregressive structure for each of the countries:

```
. xtcointtest pedroni Cpc GDPpc, lags(aic 5) ar(same) demean

Pedroni test for cointegration
------------------------------
H0: No cointegration                      Number of panels    =    12
Ha: All panels are cointegrated           Number of periods   =    18

Cointegrating vector: Panel specific
Panel means:          Included            Kernel:             Bartlett
Time trend:           Not included        Lags:               1.00 (Newey?West)
AR parameter:         Same                Augmented lags:     3 (AIC)

Cross-sectional means removed
--------------------------------------------------------------------------------
Statistic             p-value
--------------------------------------------------------------------------------
Modified variance ratio                  -2.6524              0.0040
Modified Phillips-Perron t                2.1041              0.0177
Phillips-Perron t                         1.2049              0.1141
Augmented Dickey?Fuller t                 2.8840              0.0020
--------------------------------------------------------------------------------
```

In almost all of the reported Pedroni test statistics, the null of "no-cointegration" is rejected. In other words, there is a long-run and stable linear relationship between income and consumption expenditure. This supports the permanent income hypothesis.

The results of a Kao cointegration test leads to similar results: rejecting the null of no-cointegration at the 0.10 level:

14.7 Cointegration Tests

```
. xtcointtest kao Cpc GDPpc, lags(aic 5) demean

Kao test for cointegration
--------------------------
H0: No cointegration                    Number of panels    =    12
Ha: All panels are cointegrated         Number of periods   =    17

Cointegrating vector: Same
Panel means:          Included          Kernel:             Bartlett
Time trend:           Not included      Lags:               1.50 (Newey?West)
AR parameter:         Same              Augmented lags:     5 (AIC)

Cross-sectional means removed
-------------------------------------------------------------------------
Statistic              p-value
-------------------------------------------------------------------------
Modified Dickey-Fuller t                1.6321              0.0513
Dickey-Fuller t                         1.4880              0.0684
Augmented Dickey-Fuller t              -2.6748              0.0037
Unadjusted modified Dickey-Fuller t     1.9957              0.0230
Unadjusted Dickey-Fuller t              1.9581              0.0251
-------------------------------------------------------------------------
```

A Westerlund test provides a little more nuance, allowing us to specify whether the alternative hypothesis has all countries cointegrated or merely some of them. First, we run a test where some panels may be cointegrated:

```
. xtcointtest westerlund Cpc GDPpc, somepanels demean

Westerlund test for cointegration
---------------------------------
H0: No cointegration                    Number of panels    =    12
Ha: Some panels are cointegrated        Number of periods   =    19

Cointegrating vector: Panel specific
Panel means:          Included
Time trend:           Not included
AR parameter:         Panel specific

Cross-sectional means removed
-------------------------------------------------------------------------
Statistic              p-value
-------------------------------------------------------------------------
Variance ratio                          2.0880              0.0184
-------------------------------------------------------------------------
```

The Westerlund test rejects the null of "no panels are cointegrated" in favor of "some panels are cointegrated." The test does not tell us which countries are cointegrated. Nor does it rule out the possibility that all are cointegrated. To test for this, we re-run the Westerlund test, but specify `allpanels`:

```
. xtcointtest westerlund Cpc GDPpc, allpanels demean

Westerlund test for cointegration
--------------------------------
H0: No cointegration                    Number of panels    =    12
Ha: All panels are cointegrated         Number of periods   =    19

Cointegrating vector: Panel specific
Panel means:          Included
Time trend:           Not included
AR parameter:         Same

Cross-sectional means removed
--------------------------------------------------------------------------------
Statistic             p-value
--------------------------------------------------------------------------------
Variance ratio                                  1.3182          0.0937
--------------------------------------------------------------------------------
```

The test is unable to reject the null at the 0.05 level. However, at the 0.10 level the null is rejected in favor of the alternative that all countries are cointegrated.

So, what is the long-run relationship between income and consumption expenditure? To answer this we estimate a fixed effect model with time FEs, without time FEs, and the latter again but with Driscoll-Kraay standard errors:

```
. quietly xtreg Cpc GDP i.year, fe
. estimates store TimeFE
. quietly xtreg Cpc GDP, fe
. estimates store FE
. quietly xtscc Cpc GDP, fe
. estimates store DKraay
. estimates table TimeFE FE DKraay , b(%7.3f) se(%7.3f) drop(i.year)

    ----------------------------------------------
       Variable |  TimeFE        FE       DKraay
    ------------+---------------------------------
          GDPpc |   0.150      0.240      0.240
                |   0.021      0.020      0.041
          _cons |  1.9e+04    1.7e+04    1.7e+04
                | 769.234    740.787   1682.847
    ----------------------------------------------
                             Legend: b/se
```

We find that between 15 and 24 cents of every dollar of income is spent on consumption.

14.8 Further Reading

There are currently three classic textbooks on panel data: Baltagi (2021), Wooldridge (2010), and Hsiao (2022). Wooldridge's text is the easiest to read of the three. Baltagi's text is in its 6th edition, and for good reason, it is not overly complicated, it is thorough, and it is worth reading.

Arellano (2003) provides a unified treatment of GMM estimators in static and dynamic panel models.

A more recent text is Pesaran (2015), a huge tome of over 1,000 pages. In my opinion, no one in the last 20 years has had more of an influence on panel data econometrics than Hashem Pesaran. His book is not yet old enough to be considered a classic. It soon will be.

Students are encouraged to begin with Wooldridge's and Baltagi's texts before moving on to Arellano's, Hsiao's, and Pesaran's graduate-level texts.

Pesaran (2021) has a thorough review article about testing for cross-sectional dependence in panel data.

Im et al. (2023) have published an interesting retrospective paper, discussing their difficulties in publishing their IPS paper and the subsequent success and massive influence their paper has had since then. Scholars rarely discuss the process by which they arrive at their final results; this brief paper is fascinating reading.

14.9 Homework

1. Download the dataset `Hausman_HW_1.dta`. Conduct a Hausman test for fixed effects vs random effects in the following model:

$$Y_{i,t} = \beta_0 + \beta_1 X_{i,t} + u_i + \epsilon_{i,t}$$

   Which model does the Hausman test indicate is preferred, random effects or fixed effects?
   (a) Conduct a similar test with the `Hausman_HW_2.dta` dataset.
   (b) Conduct a similar test with the `Hausman_HW_3.dta` dataset.
   (c) Conduct a similar test with the `Hausman_HW_4.dta` dataset.
2. Blundell and Bond (1998) developed the system GMM estimator for dynamic panel data. Use the Arellano-Bond data from Sect. 14.2:

   ```
   . webuse abdata, clear
   ```

   and the `xtabond2` command to estimate:

   $$n_{i,t} = \beta_0 n_{i,t} + \beta_1 w_{i,t} + \beta_2 w_{i,t-1} + \beta_3 k_{i,t} + \beta_4 k_{i,t-1} + \boldsymbol{\beta_t v_t} + u_i + \epsilon_{i,t}$$

(a) Estimate the equation using difference GMM, treating the yearly dummies as strictly exogenous, and all other variables as endogenous. (Hint: Use the `noleveleq` option to specify Differenced GMM, `robust` for the standard errors, and `small` to use small sample t test statistics rather than large sample z statistics.)

(b) Repeat the estimation above, but use system GMM. Use options `robust small H(1)`.

(c) How do your estimates compare to those given in the final two columns of Table 4 in Blundell and Bond (1998)?

3. In this problem we will look at how having too many instruments can affect parameter estimates in dynamic panel data models. Download the `Thomson2017.dta` dataset and re-estimate the final column of Thomson's Table 4 using the following command:

```
. xtabond2 lnRnD L.lnRnD L.lnValueAdded L.lnTaxPrice i.t, ///
    gmm(L.(lnRnD lnValueAdded lnTaxPrice), ///
    laglimit(. 3) collapse) iv(i.t) twostep orthog robust
```

Compare your results if you:
(a) Remove the `collapse` option
(b) Remove the `laglimit` restriction
(c) Remove both `collapse` and `laglimit`, so that you estimate the equation using the full set of available instruments.
(d) How far apart are the coefficients on the lagged dependent variable?
(e) How far apart are the coefficients on `lnTaxPrice`, the main variable of interest?

4. Estimate an LLC unit root test for the EU countries, as earlier in this chapter, on the `PanelUnitRoot.dta` dataset. This time specify that the AIC should be used to determine the number of lags in the ADF regressions. Specify that the maximum number of lags to be considered is five.
(a) What is the p-value for this new test?
(b) Does your conclusion about unit roots for EU countries change?

5. Levin Lin and Chu recommend demeaning as a means of minimizing the effect of cross-sectional dependence. Demeaning calculates the average of $X_{i,t}$ at a particular time period, over all countries, and subtracts this mean from the observation. In other words, it re-scales $X_{i,t}$ at each time period, so that the global average is zero, and each country is measured as a difference from the global mean. Doing so can sometimes minimize the effect of cross-sectional dependence.

Download the `PanelUnitRoot.dta` dataset and re-estimate the LLC test with AIC and `demean` as an option.
(a) What is your p-value for this new test?
(b) Is your conclusion different from the test without the `demean` option? If so, what does this imply?

6. Download `PanelUnitRoot.dta` and conduct a series of unit root tests on the South American countries in the dataset.

14.9 Homework

(a) Run an LLC test, allowing for trend. Allow Stata to determine the optimal number of ADF lags, choosing them by AIC with a maximum lag of 8. What do you conclude?

(b) Run an IPS test, allowing for trend, and a maximum allowable lag length of 8, as above. What do you conclude?

(c) Finally, run a Hadri test, also allowing for trend and cross-sectional dependence. What do you conclude?

(d) Are your conclusions for the Latin American countries different than those for the European countries that we calculated earlier in this chapter?

7. The CIPS test (Pesaran 2007) is one of the most popular of the so-called "second generation" unit root tests. An acronym for Cross-Sectional Im-Pesaran-Shin test, CIPS builds on the classic IPS test by allowing for the possibility of cross-sectional dependence. The user-written Stata command xtcips by Burdisso and Sangiácomo (2016) implements this test. First, install the command and download the data (from the book's website):

```
. net install st0439.pkg
. use lnXRdata.dta, replace
```

(a) Run the CIPS test on the log of the exchange rate:
```
. xtcips lnXR, maxlags(5) bglags(1)
```
What do you conclude? Is the PPP hypothesis upheld?

(b) Re-run the CIPS test as before, but allow for a deterministic trend. Is the PPP hypothesis upheld?

(c) Compare your results to the standard IPS test implemented with
```
. xtunitroot ips lnXR, lags(aic 5)
```
How does this result differ from the CIPS results?

For the next several questions, use panelVAR.dta (the data on GDP and CO2 emissions from Sect. 14.6.1).

8. Run an IPS test in Stata to see whether the pctGDP and pctCO2 variables are stationary. Use lags(2).
   (a) At the 0.05 level, is pctGDP stationary? (More accurately, is there evidence that at least some of the panels are stationary?)
   (b) At the 0.05 level, is pctCO2 stationary? (More accurately, is there evidence that at least some of the panels are stationary?)

9. Run an LLC test in Stata to see whether the pctGDP and pctCO2 variables are stationary. Use lags(2).
   (a) At the 0.05 level, is pctGDP stationary?
   (b) At the 0.05 level, is pctCO2 stationary?

10. Re-estimate the panel VAR on pctGDP and pctCO2, but estimate a 2-lag model. Keep the same instlags(1/4) instrumentation.
    (a) At the 0.10 level, does pctGDP Granger-cause pctCO2?
    (b) At the 0.10 level, Does pctCO2 Granger-cause pctGDP?

11. Re-estimate the panel VAR on pcGDP and pcCO2, but estimate a 1-lag model. Keep the same `instlags(1/4)` instrumentation.
    (a) At the 0.10 level, does pctGDP Granger-cause pctCO2?
    (b) At the 0.10 level, does pctCO2 Granger-cause pctGDP?
12. Re-estimate the panel VAR on pctGDP and pctCO2, but with the following modifications.
    (a) Run `varsoc` with a maximum of four lags, and use more distant lags as instruments: `instlags(4/7)`. According to three information criteria, what are the optimal lags? Are they consistent? Given the output, what lag should you select?
    (b) Run `pvar` with the optimal lags from the previous step and the indicated instrumentation. Then run `pvarstable`. Is the estimated panel VAR stable? Do you have any concerns about the indicated lengths of the eigenvalues?
    (c) Does pctGDP Granger-cause pctCO2 at the 0.10 level? At the 0.05 level? At the 0.01 level?
    (d) Does pctCO2 Granger-cause pctGDP at the 0.10 level? At the 0.05 level? At the 0.01 level?
13. Use the `xtcoint.dta` dataset to see whether there a long-run linear relationship between per capita CO_2 and per capita GDP?
    (a) Estimate a fixed effects regression of CO2pc on GDPpc. Does there seem to be a statistically significant relationship between GDP and CO_2?
    (b) Conduct a Pesaran cross-sectional dependence test using Stata's `xtcsd` command. Does there seem to be cross-sectional dependence?
    (c) Conduct a Pedroni test cointegration test between CO2pc on GDPpc. Specify these options: `lags(aic 2) ar(same) demean`. Are the two variables cointegrated?

Conclusion 15

We have explored some of the more common time-series econometric techniques. The approach has centered around developing a practical knowledge of the field, learning by replicating basic examples and seminal research. But there is a lot of bad research out there, and you would be best not to replicate the worst practices of the field. A few words of perspective and guidance might be useful.

First, all data are historical. A regression may only reveal a pattern in a dataset. That dataset belongs to a particular time period. Perhaps our regression used the latest data, say, 2017 quarterly back to 1980. This is a healthy sized dataset for a macro-econometrician. But when we perform our tests of statistical significance, we make several mistakes.

We claim to make statements about the world, as though the world and its data do not change. We might have tested the quantity theory of money and found that it held. But there is no statistical basis for claiming that the quantity theory will, therefore, always apply. We are inclined to believe it. And I do, in fact, believe that the quantity theory has a lot of predictive power. But it is still an article of faith to take a result based on historical data and extend it to the infinite future. The past may not be prologue.

We do have methods to test whether the "world has changed." We tested for this when we studied "structural breaks." But we cannot predict, outside of our sample dataset, whether or when a structural break will occur in the future. We don't have crystal balls. The extent to which we can make predictions about the future is limited by the extent to which the world doesn't change, underneath our feet, unexpectedly.

We economists often portray ourselves as, somehow, completely objective in our pursuits. That we let the data speak for themselves. That we are armed with the scientific method—or at least with our regressions—and can uncover enduring truths about the world. A bit of modesty is in order.

We write as though it is the data, and not us, who is talking. This is nonsense. Econometricians are human participants in this process. We do have an effect. Although we might let significance tests decide which of ten variables should be included in a regression, we did, after all, choose the initial ten. Different models with different variables give different results. Reasonable economists often differ. In fact, when it comes to econometric results, it feels as though we rarely agree.

When your final draft is finally published, you will be making a claim about the world. That your analysis of the data reveals something about how the world was, is, or will be. Regardless, you will be presenting your evidence in order to make a claim. All of your decisions and statistical tests along the way will shape the credibility of your argument. Weak arguments use inaccurate or non-representative data, have small samples, perform no statistical tests of underlying assumptions, perform the improper tests of significance, perform the tests in the improper order, and confuse statistical with practical significance. Those papers are not believable. Unfortunately, they do get published.

Why is p-hacking so prevalent? The simple answer is to get published. A deeper answer may be that econometrics is a form of rhetoric or argumentation. Dressing up a theory in mathematical clothes, and presenting statistically significant results, is how we make our cases.

It is impossible for econometricians to be logical positivists. They cannot hold an agnostic position, only taking a stance once all the data have been analyzed. Rather, they have their beliefs and ideologies. They might construct a theory. Then they might test it. But someone has to believe in the theory in the first place for the tests to be worth the effort (Coase 1982). Which means that economists are not as unbiased as they claim or believe themselves to be:

> These studies, both quantitative and qualitative, perform a function similar to that of advertising and other promotional activities in the normal products market... These studies demonstrate the power of the theory, and the definiteness of the quantitative studies enables them to make their point in a particularly persuasive form. What we are dealing with is a competitive process in which purveyors of the various theories attempt to sell their wares (Coase 1982, p.17).

This also means that econometricians don't test theories objectively as much as they try to illustrate the theories they already have. This is unfortunate. But it is not an uncommon practice. Certainly, repeated failed attempts to successfully illustrate a theory will lead one to modify their theory; but they rarely abandon them and then only if an alternative theory can replace it (Coase 1982).

Like it or not, economists engage in argumentation and rhetoric as much as they engage in science.

"Hardly anyone takes data analyses seriously. Or perhaps more accurately, hardly anyone takes anyone else's data analyses seriously" (Leamer 1983, p. 37).

Why?

"If you torture the data long enough, it will confess [to anything]" answers the famous quip attributed to Ronald Coase. Unfortunately, some scholars view the research process as a hunt for low p-values and many asterisks.

As Andrew Gelman puts it, econometrics is a so-called garden of forking paths that invalidates most hypothesis tests (e.g., Gelman & Loken 2013, 2014; Gelman 2016, 2017). The econometrician is forced, from the outset, to make a series of decisions on a set of questions. What is the research question? What variables should be considered? What level of significance should be used? What information criteria should be used for lag length selection? What to do if the estimates yield economically unintelligible results? What is the decision criteria for practical significance? Each of these decisions requires judgment from the econometician. There is no way to remove judgment or trained economic intuition from the procedure. Econometrics is ultimately a social science performed by humans. There is no way to remove the human element from the process.

In his "Econometrics-Alchemy or Science?" paper, David Hendry (1980, p. 390) quips that "econometricians have found their Philosopher's Stone; it is called regression analysis and [it] is used for transforming data into 'significant' results!"

In 1983, Edward Leamer published his influential and infamous article "Let's Take the Con Out of Econometrics" where he criticized economists for p-hacking:

> The econometric art as it is practiced at the computer terminal involves fitting many, perhaps thousands, of statistical models. One or several that the researcher finds pleasing are selected for reporting purposes. This searching for a model is often well intentioned, but there can be no doubt that such a specification search invalidates the traditional theories of inference. The concepts of unbiasedness, consistency, efficiency, maximum-likelihood estimation, in fact, all the concepts of traditional theory, utterly lose their meaning by the time an applied researcher pulls from the bramble of computer output the one thorn of a model he likes best, the one he chooses to portray as a rose. (Leamer 1983, p. 36)

Statistical tests rely on the laws of probability. But "research" of the sort Leamer described is analogous to flipping a coin, even a fair and unbiased coin, repeatedly until it lands on heads and then claiming that 100% of the flips that you report are heads!

> A dataset can be analyzed in so many different ways...that very little information is provided by the statement that a study came up with a $p < .05$ result. The short version is that it's easy to find a $p < .05$ comparison even if nothing is going on, if you look hard enough...This problem is sometimes called 'p-hacking' or 'researcher degrees of freedom. (Gelman & Loken 2013, p. 1)

In fact, one can engage in "p-hacking" without "fishing." That is, p-values should be taken with a grain of salt even if you stuck with your first regression (and didn't go on a fishing expedition). You're still fishing if you caught a fish on your first cast of the line (Gelman & Loken 2013).

Modifying a hypothesis after looking at (the results of) the data is a reverse form of p-hacking. Changing one's hypothesis to fit the data invalidates the hypothesis test (Gelman & Loken 2013).

Even if there is no p-hacking, p-values are often misused. Deirdre McCloskey and Steven Ziliak examined the articles in the *American Economic Review*, one of the most prestigious journals in Economics, and found that approximately 70% of the articles in the 1980s focus on statistical significance at the expense of economic/practical significance (McCloskey & Ziliak 1996). By the 1990s, that unfortunate statistic increased to 80% (Ziliak & McCloskey 2004).[1] The "cult of statistical significance" has caused widespread damage in economics, the social sciences, and even medicine (Ziliak & McCloskey 2008).

By 2016 the misuse of p-values became so widespread that the American Statistical Association felt obligated to put out a statement on p-values. The ASA reminds us that p-values are not useful if they come from cherry-picked regressions and that statistical significance is not the same as relevance (Wasserstein & Lazar 2016).

Some have suggested that the $p < 0.05$ standard be replaced with a more stringent $p < 0.005$. The revised threshold for significance would make it harder to engage in p-hacking (this includes the 72 co-authors of Benjamin et al. (2017)).

Too often, we mistake statistical significance for practical or economic significance. Not all statistically significant results are important. These are not synonyms. Statistical significance means, loosely speaking, that some kind of effect was detectable. That doesn't mean that it is important. For importance, you need to look at the magnitude of the coefficients, and you need to use some human/economic judgment. A large coefficient at the 10% level might be more important than a small one that is significant at the 0.0001% level. How big is big enough? It depends on your question. It depends on context. Statistics can supply neither context nor judgment. Those are some of the things that you, as a practicing econometrician, must bring to the table.

Statistical significance is not the same thing as "practical significance" or "oompf":

> [A] variable has oompf when its coefficient is large, its variance high, and its character exogenous, all decided by quantitative standard in the scientific conversation. A small coefficient on an endogenous variable that does not move around can be statistically significant, but it is not worth remembering." (McCloskey 1992, p. 360)

Statistical significance really just focuses on sample size. With enough observations any coefficient becomes statistically significant (McCloskey 1985, p. 202).

Darrell Huff (2010, p. 138), in his sarcastically titled classic, *How to Lie with Statistics*, remarked that "Many a statistic is false on its face. It gets by only because the magic of numbers brings about a suspension of common sense." You are implored to keep your wits about you. Does the number jibe with your common sense? With your trained professional intuition? If not, you should be skeptical.

So, what is to be done?

You will need to convince your readers that you have not cherry-picked a regression. Always begin by graphing your data. As anyone who has worked through Anscombe's quartet can testify, a graph can often reveal a pattern in data

---

[1] Neither I nor McCloskey and Ziliak have run the relevant hypothesis tests, but such large numbers have large practical implications: the profession has neglected to consider whether an effect is worth worrying over. For an interesting response to Ziliak and McCloskey on the usefulness of p-values, see Elliott and Granger (2004).

that standard techniques would miss (e.g., Anscombe 1973). The problem is that if you stare long enough at anything, you'll begin seeing patterns when none exist.

Don't practice uncritical cook-book econometrics. Begin with a good theory for why two variables might be related. Don't work in the other direction, letting your coefficients determine what theory you're pitching. Be able to explain why two variables might be related.

If you will report regression coefficients, you should show whether and "how an inference changes as variables are added to or deleted from the equation" (Leamer 1983, p. 38). It is now standard practice to report sets of results with slightly different sets of variables. Most journals today demand at least this rudimentary level of robustness.

Post your data and your code. Let people play with your data and models so that they can see you aren't pulling any fast ones. Let them look up your sleeve, as it were. Papers that do not invite or even encourage replication should be treated with suspicion.

Follow the advice of Coase and McCloskey and never forget to answer the most important question: so what?! Pay attention to the size of your coefficients. A statistically significant result doesn't mean much more than that you are able to detect some effect. It has nothing to say about whether an effect is worth worrying over.

I recommend the practicing econometrician practice a bit of humility. Your results are never unimpeachable, your analysis is never perfect, and you will never have the final word.

Tables of Critical Values

Table A.1 Engle & Yoo critical values for the cointegration test

Number of var's	Sample size	Significance level		
N	T	1%	5%	10%
1[a]	50	2.62	1.95	1.61
	100	2.60	1.95	1.61
	250	2.58	1.95	1.62
	500	2.58	1.95	1.62
	∞	2.58	1.95	1.62
1[b]	50	3.58	2.93	2.60
	100	3.51	2.89	2.58
	250	3.46	2.88	2.57
	500	3.44	2.87	2.57
	∞	3.43	2.86	2.57
2	50	4.32	3.67	3.28
	100	4.07	3.37	3.03
	200	4.00	3.37	3.02
3	50	4.84	4.11	3.73
	100	4.45	3.93	3.59
	200	4.35	3.78	3.47
4	50	4.94	4.35	4.02
	100	4.75	4.22	3.89
	200	4.70	4.18	3.89
5	50	5.41	4.76	4.42
	100	5.18	4.58	4.26
	200	5.02	4.48	4.18

[a] Critical values of $\hat{\tau}$
[b] Critical values of $\hat{\tau}_\mu$
Both cited from Fuller (1976, p. 373), used with permission from Wiley. Reprinted from Engle and Yoo (1987); used with permission from Elsevier

Table A.2 Engle & Yoo critical values for a higher-order system

Number of var's	Sample size	Significance level		
N	T	1%	5%	10%
2	50	4.12	3.29	2.90
	100	3.73	3.17	2.91
	200	3.78	3.25	2.98
3	50	4.45	3.75	3.36
	100	4.22	3.62	3.32
	200	4.34	3.78	3.51
4	50	4.61	3.98	3.67
	100	4.61	4.02	3.71
	200	4.72	4.13	3.83
5	50	4.80	4.15	3.85
	100	4.98	4.36	4.06
	200	4.97	4.43	4.14

Reprinted from Engle and Yoo (1987); used with permission from Elsevier

A Tables of Critical Values

Table A.3 McKinnon critical values for the no trend case (τ_{nc} and τ_c)

N	Variant	Level	Obs.	β_∞	(s.e.)	β_1	β_2	β_3
1	τ_{nc}	1%	15,000	−2.56574	(0.000110)	−2.2358	−3.627	
1	τ_{nc}	5%	15,000	−1.94100	(0.000740)	−0.2686	−3.365	31.223
1	τ_{nc}	10%	15,000	−1.61682	(0.000590)	0.2656	−2.714	25.364
1	τ_c	1%	15,000	−3.43035	(0.000127)	−6.5393	−16.786	−79.433
1	τ_c	5%	15,000	−2.86154	(0.000068)	−2.8903	−4.234	−40.040
1	τ_c	10%	15,000	−2.56677	(0.000043)	−1.5384	−2.809	
2	τ_c	1%	15,000	−3.89644	(0.000102)	−10.9519	−22.527	
2	τ_c	5%	15,000	−3.33613	(0.000056)	−6.1101	−6.823	
2	τ_c	10%	15,000	−3.04445	(0.000044)	−4.2412	−2.720	
3	τ_c	1%	15,000	−4.29374	(0.000123)	−14.4354	−33.195	47.433
3	τ_c	5%	15,000	−3.74066	(0.000067)	−8.5631	−10.852	27.982
3	τ_c	10%	15,000	−3.45218	(0.000043)	−6.2143	−3.718	
4	τ_c	1%	15,000	−4.64332	(0.000101)	−18.1031	−37.972	
4	τ_c	5%	15,000	−4.09600	(0.000055)	−11.2349	−11.175	
4	τ_c	10%	15,000	−3.81020	(0.000043)	−8.3931	−4.137	
5	τ_c	1%	15,000	−4.95756	(0.000101)	−21.8883	−45.142	
5	τ_c	5%	15,000	−4.41519	(0.000055)	−14.0406	−12.575	
5	τ_c	10%	15,000	−4.41315	(0.000043)	−10.7417	−3.784	
6	τ_c	1%	15,000	−5.24568	(0.000124)	−25.6688	−57.737	88.639
6	τ_c	5%	15,000	−4.70693	(0.000068)	−16.9178	−17.492	60.007
6	τ_c	10%	15,000	−4.42501	(0.000054)	−13.1875	−5.104	27.877
7	τ_c	1%	15,000	−5.51233	(0.000126)	−29.5760	−69.398	164.295
7	τ_c	5%	15,000	−4.97684	(0.000068)	−19.9021	−22.045	110.761
7	τ_c	10%	15,000	−4.69648	(0.000054)	−15.7315	−6.922	67.721
8	τ_c	1%	15,000	−5.76202	(0.000126)	−33.5258	−82.189	256.289
8	τ_c	5%	15,000	−5.22924	(0.000068)	−23.0023	−24.646	144.479
8	τ_c	10%	15,000	−4.95007	(0.000053)	−18.3959	−7.344	94.872
9	τ_c	1%	15,000	−5.99742	(0.000126)	−37.6572	−87.365	248.316
9	τ_c	5%	15,000	−5.46697	(0.000069)	−26.2057	−26.627	176.382
9	τ_c	10%	14,500	−5.18897	(0.000062)	−21.1377	−9.484	172.704
10	τ_c	1%	15,000	−6.22103	(0.000128)	−41.7154	−102.680	389.330
10	τ_c	5%	15,000	−5.69244	(0.000068)	−29.4521	−30.994	251.016
10	τ_c	10%	15,000	−5.41533	(0.000054)	−24.0006	−7.514	163.049
11	τ_c	1%	14,500	−6.43377	(0.000145)	−46.0084	−106.809	352.752
11	τ_c	5%	15,000	−5.90714	(0.000068)	−32.8336	−30.275	249.994
11	τ_c	10%	15,000	−5.63086	(0.000055)	−26.9693	−4.083	151.427
12	τ_c	1%	15,000	−6.63790	(0.000127)	−50.2095	−124.156	579.622
12	τ_c	5%	15,000	−6.11279	(0.000069)	−36.2681	−32.505	314.802
12	τ_c	10%	15,000	−5.83724	(0.000054)	−29.9864	−2.686	184.116

Table copyright MacKinnon (2010); used with permission

Table A.4 McKinnon critical values for the linear trend case

N	Level	Obs.	β_∞	(s.e.)	β_1	β_2	β_3
1	1%	15,000	−3.95877	(0.000122)	−9.0531	−28.428	−134.155
1	5%	15,000	−3.41049	(0.000066)	−4.3904	−9.036	−45.374
1	10%	15,000	−3.12705	(0.000051)	−2.5856	−3.925	−22.380
2	1%	15,000	−4.32762	(0.000099)	−15.4387	−35.679	
2	5%	15,000	−3.78057	(0.000054)	−9.5106	−12.074	
2	10%	15,000	−3.49631	(0.000053)	−7.0815	−7.538	21.892
3	1%	15,000	−4.66305	(0.000126)	−18.7688	−49.793	104.244
3	5%	15,000	−4.11890	(0.000066)	−11.8922	−19.031	77.332
3	10%	15,000	−3.83511	(0.000053)	−9.0723	−8.504	35.403
4	1%	15,000	−4.96940	(0.000125)	−22.4594	−52.599	51.314
4	5%	15,000	−4.42871	(0.000067)	−14.5876	−18.228	39.647
4	10%	15,000	−4.14633	(0.000054)	−11.2500	−9.873	54.109
5	1%	15,000	−5.25276	(0.000123)	−26.2183	−59.631	50.646
5	5%	15,000	−4.71537	(0.000068)	−17.3569	−22.660	91.359
5	10%	15,000	−4.43422	(0.000054)	−13.6078	−10.238	76.781
6	1%	15,000	−5.51727	(0.000125)	−29.9760	−75.222	202.253
6	5%	15,000	−4.98228	(0.000066)	−20.3050	−25.224	132.030
6	10%	15,000	−4.70233	(0.000053)	−16.1253	−9.836	94.272
7	1%	15,000	−5.76537	(0.000125)	−33.9165	−84.312	245.394
7	5%	15,000	−5.23299	(0.000067)	−23.3328	−28.955	182.342
7	10%	15,000	−4.95405	(0.000054)	−18.7352	−10.168	120.575
8	1%	15,000	−6.00003	(0.000126)	−37.8892	−96.428	335.920
8	5%	15,000	−5.46971	(0.000068)	−26.4771	−31.034	220.165
8	10%	15,000	−5.19183	(0.000054)	−21.4328	−10.726	157.955
9	1%	15,000	−6.22288	(0.000125)	−41.9496	−109.881	466.068
9	5%	15,000	−5.69447	(0.000069)	−29.7152	−33.784	273.002
9	10%	15,000	−5.41738	(0.000054)	−24.2882	−8.584	169.891
10	1%	15,000	−6.43551	(0.000127)	−46.1151	−120.814	566.823
10	5%	15,000	−5.90887	(0.000069)	−33.0251	−37.208	346.189
10	10%	14,500	−5.63255	(0.000063)	−27.2042	−6.792	177.666
11	1%	15,000	−6.63894	(0.000125)	−50.4287	−128.997	642.781
11	5%	15,000	−6.11404	(0.000069)	−36.4610	−36.246	348.554
11	10%	15,000	−5.83850	(0.000055)	−30.1995	−5.163	210.338
12	1%	15,000	−6.83488	(0.000126)	−54.7119	−139.800	736.376
12	5%	15,000	−6.31127	(0.000068)	−39.9676	−37.021	406.051
12	10%	14,000	−6.03650	(0.000074)	−33.2381	−6.606	317.776

Table copyright MacKinnon (2010); used with permission

A Tables of Critical Values

Table A.5 McKinnon critical values for the quadratic trend case

N	Level	Obs.	B(∞)	(s.e.)	β_1	β_2	β_3
1	1%	15,000	−4.37113	(0.000123)	−11.5882	−35.819	−334.047
1	5%	15,000	−3.83239	(0.000065)	−5.9057	−12.490	−118.284
1	10%	15,000	−3.55326	(0.000051)	−3.6596	−5.293	−63.559
2	1%	15,000	−4.69276	(0.000124)	−20.2284	−64.919	88.884
2	5%	15,000	−4.15387	(0.000067)	−13.3114	−28.402	72.741
2	10%	15,000	−3.87346	(0.000052)	−10.4637	−17.408	66.313
3	1%	15,000	−4.99071	(0.000125)	−23.5873	−76.924	184.782
3	5%	15,000	−4.45311	(0.000068)	−15.7732	−32.316	122.705
3	10%	15,000	−4.17280	(0.000053)	−12.4909	−17.912	83.285
4	1%	15,000	−5.26780	(0.000125)	−27.2836	−78.971	137.871
4	5%	15,000	−4.73244	(0.000069)	−18.4833	−31.875	111.817
4	10%	15,000	−4.45268	(0.000053)	−14.7199	−17.969	101.920
5	1%	15,000	−5.52826	(0.000125)	−30.9051	−92.490	248.096
5	5%	15,000	−4.99491	(0.000068)	−21.2360	−37.685	194.208
5	10%	15,000	−4.71587	(0.000054)	−17.0820	−18.631	136.672
6	1%	15,000	−5.77379	(0.000126)	−34.7010	−105.937	393.991
6	5%	15,000	−5.24217	(0.000067)	−24.2177	−39.153	232.528
6	10%	15,000	−4.96397	(0.000054)	−19.6064	−18.858	174.919
7	1%	15,000	−6.00609	(0.000125)	−38.7383	−108.605	365.208
7	5%	15,000	−5.47664	(0.000067)	−27.3005	−39.498	246.918
7	10%	14,500	−5.19921	(0.000062)	−22.2617	−17.910	208.494
8	1%	14,500	−6.22758	(0.000143)	−42.7154	−119.622	421.395
8	5%	15,000	−5.69983	(0.000067)	−30.4365	−44.300	345.480
8	10%	15,000	−5.42320	(0.000054)	−24.9686	−19.688	274.462
9	1%	15,000	−6.43933	(0.000125)	−46.7581	−136.691	651.380
9	5%	15,000	−5.91298	(0.000069)	−33.7584	−42.686	346.629
9	10%	15,000	−5.63704	(0.000054)	−27.8965	−13.880	236.975
10	1%	15,000	−6.64235	(0.000125)	−50.9783	−145.462	752.228
10	5%	15,000	−6.11753	(0.000070)	−37.0560	−48.719	473.905
10	10%	15,000	−5.84215	(0.000054)	−30.8119	−14.938	316.006
11	1%	14,500	−6.83743	(0.000145)	−55.2861	−152.651	792.577
11	5%	15,000	−6.31396	(0.000069)	−40.5507	−46.771	487.185
11	10%	14,500	−6.03921	(0.000062)	−33.8950	−9.122	285.164
12	1%	15,000	−7.02582	(0.000124)	−59.6037	−166.368	989.879
12	5%	15,000	−6.50353	(0.000070)	−44.0797	−47.242	543.889
12	10%	14,500	−6.22941	(0.000063)	−36.9673	−10.868	418.414

Table copyright MacKinnon (2010); used with permission

References

Abrigo, M. R., & Love, I. (2016). Estimation of panel vector autoregression in Stata. *The Stata Journal, 16*(3), 778–804.

Acemoglu, D., Johnson, S., & Robinson, J. A. (2000). *The colonial origins of comparative development: An empirical investigation*. Technical report, National Bureau of Economic Research.

Amisano, G., & Giannini, C. (2012). *Topics in structural VAR econometrics*. Springer Science & Business Media.

Ando, A., Modigliani, F., & Rasche, R. (1972). Appendix to part 1: Equations and definitions of variables for the FRB-MIT-Penn econometric model, November 1969. In *Econometric Models of Cyclical Behavior* (Vols. 1 and 2', NBER, pp. 543–598).

Andrews, D. W., & Lu, B. (2001). Consistent model and moment selection procedures for GMM estimation with application to dynamic panel data models. *Journal of Econometrics, 101*(1), 123–164.

Angrist, J. D., & Pischke, J.-S. (2017). *Undergraduate econometrics instruction: Through our classes, darkly*. Technical report, National Bureau of Economic Research.

Anscombe, F. J. (1973). Graphs in statistical analysis. *The American Statistician, 27*(1), 17–21.

Arellano, M. (2003). *Panel data econometrics*. Oxford University Press.

Arellano, M., & Bond, S. (1991). Some tests of specification for panel data: Monte carlo evidence and an application to employment equations. *The Review of Economic Studies, 58*(2), 277–297.

Arellano, M., & Bover, O. (1995). Another look at the instrumental variable estimation of error-components models. *Journal of Econometrics, 68*(1), 29–51.

Ashworth, J., & Thomas, B. (1999). Patterns of seasonality in employment in tourism in the UK. *Applied Economics Letters, 6*(11), 735–739.

Azevedo, J. P. (2011). *WBOPENDATA: Stata module to access world bank databases*. Statistical Software Components S457234, Boston College Department of Economics.

Bai, J., Lumsdaine, R. L., & Stock, J. H. (1998). Testing for and dating common breaks in multivariate time series. *The Review of Economic Studies, 65*(3), 395–432.

Bai, J., & Perron, P. (1998). Estimating and testing linear models with multiple structural changes. *Econometrica, 66*(1), 47–78.

Bai, J., & Perron, P. (2003). Computation and analysis of multiple structural change models. *Journal of Applied Econometrics, 18*(1), 1–22.

Bailey, M. A. (2020). Real econometrics: The right tools to answer important questions.

Baillie, R. T., & DeGennaro, R. P. (1990). Stock returns and volatility. *Journal of Financial and Quantitative Analysis, 25*(2), 203–214.

Baltagi, B. H. (2021). *Econometric analysis of panel data* (6th ed.). Springer.

Banerjee, A., Dolado, J. J., Galbraith, J. W., & Hendry, D. (1993). *Co-integration, error correction, and the econometric analysis of non-stationary data*. Oxford University Press.

Banerjee, A., Lumsdaine, R. L., & Stock, J. H. (1992). Recursive and sequential tests of the unit-root and trend-break hypotheses: Theory and international evidence. *Journal of Business & Economic Statistics, 10*(3), 271–287.

Baum, C. F. (2001). Residual diagnostics for cross-section time series regression models. *The Stata Journal, 1*(1), 101–104.

Baum, C. (2015). ZANDREWS: Stata module to calculate Zivot-Andrews unit root test in presence of structural break. https://EconPapers.repec.org/RePEc:boc:bocode:s437301

Beaulieu, J. J., & Miron, J. A. (1990). *A cross country comparison of seasonal cycles and business cycles*. Technical report, National Bureau of Economic Research.

Beaulieu, J. J., & Miron, J. A. (1993). Seasonal unit roots in aggregate US data. *Journal of Econometrics, 55*(1–2), 305–328.

Beck, N., & Katz, J. N. (2011). Modeling dynamics in time-series–Cross-section political economy data. *Annual Review of Political Science, 14*, 331–352.

Benjamin, D., Berger, J., Johannesson, M., Nosek, B., Wagenmakers, E., Berk, R., Bollen, K., Brembs, B., Brown, L., Camerer, C. et al. (2017). *Redefine statistical significance*. Technical report, The Field Experiments Website.

Blanchard, O. J., & Quah, D. (1989). The dynamic effects of aggregate demand and supply disturbances. *American Economic Review, 79*(4), 655–673.

Bloomfield, P. (2004). *Fourier analysis of time series: An introduction*. John Wiley & Sons.

Blundell, R., & Bond, S. (1998). Initial conditions and moment restrictions in dynamic panel data models. *Journal of Econometrics, 87*(1), 115–143.

Bollerslev, T. (1986). Generalized autoregressive conditional heteroskedasticity. *Journal of Econometrics, 31*(3), 307–327.

Bollerslev, T. (1987). A conditionally heteroskedastic time series model for speculative prices and rates of return. *The Review of Economics and Statistics, 69*(3), 542–547.

Bollerslev, T., Engle, R. F., & Wooldridge, J. M. (1988). A capital asset pricing model with time-varying covariances. *Journal of Political Economy, 96*(1), 116–131.

Box, G. E., & Jenkins, G. M. (1976). *Time series analysis: Forecasting and control* (Revised ed.). Holden-Day.

Brandt, P. T., & Williams, J. T. (2007). Multiple time series models. In *Quantitative applications in the social sciences* (Vol. 148). Sage.

Braun, P. A., & Mittnik, S. (1993). Misspecifications in vector autoregressions and their effects on impulse responses and variance decompositions. *Journal of Econometrics, 59*(3), 319–341.

Brooks, C. (2014). *Introductory econometrics for finance*. Cambridge University Press.

Burdisso, T., & Sangiácomo, M. (2016). Panel time series: Review of the methodological evolution. *The Stata Journal, 16*(2), 424–442.

Byrne, J. P., & Perman, R. (2007). Unit roots and structural breaks: A survey of the literature. In B. B. Rao (Ed.), *Cointegration for the applied economist* (2nd ed., pp. 129–142). Palgrave Macmillan.

Campbell, J. Y., & Mankiw, N. G. (1987a). Are output fluctuations transitory? *The Quarterly Journal of Economics, 102*(4), 857–880.

Campbell, J. Y., & Mankiw, N. G. (1987b), Permanent and transitory components in macroeconomic fluctuations. *The American Economic Review, Papers and Proceedings, 77*(2), 111–117.

Campbell, J. Y., & Perron, P. (1991). Pitfalls and opportunities: What macroeconomists should know about unit roots. *NBER Macroeconomics Annual, 6*, 141–201.

Campos, J., Ericsson, N. R., & Hendry, D. F. (1996). Cointegration tests in the presence of structural breaks. *Journal of Econometrics, 70*(1), 187–220.

Chamberlain, G. (1982). The general equivalence of Granger and Sims causality. *Econometrica: Journal of the Econometric Society, 50*(3), 569–581.

Chang, S. Y., & Perron, P. (2017). Fractional unit root tests allowing for a structural change in trend under both the null and alternative hypotheses. *Econometrics, 5*(1), 5.

Chatfield, C. (2016). *The analysis of time series: An introduction*. CRC Press.

Cheung, Y.-W., & Lai, K. S. (1995a). Lag order and critical values of the augmented Dickey–Fuller test. *Journal of Business & Economic Statistics, 13*(3), 277–280.

Cheung, Y.-W., & Lai, K. S. (1995b). Practitionar's corner: Lag order and critical values of a modified Dickey–Fuller test. *Oxford Bulletin of Economics and Statistics, 57*(3), 411–419.

Chou, R., Engle, R. F., & Kane, A. (1992). Measuring risk aversion from excess returns on a stock index. *Journal of Econometrics, 52*(1-2), 201–224.

Christiano, L. J. (1992). Searching for a break in GNP. Journal of Business & Economic Statistics, 10(3), 237–250.

Christiano, L. J., & Eichenbaum, M. (1990). Unit roots in real GNP: Do we know, and do we care?. In *Carnegie-Rochester conference series on public policy* (Vol. 32, pp. 7–61). Elsevier.

Christiano, L. J., Eichenbaum, M., & Evans, C. L. (1999). Monetary policy shocks: What have we learned and to what end?. *Handbook of Macroeconomics, 1*, 65–148.

Clarke, J. A., & Mirza, S. (2006). A comparison of some common methods for detecting granger noncausality. *Journal of Statistical Computation and Simulation, 76*(3), 207–231.

Clemente, J., Gadea, M. D., Montañés, A., & Reyes, M. (2017). Structural breaks, inflation and interest rates: Evidence from the G7 countries. *Econometrics, 5*(1), 11.

Clements, M. P., & Hendry, D. F. (1997). An empirical study of seasonal unit roots in forecasting. *International Journal of Forecasting, 13*(3), 341–355.

Coase, R. H. (1982). *How should economists choose?* (pp. 5–21). The G Warren Nutter Lectures in Political Economy, The American Enterprise Institute.

Cochrane, J. H. (1991). A critique of the application of unit root tests. *Journal of Economic Dynamics and Control, 15*(2), 275–284.

Cooley, T. F., & LeRoy, S. F. (1985). Atheoretical macroeconometrics: A critique. *Journal of Monetary Economics, 16*(3), 283–308.

Cooper, R. L. (1972). The predictive performance of quarterly econometric models of the united states. In *Econometric models of cyclical behavior* (Vols 1 and 2', NBER, pp. 813–947).

Corbae, D., & Ouliaris, S. (1988). Cointegration and tests of purchasing power parity. *The Review of Economics and Statistics, 70*(3), 508–511.

De Hoyos, R. E., & Sarafidis, V. (2006), Testing for cross-sectional dependence in panel-data models. *The Stata Journal, 6*(4), 482–496.

DeJong, D. N., Ingram, B. F., & Whiteman, C. H. (2000), A Bayesian approach to dynamic macroeconomics. *Journal of Econometrics, 98*(2), 203–223.

Dickey, D. A., & Fuller, W. A. (1979), Distribution of the estimators for autoregressive time series with a unit root. *Journal of the American Statistical Association, 74*(366a), 427–431.

Dickey, D. A., Jansen, D. W., & Thornton, D. L. (1991). *A primer on cointegration with an application to money and income*. Technical report, Federal Reserve Bank of St. Louis.

Dicle, M. F., & Levendis, J. (2011). Importing financial data. *Stata Journal, 11*(4), 620–626.

Diebold, F. X. (1998), The past, present, and future of macroeconomic forecasting. *Journal of Economic Perspectives, 12*(2), 175–192.

Ditzen, J., Karavias, Y., & Westerlund, J. (2021). Testing and estimating structural breaks in time series and panel data in Stata. arXiv preprint arXiv:2110.14550

Doan, T., Litterman, R., & Sims, C. (1984). Forecasting and conditional projection using realistic prior distributions. *Econometric Reviews, 3*(1), 1–100.

Dolado, J. J., & Lütkepohl, H. (1996). Making Wald tests work for cointegrated VAR systems. *Econometric Reviews, 15*(4), 369–386.

Driscoll, J. C., & Kraay, A. C. (1998). Consistent covariance matrix estimation with spatially dependent panel data. *Review of economics and statistics, 80*(4), 549–560.

Drukker, D. M. (2006). Importing federal reserve economic data. *Stata Journal, 6*(3), 384–386.

Durlauf, S. N., & Phillips, P. C. (1988). Trends versus random walks in time series analysis. *Econometrica: Journal of the Econometric Society, 56*(6), 1333–1354.

Dwyer, G. (2014). The Johansen tests for cointegration. http://www.jerrydwyer.com/pdf/Clemson/Cointegration.pdf

Eberhardt, M. (2012). Estimating panel time-series models with heterogeneous slopes. *The Stata Journal, 12*(1), 61–71.

Eichenbaum, M., & Singleton, K. J. (1986). Do equilibrium real business cycle theories explain postwar us business cycles? *NBER Macroeconomics Annual, 1*, 91–135.

Elliot, G., Rothenberg, T. J., & Stock, J. H. (1992). *Efficient tests for an autoregressive unit root.* Working Paper 130, National Bureau of Economic Research. http://www.nber.org/papers/t0130

Elliot, G., Rothenberg, T. J., & Stock, J. H. (1996). Efficient tests of the unit root hypothesis. *Econometrica, 64*(4), 813–836.

Elliott, G. (1998). On the robustness of cointegration methods when regressors almost have unit roots. *Econometrica, 66*(1), 149–158.

Elliott, G., & Granger, C. W. (2004). Evaluating significance: Comments on "size matters". *The Journal of Socio-Economics, 33*(5), 547–550.

Enders, W. (2014). *Applied econometric time series* (3rd ed.). Wiley & Sons.

Engle, R. F. (1982). Autoregressive conditional heteroscedasticity with estimates of the variance of United Kingdom inflation. *Econometrica: Journal of the Econometric Society, 50,* 987–1007.

Engle, R. F., & Bollerslev, T. (1986). Modelling the persistence of conditional variances. *Econometric Reviews, 5*(1), 1–50.

Engle, R. F., & Granger, C. W. (1987). Co-integration and error correction: Representation, estimation, and testing. *Econometrica: Journal of the Econometric Society, 55,* 251–276.

Engle, R. F., Granger, C. W. J., Hylleberg, S., & Lee, H. S. (1993). Seasonal cointegration: The Japanese consumption function. *Journal of Econometrics, 55*(1–2), 275–298.

Engle, R. F., Lilien, D. M., & Robins, R. P. (1987). Estimating time varying risk premia in the term structure: The ARCH-M model. *Econometrica: Journal of the Econometric Society, 55*(2), 391–407.

Engle, R. F., & Yoo, B. S. (1987). Forecasting and testing in co-integrated systems. *Journal of Econometrics, 35*(1), 143–159.

Engle, R., & Granger, C. (1991). *Long-run economic relationships: Readings in cointegration.* Oxford University Press.

Epstein, R. J. (2014). *A history of econometrics.* Elsevier.

Fair, R. C. (1992), The Cowles Commission approach, real business cycle theories, and New-Keynesian economics. In *The business cycle: Theories and evidence* (pp. 133–157). Springer.

Florens, J.-P., & Mouchart, M. (1982). A note on noncausality. *Econometrica: Journal of the Econometric Society, 50*(3), 583–591.

Franses, P. H. (1991). Seasonality, non-stationarity and the forecasting of monthly time series. *International Journal of Forecasting, 7*(2), 199–208.

Franses, P. H. (1996). *Periodicity and stochastic trends in economic time series.* Oxford University Press.

Franses, P. H., & Paap, R. (2004). *Periodic time series models.* Oxford University Press.

Frees, E. W. (1995). Assessing cross-sectional correlation in panel data. *Journal of Econometrics, 69*(2), 393–414.

French, K. R., Schwert, G. W., & Stambaugh, R. F. (1987). Expected stock returns and volatility. *Journal of Financial Economics, 19*(1), 3–29.

Friedman, M. (1937). The use of ranks to avoid the assumption of normality implicit in the analysis of variance. Journal of the American Statistical Association, 32(200), 675–701.

Friedman, M. (1969). *The optimum quantity of money and other essays.* Chicago.

Friedman, M., & Schwartz, A. J. (1963). *A monetary history of the United States, 1867–1960.* Princeton University Press.

Fuller, W. A. (1976). *Introduction to statistical time series.* New York: Wiley.

Gelman, A. (2016). The problems with p-values are not just with p-values. *The American Statistician, Supplemental Material to the ASA Statement on p-values and Statistical Significance, 10*(00031305.2016), 1154108.

Gelman, A. (2017). The failure of null hypothesis significance testing when studying incremental changes, and what to do about it. *Personality and Social Psychology Bulletin, 44*(1), 16–23.

Gelman, A., & Loken, E. (2013). The garden of forking paths: Why multiple comparisons can be a problem, even when there is no "fishing expedition" or "p-hacking" and the research hypothesis was posited ahead of time. Department of Statistics, Columbia University.

Gelman, A., & Loken, E. (2014). The statistical crisis in science data-dependent analysis—A "garden of forking paths"—Explains why many statistically significant comparisons don't hold up. *American Scientist, 102*(6), 460.

Geweke, J., & Whiteman, C. (2006). Bayesian forecasting. *Handbook of Economic Forecasting, 1*, 3–80.

Ghose, D., & Kroner, K. F. (1995). The relationship between GARCH and symmetric stable processes: Finding the source of fat tails in financial data. *Journal of Empirical Finance, 2*(3), 225–251.

Ghysels, E. (1990). Unit-root tests and the statistical pitfalls of seasonal adjustment: the case of US postwar real gross national product. *Journal of Business & Economic Statistics, 8*(2), 145–152.

Ghysels, E., Lee, H. S., & Noh, J. (1994). Testing for unit roots in seasonal time series: Some theoretical extensions and a monte carlo investigation. *Journal of Econometrics, 62*(2), 415–442.

Ghysels, E. & Osborn, D. R. (2001). *The econometric analysis of seasonal time series*. Cambridge University Press.

Ghysels, E., & Perron, P. (1993). The effect of seasonal adjustment filters on tests for a unit root. *Journal of Econometrics, 55*(1-2), 57–98.

Gleick, J. (1987). *Chaos: The making of a new science*. Viking Press.

Glosten, L. R., Jagannathan, R., & Runkle, D. E. (1993). On the relation between the expected value and the volatility of the nominal excess return on stocks. *The Journal of Finance, 48*(5), 1779–1801.

Glynn, J., Perera, N., & Verma, R. (2007). Unit root tests and structural breaks: A survey with applications. *Revista de Métodos Cuantitativos para la Economía y la Empresa, 3*(1), 63–79.

González, A., Teräsvirta, T., & Dijk, D. V. (2005). Panel smooth transition regression models. Technical report, SSE/EFI Working Paper Series in Economics and Finance.

Gonzalo, J. (1994). Five alternative methods of estimating long-run equilibrium relationships. *Journal of Econometrics, 60*(1–2), 203–233.

Gonzalo, J., & Pitarakis, J.-Y. (1998). Specification via model selection in vector error correction models. *Economics Letters, 60*(3), 321–328.

Gonzalo, J., & Pitarakis, J.-Y. (2002). Lag length estimation in large dimensional systems. *Journal of Time Series Analysis, 23*(4), 401–423.

Granger, C. W. (1969). Investigating causal relations by econometric models and cross-spectral methods. *Econometrica: Journal of the Econometric Society, 37*(3), 424–438.

Granger, C. W. (1980). Testing for causality: A personal viewpoint. *Journal of Economic Dynamics and Control, 2*, 329–352.

Granger, C. W. (1988). Some recent development in a concept of causality. *Journal of Econometrics, 39*(1–2), 199–211.

Granger, C. W. (2004). Time series analysis, cointegration, and applications. *American Economic Review, 94*(3), 421–425.

Granger, C. W., & Newbold, P. (1974). Spurious regressions in econometrics. *Journal of Econometrics, 2*(2), 111–120.

Hadri, K. (2000). Testing for stationarity in heterogeneous panel data. *The Econometrics Journal, 3*(2), 148–161.

Hall, R. E. (1978). Stochastic implications of the life cycle-permanent income hypothesis: Theory and evidence. *Journal of Political Economy, 86*(6), 971–987.

Hansen, B. E. (2001). The new econometrics of structural change: Dating breaks in us labor productivity. *The Journal of Economic Perspectives, 15*(4), 117–128.

Hansen, L. P. (1982). Large sample properties of generalized method of moments estimators. *Econometrica: Journal of the Econometric Society, 50*(4), 1029–1054.

Hansen, P. R., & Johansen, S. (1998). *Workbook on Cointegration*. Oxford University Press on Demand.

Harris, R. D., & Tzavalis, E. (1999). Inference for unit roots in dynamic panels where the time dimension is fixed. *Journal of Econometrics, 91*(2), 201–226.

Harris, R., & Sollis, R. (2003). *Applied Time Series Modelling and Forecasting*. John Wiley & Sons.

Hatemi-J, A. (2003). A new method to choose optimal lag order in stable and unstable VAR models. *Applied Economics Letters, 10*(3), 135–137.

Hausman, J. A. (1978). Specification tests in econometrics. *Econometrica, 46*(6), 1251–1271.

Hayakawa, K. et al. (2009). First difference or forward orthogonal deviation-which transformation should be used in dynamic panel data models?: A simulation study. *Economics Bulletin, 29*(3), 2008–2017.

Hendry, D. F. (1980). Econometrics-alchemy or science? *Economica, 47* 387–406.

Hibon, M. & Makridakis, S. (1997). ARMA models and the Box–Jenkins methodology. *Journal of Forecasting, 16*, 147–163.

Hlouskova, J., & Wagner, M. (2006). The performance of panel unit root and stationarity tests: results from a large scale simulation study. *Econometric Reviews, 25*(1), 85–116.

Hoechle, D. (2007). Robust standard errors for panel regressions with cross-sectional dependence. *The Stata Journal, 7*(3), 281–312.

Holtz-Eakin, D., Newey, W., & Rosen, H. S. (1988). Estimating vector autoregressions with panel data. *Econometrica: Journal of the Econometric Society, 56*(6), 1371–1395.

Hosoya, Y. (1977). On the Granger condition for non-causality. *Econometrica (pre-1986), 45*(7), 1735.

Hsiao, C. (1979). Autoregressive modeling of Canadian money and income data. *Journal of the American Statistical Association, 74*(367), 553–560.

Hsiao, C. (1981). Autoregressive modelling and money-income causality detection. *Journal of Monetary economics, 7*(1), 85–106.

Hsiao, C. (2022). *Analysis of panel data* (4th ed.). Cambridge University Press.

Hsieh, D. A. (1988). The statistical properties of daily foreign exchange rates: 1974–1983. *Journal of International Economics, 24*(1–2), 129–145.

Huff, D. (2010). *How to lie with statistics*. WW Norton & Company.

Hylleberg, S., Engle, R. F., Granger, C. W., & Yoo, B. S. (1990). Seasonal integration and cointegration. *Journal of Econometrics, 44*(1), 215–238.

Hylleberg, S., Jørgensen, C., & Sørensen, N. K. (1993). Seasonality in macroeconomic time series. *Empirical Economics, 18*(2), 321–335.

Im, K. S., Pesaran, M. H., & Shin, Y. (2003). Testing for unit roots in heterogeneous panels. *Journal of Econometrics, 115*(1), 53–74.

Im, K. S., Pesaran, M. H., & Shin, Y. (2023). Reflections on testing for unit roots in heterogeneous panels. *Journal of Econometrics, 234*, 111–114.

Ivanov, V., & Kilian, L. (2005). A practitioner's guide to lag order selection for VAR impulse response analysis. *Studies in Nonlinear Dynamics and Econometrics, 9*(1), 1–34.

Johansen, S. (1988). Statistical analysis of cointegration vectors. *Journal of Economic Dynamics and Control, 12*(2–3), 231–254.

Johansen, S. (1991). Estimation and hypothesis testing of cointegration vectors in Gaussian vector autoregressive models. *Econometrica: Journal of the Econometric Society, 59*(6), 1551–1580.

Johansen, S. (1994). The role of the constant and linear terms in cointegration analysis of nonstationary variables. *Econometric Reviews, 13*(2), 205–229.

Johansen, S. (1995a). *Likelihood-based inference in cointegrated vector autoregressive models*. Oxford University Press.

Johansen, S. (1995b). A statistical analysis of cointegration for I(2) variables. *Econometric Theory, 11*(1), 25–59.

Juselius, K. (2006). *The cointegrated VAR model: methodology and applications*. Oxford University Press.

Juselius, K. et al. (1992). Testing structural hypotheses in a multivariate cointegration analysis of the PPP and the UIP for UK. *Journal of Econometrics, 53*(1–3), 211–244.

Kao, C. (1999). Spurious regression and residual-based tests for cointegration in panel data. *Journal of Econometrics, 90*(1), 1–44.

References

Keating, J. W. (2000). Macroeconomic modeling with asymmetric vector autoregressions. *Journal of Macroeconomics, 22*(1), 1–28.

Keele, L., & Kelly, N. J. (2005). Dynamic models for dynamic theories: The ins and outs of lagged dependent variables. *Political Analysis, 14*(2), 186–205.

Khon, R. (1981). A characterization of Granger-Sims exogeneity. *Economics Letters, 8*(2), 129–133.

Kilian, L., & Lütkepohl, H. (2017). *Structural vector autoregressive analysis*. Cambridge University Press.

Kim, Y. (1990). Purchasing power parity in the long run: a cointegration approach. *Journal of Money, Credit and Banking, 22*(4), 491–503.

Kwiatkowski, D., Phillips, P. C., Schmidt, P., & Shin, Y. (1992). Testing the null hypothesis of stationarity against the alternative of a unit root: How sure are we that economic time series have a unit root? *Journal of Econometrics, 54*(1–3), 159–178.

Lanne, M., Lütkepohl, H., & Saikkonen, P. (2002). Comparison of unit root tests for time series with level shifts. *Journal of Time Series Analysis, 23*(6), 667–685.

Lanne, M., Lütkepohl, H., & Saikkonen, P. (2003). Test procedures for unit roots in time series with level shifts at unknown time. *Oxford Bulletin of Economics and Statistics, 65*(1), 91–115.

Larsson, R., Lyhagen, J., & Löthgren, M. (2001). Likelihood-based cointegration tests in heterogeneous panels. *The Econometrics Journal, 4*(1), 109–142.

Leamer, E. E. (1983). Let's take the con out of econometrics. *The American Economic Review, 73*(1), 31–43.

Leamer, E. E. (1985). Vector autoregressions for causal inference? In *Carnegie-Rochester Conference Series on Public Policy* (Vol. 22, pp. 255–304). North-Holland.

Lee, J., & Strazicich, M. C. (2003). Minimum Lagrange multiplier unit root test with two structural breaks. *The Review of Economics and Statistics, 85*(4), 1082–1089.

Levin, A., Lin, C.-F., & Chu, C.-S. J. (2002). Unit root tests in panel data: Asymptotic and finite-sample properties. *Journal of Econometrics, 108*(1), 1–24.

Lewandowski, P. (2007). PESCADF: Stata module to perform Pesaran's CADF panel unit root test in presence of cross section dependence.

Leybourne, S., Newbold, P., & Vougas, D. (1998). Unit roots and smooth transitions. *Journal of Time Series Analysis, 19*(1), 83–97.

Lintner, J. (1965). The valuation of risk assets and the selection of risky investments in stock portfolios and capital budgets. *The Review of Economics and Statistics, 47*(1), 13–37.

Litterman, R. B. (1985). *A Bayesian procedure for forecasting with vector autoregressions and forecasting with Bayesian vector autoregressions–Four years of experience*. Federal Reserve Bank of Minneapolis.

Lucas, R. E. (1976). Econometric policy evaluation: A critique. In *Carnegie-Rochester conference series on public policy* (Vol. 1, pp. 19–46). Elsevier.

Lumsdaine, R. L., & Papell, D. H. (1997). Multiple trend breaks and the unit-root hypothesis. *The Review of Economics and Statistics, 79*(2), 212–218.

Lütkepohl, H. (1982). Non-causality due to omitted variables. *Journal of Econometrics, 19*(2–3), 367–378.

Lütkepohl, H. (1985). Comparison of criteria for estimating the order of a vector autoregressive process. *Journal of Time Series Analysis, 6*(1), 35–52.

Lütkepohl, H. (2005). *New introduction to multiple time series analysis*. Springer Science & Business Media.

Lütkepohl, H., & Saikkonen, P. (1999). Order selection in testing for the cointegrating rank of a VAR process. In R. Engle, & H. White (Eds.), *Cointegration, causality, and forecasting: A festschrift in honour of Clive WJ Granger* (Chapter 7, pp. 168–199). Oxford: Oxford University Press

Lütkepohl, H., & Wolters, J. (2003). Transmission of German monetary policy in the pre-euro period. *Macroeconomic Dynamics, 7*(5), 711–733.

MacKinnon, J. G. (1991). Critical values for cointegration tests. In R. F. Engle, & C. W. J. Granger (Eds.), *Long-run economic relationships: Readings in cointegration* (Chapter 13).

MacKinnon, J. G. (2010). *Critical values for cointegration tests*. Technical report, Queen's Economics Department Working Paper.

Maddala, G. S., & Kim, I.-M. (1998). *Unit roots, cointegration, and structural change*. Cambridge University Press.

Maddala, G. S. & Wu, S. (1999). A comparative study of unit root tests with panel data and a new simple test. *Oxford Bulletin of Economics and Statistics, 61*(S1), 631–652.

Makridakis, S., Andersen, A., Carbone, R., Fildes, R., Hibon, M., Lewandowski, R., Newton, J., Parzen, E., & Winkler, R. (1982). The accuracy of extrapolation (time series) methods: Results of a forecasting competition. *Journal of Forecasting, 1*(2), 111–153.

Makridakis, S., Chatfield, C., Hibon, M., Lawrence, M., Mills, T., Ord, K., & Simmons, L. F. (1993). The m2-competition: A real-time judgmentally based forecasting study. *International Journal of Forecasting, 9*(1), 5–22.

Makridakis, S., & Hibon, M. (2000). The m3-competition: Results, conclusions and implications. *International Journal of Forecasting, 16*(4), 451–476.

Makridakis, S., Hibon, M., & Moser, C. (1979). Accuracy of forecasting: An empirical investigation. *Journal of the Royal Statistical Society. Series A (General), 142*(2), 97–145.

Mandelbrot, B. (1963). New methods in statistical economics. *Journal of Political Economy, 71*(5), 421–440.

McCloskey, D. (1992). The bankruptcy of statistical significance. *Eastern Economic Journal, 18*(3), 359–361.

McCloskey, D. N. (1985). The loss function has been mislaid: The rhetoric of significance tests. *The American Economic Review, 75*(2), 201–205.

McCloskey, D. N., & Ziliak, S. T. (1996). The standard error of regressions. *Journal of Economic Literature, 34*(1), 97–114.

McCoskey, S., & Kao, C. (1998). A residual-based test of the null of cointegration in panel data. *Econometric Reviews, 17*(1), 57–84.

McCurdy, T. H., & Morgan, I. G. (1985). *Testing the martingale hypothesis in the Deutschmark/US dollar futures and spot markets*. Technical Report 639, Queen's Economics Department Working Paper.

Meese, R. A., & Rogoff, K. (1983a). Empirical exchange rate models of the seventies: Do they fit out of sample? *Journal of International Economics, 14*(1–2), 3–24.

Meese, R. & Rogoff, K. (1983b). The out-of-sample failure of empirical exchange rate models: Sampling error or misspecification? In *Exchange rates and International Macroeconomics* (pp. 67–112). University of Chicago Press.

Merton, R. C. (1973). An intertemporal capital asset pricing model. *Econometrica: Journal of the Econometric Society, 41*(5), 867–887.

Merton, R. C. (1980). On estimating the expected return on the market: An exploratory investigation. *Journal of Financial Economics, 8*(4), 323–361.

Milhøj, A. (1987). A conditional variance model for daily deviations of an exchange rate. *Journal of Business & Economic Statistics, 5*(1), 99–103.

Mundlak, Y. (1978). On the pooling of time series and cross section data. *Econometrica, 46*(1), 69–85.

Murray, M. P. (1994). A drunk and her dog: An illustration of cointegration and error correction. *The American Statistician, 48*(1), 37–39.

Narayan, P. K., & Popp, S. (2010). A new unit root test with two structural breaks in level and slope at unknown time. *Journal of Applied Statistics, 37*(9), 1425–1438.

Naylor, T. H., Seaks, T. G., & Wichern, D. W. (1972). Box-Jenkins methods: An alternative to econometric models. *International Statistical Review/Revue Internationale de Statistique, 40*(2), 123–137.

Neal, T. (2014). Panel cointegration analysis with Xtpedroni. *The Stata Journal, 14*(3), 684–692.

Nelson, C. R. (1972). The prediction performance of the FRB-MIT-Penn model of the US economy. *American Economic Review, 62*(5), 902–917.

Nelson, C. R., & Kang, H. (1981). Spurious periodicity in inappropriately detrended time series. *Econometrica: Journal of the Econometric Society, 49*(3), 741–751.

Nelson, C. R., & Plosser, C. R. (1982). Trends and random walks in macroeconomic time series: Some evidence and implications. *Journal of Monetary Economics, 10*(2), 139–162.

Nelson, D. B. (1991). Conditional heteroskedasticity in asset returns: A new approach. *Econometrica: Journal of the Econometric Society, 59*(2), 347–370.

Nerlove, M. (1967). Experimental evidence on the estimation of dynamic economic relations from a time series of cross-section. *The Economic Studies Quarterly (Tokyo. 1950), 18*(3), 42–74.

Nerlove, M. (1971). Further evidence on the estimation of dynamic economic relations from a time series of cross sections. *Econometrica, 39*(2), 359–382.

Newey, W. K., & West, K. D. (1986). *A simple, positive semi-definite, heteroskedasticity and autocorrelationconsistent covariance matrix*. Working Paper 55, National Bureau of Economic Research. http://www.nber.org/papers/t0055

Ng, S., & Perron, P. (1995). Unit root tests in ARMA models with data-dependent methods for the selection of the truncation lag. *Journal of the American Statistical Association, 90*(429), 268–281.

Ng, S., & Perron, P. (2001). Lag length selection and the construction of unit root tests with good size and power. *Econometrica, 69*(6), 1519–1554.

Nickell, S. (1981). Biases in dynamic models with fixed effects. *Econometrica, 49*(6), 1417–1426.

Osborn, D. R. (1990), A survey of seasonality in UK macroeconomic variables. *International Journal of Forecasting* **6**(3), 327–336.

Osborn, D. R., Heravi, S., & Birchenhall, C. R. (1999). Seasonal unit roots and forecasts of two-digit European industrial production. *International Journal of Forecasting, 15*(1), 27–47.

Otrok, C., & Whiteman, C. H. (1998). Bayesian leading indicators: Measuring and predicting economic conditions in Iowa. *International Economic Review, 39*(4), 997–1014.

Ozcicek, O., & McMillin, D. W. (1999). Lag length selection in vector autoregressive models: Symmetric and asymmetric lags. *Applied Economics, 31*(4), 517–524.

Pankratz, A. (1983). *Forecasting with univariate Box-Jenkins models: Concepts and cases*. John Wiley & Sons.

Pankratz, A. (1991). *Forecasting with dynamic regression models*. John Wiley & Sons.

Pedroni, P. (1999). Critical values for cointegration tests in heterogeneous panels with multiple regressors. *Oxford Bulletin of Economics and Statistics, 61*(S1), 653–670.

Pedroni, P. (2001). Purchasing power parity tests in cointegrated panels. *The Review of Economics and Statistics, 83*(4), 727–731.

Pedroni, P. (2004). Panel cointegration: asymptotic and finite sample properties of pooled time series tests with an application to the PPP hypothesis. *Econometric Theory, 20*(3), 597–625.

Perron, P. (1989). The great crash, the oil price shock, and the unit root hypothesis. *Econometrica: Journal of the Econometric Society, 57*(6), 1361–1401.

Perron, P. (1997). Further evidence on breaking trend functions in macroeconomic variables. *Journal of Econometrics, 80*(2), 355–385.

Perron, P., & Vogelsang, T. J. (1992). Nonstationarity and level shifts with an application to purchasing power parity. *Journal of Business & Economic Statistics, 10*(3), 301–320.

Pesaran, M. H. (2006). Estimation and inference in large heterogeneous panels with a multifactor error structure. *Econometrica, 74*(4), 967–1012.

Pesaran, M. H. (2007). A simple panel unit root test in the presence of cross-section dependence. *Journal of Applied Econometrics, 22*(2), 265–312.

Pesaran, M. H. (2015). *Time series and panel data econometrics*. Oxford University Press.

Pesaran, M. H. (2021). General diagnostic tests for cross-sectional dependence in panels. *Empirical Economics, 60*(1), 13–50.

Peters, E. E. (1996). *Chaos and order in the capital markets* (2nd ed.). John Wiley & Sons.

Phillips, P. C. (1986). Understanding spurious regressions in econometrics. *Journal of Econometrics, 33*(3), 311–340.

Phillips, P. C., & Perron, P. (1988). Testing for a unit root in time series regression. *Biometrika, 75*(2), 335–346.

Plosser, C. I., & Schwert, G. W. (1977). Estimation of a non-invertible moving average process: The case of overdifferencing. *Journal of Econometrics, 6*(2), 199–224.

Qin, D. (2011). Rise of VAR modelling approach. *Journal of Economic Surveys, 25*(1), 156–174.

Quintos, C. E., & Phillips, P. C. (1993). Parameter constancy in cointegrating regressions. *Empirical Economics, 18*(4), 675–706.

Rachev, S. T., Mittnik, S., Fabozzi, F. J., Focardi, S. M. et al. (2007). *Financial econometrics: From basics to advanced modeling techniques* (Vol. 150). John Wiley & Sons.

Rao, B. B. (2007). *Cointegration for the applied economist* (2nd ed.). Palgrave Macmillan.

Roodman, D. (2009a). How to do xtabond2: An introduction to difference and system GMM in Stata. *The Stata Journal, 9*(1), 86–136.

Roodman, D. (2009b). A note on the theme of too many instruments. *Oxford Bulletin of Economics and Statistics, 71*(1), 135–158.

Runkle, D. E. (1987). Vector autoregressions and reality. *Journal of Business & Economic Statistics, 5*(4), 437–442.

Said, S. E., & Dickey, D. A. (1979). Testing for unit roots in autoregressive-moving average models of unknown order. *Biometrika, 71*(3), 599–607.

Saikkonen, P., & Lütkepohl, H. (2000). Testing for the cointegrating rank of a VAR process with structural shifts. *Journal of Business & Economic Statistics, 18*(4), 451–464.

Sargan, J. D. (1958). The estimation of economic relationships using instrumental variables. *Econometrica: Journal of the Econometric Society, 26*, 393–415.

Sargent, T. J. (1976). The observational equivalence of natural and unnatural rate theories of macroeconomics. *Journal of Political Economy, 84*(3), 631–640.

Sargent, T. J., Sims, C. A. et al. (1977). Business cycle modeling without pretending to have too much a priori economic theory. *New Methods in Business Cycle Research, 1*, 145–168.

Schaffer, M. E. (2010). egranger: Engle-Granger (EG) and augmented Engle-Granger (AEG) cointegration tests and 2-step ECM estimation. http://ideas.repec.org/c/boc/bocode/s457210.html

Schenck, D. (2016). Log-run restrictions in a structural vector autoregression. https://blog.stata.com/2016/10/27/long-run-restrictions-in-a-structural-vector-autoregression/.

Schorfheide, F. (2005). VAR forecasting under misspecification. *Journal of Econometrics, 128*(1), 99–136.

Schwarz, G. (1978). Estimating the dimension of a model. *The Annals of Statistics, 6*(2), 461–464.

Schwert, G. W. (1989). Tests for unit roots: A Monte Carlo investigation. *Journal of Business & Economic Statistics, 7*(2), 147–159.

Schwert, G. W. (2002). Tests for unit roots: A Monte Carlo investigation. *Journal of Business & Economic Statistics, 20*(1), 5–17.

Sephton, P. (2017). Finite sample critical values of the generalized KPSS stationarity test. *Computational Economics, 50*(1), 161–172.

Sharpe, W. F. (1964). Capital asset prices: A theory of market equilibrium under conditions of risk. *The Journal of Finance, 19*(3), 425–442.

Shumway, R. H., & Stoffer, D. S. (2006). *Time series analysis and its applications: With R examples*. Springer Science & Business Media.

Sims, C. A. (1972). Money, income, and causality. *The American Economic Review, 62*(4), 540–552.

Sims, C. A. (1980a). Comparison of interwar and postwar business cycles: Monetarism reconsidered. *The American Economic Review, 70*(2), 250–257.

Sims, C. A. (1980b). Macroeconomics and reality. *Econometrica: Journal of the Econometric Society, 48*(1), 1–48.

Sjö, B. (2008). Testing for unit roots and cointegration. https://www.iei.liu.se/nek/ekonometrisk-teori-7-5-hp-730a07/labbar/1.233753/dfdistab7b.pdf

Stock, J. H., & Watson, M. W. (1989). Interpreting the evidence on money-income causality. *Journal of Econometrics, 40*(1), 161–181.

Stralkowski, C., & Wu, S. (1968). *Charts for the interpretation of low order autoregressive moving average models*. Technical Report 164, University of Wisconsin, Department of Statistics.

Taylor, M. P. (1988). An empirical examination of long-run purchasing power parity using cointegration techniques. *Applied Economics, 20*(10), 1369–1381.

Teal, F., & Eberhardt, M. (2010). Productivity analysis in global manufacturing production. http://www.economics.ox.ac.uk/research/WP/pdf/paper515.pdf

Thomson, R. (2015). Replication data for: The effectiveness of R&D tax credits. https://doi.org/10.7910/DVN/BVWWOQ

Thomson, R. (2017). The effectiveness of R&D tax credits. *Review of Economics and Statistics, 99*(3), 544–549.

Thornton, D. L., & Batten, D. S. (1985). Lag-length selection and tests of Granger causality between money and income. *Journal of Money, Credit and Banking, 17*(2), 164–178.

Toda, H. Y., & Yamamoto, T. (1995). Statistical inference in vector autoregressions with possibly integrated processes. *Journal of Econometrics, 66*(1), 225–250.

Tsay, R. S. (2013). *Multivariate time series analysis: With R and financial applications*. John Wiley & Sons.

Uhlig, H. (2005). What are the effects of monetary policy on output? results from an agnostic identification procedure. *Journal of Monetary Economics, 52*(2), 381–419.

Vigen, T. (2015). *Spurious correlations*. Hachette Books.

Vogelsang, T. J., & Perron, P. (1998). Additional tests for a unit root allowing for a break in the trend function at an unknown time. *International Economic Review, 39*(4), 1073–1100.

Wagner, M., & Hlouskova, J. (2009). The performance of panel cointegration methods: Results from a large scale simulation study. *Econometric Reviews, 29*(2), 182–223.

Wasserstein, R. L., & Lazar, N. A. (2016). The ASA statement on p-values: context, process, and purpose. *The American Statistician, 70*(2), 129–133.

Westerlund, J. (2005). New simple tests for panel cointegration. *Econometric Reviews, 24*(3), 297–316.

Windmeijer, F. (2005). A finite sample correction for the variance of linear efficient two-step GMM estimators. *Journal of Econometrics, 126*(1), 25–51.

Wooldridge, J. M. (2010). *Econometric analysis of cross section and panel data* (2nd ed.). MIT Press.

Wu, S. (2010). Lag length selection in DF-GLS unit root tests. *Communications in Statistics-Simulation and Computation, 39*(8), 1590–1604.

Zakoian, J.-M. (1994). Threshold heteroskedastic models. *Journal of Economic Dynamics and control, 18*(5), 931–955.

Ziliak, S. & McCloskey, D. N. (2008). *The cult of statistical significance: How the standard error costs us jobs, justice, and lives*. University of Michigan Press.

Ziliak, S. T., & McCloskey, D. N. (2004). Size matters: The standard error of regressions in the American economic review. *The Journal of Socio-Economics, 33*(5), 527–546.

Zivot, E., & Andrews, D. W. K. (1992). Further evidence on the great crash, the oil-price shock, and the unit-root hypothesis. *Journal of Business and Economic Statistics, 20*(1), 25–44.

Zivot, E., & Wang, J. (2007). *Modeling financial time series with S-Plus®* (Vol. 191). Springer Science & Business Media.

Index

A
ACF, *see* Autocorrelation function (ACF)
ADF test, *see* Augmented Dickey-Fuller (ADF) test
Akaike Information Criterion (AIC), *see* Information criterion
ARCH, *see* Autoregressive conditional heteroscedasticity (ARCH)
ARCH-LM test, 223–227, 231
Arellano-Bond, 411, 418–423, 426, 430, 433, 443, 455
ARIMA process, 105–126, 138, 141
ARMA, *see* Autoregressive moving average (ARMA)
AR process, *see* Autoregressive (AR) process
Asymmetric GARCH model, 251–258
Asymmetric VAR, 272
Augmented Dickey-Fuller (ADF) test, 144, 145, 155–156, 160, 161, 173, 187, 188, 198, 352–355, 357, 379, 432–437, 439, 440, 449–451, 456, 457
Autocorrelation function (ACF), 34, 49–75, 77, 79, 82, 83, 119, 121, 127, 136–138, 222
Autocorrelation test, 222
Autocovariance function, 26, 52, 55–57, 63, 85, 163, 276, 305
Autoregressive conditional heteroskedasticity (ARCH)
  generalized, 233
Autoregressive moving average (ARMA)
  autocovariance function, 26, 52
  estimation, 34, 38, 47, 49
  identification, 136–138
  invertibility, 138–139
Autoregressive (AR) process
  autocorrelation function, 53, 65, 72
  autocovariance function, 57

  estimation, 233
  integrated, 415
  nonstationary, 144, 152, 155
  stable, 91, 280
  stationary, 41, 99, 101, 149–151, 284

B
Back-shift operator, *see* Lag operator
Bartlett kernel
  Bartlett, 73–75, 77, 121, 138, 163, 305, 436, 452, 453
Bayesian VAR, 265, 306
Bias, 2, 17–19, 27, 140, 157, 172, 187, 225, 264, 378, 397, 411, 413, 415–425, 429, 433, 435, 439, 443, 445
BIC, *see* Information criteria
Box-Jenkins approach, 49, 132, 141
Box-Ljung test, 222, 224, 228, 231, 238–242, 244, 261
Break-point test, 188, 198, 199

C
Capital asset pricing model (CAPM), 249, 251
CAPM, *see* Capital asset pricing model (CAPM)
Causality, 264, 266, 272, 296–303, 308, 338, 340, 377–378, 448
  See also Granger causality
Central limit theorem, 146
Characteristic function, 94
Cholesky decomposition, 311, 314–324
Cointegrating rank test
  Johansen, 360, 364–376, 378, 449, 450
  likelihood ratio, 368, 369

Cointegrating rank test (*cont.*)
  maximum eigenvalue, 365, 368, 369, 371
  trace, 365, 371
Cointegration
  definition, 344, 351, 449
  Granger's representation theorem, 349, 362
  order of integration, 339
Cointegration matrix, 362, 365, 367, 374
Companion form, 277, 310, 332
Conditional volatility, 207
Covariance stationary process, 14, 15, 86
Cross-sectional dependence (CSD), 173, 408–414, 435, 436, 439, 440, 451, 456–458
CSD, *see* Cross-sectional dependence (CSD)

D

Data, 1, 12, 49, 113, 129, 143, 175, 202, 263, 316, 356, 385, 415, 459
Deterministic trend (DT), 111–113, 143–145, 150, 152–157, 162, 172, 173, 337, 339, 366, 432, 436
Deterministic term, 435
Deterministic variables, 106, 113, 127, 128, 139, 183, 184, 339, 367, 432, 449
DF, *see* Dickey-Fuller (DF)
Dickey-Fuller (DF), 140, 144–161, 164, 172, 173, 177, 182, 186, 188, 198, 352, 357, 359, 431, 432, 434, 436, 437, 439, 440, 449, 450
Dickey-Fuller test
  distribution, 145
Differencing
  seasonal, 128, 130–132, 139
Dummy variables, 127–129, 139, 140, 178, 183, 186, 188, 192, 251, 252, 256, 299, 300, 338, 364, 389, 390, 394–396, 404–406, 408, 410, 413, 414, 426
Dynamic panel, 411, 415–458
Dynamic panel bias, 415–425, 429, 433, 445

E

EGARCH process, 253–256, 261
Endogeneity, 197, 316, 390–391, 393, 394, 410, 415–418, 420, 423, 429
Endogenous variables, 285, 311, 329, 334, 420, 462
Error correction, 348–350, 354
Exogeneity, 314, 316, 394, 427
Exogenous variables, 222, 296, 300, 328, 430, 432, 441

F

FE, *see* Fixed effects (FE)
FEVD, *see* Forecast error variance decomposition (FEVD)
Final prediction error (FPE), 268, 271, 272, 277, 300, 301, 306, 376
Fixed effects (FE), 386, 390, 393–408, 411, 415, 420, 421, 426, 430, 432, 433, 449, 454, 455, 458
Forecast
  direct, 35, 327
  error, 308, 309, 326–329, 375
  iterated, 31, 35, 292
Forecast error variance decomposition (FEVD), 269, 303, 308, 309, 326–329, 375
Forecast horizon, 258, 294
FPE, *see* Information criterion

G

GARCH-in-mean, 242, 248–251
GARCH-M, *see* GARCH-in-mean
GARCH process
  asymmetric, 242, 251, 253, 256–258
  E-GARCH, 242, 253–257
  GARCH-in-mean, 248–251
  GARCH-t, 242–248, 259
  GJR-GARCH, 242, 251–253, 256–258
  integrated (I-GARCH), 242, 258–260
  multivariate, 248
  stationary, 233, 240, 242, 276
  t-distribution, 242
  T-GARCH, 242, 256
  threshold, 256–258
Generalized method of moments (GMM), 418–424, 426, 427, 429–431, 433, 443, 445, 446, 455, 456
GLS estimation, 157, 160
GMM, *see* Generalized method of moments (GMM)
Granger-Causality, 448
  testing, 297, 299, 301–303, 340, 378, 448
Granger's representation theorem, 349, 362

H

HAC, 160
Hannan and Quinn information criterion (HQIC), *see* Information criterion
Hannan-Quinn Criterion, *see* Information criterion
Hansen J-test, 423

Hausman, J.A., 394, 396, 397
HEGY test, 172

I
Identification problem, 330
IGARCH process, *see* Integrated GARCH process
Im-Pesaran-Shin (IPS), 437, 457
Impulse response function (IRF)
    orthogonalized, 311–326, 447
Information criterion
    AIC, 81, 82, 195, 257, 270–272, 306, 376, 433, 434, 436, 444, 452, 456, 457
    BIC, 81–83, 158, 195, 224, 238–240, 257, 261, 272, 376, 433, 434, 444, 445
    final prediction error, 272, 376
    FPE, 268, 271, 300, 301, 306, 376
    HQIC, 268, 270–272, 306, 376, 444, 445
    SBIC, 268, 270–272, 306, 376
Integrated GARCH process, 259
Integrated process, 86, 113, 258
Invertible MA process, 233
IPS, *see* Im-Pesaran-Shin (IPS)

J
Johansen estimation approach, 360
Johansen test
    distribution, asymptotic, 360
    Max test, 368
    Specification of deterministic part, 366, 367
    trace test, 368–369

K
KPSS test, 162–163, 304, 305, 435
Kurtosis, 85, 201, 207–209, 216, 219, 243–245, 260, 262

L
Lagged dependent variables (LDV), 17–21, 415, 421–423, 429, 433–435, 456
Lag operator, 3, 87, 96, 100–101, 109, 134, 279, 280, 426
Lag order selection, 375, 455
Lag polynomial, 3, 87, 88, 96, 97, 99, 102, 133, 134, 136
Lagrange multiplier (LM) test, 162, 222–227, 230, 231, 307, 410
LDV, *see* Lagged dependent variables (LDV)
Long-run effects, 454
Long-run mean, 284
Long-run parameters of VECM, 340, 362
Long-run restrictions, 336–338
Long-run variance, 163, 258, 450
Lucas Critique, 175

M
MA process, *see* Moving average (MA) process
MA representation, 284, 287, 318
Markov chain, 198
Maximum eigenvalue test for cointegration, 365, 368
Minnesota prior, 265
Money demand, 264
Moving average (MA) process
    autocorrelation function, 34
    finite order, 99, 203
    infinite order, 99, 233
    invertible, 99, 101, 103, 156, 233, 325
Multivariate GARCH process, 248
Mundlak, 400–401

N
Newey-West estimator, 160, 161
Nickell bias, *see* Dynamic panel bias

O
Observationally equivalent, 264, 296
OIRFs, *see* Orthogonalized impulse responses (OIRFs)
Order of integration, 106, 107, 339
Order of variables, 313–326, 329, 334–336, 378
Orthogonalized impulse responses (OIRFs), 301, 311, 313–315, 318, 319, 333–325, 335, 375
Overfitting, 420

P
PACF, *see* Partial autocorrelation function (PACF)
Panel data, 173, 198, 348, 385–458
Partial autocorrelation function (PACF), 49, 65–75, 77, 79, 121, 122, 136–138
Phillips-Perron test, 140, 144, 160–161, 172, 432, 435, 437, 452
Portmanteau test, 228, 231, 238–240, 242, 244–248

Power, 3, 12, 54, 86, 134, 139, 140, 149, 157, 158, 161, 162, 165, 172, 173, 287, 288, 301, 321, 347, 352, 360, 375, 376, 432, 435, 439, 442, 448–460
p-value, 122, 125, 145, 148, 151–155, 158, 161, 170, 223, 224, 228, 269, 339, 340, 352, 356, 357, 398, 399, 401, 412, 423, 425, 427, 435–438, 445, 448, 452–454, 461, 462

R

Random effects (RE), 389, 393–403, 409, 411, 455
Random walk, 103, 105, 106, 108, 109, 121–126, 128, 143, 146, 148, 150, 152, 162, 166, 169, 251, 277, 343, 348, 356, 367, 370, 450
Random walk with drift, 106, 110, 112, 113, 115, 121, 143–145, 152, 153, 370
RE, *see* Random effects (RE)
Reduced form, 264, 311, 329–333, 335, 361, 362
Residual autocorrelation
    Box-Ljung test, 222, 224, 231, 238–242, 244, 246, 247, 261
    LM test, 162, 222–227, 230, 231, 260, 413, 438
    Portmanteau test, 228, 231, 238–240, 242, 244–248
Residuals, 14, 24, 26, 35–37, 49, 112, 113, 118, 123, 155, 157, 162, 164, 167, 180, 182, 184, 185, 190, 191, 211, 222, 223, 227, 239–248, 254, 262, 307, 327, 338, 351–360, 364, 365, 424, 425, 449, 450
Restrictions
    long-run, 336–338
    short-run, 265
    sign restrictions, 265
Return, 4, 5, 9, 36, 125, 201, 203, 207, 223, 225, 226, 230, 236, 240, 243, 245, 248–251, 258–262, 279, 286, 287, 308, 364, 392, 402
RMSE, *see* Root mean square error (RMSE)
Root mean square error (RMSE), 159, 170, 185, 186, 189, 190, 193, 268, 372, 380, 382

S

Schwarz criterion, 188, 270, 306
Seasonal ARIMA process, 133, 138, 141
Seasonal ARMA process, 127–141

Seasonal differencing, 127, 128, 130–133, 136, 139
Seasonal unit root test, 139, 140, 172
Shift dummy variable, 127
Shocks, 21–24, 29, 30, 34, 35, 40, 47, 140, 143, 164, 171, 173, 177–179, 182, 183, 187, 197, 242, 253, 256, 258, 269, 284–289, 292, 301–303, 308, 310–316, 319, 326–330, 332, 333, 337, 350, 365, 386, 389, 403–405, 408–411, 413, 425, 447, 451
Short-run parameters of VECM, 343, 355
Size, 14, 18, 20, 22, 80, 116, 118, 122, 140, 158, 172, 280, 352, 353, 375, 379, 396, 408, 421, 435, 462, 463, 465, 466
Skewness, 85, 201
Smooth transition, 198
Spurious correlation, 122, 124
Spurious regression, 86, 122, 124, 448, 449
Stability condition, 94, 95, 306, 307, 446, 447
Stable AR process, 91
Stable VAR, 278, 281, 282, 284, 306, 307, 310, 446, 447
Standardized residuals, 222, 240, 243, 245, 246, 248, 254, 262
Stata commands
    `ac`, 71, 79
    `ARCH`, 209, 210, 218
    `arima`, 16, 17, 28, 30, 38, 96, 122
    `corrgram`, 72, 74, 121, 122
    `dfgls`, 157–159
    `dfuller`, 148–151, 153, 154, 156, 170, 171
    `drawnorm`, 302, 312, 317, 320, 334
    `egranger`, 354, 358, 359
    `estat archlm`, 223, 226, 231
    `estat aroots`, 94–96, 122, 138
    `estat ic`, 80–82, 224, 231
    `fcast compute`, 294, 295
    `fetchyahooquotes`, 8, 9, 106, 107, 172, 188, 240, 256
    `freduse`, 8, 77, 159, 266, 297, 299, 304, 337
    `hegy4`, 172
    `histogram`, 209, 211
    `irf create`, 22, 312–314, 320, 324, 335, 336, 338
    `irf graph`, 22, 269, 312, 338
    `irf table`, 320, 321, 324, 327, 328, 335, 336
    `kpss`, 163, 305
    `pac`, 72, 73, 77, 79
    `pperron`, 160, 161, 437
    `predict`, 31–33, 35–37, 211

Index

pvar, 443, 444, 446–458
pvarirf, 447
pvarstable, 446, 458
qnorm, 209
regress, 16, 17, 27, 148, 161, 225, 389
set seed, 18, 44, 113, 123–125, 176, 179, 209, 215, 219, 234, 237, 312, 355, 369, 402
simulate, 125
sureg, 270
tabstat, 216
var, 266, 269, 270
varbasic, 269
vargranger, 340
varsoc, 271, 339, 375, 444, 458
varstable, 282
vec, 354, 375
vecrank, 369, 371
wbopendata, 8, 107
wntestq, 222
xtabond, 419
xtabond2, 419, 420, 424, 426, 455
Stationarity, *see* Stationary
Stationary, 13, 51, 85, 105, 127, 144, 176, 203, 263, 311, 343, 385, 415
Structural breaks
    dating of breaks, 118, 188–198, 378
    tests, vii, 176–189, 197–199, 378, 411, 433, 459
Structural change, 177, 184, 186, 198, 199
Structural vector autoregression (SVAR), 265, 311, 329–340, 350, 361, 362
SVAR, *see* Structural vector autoregression (SVAR)

T

t-distribution, 356
Test
    autocorrelation, squared residuals, 222
    cointegration, 252, 267, 348, 377, 378, 413, 448–454, 458, 465
    Dickey-Fuller regression, 449
    Dickey-Fuller test, 144–160
    Engle's Lagrange-Multiplier test, 307
    heteroskedasticity, 160, 201–204, 206, 223, 226, 231, 233, 242, 389, 438
    independence, 413
    Johansen test, 367, 371, 449
    Kwiatkowski-Phillips-Schmidt-Shin-tests, 144
    Phillips-Perron test, 140, 160–161, 172, 435, 437
    unit root test, 9, 94, 139, 140, 143–173, 176, 188, 194–197, 199, 352, 431, 433, 435–439, 456, 457
    white noise, 26, 43, 49, 59, 111, 119–121, 129, 157, 222, 228, 238–240, 242, 244–248, 376, 424
TGARCH process, 256
Threshold autoregressive model, 256
Threshold GARCH process, 256
Time-varying coefficients, 201–262
Trace test for cointegration, 365
Trend-stationary process, 113, 114, 116, 117, 120, 165, 173, 176, 198

U

Unit root
    annual, 166–168
    seasonal, 128, 130, 138–140, 172
Unit root test
    ADF test, 144 (*see also* Stata commands, dfuller)
    KPSS test, 144, 162–163, 304, 435
    Kwiatkowski, 144, 162 (*see also* Stata commands, kpss)
    level shift, 189
    Schmidt-Phillips, 144
    seasonal, 139, 140, 172

V

VAR, *see* Vector autoregression (VAR)
Variance, long-run, 163, 258, 450
VARMA process, *see* vector autoregressive moving-average (VARMA) process
VAR process, *see* Vector autoregressive (VAR) process
Vector autoregression (VAR)
    Bayesian VAR, 265
    correlation function, 222, 312
    covariance function, 312
    estimation, 9, 266–270
    forecast error variance decomposition, 308, 309, 326–329
    forecasting, 292–295
    form, reduced, 311, 329, 330, 332, 333, 361, 362
    form, structural, 329, 331
    lag order, 270–272, 376–378
    stability, 86, 276–282
Vector autoregressive moving-average (VARMA) process, 340

Vector error correction mechanism (VECM)
  estimation, 340
  forecasting, 375
  reduced rank estimation, 376
Vector error correction model (VEC/VECM),
  360–363, 373, 377–380
Volatility
  ARCH-in-mean model, 248
  ARCH(p) model, 223, 226, 231, 241
  asymmetric, 251
  EGARCH model, 261
  GARCH(1,1) model, 201, 238
  GARCH(p,q) model, 233, 236, 240, 241, 254, 258

Heavy tails, 259
IGARCH, 259

W
Weighting function, 202
White noise, 26, 43, 49, 59, 111, 119–121, 129, 157, 222, 228, 231, 238–240, 242, 244–248, 376, 424
White noise process, 119, 129

Y
Yule-Walker equations, 55, 56, 58

Printed in the United States
by Baker & Taylor Publisher Services